I warmly commend and welcome this excellent commentary on Ezekiel. Professor Mackay, an Old Testament and Hebrew specialist, has provided us with a readable but rich, competent commentary on the biblical text. His extended introduction is also valuable and a necessary read for grappling with the text of Ezekiel. Preachers, and all who desire to enjoy and dig into God's Word, will be enriched by using this commentary.

D. Eryl Davies
Elder of Heath Church
Research Supervisor, Union School of Theology

Over the years John L. Mackay has produced a number of carefully researched and well written commentaries on major Biblical books; these two volumes on Ezekiel are no exception. The commentary is marked by considerable scholarship with judicious comment on the relevant literature. It is also very readable and John Mackay wears his learning lightly. Pastoral and practical concerns are handled sensitively. The commentary will be of particular help to preachers and help them to tackle this often neglected book. Don't be tempted to ignore the introductory material which is as lucid an account as I have ever read of Ezekiel's life and times, and a fascinating discussion of the relationship of the Spirit of God and the human personality. It is also accessible to the general reader and not overburdened with technicalities.

Bob Fyall
Former Senior Tutor in Ministry, Cornhill Training Course, Scotland

John L. Mackay continues to make a superb contribution to the Church with his latest commentary. It is a believing work, affirming divine inspiration from the outset, and thus refreshing and vital. It is a comprehensive work; relentless, yet still accessible. This is not just another commentary; it takes its place amongst the best.

Jared Hood
Old Testament Lecturer, Academic Dean, Faculty Secretary,
Presbyterian Theological College

EZEKIEL

A Mentor Commentary

Volume 2: Chapters 25–48

John L. Mackay

All Scripture translations throughout this volume are the author's own.

Copyright © John L. Mackay 2018

paperback ISBN 978-1-5271-0110-4

First published in 2018
by
Christian Focus Publications Ltd,
Geanies House, Fearn, Ross-shire
IV20 1TW, Scotland

www.christianfocus.com

A CIP catalogue record for this book is available from the British Library.

Cover design by Daniel Van Straaten

Printed and bound by Bell and Bain, Glasgow

All rights reserved. No part of this publication may be reproduced, stored in a retrieval system, or transmitted, in any form, by any means, electronic, mechanical, photocopying, recording or otherwise without the prior permission of the publisher or a licence permitting restricted copying. In the U.K. such licences are issued by the Copyright Licensing Agency, Saffron House, 6-10 Kirby Street, London, EC1 8TS. www.cla.co.uk

CONTENTS

Figures 6
Abbreviations 7

Volume 2
VI. Oracles against the Nations (25:1–32:32) 9
VII. Restoration and Renewal (33:1–39:29) 161
VIII. Perfect Order (40:1–48:35) 349

Works Cited 551
Subject Index 562
Index of Scripture Quoted 569
Index of Hebrew Words 575

FIGURES

1. Ezekiel's World 14
2. The Temple Complex
   Revealed to Ezekiel 364
3. Ezekiel's Guided Tour (Part 1) 370
4. The Outer East Gateway 374
5. The Temple Building 398
6. Ezekiel's Guided Tour (Part 2) 426
7. North–South Cross-section of the Altar 442
8. The Central District of the Land 480
9. The Tribal Territories 524

ABBREVIATIONS

ABD	*Anchor Bible Dictionary.* D. N. Freedman (ed.). 6 volumes. New York: Doubleday, 1992.
Ag. Ap.	Josephus, *Against Apion* in Flavius Josephus, *The Works of Josephus: Complete and Unabridged*, rev. ed., trans. William Whiston (Peabody: Hendrickson, 1987).
ANET	*Ancient Near Eastern Texts Relating to the Old Testament.* J. B. Pritchard (ed.) 3rd edition. Princeton: Princeton University Press, 1969.
Ant.	Josephus, *Antiquities* in Flavius Josephus, *The Works of Josephus: Complete and Unabridged*, rev. ed., trans. William Whiston (Peabody: Hendrickson, 1987).
ASV	American Standard Version
AV	Authorised Version (King James) (1611).
BDB	F. Brown, S. R. Driver and C. A. Briggs (eds.), *A Hebrew and English Lexicon of the Old Testament.* Oxford: Clarendon Press, 1907.
BHS	*Biblica Hebraica Stuttgartensia.* K. Elliger and W. Rudolph (eds.). Stuttgart: Deutsche Bibelstiftung, 1977.
COS	Hallo, William W. and K. Lawson Younger. *The Context of Scripture.* Leiden; New York: Brill, 1997–2002.
ESV	*English Standard Version.* (Anglicized edition) London: HarperCollins, 2012.
GKC	W. Gesenius, E. Kautzsch and A. E. Cowley, *Gesenius Hebrew Grammar.* Oxford: Clarendon Press, 1910 (second edition).
GNB	Good News Bible (= Today's English Version). Glasgow: Collins/Fontana, 1976.
HALOT	*The Hebrew and Aramaic Lexicon of the Old Testament.* L. Koehler, W. Baumgartner and J. J. Stamm. 5 volumes. Brill: Leiden, 1994-1999.
HCSB	The Holman Christian Standard Bible. Nashville: Holman Bible Publishers, 2003.
Hist.	Herodotus in Herodotus, *The History of Herodotus*, trans. G. C. Macaulay (London and New York: MacMillan, 1890).
IBHS	*An Introduction to Biblical Hebrew Syntax.* B. K. Waltke and M. O'Connor. Winona Lake, Indiana: Eisenbrauns, 1990.
ISBE(1915)	*International Standard Bible Encyclopedia.* J. Orr (ed.). 5 volumes. Chicago: Howard Severance, 1915.

ISBE	*International Standard Bible Encyclopedia*. G. W. Bromiley (ed.). 4 volumes. Grand Rapids: Eerdmans, 1979–1988.
ISV	International Standard Version. Yorba Linda, CA: ISV Foundation, 2011.
Joüon	Joüon, P. *A Grammar of Biblical Hebrew*. Translated and revised by T. Muraoka. Rome: Editrice Pontificio Istituto Biblico, 1991.
LXX	Septuagint, according to *Septuaginta II*, ed. A. Rahlfs. Deutsche Bibelgesellschaft: Stuttgart, 1982.
MT	Massoretic Text (as in *BHS* above).
NASB	New American Standard Bible. LaHabra, California: The Lockman Foundation, 1995.
NEB	The New English Bible: Old Testament. Oxford University Press and Cambridge University Press, 1970.
NIDOTTE	*New International Dictionary of Old Testament Theology and Exegesis*. W. A. VanGemeren (ed.). 5 volumes. Grand Rapids: Zondervan, 1997.
NIV (1984)	New International Version. (Anglicised edition). London: Hodder and Stoughton, 1984.
NIV	New International Version. Grand Rapids, MI: Zondervan, 2011.
NJPS	*Tanakh: The Holy Scriptures: The New JPS Translation according to the Traditional Hebrew Text*. Philadelphia: The Jewish Publication Society, 1985.
NKJV	New King James Version. Nashville: Thomas Nelson, 1982.
NLT	New Living Translation. Wheaton, Illinois: Tyndale House, 1997.
NRSV	New Revised Standard Version. New York and Oxford: Oxford University Press, 1989.
REB	Revised English Bible. Oxford University Press and Cambridge University Press, 1989.
RSV	Revised Standard Version. London: Oxford University Press, 1963.
TDOT	*Theological Dictionary of the Old Testament*. G. J. Botterweck, H. Ringgren and H-J. Fabry (eds.) (15 vols.) Grand Rapids: Eerdmans, 1974-2006.
TWOT	*Theological Wordbook of the Old Testament*. R. L. Harris and G. L. Archer (eds.). Chicago: Moody Press, 1980.

VI. Oracles against the Nations

(25:1–32:32)

OUTLINE

A. Against the Ammonites (25:1–7)
B. Against Moab and Seir (25:8–11)
C. Against Edom (25:12–14)
D. Against the Philistines (25:15–17)
E. Against Tyre (26:1–28:19)
  1. Four Oracles against Tyre (26:1–21)
  2. The Downfall of Tyre (27:1–36)
  3. Indictment and Judgement of the Leader of Tyre (28:1–10)
  4. Lament over the King of Tyre (28:11–19)

F. Against Sidon (28:20–26)
  1. The Fate of Sidon (28:20–23)
  2. Israel's Return (28:24–26)

G. Against Egypt (29:1–32:32)
  1. Judgement on the Great Monster and the Splintered Staff (29:1–16)
  2. Nebuchadnezzar's Reward (29:17–21)
  3. Judgement on Egypt (30:1–19)
  4. Pharaoh's Broken Arm (30:20–26)
  5. The Lofty Cedar (31:1–18)
  6. Lament over Pharaoh (32:1–16)
  7. Descent into Sheol with the Uncircumcised (32:17–32)

VI. Oracles against the Nations (25:1-32:32)

Oracles against the nations form a recurrent feature of Old Testament prophecy. As Jeremiah remarked, 'The prophets ... from earliest times prophesied against many lands and against great kingdoms of war and of disaster and of pestilence' (Jer. 28:8). Perhaps as much as one-fifth of the prophetic record is taken up with groups of such material (Isaiah 13–23, Jeremiah 46–51, Amos 1–2, the first part of Obadiah, Nahum, Zephaniah 2–3, and this central section of Ezekiel, chs. 25–32).

Why does the LORD draw the destiny of these particular nations to the attention of Ezekiel and his audience? One answer to that question is to detect here a catalogue of conventional opponents of Israel, very much mirroring those listed in Amos 1–2 and Isaiah 13–23. However, there is more involved than that. All these states were opposed to Babylon. Indeed, Edom, Moab, Ammon, Tyre and Sidon were represented at a conference convened by Zedekiah, the last king of Judah, presumably to consider what united action they might take to counter Babylon (Jer. 27:3). However, it is not for political conspiracy that the LORD indicts them, but for their opposition to his purposes.

The interpretive key to these oracles is to be found in the brief word of promised relief and restoration inserted by Ezekiel at their centre (28:24–26). This provides the vantage point which enables us to discern the ultimate purpose behind God's dealings with other nations—the establishment and recognition of his universal rule and his provision for those who serve him. The nations whose downfall is predicted are enemies of the LORD because they oppose his purposes for his people, and have mistreated them or else revel in Babylon's mistreatment of them which they see as culminating in Israel's demise. Furthermore, these countries by encouraging anti-Babylonian sentiment or colluding in anti-Babylonian alliances are acting in opposition to the LORD's declared intention regarding the role Babylon is playing in the affairs of the nations at that juncture (Jer. 27:6–8).

So Ezekiel's oracles regarding the other nations are addressed to the exiles to remind them of the character of their God and the nature of his purposes throughout the lands.

(1) The oracles declare the impartiality of the LORD's justice. That there will be judgement of the people of God has been the theme of the book so far, but as Peter remarked, 'it is time for judgement to begin with the household of God; and if it begins with us, what will be the outcome for those who disobey the gospel of God? And "If the righteous is saved with difficulty, where will the ungodly and ˻the˼

sinner appear?" ' (1 Pet. 4:17–18). So the exiles are being urged to ponder the fact that other nations are in no way exempt from divine scrutiny and divine retribution.

(2) As a result of seeing that the destiny of the nations is determined by the LORD, the exiles are implicitly directed not to envy nations like Tyre and Egypt. Israel wants to become like them (11:12; 20:32; 23:30). Certainly two of those nations sympathetic to Judah's attempts to rebel against Babylon possess considerable worldly prestige—Tyre through her commercial power, and Egypt through her economic and military dominance. But neither wealth nor military prowess secures a right relationship with God. The announced destiny of these nations serves to warn the exiles to turn from alliances with them, and to focus on their covenant bond with the LORD.

(3) Moreover, through these oracles Israel is being assured of the sovereign control of God. No matter how powerful their enemies may be in military or economic terms, they cannot thwart his provision for his people. Indeed, so that there may be scope for the increase of God's people, he is acting to check their enemies and forcibly diminish their power. When the people under the curse of the broken covenant acknowledge their wrongdoing in repentance, then the LORD promises not only to restore them, but also to transfer to their enemies the curses and persecution they had experienced at their hands (Deut. 30:1–7). It is in this way that the LORD's rule will be advanced.

(4) The people of the LORD will experience relief not only in terms of immediate deliverance from invasion and conquest, but there is also the prospect of the full realisation of the covenant promise. Since the imposition of divine judgement in the form of the exile would engender doubts among the exiles as to what the future holds for them, they are being reminded of the LORD's basic covenant promise to Abraham. 'I will bless those who bless you, and the one who dishonours you I will curse, and in you all the families of the earth will be blessed' (Gen. 12:3). God's action in cursing their enemies shows that he is still acting in accordance with one aspect of the Abrahamic covenant, and so, despite appearances to the contrary, the exiles may have a well-grounded hope that other aspects of the covenant also remain operational and that the blessing promised to Abraham and his seed will yet be realised.

Literary Structure. The oracles are located at this juncture in Ezekiel's work for two reasons. Firstly, in terms of the literary structure of the book, their presence delays the fulfilment of the prophecies of chapter 24 until chapter 33, and so provides a measure of dramatic heightening in the presentation.[1]

Secondly, the oracles are positioned theologically so as to move from the theme of judgement upon Israel to judgement curtailing the power of her enemies, and thus there is opened up the positive prospect of a new world order involving divine restoration for Israel. The oracles are both interlude and prelude (cf. Woudstra 1968:23). Before that prospect of renewal can occur, judgement has to be imposed on Israel, and the nations which would prove hostile to a restored Israel would have to be neutralised or removed to permit the land to be occupied again in security.

> Since seven nations are named in all, and divine judgment is pronounced against them in turn, we are reminded of the command of Deuteronomy 7:1 that God will bring Israel into the land and clear away seven nations greater and stronger than themselves. These oracles are a transition to a new word of hope for Israel by establishing that God indeed controls the deeds and fates of all peoples, and has the power to reverse the loss of Israel's land and bring the neighboring hostile powers to heel. In some ways, these are part of a word of salvation to Israel by redirecting divine wrath against those nations that have helped humiliate the chosen people, and by preparing for the final decisive step: the promised return of Israel itself from exile. (Boadt 1990:4)

Many of the oracles are dated from the years when Jerusalem was under siege, and are presented in a roughly chronological sequence which is disrupted only by 26:1 and 29:17. However, their order is also influenced by their geographical location relative to Judah. First, consideration is given to Ammon to the east (25:1–7), then Moab to the south-east (25:8–11), Edom to the south (25:12–14), and Philistia to the south-west (25:15–17). See Figure 1. Philistia is the only nation of this initial group of four with which Judah did not acknowledge kinship. However, all four were traditionally hostile to Judah, and are condemned for their on-going malicious attitude.

---

1. 'The corresponding segments in chs. 24 and 33 that refer to the destruction of Jerusalem and its 'sanctuary', the Temple, are an illustration of the structural bounding device of *exclusio*, i.e., they serve to *externally* bracket the enclosed foreign judgment oracles section (chs. 25–32). The operation of *exclusio* is thus similar to that of *inclusio*, except that the former is constituted by a pair of passages that lie just *outside* the initial and final borders of the demarcated unit' (Wendland 2009:209).

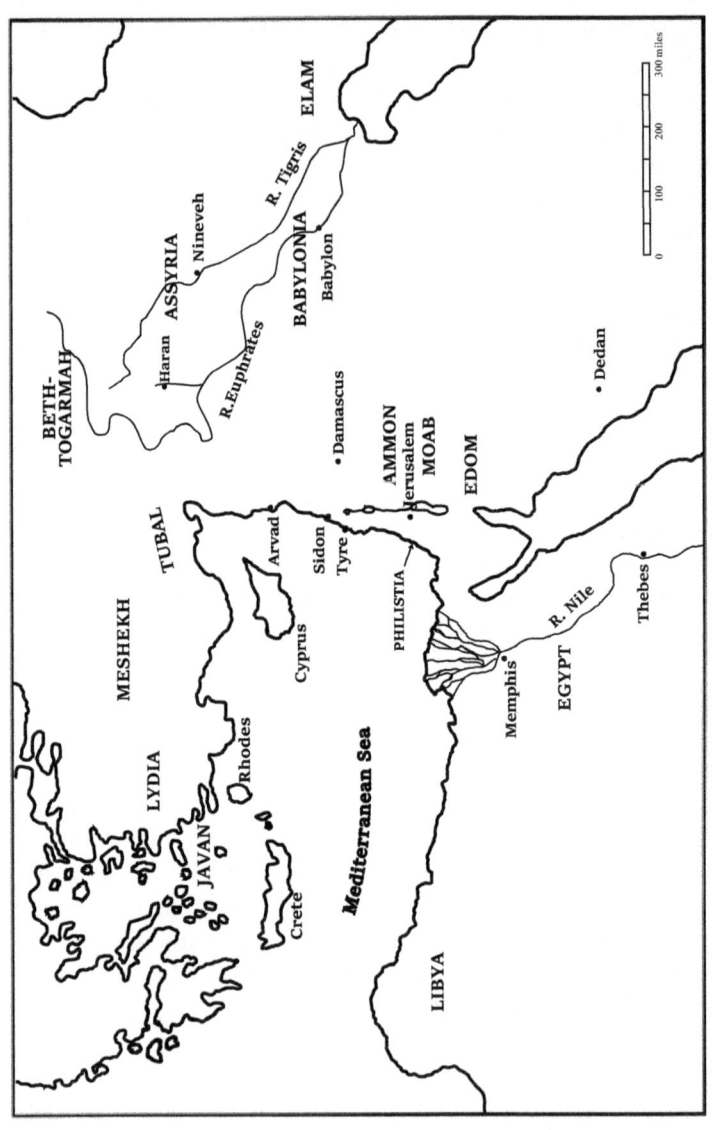

Figure 1. Ezekiel's World.

After this, two more distant nations are accorded lengthier treatments, Tyre in chapters 26–28 and Egypt in chapters 29–32. Indeed, the oracle concerning Egypt is of the same size as all the others combined. It is, however, significant that brief consideration is given to Sidon in 28:20–23. This brings the number of nations to seven, a number which may be used symbolically to convey totality and finality (cf. Amos 1–2).[2] Furthermore, there are seven sections to the material concerning Egypt (and probably also Tyre), and indeed it is possible to analyse the final oracle against Egypt (32:17–32) into seven strophes (see Introduction to that oracle). 'The recursive number seven in this section appears to emphasise the completeness of the LORD's condemnation of *all* possible forces of wickedness in the world that would oppose the execution of his gracious covenantal plan (cf. 28:24–26)' (Wendland 2009:216).

Babylon. There is, however, one problem which calls for examination: why is there no mention of Babylon? The city and the empire of which is formed the centre have already been used as the epitome of the powers of this world ranged against the kingdom of God in Isaiah 13–14. If God's rule is to be established by the overthrow of such hostile powers, why then does Ezekiel's message not highlight Babylon's fate? The answer would seem to be given by the fact that in Ezekiel's day, rather than being ranged against God's purposes, Babylon is the instrument in God's hand for the punishment of his people. Instead Tyre and Egypt—the two nations about whose destiny most is disclosed— are used as the prime illustrations of major powers of this world acting contrary to the will of God. He had determined to punish Judah by means of Babylon, and Tyre and Egypt by their opposition to Babylon are delaying Nebuchadnezzar's advance and his execution of the role which has been divinely assigned to him. Furthermore, there may be some validity in the suggestion that 'Tyre symbolizes Babylon itself, for all through its long history Babylon had been one of the greatest commercial centres of the world. ... If all Tyre's riches and commerce and the power that riches can buy could not save her in the hour of her need, then Babylon would equally go down to her fate, when her hour had struck' (Ellison 1956:100).

---

2. As noted earlier, it may be that seven was additionally associated with hostility towards Israel in that there were seven Canaanite nations which had to be defeated before Israel could occupy the land (Deut. 7:1).

A. Against the Ammonites (25:1-7)

No date is provided for the material in this chapter, but the background to the oracles presupposes the fall of Jerusalem in 586 B.C. Moreover, mention of Ammon and Moab as unscathed and acting in the manner described suggests a time before 582 when, as Josephus records, Nebuchadnezzar's fourth campaign into this area wiped Ammon and Moab out of existence (*Ant.* 10.181).

The area controlled by the Ammonites to the east of the Jordan lacked natural frontiers and varied somewhat in extent over the centuries. Traditionally their territory was bounded on the east by the Arabian Desert and on the north by Gilead, so that it lay roughly in the area of modern Jordan, the name of whose capital, Amman, reflects that of the ancient kingdom. The Ammonites had a blood connection with the Israelites through Lot (Gen. 19:36-38), but despite that (or because of it?) the history of relations between the two peoples was one of bitter conflict. Moreover, half the traditional territory of the Ammonites had been allocated to the tribe of Gad (Josh. 13:24-25), and this led to disputes with the tribes on the east bank of the Jordan. Jephthah, Saul, and David all engaged in warfare against the Ammonites (Judg. 10:7-11:33; 1 Sam. 11; 2 Sam. 8:12; 10:1-11:1; 12:26-31). Though David annexed the country (2 Sam. 10-12), the Ammonites regained their independence later. During Ahab's reign, Ammon and Israel were part of a Levantine coalition which checked the advance of Assyria at Qarqar in 853 B.C. By the time of Uzziah and Jotham, Ammon was again paying tribute to Judah (2 Chron. 26:8; 27:5). However, Amos condemned the Ammonites for the atrocities they committed in seeking to extend their territory northwards into Gilead (Amos 1:13-15; cf. Jer. 49:1; Zeph. 2:8-11).

The Ammonites submitted to Nebuchadnezzar in his sweep south after the battle of Carchemish in 605 B.C. However, their loyalty was variable. They aided the Babylonians against Jehoiakim in 598, yet they joined the intrigue against Babylon a few years later (Jer. 27:3). After the fall of Jerusalem they accepted refugees from Judah, and Baalis, king of Ammon, was involved in the assassination of Gedaliah, the Babylonian appointee as governor of Judah (Jer. 40:14). Their continuing anti-Babylonian stance led to their overthrow in 582. Whereas Jeremiah 49:6 predicts a restoration for the Ammonites, Ezekiel makes no mention of this, and later appearances of Ammonites probably refer to other peoples who moved into their devastated territory.

AGAINST THE AMMONITES

^{25:1}And the word of the LORD came to me, saying, ^{25:2}'Son of man, set your face towards the Ammonites, and prophesy against them, ^{25:3}and say to the Ammonites, "Hear the word of the Lord GOD. Thus says the Lord GOD: Because you said 'Aha!' against my sanctuary when it was profaned, and against the land of Israel when it was desolated, and against the house of Judah when they went into exile, ^{25:4}therefore, behold, I am about to give you to the people of the east as a possession, and they will place their encampments among you, and they will set their dwellings among you; they ⌊are the ones who⌋ will eat your fruit and drink your milk. ^{25:5}And I will set Rabbah as a pasture for camels and ⌊the city of⌋ the Ammonites as a resting place for flocks. And you will know that I ⌊am⌋ the LORD. ^{25:6}For thus says the Lord GOD: Because you clapped ⌊your⌋ hands and pounded with ⌊your⌋ feet, and rejoiced with all your scorn in ⌊your⌋ heart against the land of Israel, ^{25:7}therefore, behold, I ⌊am the one who⌋ shall stretch out my hand against you and shall give you ⌊as⌋ plunder for the nations and shall cut you off from the peoples and shall make you perish from the lands. I will destroy you; and you will know that I ⌊am⌋ the LORD." '

♦ **25:1–2** The chapter began with the message-reception formula and the LORD's distinctive address to Ezekiel, **Son of man.** In this way Ezekiel made clear that his message was divinely authorised, and not the product of mere nationalistic zeal on his part. **Set your face towards** occurred in eight other places with various prepositions (cf. 6:2) to indicate that the prophet was to dramatise his presentation by turning in the direction of the country named and by looking towards it with a stern countenance as he denounced those involved. **The Ammonites** was literally, 'the sons of Ammon', which was the regular form of the nation's name in both biblical and extra-biblical sources, though it is uncertain why.

♦ **25:3** Unlike the other peoples mentioned in this chapter who were only talked about, the Ammonites were to be addressed by the prophet (at least in dramatic form). **Because** also introduced other accusations of hostility towards Israel in 25:6, 8, 12, 15, with 'therefore' subsequently marking the transition to divine condemnation (cf. 5:8).[3]

---

3. 'The "because—therefore" sequence occurs earlier in the Book of Ezekiel: against Jerusalem (5:7–19; 16:36–37); against false prophets and diviners (13:8, 22–23); and against Israel (22:19–22). Now the same standard operates against the foreign nations' (Raabe 2010:198).

Various second person pronominal forms were employed in this oracle. The initial injunction, **Hear**, and also the closing 'then you will know' (25:5), were masculine plural in form (as was the introductory 'against them', 25:2). However, elsewhere in 25:3–5 'you' was feminine singular, possibly because 'the sons of Ammon' was regarded as virtually the designation of a land, which would be treated as feminine in Hebrew, or, more probably, because mention of the capital city of Rabbah (a feminine form) determined the way those being addressed are viewed. Rabbah was the only city in their territory mentioned in the Old Testament. Even so, in 25:6–7, 'you' switched to masculine singular forms, perhaps addressing the king of Ammon as the representative of the nation.

The attitude of the Ammonites towards Jerusalem reflected the period after the capture of the city. It is evident that Ezekiel did not insert these oracles into his prophecy at this point for strictly chronological reasons, but because of their thematic significance. The three clauses of the indictment against the Ammonites related to their continuing malicious relish at the fate of Judah (cf. 21:28–29). **Aha!** (cf. 26:2; 36:2) gave vent to their sense of satisfaction and gloating, while **against** conveyed the hostility which characterised their attitude.[4] This was fundamentally a religious perception. **Profaned** (cf. 13:19) expressed the defilement of the **sanctuary** through intrusion and destruction (cf. 24:21). Because of ancient associations between the prosperity of a land and the power and influence of its god, Ammonite vaunting over Jerusalem was effectively a dismissal of the God of the land as they rejoiced in their impression that the LORD's incapacity had been exposed and his purposes for his people had been stymied. Because the Ammonites had interacted with Israel over the centuries, they were aware of the basic tenets of Israel's faith, even in its later popular degraded form—and now they considered it to have been exposed as worthless. **The land of Israel** (cf. 7:2) did not just refer to the north, but to the whole of the Promised Land (cf. 9:9), whereas **the house of Judah** focused on the people of the south. Both had suffered severely.

♦ **25:4 Therefore** introduced the LORD's verdict against the gloating of the Ammonites. *I am about to give you* revealed his determination to

---

4. The preposition used three times in this verse is '*el* which may be rendered more neutrally as 'towards' or 'over'. However, its use had increasingly overlapped with that of *'al*, 'against', and the use of the latter preposition in 25:7 suggests that a hostile sense is intended here also.

weaken Ammon, either by undermining their national resolve or by depriving them of resources, so that they could not effectively resist aggression. They would shortly be dominated by *the people* (lit., 'sons') *of the east*, or Qedemites, groups of nomads who inhabited the Arabian desert and who were always ready to exploit any weakness among more settled peoples to their west. In Ezekiel's day they had expanded into Edom and presented an on-going threat to Moab. References to tents and camels supports this identification, as does Jeremiah's use of the phrase 'the sons of the east' (Jer. 49:28). Throughout this verse the feminine *you* related to the land of Ammon whose ownership would be transferred into the *possession* of these nomadic tribes. The Ammonites would therefore no longer control their traditional territory, but would have to live with nomadic *encampments* dominating the land. An encampment would have only rudimentary protection, perhaps a low stone wall, more to guard against marauding animals and to prevent their own livestock from wandering than to protect against enemy attack. The intruders would also *set their dwellings* or 'pitch their tents' throughout the land in less formal settlements. As they spread over and controlled the land, they would not hesitate to appropriate its resources. *Fruit* here stood for the agricultural produce of the land in general, and *milk* would have been a major element in the diet of these wandering herdsmen.

♦ **25:5** The destruction of the Ammonite capital was presented in parallel lines. The full title of the capital was 'Rabbah of the sons of Ammon' (see on 21:20 for its location). The LORD declared that he *will set* it as ground where camels would graze and as a place where flocks would be penned for their safety. This described a return to unsettled wilderness conditions.

As a consequence of this invasion and devastation, it was foretold that *you will know that I ⌊am⌋ the LORD.* 'You' was now masculine plural, presumably in reference to the Ammonites themselves, who would have no option but to recognise the sovereignty of the LORD in their affairs when his predicted penalty was imposed upon them.

♦ **25:6** Though the messenger formula, *thus says the Lord GOD*, marked the beginning of a second oracle against Ammon, it was closely connected to what had preceded as the initial *for* indicated. The impending catastrophe would be the result of the LORD's verdict on their conduct, which was described in general terms and cannot be identified with any specific event. 'You' was now masculine singular, and possibly addressed the king of Ammon, who as the representative of his people had taken the lead in expressing the glee they felt at Judah's overthrow. ***You clapped ⌊your⌋ hands***[5] was a gesture of pleasure (cf. 6:11), and you ***pounded with your feet*** (cf. 6:11) indicated approval. Such outward manifestations of satisfaction displayed how they ***rejoiced with all your scorn in ⌊your⌋ heart against the land of Israel.*** 'Heart' renders *nepeš*, 'soul', which described their whole inner being (cf. 24:21). The root behind 'scorn' (*šā'aṭ*) occurred only in Ezekiel (also 25:15; 36:5; but for a similar root, see on 16:57), and indicated a contemptuous dismissal. 'Spiteful contempt' (REB) and 'malice of heart' (NRSV) attempt to capture the utter malevolence with which they were filled.

♦ **25:7** ***Therefore*** again introduced the LORD's verdict on the behaviour just described. ***Behold***[6] diverted the focus of attention from the conduct of the Ammonites to the intention of the LORD, which he declared in four emphatic clauses, using prophetic perfects (Introduction §6.3b). ***I ⌊am the one who⌋ shall stretch out my hand against you.*** This was an action conveying hostile intent (cf. 6:14). Also the LORD declared that he ***shall give you as plunder***[7] ***for the nations.*** It would not be Judah which would benefit from the overthrow of Ammon, but the Arab invaders. Furthermore, God ***shall cut you off from the peoples.*** Indeed, he ***shall make you perish from the lands.*** This was a verdict of extermination, pronounced on the king ('you' was singular in this verse), but with dire implications for the nation he led.

There then followed an isolated verb, ***I will destroy you.*** It starkly summarised the preceding description and provided the basis for the

---

5. Greenberg (1997:519) notes that this verse contains many Aramaic forms, probably to give dramatic colour to what is ostensibly an address to foreign people. These include the qal infinitive form *maḥ'ăkā*, 'you clapped'.

6. The focus particle *hinənî* is unlikely to be a *futurum instans* ('I am about to stretch out', HCSB) as it is followed not by a participle, but by a perfect (cf. Introduction §6.3c). The force of the perfect *nāṭîtî* may be that of a present perfect 'I have stretched out' (cf. NASB, ESV) and still do stretch out, so that threatened judgement continued to hang over them. Alternatively, this may be an instance of a prophetic perfect where the future action is conceived of as so certain that it is viewed as already complete (Introduction §6.3b). The following perfects with conjunctive *waw* are then to be understood in a similar sense, either as *waw*-consecutive perfects after a virtual future or as a series of verbs with copulative *waw*.

7. The kethib is *ləbag*, but no one can say what that means, and so from the ancient versions onwards the qere *ləbaz*, 'as plunder', has been followed.

concluding recognition formula, *you will know that I ₍am₎ the* LORD. 'You' continued to be masculine singular (unlike the plural in 25:5).

REFLECTION
- *Schadenfreude*, or maliciously deriving pleasure from the misfortunes of another, particularly from the downfall of an enemy, is a frequent human response, but it is one which Scripture condemns. It was not David's attitude towards his opponents (Ps. 35:12–14; cf. Job 29:11–17; 31:29–30) though it was theirs towards him (Ps. 35:15–16). 'When your enemy falls, do not rejoice, and when he stumbles, let not your heart be glad, lest the LORD sees it and it is evil in his eyes, and he turns away his anger from him' (Prov. 24:17–18). 'Falls' here does not refer to falling into sin, but being affected by grievous misfortune (cf. Prov. 24:16). When others suffer, compassion is not to be withdrawn from them no matter who they are (cf. Luke 6:27). If we fail to show kindness to others, our attitude may be more reprehensible in God's sight than any of our enemy's actions. In that case the LORD may turn away his anger from our adversary and direct it against us.

B. Against Moab and Seir (25:8–11)

Moab had blood links with Ammon (Gen. 19:30–38). Its territory was centred on the elevated plateau east of the Dead Sea, with the river Zered to the south, the Dead Sea to the west, and the Arabian Desert to the east. It frequently struggled to control and extend its northern border, often in conflict with Israel (cf. Deut. 23:3–6; Isa. 16:12–14).

Moab had viewed the arrival of the Israelites from Egypt with hostility (Num. 22–25). Though David himself had Moabite connections, he treated the land harshly, forcing them to pay tribute (2 Sam. 8:2). After the break-up of the united kingdom under David and Solomon, Moab enjoyed a period of independence before it was dominated by Omri of Israel. On the death of Ahab, his son and successor, a revolt, with much subsequent skirmishing, permitted another period of autonomy until, in the time of Uzziah, Moab came under the control of Judah for a while, though later it paid tribute to Assyria. In this oracle Moab is treated as subordinate to Ammon, with its fate determined conjointly with it. Moab had been associated with Ammon in helping Nebuchadnezzar against Jehoiakim, yet had been subsequently involved in the anti-Babylonian conference under Zedekiah. It also joined in taunting Jerusalem (Jer. 48:26–35; cf. Zeph. 2:8).

²⁵:⁸Thus says the Lord GOD, 'Because Moab and Seir have said, "Behold, like all the nations ⌊is⌋ the house of Judah," ²⁵:⁹therefore, behold, I am about to open the side of Moab from the cities, from its cities, from its border, the splendour of the land, Beth-hayshimoth, Baal-meon, and Qiryathaim ²⁵:¹⁰to the people of the east along with the Ammonites. And I will give it as a possession that the Ammonites may not be remembered among the nations. ²⁵:¹¹And in Moab I will execute judgements; and they will know that I ⌊am⌋ the LORD.'

♦ **25:8** There is a text critical problem here connected with the words, *because Moab and Seir have said* (lit., 'because of saying of Moab and Seir'). Did 'and Seir' occur in the original manuscripts? 'Seir' usually referred to the land or people of Edom (cf. 35:15). If it was originally present in the text, this would have been the only oracle addressed to two different peoples (though various groups of Philistines were listed in 25:16). Furthermore, Edom was the subject of the following oracle (25:12–14). 'And Seir' did not occur in some early versions (the Septuagint and the old Latin), but it was found in others (the Vulgate, the Peshitta, and the Targum). There are therefore English translations which omit the term (GNB, NLT, NRSV), though many retain it (NASB, NIV, NKJV, ESV). It is far more likely that this surprising term has been deliberately omitted in some versions because it is difficult to see why anyone would have added it. Even so, the significance of 'and Seir' being present here is unclear, and its excision or retention unresolved.

Have said may cover inward speech, that is, thought, as well as outward utterance (cf. 20:32). The words which the LORD attributed to Moab expressed the essence of their attitude and their offence: *Like all the nations ⌊is⌋ the house of Judah.*[8] This dismissed Judah's claim to a special status which set her apart from other countries because of the LORD's covenant with her. It also incorporated a denial of God's power and faithfulness. When the Moabites witnessed the calamities which had come upon Judah and Jerusalem, they concluded that their God had been powerless to avert them. Moreover, events had clearly refuted the claims Israel made of a divinely provided security. The realpolitik of the situation was that Judah like her neighbours had to bow before the might of imperial Babylon, and who her God was

---

8. The LXX expands this to 'the house of Israel and Judah' (an addition found also in some Hebrew manuscripts). While this makes clear the theological, rather than merely political, dimensions of the situation, it is fairly certain to be a secondary expansion.

made no difference to the outcome. But this was a grossly deficient assessment in that it ignored the LORD's claim on the obedience of his people and the reality of his disciplining of their transgression. There was, however, a substantial and uncomfortable element of truth in Moab's perception. There had been a time when becoming like other nations had been just what Israel had wanted (1 Sam. 8:4-7), and ironically that was how Judah had recently been behaving (20:32). So her conduct had violated the covenant, and the LORD's actions against her did in fact treat her just like any other nation. The special relationship no longer worked to her advantage. 'You only have I known of all the families of the earth; therefore I will punish you for all your iniquities' (Amos 3:2). But God's sovereign choice meant that his discipline was a sign of his commitment to the relationship and his determination to preserve it—on his terms.

♦ **25:9** *Therefore* introduced the LORD's verdict on Moab's conduct. *Open the side of Moab* employed military language to describe outflanking Moab's defences. 'Side' may also be used of the slope of a hill, and could allude to the steep descent on the western edge of Moabite territory where it sloped down to the rift valley and the Dead Sea. *From the cities, from its cities,*[9] *from its border* is difficult to explain. 'From' may be used privatively to denote the loss of cities and territory, with the repetition forming an emphatic expression. Alternatively, 'from' may indicate direction, with the scene being one of the complete overthrow of the Moabite cities starting from the very border of its territory. Either way, Moab was to be devastated.

The splendour of the land indicated the most desirable and fruitful locations in Moab, which presumably lay in the plain to the north of the river Arnon. The location of the three cities is tolerably certain. *Beth-hayshimoth* was situated about a thousand feet (305 m) below sea level at a distance of a mile and a half (2.4 km) north-east of where the river Jordan entered the Dead Sea, and guarded the ascent to the much higher plateau of Medeba where the other two cities were set. *Baal-meon* (cf. Num. 32:38; 1 Chron. 5:8; and with a somewhat different designation, Josh. 13:17; Jer. 48:23) lay five miles (8 km) south-west of the capital, Medeba, about eight miles (13 km) east of the Dead Sea. *Qiryathaim*[10] (also transliterated as Kiriathaim, a dual

---

9. The phrase 'from its cities' is omitted in LXX, and this is followed by NRSV and NIV.

10. The kethibh, *qiryātmâ*, represents a defective spelling of the name while the qere has the usual spelling, *qiryātáymâ*.

form perhaps meaning 'double city') probably was located six miles (10 km) west of Medeba. The Mesha Stele implied that an important shrine dedicated to the Moabite god Chemosh was situated there (*COS* 2.23). These three cities were not in the Moabite heartland between the Zered and the Arnon, but further north in the territory which had been assigned to Reuben. However, by Ezekiel's time they had for centuries been under the control of Moab. They may be mentioned as places which an army attacking from the north would first capture.

♦ **25:10** The initial phrase of the verse, *to the people of the east along with the Ammonites*, is better taken as the conclusion of the preceding verse. It would thus indicate that Moab was also going to be laid open to depredations from the same desert tribes as Ammon had been (25:4). *And I will give it* (feminine, presumably the land of Moab) *as a possession* (cf. 25:4) for the invaders to hold. *So that the Ammonites may not be remembered among the nations*[11] marked their absence from the pages of subsequent history. The switch to the mention of the Ammonites reflected their political hegemony over Moab during this period. Moab disappeared from the pages of history during the period of Babylonian ascendancy.

♦ **25:11** *And in Moab I will execute judgements. And they will know that I ⌐am⌐ the LORD.* The LORD would not tolerate Moab's dismissal of him and their disparagement of his purposes. Through the imposition of his judgement (cf. 5:10), they would have to reckon with the reality of his existence and control, especially in his character as the God of the covenant who is directing the affairs of earth to accomplish his ends for his people.

REFLECTION
- Judging by appearances frequently proves erroneous, and nowhere more so than in spiritual matters. Moab was incapable of distinguishing between the LORD utterly abandoning his people and the LORD severely chastising them because of their sin. The Moabites therefore concluded that Judah was no different from any other nation (25:8)—and in terms of worldly criteria, who can blame

---

11. There is a marked lack of agreement between the third person singular verb, *tizzākēr*, 'she will be remembered', and the masculine plural subject, 'the sons of Ammon'. Presumably this title 'the sons of Ammon' was so frequently used for the nation (cf. 25:1) that there was no great difficulty in understanding the feminine noun 'land' as occurring before it. Alternatively the reference may be to the capital, 'Rabbah of the sons of Ammon'.

them for reaching that conclusion? But outward appearances may be deceptive. With good reason the prophet Micah had represented Jerusalem, when she came to her senses in captivity, as saying, 'Rejoice not over me, my enemy' (Mic. 7:8–10). She submitted to bearing the LORD's indignation against her for her sin, but waited for divine deliverance. Jeremiah also recorded the difference which the LORD made between his treatment of Jacob, his servant, and his dealings with other nations. 'I will make an end to all the nations where I have driven you, but of you I will not make an end; and I will correct you with judgement, and I will not let you go entirely unpunished' (Jer. 46:28).

C. Against Edom (25:12–14)

While these prophecies against the nations make no mention of Babylon (cf. Introduction to 25:1–32:32 above), they do mention Edom. Not much is known about its internal affairs, but it represents the world's bitter hostility to the people of God (Amos 1:11). However, the brief treatment here (as distinct from ch. 35) suggests that Edom did not pose a major threat to Judah before the fall of Jerusalem. This would fit in with the current archaeological perception that it was only a unified kingdom with a centralised administration during the period of Assyrian dominance, when it was a vassal of Assyria. When that empire collapsed, Edom probably reverted to a looser, tribal form of organisation.

Edomite territory lay in the mountainous terrain south and southeast of Judah on both sides of the rift valley south of the Dead Sea, bordering on Moab at the river Zered to the north and stretching as far south as the Gulf of Aqaba. The name Edom means 'red' and refers to the red sandstone of their hills. More closely kin to Israel than either Ammon or Moab, the Edomites were descendants of Jacob's twin brother Esau, who had taken control of the area even before Jacob returned from Paddan-Aram (Gen. 32:3; 36:5–8). There was frequent hostility between the peoples which continued the tension between the twins Jacob and Esau even when they were still in their mother's womb (Gen. 25:21–23).

At the time of the Exodus Edom refused to grant the Israelites the right of passage through their territory (Num. 20:14–21). Saul defeated Edom (1 Sam. 14:47), and David subsequently brought Edom under Israelite control with considerable loss of life (2 Sam. 8:13–14). However, during Solomon's reign the Edomites struggled against

Israel and became independent (1 Kgs. 11:14–25). To regain control of the trade routes through Arabia and especially through the Red Sea port of Ezion-geber (Elath), Ahab of Israel and Jehoshaphat of Judah again reduced the Edomites to vassal status (1 Kgs. 22:47; 2 Kgs. 3:9), but this subjugation was short-lived (2 Kgs. 8:20–22). Although Edom had participated in Zedekiah's conference (Jer. 27:3), when the Babylonians arrived, they quickly changed sides and engaged in looting the fallen city. This treachery motivated expressions of outrage (Obad. 11–14; Ps. 137:7; Lam. 4:21), though some fugitives from Jerusalem found refuge there (Jer. 40:11). Subsequent Babylonian pressure to control the trade routes through Arabia forced the Edomites from their traditional territory (cf. Mal. 1:3–4), and many moved into what had been southern Judah, where the name Idumea perpetuated their memory.

> [25:12]Thus says the Lord GOD, 'Because Edom acted by taking vengeance against the house of Judah, and has incurred great guilt in that they avenged themselves on them, [25:13]therefore thus says the Lord GOD, "I will stretch out my hand against Edom, and will cut off from it man and animal. And I will set it a heap of ruins from Teman, and to Dedan they will fall by the sword. [25:14]And I will set my vengeance upon Edom by the hand of my people Israel, and they will do in Edom according to my anger and according to my fury. And they will know my vengeance, declares the Lord GOD." '

♦ **25:12** ***Edom acted*** (lit., 'did'; cf. 25:14) ***by taking vengeance*** (*nāqam*) employed the cognate accusative construction 'avenging vengeance' (cf. 24:8). It was not specified how or when this had occurred, but it evidently referred to deliberate atrocities perpetrated in connection with the fall of Jerusalem. The divine verdict on Edom's conduct was that they ***incurred great guilt***[12] ***in that they took revenge***[13] ***on them***. When individuals or nations seek 'revenge' or 'vengeance', they generally claim to be seeking no more than what is rightfully due from one who has wronged their interests. However, human vengeance is frequently intensified and distorted by pent-up

---

12. In *wayye'šəmû 'āšôm*, 'they incurred great guilt', the infinitive absolute intensifies the extent of their blameworthiness.

13. The verb *wəniqqəmû* is not the expected *waw*-consecutive imperfect which would have implied that the taking of vengeance occurred next in sequence after they had incurred great guilt. Instead the clause functions epexegetically to identify their great guilt as being incurred in the very act of taking vengeance.

resentment and loss of self-control, and so vengeance is generally viewed negatively. Certainly individual imposition of revenge is condemned in Scripture. 'Do not say, "I will pay back evil"; wait for the LORD, and he will save you' (Prov. 20:22; cf. Prov. 24:28–29). However, there must also be taken into account the divine dimension to vengeance (see on 25:14).

♦ **25:13** *Therefore* marked the sequence whereby Edom's sin evoked divine displeasure and punishment, and the repeated messenger formula specified the divine origin of what would be imposed. *I will stretch out my hand against Edom* (cf. 25:7). Both man and beast would be wiped out when the LORD acted against Edom. *I will set it a heap of ruins* (*horbâ*) *from Teman* indicated physical devastation of the infrastructure of the land. Teman means 'south' or 'southern land', and may have been used to refer to the whole of Edom, particularly the area near its capital, Bozrah, so that the whole land would be engulfed from its centre outwards. *To Dedan they will fall by the sword,* with last word 'sword' (*ḥereb*) incorporating a play on the earlier 'heap of ruins'. Military invasion would lead to ruthless slaughter. Dedan is commonly identified as a major oasis on the trade route to Yemen, three hundred miles (480 km) south-east of Teman. If this identification is correct, it was not really under Edomite control and it may be mentioned more as a conventional place, a picture of their enemies' pursuit of the fleeing Edomites deep into the desert. Many modern translations depart from the punctuation of the Massoretic Text and read, 'And I will set it a heap of ruins; from Teman even to Dedan they will fall by the sword.' This would fit in with the suggestion based on Jeremiah 49:7–8 where Teman and Dedan are mentioned together, that the latter was also the name of a town in Edom, perhaps settled by people from Dedan.

♦ **25:14** However, *I will set my vengeance upon Edom* introduced the reality of divine vengeance which would be imposed as God's just retribution on wrongdoers. One of the reasons for merely human vengeance being prohibited in Scripture is that it infringes the sovereign rights of the LORD. In his capacity as king (which included that of a judge) it is his prerogative to demand an account from those who transgress his laws. 'Vengeance is mine' (Deut. 32:35).

In this instance, *by the hand of my people Israel* disclosed that the people of God would be involved as the instruments through whom he imposed his vengeance. A similar role reversal was foreshadowed in Obadiah 15 and 18, and would have given encouragement to the defeated and dispirited exiles that they would once more have a significant part to play in God's purposes. Since the historical record shows that it was Arabs, not Israelites, who eventually devastated Edom, it would seem that the prophet's perspective stretched forwards to the final overthrow of the enemies of God and his people. In *according to my anger and according to my fury*, the repetition of the personal pronoun 'my' (five times in total in this verse) accords with the view that what was contemplated was not a further oscillation in the politics of the region, but the final divine resolution of affairs. This is probably not to be thought of as consummated in the course of current history, but as part of the grand divine restoration which has already been anticipated in 16:60–62 (cf. 34:25; 37:26).

The oracle concluded with a modified form of the recognition formula, *they will know my vengeance*, followed by the signature formula confirming the divine prediction. The Edomites would experience the LORD's penalty on their behaviour and in this way would be forced to acknowledge his sovereignty.

REFLECTION

- Merely human revenge is ugly, high-handed, and often ill-informed. It is virtually synonymous with injustice, unbridled cruelty, and atrocities. So it is necessary to remember that the injunctions, 'Repay no one evil for evil … Beloved, never avenge yourselves, but give place to the wrath ⌊of God⌋, for it is written, "Vengeance is mine; I will repay, says the Lord" ' (Rom. 12:17, 19), remain valid.

    Divine vengeance is not, however, tainted with all that degrades human revenge, because it proceeds from one who is both just and all-knowing. Vengeance is part of God's intrinsic reaction to the sinful rebellion of mankind. He must assert his rights over against human violation of them. The retributive justice of God demands that sin be punished, no less in the New Testament than in the Old.[14] It was Jesus himself who spoke about 'days of vengeance' which would fulfil all that is written' (Luke 21:22). The time is steadily approaching when 'the Lord Jesus is revealed from heaven with his mighty angels, in flaming fire taking vengeance on those who do not know God and on those who do not obey the gospel of our Lord Jesus' (2 Thess. 1:7–8).

---

14. For a more extended study of divine vengeance, see Peels 2003:72–86.

D. Against the Philistines (25:15-17)

The Philistine pentapolis was located in south-western Palestine. Gaza, Ashdod and Ashkelon were port cities near the shore of the Mediterranean, while Ekron and Gath were situated further inland on the coastal plain. The region straddled the trade route between Egypt to the south, and Damascus and Mesopotamia to the north. The Philistines themselves were descendants of the Sea Peoples, who had maintained trading settlements in the area from the time of the patriarchs (Gen. 21:34; 26:1). However, in the thirteenth century B.C. a major influx of the Sea Peoples invaded the area from Asia Minor and then settled there, adopting much from Canaanite religion and practices. While the Philistines were hostile to Israel, they were by no means uncultured as the use of their name often suggests.

The Philistines had exerted pressure on Israel, to the point of threatening their continuing existence, both after the destruction of Shiloh (1 Sam. 4-6) and again on the death of Saul (1 Sam. 31). However, their menace was effectively neutralised by David (2 Sam. 5:17-25), though they preserved their identity for centuries. There is no evidence that they acted against Judah when the Babylonians advanced. Indeed, Philistine cities seem to have suffered at this time (Jer. 47), with the rulers of Gaza, Ashdod and Ashkelon being deported by Nebuchadnezzar in 604 B.C. Though the weakened Philistine cities played no part in the Jerusalem conference of 593 B.C. (Jer. 27), we do not know of any specific grievance which Judah might have had against them at this time. Complaints against them may just be a carry-over from the past such as when the Philistines were associated with Edom, Moab, and Ammon as enemies of Israel (Isa. 11:14).

The oracle against the Philistines has the same tripartite structure as the preceding oracles. The messenger formula introduces an indictment, beginning 'because' (25:15), followed by an announcement of the divine verdict against them, beginning 'therefore' (25:16-17a). The oracle concludes with a form of the recognition formula (25:17b).

> 25:15Thus says the Lord GOD, 'Because the Philistines acted vengefully and took vengeance with scorn in ⌊their⌋ heart, to destroy ⌊with⌋ perpetual enmity, 25:16therefore thus says the Lord GOD, "Behold I am about to stretch out my hand against the Philistines, and I will cut off the Kerethites, and I will destroy the remnant of the seacoast. 25:17And I will execute

great acts of vengeance on them with furious rebukes. And they will know that I ⌊am⌋ the LORD when I put my vengeance on them."'

♦ **25:15** There were many resemblances between these two verses and the preceding oracle against Edom. Neither contained any great detail. The Philistines had been organised in five independent cities, and so *the Philistines* did not refer to a single state, but to the various groups collectively. *Acted vengefully* (lit., 'in/with vengeance') *and took vengeance* involved a threefold repetition of the one root, *nāqam* (cf. 25:12),[15] which emphasised how intent they were on paying off old scores. *With scorn in ⌊their⌋ heart* (cf. 25:6) also portrayed the disparaging malevolence that motivated their attacks when Judah was overwhelmed by the Babylonians. *To destroy with perpetual enmity* (cf. 35:5) showed that it was not recent events which had stirred up Philistine animosity against Judah.

♦ **25:16** *Therefore* again marked the onset of the inevitable repercussions on such behaviour as *the Lord GOD* intervened in the situation with the authority that is his as supreme ruler of all and with the concern for his people that is encapsulated in his covenant name Yahweh (represented by GOD in this combination of epithets; see on 2:4). The three verbs of his pronouncement reflected those found in 25:7. *I am about to stretch out my hand against the Philistines* expressed the LORD's intention to take hostile action against them (cf. 25:13). *I will cut off the Kerethites* (*wəhikrattî ʾet-kərētîm*). The name Kerethites referred to another group of the Sea Peoples closely related to the Philistines. The distinction between them was probably no longer evident in Ezekiel's day, but the old designation provided scope for word play with the accompanying verb. As in Zephaniah 2:5, a third group from the Sea Peoples were also identified. *The remnant of the seacoast* described them as having also settled along the Mediterranean coast of Palestine. *I will destroy* decreed that they too would meet a similar end. Indeed, by New Testament times the Philistines had completely vanished from contemporary records.

♦ **25:17** The focus on divine action against the Philistines continued from the previous verse and developed the retributive equivalence of the penalty the LORD would impose on their behaviour. Twice more

---

15. 'Acted vengefully' is *wayyinnāqəmû nāqām* (cf. *IBHS* §23.2.1 for the use of the niphal with an internal accusative). There are two further occurrences of the root in 25:17.

the term *vengeance* occurred (cf. 25:15), but now it was specifically *my vengeance* (25:12) which was under consideration, which would take the form of *great acts of vengeance* (lit., 'great vengeances') and *furious rebukes* or 'chastisements'.[16]

Yet again the recognition formula emphasised that when the LORD resolved to act in retribution against his enemies, they would be left in no doubt as to who it was that was at work in their demise.

REFLECTION

- 'Enmity' (25:15) is the same term as was employed in Genesis 3:15 when the LORD God said to the serpent, 'I will put enmity between you and the woman, and between your seed and her seed.' Not only was the term the same, the attitude of the Philistines was a specific instance of that age-long animosity. Satanic hostility reached its greatest intensity at the time of the crucifixion. Though it is now checked, it remains virulent until the consummation. 'The God of peace will soon crush Satan under your feet' (Rom. 16:20).

E. Against Tyre (26:1–28:19)

The focus of the oracles now switches from the preceding, brief messages regarding Judah's near neighbours to more extended treatments of Tyre (76 verses) and Egypt (97 verses), the two major nations which continued to oppose Nebuchadnezzar after the fall of Jerusalem.

Location and History of Tyre. Tyre (*ṣôr*), whose name signifies 'a rock' (*ṣûr*), was situated on a craggy island of about 40 acres (16 ha) which lay 0.5 miles (800 m) off the Mediterranean coast, about 30 miles (48 km) north of mount Carmel, in an area corresponding to the south of modern Lebanon. The island had two harbours, one facing north and the other south, and was in a highly advantageous situation for maritime trading. At its peak the city may have held a population of 30,000 in its densely packed site. Tyre enjoyed considerable security, not only from its off-shore location but also from the massive fortifications round the island. Furthermore, there was an earlier settlement on the mainland, known as Ushu in Egyptian and Assyrian texts, and as ancient Tyre to the Romans. Mainland Tyre kept the island city supplied with water and natural resources. It was Ushu which would be taken and devastated by external aggression.

---

16. The phrase is omitted in the LXX, but it is typical of Ezekiel's style.

Tyre was a Phoenician settlement. The Phoenicians were not a unified nation, but a series of city states characterised by their interest in trading around the Mediterranean Sea. Initially Sidon, 25 miles (40 km) further north, was the more prominent city, but Tyre became dominant after 1200 B.C.

Tyre played a major role in the commerce of the ancient Near East. Its craftsmen and artisans produced luxury items, including the well-known purple dye, which they traded for raw materials. They also exported timber from the hills of Lebanon, built ships, and were master mariners who amassed great wealth as merchants and middlemen in the trade flows throughout the Mediterranean and its hinterland. The Phoenicians, and particularly the Tyrians, established many coastal colonies around the Mediterranean, most notable of which was Carthage, Rome's arch-enemy in north Africa, but their zone of influence extended at least as far as Spain. These colonies were largely trading depots, for the Phoenicians were not interested in building up a land-based empire, whether near or far.

Since the Phoenicians were disinterested in military conquest of neighbouring peoples, and since the Israelites were largely averse to seafaring, there is no record of warfare between Tyre and Israel. Indeed, in the time of David and Solomon good relationships had been established, probably influenced by David's defeat of the Philistines who had competed with the Phoenicians as traders. Hiram of Tyre assisted Solomon in the construction of the Temple (1 Kgs. 5). Later, however, the religion of the northern kingdom was debased through the impact of alliances with Phoenicia (e.g., 1 Kgs. 16:30–33).

Because of its wealth and commercial significance, Tyre was a lucrative prize for invaders. Though it was never captured by the Assyrians, the stranglehold they established over its land-based supply lines compelled it to negotiate and come to an arrangement with Assyria. A similar outcome prevailed when, beginning shortly after the fall of Jerusalem, Nebuchadnezzar besieged Tyre for thirteen years, for he too was unable to capture the island fortress. However, the attrition of the prolonged siege exhausted the Tyrians and forced them into subjection to Babylon. A king favourably inclined to Babylon was installed and kept under close supervision. Archaeological evidence shows that Tyre, however, continued to exist and to engage in trading.

As a detached island, Tyre resisted capture until the arrival of Alexander the Great in 332 B.C. He overwhelmed the mainland settlements and used the fabric of their buildings to construct a stone causeway out to the island. This enabled him to overcome the island's defences. Over subsequent centuries there was a gradual build-up of silt along this causeway, so that Tyre became permanently linked to the mainland through the formation of a peninsula. After the fall of Tyre, Sidon regained its former prominence, but Tyre itself continued to exist and was still a leading city and port in Roman times. By the late twelfth century A.D. it had been captured by Muslim forces and obliterated.

Structure. The most significant structural indicator is the presence of the message-reception formula in 26:1; 27:1; 28:1, 11. This suggests four major blocks of material, which may be further analysed as consisting of two parallel oracles, one against the city (26:1–21) and the other against its king (28:1–10), each of which is followed by a lament, over Tyre (27:1–36) and over the king of Tyre (28:11–19). The recurrence of 'dire terror' in 26:21; 27:36; 28:19 reinforces the appropriateness of this analysis to some extent.

It is also possible to use the occurrence of the messenger formula in 26:7, 15, 19 to divide the initial oracle into four segments, and in this way to reckon that there are seven oracles in total, so that their number reflects the complete destruction which is foretold for the city. (See the Introduction to chs. 25–32.)

Biblical Connections. Tyre is also the subject of prophetic diatribes in Isaiah 23, Joel 3:4–8, Amos 1:9–10, and Zechariah 9:2–4. In the New Testament many features of this section are echoed in John's description of the fall of Babylon, e.g., throwing of dust on the head (27:30, compare Rev. 18:19), an end to music and dancing (26:13; Rev. 18:22), cry of amazement (27:32; Rev. 18:18), and especially the lists of luxury items (cf. 27:12–25), though the inventory of Revelation 18:11–13 is updated to fit later trading patterns.

(1) Four Oracles against Tyre (26:1–21)

Since chapter 27 clearly consists of a separate oracle, it is appropriate to consider the four sections of this chapter together. They portray various aspects of Tyre's downfall. In the first section (26:1–6) the reason for Tyre's punishment is set out in terms of her exultant glee over Jerusalem's fall—a basis for condemnation which is similar to that found in the four oracles of chapter 25. This provides the background for the subsequent, more detailed sections. The second oracle (26:7–14) sets out the role Nebuchadnezzar will play in the downfall of Tyre: he will act as the agent of the LORD, wreak havoc on the city, and massacre its inhabitants. The reaction to the fall and devastation of Tyre from its many trading contacts around the Mediterranean is then dramatised in the form of a lament they will utter (26:15–18). The concluding oracle (26:19–21) sums up the finality of the sentence imposed on Tyre when the LORD completely wipes it out.

Fulfilment of Prophecy. This passage has proved to be a key text in discussions about the nature of biblical prophecy. The standard critical interpretation argues that 26:1–14 predicts that Tyre will be taken by Nebuchadnezzar, that he will carry off much plunder from it, and that he will utterly obliterate its site. It is also contended that, after this forecast proves to be wrong, sixteen years later Ezekiel presents a correction and apology in 29:17–20, in which plunder from Egypt is offered as compensation for what had not been pillaged from Tyre.

There are many who consider that this situation falsifies the doctrines of Scripture inspiration and infallibility. Others, while not denying the divine origin of Scripture, consider that the passage challenges the traditional Christian understanding of the nature of biblical prophecy. It is argued that prophetic genuineness did not depend on unvarying accuracy of prediction. 'The emphasis is not on God's ability to let his people know beforehand what would happen, but on his power to change world history for the sake of his people' (Renz 2000:21). 'The prophet foretold what God actually intended at the time, but subsequently recounted that God settled for a lesser outcome, despite the fact that he could have enforced fulfilment had he wished to do so' (Udd 2005:36). These approaches are, however, in apparent tension with the requirements of Deuteronomy 18:22, 'when a prophet speaks in the name of the LORD, if the word does not come to pass or come true, that is a word that the LORD has not spoken.'

Moreover, there are a number of further considerations which support the traditional view of the interpretation of prophecy. For instance, prophecy is not to be conceived of as simply history written beforehand. What is revealed is not set against a dated timeline and described in prosaic detail. The language employed uses stock metaphor and a generic, impressionistic style of presentation, which is not properly interpreted by uniformly seeking a one-to-one correspondence between the hyperbolic and allusive scenario of the prophecy and the facts of history. But the definite mention of Nebuchadnezzar in 26:7 militates against treating the whole of this passage in such a generalised fashion.

Furthermore, many prophecies which seem to be absolute in their nature are in fact uttered with an implicit condition: 'This will happen if you do not do something (generally, repent)'. This is not an unwarranted imposition on the text to make it fit the facts of history. Rather it recognises the intrinsic nature of prophetic communication. It is not to provide a preview of history to satisfy human curiosity, but to induce spiritual change. The analogy with Nineveh in the days of Jonah may be adduced, where the repentance of the city modifies the stark and seemingly absolute warning of 'Yet forty days and Nineveh will be overthrown' (Jonah 3:4). Again, there is the categoric warning to Hezekiah of his impending death (Isa. 38:1) which, after his repentance, is commuted to an additional fifteen years of life (Isa. 38:5). The divine logic behind this is clearly spelled out in Jeremiah 18:5–10. For the relevance of conditionality to the interpretation of the prophecies against Tyre, see the Reflection on 26:7–14.

Another approach to prophetic interpretation argues that the view presented to the prophet's inner eye frequently involves flattening the time perspective on future events so that it is not possible to distinguish the precise temporal interrelationships of what is foretold. The classic example of this is Christ's address in the Nazareth synagogue (Luke 4:16–30) where he separates into two what had seemed originally to be a seamless Messianic prophecy from Isaiah 61:1–7. By stopping the reading after 'to proclaim the year of the Lord's favour', Jesus is able to announce, 'Today this Scripture has been fulfilled in your hearing', and to postpone the following line, 'and the day of vengeance of our God' until his Second Coming.

Taking the possibility of a multi-staged fulfilment into account, this prophecy concerning Tyre may be understood as a meaningful and accurate communication to Ezekiel and his original audience regarding divine opposition to Tyre and the judgement which would be imposed on it. That this doom did not occur immediately does not falsify or undermine the prophecy (see on 29:17–20). Enough did happen to corroborate the LORD's intention and to encourage waiting for complete realisation of the prediction. Multi-staged fulfilment only becomes evident with the benefit of hindsight in the light of subsequent progress in the cumulative process of divine revelation and salvation.

So some features of the prophecies against Tyre are related to Nebuchadnezzar's attack on the city, while others await subsequent fulfilment (Ferguson 2006). In addition to the literary structure of the oracles, Ferguson identifies a further framework (which might be termed a prophetic structure) in the first two oracles, in which two 'they' sections deal with the actions of the 'many nations' against Tyre (26:3-6, 12-14), and surround a centrepiece (26:7-11) that is concerned with Nebuchadnezzar's siege of the city. While this last perspective is largely adopted below as being generally plausible, it must be admitted that no treatment is clear of all difficulties.

(a) Tyre's Destruction (26:1-6)
This oracle follows the same pattern as is found in chapter 25. First, the reason for the LORD's impending action is given in terms of Tyre's misconduct (26:2). This is followed by a statement of the penalty which will be imposed (26:3-6a), and by a concluding recognition formula (26:6b) setting out the LORD's purpose in his action. In this section the aggressors are 'many nations' (26:3), and there is no specific mention of the Babylonians.

> 26:1And it came about in the eleventh year, on the first of the month, ⌊that⌋ the word of the LORD came to me, saying, 26:2'Son of man, because Tyre has said against Jerusalem, "Aha! broken is the gate of the peoples; it has been turned over to me; let me prosper ⌊while⌋ she has been laid waste", 26:3therefore thus says the Lord GOD, "Behold, I ⌊am⌋ against you, O Tyre, and I will bring up many nations against you as the sea brings up its waves. 26:4And they will destroy the walls of Tyre and raze its towers. And I will sweep away its dust from it and set it like bare rock. 26:5It will be a site for spreading nets to dry in the midst of the sea, for I have spoken, declares the Lord GOD, and it will become plunder for the nations. 26:6And her daughters which are in the field will be slain by the sword. And they will know that I ⌊am⌋ the LORD."'

♦ **26:1** *On the first of the month* did not specify which month, and even more puzzling is the fact that, while in the oracle itself Tyre was seen to be rejoicing over Jerusalem's fall, *in the eleventh year* would date this oracle before the fall of the city in the fourth month of the twelfth year of their captivity, with Ezekiel being informed of the capture of Jerusalem in the tenth month of the twelfth year (33:21). Neither textual emendation nor the employment of different dating systems seems to provide an adequate answer. More probable is Greenberg's suggestion (Greenberg 1997:530) that after two years of siege the downfall of Jerusalem was being taken as a foregone conclusion. The absence of a numeral for the month meant that the date could fall between spring 587 and spring 586, with a later date more probable than an earlier one.

♦ **26:2** The LORD informed Ezekiel in his capacity as a prophet (*Son of man*, cf. 2:1) that he was going to act against Tyre because of its hostile disposition towards Jerusalem. Tyre's attitude was one of anticipatory, gloating glee over Jerusalem's coming misfortune. The mocking *Aha!* formed a link with the oracle against Ammon (25:3), which was also reflected here in that in 26:3 this oracle as well took the form of direct address to the nation concerned.

Broken is the gate (lit., 'door leaves'[17]) *of the peoples* may have anticipated the destruction of the literal gates of the city, but it more probably referred to Jerusalem's key location on trade routes used by Tyrian merchants to venture further east (cf. 'wheat from Minnith', 27:17). The perception of Jerusalem as an important staging post may well have been a carry-over from earlier times when Judah's control of the area was greater, rather than what prevailed in the sorry circumstances of Zedekiah's day. Though *it has been turned over to me*[18] could refer to transfer of ownership (cf. Jer. 6:12) of 'it', a feminine form agreeing with the Hebrew gender of 'city', what was in view was not physical occupation of Jerusalem, but control of the trade routes which passed through Judah. With the defeat of the city these would become open to Tyrian exploitation, and her traders would be able to pass through the area without having to pay an additional set of tariffs on their goods.

Tyre's commercial focus was evident in her concluding two statements. Though they were not explicitly connected, it seems clear that *let me prosper* (lit., 'be filled') summarised Tyre's intention to take full trading advantage of the circumstances while *she has been laid waste*, that is, while Jerusalem's power and prestige were devastated. Unlike the earlier condemnation of Ammon, no mention was made of any exultation on Tyre's part because of the destruction of the Temple or the deportation of the people. Tyre's motivation was to extract the maximum profit from any situation, and this was the principal angle from which she assessed the impact of Jerusalem's fall.

---

17. There is a lack of concord between the feminine singular verb *nišbərâ*, 'she/it has been broken', and the feminine plural subject *daltôt*, 'doors of'. There are other instances of such a lack of agreement, probably helped here by the double gates being thought of as a single entity. Alternatively the subject of the verb may be 'she', that is the city, which is then further described as 'the gateway to the peoples' (cf. AV, ASV, NKJV, NLT).

18. The verb may, however, be rendered, 'it has swung open to me' (RSV, NIV, ESV), which would keep the figure of the gate in the foreground, but the meaning is much the same.

♦ **26:3** Tyre's programme for economic advancement had, however, been scrutinised and found wanting. *Therefore thus says the Lord GOD* introduced the divine verdict on Tyre's profiteering self-advancement. The LORD's employment of the opposition formula (5:8), *Behold, I ⌊am⌋ against you, O Tyre*, anticipated his personal intervention to reverse Tyre's expectations and frustrate her trading ambitions. Divine opposition would work itself out through God's control of the political fluctuations in the area. *I will bring up many nations against you as the sea brings up its waves.*[19] Though this statement did not indicate the time scale for such action, it did emphasise the LORD's control over the situation. While 'many nations' could indeed reflect the multinational composition of the imperial army (cf. 'many people', 26:7), the comparison with the force of the sea suggests that what Ezekiel envisioned was not the arrival of a single tsunami wave to crush the city with one blow, but a succession of assaults on it. Ferguson (2006:53) cites a key study of Newsom regarding the metaphor of the waves.

> 'The significant connotation of the phrase "as the sea brings up its waves" is not difficult to define. It is the utter relentlessness of the ocean. No one wave may bring full destruction, but it does not matter. It is the unending succession of waves which destroys even the strongest rock. ... The apparent solidity and security of the island is revealed as an illusion of perspective, not a contradiction of Yahweh's power. Equally, the Babylonian opponents of Tyre, included as the "many nations", are imaged in such a way that they do not appear as independent powers but merely as episodes in Yahweh's patient, powerful sovereignty.' (Newsom 1984:156)

In this way it was apparent from the start that the vision afforded Ezekiel stretched over a long period of time and involved more than Nebuchadnezzar's activity against the city. The comparison with the crashing of the waves was a fitting description of the end of the nation which depended so much on its maritime empire.

♦ **26:4** *They will destroy the walls of Tyre* might possibly have retained 'waves' as its subject, but the plural more probably looked back to the 'many nations'. *Raze its towers* referred to towers placed at intervals on city walls both as lookout posts and as platforms whose height permitted missiles to be hurled further. The island fortress of

---

19. The preposition in *ləgallayw*, 'to its waves', is probably an Aramaic-style marker of an accusative, after a transitive hiphil verb.

Tyre had a massive wall round it incorporating such towers, but they would all be reduced to rubble.

Though the 'many nations' would inflict this destruction on Tyre, they would be acting as instruments of the LORD. He presented himself as being personally involved: *I will sweep away its dust from it.* This was not an act to promote the tidiness of the amenities of the city. The dust stood for the ruins left after the demolition of the city (cf. 26:14) rather than 'soil' (ESV). Presumably the whole island would be scoured clean by the sea. *Set it like bare rock* (cf. 24:7) envisaged no trace of human construction being left as the site of Tyre was returned to its original state. Though 'rock' was not the same term as gave rise to the name of Tyre, the prediction clearly reflected on its name: 'Rock you are and to rock you will return.'

♦ **26:5** Further graphic detail was added to show how completely Tyre would be annihilated. Where once cargoes from the nations had been piled high as merchantmen from throughout the known world brought their wares to trade them, all that would be left was deserted rock. *It will be a site for spreading nets to dry in the midst of the sea.* The offshore island on which Tyre had been erected would remain accessible to fishermen who would use the empty space to dry their nets on its rocks. *For I have spoken, declares the Lord GOD* affirmed the certainty of what was predicted. Moreover, in a clause which was closely connected with the following verse, the LORD asserted that *it will become plunder for the nations.* Those who would conquer Tyre would reap the advantage of pillaging her wealth. This would be just requital for the way in which she had exploited other nations to her own commercial advantage.

♦ **26:6** The downfall of the city would be accompanied by disaster in the territory dependent on Tyre. *And her daughters which are in the field will be slain by the sword.* 'Daughters' was often used to describe economically and politically dependent settlements which arose in the immediate vicinity of a major city (cf. 16:27). Because of Tyre's island situation her 'daughters' were towns and villages 'in the field', that is, on the mainland. When her enemies were frustrated by their inability to capture Tyre, they would vent their vexation on these settlements which could be more easily captured. Here mention of 'the sword' indicated the slaughter of their populations by the invading forces..

The concluding recognition formula, *And they will know that I ⌊am⌋ the LORD,* set out the divine purpose in the imposition of these punishments: the LORD would force Tyre,[20] which vaunted itself on its invulnerability, to acknowledge his sovereign rule. This was the only occurrence of the recognition formula in the prophecies against Tyre whereas it occurred eight times against Egypt and a further eight times elsewhere in this division of the prophecy.

REFLECTION

- 'Aha!' (26:2) gave voice to Tyre's profit-oriented temperament at the removal of a competitor. But in business as in every sphere of life, 'he who is rejoices at disaster [or, calamity] will not go unpunished' (Prov. 17:5). It would only be a matter of months before Tyre itself would experience the rigours of siege warfare. What would then become of her confident assertion, 'Let me prosper while she has been laid waste' (26:2)? Those who 'go into such and such a city and spend a year there and do business and make a profit' have always to be reminded, 'You do not know what tomorrow will bring' (Jas. 4:13–14).
- While faith possesses an indestructible source of confidence in being able to say, 'If God ⌊is⌋ for us, who ⌊can be⌋ against us?' (Rom. 8:31), how dire is the situation of those to whom God says, 'I am against you' (26:3)! Neither the opulence and grandeur of a city like Tyre nor its far-flung fleet would constitute a defence when they incurred the wrath of God by their misconduct. What then will befall our lands which have adopted a post-Christian culture and have thereby provoked the anger of God?

(b) The Intervention of Nebuchadnezzar (26:7–14)

The judgement on Tyre is next presented in even more stark and shattering terms as being imposed by Nebuchadnezzar, the Babylonian emperor, whom God will use as his agent. However, in 26:12 there is a switch from a third person singular description of the aggressor to a plural description, from 'he' and 'his' to 'they'. Those who argue for a multi-stage fulfilment of this prophecy argue this indicates a change in perspective back to that of the first oracle. There is thus a merging of the time horizon in terms of what is disclosed to the prophet.[21]

---

20. Many scholars argue for the recognition formula here being a secondary insertion. Certainly the plural 'they will know' has as its grammatical antecedent the 'daughters' of Tyre rather than Tyre itself, but this does not provide sufficient grounds for rejecting the clause.

21. Such blending of elements from various time frames may be detected, for instance, in Ahijah's prophecy in 1 Kings 14.

AGAINST TYRE 41

²⁶:⁷For thus says the Lord GOD, 'Behold, I am about to bring to Tyre from the north Nebuchadnezzar, king of Babylon, king of kings, with horses, chariots and horsemen, and an assembly and many people. ²⁶:⁸Your daughters in the field he will slay with the sword, and he will set a siege-wall against you, and he will pour out an assault-ramp against you and raise shields against you. ²⁶:⁹The blows of his battering rams he will set against your walls, and your towers he will demolish with his crowbars. ²⁶:¹⁰Because of the abundance of his horses, their dust will cover you; at the noise of his horsemen, wagons, and chariots, your walls will quake as he enters your gates like entrances made into a city that has been breached. ²⁶:¹¹With the hoofs of his horses he will trample all your streets; he will slay your people with the sword and your strong pillars will come down to the ground. ²⁶:¹²They will plunder your wealth and pillage your merchandise and raze your walls and they will demolish your desirable houses; your stones and your timber and your dust they will put in the midst of the waters. ²⁶:¹³And I will make an end to the roar of your songs, and the sound of your harps will be heard no longer. ²⁶:¹⁴And I will set you a bare rock; she will be a place for spreading nets to dry. She will not be rebuilt again, for I ⌊am⌋ the LORD, I have spoken, declares the Lord GOD.'

♦ **26:7** Repetition of the messenger formula marked the start of a new oracle, with *for* indicating that what followed amplified the foregoing pronouncement. The LORD was *about to bring ... from the north* the agent through whom he would impose his punishment, and who was named here for the first time in the book. Although **Nebuchadnezzar** is the better known spelling of the Babylonian emperor's name, Ezekiel used here (and in 29:18–19; 30:10) the form Nebuchadrezzar, which is technically a more accurate transliteration of 'Nabu-kudurru-uṣur', 'May Nabu [the Babylonian god] protect the heir'. (This form is also found frequently in Jeremiah.) *From the north* indicated the direction from which the armies would arrive. Babylon was due east of Tyre and Jerusalem, but separated from them by trackless and inhospitable desert, and travellers ordinarily proceeded northwest from Babylon following the course of the Euphrates before turning southwards inland from, but parallel to, the line of the Mediterranean coast. It is unlikely that 'north' here had any of the ominous overtones that it had in Jeremiah's 'foe from the north' (cf. Jer. 1:14; 6:1).

King of Babylon (cf. 17:12; 19:9; 21:19, 21; 24:2) seems to have been Nebuchadnezzar's preferred self-designation, whereas **king of kings** was also employed as a title of the Babylonian god Marduk. Its use here may have reflected the divine pretensions of the king, but it was more probably a vestige of Assyrian practice, where it is attested as a title accorded to several of their monarchs, and was equivalent to 'emperor'. ***An assembly and many people*** was an instance of hendiadys (a single reality expressed using two terms) implying an assembly consisting of many people, that is, a large army. Notice that in this context 'people' was employed rather than the more politically charged 'nations' (as in 26:3, 5). Ezekiel proclaimed just as clearly as Jeremiah that Nebuchadnezzar was God's instrument of judgement.

♦ **26:8** The LORD then again (26:3) addressed Tyre directly, personifying the city using feminine singular forms as was common in such address because of the gender of the underlying Hebrew noun for a 'city' (see on 5:5). ***Daughters in the field*** refers to the dependent towns and villages of Tyre (cf. 26:6). This was the obvious strategy in besieging Tyre. The cities on the mainland were vulnerable to military assault, and capturing them forced the island fortress of Tyre to use much longer supply lines to obtain provisions, particularly adequate water supplies. It could be done, but it was obviously a drain on resources and morale.

There then followed a very detailed description of ancient siege warfare, which raises the problem that Nebuchadnezzar did not, indeed could not, implement these procedures against the island city of Tyre. That did not occur until centuries later when Alexander the Great built a causeway out to the island and thus could deploy implements such as battering rams against it. Nebuchadnezzar weakened Tyre and gained political hegemony over it, but he never assaulted it in this fashion. While the description may be explained as using stereotypical imagery to set out the overthrow of the city and the slaughter of its population—and thus not require a one-to-one correspondence with historical data—it is more probable that this was intended to describe what Nebuchadnezzar would do to mainland Tyre rather than to the island city.

The ***assault-ramp*** and the ***siege-mound*** (cf. 4:2) were standard implements of siege warfare, but the exact significance of ***raise shields against you*** is problematic. There is no evidence from this period of the later Roman 'testudo' or tortoise-shell, a roofed structure used to cover and protect besieging troops as they undermined a city wall. Possibly large body shields used for individual defence were intended.

♦ **26:9** ***The blows of his battering rams*** involved two words not found elsewhere, and the translation is speculative. It did not employ the normal Hebrew word for battering-ram found in 4:2; 21:22, and may well have related to specific items of ancient military hardware which can no longer be precisely identified. *Your towers* referred to those on the city walls (cf. 26:3). If those towers were demolished, then the city (here Ushu, mainland Tyre) had been captured. *Crowbars* is ordinarily rendered 'swords' but may refer to other similar items (cf. 5:1). It is known that short swords and similar metal implements were inserted between the stones of fortifications to prise them loose.

♦ **26:10** The strength of the invading forces was presented in terms of the massive clouds of dust stirred up by the advancing forces. ***Because of the abundance of his horses, their dust will cover you.*** They would be unable to ignore the dire warning given by the dust settling on them. ***At the noise of his horsemen, wagons, and chariots your walls will quake as he enters your gates.*** There would not be just the suffocating effect of the dust when Nebuchadnezzar and his immense military force entered mainland Tyre's gates; the ground itself would tremble as in an earthquake.

The final clause raises an interesting problem: ***like entrances made into a city that has been breached.*** On the one hand, this comparison may be taken as a reference to island Tyre which could not be entered in quite the same way as a mainland city might. On the other hand, there was a Hebrew idiom in which the particle of comparison was used to assert a fundamental identity, 'just like such entrances'. So it is more probable that this declared that the fate of mainland Tyre would parallel that of any other captured city.

♦ **26:11** ***With the hoofs of his horses he will trample*** (*bəparsôt sûsawy yirmōs*) was an instance of repeated sibilants to provide assonance. Nebuchadnezzar would completely swamp the captured city with his invading forces. ***Your strong pillars*** (lit., 'pillars of your strength'[22]) may not simply be parts of any building, but specifically those standing before the temple of their god Melqart (cf. Jachin and Boaz erected by Tyrian craftsmen before Solomon's Temple, 1 Kgs. 7:15–22). If they symbolised the presence of their god and the protection he extended to their city, then the demolition of these pillars brought down not just a physical structure, but a belief system as well.

---

22. The term *maṣṣəbôt*, 'pillars', is here followed by a feminine singular verb *tērēd*, 'she will come down'. Greenberg (1997:534) suggests that originally the noun may have ended with the Phoenician feminine singular termination *-at*, which has been later misunderstood. If so, then the situation would not have been so readily comparable with the two Temple pillars.

♦ **26:12** There is significant debate regarding the plural verbs found here. Do they picture the many soldiers or the many nations which comprised Nebuchadnezzar's multi-national army swarming over the fallen city as they looted it? Although there was no immediate antecedent for 'they', such a switch from singular to plural was not uncommon in Hebrew as the author's perspective altered.[23] Another possibility is that the plural presented a general summary of succeeding generations and invaders. It is a weak point of taking this verse as parallel to 26:3–6 that there is no textual indication of a change of focus, and therefore the proposal is open to the objection that it is overly subtle, and to be dismissed on that account.

Your stones and your timber and your dust ('rubble', cf. 26:4) *they will put in the midst of the waters*[24] might describe the invaders throwing whatever impeded their search for booty into the sea. Ferguson argues, however, that 'the fact that rubble would be *put* in the sea implies greater care and purpose than when invaders do it in a frenzied victory celebration' (2006:54). This fitted in better with Alexander's capture of Tyre than with events under Nebuchadnezzar, in which case it would correspond to the general description of 26:4.

♦ **26:13** There is a similarity with Amos 5:23 in that silencing music was a sign of the absence of rejoicing, which was here caused by loss of population. The vibrant commercial city would no longer resound with entertainment.

♦ **26:14** *I will set you a bare rock* (cf. 26:4) reiterated the severity of the LORD's judgement on the city. The LORD then ceased to address Tyre, treating it as something belonging to the past, already dismissed from reality. *She will be*[25] *a place for spreading nets to dry* (cf. 26:5), merely used by fishermen and of no great economic significance.

Furthermore, *she will never be rebuilt.* This was not simply a matter of physical recovery and buildings, but of national prominence and

---

23. In 26:12 the LXX continues the preceding singulars, but this probably arose as an attempt to simplify the reference of the text. The Targum, Vulgate and Peshitta preserve the plurals of the MT.

24. Although LXX has 'sea' rather than 'waters', it is probable that English translations which render 'sea' are simply translating dynamically.

25. The two verbs *tihyeh* and *tibbāneh* are in form either third person feminine singular or second person masculine singular (cf. 21:32). Though it might be maintained that Tyre continues to be addressed directly but using masculine forms, the consistent feminine usage elsewhere makes this implausible.

economic domination. The picture was not necessarily that of no settlement at all, but of no walled settlement. The Babylonians weakened Tyre by depriving it, for instance, of control over the cedar forests on the mainland. The city continued to exist but from that time on its trade largely created wealth for foreign overlords. It was devastated by Alexander the Great when in 332 B.C. he built a causeway out to the city and ended its isolation. The city continued to decline over subsequent centuries. *I ⌊am⌋ the LORD, I have spoken, declares the Lord GOD* emphasised the irrevocable nature of the LORD's decision and decree (cf. 12:25).

REFLECTION

- How should we interpret prophecy? To say it will not be fulfilled in detail might seem to be tantamount to saying it will not be fulfilled at all. Block (1998:147–149) considers this to be a conditional prophecy and that Tyre's submission constituted resignation to the will of God so that implementation of the threats was suspended until the time of Alexander the Great. Instances of such conditionality are to be found in the delayed implementation of Micah 3:12 through Hezekiah's repentance (Jer. 26:17–19), as well as the impact of Jonah's preaching in Nineveh (Jonah 3:4, 10).[26]

But what occurred to permit such a suspension of the divine threat in the case of Tyre? While there was no Jonah sent to Tyre, there had in fact been a divine message relayed there through Jeremiah and the Tyrian representatives at the Jerusalem conference (Jer. 27:3). Tyre knew that it was the LORD's decree, 'Now I myself have given all these lands into the hand of Nebuchadnezzar, king of Babylon' (Jer. 27:6). Moreover, there was also the divine promise, ' "But as for the nation which will bring its neck under the yoke of the king of Babylon and shall serve him, I shall let it remain in its land," declares the LORD, "and they shall till it and shall inhabit it" ' (Jer. 27:11). Tyre knowingly defied the LORD's will for thirteen years in its resistance to Nebuchadnezzar, but it seems highly probable that after thirteen years of hardship and deprivation it sued for peace. No matter that this was done with great reluctance on their part (and probably without acknowledgement of the warnings given to it earlier), it may well have been that the LORD saw grounds even in that grudging submission to his will sufficient to warrant a stay of the full execution of his wrath.

---

26. A comprehensive analysis of the phenomenon of conditional prophecy is provided by Fairbairn (1964:58–82).

(c) Dismay of the Rulers of the Sea (26:15–18)
The impact of Tyre's overthrow is not confined to the city and its close surroundings. Her trading partners round the Mediterranean are also affected. This is foretold in a direct address of the LORD to Tyre in which he predicts the mournful reaction of such city-states to her fall.

> ²⁶:¹⁵Thus says the Lord GOD to Tyre, 'At the sound of your downfall, when the wounded groan, when slaughter takes place in your midst, will not the coastlands quake? ²⁶:¹⁶And all the rulers of the sea will come down from their thrones and strip off their robes and take off their colourful clothes; they will clothe themselves with trembling, they will sit upon the ground, they will tremble time and again, they will be appalled at you. ²⁶:¹⁷And they will take up a lament over you and say to you,
> "How you have perished,
>   O one inhabited from the seas,
>   O renowned city
>   who were strong on the sea,
>   she and her inhabitants
>   who set their terror on all her inhabitants!
> ²⁶:¹⁸ Now the coastlands will tremble
>   ⌊on⌋ the day of your downfall,
>   and the coastlands which are on the sea
>   will be dismayed because of your departure."'

♦ **26:15** Beginning with the messenger formula, the LORD continued to address Tyre using second person feminine singular forms. He employed an extended rhetorical question to convey an emphatic affirmation of what would occur *at the sound of your downfall* (cf. 26:18; 27:27; 31:13, 16; 32:10). *The wounded* were those who had been pierced, that is, mortally injured, but they were not yet dead as they were heard to *groan* in agony. *Slaughter takes place in your midst* is less horrific than the Hebrew which used a verb and a cognate noun, 'slaughter is slaughtered'. The sounds emanating from Tyre's collapse would be so loud that they would carry far and wide, and as a consequence, *Will not the coastlands quake?* The quaking in Tyre (26:10) would send out shockwaves as the economic repercussions of the collapse of such a major commercial power impacted on these coastal cities. 'Coastlands' was virtually a technical term for settlements on the shore of the Mediterranean. They would be gripped by fear regarding their own survival, for all would experience a loss of prosperity through Tyre's demise.

♦ **26:16** *All the rulers of the sea* described the leaders of the Phoenician colonies. They would have held a stake in the trading enterprises that functioned locally. The *thrones* of the ancient world were typically elevated to signify rank (hence the need for footstools to get onto them with a measure of dignity), and so *come down* (rather than 'come off') was the appropriate verb for abasement. *Robes* renders a term for a sleeveless garment, which probably indicated their rank. *Colourful clothes* were made from material in which threads of many colours were intricately woven in an extended pattern. Only the most wealthy could have afforded such costly garments, and rather than tearing their clothes in the customary gesture of grief (cf. the king of Nineveh in Jonah 3:6), they would remove them.

These merchant princes would also display their dismay in that *they will sit upon the ground*, a posture of humiliation and distress (Job 2:13; Isa. 3:26; 47:1; Jer. 14:2). Also, *they will clothe themselves with trembling* (lit., 'tremblings'). While Hummel (2007:804) suggests this was a use of the abstract for the concrete, and that special mourning garments were referred to, it was more probably an uncontrolled exhibition of the emotion which would overwhelm them. *Time and again* they would be convulsed with grief as they are *appalled* (*šāmam*, cf. 12:19) at what has happened to Tyre.

♦ **26:17** The leaders of Tyre's trading partners and colonies were presented as taking up a lament over the city. *Lament* was technically a funeral lament or a dirge (cf. 2:10; ch. 19), and here there was exhibited the 'once—now' format characteristic of that literary genre. Tyre's former achievements were looked back on (26:17) and contrasted with the state which had befallen her (26:18). *How!* resembled the beginning of the book of Lamentations, where the verb 'to inhabit' or 'to dwell' also occurred (Lam. 1:1). *Inhabited* here was a passive form, meaning that the city was settled and populated by those who arrived by sea. The plural *seas* conveyed the vastness of the extent from which her population and her wealth were drawn. Many scholars propose to read, 'O one who has vanished/been destroyed from the seas' (cf. RSV, NRSV),[27] but this seems unnecessary since talking of the origins of Tyre fitted the context well at this point. *Renowned city* brought out how Tyre was praised for her wealth,

---

27. This change follows the LXX, 'you were destroyed', and is explained by reading *nišbatt*, 'you were brought to a finish' (a niphal from the root *šābat*) instead of *nôšebet*, 'inhabited one', 'settled one' (a niphal participle from *yāšab*).

architecture, and security. ***Strong on the sea*** might be rendered by a superlative to bring out Tyre's unchallenged grip on maritime power.

She and her inhabitants referred to Tyre and her citizens whose power was such as to induce terror in others. ***On all her inhabitants*** is somewhat obscure. The feminine 'her' can only refer to Tyre, but the thought of terrorising themselves is convoluted to say the least (cf. NASB, NKJV, ESV). Possibly (Greenberg 1997:537–538) the preposition 'on' was intended as a further specification of the previous 'she and her inhabitants' so that the lines should be rendered:

> She and her inhabitants who imposed their terror,
> Yes, she and all her inhabitants.

The emphasis was that her whole population were instrumental in inducing in others the reaction of ***terror*** (*ḥittît*), the demoralising impact of being confronted by a superior and hostile power. Tyre's commercial empire was obviously no benign arrangement.

♦ **26:18** ***Now*** introduced the changed state of affairs which would be occasioned by with Tyre's downfall. ***The coastlands***[28] (cf. 26:15) were the sites round the Mediterranean where the Phoenicians had their vast maritime commercial network. ***Will tremble*** (cf. 26:16) reflected the same emotion as 'quake' in 26:15, which was also a prominent feature in ***be dismayed***, being overwhelmed by intense shock and dread at a sudden, threatening occurrence. Tyre's ***departure*** from the commercial world would undoubtedly have a destabilising and devastating impact on her dependent territories.

REFLECTION

- The merchant princes of the various settlements throughout the distant coastlands were well aware that Babylon had no interest in invading their territory. What they trembled at was the collapse of the commercial network of which Tyre had been the linchpin. No longer would Tyrian craft transport their exports of raw material to distant lands, and bring back from there manufactured items and precious goods. Their trading network had collapsed with Tyre; the connections upon which their prosperity depended had gone. They were reminded that they were living in an uncertain world, and there is nothing that the business world dislikes more than uncertainty. The world they had known and profited from had been turned upside down, and so they bewailed their lot.

How different is the reaction of the one who fears the LORD. 'He

---

28. 'The coastlands' (*hāʾiyin*) has here an Aramaic plural ending, though later in the verse the normal Hebrew form is employed (cf. *IBHS* §7.4b).

does not fear evil tidings; his heart is steadfast, trusting in the LORD' (Ps. 112:7). It is not promised that in the vicissitudes of this life he will not receive word of wars and rumours of wars, of international tension, and of famines and earthquakes (cf. Matt. 24:6–7). However, he has a different perspective on life and its setbacks because his hope is grounded on the certainties of God and his revelation. He knows whom he has believed and is convinced that he is able to guard until the Day of Judgement the deposit which has been entrusted to his keeping (cf. 2 Tim. 1:12). This provides certainty whatever the challenge which has to be faced (cf. Rom. 8:35–39).

(d) *Submerged in the Deep (26:19–21)*
The emphasis throughout this concluding oracle is on the inevitable outcome for Tyre when the LORD will take action against her. When the LORD judged Jerusalem, there was always a prospect of future recovery because of his refusal to violate his covenant commitment. No possibility of restoration is held out for Tyre once judgement has come upon her.

> ²⁶:¹⁹For thus says the Lord GOD, 'When I set you a desolated city like the cities which are not inhabited, when ⌊I⌋ bring up upon you ⌊the⌋ deep and the many waters cover you, ²⁶:²⁰then I will bring you down with those who ⌊have⌋ gone down to the pit, to the people of old; and I will make you dwell in ⌊the⌋ land of lowest places like the ancient ruins with those who ⌊have⌋ gone down to the pit, so that you will not be inhabited, but I will set beauty in ⌊the⌋ land of ⌊the⌋ living. ²⁶:²¹A dire terror I will set you, and you will be no more. ⌊Though⌋ you are sought for, you will no longer ever be found, declares the Lord GOD.'

♦ **26:19** *For* connected this oracle with the preceding lament by setting out the factors which justified the lament of the coastlands: the LORD had pronounced a death sentence against Tyre. This was presented in terms of two descriptions. Firstly, the LORD would set Tyre as *a desolated city* which was *not inhabited*. There were many such ruined and abandoned settlements throughout the ancient Near East from earthquakes or enemy incursions. Secondly, the LORD would swamp Tyre. The rendering of ⌊*the*⌋ *deep* (*təhôm*; cf. 31:4) is problematic. While some treat it as a term originating in pagan mythology for 'the primeval ocean' (REB), in Scripture it did not have mythological overtones and was used merely for the 'ocean depths'. *The many waters* may point to destructive, life-threatening forces (cf. 1:24;

Pss. 18:16; 32:6; 144:7), and again there is no need to assume a mythical origin for the expression. In the present context two scenarios are possible. Either the LORD was announcing that he would overwhelm the site of Tyre with inundations from the sea, or else the language of the deep and many waters was used metaphorically to describe the armies that the LORD would bring against Tyre (cf. 26:3).

♦ **26:20** Once the LORD began to act against Tyre, there would be no reprieve. *I will bring you down with those who ⌊have⌋ gone down to the pit.* The city was depicted as an individual descending into the realm of the dead (cf. 31:14-18; 32:17-32). In ordinary use a *pit* (*bôr*) was a well, a cistern (possibly dry), or a cavity of some kind in the ground. The term was extensively employed as a metaphor for the grave, though it is not totally clear here if an individual grave was intended or the realm of the dead as a whole. *The people of old* were those who lived in former times, and who had already been interred. Tyre would join them.

In the second part of the verse a contrast was drawn between what would prevail *in ⌊the⌋ land of lowest places* (or, 'the world below'; cf. 32:18, 24) and *in ⌊the⌋ land of ⌊the⌋ living.* The former term described the netherworld as the place to which the dead had been consigned. It was viewed as being *like the ancient ruins.* The comparison was with cities such as those mentioned in 26:19, which had suffered from a natural disaster or enemy devastation. After a catastrophe, it was common practice to flatten the debris and erect new buildings on top of it. Consequently, if at a later stage a hole was being dug in a settled site, the remains of buildings from a previous settlement might well have been found. 'Ancient' (*'ôlām*) did not here indicate 'eternal', but it may have connoted 'hidden'. Just as the ancient ruins lay under rebuilt cities, so the land of lowest places lay beneath the surface of the ground, and there would be found *those who ⌊have⌋ gone down to the pit.* When Tyre would be consigned there also, the result would be that the city would *not be inhabited.*

It is difficult to be certain what was intended by the words, *and I will set beauty in the land of the living.* While they may set out another aspect of God's provision, that thought is intrusive and not well-motivated in this context. An alternative, which has won a measure of acceptance (Block 1998:47; Hummel 2007:809), is to take the verb as an archaic second person feminine form and to assume that the force of the 'not' in the preceding clause extends to this one, to yield , 'and ⌊so that⌋ you will not give glory in the land of the living'.

AGAINST TYRE

♦ **26:21** *I will set you a dire terror.* The noun 'dire terror' (*ballāhâ*) was a plural form, reinforcing the suddenness, duration, or intensity of the experience. The thought was 'I will assign to you a dreadful end' rather than 'I will render you an instance of intense terror to others', that is, 'a terrifying example' (GNB), causing alarm and fearfulness in other commercial centres. Set alongside *you will be no more*, the idea may be of existence in the underworld. ⌈*Though*⌋ *you are sought for, you will no longer ever be found* echoed the finality of the verdict as in 26:14.

REFLECTION
• In the midst of prosperity it can be difficult to grasp how unreliable security derived from this world's possessions and strength in fact is. While the disasters and catastrophes of life are constant reminders of how precarious our existence is, it is easy to insulate ourselves from such reminders because they occur somewhere else or to someone else. But Jesus clearly told us that the lesson we are to learn from tragedies affecting others is, 'Unless you repent, you will all likewise perish' (Luke 13:3, 5).

(2) The Downfall of Tyre (27:1–36)

This chapter gives fascinating glimpses into the construction of ancient ships and patterns of international trade. It includes many specialist terms whose meanings can only be guessed at, so that it provides considerable material for the lexicographer to analyse. It is also a skilfully constructed piece of literature, which testifies to the comprehensive knowledge of its human author. But what of its theological significance? There is no mention of God after 27:3, and no overt theological reflection either. What message did it convey to Ezekiel and his contemporaries?

An answer may be hazarded by supposing that this material originates during, or shortly after, the siege of Jerusalem when the exiles are looking with admiration at Tyre because, unlike Jerusalem, its economic strength and impregnable location are giving it the ability to withstand Nebuchadnezzar's forces. The prophet's mission is concerned with correcting such an attitude of reliance on military resources and, more especially, on economic prowess for security. Tyre's downfall is no longer linked to its attitude towards Jerusalem. Rather both cities experience a fall from a privileged position because they focus on self and fail to acknowledge God's role in their success.

There are three sections in the presentation. The first (27:1–11) gives a graphic description of Tyre's power and prowess by aptly comparing it to a splendid merchant ship. The poem is described as a lament, and these verses comprise the 'once' section of this genre by setting out the former glory of the departed. The poetic structure is interrupted in 27:12–25 by a prosaic directory of Tyre's trading partners, which constitutes an imposing list of places and their exports, and accentuates the city's strategic economic importance and fabulous wealth. Then the lament resumes with the 'now' section which switches to consider the present condition of Tyre (27:26–36). The merchantman has suffered shipwreck (27:26–27), and others are envisaged as taking up a lament over its loss.

(a) A Stately Merchant Ship (27:1–11)

^{27:1}And the word of the LORD came to me, saying, ^{27:2}And ⌞as for⌟ you, son of man, take up a lament over Tyre, ^{27:3}and say to Tyre which dwells by the entrances of the sea, ⌞which⌟ trades with the peoples to the many coastlands, "Thus says the Lord GOD:

    O Tyre, you yourself have said,
        'I ⌞am⌟ perfect in beauty.'
^{27:4}   Your boundaries ⌞are⌟ in the heart of the seas;
        your builders have made perfect your beauty.
^{27:5}   Of cypress trees from Senir they shaped for you
        all your planks;
    a cedar of Lebanon they took
        to make a mast for you.
^{27:6}   ⌞From⌟ oaks of Bashan
        they made your oars;
    your deck they made of ivory ⌞inlaid⌟ in boxwood
        from the coastlands of Kition.
^{27:7}   ⌞Of⌟ colourful linen from Egypt
        was your sail, to be your banner;
    ⌞of⌟ blue and purple ⌞cloth⌟ from the coastlands of Elishah
        was your awning.
^{27:8}   The inhabitants of Sidon and Arvad
        were your rowers.
    Your skilled men, O Tyre, were in you;
        they ⌞were⌟ your pilots.
^{27:9}   The old ⌞hands⌟ of Gebal, even its skilled ⌞men⌟, were in you,
        repairing your damage;
    all the ships of the sea and their seamen were in you,
        to bring your imports.
^{27:10} Persia and Lud and Put were in your force,
        ⌞as⌟ your men of war.

>   They hung shield and helmet on you;
>   they gave you grandeur.
> 27:11 The people of Arvad and Helekh ⌊were⌋ on your
>   walls round about;
>   the Gammadites were in your towers.
>   They hung their quivers upon your walls round about;
>   they ⌊were the ones who⌋ perfected your beauty." '

♦ **27:1-2** The chapter began with the message-reception formula and the characteristic divine address to Ezekiel who was commanded to *take up a lament*. This referred to a dirge such as would give expression to grief over the death of an individual (cf. 26:17). So Ezekiel was to act as if he were conducting a funeral service *over Tyre*.

♦ **27:3** The poem about Tyre did not begin in a condemnatory tone; indeed it celebrated Tyre's greatness. That, however, would intensify the sense of tragedy and loss when mention was later made of her ruin (27:26). Both Tyre's situation and her commerce were described.

(1) *Which dwells*[29] *by the entrances of the sea* incorporated an accurate description of Tyre which had two harbours, the original, natural harbour to the north of the island, and a later, artificial one to the south. Although this second harbour was developed as the main base for Tyre's trading, it was subsequently neglected and no longer exists.

(2) Tyre made good use of her situation for maritime activity: ⌊*which*⌋ *trades with the peoples to many coastlands*. 'Trades' introduced a root (*rākal*) which occurred ten times in the chapter. It signified the activity of one who bought goods at one site and transferred them to another site where they were sold, with the price differential between the two markets generating a profit for the merchant. Tyre was not primarily a manufacturing power, but one whose income was derived from transporting and trading commodities in this way. 'The many coastlands' were initially those round the Mediterranean, but the extent of Tyre's commercial reach was so great that it impinged on virtually every territory of the known world.

In the second part of the verse the messenger formula introduced a

---

29. The qere *hayyōšebet*, 'the dwelling one', is the normal form of the feminine qal participle. The kethib has the form *hayyōšabtî*, with an additional final *yodh*, which is styled a 'hireq compaginis' (GKC §90 m-n). It is uncertain how it may have arisen. The Massoretes recommended the same change in Jer. 10:17; 22:23; Lam. 4:21. The meaning is the same.

poem in which Tyre was fittingly likened to a trading ship, though the term 'ship' was not in fact directly applied to her.[30] Tyre had a conceited opinion of herself. *You yourself have said, 'I am perfect in beauty.'* The term 'beauty' (*yŏpî*) was repeated in 27:4, 11. 'Beauty' and 'perfect', that is, 'complete' or 'flawless', had been applied to Jerusalem's splendour in 16:14, and 'perfect in beauty' was also used of Tyre's king in 28:12. While the language would initially have conjured up a picture of the island city, as the poem progressed the mental imagery would change to that of a splendid ship under full sail making its way across the ocean.

♦ **27:4** The terms used in this verse could apply equally to Tyre the city and to Tyre the ship which symbolised the city's pre-eminence. *In the heart of the seas* could just be a poetic expression for 'in the water' in relation to Tyre's offshore location, but in 27:26, 27 it was used twice as equivalent to 'on the high seas', and that could also be the case here in reference to the extensive commercial empire to which Tyre the ship sailed. The term, *your builders,* fitted equally well shipwrights who constructed the craft (as the following verses showed), and construction workers who erected the city and its harbours.

♦ **27:5** The text then became clearly metaphorical in the description of a boat built from the best available materials. Our knowledge of what was meant by many of these terms is uncertain. However, Tyrian craftsmanship led the world in those days, and we may be sure that the ship was soundly built, using timber of the highest quality, much of which would have been obtained from the heavily forested hinterland of Tyre in the mountains of Lebanon. It is uncertain which tree was involved: *cypress* (cf. NLT), fir (AV, ESV), pine (NIV, HCSB), or juniper. However, whichever it was, it was highly regarded for construction purposes, having been used in Solomon's Temple along with cedar (1 Kgs. 5:8, 10; 6:34; 9:11). **Senir** was an Amorite name for mount Hermon (cf. Deut. 3:8–9; 1 Chron. 5:23), and it was also related to the Assyrian term for the area. **Planks** was a dual form, and was probably applied to some doubled feature of the vessel, either two sets of ribs for the ship, or else it was of a two-decked construction, in which

---

30. Though the MT is not difficult to interpret, critics are often in favour of reading *'ŏnî*, 'ship', instead of *'ănî*, 'I', and deleting 'you have said' as a secondary insertion, so as to render the start of the lament as 'O Tyre, you are a ship, perfect in beauty' (e.g., Zimmerli 1983:42). Such speculation is without versional support and quite unnecessary.

rowers occupied the lower deck and sailors the upper (Hummel 2007:820). The famed *cedar of Lebanon* provided a sufficiently long and stout piece of wood to serve as the *mast* of the vessel.

♦ **27:6** *Oaks* seems to be a generic term rather than a specific tree, which may also be identified with the 'terebinth'. *Bashan* was famed for this sort of wood (Isa. 2:13; Zech. 11:2), which here provided *oars* for the craft. Hummel (2007:820) raises the possibility that there may have been two rows of oarsmen, one on the lower deck, and the other in the hull with oars projecting through slits. *Your deck* may refer either to boards placed underfoot or to the sides of cabins (the term is used for the wooden framework of the tabernacle, Exod. 26:15–29; Num. 3:36), the latter being more probable if the following word is retained in the text. The notion of *ivory* (lit., 'tooth', and subsequently employed with reference to an elephant's tusk) being used in the construction of such a craft has seemed so preposterous to many that its deletion has been advocated. However, this was the description of a luxury 'East Indiaman', and such extravagant panelling would not have been incongruous. *Boxwood*[31] (Isa. 41:19; 60:13) may also be rendered 'cypress', and was imported from *Kition* (Isa. 23:1, 12), an important Phoenician colony (modern Lanarka) on the south-east of Cyprus.

♦ **27:7** This splendid craft had a sail worthy of its grandeur. This provided an additional source of propulsion should the wind be blowing from the right quarter. Egyptian *linen* was a valuable fabric in antiquity, and rather than being dyed it was made *colourful* by means of embroidery, as was the case with the temple barges on the Nile. With such a design on it, a sail would also act as a *banner*, by which the identity of the craft could be established from a distance. *Blue and purple* were the colours of two much admired dyes. Indeed it was the dye from a shellfish found on the Phoenician coast that gave rise to the Greek name for the Phoenicians. Here it would seem that there was an even more highly regarded dye from *Elishah.* The name is found in Assyrian sources, and Elishah was listed as a son of Javan in Genesis 10:4, but its location is unknown. Modern scholarship favours a reference to the east coast of Cyprus, but no association with dyed

---

31. The Massoretic text reads *bat-ʾăššurîm*, 'daughter of the Assyrians', from which no plausible meaning can be derived. The ancient versions (with the exception of the Targums) obviously vocalised the consonants differently to read *biťaššurîm*, the preposition 'with' followed by the name of a tree.

fabric has been established. The *awning* was erected over a portion of the deck to provide shade from the sun.

♦ **27:8** Attention then turned from the magnificent ship to its highly skilled crew. *The inhabitants of Sidon and Arvad* referred to two Phoenician cities. Although of diminished status in Ezekiel's time, Sidon had surpassed Tyre in the past and would do so again. It was located on the coast 25 miles (40 km) north of Tyre. Arvad, the most northerly Phoenician settlement, was an island nearly 2 miles (3 km) off the coast, and 110 miles (177 km) north of Tyre.

Although RSV and NRSV emend *Tyre* to identify here a reference to a further Phoenician city, Zemer (cf. Gen. 10:18), there is no need to alter the text. *Your skilled* (lit., 'wise') *men* were the same group as *your pilots* (or 'ropemen'), highly skilled seamen who knew how best to trim the craft to take advantage of whatever breeze was blowing and to control the direction it was taking. These mariners were from Tyre itself, as outsiders were seemingly avoided for this key role.

♦ **27:9** *Gebal* was located 60 miles (97 km) north of Tyre, and was an ancient and significant Phoenician port dating back to the third millennium B.C., which later became known by its Greek name, Byblos. Its *old ⌊hands⌋* were not 'elders' in the sense of being leaders in the community, but those who had gained valuable experience over the years. They were the same group as *its skilled* (lit., 'wise ones') ⌊*men*⌋ who served to maintain the craft by *repairing your damage*, literally, 'making strong your breach', that is, keeping the craft watertight and remedying any other deficiency.

On this third occurrence of *were in you* in the second part of 27:9 the focus has clearly shifted from Tyre the ship to Tyre the city. Its harbour was viewed as filled with *all the ships of the sea and their seamen.* The market of Tyre acted as a magnet for merchants from all nations as they came *to bring your imports.* The precise nature of the transaction described by the verb and its cognate noun is not certain, but the picture of a thriving commercial centre is clearly established. For further details, see on 27:12.

♦ **27:10** The picture of Tyre's bustling harbours and thriving markets concluded with a reference to the security put in place for their protection. *Persia and Lud and Put were in your force,* ⌊*as*⌋ *your men of war.* These men were mercenaries coming from far and wide. Persia had not yet achieved greatness, and in Ezekiel's day was a minor state located east of the Persian Gulf. Lud is mentioned in two contexts in

Genesis 10, one favouring an African location (Gen. 10:13), while the other connects the name with Semitic peoples (Gen. 10:22), and favours an identification with Lydia in Asia Minor. The latter was a significant power in this period, but there was no suggestion here of any formal alliance with Tyre. It is generally accepted that Put refers to at least part of the area we now know as Libya. In 30:5 Put and Lud were among the mercenary forces trying to defend Egypt. That members of these three peoples were present demonstrated how Tyre was able to attract men from every corner of the globe to serve in its army; the pay and prospects of booty were good. Economic dominance had led to political and military leadership.

They hung shield and helmet on you described the practice of decorating walls with these implements of war (cf. 27:11; Song 4:4), and probably this was also the case on such space as was available on board ships. ***They gave you grandeur.*** The presence of these mercenaries contributed to the glamour and prestige of Tyre. While Tyre was prepared to defend itself, it was not interested in territorial expansion. The role of these mercenaries was probably to act as marines to guard the merchant fleet from pirates.

♦ **27:11** For ***Arvad***, see on 27:8. It is now generally accepted that ***Helekh*** was also a place name referring to Cilicia (cf. RSV, NIV, ESV, HCSB) rather than being a reference to 'your army' as the same word is rendered in 27:10 (cf. AV, NKJV, NASB). That ***the Gammadites*** came from Gammad is fairly certain, but its location is unresolved, possibly a town in Syria. These soldiers served as watchmen ***in your towers***, ready to defend Tyre.

They hung their quivers upon your walls round about was another reference to a display of arms similar to that of 27:10. The final line echoed 27:3 as an inclusion round the poem, celebrating the consummate ***beauty*** of Tyre.

(b) Tyre's Trading Network (27:12–25)
There is then inserted into the lament a directory of Tyre's trading partners and the goods they made available. The origin of the information is not stated. While it may be covered by the rubric, 'Thus says the Lord GOD' (27:3), it is more probable that the Spirit guided Ezekiel to incorporate items from a list with which he was already familiar. In this way further substantial proof is provided of the extent of Tyre's commercial empire. Many of the commodities traded are found in a similar catalogue of Babylon's activities (Rev. 18:12–13).

The list goes full circle, beginning and ending with Tarshish (27:12, 25), to indicate the worldwide reach of Tyre. According to Greenberg (1997:566–567), Ezekiel first mentions trading partners, west and north of Tyre (27:12–15), then those near Tyre to the east or north-east (27:16–19), next Arabian partners to the south-east (27:16–19), and finally those in the more distant east (27:23). (See Figure 1.) For each nation or group of nations, details are given of the goods traded, and whether they are exports or imports. Tyre is presented as controlling and exploiting a vast trading zone on land and sea.

> ²⁷:¹²Tarshish dealt with you because of the abundance of all ⌊your⌋ wealth; for silver, iron, tin, and lead they exchanged your exports. ²⁷:¹³Javan, Tubal, and Meshekh—they were trading with you; for human lives and articles of bronze they exchanged your imports. ²⁷:¹⁴Those from Beth-togarmah exchanged horses, chariot teams and mules ⌊for⌋ your exports. ²⁷:¹⁵The sons of Dedan were trading with you; many coastlands were dealers of your hand. They brought back ivory tusks and ebony as your payment. ²⁷:¹⁶Aram dealt with you because of the abundance of your produce; emeralds, purple dye, colourful fabric, fine linen, coral and ruby they exchanged for your exports. ²⁷:¹⁷Judah and the land of Israel—they were trading with you; wheat of Minnith and millet and honey and olive oil and balm they exchanged for your imports. ²⁷:¹⁸Damascus was trading with you because of the abundance of your goods, because of the abundance of ⌊your⌋ wealth, with wine from Helbon and wool from Zahar. ²⁷:¹⁹And Dan and Javan from Uzzal exchanged for your exports: wrought iron, cinnamon and sweet cane were for your imports. ²⁷:²⁰Dedan was trading with you in saddle-cloths for riding. ²⁷:²¹Arabia and all the chieftains of Qedar were dealing at your hand: with lambs and rams and goats they were dealing for you in them. ²⁷:²²The traders of Sheba and Raamah—they were trading with you; the best of all balsam and every kind of precious stone and gold they exchanged for your exports. ²⁷:²³Haran and Kanneh and Eden, traders of Sheba, Asshur, Kilmad ⌊were⌋ your traders. ²⁷:²⁴They were trading with you in ornate clothes, in cloaks of bluish purple and embroidered cloth, in coloured rugs, and in tightly twisted cord in your place of trading. ²⁷:²⁵The ships of Tarshish were carrying your imports; so you were filled and heavily laden in the heart of the seas.

♦ **27:12** The list began with *Tarshish*, a settlement on the western shore of the Mediterranean, probably in modern Spain (cf. Jonah 1:3), where there were deposits of various metals (cf. Jer. 10:9). ***Dealt with you*** (lit., '⌐was¬ your dealer') used a form derived from the root *sāḥar*, which occurred six times in a number of terms found throughout the chapter (cf. 27:15, 16, 18, 21, 36). It had the sense of 'acting as a middleman' in a trading process, and of course making a profit for oneself at the same time. Here it is translated with a form of 'deal'. A related term was *rākal*, 'to trade', which occurred seven times (cf. 27:3). ***Because of the abundance of all your wealth.*** For 'wealth', see on 27:18, 27, 33. Other places were willing to trade with Tyre because it was ready to purchase any commodity. ***They exchanged*** (lit., 'gave') occurred seven times in the passage (cf. 27:13, 14, 16, 17, 19, 22) for the process by which peoples bartered local produce for ***exports*** shipped through Tyre. 'Exports' were viewed as items which were 'left' or 'relinquished' for someone else to use (cf. 27:14, 16, 19, 22, 27, 33). The goods imported into Tarshish were exchanged for partially refined ores of various metals: ***silver, iron, tin, and lead.***

♦ **27:13** ***Javan*** described the Greek people of Ionia in western Asia Minor and its associated islands. ***Tubal and Meshekh*** were located in the interior of Asia Minor (the names recur in reverse order in 32:26; 38:2–3; 39:1). These nations were involved in the slave trade (they were far from alone in this, cf. Joel 3:4–6; Amos 1:6, 9). ***Human lives*** (lit., 'soul/life of mankind'; cf. Rev. 18:13) and ***articles of bronze*** were used to acquire the ***imports***, that is, the goods which the Tyrians brought to their lands. Tyre therefore played a major role in the slave trade round the Mediterranean.

♦ **27:14** Togarmah was mentioned in Genesis 10:3 as one of the sons of Gomer, and here ***those from Beth-Togarmah*** would indicate his descendants. The name also occurred in Assyrian lists of people who paid them tribute, and in 38:6 it is located in the distant north. Trading in ***horses*** and ***mules*** was a common practice in the ancient world. ***Chariot teams*** renders a word usually taken as 'horsemen'. It might refer to horses and those who had trained them and could ride them skilfully, but it may well just be animals trained to work together.

♦ **27:15** ***The sons of Dedan*** is often understood as a spelling error for 'the sons of Rhodes' (LXX, NIV, NRSV). Dedan will occur later in 27:20, and the similarity of the Hebrew letters corresponding to *d* and *r* could easily have given rise to the error. Mention of Rhodes, a large island off south-west Asia Minor, certainly fitted in with ***many coastlands. Dealers of your hand*** is literally 'dealing of your hand', but the abstract term conveyed the thought that they acted as accredited agents of the Tyrians. ***Ivory tusks and ebony***[32] were exotic goods which had reached the Mediterranean by various routes from Africa or India. The word ***payment*** was a loan word from Sumerian, probably with the sense of a contractual payment (Greenberg 1997:555).

♦ **27:16** ***Aram*** (Syria) referred to the state which had Damascus as its capital. However, that city was mentioned separately in 27:18, and this has led many to favour reading Edom instead (cf. RSV, NRSV). This mistake would involve confusing the same letters as are involved in the proposal in 27:15. Hebrew scribes might have been more prone to slips of the pen while copying lists with many unfamiliar words. It certainly gives a more logical sequence from south to north as regards the countries listed in 27:16–18, but early supporting evidence is sparse, being limited to the Greek translation of Aquila and the Peshitta. Many of the traded items are no longer clearly identifiable: ***emeralds*** may perhaps be 'turquoise'; ***purple dye*** may also refer to fabric dyed with that colour; ***ruby*** is understood by some to refer to 'pearls'. ***Fine linen*** is at least certain. Though the term differed from that in 27:7, it was a later equivalent.

♦ **27:17** ***The land of Israel*** no longer existed as a political entity, and its use alongside ***Judah*** was contrary to Ezekiel's usual idiom (cf. 9:9). Here it referred to the trading patterns of previous centuries or to trade with those still living in that area (hence the insertion of *'ereṣ*, 'land'; cf. 40:2). Both north and south generated surplus agricultural produce which could be used in international trade. ***Wheat of Minnith*** seems to refer to grain coming from a site in Transjordan, and implied that Judah and Israel were acting as middlemen in trading such grain (possibly of high quality and so with a ready international market) with Tyre. The next item is quite obscure. It was simply transliterated as a place name Pannag in the AV, and more recent renderings such as 'cakes' (NASB), 'meal' (ESV), 'confections' (NIV), ***millet*** (NKJV, NRSV), and 'olives and early figs' (RSV) reveal by their variety the uncertainty surrounding the term for some sort of foodstuff. ***Balm*** was a medicinal resin associated with Gilead (cf. Jer. 8:22; 46:11; 51:8).

---

32. The qere is *wəhobnîm* while the kethibh has the variant spelling *wəhôbənîm*, 'and ebony'. The noun, which is an Egyptian loan word, does not occur elsewhere in the Old Testament, but it was used by the Greeks and from there made its way into English as 'ebony'.

♦ **27:18** The repeated *because of the abundance of your goods, because of the abundance of ₍your₎ wealth* was indicative of the key role Damascus and the Aramean city-states played in the economy of Tyre. *Helbon* was about 10 miles (16 km) north of Damascus, and its wine was noted in both Babylonian and Persian sources. *Wool from Zahar* is a more problematic term. It may refer to an area north-west of Damascus, or it may be a generic term for 'white wool' (Greenberg 1997:557).

♦ **27:19** It is difficult to know how to treat the second part of 27:18 and the first part of 27:19. One way is to disregard the verse division, to take the last two phrases of 27:18 'with wine from Helbon and wool from Zahar' with verse 19 and to emend *And Dan and Javan from Uzzal* to read as 'wine casks from Izalla'[33] so as to obtain 'wine from Helbon, and wool from Zahar, and wine casks from Izalla they exchanged for your exports.' This is justified on the grounds that it is difficult to find any connection between Dan in the far north of Israel and Javan (Ionia) in western Asia Minor—and Javan has been mentioned already in 27:13. Izalla (or Uzal, NIV, ESV) was a town in the foothills of eastern Anatolia, north of Haran, and it was a well-known producer of wine. This would then summarise what Damascus gave for imports from Tyre. The trade flow in the other direction consisted of *wrought iron* or 'worked iron', perhaps a more malleable form, *cinnamon* (or 'cassia', an expensive perfume from east Asia), and *sweet cane*, a spice prepared from an aromatic grass and used in medicine and flavouring.

♦ **27:20** There is no explanation for the brevity of this verse. No mention was made of what was received in exchange from Tyre. *Dedan* (cf. 25:13) was a major oasis in the Arabian desert on the trade route from southern Arabia (cf. the connection with Sheba in 27:22). What they traded in is not quite clear. *Cloths* would usually signify 'clothes' and it was accompanied by a word which may be connected either with an Arabic term for a blanket or an Akkadian word for 'woollen material' (*HALOT* 341). It is the addition of *for riding* that suggests a rendering such as 'saddle-cloths'. It may, however, have been special clothing for riding.

---

33. The changes involved are twofold. First, in place of *wədān wəyāwān*, 'and Dan and Javan', there is read *wədannê yayin*, 'and casks of wine', and then repointing *məʾûzzāl* as 'from Uzzal'. The NASB found the mention of Dan here so puzzling that it read it as another place name 'Vedan'.

♦ **27:21** *Arabia* was a general term for the area inhabited by the bedouin of the desert who were from various ethnic backgrounds quite distinct from modern Arabs. *All the chieftains* ('rulers' or 'sheikhs') *of Qedar* suggested that these people were descendants of a son of Ishmael (cf. Gen. 25:13; 1 Chron. 1:29) who were organised in some form of tribal federation, presumably based round their main settlement at the oasis of Dumah in the heart of the Arabian desert, 270 miles (430 km) to the north of Dedan. *Were dealing at your hand* (lit., '⌐were⌐ dealers of your hand', cf. 27:15) implied that they were acting as Tyre's agents in the area.

♦ **27:22** While *Sheba* was a well-known Old Testament name and *Raamah* (which is otherwise unknown) was also connected with it in Genesis 10:7 and 1 Chronicles 1:9, it may have been the case that Sheba originated in the north, and after migrating into the southern Arabian desert, founded a kingdom there while retaining trading links with further north. By the time of the Queen of Sheba in Solomon's day (1 Kgs. 10) it seems to have become a prosperous kingdom through its control of the trade route through the narrow strait between Arabia and Africa, and through local production of spices. *The best of all balsam and every kind of precious stone and gold* reflects the list of the items brought by the Queen of Sheba (1 Kgs. 10:10).

♦ **27:23** The list then reviewed links with the area to the north-east of Tyre. *Haran* was on the river Balikh, 60 miles (97 km) north of its confluence with the Euphrates, and is well known from its connection with Abraham (cf. Gen. 11:31–32; 12:4–5). *Kanneh* was probably located east of Haran, while *Eden* was a shortened form of Beth-Eden, a significant Aramean state west of Haran. *Traders of Sheba* seems misplaced in that trade relations with Sheba were discussed in the previous verse. There is no corresponding term in the Septuagint. *Asshur, Kilmad* is a curious collocation. Asshur may indeed refer to one of the main cities of Assyria (as well as to the country itself), but Kilmad is quite unknown. It has been proposed that it should be read as a reference to the 'whole of Media' (Zimmerli 1983:68).

♦ **27:24** Right to its end this trade directory contained a number of unique terms which puzzle the modern reader. *Ornate clothes* occurred only here, and its precise significance is uncertain. Cognate terms to the unique word *cloak* offer some clue as to it being used to wrap round the body (*HALOT* 192), and a similar methodology is used to suggest the rendering *coloured rugs* or 'carpets with coloured edging'. While ***tightly twisted cord*** (lit., 'cords wound and compacted') may have been the material with which the foregoing rugs were made, it is somewhat more probable that it constituted the final item of trade. ***In your place of trading*** ('bazaar'?) also involved a unique term which might also mean 'for your trading'.

♦ **27:25** To indicate completion of the catalogue ***the ships of Tarshish*** were mentioned, recalling the start of the list in 27:12. This was not simply a term for ships originating from Tarshish, but had become a technical term for the finest trading ships whatever their port of origin.

While it is possible to take ***so you were filled and heavily laden in the heart of the seas*** with 27:26 as resuming the lament, it is more likely that Ezekiel inserted it as a transitional summary. Though the preceding catalogue showed how much of Tyre's trading was overland with peoples to its east, the image of Tyre as a ship was again invoked. The Tyrians did business in so many goods and with so many partners that their ship lay low in the water with all the freight it contained. In itself this was indicative of the great wealth that Tyre possessed. But such weighty cargo also constituted a potential hazard—a possibility which was exploited when the lament was taken up again.

(c) Shipwreck and Lament (27:26–36)

It is best to treat 27:12–25 as material which Ezekiel deliberately intruded into the lament to emphasise the magnitude of Tyre's wealth and trade. Now the lament resumes from 27:11, and the speaker is the LORD, who sets out the situation which will engulf Tyre, and which itself will involve a further lament (27:32–36).

> 27:26 Into the great waters
>   your rowers have brought you;
> the east wind has broken you
>   in the heart of the seas.
> 27:27 Your wealth, that is, your exports ⌞and⌟ your imports,
>   your seamen and your pilots, those who repair
>   your damage,
> those who bring you imports,
>   and all your men of war who are in you—
> indeed, all your assembly which is in your midst,
>   will fall in the heart of the seas
>   in the day of your downfall.
> 27:28 At the sound of the cry of your pilots
>   the pasturelands will quake.
> 27:29 And they will come down from their ships
>   all who handle the oars;

        seamen ⌊and⌋ all the pilots of the sea
           will stand on the land.
27:30 And they will make their voices heard over you,
           and they will cry out bitterly.
        And they will throw up dust on their heads;
           in the ashes they will roll.
27:31 And they will shave themselves bald because of you,
           and they will put sackcloth round their waist;
        and they will weep because of you with bitter anguish
           ⌊with⌋ bitter mourning.
27:32 And they will take up a lament because of you
           in their dirge;
        and they will lament over you:
        "Who ⌊was⌋ like Tyre,
           like ⌊the one⌋ destroyed in the midst of the sea?
27:33 When your merchandise came out from the seas,
           you satisfied many peoples;
        with the abundance of your wealth and your goods
           you enriched the kings of the earth.
27:34 ⌊At⌋ the time of your being broken by the seas,
           in the depths of the waters,
        your merchandise and all your crew
           fell in your midst.
27:35 All the inhabitants of the coastlands
           were appalled because of you;
        and their kings shuddered greatly,
           ⌊their⌋ faces were troubled.
27:36 Dealers among the peoples hissed at you;
           you have become a dire terror
           and will be no more for ever." '

♦ **27:26** The lament over Tyre resumed from 27:11, and the city was again compared to a splendid merchant ship, but the metaphor was transformed from one of success into one of fragility (Newsom 1984:157). The ship had left harbour. ***Your rowers have brought you into the great waters.*** Presumably the rowers were employed because there was not enough wind for the sail. However, once the ship was out at sea, ***the east wind has broken you in the heart of the sea.*** Conditions abruptly and unexpectedly changed, and the ship was irretrievably damaged and sank (cf. Ps. 48:7). The mountains come down close to the sea at the site of Tyre, and sudden ferocious winds sweep down from them and raise great waves close to the shore. 'Wind' was the only occurrence of *rûaḥ* in the oracles against the nations, and was obviously used of the natural phenomenon, as it was in the two earlier occurrences of 'east wind' (17:10; 19:12). However, this was not simply a 'natural' occurrence, but one that was divinely controlled to transform the location which had been the basis of Tyre's prosperity into its grave.

♦ **27:27** The catalogue which followed was different from that in earlier verses. It listed not the outcome of successful trading, but of what was lost at sea—cargo, crew, and passengers. It was perhaps a reflection of Tyre's materialistic outlook that the list began with the cargo which perished: *your wealth, that is,*[34] *your exports ⌊and⌋ your imports.* These terms were also incorporated in the trade catalogue (27:12–13), while *seamen, pilots, those who repair your damage, those who bring you imports,* and *your men of war* drew on the description found in 27:8b–10. This feature indicated the close relationship between the three divisions in this chapter. *Indeed, all your assembly,* crew and passengers alike, would be engulfed in the tragedy. *Will fall in the heart of the seas* portrayed them as being drowned. Since the sinking ship symbolised the destruction of the city, 'your assembly' ultimately referred to the whole population of Tyre and its destiny *in the day of your downfall.*

♦ **27:28** *At the sound of the cry of your pilots* poetically envisaged their shouts of distress as being sufficiently loud that not only would they reach the shore but *the pasturelands will quake.* 'The pasturelands' were the fields immediately surrounding a city where animals were grazed. Here the reference is to Tyre's mainland settlements, which 'quake', that is, reverberate with terror as they become aware of the drama which was unfolding out at sea.

♦ **27:29** The loss of the ship Tyre would evoke a response from other mariners. *All who handle the oars* would disembark from their vessels, and *seamen* (27:9) and *all the pilots of the sea* (27:8, 27, 28) *will stand on the land.* The phrase was literally 'stand to the land', and one wonders if it represented making towards the shore in smaller craft to gain safety of shallower waters, or if it was a gesture of respect.

♦ **27:30–31** The other mariners (presumably, the other Phoenician cities) would bewail the loss of Tyre, giving vent to their grief when *they will cry out bitterly* and engage in customary expressions of grief, of which *they will throw up dust on their heads* would be one (cf. Josh. 7:6; Job 2:12) and *in ashes they will roll,* or perhaps 'they will sprinkle themselves with ashes', would be another (cf. Jer. 6:26). The

---

34. 'That is' treats *wəʿizbônayik* as an instance of explicative *waw*.

intensity with which they would feel their loss was brought out by listing further mourning rituals in which they would engage. ***They will shave themselves bald*** (cf. 7:18; Isa. 22:12). They will ***put sackcloth round their waist*** (cf. 7:18). And this would occur ***because of you*** (or, 'over you'). Tyre would be utterly lost, and this would occasion weeping ***with bitter anguish*** (lit., 'with bitterness of soul'). Indeed, the whole scene would be characterised by ***bitter mourning***, that is, by engaging in conventional rituals to express their deep emotion.

♦ **27:32** ***They will take up a lament because of you*** (or, 'over you') ***in their dirge.***[35] So next there was recorded a lament within a lament (27:2), but whereas the lament uttered by the prophet anticipated Tyre's demise, this lament of the other Phoenician communities would be conventionally timed to follow her overthrow. The 'once' section of the lament, looking back to Tyre's glorious past, is in 27:32–33, while the 'now' section (27:34–36) sets out the reversal of her fortunes.

Who ⌊was⌋ like Tyre? celebrated her former incomparable glory with an aghast question at the destruction of such a great empire. In the last line of the verse the Hebrew root *dāmâ* is rendered either 'being put to silence' (ASV, HCSB, NIV), or ⌊*the one*⌋ ***destroyed*** (AV, ESV). No other city had met a fate like hers ***in the midst of the sea.***

♦ **27:33** The speakers continued their lament in customary fashion by addressing the departed, using second person singular feminine forms to speak to Tyre. They described the former greatness of the economic superpower ***when your exports came out from the seas.*** When her ships had unloaded their wares, she had ***satisfied many peoples***, not just her own population. Moreover, ***the abundance of your wealth and your imports*** had generated riches for ***the kings of the earth***, who had been able to sell local products and who would also have imposed tariffs on traded goods.

♦ **27:34** Tyre's former greatness contrasted with the disaster which had overwhelmed her ⌊*at*⌋ ***the time of*** ⌊*your*⌋ ***being broken by the seas.*** For ⌊*at*⌋ ***the time of*** (cf. AV, ASV) most modern translations read an adverb 'now'.[36] 'Being broken' reused the verb 'has broken' (27:26) at the start of the lament. Only ***imports*** were mentioned in this verse, but

---

35. *bənîhem* seems to be the preposition *bə*, 'in', followed by *nəhî*, 'dirge', with syncopation of the *he*, and a third person masculine plural suffix.

36. The initial *ʿēt*, 'time', is considered a defective spelling of *ʿattâ*, 'now', with the subject 'you' being understood from the context: 'Now ⌊you⌋ are broken'.

they stood for all the merchandise in which Tyre traded. When the ship was wrecked, *your imports and all your crew* (lit., 'assembly'; cf. 27:27) *fell in your midst*, that is, they sank into the depths along with the fabric of the vessel.

♦ **27:35** The reaction to Tyre's overthrow spread throughout *the coastlands* of the Mediterranean (cf. 26:15). The general population *were appalled* (*šāmam*, cf. 12:19; 26:16), overwhelmed and disoriented by the loss of Tyre. *The kings shuddered greatly* was literally 'the kings haired hair', that is, their hair stood on end with shock (cf. 32:10; Jer. 2:12). These leaders of the Phoenician colonies (26:16) *were troubled*, that is, they were agitated and suffered inner confusion at this disaster and what it portended for their own future.

♦ **27:36** The trading community was also affected. *Dealers* (from *sāḥar*, 'to deal, do business', cf. 27:12), or 'merchants', *among the peoples* who were within Tyre's zone of influence, *hissed* (*šāraq*, 'to whistle'). This did not indicate production of a musical tune, but of a sibilant sound used to attract attention. The significance of such sounds varies with situation and culture. When the verb was used in connection with a scene of horror or desolation, it indicated derisive amazement (cf. 1 Kgs. 9:8), or possibly intense shock (cf. Jer. 18:16; 19:8). For *dire terror*, see on 26:21. The commercial community were left overwhelmed as they tried to adjust to the shock to the economic system arising from the fact that Tyre *will be no more for ever*.

REFLECTION
- God is not mentioned after the introductory rubric of 27:3, but absence of mention is not to be equated with absence of presence. Though Tyre's achievements and global trading network are not played down, it is made perfectly clear that abundance of wealth and massive trade surpluses are no bulwark against the east wind blowing (27:26). And who controls the east wind but the LORD? 'By the east wind you broke the ships of Tarshish' (Ps. 48:7).
- While the east wind is a reminder of power that cannot be humanly tamed and which can wreak havoc, it also pictures the swiftness with which circumstances can change. The rowers no doubt pulled hard on their oars to being the craft out of harbour (27:26), but the sudden onset of an east wind transformed their voyage from one of commercial prosperity to one involving loss of cargo and life. The chilling description of Tyre's shipwreck very effectively presents the transience of human achievements. We never know when we will be

called to account. 'But God said to him, "⌊You⌋ fool! This night your soul is required of you, and the things you have got ready, whose will they be?" So is the one who stores up wealth for himself and is not rich towards God' (Luke 12:20–21). How difficult it is in a materialistic age to avoid the trap Tyre fell into! It is eternal folly to store up earthly treasure and devote one's life to advancing one's career and amassing earthly resources (Matt. 6:19–24).

(3) Indictment and Judgement of the Leader of Tyre (28:1–10)

The closing two oracles concerning Tyre do not add appreciably to what has already been said, but they come at matters from a different angle by focusing on the king of Tyre and addressing him. As an absolute ruler he determines the character of the kingdom he rules over, and his policies shape the destiny of the land, for good or for ill. When he is defeated, his subjects suffer along with him. And for any of the exiles who imagine that Tyre will successfully resist Babylon and in that way indirectly help their own situation, the message is unambiguously delivered that pride leads to a fall and that, because of his overweening pride, the king of Tyre will experience a precipitate and ignominious fall—and his city along with him.

The section displays the standard prophetic form of divine accusation (28:1–5) followed by sentence (28:6–10). The focus is on the king of Tyre as the embodiment of his nation. This oracle and the next date from the time of the fall of Jerusalem when Tyre was ruled by Ittobaal (Ethbaal) II (c.590–c.575 B.C.). He is not, however, mentioned as an individual. The depersonalised figure of the king epitomises the disposition of his people as a whole, and both share the same fate.[37]

There are connections with other material in Ezekiel: the reference to trade in 28:5 looks back to chapter 27; and the references to Sheol in 28:8–10 are similar to those in 32:18–32.

> ^{28:1}And the word of the LORD came to me, saying, ^{28:2}'Son of man, say to the leader of Tyre, "Thus says the Lord GOD:
> Because your heart is haughty,
> and you have said, 'I ⌊am⌋ a god.
> On a divine throne I sit
> in the heart of the seas'—

---

37. 'It is not clear whether these passages also attempt to refute the ideology of divine kingship. It is more likely that the ruler stands as a symbolic figure for the city-state' (Renz 1999:96).

　　　　　but you ⌊are⌋ human, and not a god—
　　　　　and you have set your heart as the heart of gods.
28:3　　Behold, you ⌊are⌋ wiser than Daniel;
　　　　　no secret can be hidden from you.
28:4　　By your wisdom and by your understanding
　　　　　you have made wealth for yourself,
　　　　　and have made gold and silver
　　　　　in your treasuries.
28:5　　By the greatness of your wisdom in your trading
　　　　　you have multiplied your wealth;
　　　　　and your heart has become haughty in your wealth.

28:6Therefore thus says the Lord GOD:
　　　　"Because you set your heart
　　　　　like the heart of a god,
28:7　　therefore, behold, I am about to bring strangers
　　　　　against you,
　　　　　violent ones of nations;
　　　　and they will draw their swords against the beauty
　　　　　of your wisdom,
　　　　and they will profane your splendour.
28:8　　To the pit they will bring you down,
　　　　and you will die the death of the slain
　　　　　in the heart of the seas.
28:9　　Will you really say, 'I ⌊am⌋ a god,'
　　　　　in the presence of the one who slays you?
　　　　but you ⌊are⌋ human, and not a god,
　　　　　in the hand of those who profane you.
28:10　The death of the uncircumcised you will die
　　　　　at the hand of strangers—
for I have spoken, declares the Lord GOD." '

♦ **28:1–2** The section began with the message-reception formula and the characteristic form of direct divine address to the prophet so that there was no doubt regarding the divine origin of the communication and Ezekiel's warrant for delivering it. ***Say to the leader of Tyre*** instructed him how he was to present the oracle to his exilic audience in Babylon; it did not require him to travel to Tyre (his captors would not have permitted that) and confront the king personally. The ruler of Tyre was styled a ***leader*** (*nāgîd*; found only here in Ezekiel) rather than a 'king' (*melek*, contrast 28:12). 'Leader' described an individual of high status, and was used of Saul (1 Sam. 9:16) and of David (1 Sam. 13:14). Though 'leader' and 'king' were treated as parallel expressions in Psalm 76:12, there does seem to have been a difference of emphasis. 'Leader' was used in earlier texts for the first rulers of

Israel, where it probably indicated the subordinate status of one who acknowledged the supreme rights of God over the nation, whereas 'king' had associated with it notions of absolute power and control. 'Leader' was never used of God, whereas 'king' was applied to both divine and human rulers. While it is not known how the king of Tyre at this period styled himself, using 'leader' here to refer to him was not just a matter of stylistic variation, but served to undermine right from the start any pretensions he entertained as to his personal status.

The LORD's actions are never arbitrary or whimsical, and so his proceedings against the king began with *because* to introduce the basis on which divine action would proceed. The charge brought against the king (and through him against Tyre as a whole) was: ***Your heart is haughty*** (cf. 28:5, 17). 'Is haughty' (*gābah*) used physical height as a metaphor. While this root could indicate the incomparable superiority of God (Ps. 113:5), it was generally employed negatively for conceited human self-elevation (16:50; 31:5). The LORD's humbling of such vanity constituted a major theme of this address. 'Heart' was also a key concept, occurring nine times in 28:1–19 in two forms of the word. In Hebrew thought the scope of 'heart' included an individual's entire inner disposition: mind, emotions, and will (see on 11:19).

It was adduced as evidence to support the charge of arrogance that the king had ***said*** (or perhaps 'thought' as the verb was also used of the inner speech of the mind; 20:32), ***I ⌊am⌋ a god*** (*'ēl*). Though this term also designated El, the head of the Canaanite pantheon, it is improbable that the king considered himself to be El, or indeed to be Melqart ('king of the city'), the chief Tyrian god. However, in the ancient Near East (apart from Egypt) the king was considered to be the appointee of the god of the nation, and in some sense to act with the authority of that god. From that basis it was no great step to consider oneself to be a god. Indeed, in Egypt Pharaoh was divinised, and Tyre had extensive trading contacts with Egypt. So it was entirely plausible that the inflated ego of the Tyrian king regarded himself as 'a god', that is, as a member of the divine council which played a prominent role in polytheistic thinking. The king was thus espousing an attitude similar to that presented in 'you will be like God' (Gen. 3:5), and such pretension marked him out for punishment.

In addition, the king claimed that ***on a divine throne I sit*** (cf. Isa. 14:13). The verb 'sit' (here 'I have sat down' and therefore 'am sitting') may also bear the sense 'sit enthroned'. In 'a divine throne' (lit., 'seat of gods') the noun 'throne' is from the same root as the verb 'to sit', and may refer more generally to a 'dwelling place', but here the focus is on the king's claim to rule with the unchallengeable authority of a god. *In the heart of the seas* referred to Tyre's island situation and the impregnability it conferred on this absolute monarch. This phrase did not employ the expression 'in the midst of', which is repeated throughout Ezekiel (cf. 1:1), but a synonymous idiom incorporating the term 'heart' to highlight the theme of the oracle. The king with the spiritual heart disease would perish in the heart of what gave rise to his malady (cf. 28:8).

Not for a moment were the king's boastful pretensions allowed to stand unchallenged. The LORD directly contradicted them: *but you ⌊are⌋ human, and not a god.* 'Human' renders *'ādām*, 'man, mankind', and clearly categorised the king as mortal by denying him the divine status of a 'god' (*'ēl*). However, the charge was levelled against the king that, at odds with his true status, *you have set your heart as the heart of gods.* Wisdom was recognised as a divine attribute, but the king considered his ability to formulate policies and to act wisely in his own interest and that of his nation as a match for anything the gods could exhibit. The theme was taken up in the next verse.

♦ **28:3** The NIV and REB follow the approach of the Septuagint and the Peshitta in rendering the two clauses of this verse as questions, and thus they indicate that the claim to surpassing wisdom implicit in the assumption of divine status was unwarranted. Others read this and the following two verses as sarcastically setting out the implications of the king's claim to deity, so as to show how presumptuous they were. However, it seems best to take these verses as conceding the reality of Tyre's achievements before pointing out the flaw which poisoned them. At one level the king of Tyre did possess considerable acumen, particularly in trading skills. For *Daniel,*[38] see on 14:14, 20. Taking him as the epitome of human wisdom was borne out by the book which bears his name (cf. Dan. 1:4, 17, 20; 2:23; 5:11, 14), since 'no mystery is too difficult for you' (Dan. 4:9). *No secret can be hidden from you*[39] used several rare words, but the sense is clear. 'Secret'

---

38. The kethib has the defective spelling of the name *dāni'ēl*, for which the qere recommends the full spelling *dānî'ēl*, which is found elsewhere, including the book of Daniel. It is this variation in spelling which has given rise to the proposal that someone other than the biblical character is in view here.

39. This understands the plural verb in 'with respect to every hidden thing they do not keep you in the dark' as an impersonal usage, equivalent to an English passive construction.

referred to what had been deliberately concealed, while 'hidden' pictured something lying in the dark and therefore escaping observation and knowledge. It was considered to be a mark of true wisdom to be able to unravel the obscure and mysterious (1 Kgs. 10:3). So the king was credited with genuine talent.

♦ **28:4** *Wisdom* and *understanding* were a conventional pair, used here to describe the business acumen of the king. His prosperity and that of his realm were not accidental, but came about through the application of his God-given abilities. He was a skilful operator who could assess market trends and business opportunities, and so *made wealth* (and the power and prestige which accompanied it) for himself and *made silver and gold* which boosted the royal coffers. Commercial success puffed up the self-importance of the ruler of what was, in terms of area, a very small kingdom.

♦ **28:5** *Wisdom* continued to describe the king's practical ability as an entrepreneur in the world of *trading* (*rākal*, cf. 27:3) and commerce. By using his skills he considerably *multiplied* (from the same root as 'greatness') his *wealth*. It was openly acknowledged that the king of Tyre had been vastly successful in economic terms.

However, there was a major flaw in the prosperity and power that the king enjoyed. It had distorted his estimate of his own competence and ability, and had inflated his self-esteem. *Your heart has become haughty in your wealth.* This repeated the thought of 28:2 to form an inclusion round this indictment of the pride displayed by the king, which formed the basis for his condemnation.

♦ **28:6** *Therefore*, corresponding to the 'because' of 28:2, marked the transition from the accusation to the announcement of the divine verdict, introduced by the messenger formula. The lengthy parenthesis of 28:3–5 necessitated summarising the earlier indictment: *because you set your heart like the heart of a god*, reflecting the last clause of 28:2.

♦ **28:7** *Therefore* corresponded to the same term at the start of the previous verse. The punishment the LORD had decided on was *to bring strangers against you*. 'Strangers' were not just those the king had not previously encountered. They were also 'alien' in that he would be unable to understand them. The reference had both a broader and a narrower application. *Violent ones of nations* suggested military forces from various countries, selected for their ferocious cruelty. The following oracle focused more specifically on the Babylonians (cf. 30:11; 31:12; 32:12), but ruthless use of cruelty was by no means limited to them. ***The beauty of your wisdom*** referred to the splendid buildings and fleet erected and maintained by Tyre's opulence, as well as to the state resources which had been garnered by royal skill. Divine judgement would also expose the pretentious claims of the monarch to be divine. ***Your splendour*** comes from a root meaning 'to shine forth' and may well refer to the aura (Akkadian *melammu*) which ancient Near Eastern thought supposed radiated from a god or an outstanding king. The religious associations of the term fitted in with the description of the action taken against it as ***they will profane.***[40] Enemy action would devastate Tyre's beautiful resources. Their ruins would leave no scope for supposing the king of Tyre to be endowed with divine power and acumen. The invalidity and illegitimacy of his claims would be exposed for all to see.

♦ **28:8** The divine sentence then concentrated on the personal destiny of the king. ***They will bring you down to the pit.*** 'Pit' (*šaḥat*) here was the same term as was found in 19:4, 8 for a hole to trap an animal, rather than the more common term for a pit or cistern (*bôr*, cf. 26:20; 31:14), but both were synonyms for the grave. ***You will die the death***[41] ***of the slain*** was a Hebrew idiom for meeting a violent end. That this was the fate of a mortal, not of a god, further debunked the king's pompous claims. ***In the heart of the seas*** was added here to convey the thought that even though the king was dwelling securely in his island fortress, he would not escape the fate brought on by the advancing enemy (cf. 28:2).

♦ **28:9** The rhetorical question expecting a negative answer asserted sarcastically that, when the king was defeated, he would be forced to acknowledge his own mortality. ***I ₍am₎ a god*** repeated the claim of 28:2, but this time used the plural term for God (*'ĕlōhîm*), which was generally used for the one, true God. While this might warrant the

---

40. In 28:7, 9 there was a wordplay between *ḥālal* (II), 'to pierce', 'to slay' and *ḥālal* (I), 'to profane'. After the occurrence of 'draw their swords' (28:7) or 'the one who slays you' (28:9), there would be an expectation that the root 'pierce'/'slay' would occur, and commentators often emend the text accordingly (e.g., Zimmerli 1983:2.75). But Newsom argues this expectation had been deliberately created to emphasise that once the king of Tyre was killed, his corpse would defile the city (1984:159–160).

41. The term *māmôt* is plural in form, but there is no corresponding singular and it is probably unwarranted to find in it an intensificatory notion and translate 'violent death' as Ellison recommends (1956:109).

translation, 'I ˻am˼ God', it is more probable that it was here employed generically, 'a god' or 'divine'. This claim could not be maintained *in the presence of the one who slays you.* While the participle is singular in the Massoretic Text, some manuscripts and also early versions have a plural form (cf. NIV, NRSV, ESV), but the difference in meaning is slight.

The fact that *you are human* (*'ādām*, perhaps anticipating the next section) *and not a god* (*'ēl*, cf. 28:2) was established by the king's physical death which simultaneously gave the lie to his claims of deity. *Those who profane you*[42] probably embodied a word play with an associated meaning usually represented in English translations, 'those who slay/wound you'. The king of Tyre was also the chief priest of the local god, and his death in his sanctuary in the heart of the seas defiled that sanctuary where the king resided (28:2; Newsom 1984:159–160).

♦ **28:10** *The death of the uncircumcised* further belittled the king of Tyre. Since Herodotus records (*Hist.* 2.104) that the Phoenicians practised circumcision (at least at some period), the speech was metaphorical. 'Uncircumcised' referred to one outwith the covenant community, who would therefore die unreconciled to God (cf. 32:21). *At the hand of strangers* added to the debased and shameful degradation of such a death. But it was what would surely overtake Tyre and its king, *for I have spoken, declares the Lord GOD.*

REFLECTION

• Ancient Greek thought often examined the reality of hubris, such overweening human arrogance, particularly against the gods, that inevitably drew down on itself disaster and ruin in the form of nemesis, divine punishment. There was much truth in such pagan thinking. The king of Tyre 'was puffing himself up, bringing attention to himself, but his larger than life image of himself that he was reflecting was but an empty bubble that would be popped suddenly by judgment from the true God's hand' (Beale 2008:139). But such spiritual self-assertion is not confined to kings and rulers. It has infected human thinking ever since the insinuation of Satan, 'You will be like God' (Gen. 3:5). Such thinking involves a

---

42. The piel participle *məḥallêkā*, 'those who profane you', reflects the piel of *ḥalal* (I), the same verb in 28:7. The parallelism with 'the one who slays you' suggests the root *ḥālal* (II) (which lies behind the term 'slain' in 28:8), though that would ordinarily require a polel form to convey the meaning 'to pierce, to wound', hence the recommendation to repoint the verb to *məḥōləlêkā*, 'those who pierce you'.

fundamental misperception of created reality. Only one is divine—the LORD. And he will not share his glory with any other.
- 'Everyone who is haughty of heart is an abomination to the LORD. Rest assured, he will not remain unpunished' (Prov. 16:5). The only antidote to the presumption of the fallen heart is the fear of the LORD, which is the beginning of wisdom, both its start and the foundation on which it must always rest (Prov. 9:10). It is all too easy to join with those 'who are wise in their own eyes, and discerning in their own estimation' (Isa. 5:21), and so think of themselves more highly than they ought (Rom. 12:3). Awed respect for God and his will curtails and extinguishes human arrogance (Rom. 12:2).
- A close parallel to the conduct of the king of Tyre is to be found in that of Herod Agrippa who 'did not give God the glory' when he revelled in the blandishments and ovation of the people of Tyre and Sidon as they cried out, 'The voice of a god, and not of a man!' (Acts 12:20–23). His sudden and sorry end serves as a permanent warning to all those who cultivate popular applause.

(4) Lament over the King of Tyre (28:11–19)

The final oracle in the sequence concerning Tyre is closely linked to the preceding section as is evident from the verbal connections which exist between them: 'your heart ... haughty' (28:2, 17), 'wisdom' (28:4, 12), 'beauty' (28:7, 12), and 'trading' (28:5, 16). Balancing the accusation and verdict pronounced in the previous section, this oracle is styled a lament over the king of Tyre (28:12a). As is typical in a lament, the past glory of the king is stressed (28:12b–15), and contrasted with his later fate (28:16–19), but there are variations from the conventional style in that there is an emphasis on the king's sin and its punishment, and there are no expressions of grief over his death.

The main theme of the passage is readily identified as the way in which one who has enjoyed high status and prosperity can lose it all through sinning against God and incurring his judgement. However, there are differing views as to the nature of the comparison by which this subject is illustrated. The reference to Eden in 28:13 establishes that the biblical background is drawn from the narrative of Genesis 2–3 regarding Adam and Eve in the garden. Even so, there are two areas of dispute. Many things are said which have no parallel in Genesis. Are they to be regarded as drawn from Tyrian mythology and incorporated into the lament to expose how inadequate that system of thought was? Also, precisely which figure is being used to implement the comparison? Is it Adam? Or is it a cherub, who in fact turns out to be Satan?

As regards the first question, it is obvious that many modern scholars point to parallels between elements in this account and what is now known about ancient Near Eastern mythological beliefs. Indeed, it is commonplace to argue that Ezekiel developed material from surrounding cultures in composing this lament. Such an approach is to be regarded with considerable caution. Although our knowledge of the religious thought of other nations in Ezekiel's day has increased significantly, it is still the case that we do not possess anything like full knowledge of what was prevalent in Tyre.[43] Furthermore, most arguments concerning mythological allusions presume that the biblical material is derived from the thought world of Israel's neighbours. It is far more theologically robust to contend that, if parallels can be identified between the two bodies of literature, priority should be assigned to the biblical version.[44] Heathen beliefs either contained a distorted and polluted adaptation of the truth, or were outright denials of it. Furthermore, to the extent that there are allusions to purely pagan beliefs, the text does not concede any reality to them. The funeral dirge does not reinforce the tenets of heathen religion, but rather subverts them and throws them back at the king of Tyre.

As regards the second question, regarding which figure in Eden the king is being compared with, it should be noted that both styles of interpretation may be brought into accord with biblical revelation. As far as Ezekiel's message is concerned, it is supported on either approach by identifying a parallel between the king of Tyre who enjoyed great status and blessings, and lost all through sin, and another figure who similarly lost the good which had been divinely bestowed on him. Much of the discussion which the passage has generated has not been primarily shaped by a desire to understand what Ezekiel was saying to his contemporaries, but to see if what he said can be made to throw light on the career of Satan, a theme about which Scripture is

---

43. Darr comments that 'not only is the text difficult at points, but also one may be certain that its motifs and imagery exceed our knowledge of ancient Near Eastern mythology' (2001:1391). It is therefore more satisfactory to curtail the use of pagan mythology in explicating the passage.

44. Ellison sagely remarks, 'In our justifiable rejection of the modern view that the early stories of Genesis are merely pagan myths purified of their polytheism we tend to forget the far truer view of our fathers that the pagan myths represent a polytheistic corruption of the truths of the Bible' (1956:110).

largely silent (cf. 2 Pet. 2:4; Jude 6; Rev. 20:10). To read this passage along with Isaiah 14 as providing material for constructing an account of the career of Satan as an angel who rebelled against God is to interpret the presentation in too literal a fashion. It is evidently just as much a literary construction as the preceding metaphor of the merchant ship, Tyre.

It is interesting to compare two modern treatments of the question, neither of which was advanced to address Ezekiel 28 directly, but both of which illustrate the different approaches taken.

Heiser (2015) develops an extensive and thoroughly researched analysis of passages in Scripture which may be interpreted as referring to the divine council consisting of subordinate angelic figures, who were also known as 'gods'. In the course of this discussion Heiser understands the king of Tyre's claim, 'I am a god' (28:2), to assert his membership of that divine council, and that the background to the comparison in this chapter is that of the rebellion in Eden of an angelic being against God, and the only such rebel in Genesis 3 is the serpent (2015:78). This approach, he claims, has more comprehensive explanatory power than the traditional identification of the comparison involved as being that with Adam. It should be noted that rejection of Heiser's understanding of this oracle need not imply rejection of every aspect of his thesis.

On the other hand, Beale (2004; 2008:135–140) has also shed much light on this portion of Scripture in elaborating his thesis regarding the pervasive nature of temple imagery throughout Scripture. He argues that Eden was the first sanctuary where God made his presence known to Adam, who had charge over it as a priest and a king. In this way there is an obvious parallel with Christ as the second Adam who fulfils the same dual role. On this basis Beale interprets the comparisons in this section as between the king of Tyre (who probably also functioned as a king and a priest) and Adam, both of whom engaged in idolatry in the form of self-worship, arrogating to themselves a status which rightfully belongs to God alone.

The following exposition largely adopts Beale's standpoint. However, it should not be supposed that the lament is to be read as an historical account. Fairbairn rightly characterised it as an historical parable, in which the kings of Tyre were collectively personified as an ideal man such as might have been found in Eden (1851:314). What is being presented is not simply the tragedy of a single king of Tyre, or even of a dynasty there. Such a sequence of events is one that has been repeated throughout human history whenever individuals have lived without recognition of God, and particularly in respect of the careers of those political leaders who have dominated lands and nations..[45]

^{28:11}And the word of the LORD came to me, saying: ^{28:12}'Son of man, take up a lament over the king of Tyre and say to him, "Thus says the Lord GOD:
>   You ˻were˼ a seal of perfection,
>   full of wisdom and perfect in beauty.
> ^{28:13} You were in Eden, the garden of God;
>   every precious stone ˻was˼ your covering—
>   carnelian, peridot and moonstone,
>   beryl, onyx and jasper,
>   sapphire, turquoise and emerald;
>   and the workmanship of your mountings and settings
>   ˻was˼ gold.
>   In the day you were created, they were prepared.
> ^{28:14} You ˻were˼ an anointed cherub who protects,
>   and I appointed you.
>   You were on God's holy mountain;
>   in the midst of the stones of fire you moved around.
> ^{28:15} You ˻were˼ blameless in your ways
>   from the day you were created
>   until perverse misconduct was found in you.
> ^{28:16} Through the abundance of your trading
>   you were filled with violence in your midst,
>   and you sinned;
>   so I cast you as profane from the mountain of God,
>   and I destroyed you, O cherub who protects,
>   from the midst of the stones of fire.
> ^{28:17} Your heart was haughty because of your beauty;
>   you corrupted your wisdom for the sake of your
>   splendour;
>   Upon the earth I have thrown you;
>   before kings I have set you that they may see you.
> ^{28:18} By the abundance of your iniquities,
>   by the injustice of your trading
>   you profaned your sanctuaries;

---

45. Fairbairn argues that Ezekiel's presentation 'clothes the ideal according to the usage of our prophet in an historical drapery, and beholds the past revived again in the personified existence of which it treats. But it is no wild play of fancy, or arbitrary indulgence of a lawless imagination. A sublime moral runs through the parable. It reads over again the great lesson of man's weakness and degeneracy, and shows how inevitably the good, when unaccompanied by a really Divine element, turns in him to corruption and ruin' (1851:315).

>   and I brought out fire from your midst—
>   it consumed you—
>   and I set you as ashes upon the ground
>   before the eyes of all who saw you.
> 28:19 All who know you among the nations
>   have been appalled because of you;
>   and you have become a dire terror
>   and will not be for ever."'

♦ **28:11-12** The use of the message-reception formula and the characteristic mode of divine address to the prophet marked this as the start of a new oracle. In directing Ezekiel to ***take up a lament*** (cf. 19:1; 26:17; 27:2; 32:2), the LORD used the expression in a somewhat extended sense of a sorrowful critique. Employment of this term constituted a warning that the initial commendatory statements regarding the king would be subsequently modified in the light of the inevitable conclusion of any lament: the death of the one celebrated in it. ***The king of Tyre*** was now titled as 'king', unlike 28:2 where 'leader' had been used. This change was probably motivated by the arrogance which the king had been observed to display. ***And say to him***[46] indicated that the ostensible addressee of the following verses was the king of Tyre, though it remained clear that these words were intended for Ezekiel's fellow exiles to inform them about the destiny of the king of Tyre.

The supplement in ***you ₋were₋*** is based on the explicit statement of the following verse. But who was the 'you' who was being addressed? In the light of the preamble it would be natural to identify this figure as ***the king of Tyre***, but considering what was said regarding him, the figure in the foreground was more probably Adam (or Satan, on the alternative reading of these verses) up to the transition around 28:16. So the past career of the Tyrian king was presented as a recapitulation of that of Adam—and with the same outcome.

Three epithets were used to describe Adam, and with him the king of Tyre. The first of these, ***a seal of perfection***, is problematic. The Massoretic text reads a participle 'one who seals' (cf. AV, ASV, NASB margin), but ancient versions and most modern translations understand

---

46. There are two features of *wəʾāmartā lô*, 'and say to him', which are noteworthy but do not affect the translation. The first is that the *waw*-consecutive is not finally accented as it normally would be in this construction, probably to avoid the collocation of two stressed syllables (cf. GKC § 29e); the other is the conjunctive daghesh in the *lamed* (cf. GKC §20f).

it as a noun denoting 'a seal' or 'a signet ring'.[47] The designation of a human ruler as a signet was found elsewhere in Scripture (of Jehoiachin, Jer. 22:24; of Zerubbabel, Hag. 2:23). The second word in the epithet occurred elsewhere only in 43:10 where it referred to the 'plan' or 'pattern' of the temple, perhaps more precisely its perfect proportions. The expression might therefore mean 'one who seals a plan' in reference to the exercise of personal wisdom and skill. However, it is more plausible to take the expression in the light of the following reference to Eden. Adam as the seal of perfection acted as God's duly appointed representative with authority over the garden and with the duty of maintaining it and acting as guarantor for the realm God had placed him over. This role was emulated by the king of Tyre as regards the kingdom of which he had been given charge.

The second epithet, *full of wisdom*, continued the earlier use of wisdom as the practical sagacity required to conduct affairs successfully (cf. 28:3–5). A connection between the first man and wisdom is perhaps reflected in Job 15:7–8. The third expression, *perfect in beauty* (*yŏpî*), also reflected earlier language (27:3, 11). This praise, which initially referred to Adam, was reminiscent of the description of the beauty of Tyre as a merchant ship (27:2–9). The LORD did not dispute that the king of Tyre had possessed wisdom and splendour which rivalled Adam's primeval endowments, though no concessions were made to the king's pretensions to be divine.

♦ **28:13** *You were in Eden* specified the abode of primal humanity. *The garden of God* (cf. 31:8–9; Isa. 51:3) referred to the superb provision which God had made as Creator, and where he had presenced himself in fellowship with mankind. It may be justly asserted that Eden was the divine abode on earth, the prototypical sanctuary after which the Tabernacle and Temple were subsequently patterned (cf. Beale 2004:66–80).

Your covering was the rendering of the early versions, and is followed by most modern translations. If Eden was a temple, then Adam was the priest who had charge of its maintenance, as well as being the LORD's vassal given royal dominion over the created realm. In that case the following list of gem stones conjured up images of the high priest's breastpiece—which was not made of metal as the older rendering 'breastplate' might suggest, but of fabric—and which had

---

47. The consonantal text remains the same. Whereas the MT reads a qal participle *ḥôtēm* from the verb *ḥātam*, 'to seal', 'to confirm', the versions pointed it as the construct noun *ḥôtam*, 'a seal'.

gem stones attached to it (Exod. 28:17–20). That would reflect Adam's role as priest-king in Eden, and constitute a parallel with the status of the king of Tyre, though neither need have actually worn such a garment. After all, prior to the fall, Adam was naked (Gen. 2:25).[48]

However, the root behind the term 'covering' (*məsukâ*, from *sākak*) recurred in 28:14, 16 where it is ordinarily rendered 'protects', and it is plausible that the term which occurred only here has the sense of 'protection'. Though Hummel (2007:851) retains 'your covering' in his translation, he notes the arguments for the possibility that it means 'your fence' or 'your wall' as that which marked the boundary of a sacred area. This reflects the assessment of Greenberg (1997:581–582). So it may be that what was described was a jewel-encrusted wall (cf. Rev. 21:18–20). Again, this need not assert the historical existence of this artefact; it was symbolic of Eden's resplendence and security.

The precise identity of the precious stones is uncertain. ***Jasper*** (*yāšpēh*) is usually translated in this way because the English noun is derived from the Hebrew word. The same is true of ***sapphire*** (*sappîr*), but as that gemstone was virtually unknown in antiquity, 'lapis lazuli' is often the preferred modern rendering. Though the stones involved cannot be easily recognised, the varieties of colour made for a display of dazzling splendour: the dark red ***carnelian***, the pale green ***peridot***[49] from Egypt, the white ***moonstone***, the green ***beryl***, the reddish-brown and white tinged ***onyx***, the green ***jasper***, the blue ***sapphire***, the greenish-blue ***turquoise***, and the green ***emerald***.

The presence of the conjunction 'and' showed that the stones were listed in three groups of three, as compared to four rows of three in which the jewels on the high priest's breastpiece were arranged in Exodus 28. The first two stones in the first row were the same in both texts, and Ezekiel's second group of three corresponded to the final row in Exodus. Though the other stones mentioned in Ezekiel were also found in Exodus, the third row in Exodus was not present here. It is unclear if it has been omitted in the transmission of the Hebrew text, or if it was never present and mistakenly restored in the Septuagint.

---

48. The fact that Adam was naked before he fell does not rule out the rendering 'covering' for a piece of clothing in an ideal description of the sort found here. It was symbolic of Adam's status, not an historical delineation of his condition at that time.

49. The usual translation is 'topaz' following the LXX, but it is probable that the LXX translators were not referring to the modern topaz but to a yellow stone, chrysolite (cf. NRSV, NIV11). Even so, the peridot is known from ancient Egyptian jewellery and seems more probable here.

The Massoretic punctuation lists 'gold' along with the precious stones, but this seems improbable. Taking the word with the following phrase, which is itself abstruse, yields a sense such as *the workmanship of your mountings and settings ⌊was⌋ gold.*[50] However, as 'mountings' renders a term elsewhere understood as 'hand drums' or 'tambourines', it is possible to understand 'settings' (which occurred only here and was related to a root meaning 'to pierce') as another musical instrument such as 'pipes', which are hollow. The variety of translations again evidences the obscurity, and no rendering can claim any great certainty.

In the day you were created clearly assigned Adam as the ideal man (and hence also the ideal king) a subordinate status as part of God's creation. *They were prepared* referred to the stones. If at one level they formed a protective wall for the garden, then at another level what was in view were the natural defences with which Tyre was endowed. Though the king's life and the advantages possessed by his realm were both divine gifts, he did not recognise the true origin of either.

♦ **28:14** Resolution of the textual and translational conundrums posed by this verse impacts significantly on the understanding of the passage as a whole. The initial *you* (*ʾatt*) in the Massoretic text is pointed as a feminine singular form, which is, to say the least, problematic in address to Adam or to a king. There are two ways of the handling this difficulty. One is to follow the Septuagint and read *ʾēt*, 'with', which produces a translation such as, 'With an anointed cherub as guardian I placed you' (NRSV; cf. GNB, REB). The 'and' is then deleted as a later adjustment. As well as the functions attributed to the cherubim in Scripture, archaeology attests that in Tyrian art they featured as royal attendants.

Alternatively, the initial *you* may be understood as a rare masculine form, which was attested elsewhere (Num. 11:15; Deut. 5:24; cf. GKC §32g). It is much more probable that this unusual form was misunderstood by later scribes and changed to the easier 'with', so that Adam was originally identified as a *cherub*. This was the term used in chapter 10 for the throne attendants of the LORD, and here a similar role was assigned to Adam in Eden which was the primal sanctuary and earthly residence of God. Adam had been allotted the duty of

---

50. This rendering omits the *bāk*, 'in you', which the MT treats as the last word of this clause. It is difficult to determine its significance whether with what precedes it or what follows.

working the garden and keeping/guarding (*šāmar*) it (Gen. 2:15).[51] So it was implied the king of Tyre had been allocated a similar role. ***Anointed*** described Adam/the king as duly installed in office as a priest-king.

Who protects (*sākak*) translates the same verb as was used of the role of the cherubs 'overshadowing' the mercy seat (cf. Exod. 25:20; 37:9; 1 Kgs. 8:7), and there are translations which render in that fashion (cf. AV, ASV, NASB, NKJV). However, there was nothing in this context to which such 'covering' might refer, and it is more likely that a general role such as protector or guardian was referred to here and in 28:16 (see also on 'covering', 28:13).

Although the Massoretic accents read ***and I appointed you*** with what followed, the phrase might have reinforced what preceded by pointing out that the anointing was to a divinely assigned role. The fundamental assertion was that, however elevated a cherub might be, it was still created, not divine, and its function was assigned by God. This also applied both to Adam and to the king of Tyre.

You were on God's holy mountain. Many scholars consider this phrase to reflect Canaanite ideas of the seat of the gods being on a high mountain. However, Canaanite myths incorporated many distorted elements of truth. While Scripture did not directly assert that the garden of Eden was located on a mountain, the river flowing out of it to water the earth suggested it occupied an elevated site (Gen. 2:10–14). It was also the case that sanctuaries/temples of God were associated with mountains. This was certainly true of Ezekiel's temple (40:2; 43:12; cf. Rev. 21:10), and also more generally (Beale 2004:146). ***Holy mountain*** was employed frequently in connection with the divine presence (20:40; Ps. 48:1; Isa. 2:2–4; 27:13; Jer. 31:23; Zech. 8:3). So this is a description of the privileged access to God that was available in Eden.

Although guesses abound as to the precise reference of ***in the midst of the stones of fire*** (cf. 28:16), all agree that what was pictured enhanced the majestic status of the king. Heiser argues that these stones of fire 'not only describe an abode, but also divine entities in that abode' (2015:80). However, the simplest understanding is that 'the stones of fire' depicted the coruscation of the jewel-encrusted

---

51. 'When Adam failed to guard the temple by sinning and letting in a foul serpent to defile the sanctuary, he lost his priestly role, and the cherubim took over the responsibility of "guarding" the Garden temple' (Beale, G. K. 2004:70).

protective wall (28:13). Moreover, ***you moved around*** (*hālak* hithpael) was also used of God's progress through his realm (e.g., Gen. 3:8; Lev. 26:12; Deut. 23:15; Job 22:14). Likewise Adam/the king of Tyre walked in state through the territory which had been placed under his control.

♦ **28:15** At this point the description of the original blessed state of Adam/the king of Tyre began to merge with divine critique and judgement. ***Blameless in your ways*** need not have implied total absence of sinful conduct, but it did require a high level of moral integrity and probity (cf. Gen. 6:9; 17:1; Job 1:1), and in the present context was intended to be taken absolutely to convey the moral perfection which existed in Eden before the fall. ***From the day you were created*** referred back to the last line of 28:13, and asserted that Adam and the king alike owed their existence and privileged position to God.

But there came a change to that primordial bliss. It had only lasted ***until perverse misconduct was found in you.*** 'Perverse misconduct' (*'awlâ*, a feminine form corresponding to *'āwel*, 'injustice'; cf. 3:20) denoted action that was contrary to what is right and equitable. But no clear indication was as yet given regarding what constituted that unrighteous activity.

♦ **28:16** As the reference to 'trading' made clear, at this point Eden began to fade from consideration and the focus fell increasingly on the conduct of the king of Tyre. This and the following two verses each incorporated the 'once—now' pattern characteristic of a lament, with the first part of each verse looking back to former success, and the second part setting out the divine verdict. ***Through the abundance of your trading*** referred to Tyre's international commercial success. Its zone of influence was vast as regards its geographical spread, and it traded in any commodity for which there was a market. But this was not without consequences for its behaviour. ***You were filled***[52] ***with violence in your midst*** conveyed a picture of ruthless, unscrupulous trading which had no compunction as regards violating the rights of others if there was profit to be had (for 'violence', see on 7:11, 23). The description was reminiscent of the degenerate behaviour of the pre-flood world (Gen. 6:11, 13). There could be no doubt that ***you***

---

52. In the verb *mālû*, 'they filled' the *aleph* has been omitted as is common in later Hebrew. The third person plural form is impersonal and equivalent to a passive.

sinned as the king remorselessly pursued commercial gain—and took his subjects along with him.

Such conduct incurred the judgement of God: *so I cast you as profane* (lit., 'I profaned you', though the following 'from' requires a more dynamic understanding). It must be remembered that the standpoint of this lament was after the downfall of the Tyrian king, but the funereal words were first uttered by Ezekiel as a prophetic diatribe against the king while he was still alive. No longer was the king the blameless cherub, the priest-ruler with due authority over Tyre. He had defiled his conduct, and was treated accordingly. *From the mountain of God* (28:14) implied banishment from the holy place because of pollution. He was addressed as *O cherub who protects* and reminded of his privileged domain in *the midst of the stones of fire* (see on 28:14), but his conduct had rendered him unfit to inhabit such a sanctuary. *I destroyed you* may here have had the sense 'to cause to be removed', that is, banished as Adam was from a former place of security (Gen. 3:23–24).[53]

♦ **28:17** The condemnation of the king of Tyre reverted to his pride (28:2, 5). *Your heart* covered the whole of his inner motivation and desire (28:2). *Haughty* (28:2) captured the unwarranted conceit of the swollen-headed king, while *because of your beauty* (*yŏpî*, 28:12) showed how outward appearances dominated and distorted his judgement. *You corrupted* (cf. 16:47) *your wisdom* implied misapplying his practical ingenuity and insight to wrong ends.

As a result, through this lament the LORD foretold that he would dethrone the Tyrian king. *Upon the earth I have thrown you* pointed to complete loss of royal status—indeed to overthrow and destruction of the kingdom along with the king. Modern commentators are inclined to recognise 'underworld' as another meaning for the term rendered 'earth' on the basis of use in cognate languages. Hummel (2007:856) accepts that conclusion in this passage and compares it with 32:18, 24, but no more may be implied than 'to the ground'

---

53. The NRSV translation, 'the guardian cherub drove you out from among the stones of fire' (cf. RSV), follows the LXX and Peshitta. It involves emending *wāʾabbedəkā*, 'and I destroyed you' to *wayʾabbedeka*, 'and he destroyed you.' This change fits in with rendering 'with' in 28:14 which would then have both the cherub and the king of Tyre on the holy mountain. However, the Genesis 3 account has the cherubim installed as guardians of Eden only after Adam was no longer qualified for that role and had been banished.

(19:12).[54] ***Before kings I have set you*** denoted the humiliation of the king in the sight of rulers who had previously been his subordinates. ***That they may see you*** pointed not just to their awareness of what had happened to him, but suggested that they would gloat and rejoice over his ignominious downfall.

♦ **28:18** Again it was stressed that the king's conduct had led to his undoing. ***By***[55] ***the abundance of your iniquities*** may be a general accusation which was made more specific by the following phrase in apposition to it, ***by the injustice*** ('*āwel*; cf. 3:20) ***of your trading***. The commercial activity for which Tyre was renowned had been pursued using unfair means (cf. 28:15–16). ***You profaned*** (see on 13:19) ***your sanctuaries*** probably declared that the king's moral misconduct in commercial activities polluted the sanctuary where he served in his capacity as priest-king. While the plural 'sanctuaries' might refer to the many temples/shrines which would be found in a pagan city such as Tyre, probably only the main sanctuary was in view (cf. 7:24; 21:2).

I brought out fire from your midst. While this clearly described divine judgement being imposed on Tyre through fire, it is far from clear how this was envisaged as occurring. 'Your midst' could hardly apply to the king himself; perhaps it covered the king and his domain. Certainly ***it consumed you*** could refer to the king and the city, which was thus ***set as ashes upon the ground***. Furthermore, ***before the eyes of all who saw you*** (cf. 28:17) emphasised that the public imposition of justice added to the humiliation of the king and his city, and also set them as a warning before others.

♦ **28:19** The closing thought of the preceding verse was continued in ***all who know you among the nations have been appalled*** (*šāmam*, cf. 27:35) ***because of you***. They were aghast as they witnessed the overthrow of Tyre and its king. ***You became a dire terror and will not be for ever*** repeated the thought of 27:36. 'Dire terror' (an intensive plural; see on 26:21) referred to what the king of Tyre would himself experience, far removed from his initial privilege and prosperity.

---

54. Heiser argues that this description does not fit Adam, who was already on earth, and who did not end up in the underworld. Instead he argues that 'this is the sort of language we would expect if the point was the expulsion of a heavenly being from the divine council' (Heiser 2015:81). At this point, however, it would seem that only the king of Tyre is in view.

55. An instance of causal *min*, 'from' (cf. *IBHS* §11.2.11d), but Renz (1999:170) disputes this and argues that it points to the means by which the shrines have been profaned, not the reason.

REFLECTION

- Hubris or overweening pride is occasioned by mankind putting self in place of God when determining their course of conduct. That was the archetypal sin of Adam which has been perpetuated ever since. Whenever mankind seek to recreate paradise without first centring their thinking on God, their enterprise is doomed to failure because it replicates Adam's sin. There will inevitably come the time when 'perverse misconduct was found in you' (28:15).
- In our current culture where business success is rated so highly, it is especially pertinent to note that 'the abundance of your trading' (28:16) was singled out as the cause of the king's downfall—not his pagan beliefs. Being dominated by a desire for success and profit is the source of corruption. It led to 'violence in your midst', perhaps especially the suppression of the rights of others in the slave trade in which Tyre and Sidon played such a prominent part (Joel 3:6).
- Perfect humanity is only found in Christ. The second Adam was needed to achieve what the first Adam could not, and what all human pretenders to occupy the place of Adam fail to accomplish. To enter the new Eden from which there will be no expulsion requires a living relationship with the last Adam (Rom. 5:14; 1 Cor. 15:42–50).

F. Against Sidon (28:20-26)

Nestling between the extended treatments of Tyre and of Egypt, the oracle concerning Sidon is easily overlooked, but it is of strategic significance as regards both the literary structure of this division of the prophecy and its theological significance.

Sidon (*ṣîdôn*, probably 'Fishertown') was another Phoenician settlement, which lay about 25 miles (40 km) north of Tyre. In earlier times it had been more dominant than Tyre (cf. Gen. 10:15), and it would become so again during the Persian era. In the intervening centuries it was destroyed by the Assyrians, but regained a measure of prosperity as their empire went into decline. Sidon participated in the anti-Babylonian conference which was convened by Zedekiah (Jer. 27:3). Though its king was deported by Nebuchadnezzar (*ANET* 308), the city itself did not suffer extensive destruction and recovered quite quickly from Babylonian aggression.

The inclusion of this brief and unspecific prophecy about Sidon was apparently motivated by the desire to have seven items in this collection of oracles against the nations, and so to indicate the LORD's total control over the affairs of the nations. Including the oracle at this point, however, went beyond acquiring a total of seven, or locating the treatment of Sidon next to its neighbour, Tyre. Block (1998:122–123) notes that the mention of the house of Israel in 28:24–26 divides the oracles against the nations into two blocks, each consisting of 97 verses (25:1–28:23 and 29:1–32:32). This central placement also suggests that more than geography or literary considerations dictate its position. It is a theologically fundamental declaration of the core factors motivating God's providential dealings with this world: the need for due recognition of divine sovereignty; and his desire to promote and secure the well-being of his covenant people.

On the one hand, the LORD exercises control over the international political scene so that he might reveal who he is. Four times in seven verses the recognition formula is repeated, 'And they will know that I ⌊am⌋ the LORD' (28:22, 23, 24, 26). Though mankind consider themselves to be in charge of their own destiny, divine intervention will disabuse them of that thought, and they will be forced to recognise not only the supremacy and power of the LORD, but also his 'glory' and his 'holiness' (28:22).

On the other hand, the LORD's control advances his sovereign purposes for his covenant people. When their enemies are subjected to divine judgement and are consequently rendered incapable of interfering in the affairs of the house of Israel, this opens the way for the fortunes of the people to be securely established. The character of the LORD will also be perceived in the manner in which he restores his people and re-establishes them in the land (28:24–26). In this fashion the two parts of this section are linked because both in the LORD's treatment of Sidon and in his restoration of his people he reveals his holiness (28:22, 25).

(1) The Fate of Sidon (28:20–24)

> ^{28:20}And the word of the LORD came to me, saying, ^{28:21}'Son of man, set your face towards Sidon and prophesy against her, ^{28:22}and say, "Thus says the Lord GOD:
> > Behold, I am against you, O Sidon,
> > and I will display my glory in your midst,
> > And they will know that I ⌊am⌋ the LORD
> > when I execute judgements in her
> > and display my holiness in her.
> ^{28:23} And I will send pestilence into her
> > and blood into her streets;

and the slain will fall in her midst
by the sword ⌊which will be⌋ against her from
round about;
And they will know that I ⌊am⌋ the LORD." '
28:24ʹAnd there will no longer be for the house of Israel a thorn to cause pain or a thornbush to scratch from all those round about them who scorn them. And they will know that I ⌊am⌋ the Lord GOD.

♦ **28:20–21** The nature and structure of this oracle were similar to those in chapter 25, with the message-reception formula, followed by the usual divine address to Ezekiel, the hostile-orientation formula, a command to prophecy and an oracle beginning with the messenger formula (compare 25:1–3, which also had a call to listen). *Set your face towards Sidon* denoted the assumption of a stern and threatening gaze in that direction (cf. 4:3) as the prophet delivered the message entrusted to him *against her.* The personified city was the ostensible addressee, but Ezekiel's fellow exiles were the real audience.

♦ **28:22** The message proper was preceded by the messenger formula to attest its genuinely divine origin. *I am against you* set out the LORD's opposition to Sidon's conduct (cf. 6:2), though the reason for her condemnation was not stated. Then the LORD asserted his aim in his forthcoming intervention: *I will display my glory* (*kābēd* niphal; cf. 39:13). This niphal verb (as also 'display my holiness' later in the verse) had a reflexive rather than a passive significance. The thought was not simply, 'I will be glorified', when others acknowledge the grandeur and absolute dominion of the LORD by extolling his name. That would be a consequential aspect of the situation. Primarily the LORD would take the initiative to disclose, assert, and vindicate his resplendent authority and power. By acting in judgement *in your midst*, his overthrow of evil would be an unmistakable demonstration of his sovereign control. Such a revelation had a precursor in the LORD's dealings with Egypt (Exod. 14:4, 17–18), a passage where there was also repetition of the recognition formula (Exod. 14:4, 18).

Thus the result of divine action would be human acknowledgement of the LORD as expressed in the recognition formula, *And they will know that I ⌊am⌋ the LORD.* 'They' was ambiguous, but probably referred to the people of Sidon, who would be forced by God's overwhelming intervention to recognise his supreme jurisdiction and might. *Judgements* were the verdicts of the divine King by which he enforced his decrees against the city (cf. 5:10). *Display my holiness* (*qādaš* niphal; cf. 20:41) was also an act of divine initiative. Although holiness often referred to the inaccessible being of God which was outwardly exhibited in glory (Isa. 6), here there would be a public demonstration of divine 'holiness' which would vindicate God's righteous character (cf. 20:41; 28:25; 36:23; 38:16; 39:27).

♦ **28:23** The form of the verb *send* may have conveyed the thought of 'give free rein to' (*HALOT* 1514) as though these evil forces had been straining to be let loose and the LORD removed whatever held them in check. No mention was made here of human instrumentality; all is attributed to divine action. The means which God would use were described in familiar terms: *pestilence* (cf. 5:12), *blood* (cf. 5:17), and *sword* (cf. 5:12). The result would be death in Sidon: *the slain will fall in her midst* (cf. 6:7). The details of Sidon's history at this point are no longer extant. Since it was not so easily defended as Tyre, presumably it soon fell to Nebuchadnezzar, who then deported its king.

Again, it was emphasised that the result of divine intervention would be that *they will know that I ⌊am⌋ the LORD.*

♦ **28:24** The reversion to prose at this point indicated that this verse was not part of what was addressed to Sidon. It functioned as a transition to the separate oracle contained in the closing two verses of the chapter, where the consequences of the LORD's intervention for the covenant community, *the house of Israel*, were developed more fully. Here the emphasis was on the negative aspects of divine imposition of judgement against *all those round about them who scorn them* (*šûṭ*, cf. 16:57). The contemptuous dismissal of Judah by her neighbours was compared to *a thorn* (cf. 2:6) *to cause pain or a thornbush to scratch* (cf. a similar thought occurred in Num. 33:55). *No longer* pointed to the state of affairs which would prevail after the LORD had acted to dispose of such irritants. He would remove this source of difficulty and hostility from his people—something they could not do for themselves.

The verse (and the brief oracle) concluded with the recognition formula: *and they will know that I ⌊am⌋ the Lord GOD.* But who would gain this knowledge? At one level, the echo of 28:23 reinforced the perception that it would be the people of Sidon, along with others who had previously belittled and despised Israel. However, the nearest antecedent is 'the house of Israel' who were subsequently twice referred to as 'them'. It is therefore probable that the protection afforded to Israel would heighten their awareness of the goodness of the LORD who was their Sovereign.

REFLECTION
- 'Display my glory ... display my holiness' (28:22). If these expressions were uttered by any other being, they would be tainted by narcissism. But this is the Creator of the universe speaking, and it is part of the inherent moral order of his realm that there be due acknowledgement of the character and majesty of the one who brought it all into existence and who continues to maintain and sustain it.

(2) Israel's Return (28:25–26)

Ezekiel appended to the foregoing oracle another prose supplement. From the positive tone of its message of restoration many suppose that it originated some time after the fall of Jerusalem. While the possibility undoubtedly exists that the prophet included these verses when, in his later years, he was organising the final form of his prophecy, it must be remembered that throughout the earlier part of the book there are a number of brief vistas of the divine relief which will be extended to God's people (11:14–21; 16:59–63; 20:33–44), and that may well be the case here also. Renz insightfully comments that this section 'is the first promise of salvation that is not explicitly set in a polemical context against the present failure of Israel ... It is probably for this reason that the patriarchal traditions, regularly disregarded by Ezekiel, can be brought into play here' (Renz 1999:175).

> 28:25 Thus says the Lord GOD, "When I gather the house of Israel from the peoples among whom they have been dispersed and display my holiness in them before the eyes of the nations, then they dwell upon their land which I gave to my servant Jacob. 28:26 And they will dwell securely upon it, and build houses, and plant vineyards; and they will dwell securely when I execute judgements on all those who scorn them from those round about them; and they will know that I ⌊am⌋ the LORD their God."'

♦ **28:25** The messenger formula introduced a final section, which developed the theme of the prose comment of 28:24. The LORD's intervention would not only remove the hostility displayed by Israel's adversaries; it would positively advance his people's cause, primarily because he would *gather the house of Israel*, the covenant community. The exiles would be taken *from the peoples among whom they have been dispersed* in divine judgement, and they would be restored to their land (cf. 36:16–32). In the Old Testament perspective the only land which could be described as *their land* was that promised to the patriarchs (Gen. 12:7; 26:3; 28:13). Being brought back there was evidence that the covenant relationship was being restored. But why was it described as *their land which I gave to my servant Jacob* with no mention of Abraham or Isaac? Hummel (2007:871) cites the traditional answer that whereas all of Jacob's sons were included in God's blessing, that was not true of the offspring of Isaac or Abraham.

But there was another aspect to Israel's restoration in that through it the LORD committed himself to *display my holiness in them* and so give evidence of his unique superiority (cf. 28:22). This would again be done openly *before the eyes of the nations,* to reverse the public humiliation of Israel's punishment. The people would then *dwell* in the territory provided for them by their covenant Overlord. There is an air of permanence about these arrangements.

♦ **28:26** The security of their resettlement in the land was emphasised, not only by the repeated divine declaration, *they will dwell securely* (cf. 34:25)—a blessing derived from covenant obedience (Lev. 26:5)—but also by a first glimpse of restored Israel's renewed activity and enjoyment of the LORD's provision. They would *build houses and plant vineyards,* activities which require a world where there would be adequate safeguards from hostile forces (e.g., Deut. 20:5–6; Isa. 65:21). Moreover, the people could be assured of the permanence of their occupation. No external threat would disturb their occupation of the land since the LORD would *execute judgements* (cf. 5:10; 28:22) on those neighbouring countries which had previously derided them (28:24). This time there could be no doubt as to the subjects of the recognition formula: *they will know that I ˻am˼ the LORD their God.* This was no longer an enforced recognition of the LORD from those whose hearts remained alienated from him. The covenant people would readily and gratefully acknowledge the LORD's goodness and power in the sovereign provision he made for them.

REFLECTION

- At the centre of this extended presentation of the LORD's power over the nations (chs. 25–32), there is included this declaration of his restoring grace. Though his people had been justly subject to his judgement, the measures he took against them were not merely punitive. He continued to recognise the bond he had instituted between himself and them, and so his discipline was designed as restorative. In the midst of the suffering of the exiles they were granted this vision of return and re-establishment in the land to give

hope to the faithful and enable them to persevere through the dark days which still lay ahead. They were not in the grip of blind fate or an irreconcilable God, but one who was still working for their good and who was urging them to respond correctly to his chastisement. 'As many as I love, I reprove and discipline; therefore be zealous and repent' (Rev. 3:19).
- When the Jews were restored to the land under Cyrus (Ezra 1:1–4), this prophecy was in measure fulfilled. The LORD did bring Israel back to the Promised Land, and their enemies were restrained. Even so, what they experienced fell short of the full extent of the bliss here described. That awaits the time when the whole 'Israel of God' (Gal. 6:16), comprising believing Jew and Gentile alike, come as Abraham's offspring and heirs according to promise (Gal. 3:29) into enjoyment of the new Jerusalem. Just as this vision of restoration gave hope to the Jews in exile, so the promise of the 'inheritance that is untouched by death, unstained by evil, and unimpaired by time' (1 Pet. 1:4; Beare 1970:83–84)—the ultimate experience of immortality, purity, and beauty—encourages those who are now 'the elect exiles of the dispersion' (1 Pet. 1:1) as they struggle to maintain their witness on earth.

G. Against Egypt (29:1–32:32)

The central division of Ezekiel's prophecy (chs. 25–32) is deliberately structured in terms of seven oracles against the nations, and in the seventh oracle, that against Egypt, there are seven sections. These sections, which are complete divine speeches in their own right, are dated (apart from the third, 30:1–19), and are in chronological order apart from the second (29:17–21). The first oracle (29:1–16) was revealed a year after the Babylonians began the final siege of Jerusalem, and two years before Ezekiel and his fellow exiles received news of the fall of the city (33:21). It is the earliest of all Ezekiel's oracles against the nations.

The short second oracle (29:17–21) is in fact the latest dated prophecy in the book. It is brought forward out of sequence probably because of its thematic link with Tyre. Nebuchadnezzar has been unable to benefit from the siege of Tyre as he expected, but God will give him booty from Egypt as a consolation prize. The third oracle (30:1–19) is undated but takes up from 29:19 the theme of Egypt's multitude (30:4, 10, 15), which will face defeat at the hands of Nebuchadnezzar. The fourth oracle (30:20–26) emphasises how the

LORD will use the Babylonians to break the power of Egypt thoroughly. The fifth oracle (31:1–18) employs Assyria as an object lesson to teach Egypt regarding the fate that she will share because of her sinful pride.

Although Pharaoh is not directly named, three of the seven oracles (1, 5, 6) are addressed to him in his capacity as king of Egypt and the embodiment of the nation. In many respects the final two oracles, a lament over the fall of Pharaoh, king of Egypt (32:1–16) and Pharaoh's descent into Sheol (32:17–32) recapitulate the message already delivered: the Babylonians will invade and defeat Egypt, as a result of which Pharaoh himself will perish.

Egypt had been one of the great empires of the ancient world, and it remained a formidable force even though it was no longer as powerful as in previous millennia. Since Syria-Palestine formed a buffer zone between it and the Mesopotamian powers, Egypt desired to keep it within its zone of influence, and was prepared to intervene in the area if it felt its interests were under threat through encroachments from the north.

Throughout the period of Assyrian and Babylonian domination of the ancient Near East, the Egyptians encouraged rebellion by the vassal states of Syria-Palestine which had been incorporated into the Mesopotamian empires (cf. Isa. 30:1–5; 31:1–3). However, after the fall of Nineveh in 612 B.C., when Egypt tried to prop up the remnants of the Assyrian empire, it was soundly defeated by the Babylonians at Carchemish in 605 B.C. Though it could not be easily seen at the time, that rout marked the start of a long period of decline for Egypt. The Babylonians, however, continued to view Egypt as a major challenge to their hegemony, as well as a tempting prize. Consequently, many of the references to Pharaoh in these chapters are probably to Hophra (Apries, 589–570 B.C.), who did challenge the Babylonian army when it began to besiege Jerusalem (Jer. 37:5–8). This may just have been a token effort, for it was soon seen off by the Babylonians.

The extent to which the prophet's ministry dealt with Egypt is testimony to the allure which this major power in north-east Africa possessed for Judah as a counterbalance to incursions from the north. Political expediency repeatedly promoted the desirability of an alliance with Egypt (e.g., Isa. 30:1–2), and this led to trouble, not only because it violated covenant trust in the LORD, but also because Egypt was liable to renege on its commitment to provide assistance. That was why it had been accorded the epithet, 'Rahab who sits still' (Isa. 30:7).

Surprisingly, mention is also made of restoration for Egypt despite its hostility to Israel (29:13–14; cf. Isa. 19:18–25). This is a presentation in Old Testament garb of the reality of the ingathering of the Gentiles into the one church of Jesus Christ, where Jew and Gentile alike comprise the 'one fold' encompassing 'the Israel of God' (Gal. 6:16).

(1) Judgement on the Great Monster and the Splintered Staff (29:1–16)

The limits of this oracle are determined by a new date formula in 29:17 along with the introductory formula, 'the word of the LORD came to me'. The number of sub-divisions which should be identified within the present oracle is less certain. A form of the recognition formula, 'then they will know that I ⌊am⌋ the LORD', occurs in 29:6a, 9a, 16, each marking the end of a section, but thematic considerations argue for a further break after 29:13.

This section once more raises questions regarding the nature of prophetic language and the fulfilment of prophecy. The doom awaiting Egypt is conquest by Nebuchadnezzar which will apparently involve the ignominious death of the Pharaoh, considerable loss of life, and deportation from the land. The extant records are scant regarding what happened in this period towards the end of Nebuchadnezzar's reign.

Jeremiah predicted that Pharaoh Hophra would be given into the hands of his enemies, those who sought his life (Jer. 44:30). In the event these foes were Egyptian as well as Babylonian. After trouble had arisen in Libya, Hophra sent a courtier, Ahmose (also known as Amasis, 570–526 B.C.), to take charge of the Egyptian forces and suppress the revolt. But his troops acclaimed Ahmose as Pharaoh. For a while he seems to have shared control of the land with Hophra, but eventually defeated him, and procured his death. At this time of internal confusion and weakness, Nebuchadnezzar invaded Egypt (Jer. 43:13). Josephus reported that Nebuchadnezzar campaigned in Libya (*Ant.* 10.227), which certainly implied a prior measure of success in Egypt itself. Josephus also recorded that Nebuchadnezzar slew Pharaoh (*Ant.* 10.182; see on 30:26), whereas Herodotus stated that Ahmose played in leading role in the death of Hophra (*Hist.* 2.169).

So, while the Babylonians did raid Egypt, the extent of their victory remains unclear. Possibly the language of this prophecy is hyperbolic. Alternatively, the prophecy has an implicit condition which limits the extent to which Egypt would in fact be devastated, but it is far from obvious what that condition might have been.

(a) The Great Monster (29:1–6a)

29:1 In the tenth year, in the tenth ⌐month⌐, on the twelfth of the month, the word of the LORD came to me, saying, 29:2'Son of man, set your face against Pharaoh, king of Egypt, and prophesy against him, and against Egypt, all of it. 29:3Speak and say, "Thus says the Lord GOD:

 Behold, I am against you
  Pharaoh, king of Egypt,
 ⌐you⌐ great monster which lies
  in the midst of its streams,
 that has said, 'My Nile is my own;
  I made ⌐it⌐ for myself.'
29:4 And I will set hooks in your jaws,
 and will make the fish of your streams stick
  to your scales;
 and I will bring you up out of the midst of your streams,
  and all the fish of your streams will stick to your scales.
29:5 And I will throw you out into the wilderness,
 you and all the fish of your rivers.
 Upon the surface of the open country you will fall;
  you will not be brought together and you will not
   be gathered.
 To the beasts of the earth and to the birds of the heavens
  I have given you as food.

29:6Then all the inhabitants of Egypt will know that I ⌐am⌐ the LORD." '

♦ **29:1–2** The date *the tenth year, in the tenth ⌐month⌐, on the twelfth of the month* corresponds to 7th January 587 B.C. and so this oracle was the earliest in the collection against the nations. The siege of Jerusalem had begun a year earlier (24:1). The oracle was given a full, formal introduction beginning with the message-reception formula, followed by *Son of man* (cf. 2:1), the usual form of divine address to the prophet, and by the hostile-orientation formula, *set your face* (cf. 6:2). Here the preposition was explicitly *against*, so that Ezekiel's gesture led into an announcement of impending woe.

 Pharaoh (from an Egyptian expression meaning 'great house') originated as a term for the royal palace, which came to be applied to its occupant. It was hardly necessary to add *king of Egypt*, but this did emphasise his status and, with the use of 'king' (cf. 7:27), brought his absolute rule into prominence. The addition of *and against Egypt, all of it* exemplified a feature of the prophecies against Egypt: the fortunes of Pharaoh, his people, and his land were explicitly interwoven. Though at any juncture the spotlight may fall on one of them in particular, the other two were always implicated to some extent. This perspective was more noticeable in Hebrew than it is in translation because the inflected nature of the language made evident the frequent changes in person and number.

♦ **29:3 *Speak and say*** (cf. 14:4; 20:3, 27; 33:2) seems to involve redundancy, but was probably an idiom for deliberate formal speech. The opposition formula, ***I am against you*** (cf. 5:8), repeated what is found against Tyre (26:3) and against Sidon (28:22), and expressed general divine opposition to ***Pharaoh, king of Egypt***.

Great monster was another telling metaphor, though it is difficult to convey its overtones in English.[56] At one level it originated as a description of the crocodile (note 'scales' 29:4; 'feet' 32:2), which, though pictured as lazing at the side of the Nile, remained a formidable threat to others. In parts of Egypt, especially in the delta, the crocodile was worshipped as a god, Sohek. Moreover, the term also possessed mythological associations, though 'dragon' (AV, NRSV, ESV) overemphasises this dimension. When Scripture graphically portrayed malign powers and used terms, such as 'monster', which were possibly drawn from the ancient Near Eastern myth of the chaos monster, it did not endorse these myths. Instead, it exposed their falsity and inadequacy, generally by asserting in the same context the absolute superiority of the LORD over all the demonic gods of the heathen (cf. Isa. 27:1; 51:9; Pss. 74:13–14; 89:10).

Which lies described an animal at rest, or lurking in ambush for prey. It was the term used in Genesis 4:7 for sin as a monster lying in wait to waylay Cain. There may well have been such demonic overtones in the use of the word here. Given that it was in ***its streams***, that is, in its own waters, that the crocodile was lying, the imagery seems to be that of contentment, security, and repletion. 'Streams' was the plural of the term rendered ***Nile*** (*yəʾōr*) in the following line. Though originally an ordinary Egyptian term for 'a river', as there was really only one river in Egypt, it came to designate the Nile. The plural form presumably referred to the various branches of the Nile found in

---

56. Although *tannîm* appears to be plural in form, the accompanying adjective *gādôl* proves that it is singular, and therefore is not the similarly spelled plural of *tan*, 'jackal', but rather the spelling found in Ezekiel (also in 32:2) for the term *tannîn*, 'monster' (cf. Ps. 74:13; Isa. 27:1; 51:9). Perhaps this reflects an inaccurate correction of what looked like an Aramaic plural ending to the corresponding Hebrew form, when no change was needed at all.

the delta. The Twenty-sixth Dynasty of Egypt, which was in power at this time, had its capital at Sais, in the west-central part of the delta. Pharaoh boasted, *My Nile is my own; I am the one who made it.* This was a claim to deity, exhibiting the same arrogance which the king of Tyre had openly displayed (28:2). *For myself*[57] revealed his absorption with his own interests. The annual flooding of the Nile was central to the fertility and prosperity of Egypt, and hence to the revenues flowing into the royal treasuries. And in Egyptian religion Pharaoh was considered to control the Nile without which Egypt would have been totally desert.

♦ **29:4** Those whose expectations for Jerusalem were based on Egyptian help might initially have found the portrayal of Pharaoh as the great crocodile an encouraging comparison, but their calculations were abruptly confounded, for the LORD could not let Pharaoh's infringement of his sovereignty pass unnoticed. Crocodiles were not exempt from capture and slaughter. *I will set hooks*[58] *in your jaws* (cf. 19:4; 38:4) pictured a technique which Herodotus (*Hist.* 2.70) attested was used in Egypt to hunt them. An animal carcass attached to strong metal hooks was floated in the river, and when the crocodile swallowed the bait, it was pulled to land by means of the hooks which would become wedged within it. This intrusive coercion by the LORD exposed how illusory the military security and bureaucratic control were which sustained pharaonic complacency.[59]

The threefold repetition of *your streams* (with an emphasis on 'your') was probably intended as an ironic rejection of the claims made regarding ownership and control of the Nile in 29:3. *And all the fish of your streams will stick to your scales.*[60] Though zoologically

---

57. The form *'ăśîtinî* seems to mean 'I made myself', but it is increasingly recognised that the pronominal suffix may be used in a datival sense (Joüon §125ba; *IBHS* §10.2.1i).

58. The kethib *ḥaḥîyîm* is the plural of *ḥāḥ*, 'hook', with the *yodh* written twice. The qere gives the regular spelling *ḥaḥîm*.

59. 'With v. 4, Ezekiel, in effect, flips the crocodile metaphor over to reveal its soft underbelly' (Darr 2001:1404).

60. The presence of the *wᵉēt* rather than simply the conjunction constitutes a problem. It might function to indicate a second object after the preceding verb, 'I will bring you up and all the fish of your streams' followed by an unmarked relative clause, '⌊which⌋ stick to your scales'. Alternatively, *'ēt* may be analysed as the preposition 'with' (though the presence of the conjunction is then puzzling), but most probably it is used as an emphatic particle whose force need not be brought out in translation (cf. Joüon §125j).

implausible, this cartoon image conveyed a vital message. When the crocodile was caught, all the smaller fish which depended on it and were to be found clinging to its scales would be involved in the same doom. These fish represented either the Egyptian army, or the population as a whole, but the lesson could be readily extended to apply to the smaller nations of Syria–Palestine which were looking to Egypt for assistance.

♦ **29:5** Pharaoh would be cut down to size, because on his death he would not have a grand state funeral, but his corpse would be discarded to rot in the desert and become carrion. Although some translations prefer 'leave' (e.g., NIV, HCSB) or 'abandon' (e.g., NASB), the more dynamic sense of ***throw*** or 'hurl' seems to be appropriate here. The AV attempts to cover both options with 'I will leave thee *thrown*'. Crocodiles can travel some distance out of water, but what was envisaged by ***open country*** (or 'field') was not cultivable land, but the deserts outwith the congenial environment of the Nile valley. ***Not brought together or gathered***, probably with a view to burial, portrayed an ignominious end (cf. 39:4; Deut. 28:26; Jer. 34:20), especially for an Egyptian monarch who would lavish state resources on erecting a suitable tomb for himself.[61]

♦ **29:6a** ***Then all the inhabitants of Egypt will know that I ⌊am⌋ the LORD*** functioned here, as elsewhere, to conclude the preceding oracle, so that the verse division was inappropriate. When the predicted calamity befell Pharaoh and his realm, his subjects would relearn the lesson of the Exodus (Exod. 7:5, 17). With the trappings of power stripped from Pharaoh and his arrogance undermined, the Egyptians would come to appreciate that the real motivating and controlling force in their land was none other than the LORD himself.

(b) The Splintered Staff (29:6b-9a)
The focus in this section is on another metaphor which is used to bring out the implications of the way Egypt is meddling in the affairs of the LORD's people. The thought moves from the arrogance of Pharaoh to

---

61. Translations such as RSV and NRSV which render 'not be gathered and buried' have probably accepted the emendation of *tiqqābēṣ*, 'you will be gathered', to *tiqqābēr*, 'you will be buried', on the evidence of the Targum and several Hebrew manuscripts. But the use of the former verb in the fulfilment recorded in 29:13 indicates that the change is not necessary. Moreover, the proposed emendation does not really affect the sense of the passage.

the delusive alliance and support he extends to Judah by alluring them into opposing Babylon contrary to the announced will of God. The comparison with a reed had been employed earlier by the Assyrian Rabshaqeh when Jerusalem was besieged in 701 B.C. 'Behold, you have put your trust in this staff of a broken reed, in Egypt, which ⌊if⌋ anyone leans on it, it will go into his hand and pierce it; so is Pharaoh, king of Egypt, to all who are trusting in him' (Isa. 36:6). Similarly when, over a century later, Zedekiah seeks Egyptian help (17:15–18), despite the assurances Egypt gives, the promised assistance proves to be no more than a token gesture (Jer. 37:5–7). Once more Egypt is exposed as all words, and little or no action. So it is a delusion to treat it as a potential source of protection and defence rather than the LORD.

> 29:6b⌐ "Because they have been a staff of reed to the house of Israel—29:7when they seized you by the hand, you would splinter and tear all their shoulders, and when they supported themselves upon you, you would break and cause to stand for them all hIps—29:8therefore thus says the Lord GOD: Behold, I am about to cause a sword to come against you, and I will cut off from you man and animal, 29:9and the land of Egypt will become a desolation and a ruin. And they will know that I ⌊am⌋ the LORD." '

♦ **29:6b** *Because they have been* is often changed to 'because you (singular) have been',[62] looking back to the previous description of Pharaoh and to the following verse. However, Hebrew use of pronouns was flexible, and a third person plural reflecting 'all the inhabitants of Egypt' presents no real difficulty. *A staff* was a stick used to support oneself while walking. Unfortunately *the house of Israel*, the covenant people of God, had not chosen a stout stick, but were relying on a *reed*. One thinks of a hollow reed growing by the Nile. Outwardly it looked sufficient for the task, but once it was put to the test and made to bear a load, it inevitably crumpled and failed. So Egypt's condemnation arose—as had that of the nations whose downfall was predicted earlier—from its relationship with Judah, in this case because they did not provide the support they had pledged to them.

♦ **29:7** This verse was a parenthesis in which Pharaoh was directly addressed ('you' was masculine singular). His inadequate response was described in two parallel statements, in each of which a set of circumstances produced a similar outcome. In *when they seized you by*

---

62. This is the rendering of the LXX, Peshitta, and Vulgate.

the hand, 'seized' or 'grasped' referred to the action of Judah. It was wrong for them to compromise their loyalty to the LORD by abandoning their reliance on him and substituting merely human support in his place. This proved to be a disastrous course of action because the reed, that is, Pharaoh as the leader of his nation, could not take the strain: *you would splinter and tear all their shoulders*. The verb form implied that this happened on more than one occasion.[63] The exact nature of the injury received is unclear, but was apparently more serious than the piercing of the hand which the Rabshaqeh had predicted (Isa. 36:6 || 2 Kgs. 18:21). 'Shoulder' in Hebrew may refer to the whole upper torso,[64] and so the thought might be that the sharp splinter of the snapped reed thrust upwards into their armpit (cf. Hummel 2007:879). Reliance on the expected source of help resulted in injury, not relief.

The second scenario was a virtual repeat of the first, though the focus of the injury was lower in the body. When Judah required support and sought it from Pharaoh, the reed broke and left them to fall to the ground. The outcome expressed by *cause to stand for them all hips* is obscure, and, if anything, seems to yield a sense the opposite of what is expected in this context. While it might mean 'leave them to stand on their own', most translations assume that two consonants have been reversed and render 'make all their hips/loins shake', a fumbling, unsteady response in an unexpected situation (cf. Ps. 69:23).[65] This was what happened shortly after these words were uttered when Egypt aborted its attempt to come to Jerusalem's assistance (Jer. 37:7).

♦ **29:8** After the parenthesis of the preceding verse, the 'because' of 29:6 is resolved by *therefore* introducing the divine verdict. *You* was feminine singular, anticipating the feminine gender of 'land of Egypt' in the next verse. The LORD's penalty on Egypt was expressed using two stereotypical forms of doom. While *a sword* depicted enemy

---

63. The verbs *tērôṣ*, 'you will snap', and later in the verse, *tiššābēr*, 'you will break', are imperfect forms used of repeated occurrences in the past. Both verbs are followed by *waw*-consecutive perfects with a similar force.

64. The NASB favours 'hands' in line with the LXX and Peshitta which obviously read *kap*, 'hand', rather than *kātēp*, 'shoulder'. This reading was probably influenced by the similar, and better known, thought found in Isa. 36:6.

65. *BHS* proposes reading *wəhimʿadtā*, 'and you will cause to shake' (cf. Zimmerli 1983:704), in place of *wəhaʿămadtā*, 'and you will cause to stand'. The support of the LXX, Peshitta, and Vulgate is cited for this change.

invasion (cf. 5:17; and extensively in ch. 21), it did not yield any specific information about who would hold it. ***Cut off from you man and animal*** employed hyperbole to depict the devastating impact of the LORD's judgement on all forms of life in Egypt (cf. 14:13). This intensification of events at the Exodus when the LORD had struck the firstborn of man and animal (Exod. 12:12) would have stirred memories for Ezekiel's audience.

♦ **29:9a** ***A desolation and a ruin*** may well have been an instance of hendiadys for an 'utter desolation' (Greenberg 1997:605). The recognition formula asserted that in the light of this display of the LORD's power the people of Egypt would be compelled to acknowledge his existence and sovereignty.

(c) Coming Desolation (29:9b—12)

> 29:9b "Because he said, 'The Nile is mine, and I ⌐am the one who⌐ made ⌐it⌐', 29:10therefore, behold, I ⌐am⌐ against you and your streams, and I will set the land of Egypt as a site of ruins, waste, desolation, from Migdol to Syene, even as far as the border of Cush. 29:11There will not pass through it any human foot, nor will any animal's foot pass through it; and it will not be inhabited for forty years. 29:12And I will set the land of Egypt a desolation in the midst of the lands which have been desolated, and its cities in the midst of cities which have been laid waste will become a desolation for forty years, and I will disperse Egypt among the nations and scatter them among the lands." '

♦ **29:9b** The verse division was again misleading. The concluding part of 29:9 took up a different theme, resuming consideration of Pharaoh's boastful utterance in 29:3, ***Because he said,***[66] ***The Nile is mine, and I*** ⌐***am the one who***⌐ ***made*** ⌐***it***⌐***.*** Both statements were slightly less sweeping than before, but they embodied essentially the same claim of ownership of the Nile through having formed it. But this was bluster without substance. Rulers have a legitimate role in God's purposes of common grace, but if they exceed this, they dupe themselves as to their own significance.

♦ **29:10** ***Therefore*** again introduced the LORD's verdict, which was

---

66. 'You said' (cf. LXX, Peshitta, Vulgate) is often read in English versions instead of 'he said', but again this is most probably a stylistic adjustment introduced by the translators. The sense is unaffected.

expressed using the opposition formula (cf. 5:8; 29:3) and employed Pharaoh's self-perception to indict him. ***Against you and your streams*** ('you' was masculine singular) referred both to Pharaoh and to the various distributaries and irrigation channels which flowed from the Nile in the delta region (cf. 29:3–4). These stood for the vast array of physical resources to be found in Egypt. The three nouns ***ruins, waste, a desolation*** may be variously combined, but taking the first two as an intensificatory repetition of the same root yields the sense 'utter ruins' (*ḥorbôt ḥōreb*) with ***desolation*** in apposition as a further explanation. Subsequent verses elaborated on this threat against the land of Egypt. There was no further mention of Pharaoh in this oracle; he had been effectively sidelined by divine opposition.

The magnitude of the impending destruction was set out using what was probably a traditional expression for the full extent of Egypt from north to south. ***Migdol*** was a city located round a border watchtower or fortress in the north-east of the delta region (cf. Jer. 44:1; 46:14), near the trade route north along the Mediterranean coast. ***Syene*** was the modern Aswan in the far south, near the first cataract of the Nile. Both sites are known to have had Jewish communities employed as mercenaries in Egyptian service. ***Even*** (an explicative use of 'and') ***as far as the border of Cush*** pointed to territory which lay south of Aswan, corresponding to modern Sudan.

♦ **29:11** ***There will not pass through it any human foot, nor will any animal's foot pass through it*** was a finely balanced Hebrew expression to depict the emptiness of the land. ***It will not be inhabited for forty years*** probably employed 'forty years' to express a full generation (this is similar to the forty years of 4:6). The threefold repetition of this time phrase formed a significant aspect of the message. If it is taken as a realistic, rather than a symbolic, presentation, it might stretch from Nebuchadnezzar's incursion in 568 B.C. to the conquest of the land by the Persian Cambyses in 525, after which the Persians probably encouraged a measure of recovery in Egypt as one of the provinces in their empire.

♦ **29:12** ***In the midst of the lands*** indicated that Egypt was itself a land, and that it would not be exempt from the doom which had overtaken other lands, or its cities from being laid waste as other cities had been (cf. 30:7). Moreover, the LORD promised, ***I will disperse*** (cf. 11:16) ***Egypt ... and scatter*** (cf. 5:2) ***them.*** This was what had been earlier prophesied regarding Judah (12:15). Jeremiah gave greater detail regarding the way Nebuchadnezzar dealt with Egypt

(Jer. 43–44). Though dispersing populations was a standard procedure in dealing with a conquered nation, no record is extant relating such action in respect of Egypt.

(d) Egypt Restored (29:13–16)

> 29:13'For thus says the Lord GOD, "At the end of forty years I will gather Egypt from the peoples where they have been dispersed. 29:14And I will restore the fortunes of Egypt, and I will cause them to return to the land of Pathros, to the land of their origin, and there they will be a lowly kingdom. 29:15It will be the lowliest of the kingdoms, and it will no longer raise itself above the nations, and I will make them few in number so that they cannot rule over the nations. 29:16And it will no longer be the trust of the house of Israel, a reminder of iniquity when they turned after them. And they will know that I ⌊am⌋ the Lord GOD." '

♦ **29:13** *For* may here have had a contrastive force, 'but'. It introduced a clarification of why 'forty years' were mentioned—there was restoration to follow! This was an utterly unexpected development. It is not immediately evident why Egypt was to be treated in this way, when other nations were not. One perceptible difference was that Egypt had not gloated over Judah's misfortune in the way the others had done. Perhaps Pharaoh's claim to deity had been less crass than that of Tyre's king, but the beneficiary of this blessing would be the land rather than Pharaoh himself. Indeed, Egypt had attempted to come to Judah's aid. This mitigated outcome was not, however, mentioned in 30:23, but in Jeremiah 46:26b and Isaiah 19:18–25 a positive future was foretold for Egypt.

♦ **29:14–15** *I will restore the fortunes of Egypt*. For the idiom involved, see on 16:53; 39:25. The LORD promised to reinstate Egypt, but not on a grand scale. *Pathros* referred to upper Egypt, that is, the Nile valley as distinct from the delta region of lower Egypt. The restoration would therefore be a partial one, in which the loss of territory to the north would effectively distance Israel from Egyptian influence. *The land of their origin* reflected the Egyptian belief that it had been from the south that the land had been unified, and indeed on a number of occasions it was rulers from the south that brought the land back together. *A lowly kingdom* need not have implied an independent existence. It was concerned rather with political organisation under a king, but whether he was an autonomous monarch or a vassal of an overlord was not asserted (compare 17:14 as regards Zedekiah's status under Nebuchadnezzar). However, *the lowliest of the kingdoms* certainly pointed to subordinate status. *I will make them few in number* probably emphasised their military capabilities rather than their economic capacity or population size. Their reduced potential would mean that *they cannot rule over the nations*. 'Rule' (*rādâ*; cf. 34:4) pointed to a superior's dominance, using force if necessary. Egypt's empire building days would be over.

♦ **29:16** *No longer* (cf. 12:24) anticipated the time when the LORD would have intervened to effect change. In *it will no longer be*, 'it' referred to Egypt and its Pharaoh—the whole regime which the Israelites had made the object of their *trust* rather than the LORD—but the possibility of such reliance would be removed. It is unclear how *a reminder of iniquity* (lit., 'one bringing iniquity to mind') was intended to operate. Possibly the thought was that, in the absence of the Egyptian regime, Israel would regretfully recall how they had erred *when they* (the Israelites) *turned after them* (the Egyptians). Greenberg (1997:607) argues that Psalm 40:4 provided the background for the expression here. 'Blessed is the man who sets the LORD [as] his trust and does not turn to the proud', where 'the proud' was literally, the 'upsurgers', or the Rahabs, the plural of a term which was used to describe Egypt (Ps. 87:4; Isa. 30:7).

REFLECTION

- The allure of wealthy and powerful Egypt proved delusive for the people of Judah and Jerusalem when they sought help. There is no shame in needing assistance, but it is a course of folly to look for help from those who have set themselves in opposition to God. 'Now the Egyptians are human, and not God, and their horses are flesh, and not spirit. When the LORD stretches out his hand, he who helps will stumble and he who is helped will fall; they will all perish together' (Isa. 31:3; cf. Ps. 146:3–4; Jer. 17:5).
- 'A friend loves at all times' (Prov. 17:17), but Egypt's friendship was a pretence. In all that he did, Pharaoh was motivated solely by self-interest. Whenever his promises to Judah were liable to prove awkward or too costly, he promptly abandoned them, leaving Judah to fend for itself before the might of Babylon (cf. Prov. 25:19). 'All her friends have dealt treacherously with her' (Lam. 1:2). 'One who has unreliable friends soon comes to ruin, but there is a friend who sticks closer than a brother' (Prov. 18:24 NIV). Nowhere is that seen more clearly than in Jesus himself. 'No one has greater love than this, that one would lay down his life for his friends' (John 15:13).

- There would come a time when Egypt would enjoy renewed prosperity, albeit on a limited scale. This is part of God's merciful dealings even with those who oppose him, for 'he makes his sun rise on evil ⌞persons⌟ and on good, and sends rain on just ⌞persons⌟ and on unjust' (Matt. 5:45).

(2) Nebuchadnezzar's Reward (29:17–21)

This section is much later in its origin. The first four verses (29:17–20) are concerned with Nebuchadnezzar being given Egypt in return for his unprofitable activity against Tyre. As this is of obvious relevance to the future of Egypt, it is included in this set of seven oracles. It is probable that shortly after receiving this oracle, Ezekiel gathered together the records of his ministry to preserve them in the form in which we now have them. It is noteworthy that no mention is made of the Pharaoh involved. The focus is on Egypt as a whole. Theologically the matter which is brought to our attention is the fact that God rewards those who are his instruments in providence, even though they are unwitting in the role they are playing. Given, however, God's dealings with Nebuchadnezzar through Daniel, it may well be going too far to call him 'unwitting' (Dan. 4:34–37).

That this is the only dated oracle of Ezekiel which is placed out of historical sequence undeniably reflects an editorial decision. While some see the decision as made by a later figure(s), probably intending to cope with a situation in which an earlier prophetic prediction had not been realised, there is nothing to rule out that it is the prophet himself who has edited his work, and placed this oracle early in the Egyptian collection because it also involves Tyre. It should be noted that the text does not state that the earlier predictions regarding Tyre had not been realised—that is read into it by taking the sparse plunder carried off from Tyre (29:18–19) as equivalent to no plunder at all, and finding in that a contradiction to 26:12. It would seem that the judgement of Tyre was provisional, part of a complex set of divine interventions which culminates in the final resolution of earth history.

The final verse of the chapter (29:21) contains no translational difficulties, but its meaning is far from clear. If it is a messianic prophecy, its connection with the preceding verses is not immediately obvious. It may function to extend the timescale of the prophecy into the more distant future when the LORD would act to bless his people.

29:17And it came about in the twenty-seventh year, in the first ⌞month⌟, on the first of the month that the word of the LORD came to me, saying, 29:18'Son of man, Nebuchadnezzar, king of Babylon, has made his force labour hard against Tyre; every head was made bald and every shoulder was rubbed bare; yet neither he nor his force had any reward from Tyre for the labour which he had expended on it. $^{29:19}$Therefore thus says the Lord GOD, "Behold, I am about to give to Nebuchadnezzar, king of Babylon, the land of Egypt, and he will carry off its wealth and despoil its spoil and plunder its plunder, and it will be a reward for his force. $^{29:20}$As his wage for which he has worked I have given him the land of Egypt which they made for me, declares the Lord GOD.

$^{29:21}$On that day I will cause to sprout a horn for the house of Israel, and to you I will give an opening of your mouth in their midst. And they will know that I ⌊am⌋ the LORD." '

♦ **29:17** *In the twenty-seventh year, in the first ⌊month⌋, on the first of the month* refers to 26th April 571 B.C. This oracle therefore is dated two years after Ezekiel's vision of the ideal temple and city (40:1) and about 16 years and 4 months after the previous oracle (29:1). It seems to have been written not long after Nebuchadnezzar eventually accepted a compromise with Tyre and gave up his siege. This oracle was then incorporated here to be along with the other material concerning Egypt. The message reception formula occurred as usual, and was followed in the next verse with God's characteristic title for the prophet.

♦ **29:18** The subject of the oracle was the Babylonian emperor (rather than Egypt), and this verse set out the reasons for the LORD's intervention in the situation. *Has made his force labour hard* was literally 'has made his force labour with great labour'. For thirteen years Nebuchadnezzar went to great lengths to capture the island fortress of Tyre. *Every head was made bald* probably referred to chafing of soldiers' skin from being at the ready for a long time wearing a helmet, though it might have been the case that some loads were carried on the head. Carrying of loads seems the obvious explanation for *every shoulder was rubbed bare*. Whatever means Nebuchadnezzar employed to besiege the city (there is no record to support the supposition that he tried to build a causeway such as Alexander successfully constructed years later), they involved great effort, but proved unsuccessful. Possibly the military activities were focused on preventing supplies being taken from the mainland to Tyre; instead they had to be shipped in to the island from afar, perhaps from as far away as Egypt. *The reward* the besieging forces expected was the booty they would acquire from capturing the city. When the

Babylonians overran mainland Tyre, the inhabitants would have transported any moveable goods to the island fortress for security, so that no significant booty would have been present for the raiders to loot. In the resolution of the siege, probably through a negotiated settlement, the Tyrians may have made some payment to lift the siege, but they were impoverished by that time and their tribute could not have amounted to much.

♦ **29:19** *Therefore* introduced the LORD's proposed course of action to reward Nebuchadnezzar. *I am about to give* showed his absolute control in disposition of the kingdoms of this world. In place of Tyre the LORD was going to give Nebuchadnezzar *the land of Egypt. He will carry off its multitude.* The term 'multitude' (*hāmôn*) was multivalent, and could refer to population as well as to abundance of wealth or riches. 'Multitude' was used sixteen times in the oracles against Egypt (out of 84 occurrences in the Old Testament as a whole), and on many of these occasions it may be more suitably taken to refer not to material wealth but to people, especially prisoners of war forced into slavery.

♦ **29:20** *I shall give him* was an instance of a prophetic perfect, a future action regarded as so certain that it was presented as already complete (Introduction §6.3b). *Which they made for me* is absent in the Septuagint and the Peshitta. It may be that the relative term 'which' (*'ăšer*) had here a causal sense, 'because they made it for me', that is, the work he had done in besieging Tyre.

♦ **29:21** Interpreters express considerable hesitation regarding this verse, for which two main styles of explanation have been advanced.

(1) Taking *on that day* as linked to the preceding four verses, the prophecy may be viewed associated with the day of Egypt's impending despoliation at the hands of Nebuchadnezzar. *I will cause to sprout a horn* used a metaphor frequently employed for strength and power to predict an upturn in Israel's fortunes. The phrase is 'a general reference to an approaching deliverance for Israel' (Zimmerli 1983:120). *I will give an opening of your mouth in their midst* related to a renewal of Ezekiel's ministry in the community, possibly with greater impact and acceptance.

(2) However, the verse did not commence with the ubiquitous Hebrew conjunction 'and', which at least opened up the possibility that it was not to be read too closely with the preceding verses. *On that day* was obvious eschatological language, and may be taken as

referring to an aspect of the divine reordering of human affairs. Just as Babylon's destiny and that of Egypt were under his control, so too was that of *the house of Israel.*

Moreover, the phrase *I will cause to sprout a horn* was employed particularly in relation to God and his salvation (2 Sam. 22:3 || Ps. 18:2; Pss. 89:17, 24; 112:9; 148:14). More specifically, it pointed to a ruler God would provide for his people, through whom they would enjoy prosperity and security. The noun derived from the root 'sprout' was used of the messianic king, the Branch (Jer. 23:5; 33:15; Zech. 3:8; 6:12, and from a different root, Isa. 4:2; 61:11). So Israel's prosperity was ultimately associated with the coming of the Messiah, who is truly 'a horn of salvation for us in the house of his servant David' (Luke 1:69). This was in fulfilment of the divine promise, 'There I will cause to sprout a horn for David; I have got ready a lamp for my Anointed' (Ps. 132:17).

Consequently, it is not far-fetched to conclude 'this is a verse of "messianic" hope' (Joyce 2007:182), though one would wish to demur from Joyce's additional characterisation of the verse as 'isolated in the midst of the oracles against Egypt'. Rather it is an instance of the foreshortening of time horizons in which the LORD would not speak of providing an earthly reward for Nebuchadnezzar without reminding his people of his promise of the far greater reward that he held in store for them.[67]

The LORD also had a word of consolation for the prophet: *to you I will give an opening of your mouth* (cf. 16:63) *in their midst.* This did not reflect the prophet being rendered dumb (3:26–27) because that was linked to the fall of Jerusalem, and had already been reversed in 33:21–22, fourteen years before this oracle. Most probably it indicated that Ezekiel's prophecies would be verified and his credibility vindicated (Greenberg 1997:616). The thought may indeed have been that this would take place posthumously. Whenever it occurred, it would lead to the desired response on Israel's part, expressed by the recognition formula: *they will know that I ₌am₌ the LORD.*

---

67. 'The fact that the fulfilment of the prophecies against Tyre has been delayed for more than a decade does not mean Yahweh has forgotten his promises to Israel or his debt to Nebuchadnezzar. When the prophet and his people see him settling this outstanding account they may take heart that Yahweh's long-standing account with Israel (albeit of a different nature) will also be settled' (Block 1995:169).

REFLECTION

- In the flow of history God has not been pleased to use angelic armies to enforce his purposes. He has preferred to work through human agents, even though they did not acknowledge his authority and remained unaware of the role they were playing. It was in that sense that the LORD had called Nebuchadnezzar 'my servant' (Jer. 27:6). A servant need not know what his master is doing; his duty is to obey (cf. John 15:15). Nebuchadnezzar's actions were, however, motivated by his own ambition and greed, for which he would be held accountable. It is the intention behind an individual's action which determines its moral character (cf. Luke 12:47–48). This had been notably exemplified in the case of the king of Assyria who came against Judah as the rod of the LORD's anger (Isa. 10:5), but he did not appreciate this and acted for other reasons (Isa. 10:7–11), for which he was divinely judged (Isa. 10:12–19).

  However, the LORD will be indebted to no human being. Even those who are not aware of their role in his purposes will be rewarded when what they have done conforms to the LORD's will, despite the fact that their own motives are corrupt.

(3) Judgement on Egypt (30:1–19)

In terms of its content this third oracle against Egypt adds little to what has already been said in chapter 29, particularly 29:8–12. For this reason many critics assign it to a later disciple of Ezekiel (Zimmerli 1983:127–128; Eichrodt 1970:415). The grounds for doing so, that it contains nothing new, are insufficient to justify such a move. Others suspect the authenticity of these verses because they consider their literary quality to be inferior to that of Ezekiel. That in itself is highly subjective, and forms an inadequate basis for a verdict regarding authenticity in the face of a direct claim to the contrary (30:1).

There are four sections to the oracle: (a) an initial announcement of the LORD's judgement coming on Egypt, 30:1–5; (b) the impact of the judgement on Egypt upon her allies, 30:6–9; (c) the announcement of Nebuchadnezzar as the LORD's agent, 30:10–12; (d) the comprehensive scope of what will befall Egypt, 30:13–19.

This oracle is undated and its content general. It is consequently difficult to establish when the material found here originated, though its location after 29:1–16 and before 30:20 may reflect the time of Hophra's attempt to aid Jerusalem during the final siege. Alternatively, but less probably, because it follows 29:17–21, it may be connected with the period when Nebuchadnezzar raised the siege of Tyre and turned his attention to Egypt. It repeats the content of the first oracle in the form of a lament.

(a) The Day of the LORD (30:1–5)
This oracle takes up the theme of the day of the LORD, a term used to describe a significant intervention by the LORD in human affairs (see Introduction to ch. 7). Originally this had been viewed as a time of relief for Israel from their opponents, but the prophet Amos had been used to turn such traditional expectations upside down in his day. The internal injustices perpetrated within the northern kingdom of Israel had become so heinous that divine intervention would not bring deliverance to the land but imposition of penalty on it (Amos 5:18–20; 8:9–10). That was the way this theme was employed in chapter 7, but here it reverts to its original focus—divine intervention will be the occasion for scrutiny of the conduct of other nations and for demanding a reckoning from them. This will result in the overthrow of Egypt and her allies. Ironically, these were the very people so many in Judah had placed their hopes for deliverance on, and indeed a significant number from Judah were serving as mercenaries in the Egyptian army. The day of the LORD will be one of darkness for the expectations of those who no longer put their trust in the LORD.

This poem is not technically a lament occasioned by the death of an individual; rather it is a dirge, an expression of grief and distress at an impending calamity. Joyce (2007:182) explains that no date was included because 'it would be awkward to have a dating formula alongside reference to an indeterminate eschatological day.'

^{30:1}And the word of the LORD came to me, saying, ^{30:2}'Son of man, prophesy and say, "Thus says the Lord GOD:
    Wail, 'Alas for the day!'
^{30:3} For a day ⌊is⌋ near,
    even a day of the LORD ⌊is⌋ near;
  a day of clouds,
    a time for the nations it will be.
^{30:4} And a sword will come against Egypt,
    and anguish will be in Cush.
  When the slain fall in Egypt,
    they will take its abundance,
  and its foundations will be razed.
^{30:5}Cush and Put and Lud and all the mixed multitude and Kub and the people of the allied land will fall with them by the sword." '

♦ **30:1** The oracle began with the message-reception formula (cf. 3:16), but with no indication of a date. However, the date given in 30:20 probably indicated the general time period of the oracle. The repeated message-reception formula there also established the literary extent of this oracle.

♦ **30:2** For *Son of man*, the conventional divine address to the prophet, see on 2:1. Ezekiel was commanded to *prophesy*, presumably to his fellow exiles, and to introduce his communication with the messenger formula. Unlike 21:12 where *wail* was used to direct the prophet himself to lament, here a plural imperative was addressed to those who would be adversely affected by the day, particularly the Egyptians, but also their allies (30:5). This information regarding the impending day and its implications constituted a warning to them, calling them to repent. *Alas!* (*hāh*, an abbreviated form of *'ăhāh*, 'Oh no!', 11:13; 20:49). *For the day*, see on 7:7. This would be a time of divine intervention in judgement which anticipated the final day. Though this warning was ostensibly directed to the Egyptians, in effect it cautioned the covenant community not to rely on Egypt's assistance because that country would itself be soon engulfed by disaster.

♦ **30:3** *For* (*kî*) may have had asseverative force, 'indeed', but most probably it introduced the reasons why Egypt and its allies were directed to wail. *A day of the LORD* clarified what was being referred to as 'a day'. Though the phrase was not expressed in quite its usual form, its significance was similar, a time of divine scrutiny and reckoning. That it *is near* was often asserted in the prophets (Isa. 13:6; Joel 2:1; 3:14; Zeph. 1:7, 14), but it was not easy to translate this imminence into a precise time span. All depended on the sovereign timing of God, but the conditions giving rise to his visitation in judgement already existed and so there were no grounds for presuming there would inevitably be a delay.

The singular noun 'cloud' was evidently used in a collective sense to presage impending doom (cf. Joel 2:2; 3:15; Zeph. 1:15). *A time for the nations* referred to the imposition of divine judgement (cf. 21:25, 29 where 'end' also occurs). It would no longer be just his own people whom the LORD would summon to hear his verdict, but the world as a whole, because the doom which would be imposed on Egypt had implications for all mankind.

♦ **30:4** The reason for the lament was the penalty about to be inflicted on Egypt. It was expressed in stark terms. *A sword* was described in almost personal terms (***will come***) as the agent of the LORD's punishment through external military intervention and conflict (cf. 5:17). ***Anguish*** (*ḥalḥālâ*) may be too weak a rendering for this reduplicated form (Greenberg 1997:621), which denoted writhing with sudden and gripping pain as in childbirth (Isa. 21:3; Nah. 2:10). The term was also assonant with 'slain'/'pierced' (*ḥālāl*) in the following line, suggesting the panic was related to the extent of the slaughter.

Cush was the region to the south of Egypt (roughly modern Sudan). Its fortunes depended upon Egypt. Indeed the pharaohs of the twenty-fifth dynasty of Egypt (710–663 B.C.) originated in Cush. Whereas the first line of the verse predicted slaughter in Egypt, all that was said regarding Cush was that it would be seized with consternation at events to its north.

Fall was repeated in 30:5 and twice in 30:6, linking these verses and emphasising the widespread nature of the slaughter which would overwhelm the Egyptians. ***They will take*** had an unspecified subject which was obviously enemy forces. ***Abundance*** (*hāmôn*, cf. 29:19) was a key word in the Egyptian texts, and here it probably pointed to the wealth of material resources in Egypt. ***Its foundations will be razed*** possibly went further than levelling the structures of buildings to unearth and destroy the massive stones at the base of buildings. This was a picture of a nation mercilessly wiped out of existence and deprived of any hope of recovery.

♦ **30:5** Those who treat this verse as prose often consider it to be a pedestrian insertion into the text, but it did form a link with the downfall of Egypt and her allies along with her in 30:6–9. Six groups were identified. ***Cush and Put and Lud*** were three lands whose location is well established: Cush (Nubia) on the Nile to the south of Egypt; Put (Libya) to the west; and Lud (Lydia) in Asia Minor. The last two places were also mentioned in 27:10. All three had contributed men to the army of Pharaoh Neco which had lost to the Babylonians at Carchemish in 605 B.C. (cf. Jer. 46:9).

All the mixed multitude denoted a group drawn from a variety of racial backgrounds (cf. Exod. 12:38; Neh. 13:3). In this context they were mercenaries enlisted in the Egyptian army.[68] It is unclear what ***Kub*** referred to, as the term did not appear elsewhere. The Septuagint

---

68. The Peshitta evidently vocalised *ʿēreb*, 'mixed multitude', as *ʿărab*, 'Arabia', and this is followed by NIV, NRSV, ESV. However, Arabs were not present in Egypt in any significant numbers before the sixth century A.D., and this understanding is less probable.

rendering 'Libyans' suggests that there may have been a scribal error for 'Libya' (for which the Hebrew might have been *lûb*). Possibly Put and Kub/Lub were two areas in the region we now know as Libya, though the term may have been used for north Africa generally. In Nahum 3:9 Put and Libya were associated as allies of Egypt.

The people of the allied land (lit., 'the sons of the land of the treaty/covenant') is an equally puzzling reference. The group referred to might have been allies from an unnamed territory adjacent to Egypt, but it is unclear why they would have been mentioned separately from 'the mixed multitude' and in such an anonymous fashion. Although the term 'the land of the covenant' was not found elsewhere in the Old Testament in reference to Israel,[69] it is possible that was its scope here to avoid classifying them as part of the 'mixed multitude'. If the reference was to groups from the northern or southern kingdoms who had settled in Egypt (cf. Jer. 24:8), many serving as mercenaries in Egyptian armies, this oblique form of identification might have conveyed a measure of suspicion as to their religious loyalty. Another possibility is that they were military contingents sent to Egypt by Zedekiah as part of the arrangements for an alliance (cf. 17:13–21).

(b) Egypt's Allies (30:6–9)

The LORD's judgement on Egypt has serious implications for those who are its allies. And that is a warning for all those in Judah and among the exiles who groundlessly place their hopes there.

> 30:6 "Thus says the LORD:
> Those who support Egypt will fall,
>   and the pride of its strength will come down.
> From Migdol to Syene
>   they will fall in it by the sword,
>   declares the Lord GOD.
> 30:7 And they will be desolate in the midst of desolate lands,
>   and its cities will be in the midst of cities that have been
>   laid waste.
> 30:8 And they will know that I ⌊am⌋ the LORD,
>   when I set fire in Egypt
>   and all its helpers are broken.
> 30:9 On that day messengers will go out from before me in ships to startle complacent Cush, and anguish will be on them on the day of Egypt, for, behold, it is coming!"'

---

69. That interpretation is found in the LXX which reads 'sons of *my* covenant'.

♦ **30:6** The shorter messenger formula (with the LORD rather than Lord GOD) also occurs at 11:5 and 21:3, and unusually the verse also includes a terminal signatory formula, ***declares the Lord GOD*** (cf. 5:11), where the double designation occurs. This emphasised that what was being revealed was the fixed resolve of the sovereign God.

Support was used to refer to assistance extended to an individual, frequently by the LORD (cf. Pss. 3:5; 37:17, 24; 54:4; 119:116), but here it described those who extended military aid to Egypt. ***The pride of its strength*** was a Hebrew idiom for 'its/her proud strength', the extent of the land's self-assured reliance on military might and economic prowess. These would be to no avail since ***will come down*** predicted the overthrow of Egypt's armies, even though bolstered by allies and mercenaries.

For ***from Migdol to Syene***, that is, throughout the whole land from north to south, see on 29:10.

♦ **30:7** This verse reflected the prophecy of 29:11. The cities of Egypt which functioned as the administrative centres of the land ***will be desolate***, ruined and without population (cf. 6:4), because of the invasion they were unable to repel. Possibly, ***in the midst of desolate lands*** suggested that they would become like the desert which surrounded the Nile valley. ***Its***[70] ***cities ... in the midst of cities*** pictured not just the destruction of one city, but of all that lay along the Nile. Such extensive devastation occurred only rarely in Egyptian history.

♦ **30:8** The recognition formula, ***they will know that I ⌞am⌟ the LORD***, was expanded to disclose that the goal of the LORD's action against Egypt and its allies was to compel them to acknowledge his sovereign control when he ***set fire in Egypt and all its helpers are broken***. There was no hint of this acknowledgement being positive, as for instance that their recognition involved submission to him.

♦ **30:9 On that day** linked the additional information in this verse into the previous scenario. ***From before me*** pointed to the ***messengers*** being sent by divine mandate, but their mode of travel indicated that angels were not in view. ***In ships*** used an Egyptian loan word (cf. Num. 24:24; Isa. 33:21; Dan. 11:30), which probably did not refer to a

---

70. The pronominal suffix on 'its cities' (*'ārāyw*) is masculine as distinct from the feminine references to Egypt so far. Possibly the thought is 'his cities', that is, Pharaoh's.

small trading boat but to a more robustly constructed military vessel. Since **Cush** (Nubia; cf. 30:5) was upstream from Egypt, what was pictured here was a reversal of the scene in which ambassadors from Cush had come down the Nile in papyrus craft (Isa. 18:1–2). Here emissaries would advance upstream in sturdy craft to *startle complacent Cush* with the news of what had happened to Egypt. Because in this context the outlook of the Cushites was not soundly based on the facts of the situation, 'security' or 'securely' (*beṭaḥ*; cf. 28:26; 34:25) is rendered 'complacent'. No longer could they rely on their remoteness to insulate them from events in Egypt; indeed, they would have a significant impact on their fortunes.

Anguish (30:4) would grip Cush, Egypt's ally, when it learned of the downfall of its northern neighbour. *On the day of Egypt* (cf. 'day of Midian' in Isa. 9:4) referred to the same time as the initial phrase in the verse, that is, when the LORD imposed his judgement on Egypt. This was no remote possibility, *for, behold, it is coming!* Ezekiel's audience too should give heed to the warning and adjust their expectations because of the imminent disaster.

(c) Egypt Devastated by Babylon (30:10–12)
This and the following section are often treated as secondary miscellaneous compilations drawn together by Ezekielian tradents. But there is no particular reason why the prophet should not have presented a compendium of the disclosures God had made to him when he proclaimed the divine message on a variety of occasions.

The major theme is that in the ruination of Egypt the LORD will work through the agency of Babylon and, in particular, through its emperor, Nebuchadnezzar (cf. 29:18–20).

> 30:10ᵛ "Thus says the Lord GOD:
> I will make an end to the abundance of Egypt
> by the hand of Nebuchadnezzar, king of Babylon.
> 30:11 He and his people with him, violent ones of nations,
> will be brought to destroy the land,
> and they will draw their swords against Egypt,
> and they will fill the land with the slain.
> 30:12 And I will make the rivers dry,
> and will sell the land into the hand of evildoers;
> and I will make the land and its fulness desolate
> by the hand of strangers.
> I ⌊am⌋ the LORD; I have spoken." '

♦ **30:10** The focus was on the individual whom the LORD would employ as the instrument (*by the hand of*) to accomplish his purposes. He was named as *Nebuchadnezzar, king of Babylon* (cf. 29:19). While the king acted on his own initiative, the LORD would use him to reverse Egypt's prosperity. *I will put an end* (cf. 26:13) stressed the sovereign and irreversible imposition of the LORD. *Abundance* (*hāmôn*, 29:19) referred to Egypt's population, its wealth, or both.

♦ **30:11** *Will be brought* with its passive form showed that the ultimate determinant in the situation was not the will of the Babylonian king. All was controlled by the LORD (cf. 28:7) who disposes of human kings as he pleases. Moreover, when God brought Nebuchadnezzar, he would not come simply on his own. *His people* referred to the army of Babylon, who were described as *violent ones of nations* (cf. 28:7), formidable adversaries drawn from throughout the empire. Without compunction they would press home the advantage of their superior strength. *Will draw their swords* was literally 'will empty their swords', that is, empty their scabbards of their swords. This contrasted effectively with the result, *they will fill the land with the slain.*

♦ **30:12** Throughout this verse the verbs were first person singular as the emphasis fell on the direct action of the LORD. *I will make the rivers dry* showed him in control of the climate so as to bring dire conditions of drought upon Egypt. Agriculture and the prosperity of the nation were utterly dependent on the Nile for water. When the Nile failed to flood and the irrigation channels which led off it lacked water, famine was inevitable, and the economy collapsed. Through his control of natural phenomena, the LORD would make Egypt uninhabitable.

I will sell the land into the hand of evildoers indicated that the LORD would also act to bring Egypt under the control of those who would inflict evil/calamity on the land (see on 6:10) rather than those who would act without regard for moral standards. *I will make the land and its fulness desolate* (cf. 30:7), rendering it without population, without resources, and with a ruined infrastructure. This was a summary of all that the LORD would impose *by the hand of strangers*, the intermediaries through whom he would work. Strangers, especially when present in large numbers, generally constituted a threat, and hence the implications of hostility in the term. The announcement formula, *I ₍am₎ the LORD*, with the addition of *I have spoken,* expressed the divine guarantee that this prophetic word would certainly be fulfilled (cf. 5:15).

(d) Widespread Devastation (30:13-19)

The extent of the judgement which will come upon Egypt is emphasised by revealing that it will encompass the idols at the centre of the nation's religious life and also the major cities which were at the centre of its political and social fabric. The confused welter of names in Egypt, which are listed without any discernible geographical order, evokes scenes of turbulence and upheaval in the land. Ezekiel's statements reveal that he possessed considerable knowledge of Egypt.

> 30:13ᵛ "Thus says the Lord GOD:
> And I will destroy ⌊the⌋ idols
>   and will make an end of images from Noph;
> and there will no longer be a ruler from the land of Egypt,
>   and I will set fear in the land of Egypt.
> 30:14 And I will make Pathros desolate,
>   and will set fire in Zoan,
>   and execute judgements in No.
> 30:15 And I will pour out my fury upon Sin, the stronghold of Egypt,
>   and cut off the multitude of No.
> 30:16 And I will set fire in Egypt;
>   Sin will writhe in pain,
>   and No will be breached,
>   and Noph ⌊will face⌋ adversaries daily.
> 30:17 The young men of Awen and Pi-beseth will fall by the sword,
>   and these ⌊women⌋ will go into captivity.
> 30:18 And at Tehaphnehes the day shall hold back ⌊its light⌋
>   when I break there the yokes of Egypt;
>   and the pride of her power will come to an end in her.
>   She will be covered by a cloud
>   and her daughters will go into captivity.
> 30:19 And I will execute judgements in Egypt;
>   and they will know that I ⌊am⌋ the LORD."'

♦ **30:13** The LORD's action against Egypt would extend to *the idols* (*gillûlîm*, see on 6:4). *The images*, 'the little gods' (*ʾĕlîlîm*), did not occur elsewhere in Ezekiel but was a favourite term of Isaiah, and was also found earlier (Lev. 19:4; 26:1). Probably its incorporation of root for God (*ʾēl*) led to Ezekiel's avoidance of the term (cf. 6:4).[71] In

---

71. The LXX omits 'I will destroy the idols'. Also, the LXX reads in place of *ʾĕlîlîm*, 'little gods', *ʾēlîm*, 'mighty ones', 'leaders' (cf. 31:11), which yields 'I shall make an end of the petty rulers and wipe out the chieftains of Noph' (REB). But the MT is clear and no change is needed.

ancient thinking destruction of a country meant the impotence of its gods (cf. 'against all the gods of Egypt I will execute judgements', Exod. 12:12). So here the overthrow of Egypt exposed the worthlessness of the gods the Egyptians trusted in. *Noph*, otherwise known as Memphis, lay 15 miles (24 km) south of the Delta, just south of modern Cairo, at the boundary between Upper and Lower Egypt. It was an important city in ancient times, sometimes functioning as the capital. As a cultural and religious centre, destruction of its gods was a devastating event in the affairs of Egypt.

There will no longer be a ruler from the land of Egypt. This is not easy to interpret, but 'ruler' (*nāśî'*, 7:27) seems to be contrasted with Pharaoh, the king of Egypt who was acclaimed as divine. Now not even one with less pretentious status would arise from the land. The implication seems to be that the land would lack native rulers, and this was in fact the case as after 525 B.C. Egypt succumbed in turn to the Persians, Greeks, Ptolemies, and Romans, before being overwhelmed by Muslim forces.

Without idols to worship or a ruler to direct them, the Egyptians would be subject to divinely imposed *fear*. This was an unusual use of the term in the Old Testament, being neither the fear of what is awesome (cf. 1:18) nor the reverential attitude that should characterise those who approach God. Rather it referred to the terror of anarchy that gripped a society when it was deprived of fixed institutions that provided stability for their land.

♦ **30:14** The damaging toll of the foreign invasion was presented by means of its impact on a catalogue of sites in Egypt, of which the first three were listed in this verse. *Pathros* was not a city but a region in Upper Egypt, stretching south to Syene (Aswan; cf. 29:10, 14). The LORD would *make* it *desolate* (cf. 30:7). *Zoan* (known to the Greeks as Tanis) was situated in the eastern Delta, about 30 miles (48 km) from the sea, and was often a royal residence. Fire would destroy it.

No, in full No-Amon (Nah. 3:8), the city of the god Amon, is better known by its Greek name, Thebes, and lay 450 miles (725 km) south of the Mediterranean. It was often the political centre of Egypt and many impressive buildings were located there, whose ruins can still be seen at Karnak, Luxor, and the Valley of the Kings. But despite all its splendour and influence the LORD would *execute judgements* there (cf. 5:10).

♦ **30:15** Yet another Egyptian site was mentioned in this verse, *Sin*. The meaning of the Egyptian name is *stronghold*. It is normally identified as Pelusium, a fortress town in the far north-east of Egypt on the road to the land of the Philistines, where it functioned as an important border control point for movement to and from Syria-Palestine and all points north of that. For a second time *No* was spoken about, as the LORD announced his determination to *cut off the multitude* (or 'abundance'; cf. 29:19) of No/Thebes when divine judgement was imposed through premature death.

♦ **30:16** The devastation would extend throughout Egypt as the LORD *set fire*, probably as a consequence of enemy pillaging, throughout the land. Consequently, *Sin will writhe in pain* (cf. 30:4).[72] For 'Sin' (Pelusium) the Septuagint read 'Syene' (Aswan, as in 29:10; 30:6), switching the scene from north to south. Migdol and Pelusium were probably quite close together.

The walls of *No will be breached* as the enemy overwhelmed the besieged city. There was no verb in the last line of the verse, and many emendations have been proposed. It is, however, not difficult to understand the description as one of Noph (30:13) under daily siege, or else openly ('by day') attacked by others.

♦ **30:17** *Awen* was a deliberate distortion of the name of the city of On, so that it was read as a Hebrew noun for 'wickedness' or 'injustice'. The city had been the residence of Potiphera, priest of On, Joseph's father-in-law (Gen. 41:45), and was located 6 miles (10 km) north of modern Cairo. It was also known as Beth-Shemesh ('house of the sun', Jer. 43:13, equivalent to the Greek Heliopolis), because it was the centre of worship of the Egyptian sun gods, Ra and Atun.

Pi-beseth ('house of the goddess Bastet', known to the Greeks as Bubastis) was about 40 miles (64 km) north of Cairo on the easternmost distributary of the Nile, and had been a capital city during the twenty-third and twenty-second dynasties (950–725 B.C.). Bastet was a major Egyptian cat/lioness goddess, in whose worship women played a major role. This may have been the reason for the two feminine plural forms, *these*, and *will go into captivity* (cf. 30:23, 26). Mention of the women (cf. LXX, RSV, NLT) also balanced the earlier

---

72. In *ḥûl tāḥîl* (kethib) the qere substitutes *tāḥûl* for the second word, but the meaning is unaffected, 'will writhe in pain', as the two verbs *ḥîl* and *ḥûl* are of similar meaning. The former denoted turning round and round whereas the latter, which occurs more frequently, refers to being in labour and is used extensively for pain and trembling such as that associated with childbirth. The preceding infinitive absolute would ordinarily be *ḥôl* for either root, but is here spelled by attraction to the following qere form.

young men, who would be killed. Alternatively, the feminine forms may reflect the grammatical gender of the Hebrew word for 'city', so that what was being asserted was that the surviving population of both of these places would be enslaved (cf. AV, NIV, NRSV).

♦ **30:18** *Tehaphnehes* was an alternative spelling of Tahpanhes (cf. Jer. 43:7-9). It was situated inland about 15 miles (24 km) south-west of Pelusium, and known to the Greeks as Daphnae. It was a major border town on the route from Egypt through Sinai into either Palestine or Arabia. *The day shall hold back* was probably an ellipsis with the supplement 'its light' requiring to be understood, a picture of darkness corresponding to that mentioned later in the verse. Another reading involves a slight change in the pointing of the Hebrew verb to yield a word meaning 'to be/grow dark'.[73] In either event the picture was the same (cf. 32:7-8; Amos 5:18-20), and the verb was a prophetic perfect envisaging the action as completed because divinely determined (Introduction §6.3b).

The yokes of Egypt[74] was a metaphor for political subservience drawn from everyday life. A yoke was the wooden pole which was bound to an animal's neck to constrain its movements so that it could haul a farming implement or a cart wherever its owner desired. The picture was one of load-bearing and loss of free movement. The plural 'yokes' may have referred to a yoke constructed of two pieces of wood, with one bar above and another below the neck, or the thought may have been of the numerous burdens imposed by Egypt on conquered nations. When the LORD broke the yoke of Egyptian hegemony, these peoples would go free. Furthermore, Egypt's loss of power and prestige would not just be over other nations, but *in her*, that is, in the land itself. The LORD would not allow the *pride of her power* to stand.

Instead *she will be covered by a cloud* (cf. 30:3), experiencing gloom and depression. *Her daughters* may refer in reality to the women of Tahpanhes, but it was more probably an instance of

---

73. The change involved is from *ḥāśak*, 'to keep back, withhold' to *ḥāšak*, 'to be/grow dark', which involves reading the letter *šîn* in place of a *sin*, a difference which would not have been marked until quite late in the transmission of the text. The alternative reading has widespread early support.

74. The LXX obviously read *maṭṭôt*, 'stick, support', rendering it 'sceptres', rather than *mōṭôt*, 'yokes'. The LXX reading is followed by RSV and NRSV, 'dominion'. The use of the plural might also point to those nations who were allied to Egypt. All readings point to a loss of Egyptian power.

'daughter' being used for a dependent settlement (cf. 26:6). So the population of the surrounding area would also *go into captivity*.

♦ **30:19** This summary statement repeated the thought of 30:14, and probably also reflected the use of the plural *judgements* in the LORD's verdict against Egypt in Exodus 12:12. As a result of this renewed experience of the LORD's sovereign power, *they will know that I ₌am₌ the LORD*.

REFLECTION

- While the binding nature of physical laws embedded in the structure of the universe is widely recognised, fallen mankind refuse to accept that it is equally the case that we live in a moral universe where the principle of retribution is operative. 'Because the sentence against an evil deed is not carried out speedily, therefore the heart of the sons of mankind is fully set in them to do evil' (Eccl. 8:11). Scripture teaching about the day of the LORD reminds us that God's forbearance is not infinitely elastic. While he gives 'time to repent' (Rev. 2:21; cf. Rom. 2:4; 2 Pet. 3:9), such longsuffering will come to an end, and then he will step in to maintain the moral balance of his universe in 'a time for the nations' (30:3) when he will exercise his universal authority. There will be occasions of limited intervention prior to the ultimate intrusion of the Great Day when Jesus Christ will come on the clouds of heaven, 'and every eye will see him, even those who pierced him, and all tribes of the earth will wail on account of him' (Rev. 1:7).
- All who had supported and benefited from Egypt's exercise of power will be impacted by her judgement, whether her citizens within her land (30:6, 13–18) or her allies from further afield (30:5, 9). Those who aligned themselves with Egypt's wickedness will be implicated in her downfall. Similarly, those who wish to be welcomed by the Lord should not try to forge an alliance with lawless darkness (2 Cor. 6:14–18).
- When the focus turned to the idols and images (30:13), there was disclosed the basic reason for divine intervention in fury against Egypt. They had substituted idol worship for trust in the one true God. While displaying reverence towards physical images has diminished in western society, its modern equivalent is no less offensive to God: elevating 'self' or 'mankind' to the throne of one's heart. 'I am the LORD, that is my name, and my glory I will not give to another, or my praise to idols' (Isa. 42:8).

(4) Pharaoh's Broken Arm (30:20–26)

This brief oracle constitutes the fourth element of Ezekiel's presentation concerning Egypt. As with 29:17–21 the divine disclosure is given to the prophet without an explicit command to deliver this message to the exiles. It serves as an appendix to the preceding oracle with special reference to the impact of the impending judgement on Pharaoh. Here Nebuchadnezzar is not named, but is referred to three times as 'the king of Babylon'. He will be used by the LORD to inflict a crushing defeat on Egypt. This will deal a further blow to any who had hoped that Jerusalem would receive assistance from there. The oracle has as its principal theme the power and control of the LORD.

> ³⁰:²⁰And it came about in the eleventh year, in the first ⌊month⌋, on the seventh of the month, that the word of the LORD came to me, saying, ³⁰:²¹'Son of man, I have broken the arm of Pharaoh, king of Egypt, and behold, it has not been bound up to give healing or put in a bandage to bind it so that it might become strong ⌊enough⌋ to wield a sword. ³⁰:²²Therefore thus says the Lord GOD, "Behold, I am against Pharaoh, king of Egypt, and I will break his arms, both the strong ⌊arm⌋ and the one that was broken, and I will cause the sword to fall from his hand. ³⁰:²³And I will disperse Egypt among the nations and scatter them among the lands. ³⁰:²⁴And I will strengthen the arms of the king of Babylon and I will set my sword in his hand, and I will break the arms of Pharaoh and he will groan before him with the groanings of a wounded man. ³⁰:²⁵And I will strengthen the arms of the king of Babylon, but the arms of Pharaoh will fall. And they will know that I ⌊am⌋ the LORD when I set my sword in the hand of the king of Babylon and he stretches it out upon the land of Egypt. ³⁰:²⁶And I will disperse Egypt among the nations, and I will scatter them among the lands. And they will know that I ⌊am⌋ the LORD."'

♦ **30:20** The date of this oracle was 29th April 587 B.C., about the time when Pharaoh Hophra was making an abortive attempt to relieve besieged Jerusalem. It therefore originated four months after the oracle of 29:1–16, and sixteen months after the siege of Jerusalem had commenced. The oracle began with the customary message-reception formula, followed in the next verse by the usual divine mode of address to the prophet.

♦ **30:21** The LORD informed Ezekiel of what had already happened to Pharaoh's army, probably when it had made the gesture of coming to relieve Jerusalem (Jer. 37:5–7). *I have broken the arm of Pharaoh* did not refer to bodily damage, but to the LORD's causing Pharaoh to lose his ability to act aggressively and effectively. 'Arm' was used six times as a keyword in the oracle, along with 'hand' (three times), both being metaphors for power. Possibly this focus was an ironic reflection on a title that Hophra often used for himself, 'possessor of a strong/muscled arm'. Once the LORD intervened that was no longer the case. This would repeat the scenario from the time of the Exodus when the LORD's mighty hand and stretched out arm had defeated Pharaoh (cf. 20:33).

And behold drew particular attention to the fact that the injury inflicted had not been remedied. Egypt was apparently incapable of making good the damage which had been inflicted on it. *Bound up* was used of dressing a wound and applying some covering to permit recovery, but that had not occurred in this instance. *Put in a bandage to bind it* repeated the earlier verb. Possibly 'bandage', which occurs only here, means 'splint' (NIV), but cognate terms suggest being wrapped in something. If the arm had recovered, it would have been possible *to wield a sword*, grasping it by the hand and using it as a weapon. Without such recovery Egypt remained a wounded warrior, incapable of engaging in any fighting in the near future, and thus unable to intervene on behalf of Jerusalem, even had it been willing to do so.

♦ **30:22** There was then a significant change of tense from past action against Pharaoh to what the future held. *Therefore* pointed to an inference from what had just been stated, and the messenger formula was used to introduce further divine action against Egypt. The implication of the opposition formula, *Behold, I am against Pharaoh, king of Egypt,* was that, since Pharaoh had not responded to previous action against him, he would come under intensified pressure. *I will break his arms, both the strong ⌊arm⌋ and the one that was broken.* One arm, his usual fighting arm, had already been broken, now the other one which was still strong would also suffer injury and *cause the sword to fall from his hand.* While the first reverse was sustained when Egypt came to help Jerusalem, there is insufficient information to identify what constituted the second repulse, but it may not have happened until some years later.

♦ **30:23** This verse repeated the thought of the closing clauses of 29:12 regarding the dispersal of the Egyptians.

♦ **30:24** The first person verbs presented the LORD as controlling what would happen. Just as he had acted to weaken Pharaoh and leave him unable to defend himself, so the LORD would *strengthen the arms of the king of Babylon* so that he would be capable of acting as the LORD's *sword* of judgement. For *my sword*, see on 21:3–5. Pharaoh was viewed as an injured individual who *will groan before him*, that is, before Nebuchadnezzar. That did not assert that Pharaoh personally would become a casualty from combat, but that in the face of the overwhelming catastrophe which had come upon his regime he would act in a way similar to a wounded soldier.

♦ **30:25** The message regarding Nebuchadnezzar was repeated. To *strengthen the arms of the king of Babylon* enabled him to act powerfully and successfully. The absence of his personal name probably stressed his official position as leader of his nation rather than his individual competence. By way of contrast, *the arms of Pharaoh will fall* indicated a lack of resolve and strength to engage militarily.

An expanded form of the recognition formula clarified the LORD's purpose in these dealings. It was so that *they will know that I ₊am₊ the LORD*. 'They' primarily referred to the Egyptians who would be brought to acknowledge the power of the LORD as the one promoting Nebuchadnezzar's success *when I set my sword in the hand of the king of Babylon and he stretches it out upon the land of Egypt*, inflicting death and destruction.

♦ **30:26** Again it was foretold that Egypt would be dispersed *among the nations* (cf. 29:12; 30:23). The subject of *then they will know* was not specified, but once more it would seem to have been the Egyptians who were in view.

When was this prophecy fulfilled? Partial fulfilment may be traced in a number of events throughout history, but if what was being presented here foreshadowed the final day of divine intervention the picture painted on this prophetic canvas has still to be completely realised.

Though Jeremiah also anticipated that Nebuchadnezzar would invade Egypt, set up his throne in the delta region, and spread havoc throughout the land (Jer. 43:10–13), the evidence from secular records of this happening is scanty, so that many historians do not accept that it occurred, and there is a propensity to treat these passages as instances of false prophecy. However, Josephus relates that Nebuchadnezzar slew the king of Egypt and installed another king

(*Ant.* 10.182).[75] Moreover, a small fragment of a Babylonian chronicle shows Nebuchadnezzar attacking Egypt in his thirty-seventh year, 568 B.C. (*ANET* 308).

REFLECTION

- It is not the scheming of politicians which determines the course of the history of the nations. One nation rises and another falls through the fall of mankind. In this way he suppresses and punishes those who persist in withstanding his will.

(5) The Lofty Cedar Tree (31:1–18)

After the date and message-reception formula in 31:1, the address 'Son of man' (31:2a) introduces an oracle which has three divisions. The first employs a massive cedar tree as a metaphor for the former Assyrian empire in its vast extent (31:2b–9), but then it is declared that the tree, whether Assyria or Egypt, would be destroyed because of its pride (31:10–14). Finally, the tree which had been the Assyrian empire is envisaged as descending into Sheol (31:15–17), and the implications of this for Pharaoh and his forces are spelled out (31:18). The divisions between these subsections are clearly marked by the messenger formula, 'Thus says the Lord GOD' (31:10, 15).

Though critics maintain that the chapter (and especially 31:5 and 31:9) do not come from Ezekiel, this is based on their particular presuppositions. There is no real reason for denying it to the prophet.

(a) Assyria, An Object Lesson (31:1–9)

Throughout this section the image of a tree is used to portray widespread political dominance over many subject peoples dependent on the shelter and provision of an imperial power. While there are some ancient Near Eastern texts which employ the idea of a cosmic, or world, tree (Block 1998:187–189), the usage here is quite distinct and does not have mythological overtones. The description of the tree is lavish and unrestrained in extolling its qualities, with the tree being explicitly labelled as a cedar, which in turn is identified as an emblem for Assyria. Through the magnificence of the tree and the magnitude

---

75. This is often taken to have occurred 'on the fifth year after the destruction of Jerusalem' (*Ant.* 10.181) and therefore to be misdated in that there is no break in the reign of Hophra (598–570 B.C.) around 582. However, Josephus is probably to be understood as dating the event by the intervening, vaguer expression 'after he [Nebuchadnezzar] had brought all those nations [of Syria–Palestine] under subjection [which could include a settlement with Tyre]' (*Ant.* 10.182).

of its fall, Pharaoh is given a history lesson about what arrogant rulers can expect will happen to them.

³¹:¹And it came about in the eleventh year, in the third ⌊month⌋, on the first day of the month, that the word of the LORD came to me, saying, ³¹:²'Son of man, say to Pharaoh, king of Egypt, and to his multitude,
  "To whom are you like in your greatness?
31:3 Behold, Assyria ⌊was⌋ a cedar in Lebanon,
    beautiful ⌊as regards its⌋ branches,
    and a forest giving shade,
    and of great stature,
    while its top was among leafy boughs.
31:4 The waters made it great;
    the deep set it on high,
    making its rivers go round about its place of planting,
    while sending out its channels to all the trees of the field.
31:5 On account of this its stature was higher
    than all the trees of the field,
    and its boughs became large
    and its branches grew long
    from many waters when it spread out.
31:6 In its boughs all the birds of the heavens nested,
    and under its branches all the beasts of the field
        gave birth;
    and under its shadow all the great nations dwelled.
31:7 It was beautiful in its greatness,
    in the length of its foliage,
    for its root was to many waters.
31:8 Cedars could not shade it in the garden of God;
    cypress trees were not like its boughs;
    plane trees were not like its branches—
    no tree in the garden of God was like it in its beauty.
31:9 I made it beautiful
    in the abundance of its foliage;
    and all the trees of Eden envied it,
    which were in the garden of God." '

♦ **31:1** The date was 21st June 587 B.C., not quite two months after the previous oracle (30:20) and about five and a half months after the first oracle against Egypt (29:1). Nothing of particular significance is known about the date. Once more the message-reception formula was followed in 31:2 by the usual form of divine address to the prophet.

♦ **31:2** Ezekiel was commanded to use an obvious rhetorical technique and speak to Pharaoh and his forces, while his immediate audience remained his fellow exiles. The rendering ***multitude*** rather than 'abundance' (cf. 29:19) is appropriate here since his army was addressed along with Pharaoh, who, however, remained the focus of attention.

Pharaoh was confronted with the challenging question, ***To whom are you like in your greatness?*** This was not a straightforward rhetorical question expecting the answer, 'no one', for it was immediately followed by a comparison with another notable ancient regime. However, it was undoubtedly the case that Pharaoh considered none to be his equal. The message of the chapter was that the Pharaoh, despite his ***greatness*** (cf. 31:7, 18), could not escape the judgement of God, and so could expect no destiny different from any other monarch, even one as great as the Assyrian emperor, whose power and sway had equalled, indeed surpassed, that of Egypt. Egypt had been conquered by Assyria for a time in the mid-seventh century B.C. The question asked here was echoed at the close of the oracle, 'To whom are you like?' (31:18), and there was also a bracketing use of 'This is Pharaoh and all his multitude' at the end of the same verse, corresponding to the address here. Somewhat surprising is the fact that the intervening verses mention directly neither Pharaoh nor Egypt!

♦ **31:3** This verse supplied the LORD's answer to the question which had just been posed. It was possible to find a valid and relevant nation to compare Egypt to. Although the ancient versions read ***Assyria*** here, some translations (e.g., RSV, GNB) and many commentators (e.g., Zimmerli 1983:141–142) think such a reference is intrusive in an oracle against Egypt, and either omit the word or emend it into another tree, and take what follows to refer directly to Egypt.[76] However, only the initial and final inclusion focused on Egypt; the body of the oracle concentrated on Assyria as providing a recent object lesson in the transience of worldly greatness.

Behold [77]rhetorically drew Pharaoh's attention to the well-known history of Assyria, and invited consideration of its former dominance.

---

76. In this approach ʾaššûr, 'Assyria', is emended into təʾaššûr, 'cypress' (a word found in Isa. 41:19; 60:13). This may also involve treating 'a cedar in Lebanon' as a later explanatory gloss. The description is then one of Egypt rather than of Assyria (cf. Zimmerli 1983:141–153).

77. Block's analysis (1998:184) that 'Behold, Assyria' was Pharaoh's response to the question in 31:2 is unconvincing. No self-assured ruler would compare his regime to a defeated and defunct empire. Furthermore, it is not Pharaoh's self-image which is under consideration, but his impending doom.

There would be a measure of imbalance in likening a person, Pharaoh, to a country, Assyria, were it not that the absolute monarch of an ancient regime personified in himself the nation he ruled over. So, Assyria stood for all the emperors of that nation, and Pharaoh represented Egypt in its might.

Of course, Ezekiel's audience was not Pharaoh, but his fellow exiles, many of whom still cherished the hope that Egyptian intervention would reverse the catastrophe which was engulfing Jerusalem. It was therefore a suitable reminder to them of the way in which the mighty, self-assured Assyrian empire had fallen so precipitately within their lifetime.

Assyria had dominated the Near East from the accession of Tiglath-pileser III in 745 B.C. until the collapse of its empire with the fall of Nineveh in 612. Although Egypt then tried to assist the remnants of the Assyrian empire to assert itself against the rising power of Babylon, the battle of Carchemish in 605 had decisively settled that contest in Babylon's favour. However, Egypt did not totally abandon its expansionist ambitions, and was ready to exploit any sign of Babylonian weakness to regain sway over Syria-Palestine. But the memory of Assyria lived on, and in the following chapter it headed the list of those regimes which greeted Pharaoh on his arrival in Sheol (32:22–23).

The *cedar in Lebanon* was an acknowledged symbol of majesty (cf. Isa. 35:2), though there is no evidence of it being one that had been adopted by the Assyrian emperors themselves. A date palm was a more probable candidate as the emblem they favoured. However, the durability and majesty of the cedar were well-known throughout the ancient world. Here four phrases were used to bring out the stately grandeur of this tree.

(1) *Beautiful ⌊as regards its⌋ branches.* In this passage there were quite a number of terms for branches of a tree. That found here (*'ānāp*) occurred also in 17:8, 23; 36:8.

(2) *A forest giving shade.* This was probably a metaphor, 'like a forest', because the following description presented Assyria as a single tree of such luxuriant growth that it was capable of providing shelter equivalent to that from a number of other trees.

(3) *Of great stature*, literally 'height of towering height' (31:3, 5, 10, 14), where 'height' (*gābēaḥ*) is from a root often applied metaphorically to human pride (16:50; 28:2).

(4) The clause of attendant circumstances, *while its top was among leafy boughs* (cf. AV, NKJV, NIV) has also been understood as referring

to being 'among clouds' (cf. LXX, NRSV, ESV; cf. 19:11). Both approaches yield an acceptable sense, though the latter involves some textual adjustment.[78]

Many pagan mythologies used the image of a 'world tree' or 'cosmic tree' to picture the universe.[79] The tree had its roots below the ground in the underworld, and its branches reached heavenwards and provided shelter for all living creatures. There is no evidence that Canaanite religion employed this imagery, though it has been detected in Mesopotamian mythology. It is, however, a matter of dispute as to the extent of any connection between the presentation here and the 'cosmic tree'. There are no mythological overtones in this chapter, and understanding the metaphor of the great tree as a symbol for political interdependence can be interpreted without recourse to pagan analogies. Indeed, what throws more light on it is the similar comparison in chapter 17, and especially the description of Nebuchadnezzar's dream (Dan. 4:10–12). Also, in the parable of the mustard seed (Matt. 13:31–32; Mark 4:30–32; Luke 13:18–19), the protection provided by the branches of the tree was not unlike aspects of the portrait here.

♦ **31:4** The tree grew and became *great* because of an abundant water supply. *The waters* was the ordinary Hebrew word for 'water', but the parallelism with 'the deep' leads to a plural translation (even in the AV). Were there mythological overtones here? While 'waters' can imply ocean depths (Jonah 2:5), it is more probable that a contrast was drawn between rainfall (for 'water' as rain, cf. Judg. 5:4; 2 Sam. 21:10) and subterranean springs (cf. Gen. 8:2). *The deep* then represented the subterranean waters believed to lie beneath the earth. There were no residual mythological overtones in the use of 'the deep' (*təhôm*), even though scholars often allege that the term is connected with the Mesopotamian creation monster Tiamat. What was presented here was a great tree drawing water from deep in the earth, and so

---

78. The term *ʿăbôtîm*, 'leafy boughs', which occurs also in 31:10, 14, may be the plural of either of the homonyms *ʿăbôt* identified by *HALOT* (778). The first is glossed as 'branch' and the second as 'mass of branches' in reference to a tree with thick intertwining branches (translated as 'leafy', 6:13; 20:28). However, following the LXX, many relate the word to *ʿāb* (II), 'cloud, clouds', and propose emending the text to *ʿābôt* (*HALOT* 773).

79. The imagery of the cosmic tree and of the tree of life do not seem to overlap, even though the latter does occur in pagan literature. The tree of life is evidently not under consideration in this passage.

being able to survive heat and climatic variations. Assyria commanded resources from far and wide, and so could cope with shocks and difficulties.

The subject of the second part of the verse was the deep which caused *its rivers* to *go*[80] *round about its place of planting*, where 'its place' presumably referred to Assyria or to the cedar,[81] and 'its rivers' might hint at the Tigris and Euphrates, the mighty rivers of Mesopotamia. The deep also provided a lesser flow of nourishment by *sending out its channels to all the trees of the field.* 'Channels' might denote man-made water trenches, but the thought here is probably of streams going to all the other trees/nations as distinct from the rivers which nourished Assyria.

♦ **31:5** *On account of this*, that is, the abundant provision of water to the tree, *its stature was higher*.[82] This phrase reused the two roots found in 'of great height' in 31:3, and took up the third aspect of the tree from there in that the well-nourished tree was stronger than any other.

In the second part of the verse the focus switched from the height to the width of the tree (cf. 'a forest giving shade', 31:3). The term *boughs*[83] pointed to the main branches of the tree, whereas *branches* need not have been so stout. The whole tree benefited from the *many waters* which sustained it (cf. 31:4). *When it spread out*, literally 'in its sending', might possibly refer to 'the deep', but more probably it described the tree sending out branches and roots (Keil 2002:260).

---

80. The form *hōlēk* appears to be a masculine singular qal participle whereas its obvious reference is to *təhôm*, 'the deep', a feminine noun, as attested in the preceding and following verb forms. Furthermore in the qal the verb *hālak*, 'to go', is intransitive. Following Greenberg (1997:638), it is more appropriate to take *hōlēk* as written defectively for *hôlēk*, the hiphil infinitive absolute, used to continue the thought of the preceding finite verb. See also Block (1998:182); Hummel (2007:911).

81. The switch in the pronominal reference in *maṭṭāʿāh*, 'her place of planting', from 'the deep' to either the land (of Assyria) or the cedar, both of which are feminine, is surprising, but not impossible.

82. The form *gābəhāʾ*, 'she was great', is an Aramaic-style variant of the expected Hebrew form *gābəhâ*, which retains the final root letter of *gābah*.

83. Here 'bough' is spelled *sarʿappâ* in Aramaic fashion, whereas, when it recurs in 31:6, 8, it has its normal Hebrew spelling, *səʿappâ*. The Aramaic form has suggested to some that this prose verse is a later addition to the text, but quite apart from the ensuing disruption of the flow of the text, Ezekiel's location is more than sufficient to account for Aramaic influence.

♦ **31:6** The triple occurrence of *all* in this verse served to emphasise the comprehensive nature of the provision made by the great tree. Initially, it was presented as affording shelter and protection to wild life. Not unnaturally a tree was envisaged as supplying perches and nesting space for *all the birds of the heavens*, but this tree also provided shade and shelter *under its branches* for *all the beasts of the field*, that is, wild animals (cf. 34:5). There they could find a lair in which they felt secure to have and raise their young.

Then the metaphorical presentation momentarily slipped. At one level *under its shadow* pointed to the shade that a tree could afford, but at another level 'shadow' described protection and relief provided either by mankind (Isa. 30:2; Lam. 4:20) or by God (Pss. 17:8; 91:1; Isa. 49:2; 51:16). It therefore applied easily to the hegemony exercised by Assyria in its domination of lesser nations. Consequently, it was directly declared that *all the great nations were dwelling* under Assyrian overlordship. 'All the great nations' may also be rendered 'all the many nations' (cf. 26:3; 38:23; 39:27), but the addition of 'many' after 'all' seems redundant, and it is probable that the thought here was rather 'great' or 'powerful'. Assyria dominated nations large and small. 'Were dwelling' was an imperfect verb in the midst of perfects. While this might have been merely a poetic variation, it did suggest on-going existence in this state.

♦ **31:7** Various features of the tree were then repeated. *Beautiful in its greatness* took up the thought first expressed in 31:3, and *the length of its foliage* expanded on this theme. Also, the tree grew ever larger because its roots reached to *many waters* (cf. 31:5).

♦ **31:8** *Cedars could not shade it* because, cedar though it was, it grew taller than any other of the species. The identity of *cypress trees* is not well established (cf. 27:5). Repeated mention of *the garden of God* imparted a more theological turn to the description (cf. 'Eden' in next verse). The reference was undoubtedly to the garden of Genesis 2, and so what was in view were not later trees whose growth had possibly been inhibited, but perfect specimens from the garden of paradise. The tree (and therefore Assyria) surpassed even such illustrious specimens *in its beauty* (*yŏpî*, cf. 28:12).

♦ **31:9** *I made it beautiful* asserted the control and direction of the LORD in all this. The provision of beauty and abundance meant that the tree had no reason to object to its destiny on the ground that God had grudgingly provided for it. Since it lacked nothing, there was every reason for it to acknowledge God and return thanks for his goodness. Whatever went wrong in the story of the tree could not be attributed to a lack of favourable divine provision. *All the trees of Eden* were beautiful and prolific. 'And the LORD God made to sprout out of the ground every tree ⌊which is⌋ pleasant to sight and good for eating' (Gen. 2:9). Yet the personified trees *envied it* because of the surpassing beauty of the great tree which was Assyria.

(b) The Tree Cut Down (31:10–14)
The lavish description of the tree, and therefore by implication of Assyria, is introduced as a means of establishing a parallel between Egypt's greatness and that of Assyria. However, such grandiose terms are employed only to be turned into a further instance of pride receiving its comeuppance (cf. Prov. 16:18). The divine accusation is levelled not against Egypt's greatness as such, but against the arrogance it engendered (31:10). Pharaoh thinks he can determine the destiny of the known world by supporting Judah and other nations against Babylon, whereas Babylon is the LORD's appointed and announced instrument for the chastisement of his people. Therefore the power of Egypt will be divinely overwhelmed (31:11–14).

^{31:10}'"Therefore thus says the Lord GOD: Because you were high in stature and it set its top among leafy boughs, and its heart was lifted up because of its height, ^{31:11}And I will give it into the hand of a mighty one of the nations; he will surely deal with him; according to his wickedness I have driven him out. ^{31:12}Strangers, violent ones of nations, have cut it off, and left it. Upon the mountains and in all the valleys its foliage has fallen, and its branches have been broken by all the streams of the land; and all the peoples of the earth have gone down from its shadow and left it. ^{31:13}On its fallen trunk all the birds of the heaven will settle, and on its branches were all the beasts of the field. ^{31:14}⌊This happened⌋ in order that all trees of water would not make themselves high in their stature, and would not set their tops among leafy boughs; and that their mighty ones would not stand in their height—all who drink water. For all of them are given over to death, to the world below; in the midst of the sons of mankind to those who go down to the pit."'

♦ **31:10** *Therefore* marked the transition to the divine verdict on the situation previously described. However, it was unusual for the charges not to be more clearly specified in what preceded 'therefore', and consequently the divine speech began with *because* to show that the LORD's action was not arbitrary.

The passage contained various unclear pronominal references and frequent changes of person, as here where the address to the tree *you were high in stature* (cf. 31:3) was followed by *it set its top*. This was a feature of Hebrew style, not something that calls for the text to be emended, though translations may well seek to smooth matters out in the interests of English style to 'it was high' (cf. the Peshitta and the Vulgate). For *leafy boughs*, see on 31:3.

At one level the verb, 'be high' (*gābah*), referred to the physical dimensions of the tree, but the term could also mean 'to be proud' (28:2; cf. 28:5, 17) and so portrayed the unwarranted self-exaltation of arrogance. *Its heart was lifted up because of its stature* was easily seen to relate to Assyria as the referent of the metaphor.

♦ **31:11** *And I will give it*[84] related to the penalty the LORD would impose on Egypt, rather than what had already happened to Assyria, which did, however, provide the template for what would also apply to Egypt. *Into the hand of a mighty one of the nations* used the standard metaphor of a ram for a powerful leader, but the difference here was that this leader's dominance was not confined to one herd or people but, as the plural 'nations' indicated, was international in its scope.

He will surely deal with him (lit., 'do ͺtoͺ'). The subject of the verb was 'a mighty one', presumably Nebuchadnezzar, but nothing specific was said of the action he would take with regard to Pharaoh. Rather it was the reason for the LORD's action which was emphasised: *according to his wickedness I have driven him out.* At this point the past tense of the verb probably indicated that the focus reverted to the LORD's treatment of Assyria. On that basis, Pharaoh too could expect to be deposed from his throne by divine imposition.

♦ **31:12** For *violent ones of nations* as a reference to the Babylonians, see on 30:11. *Left it* conveyed a picture of discarding something as no longer of value or significance. A coalition of nations had been responsible for the destruction of the Assyrian capital, Nineveh, and portions of its former empire came under the control of other nations,

---

84. The verb *wəʾettənēhû*, 'and I will give', has ordinary *waw* (not *waw-consecutive*), and so merits a future translation. The following verb *yaʿăśeh*, 'he will deal', is an imperfect with obvious future denotation. However, the LXX (followed by NIV, NRSV) rendered the verbs as past tenses and took them to refer to Nebuchadnezzar's subjugation of Assyria, which will be paralleled in the forthcoming overthrow of Egypt. This does not seem to be warranted, though alternation of perfects and imperfects may occur in Hebrew poetry without affecting the tense value of what is presented.

but principally Babylon. The picture of the fallen tree, *its branches ... broken*, conveyed the disintegration of the Assyrian empire. *Mountains ... valleys ... streams* emphasised that this overthrow was not partial, but affected every part of the land. While mention of these physical features might seem to favour an Assyrian reference and setting, it must be noted that mountains and valleys were explicitly mentioned in connection with Pharaoh's doom in 32:5–6. *Have gone down from its shadow* rather than its branches creates somewhat of a puzzle unless the tree itself was situated on a hillside, as could be indicated by the mention of mountains and valleys. The branches may have represented the peoples of the empire.

♦ **31:13** *On its fallen trunk* was literally, 'on its downfall' (cf. 26:15; 27:27). *Will settle* was unexpected if the picture was still that of the fallen Assyrian empire, as suggested by the following past tense *were*. It may have been a frequentative usage, 'kept settling'. Both birds and wild animals exploited the tree for shelter, and in the same way other nations took advantage of the downfall of Assyria. But the toppled tree now lay on the ground so that *all the beasts of the field* no longer settled under its shade (cf. 31:6), but *on its branches*.

♦ **31:14** Some supplement such as ⌊*this happened*⌋ is required to bring out the sense. The verse incorporated the moral of the entire passage that, even though a tree (empire) enjoyed great growth and dominance, it still would not escape retribution and eclipse from the world stage. For *leafy boughs*, see on 31:3. *All trees of water* was a way of expressing 'all well-watered trees'. They should not misinterpret the growth that they had experienced, and *make themselves high in their stature* as if it had been achieved through their prowess.

Their mighty ones[85] *would not stand in their height* pictured the leaders of the nations (cf. 31:11) drawing themselves up in pride because they had benefited from their nation's good fortune—*all who drink water*.

Yet you will be brought down with the trees of Eden to the world below. It was an unusual metaphor to have trees being consigned to the underworld, but it was obviously the human figures for whom they stood which were in view. The multiple terms for death and the afterlife constituted a reminder of the inevitable terminus of every

---

85. The LXX read ʾălêhem, 'to them', rather than ʾēlêhem, 'their rams, mighty ones', and this is reflected in many English translations which generally present a paraphrase of the verse.

human life, no matter how great or powerful. This introduced a theme which permeated the remaining oracles against Egypt.

The expression *the world below* (cf. 31:16, 18) was similar to 'the world of lowest places' (26:20; 32:18, 24). The afterlife was viewed as occurring below the earth. *Sons of mankind*/Adam referred to all humanity, viewed as liable to the curse of death incurred by sin. It was a plural form of the expression 'son of man' used to describe Ezekiel (cf. 2:1). In *those who have gone down to the pit* (cf. 32:18), 'pit' referred to the afterlife as one grave shared alike by all (cf. 26:20).

(c) The Great Leveller (31:15–18)
The message of the history lesson is now clearly set out by presenting the effect of the fall of the great tree which in the first instance represents Assyria. Its overthrow led to divinely induced gloom and loss of nerve among the nations of the world (31:15–16a). There is also pictured the relieved reaction of those already in the world below at the collapse of the empire and its entry into Sheol (31:16b–17). A concluding verse makes clear that this destiny will befall Egypt as well as Assyria (31:18).

> 31:15 "Thus says the Lord GOD: On the day it went down to Sheol, I caused mourning; I covered the deep because of it. And I held back its rivers and many waters were restrained; and I clothed Lebanon in darkness because of it, and all the trees of the field wilted because of it. 31:16At the sound of its downfall I made nations quake, when I made it go down to Sheol, with those who go down to the pit; and all the trees of Eden, the choice and best of Lebanon, all that drink water, were comforted in the world below. 31:17They also went down with it to Sheol, to those slain by the sword, even its arm, those who had dwelt in its shade in the midst of the nations. 31:18To whom are you thus like in glory and in greatness among the trees of Eden? Yet you will be brought down with the trees of Eden to the world below. You will lie in the midst of the uncircumcised, with those who have been slain by the sword. This is Pharaoh and all his multitude, declares the Lord GOD." '

♦ **31:15** *On the day it went down to Sheol.* Since the illustration involving trees was still clearly being employed at the end of this verse, the 'it' here referred in the first instance to the tree, but in reality to Assyria—and by extension to Pharaoh, and indeed to any and every pretentious human empire. Sheol (see also on 32:21) was a place under the control of God, though he himself was not there (cf. Hades in Rev. 1:18). The term could refer to the grave as the common destiny of all humanity, but in other texts it was particularly the realm to which those eternally condemned by God were consigned (e.g., Num. 16:30). The Old Testament did know of God as the one who could deliver from Sheol in life-threatening situations (1 Sam. 2:6; Jonah 2:2), and this reality anticipated the eternal deliverance effected by the power of the new creation which God makes possible in Christ (Ps. 16:10; Acts 2:27, 31).

I caused mourning.[86] It is not immediately evident who was affected by this divine action. It might have been those already in Sheol, but more probably the thought was one of universal mourning. *I covered the deep because of it.* Though the last phrase might mean 'over it', it is repeated twice more in the verse with the sense 'because of it', indicating the extensive impact of the fall of the great cedar on the world order. The LORD covered the deep as a mark of mourning and respect at the loss which had been suffered so that the deep could not function normally as a reservoir providing water for the trees/nations *when I held back its rivers and many waters* (cf. 31:5) *were restrained.*

I clothed Lebanon in darkness for it. 'Darkness' evoked the desolation of grief (cf. 32:7–8). Mention of Lebanon, renowned for its forests, fitted in with the metaphor of the great tree/cedar which informed this passage. *All the trees of the field wilted because of it.* The withered trees were an emblem of the leaders of other nations losing power and resilience as the impact of the demise of the great cedar hit home.[87] The language of reversal was used to depict the impact of God's judgement as the description of 31:2–5 was inverted.

♦ **31:16** The description of the international impact of divine intervention continued in the first part of the verse. *At the sound of its downfall* envisaged the great tree crashing to the ground, and through

---

86. The LXX does not have the following verb, 'I covered', which leads to a translation such as 'I made the deep mourn' (cf. RSV, NLT). Another approach is to identify the root of the verb *he'ĕbaltî*, 'I caused mourning', not as *ʾābal*, 'to mourn' but as a homonym associated with an Akkadian noun meaning 'gate', and so render 'I gated/closed the deep over it and covered it' (cf. NRSV). The NIV offers 'I covered the deep springs with mourning for it', achieved by taking the two verbs together as a hendiadys.

87. There is in fact no verb in the clause, only a noun 'a faint' or 'a swoon'. English idiom requires the use of a verb, but to say 'all the trees of the field a faint' is acceptable Hebrew and there is no need to emend the text.

this, that is, through the humiliating collapse of the superpower, God spread terror. *I made nations quake* with fear as at an earthquake (cf. 38:19–20) because the transience of even the most impressive of earthly power structures was starkly exposed. *When I made it go down to Sheol* (cf. 31:15), *with those who go down to the pit* (cf. 26:20) emphasised that this was not a state of weakness, but utter and complete dissolution which occurred by God's sovereign imposition.

In the middle of the verse the description switched from the divinely imposed overthrow which consigned the regime to the fate that was its due. The focus is on the world below and, continuing the arboreal metaphor, there were three descriptions of those who had already been divinely consigned to Sheol. *All the trees of Eden* were the powerful rulers and their empires which had preceded Assyria and Egypt, characterising them by their finery and grand endowments. Also, *the choice and best of Lebanon*[88] was a further portrayal of the same figures, emphasising their status and productivity. *All that drink water* again referred to this group of trees/nations but denoted them as reliant on resources made available to them, and not as self-made powers.

But what was intended by the statement that they *were comforted in the world below*? They derived a sense of satisfaction from the fact that those who followed them were ultimately no more successful than they had been. Their own failure was to that extent not their fault or due to some deficiency of theirs (cf. 32:31) because the powerful cedar they had envied (31:9) had met the same end as they themselves. Possibly the presentation reflected that of Isaiah 14:10–17.

♦ **31:17** It is difficult to be certain of what was being said in this verse.[89] *They also* was probably proleptic, and anticipated the category specified in the rest of the verse. In addition to the former inhabitants of Sheol, there were also present there the nations who had been Assyria's allies and who *went down with it to Sheol.* In the downfall of the empire they too were swept into the grave, where they joined *those slain by the sword* previously.

These satellite powers were described as *its arm*. They had been conscripted into the Assyrian armies and had fought in its extensive

---

88. Unusually here there are two construct forms before one substantive in the absolute (cf. *IBHS* §9.3b).

89. Emendations of 31:17 have aligned it in some way with the LXX rendering, 'and his seed, they who dwelt under his shade, perished in the midst of their life', but there is no obvious link between the texts where they differ.

campaigns. But this had not been a one-sided arrangement, for they were also portrayed as ⌊*those who*⌋ *had dwelt in its shade in the midst of the nations*. They had enjoyed Assyrian protection and had benefited from the trading opportunities provided by the empire. But the collapse of the superpower had brought down the regimes which had been allied with it.

♦ **31:18** *To whom are you like?* reiterated the divine inquiry of 31:2 to form an inclusion. The addition of *thus* pointed to the exposition of Assyria's fate in the preceding verses. This question was directed to Pharaoh who was invited to trace the fate that awaited him in terms of the destiny which had already engulfed Assyria. Those whom he had looked down on with disdain as lesser mortals, *the trees of Eden*, would be there. He would be forced to *lie* in death (cf. 32:19) and ignominiously share his destiny with those whom he had despised, *the uncircumcised* who did not enjoy divine favour (cf. 28:10). The final declaration removed all doubt as to the ultimate reference in the matter: *Pharaoh and all his multitude*, which formed an inclusion with 31:2.

REFLECTION
- 'Before destruction ⌊goes⌋ pride, and before a fall a haughty spirit' (Prov. 16:18), and that applies to nations as well as to individuals. Those who attain worldly eminence and acclaim rarely appreciate the impermanence of their situation, and history clearly shows that the dominance of a superpower is transient. Even so, a strange forgetfulness envelops the successful so that they take the status quo for granted and presume that it will be maintained contrary to every precedent.
- Each judgement of God in the flow of earth history anticipates in measure the final settlement of the day of the LORD. This will not create a division among mankind; it will merely reveal the fundamental divide which already exists, and which will on that day become irrevocably fixed. The solemn warnings of Scripture urge us to make sure of the side on which we are to be found before it is too late to remedy matters.

(6) Lament over Pharaoh (32:1–16)

It took six months for a messenger with the news of Jerusalem's fall to reach Tel-abib (33:21). A further two months passed before Ezekiel delivered the two oracles against Egypt which are to be found in this chapter (cf. discussion on 32:17). Most of the material in this oracle elaborates on what was disclosed earlier, particularly regarding the fall of Pharaoh (29:1–16).

While the contents of this oracle may not satisfy modern definitions of a lament, both the initial command to the prophet (32:2) and the concluding note (32:16) identify it as such. In place of an acknowledgement of the former prowess or achievements of the deceased, the focus is instead on what Pharaoh considers himself to be, and it is this erroneous self-assessment which constitutes the basis for proceeding against him. The Egyptian king is likened to a monstrous crocodile which will be captured and its carcass exposed as carrion for wild animals (32:3–8). The prose verses (32:9–10) develop this imagery in terms of the international impact of the overthrow of Pharaoh. The concluding section (32:11–15) introduces the king of Babylon as the instrument the LORD will employ to punish Egypt. A final verse (32:16) predicts that this poem will be used among the nations as a dirge over Egypt's downfall.

Of what relevance to Ezekiel's audience is this repeated elaboration of the fate awaiting Egypt? It would seem that, in the period after they know that Jerusalem has fallen, at least some of the exiles are still casting about for something to latch onto to give them hope for the future—a future shaped in accordance with their vision of what would constitute a way forward for their nation. Revision of their expectations and acceptance of Ezekiel's message takes some time to occur. Meanwhile, their thinking still runs in its previous rut, and Egyptian intervention seems to provide a possible alternative for the nation rather than acknowledging the error of their outlook and trusting in the LORD. The message is therefore hammered home that there is no relief for the people of God in earthly political strategies. It is only from the LORD himself that true and lasting deliverance can come.

(a) The Monster Trapped and Slain (32:1–10)

> ³²:¹And it came about in the twelfth year, in the twelfth month, on the first of the month, that the word of the LORD came to me, saying, ³²:²'Son of man, take up a lament over Pharaoh, king of Egypt, and say to him,
> "You consider yourself to be like a young lion among
>   the nations,
>   but you ⌊are⌋ like a monster in the seas.
> And you have burst forth in your rivers,
>   and have churned the waters with your feet,
>   and have muddied their streams.

AGAINST EGYPT

^{32:3}Thus says the Lord GOD:
>   And I will spread my net over you
>   by an assembly of many peoples,
>   and they will bring you up in my dragnet.
> ^{32:4} And I will throw you down on the ground;
>   upon the surface of the field I will toss you.
>   And I will cause all the birds of the heaven to settle
>   upon you,
>   and I will cause the beasts of all the earth to satisfy
>   themselves from you.
> ^{32:5} And I will set your flesh upon the mountains
>   and I will fill the valleys with your carcass.
> ^{32:6} And I will drench the land of your flood
>   with your blood, ⌊even⌋ to the mountains;
>   and the riverbeds will be filled from you.
> ^{32:7} And when ⌊I⌋ extinguish you, I will cover the heavens,
>   and I will darken their stars;
>   I will cover the sun with a cloud,
>   and the moon will not give its light.
> ^{32:8} And ⌊as for⌋ the bright lights in the heavens
>   I will darken them over you,
>   and I will set darkness over your land,
>   declares the Lord GOD.
> ^{32:9}And I will disturb the heart of many peoples when I bring your disintegration among the nations, to lands which you have not known. ^{32:10}And I will make many peoples appalled because of you, and their kings will shudder because of you, when I swing my sword before them, and again and again each of them will tremble for his life in the day of your sudden downfall."'

♦ **32:1** The oracle was introduced by a date formula: *in the twelfth year*[90], *in the twelfth month, on the first of the month*, which is equivalent to 3rd March 585 B.C. Two months before this Ezekiel had received word that Jerusalem had fallen in the previous summer (33:21). It had been nearly two years before this that the preceding oracle was issued (31:1). The familiar message-reception formula in this verse was followed by the usual address to the prophet in 32:2.

♦ **32:2** Ezekiel was again commanded to *take up a lament* (cf. 28:12). 'Lament' here formed an inclusion round the oracle (cf. 32:16). While

---

90. The following oracle (32:17–32) is dated earlier than this, and that may explain the reading of many Hebrew manuscripts, the LXX, and the Peshitta, 'in the eleventh year', but 'twelfth' is undoubtedly the more unexpected, and therefore more probable, reading.

the scope of the term was wider than simply a funeral dirge, it always had melancholic overtones, and in prophetic discourse it was employed prospectively to indicate the impending demise of its subject. For *over Pharaoh*, see on 29:2.

The 'once–now' lament pattern was considerably truncated in this instance, with only the accusation of this verse embodying 'once' material, which was here critical rather than laudatory. The message to be delivered contrasted Pharaoh's self-perception with the reality of his situation. *You consider yourself to be like*.[91] The verb may indicate either a passive sense 'you are likened to' by others, or a reflexive one, 'you set yourself as equivalent to'. Probably here it was Pharaoh's self-evaluation which was being criticised. *A young lion among the nations* presented a picture of virility and power, vigour and success— an animal to be respected because of the threat it posed to life and limb. 'Lion' was a widely recognised characterisation of a king (cf. 19:2), which could almost amount to a claim to deity, certainly to a more than human status. The metaphor was also used of the LORD (cf. Isa. 31:4; Hos. 5:14; 13:7; Amos 3:8). 'Nations' was picked up again in 32:16 to form an inclusion. Note also that 'nations' was used in 32:9, 12 and 'peoples' in 32:3, 9, 10, so that the international implications of what was being said were clearly kept in view.

Over against the positive self-image of the ruler of Egypt, *but* introduced the divine verdict. Rather than Pharaoh being an individual to be held in awed respect, in reality he was *a monster in the seas*. His overweening claims were so ludicrous that a crocodile, not a lion, would be a more fitting emblem. 'Monster' (*tannîm*, cf. 29:3) may have had vague mythological overtones, but in this context the monster was clearly a crocodile and 'the seas' referred principally to the waters of the Nile.

Pharaoh's pretentious assessment of his achievements was put down in three clauses which pictured his actions in reptilian terms. *You have burst forth in your rivers,* that is, the channels of the Nile (cf. 31:4). This was a picture of sudden action, yet confined to a very specific area. It implied that Pharaoh could make a great impression in his native habitat, but for all his froth and fury his conduct was really rather futile. *And have churned the waters with your feet.* A crocodile cannot travel very far, and despite the appearance of much activity it

---

91. Another rendering is 'young lion of the nations, your end has come' (REB; cf. NJPS), which understands the verb as the niphal of *dāmâ* III, 'to be destroyed' rather than from *dāmâ* I, 'to be like', niphal 'to present oneself as'.

really only succeeds in setting the waters in turmoil. ***And have muddied their streams*** with the result that the waters were no longer suitable for humans or animals (cf. 34:18-19). 'Their' probably referred to the waters as they were directed into irrigation channels from the river.

♦ **32:3** The messenger formula introduced the LORD as a hunter (cf. 12:13; Hos. 7:12; Lam. 1:13), who proposed to trap crocodile Pharaoh like a wild animal. This was no easy task but one which would require to be effected ***by an assembly of many peoples***, where 'many' may also be rendered 'great' or 'mighty' (cf. 31:6). Though the preposition is often rendered 'with', it was not picturing the peoples as also caught in the net, but as those through whom the spreading of the net would be carried out. The next clause made that clear: ***they will bring you up***.[92] However, the captors would be no more than instruments in the LORD's control. What they would use was ***my net***, an implement used in a variety of contexts, and ***my dragnet***, a term more suited to fishing. In this way the LORD would exercise control over the forces of the nations so that they accomplish what he has planned.

♦ **32:4** For ***throw***, see on 29:5. Having dragged the crocodile up from a watery lair where it was more at home, the LORD would hurl the captured animal down on the ground and then discard its carcass in the open where birds and scavenging animals would treat it as carrion, and gorge themselves on it. ***I will cause*** may equally well have conveyed the sense, 'I will permit'. The emphasis was that all that took place was divinely sanctioned, and the monster would be helpless before the action initiated by the LORD. ***The beasts of all the earth*** more than hinted at the enormous size of the carcass that was to be consumed.

♦ **32:5** The scale of what would occur when Egypt fell was developed further in 32:5-7. Mention of ***the mountains*** and ***the valleys*** was reminiscent of the description of the felling of the great cedar in 31:12. The term rendered ***carcass*** occurs only here, and its meaning is uncertain. One plausible derivation suggests the idea of 'height' (AV; BDB 928), while another connects the term to what is cast aside as 'refuse' (NASB) or 'remains' (NIV). Possibly we are to envisage the crocodile's carcass as being as large as a raised heap of dead bodies.

---

92. The substitution of 'I' as the subject of the verb in RSV and NRSV is based on the LXX, but there is no need for this change to give both verbs the same subject. It is joint action which is in view.

♦ **32:6** Hummel (2007:928–929) points out that translations such as 'I will drench the land with the flow of your blood' neglect the link indicated by the Massoretes between 'land' and 'flow', and he proposes instead that the phrase ***the land of your flood*** be understood as the flood plain of the Nile. It was predicted that there was going to be an inundation of the flood plain, not with water, but with ***your blood.*** Hummel further suggests that ***to the mountains*** indicated the drastic impact of this flood which would stretch up to the cliffs at the side of the river valley. ***The riverbeds*** would then be not those of the Nile, but those of tributaries or canals flowing into the river. Ordinarily their source of water would be the overflow of the annual flood, but here it was envisaged that the blood of the slain would drain back down them into the main river. The whole picture was equivalent to a surreal cartoon depiction of the overwhelming disaster which would come upon the land of the proud young lion.

♦ **32:7** The subject of the subordinate verb ***extinguish*** or 'snuff out' was not stated. It is probably 'I', though an impersonal usage with a passive force is possible, 'when one snuffs you out', that is, 'when you are snuffed out' (cf. Greenberg 1997:653). 'Extinguish' ('be quenched', 20:47, 48; cf. 2 Chron. 29:7; Isa. 42:3; 43:17; 66:24) may refer to putting out a fire or a lamp—it would take no more effort than that for God to remove Pharaoh.

On Pharaoh's demise, God would plunge his land into deep, dark mourning since he would ***cover the heavens*** and so ***darken their stars.*** This gloom would prevail by day when God would ***cover the sun with a cloud*** and by night when he would ensure that ***the moon will not give its light.*** The scene was reminiscent of the penultimate plague upon Egypt (Exod. 10:21–23).

♦ **32:8** ***Over you*** and ***over your land*** repeated the same preposition which already occurred in 31:15 where the sense 'because of' was preferred. Here, 'because of you' is possible, but 'because of your land' is less compelling. ***The bright lights in the heavens*** referred to the sun, moon, and stars as in 32:7, which God would ***darken over you.*** Pharaoh's remains would not be entombed with elaborate funeral rites but would lie on the ground in a scene of murky obscurity, which was further intensified by ***I will set darkness over your land.*** This pictured darkness enshrouding the land because the light from heaven had been divinely closed off, and again recalled the plague of darkness upon Egypt (cf. 32:7). This in turn foreshadowed the end of the world (Joel 2:10; 3:15). ***Declares the Lord G***OD emphasised the certainty of

♦ **32:9** This and the following verse were in prose and extended the scene from 'your land' (32:8) to 'many peoples'. *I will disturb* (*kāʿas*) *the heart of many peoples* employed the verb elsewhere rendered 'provoke' when it described others stirring up the LORD's anger (cf. 8:17). Here it denoted intense emotional agitation which would afflict the peoples as they considered what was involved in the imposition of the LORD's judgement. *When I bring your disintegration among the nations* did not refer to the LORD bringing the remnants of Pharaoh's shattered people into exile (so RSV, NRSV, following LXX), but to the LORD making internationally known the news of Pharaoh's calamitous fall and the 'disintegration' (lit., 'breaking apart') of his power. *To lands which you have not known* showed that even the most distant lands, hitherto unknown even to Pharaoh, would be impacted by the traumatic news of his downfall and the overthrow of Egypt.

♦ **32:10** *I will make many peoples appalled* (*šāmam*, cf. 27:35) conveyed the shock of other nations on learning of the fate of Pharaoh and his land. Also *their kings will shudder because of you*, which used imagery based on causing one's hair to stand on end (cf. 27:35). This reaction mirrored that at the collapse of Tyre (26:15, 18; 27:28) or of the mighty cedar which was Assyria (31:16). Here it was specifically linked to their awareness of the threat they personally faced. *When I swing my sword* (lit., 'when I cause my sword to fly to and fro') described the widespread incursions of Nebuchadnezzar into whose hand the LORD had set his sword (30:24). *Time and again each of them will tremble* repeated the expression of 26:16 as other rulers were fearful for their own lives. If *sudden downfall* had come upon such a towering figure as Pharaoh, they might well wonder at the possibility of their own survival before the incursions of Babylon.

(b) The Desolation of Egypt (32:11–16)

> 32:11 "For thus says the Lord GOD:
> The sword of the king of Babylon will come upon you.
> 32:12 By swords of warriors
> I will cause your multitude to fall—
> violent ones of nations, all of them.
> They will ravage the pride of Egypt,
> and all its multitude will be annihilated.
> 32:13 And I will destroy all its animals
> from beside many waters;

> and a human foot will no longer churn them,
> and the hoofs of animals will not churn them.
> ³²:¹⁴ Then I will make their waters settle,
> and make their rivers flow like oil,
> declares the Lord GOD.
> ³²:¹⁵ When I set the land of Egypt a desolation,
> and ⌊when⌋ the land is desolate of what fills it,
> when I strike down all who inhabit it,
> then they will know that I ⌊am⌋ the LORD."
> ³²:¹⁶This is a lament, and they will lament it. The daughters of the nations will lament it; over Egypt and over all its multitude they will lament it, declares the Lord GOD.'

♦ **32:11** The occurrence of the messenger formula, *For thus says the Lord GOD* (cf. 2:4), marked the start of a new strophe in the oracle, giving further depth to what has been said. 'My sword' (32:10) was now presented as realised when *The sword of the king of Babylon will come upon you* (a masculine singular form designating Pharaoh). The image of the sword occurred frequently in Ezekiel (see on 21:3), and here it was viewed as almost possessing a life of its own ('will come') in the form of the military might at Nebuchadnezzar's disposal.

♦ **32:12** The king of Babylon would not arrive on his own. *Swords of warriors* pointed to the size and power of the Babylonian army. Through them the LORD would *cause your multitude to fall*, where 'multitude' (*hāmôn*, cf. 29:19) described Pharaoh's army rather than Egypt's wealth. *Violent ones of nations* (cf. 28:7; 30:11; 31:12) pointed back to *warriors*, and emphasised the ferocity of those who served in the Babylonian army.

The invading forces would *ravage the pride of Egypt.* 'Ravage' (*šādad*) denoted violent destruction which would lay waste the resources and monuments of which Egypt was proud. The active verb 'will ravage' (*wəšadədû*) balanced in sound the contrasting passive verb *will be annihilated* (*wənišmad*) in the following line. *Its multitude* was probably again the Egyptian army which would be utterly devastated.

♦ **32:13** The LORD would also wipe out livestock as well as the human population. *From beside many waters* obviously refers to the Nile, but the expression 'many waters' may have overtones suggestive of the Exodus (Ps. 89:9–10; Isa. 51:9–10). *Churn* repeats the verb of 32:2, in reference to troubling or disturbing the waters so as to make them muddy. In the devastation which would overwhelm Egypt there would be no humans and animals left to make the waters undrinkable.

♦ **32:14** Only here in Ezekiel was the word *then* (*'āz*) used, and this may indicate that these lines were cited from an existing source. In this context, 'then' indicated the point at which the desolation of Egypt had taken place. At that time the LORD would act to transform the judgemental devastation of Egypt, and would reclaim the land. *I will make their waters settle* envisaged the silt which had been stirred up by the earlier thrashing about of the crocodile (32:2) and others, and by human and animal feet (32:13), sinking to the river bed so that the waters became clear and drinkable.

Rivers flow like oil may just have been a picture of steady, unruffled waters, but it probably did hint as a time of blessing. The oil in view was, of course, olive oil, not a petroleum product, but Egypt did not naturally have olive trees. What was envisaged was the provision of copious and rich benefits. It was certainly not a picture of a depopulated and ruined land.

♦ **32:15** But the prophet's attention was then drawn back to what would happen before Egypt participated in this time of intense blessing. There would first be a process of divine judgement and spiritual reappraisal. *Desolation* and *desolate* come from the same root (*šāmam*; cf. 6:14) and contribute a psychologically sinister note to the destruction. *What fills it* was both its people and its wealth. When the LORD inflicted on Egypt population loss and economic decline, *then* (lit., 'and', introducing an apodosis) *they will know that I ₒamₒ the LORD*. Did the recognition formula express true repentance, or did it stop short with some lesser response? Perhaps, even without repentance, they would at least recognise the supremacy of the LORD (cf. Phil. 2:10–11). Greenberg (1997:658) suggests a parallel with Leviticus 26:34–35 by which enforced limpidity of the Nile became a substitute for enforced sabbaticals for the land of Israel.

♦ **32:16** This verse provided a conclusion similar to that found in 19:14b. After Ezekiel uttered this prospective *lament* (an inclusion with 32:2), mourners throughout the nations would learn it to bewail the dead. Professional mourners, generally women (hence *the daughters of the nations*), were a feature of contemporary culture (cf. Jer. 9:17). Here they were viewed as participating in funereal rites *over Egypt and over all its multitude*, referring back to 32:12. The fourfold occurrence of the root 'lament' (*qîn*) reinforced the solemn finality of this verse. Such a lament over those who obstinately set themselves against the divine purpose was the obverse of songs of praise to celebrate the LORD's victory over his enemies.

REFLECTION

- Pharaoh's self-image was that of 'a young lion among the nations' (32:2)—fierce, regal, invincible. This reinforced his spiritual blindness to his real condition which, of course, is defined by how God saw him—and that was quite different, 'a monster in the seas'. It is in the light of such dangers that Paul advised the Romans not to think of themselves more highly than they ought, but that each should have a self-image formed by sound judgement regarding who they were (Rom. 12:3). That this was to be done in accordance with the measure of faith that God had assigned to each one of them implied that such a realistic assessment would begin with the fact of their new standing in Christ, and how God consequently regarded them in him. The fundamental truth about any human being has always been where God assesses they stand in relation to him.

(7) Descent into Sheol with the Uncircumcised (32:17–32)

Like the preceding oracle delivered a fortnight earlier, Ezekiel's final declaration against Egypt also elaborates on earlier material, which in this case is principally that found in 31:14c–18. The prophet is commanded to wail over Egypt and so consign it to reside with other nations in Sheol. This section provides a measure of insight into the prevailing views of existence after death (see on 32:21), but care must be taken to make appropriate allowance for the literary nature of this description of an underground graveyard which houses the remains of defunct empires. The rhetoric is concerned with evoking the fate and failure of the wicked, not with expounding a complete eschatology.

The thematic coherence of the oracle is obvious, and its overall structure is easily analysed. After the introductory material in 32:17, two paragraphs (32:18–21; 32:31–32) describe Pharaoh and his warriors in Sheol—which fits in with the overall focus of the Egyptian oracles. The descent into Sheol and the visualisation of conditions there match the description given in Isaiah 14. Between these paragraphs there is a roll call of the nations which are also found in Sheol (32:22–30), again omitting Babylon (see Introduction to 25:1–32:32). In some respects this list functions as a conclusion to the oracles against the nations as a whole. Here is the ultimate destiny of those who are confident in their own abilities and power, but who fail to give due respect to the LORD, the one true God. There is no escape from him for them even in death, for his sway extends over the afterlife just as it does over affairs in the present world.

Another form of structural analysis has been proposed in which it is argued that in this seventh oracle against Egypt, the seventh country of a 'religious rogues' gallery', it is possible to detect a third level of sevens in the seven strophes of the oracle (Wendland 2009:215–216). On the basis of repeated opening and closing key expressions, Wendland identifies these as 32:17–21, 22–23, 24–25, 26–27, 28 + 31–32, 29, and 30. The delineation of six of these units is incontestable, but the fifth is problematic. Though Wendland designates the fifth strophe as 'a disjunctive judgment against Pharaoh', it is clear that its distributed nature is the weak point in this analysis because it would blur the presence of a sevenfold presentation for Ezekiel's hearers. Still, the device may have been deliberately adopted to mark the conclusion of these oracles. It is not difficult to align the following remarks based on a tripartite division with Wendland's approach.

(a) Pharaoh Consigned to Sheol (32:17–21)

> 32:17 And it came to pass in the twelfth year, on the fifteenth of the month, that the word of the LORD came to me, saying, 32:18 'Son of man, wail over the multitude of Egypt, and bring it down, her and the daughters of majestic nations, to the world of lowest places, with those who have gone down to the pit: 32:19 Than whom are you more favoured?
>   Go down and be laid with the uncircumcised.
> 32:20 In the midst of those slain by the sword they will fall; a sword has been given; they have carried her off and all her multitudes. 32:21 Mighty ones of warriors will speak to him from the midst of Sheol, with his helpers; they have come down, they have lain ⌊with⌋ the uncircumcised, those slain by the sword.'

♦ **32:17** The incomplete date formula, *in the twelfth year, on the fifteenth of the month*, probably related to the same month as the preceding date ('twelfth month', 32:1), and so corresponds to 17th March 585 B.C.[93] The message-reception formula was followed in the next verse by the LORD's usual form of address to the prophet.

---

93. Some Hebrew manuscripts, a major LXX manuscript, and the Peshitta read 'the eleventh year' in 32:1, and some Hebrew manuscripts and the Peshitta read 'the eleventh year' in 32:17. In 32:17 the LXX takes the month as the 'first', not the twelfth, and this is followed by RSV, NRSV. There is no definite evidence either way, but the LXX reading was probably the result of a desire to place this date before that of 33:21.

♦ **32:18** The command issued to Ezekiel was to *wail,* that is, to give vent to an expression of grief uttered in situations similar those where a 'lament' (cf. 32:2) would be used, but possibly less articulate in its content. *The multitude of Egypt* pointed to Egypt's troops (cf. 31:2), and it was that army which was in view in the command, *bring it down.* For 'bring down' and 'go down', see on 26:11, 16, 20; 31:12–18. Ezekiel was to usher the Egyptians into Sheol, and accompany their departure there with sorrowful cries. In this way he would provide the sound track to accompany Egypt's interment.

Her and the daughters of majestic nations is grammatically difficult after the preceding masculine/neuter references to Egypt. One possibility is to emend 'her' (*'ôtāh*) to 'you' (*'attâ*) in reference to Ezekiel, and to envisage the combination of 'you and the daughters of the majestic nations' as professional mourners who would join Ezekiel in this parody of the elaborate Egyptian rituals performed when a pharaoh was escorted to his pyramid tomb (Hummel 2007:934). More probably, the text should be retained as spelling out the comprehensive, international consequences of the fall of Egypt. Catastrophe would also engulf her satellite states (cf. the use of daughters in 26:6). No matter how *majestic* (the same term as 'splendid' in 17:8) they might be, it would be of no avail in diverting their descent *to the world of lowest places* (cf. 26:20), where Egypt and her allies would join past generations and empires: *with those who have gone down to the pit.*[94] For 'pit' (= 'the grave', see on 26:20.

♦ **32:19** This verse set out words Ezekiel was to utter as he wailed. Since the verbs have singular subjects, Pharaoh was probably the one addressed, and challenged with a question in a similar fashion to 31:2 and 31:18. Although Ezekiel's question has been frequently translated along the lines of 'Than whom are you more beautiful?', that does not really fit the present context, and *favoured* (cf. NIV) is a more appropriate rendering (cf. Ps. 90:17). If 'favour' was also a title for Tammuz (Adonis) whose cult Ezekiel witnessed in Jerusalem (8:14), then this might incorporate a sarcastic comment on the emptiness of Pharaoh's claim to elude Sheol.

The singular imperative, *go down,* mockingly commanded Pharaoh to depart. The root *yārad* ('go down', and in the hiphil 'bring down')

---

94. The verb *yārad,* 'to go down', here functions with stative force, 'to be down', and so the participial phrase *yôrədê-bôr* (lit., 'going down of pit ʟonesʃ') may be rendered with a present perfect 'those who have gone down' (so also 32:24, 25, 29, 30).

occurred 18 times in chapters 31–32, and reinforced the LORD's dismissal to the grave of those whom he had condemned. ***Be laid***[95] was a euphemism for 'burial' (repeated in 32:21, 27, 28, 29, 30, 32), representing the deceased as stretched out in the tomb. ***With the uncircumcised*** portrayed an ignominious end (cf. 28:10; 31:18), and 'uncircumcised' was repeated ten times in this section. While the description may simply be a conventional expression for those who, from an Israelite point of view, were excluded from the covenant community, it is known that Egyptian priests and kings practised circumcision, as did Edom and Sidon. So it is possible that the Egyptian hierarchy also viewed the uncircumcised as belonging to a lower caste, which would intensify the degradation of being consigned to the same fate as them.

♦ **32:20** This verse and the following contain several grammatical anomalies for which no certain resolution can be proposed. ***They will fall*** applied to the Egyptians. Block argues that ***those slain by the sword*** were not war casualties, but executed criminals, who were not given an honourable burial, and so they were also consigned to a separate, less favoured existence in the afterlife (1998:218). The clause, ***a sword has been given***/'appointed', does not appear in the Septuagint, and so is omitted in the RSV. The NRSV, however, adopts a different approach and takes the subject of the feminine verb, not as 'a sword' but as a reference to the 'land' of Egypt: 'Egypt has been handed over to the sword' (cf. AV, NKJV, ESV). However, it is surprising that there is no preposition corresponding to 'to', and on balance it is more probable that the thought is that the LORD has appointed the sword as the weapon the Babylonians will wield when acting as his agents (cf. 30:24). ***They have carried her off and all her multitudes***, or possibly, 'Carry her off and all her multitudes.'[96] Only here does the plural 'multitudes' occur in Ezekiel. It may refer to Egypt's army and those of her allies.

♦ **32:21** ***Mighty ones of warriors*** used the term 'rams' (cf. 31:11), which were both strong and leaders of the flock, to describe the first-

---

95. A hophal imperative is 'a semantic anomaly', used to convey the idea of compulsion 'be caused (against your will) to be laid', possibly an ad hoc literary creation (*IBHS* §28.5a).

96. The variation arises from difficulty in identifying the initial vowel: is the word a qal perfect, *māšəkû*, or is it a qal imperative, *moškû*, with a rare, but possible, form (cf. Judg. 9:10; Jer. 2:12; GKC §46d)? Jewish tradition favoured the latter (cf. Keil 2002:271).

rate soldiers who were already in Sheol. There they would **speak to him from the midst of Sheol with his helpers**. They addressed Pharaoh and his allies in a manner reminiscent of the taunt uttered by the shades in Isaiah 14:9–10. ***They have come down, they have lain ⌊with⌋ the uncircumcised, those slain by the sword***. Though these words may have been a further description of how the 'mighty ones of warriors' themselves had arrived in their situation, it is more probable that this was a speech of 'welcome' of the fallen heroes to Egypt and her allies. In their day they had seemed invincible warriors, but they had no means of resisting the prophetic word: 'Go down and be laid with the uncircumcised'.

Mention of **Sheol** raises the question of Israel's understanding of the afterlife, but caution is required in drawing definitive conclusions from an imaginative, rhetorical passage such as this. However, there can be no doubt that the fact of life after death had been divinely disclosed to Israel, though at this stage of revelation not much light had been shed on the conditions which what prevailed after death (see Johnston 2002).

Sheol was a uniquely Israelite term which Ezekiel and his contemporaries used to describe the abode of the dead as a place. It may have been that they envisaged reality as having a three-tier structure with heaven as the upper layer, the earth, 'the land of the living', as the middle tier, and Sheol as the lowest level. Sheol was generally viewed as the common destiny of the righteous and the wicked, but the rhetoric of this passage did not touch on the lot of the righteous. The focus was on the destiny of the wicked. They were depicted both as conscious and as corpses in a massive cemetery with national areas centred round royal figures. While the corpses were not described as undergoing punishment, they were envisaged as living in various degrees of debasement and humiliation reflecting their earlier conduct (compare, for instance, 'in the midst of Sheol', 32:21, with 'the uttermost parts of the pit', 32:23).

(b) Roll-call in Sheol (32:22–30)

> 32:22 Assyria ⌊is⌋ there and all her assembly, ⌊with⌋ her graves round about her; all of them ⌊are⌋ slain, those who have fallen by the sword, 32:23 ⌊to⌋ whom her graves were set in the uttermost parts of the pit, and her assembly is all round about her grave, all of them ⌊are⌋ slain, those fallen by the sword, who set terror in the land of the living.

AGAINST EGYPT

^{32:24}Elam ⌐is¬ there and all her company round about her grave; all of them ⌐are¬ slain, fallen by the sword, who went down uncircumcised to the world of lowest places, who set their terror in the land of the living, and they bore their disgrace with those who have gone down to the pit. ^{32:25}In the midst of the slain they have set a bed for her with all her multitude; her graves ⌐are¬ round about her, all of them uncircumcised, slain by the sword, for terror of them was set in the land of the living, and they bore their disgrace with those who have gone down to the pit; it is set in the midst of the slain.
^{32:26}Meshekh-tubal ⌐is¬ there and all her multitude; her graves ⌐are¬ round about her, all of them uncircumcised, slain by the sword, for they set their terror in the land of the living. ^{32:27}But they do not lie with warriors, those fallen from among the uncircumcised who went down to Sheol with their weapons of war, and they set their swords under their heads, and their iniquities were upon their bones, for terror of the warriors ⌐had been¬ in the land of the living.
^{32:28}But ⌐as for¬ you, in the midst of the uncircumcised
    you will be broken,
    and you will lie with those slain by the sword.
^{32:29}Edom ⌐is¬ there, her kings and all her chieftains, who despite their might have been set with those slain by the sword; they lie with the uncircumcised and with those who have gone down to the pit.
^{32:30}The princes of the north ⌐are¬ there, all of them, and all the Sidonians who have gone down with the slain—ashamed despite their terror caused by their might; and they have lain down uncircumcised with those slain by the sword, and have borne their disgrace with those who have gone down to the pit.

♦ **32:22** *Assyria.* In this and following verses (32:22–30) the nations which were to be found in the pit were listed. Leading place was accorded to *Assyria*, which was hardly surprising in view of the prominent role conferred on it as the great cedar in chapter 31. Furthermore, though Assyria had been overthrown, the people of Ezekiel's day, both in Judah and more generally in the surrounding nations, retained a very vivid memory of the brutality of that regime. *Assembly* was used to refer to the Assyrian army, whereas 'multitude' or 'horde' was applied to Egypt, Elam, and Meshekh-tubal in the repetitive rhetoric employed in these verses. Hummel suggests it might imply that the Assyrian forces were more disciplined (2007:937).

***Her*[97] *graves* were those provided for her *slain* soldiers, *those who have fallen by the sword*.** Possibly the reference was to a complex of graves centred on the grave of the king who represented the land as a whole. This was a figurative presentation of a disgraced and defunct empire, in which all its former heroes lay motionless in death.

◆ **32:23** It was only of Assyria that it was said that its ***graves are set in the uttermost parts of the pit***, as deep as can be imagined, which was a sign of intense debasement and rejection. This was also the destiny of the Babylonian king in Isaiah 14:15, where the location was explicitly contrasted with the heights where the gods live. The higher the arrogant exalt themselves, the further they will be brought down. ***Her assembly*** was gathered in a lifeless tableau round the grave of the Assyrian king.

It was also the case that the Assyrians had ***set terror in the land of the living*** (cf. 26:17). This described the way in which Assyria deliberately employed terror tactics to intimidate subject peoples and their kings. It was this former brutality which accounted for the treatment subsequently meted out to them—a thought which echoed throughout this passage (32:24, 25, 26, 30, 32).

◆ **32:24** *Elam*. The second entry in the catalogue of departed empires was ***Elam***, which lay east of Babylon and whose capital was often located at Susa. It was an ancient civilisation dating from around 3200 B.C. Since its earliest epigraphic remains have not been deciphered, not much is known about it. It was mentioned in the table of nations (Gen. 10:22) and its king appeared in Gen. 14:1, 9. It continually provoked reprisals from the Assyrians because of its interference in their empire which lay to the west and south of their country. Eventually it was conquered by the Assyrian emperor Ashurbanipal in 640 B.C., and some of its peoples were transported to the territory of the former northern kingdom of Israel (cf. Ezra 4:9–10), while there were also Israelites in Elam (Isa. 11:11). Jeremiah directed one of his oracles against it (Jer. 49:34–39). Elam was incorporated as a province of the empire of the Medes and Persians, and was no longer a political force after Alexander the Great's conquest in 331.

What was said about Elam largely repeated what had been said

---

97. The feminine form used here and in connection with the following countries arises from the influence of the suppressed headword ’*ereṣ*, 'land of', a feminine noun in Hebrew. It does not convey the thought that these nations and their armies were conceived of as female.

about Egypt. Elam's army had been slain in battle and had descended to the underworld. They were described as *uncircumcised*. It is not known if circumcision was practised in Elam, and possibly all that was implied was that they met a disreputable end. *Terror of them* was the terror they had caused, not what they themselves had experienced. Their armies too had engaged in cruel and intimidating practices *in the land of the living*, and so they were penalised in death. *They bore their disgrace with those who have gone down to the pit.*

♦ **32:25** *They have set a bed* was an impersonal construction equivalent to 'a bed has been set for her.' 'Bed' described a couch or resting-place. The root of the term was the same as that in 'be laid' (32:19), so that this bed was a bier. Often the deceased were interred by being placed on a stone bed within a hillside tomb. *For her* referred to the nation as a whole, and round her all her slain army had their final resting-place. The concluding *it is set in the midst of the slain* reflected the introductory words of the verse, with 'it' being used collectively to refer to the multitude. Even though most of the verse was omitted in the Septuagint, its repetitious nature did not indicate a need for emendation, but was a feature of Ezekiel's style, here used to good effect to convey time and again the solemn finality of the scene.

♦ **32:26** *Meshekh-tubal.* Elsewhere Meshekh and Tubal were mentioned together but as separate peoples.[98] For instance, they were listed in the opposite order in 27:13 as trading with Tyre. Here, however, *Meshekh-tubal* was a compound name, as the subsequent use of 'her' indicated. Both nations were located in Anatolia, and often cooperated with each other, though there were times when hostility prevailed between them. Their geographical location meant that they had to contend with population pressures from the north and Assyrian expansionism to the south. No direct interaction with Israel is known about (but see chs. 38–39), and they were included here probably because of their contacts with Assyria. When they were subsequently incorporated into the Persian empire, they lost their identity.

The conduct and destiny of these ferocious fighting nations were described using expressions found in the two earlier entries in this catalogue, though *slain by the sword*[99] embodied a slight variation.

---

98. For a possible structural significance of the mention of these names, see on 38:2.

99. 'Slain' renders *məḥuləlê*, a pual participle whose sense 'ones made to be pierced' is similar to the standard phrase 'pierced/slain by the sword'.

Their fate too had been determined by their previous behaviour when they had employed terror tactics to overwhelm and subjugate their adversaries.

♦ **32:27** The precise sense of this verse is uncertain. ***But*** (lit., 'and', though the following negative suggests a measure of disjunction) apparently introduced a contrast between the fallen of Meshekh-tubal and another group who had been accorded a more honourable burial. If the thought was that ***they do not lie with warriors***, the distinction may be that some warriors were honoured by being buried ***with their weapons of war***, whereas the warriors of Meshekh-Tubal were buried without such honour. Alternatively, this elite group of warriors were laid to rest at a higher level (Greenberg 1997:665).

However, the NIV (1984) follows the Septuagint by treating the initial clause as a rhetorical question (as does Hummel 2007:938): 'Do they not lie with the other uncircumcised warriors?' On that understanding Meshekh-tubal shared the same fate as the other nations—an interpretation which obviates a number of difficulties. Though the 2011 NIV reverted to translating this clause as a statement, it introduced another reading from the Septuagint by substituting 'from of old' (*mēʿôlam*) rather than 'from among the uncircumcised' (*mēʿărēlîm*; cf. GNB, NRSV). This invites reading the description as that of fallen warriors from earlier generations (such as the Nephilim, Gen. 6:4, or Nimrod, Gen. 10:8), but this is hardly necessary.

They set their swords under their heads referred to an otherwise unattested interment practice, though burying a warrior with his weapons was of frequent enough occurrence. 'They' was an impersonal plural usage, and the clause could be rendered using a passive verb: 'their swords were set under their heads'. It is not certain what sense ***their iniquities were upon their bones*** was intended to convey. Many translations adopt the emendation of 'iniquities' (*ʿăwōnōtām*) to 'shields' (*ṣinnôtām*), and find here a parallel description of the way they were buried with their shields placed over their bodies corresponding to their swords under their heads (cf. GNB, NRSV, NLT, NIV 2011). However, 'iniquities' may well have had the sense 'the punishment for their iniquities' (cf. NIV 1984, HCSB), so that their buried corpses were evidence of the death brought on them by their behaviour. This fitted in well with the final clause of the verse which explained the penalty imposed on them in terms of ***terror of the warriors*** that is, the terror they themselves had caused ***in the land of the living***.

♦ **32:28** This verse was in the form of a parallel bicolon, with assonance between *you will be broken* (*tiššābar*) and *you will lie* (*tiškab*; cf. 32:19). It was addressed directly to Pharaoh ('you' is masculine singular), who would be overwhelmed in battle and be given an ignoble burial *in the midst of the uncircumcised.* Here was a reminder to Pharaoh and Egypt that their names had not been left off this roll-call of the nations.

♦ **32:29** *Edom.* The catalogue of the defunct regimes then looked at Judah's nearer neighbours. It is unsurprising that mention was made of Edom, an inveterate foe of Israel (25:12–14), though there was no mention here of 'terror' caused by her soldiers. Although *there* was strictly 'to there', the directive force of the word is frequently absent in later writing (cf. 23:3; 48:35). *Edom* had no 'multitude', that is, an organised army, but she did have *her kings and all her rulers.* Edom's kings were mentioned from early times (Gen. 36:31–39), but 'kings' was probably used here in the sense of 'chieftains' of various clans, rather than of a single dynasty lasting for a number of generations, and 'rulers' (*nāśî*; cf. 44:3) were secondary officials in the political structure of the community. However, not enough is known about the affairs of Edom to work out more precisely what was intended. *Despite their might* (rather than 'terror' as in 32:30) may alternatively have the sense 'with their might', and this would certainly fit in with the meaning of the passage. *Lie with the uncircumcised* would be an outcome which added to the shame of the Edomites who did practise circumcision (cf. Jer. 9:25–26). In chapter 35 Edom's future destruction is prophesied, but here it would seem that it was past generations of Edomites who *have been set*, that is, allocated their position, and so *they lie* among *those who have gone down to the pit.*

♦ **32:30** *Phoenicia.* The rare term *princes* (*nāsîk*) is difficult to pin down in terms of its precise function. They may well have been local chieftains of some sort. Certainly *all of them* indicated there were a number of persons holding this status, and that none of them were exempt. It is also unclear what geographical reference was intended by *of the north*, possibly the Phoenician coastal settlements. *All the Sidonians* (lit., 'totality of Sidonian'; for Sidon, see on 28:20–24) reinforced the inference that the general area contemplated was the zone controlled by the Phoenician city states. *Who went down with the slain despite their terror* demonstrated that, despite their capacity to cause terror in others, their power was unable to extricate them from the descent into Sheol. *Ashamed* described their reaction when they realised that, ***despite their terror caused by their might*** when they forced their wishes on those who opposed them, their previously formidable strength was incapable of delaying or deflecting the final enemy from them.

Consequently, ***they have lain down*** in death. Since the Phoenicians evidently practised circumcision, ***uncircumcised*** was used here as equivalent to 'not being really circumcised, and so being outside the covenant community', or 'separated from divine blessing because of their lack of faith' (cf. 28:10; 32:19). Again, the stock phrases ***with those slain by the sword*** (cf. 32:20), ***have borne their disgrace*** (cf. 32:25), and ***those who have gone down to the pit*** (cf. 32:18) were used to associate the Phoenicians with the others whose strength and resources had proved ineffective in the face of death.

(c) The Demise of Pharaoh (32:31-32)

> ³²:³¹Them will Pharaoh see and will comfort himself for all his multitude; slain by the sword ⌊will be⌋ Pharaoh and all his force, declares the Lord GOD. ³²:³²For I have set my terror in the land of the living, and he will be laid down in the midst of the uncircumcised, with those who are slain by the sword—Pharaoh and all his multitude, declares the Lord GOD.'

♦ **32:31** The concluding two verses of the oracle moved from an initial ***them***, the other nations, back once more to ***Pharaoh***, who would observe their fate—but as one who was himself sharing in it. As he would do so, ***he will comfort himself for all his multitude*** (*hāmôn*; cf. 29:19)¹⁰⁰ extended a bitter measure of solace in that he was not the only monarch to have seen his forces wiped out in this way (cf. 31:16). The company he would be alongside in Sheol had suffered the same fate for their unwarranted delusions of self-sufficient power and grandeur, though they need not have been guilty of claiming divine status.

The LORD declared that ***Pharaoh and all his force*** (*ḥayil*) would be ***slain by the sword*** of divine justice. 'Force' emphasised the military might of his army, whereas 'multitude' conveyed instead the din and activity associated with them. Objectively the reference was the same. ***Declares the Lord GOD*** would often indicate the conclusion of an oracle, but on this occasion there was a significant postscript.

---

100. It is merely a difference in spelling which distinguishes the kethib, *hămônōh*, 'his multitude', with a final *he*, and *hămônô*, which has the expected spelling.

♦ **32:32** Translators vary in their interpretation of what the LORD finally said. The initial word (*kî*) may be rendered as 'for' or 'although'. The Massoretes themselves recorded in the margin *ḥittîtî*, 'my terror', as a recommended replacement for *ḥittîtô*, 'his terror', which occurred in the main text. The NRSV favours correcting the text so that it reads 'he spread his terror', which the NIV shades down to 'I had him spread terror'. If this is coupled with 'although', the message contrasted how Pharaoh had spread terror *in the land of the living* with the fate which awaited him *in the midst of the uncircumcised, with those who are slain by the sword.*

Alternatively, and perhaps more probably, the LORD then spoke by way of explanation (*for*) by going behind purely human reactions to emphasise the divine control over all events. While 'I have set his terror' would have declared that all Pharaoh had carried out had been by divine permission, reading with the margin, *I have set my terror*,[101] pointed to a terror which was divinely dispensed and which far exceeded that caused by human exercise of power (32:23, 24, 25, 26, 27, 30). That was the dread divine dispensation of justice, foreshadowed in the fate of these ancient kingdoms, and fully to be revealed at the great day (cf. 32:10).

As in 31:18, *Pharaoh and all his multitude* was added in conclusion to make clear who was being spoken about. *Declares the Lord GOD*, which was repeated one more time, added a solemn note of finality to this display of the ultimate impotence and transience of the power structures of humanity before the reckoning that the Sovereign of the universe would require.

REFLECTION

- When Ezekiel intoned his funereal dirge over the multitude of Egypt (32:18–19), its power did not inhere magically in the prophet's pronouncement or in the words themselves. What gave it its efficacy was that it was the word of the LORD which always accomplishes his purposes and therefore does not return to him having proved to be ineffective (Isa. 55:10-11).
- A motif which runs with quiet, but chilling, insistence throughout the oracles against the nations is that of the sword (25:13; 26:6, 8, 11; 28:23; 29:8; 30:4, 5, 6, 11, 17, 21, 22, 24, 25; 31:17, 18; 32:10, 11, 12, 20 [2×], 21, 22, 23, 24, 26, 27, 28, 29, 30, 31, 32). Here is a

---

101. Another possible variation would be to argue that *nātattî* is to be treated as a prophetic perfect (Introduction §6.2b), and should be rendered 'I shall set'.

solemn illustration of the words of Christ, 'All who take up a sword, by a sword they will perish' (Matt. 26:52; cf. Ezek. 35:5–6). How often the pages of history record that those who by the force of arms subjugate others find themselves overwhelmed in the same way! For a while the empires of this world are divinely permitted to indulge themselves in the conceit that they are invincible and their rule will last a thousand years, but inevitably divine justice exacts the penalty appropriate to their conduct. 'Whoever sheds human blood, by a human his blood is to be shed, for in the image of God he made humankind' (Gen. 9:6).

- Pharaoh was bidden depart in language which as a whole was mocking and sarcastic. No matter who he thought he was and with what pretentious trappings he surrounded himself, he could not escape death. Despite the extensive and elaborate preparations that pharaohs made to ensure their continued luxurious existence in the afterlife, what awaited him was the same as that which came on others. Death was, and is, the great leveller.
- While we are not to read arbitrarily into the Old Testament, it is the case that there is an underlying unity with the New. It has long been recognised that there was an awareness of life after death with God for his people throughout the Old Testament era. The reality of death could not be gainsaid, but the LORD had already allowed sufficient chinks of light to permeate the dark shroud of death to permit them to entertain that hope, while not yet being in a position to articulate how or when it might be possible to envisage more than Sheol as the destiny of the righteous. For instance, David, aware of the spiritual security he enjoyed in the LORD, was able to say, 'You will not abandon my soul to Sheol, or let your holy one see the pit' (Ps. 16:10). He knew of 'the path of (eternal) life' (Ps. 16:11), but he did not yet possess the New Testament insight which required that path to be opened up decisively and effectively through the death and resurrection of the Messiah (Acts 2:24–32).

VII. Restoration and Renewal

(33:1–39:29)

OUTLINE

A. News of Jerusalem's Fall (33:1–33)
  1. The Watchman's Duties (33:1–9)
  2. The Watchman's Message (33:10–20)
  3. The News Arrives (33:21–22)
  4. Unrepentant Judah (33:23–29)
  5. The Exiles' Reaction to Ezekiel (33:30–33)

B. The Shepherds of Israel (34:1–31)
  1. Condemnation of the Corrupt Shepherds (34:1–10)
  2. The Good Shepherd (34:11–16)
  3. Judgement within the Flock (34:17–22)
  4. The Messianic Shepherd (34:23–24)
  5. The Covenant of Peace (34:25–31)

C. Mount Seir and the Mountains of Israel (35:1–36:15)
  1. Denunciation of Edom's Treachery (35:1–15)
  2. Reversal of the Depredations of Israel's Enemies (36:1–15)

D. A New Heart and a New Spirit (36:16–38)
  1. For My Holy Name (36:16–21)
  2. My Spirit Within You (36:22–32)
  3. Eden Restored (36:33–36)
  4. The Flock Increases (36:37–38)

E. The Vision of the Dry Bones (37:1–14)
  1. Restored from Death (37:1–10)
  2. Interpretation of the Vision (37:11–14)

F. Reunion and Restoration (37:15–28)
  1. One in My Hand (37:15–20)
  2. One Nation, One King, One Shepherd (37:21–28)

G. Gog and Magog (38:1–39:29)
  1. The Invasion of the Armies of Gog (38:1–9)
  2. Gog's Plot to Plunder (38:10–13)
  3. The Divine Purpose (38:14–16)
  4. The Wrath of the LORD (38:17–23)
  5. The LORD's Defeat of Gog (39:1–16)
  6. Invitation to a Victory Banquet (39:17–24)
  7. Restoration of Israel (39:25–29)

VII. Restoration and Renewal (33:1–39:29)

A major transition in the book occurs at this juncture, from dark words of condemnation and impending judgement to bright pictures of reformation and revival. Though there are certain significant continuities across the divide, particularly the determinative role of the LORD in Israel's destiny, in the aftermath of the catastrophic fall of Jerusalem (33:21) the balance of Ezekiel's ministry moves decisively towards Israel's restoration. However, this will not be accomplished through those who survive the debacle and conflagration to remain in Judah. They are viewed for a last time in 33:23–29, where they are sentenced to further ruin, and then pass out of view. The future of the covenant community lies with those in exile, and to them the prophet is to extend a message of exhortation and encouragement. His presentation is designed to induce his compatriots to trust in the LORD and to conform their outlook and conduct to the promises God is making to them. They will still be living in a hostile world, but they will be aware of the overarching purpose of God for their good.

Two dates, found in 33:21 and 40:1, provide key markers for the structure of the closing divisions of the book, but both of these divisions continue to have as their target audience the community in exile after the fall of the city. Within chapters 33–39 the message-reception formula occurs at 33:1, 23; 34:1; 35:1; 36:16; 37:15; 38:1, and sets the basic structure of the division. That the formula is not found in 37:1 is readily explained by the visionary nature of what immediately follows. See on 36:1 and 39:1 for its absence there. The Introduction to chapter 33 discusses its distinctive structure.

The present division begins with a transitional chapter (ch. 33) which restates the prophet's commission in the light of the changes which occur when the exiles are definitively informed that Jerusalem has fallen (33:21). Though this authenticates Ezekiel's status as a prophet of the LORD, there is still much that needs to be improved in the attitude of the community (33:30–33). The challenge to bring about this change is approached by disclosing how the LORD will provide for the people's well-being and the vanquishment of all those who are hostile to them (chs. 35; 38–39).

The problem of the failed leadership of the people is tackled in chapter 34 by the LORD intervening directly as the divine Shepherd who will provide for his flock, and set over them the true David, who will be their shepherd and ruler (34:23–24; 37:24–25). There will then be a Spirit-induced harmony among the people (36:26–28; 37:14;

39:29). The defeat of their enemies, here represented by Edom, Judah's ancient antagonist (ch. 35), establishes conditions of safety which open up the way to renewed prosperity for God's covenant people as he works to transform the land of Israel itself (36:1–15), and then to transform the people (36:16–38), who are purified and endowed with the Spirit. These themes are further developed in two scenarios. The first is a visionary presentation of new life being imparted by the Spirit to the otherwise lifeless remains of Israel (37:1–14), and the second centres on a symbolic act which points forward to the divided people being reunited and brought back to the land under the rule of their Davidic king (37:15–28).

Israel's problems will, however, be far from over. The nations of the earth will advance against them in an assault which will be decisively quelled by the LORD (chs. 38–39). Only then will Israel be blessed with true peace and the full enjoyment of God's presence with them (39:25–29). The basis is thus laid for the closing scenes of restored Israel's worship and fellowship with God in Jerusalem (chs. 40–48).

There are promises here regarding the near and the distant future. The near future is unmistakably that of the community in exile returning to Jerusalem, but what of the implications of these prophecies for the distant future? They 'may be posited on the basis of earlier prophets such as Isaiah as a prediction of the incorporation of individuals from all nations into the holy people of God, that is, "Israel" of Messianic (neo-"Davidic") times (e.g., 34:11–16; 36:24; 37:21–23—cf. Isa. 11, John 10)' (Wendland 2009:209–210).

A. News of Jerusalem's Fall (33:1–33)

The unthinkable has happened. Jerusalem has fallen. When news of this reaches the exilic community in Babylon, the hopes which so many of them still obstinately cherish are irrevocably shattered. But the traumatised community is not left to its own devices as to how they are to cope now that their world has fallen apart. The LORD has already made provision for their guidance into the future. The very prophet who foretold what has engulfed them is recommissioned to show them the way forward. So in this transitional chapter, information is given about how the fall of Jerusalem impacted on the prophet, on those who were left in Judah, and on the community in exile.

Structure. Ezekiel's habit is to insert date formulas to punctuate his record of the various periods of his ministry. He usually places this information in a heading to the message he is given to deliver. The absence of an initial date formula is therefore a distinctive feature of chapter 33. The chapter contains five sections (33:1–9, 10–20, 21–22, 23–29, 30–33), and delaying recording the date until 33:21 highlights the pivotal nature of the information supplied in the central paragraph: 'The city has been struck down!' This marks the start of a new era and sets the agenda for the remainder of Ezekiel's ministry.

Different views exist regarding the first two sections of this chapter. For instance, Joyce (1989:144; cf. Greenberg 1997:680) considers that the two sentinel passages form 'bookends' around the judgement prophecies, and argues that 33:1–20 should be understood not as inaugurating a new period of the prophet's ministry, but as a recapitulation of the themes in chapters 1–24. It is only with the new date formula in 33:21 that the turning point in Ezekiel's ministry arrives. However, there is a decided break after the oracles against the nations. Moreover, the LORD has been preparing the prophet for this moment (24:26–27), and has acted the night before. It is quite plausible to understand 33:1–20 as material revealed to Ezekiel prior to the messenger's arrival, although not delivered to the people until after that has occurred. Indeed, the very fact that Ezekiel is directed to communicate these oracles to the people (33:2, 10) distinguishes them from his earlier appointment as a watchman (3:17–21) about which no corresponding command was issued. Now they are fully informed, and the focus of what is said oscillates between the responsibilities of the prophet and those of his audience.

Ezekiel's role as a prophetic watchman is broader than proclamation of an alarm concerning the impending capture and destruction of Jerusalem, and so does not terminate with the fall of the city. He has now to counsel and alert the exilic community regarding the way forward. The beginning of the chapter relates to how he is to function in these changed conditions. First, there is a reminder of the need for on-going faithfulness in carrying out his task (33:2–9), but that is coupled with the requirement that the people respond appropriately to the watchman's message (33:10–20). They are not to give way to despair (33:10). Instead they are reminded of the benevolence of God, and exhorted to repent (33:11).

After the epochal communique that Jerusalem has fallen (33:21–22), there are two oracles which serve to correct misunderstanding of the new situation. The first is directed against the defiance of those left behind in the land (33:23–29). The second concerns Ezekiel's situation in Babylonia. He now has a more open audience, but it is not a perceptive or spiritually alert one (33:30–33). Ezekiel's struggle to have his message accepted is by no means over, and the people are still far from forming a community ready to receive and obey God's word.

(1) The Watchman's Duties (33:1–9)

Much of the material here is similar to that found in 3:16–21. Why then is it repeated? There are many who consider this a duplicate which arose in the subsequent redaction of the book. More significantly, the whole chapter ought to be read in the light of the epochal event announced in 33:21, 'The city has been struck down!' The falsity of the consensus religion of Judah and Jerusalem has been decisively exposed by the stark facts of history. The prophet who foretold that collapse now receives a renewed prophetic commission to minister in the changed circumstances of the new order. However, Block argues that 'the chapter contains no hint at all that a new era in Ezekiel's preaching is about to begin' (1998:235).

Though the people have no option but to accept that the city has fallen as Ezekiel foretold, this irrefutable authentication of Ezekiel's message did not of itself reshape the outlook of his audience. The people were still as they had been spiritually. They were still unrepentant. Their inner life was virtually non-existent. They were beset with immoral motives, words and conduct. Further deep change was needed for them to become the people of God, and enjoy the blessings of that relationship.

So, in response to the people's perplexity, 'How then can we live?' (33:10), the LORD gives public expression to what has only been communicated as a warning and encouragement to Ezekiel previously. The prophet is required to set before the exiles the whole scope and purpose of his ministry.

The declaration of Ezekiel's responsibilities as a watchman is accompanied by a statement of the need for the people to respond. First, there is described the outcome when a watchman does warn the people (33:2–5), and then when he does not (33:6). In 33:7–9 the focus is specifically on Ezekiel as the watchman. The watchman sounds a general alarm to which each individual should respond. Then the possible outcomes are reviewed in reverse order: when the prophet does not warn (33:7–8), and when he does (33:9).

> 33:1And the word of the LORD came to me, saying, 33:2'Son of man, speak to the sons of your people and say to them, "As for a land, if I cause to come upon it a sword, and the people of the land take a man from their border and set him as their

watchman, ³³:³and ⌊if⌋ he sees the sword coming upon the land and blows the horn and warns the people, ³³:⁴and ⌊if⌋ anyone hearing the sound of the trumpet hears but does not take warning, and ⌊the⌋ sword comes and takes him, his blood will be on his own head. ³³:⁵The sound of the trumpet he had heard but he had not taken warning; his blood will be on himself. But ⌊if⌋ he had taken warning, he would have saved his own life. ³³:⁶But ⌊as for⌋ the watchman, if he sees the sword coming and does not sound the trumpet and the people are not warned, and the sword comes and takes from them a life, he has been taken for his own iniquity, but his blood I will inquire for from the hand of the watchman.

³³:⁷But ⌊as for⌋ you, son of man, I appoint you a watchman to the house of Israel. When you hear a word from my mouth, you will warn them from me. ³³:⁸When I say to the wicked ⌊person⌋, 'O wicked ⌊one⌋, you will surely die,' but you have not spoken to warn a wicked ⌊person⌋ ⌊to turn⌋ from his way, that one, ⌊as⌋ a wicked ⌊person⌋, will die for his iniquity, but his blood I will require from your hand. ³³:⁹But ⌊as for⌋ you, if you have warned a wicked ⌊person⌋ ⌊to go⌋ from his way, to turn from it, but he has not turned from his way, he ⌊for his part⌋ will die for his iniquity but you ⌊for your part⌋ will have delivered your life." '

♦ **33:1** The prophetic message-reception formula (here without a date, which was not needed in the light of 33:21, to which it was postponed for special emphasis) marked the beginning of a new section, which was accompanied in the next verse by *Son of man* (cf. 2:1), the form of address used by the LORD for the prophet when he issued instructions to him.

♦ **33:2** Apart from this chapter, the phrase *the sons of your people* was employed only in 3:11 and 37:18 (cf. 13:17), and this has suggested that it occurred here to form an inclusion with 3:11 round the record of the earlier period of Ezekiel's ministry. But it was used in this context four times (also in 33:12, 17, 30). It probably did not point to the estrangement of the LORD from the people; rather its significance lay in the bond between Ezekiel and the exiles, and his consequent responsibility towards them. Indeed, there was also a hopeful aspect to the use of the term: the exiles remained as an identifiable and distinct people. Even though their land had been captured and ravaged, they were not going to be permitted to fragment and become absorbed into the undifferentiated mass of enslaved subjects of the Babylonian regime.

So the prophet was given a message for his fellow countrymen. This was presented in generalised legal style: *⌐As for⌐ a land, if I cause to come upon it a sword* (cf. 18:5). The subject under consideration was first specified, 'a land', and then various circumstances were set out (33:2b–4a), before the scenario was resolved (33:4b). 'I cause to come' envisaged God exercising his sovereign control over events. Though it was not asserted that this particular scenario would occur, if it did, then it was clear that it was not to be regarded as a fortuitous happening that 'a sword', that is, an enemy attack (cf. 5:17), had been launched against the land.

It was further envisaged that *the people of the land* took communal action in face of this assault by taking *a man from their border*,[1] not merely a fellow countryman, but one appropriately situated near their frontier, and by appointing him *as their watchman* (cf. 3:17). His task was to be on the outlook for invading forces, and raise the alarm as soon as he became aware of their approach.

♦ **33:3** When the watchman detected *the sword coming*[2] *upon the land* as the enemy advanced, it was expected that he would employ *the horn* with which he was equipped. This would most probably be a ram's horn, which was used in liturgical contexts as a means to summon the congregation, and also in military contexts, as here, to muster the army and issue commands. By blowing the horn, the watchman would discharge his duty and *warn* (cf. 3:17–21) *the people* of the peril that was confronting them.

♦ **33:4** But to achieve its intended result an alarm must not be ignored, and so a further condition was added regarding *anyone hearing the sound of the trumpet.* Now *hears* ($\check{s}\bar{a}ma^c$) may merely denote perception of a sound, but it also described taking appropriate action in response to the message it conveyed, that is, 'to listen' to it, or in more archaic language 'to heed' it. It was also the case that while the appointment of the watchman was viewed as community action (33:2) and while the watchman's warning was similarly addressed to the people at large (33:3), here the required response was expressed as an individual reaction.

---

1. Although the form *miqṣêhem* appears to have a pronominal suffix appropriate to a plural noun, in fact the noun is singular, *qāṣeh*, and the *yodh* which appears is the original final root letter.

2. The final accent on $b\bar{a}^{\,}\hat{a}$, 'coming', shows that the Massoretes read it as a feminine participle (agreeing with 'sword', which is feminine), not as a perfect form which would have penultimate stress.

The need for an appropriate reaction was also conveyed by the form of the following verb, *take warning*.[3] This would be achieved by arming oneself to repulse the attacker, or by seeking appropriate protection. If that was not done *and the sword comes*,[4] then the upshot would most probably be that the sword *takes him*, that is, he was killed by the invading forces.

At last the scenario was resolved by an attribution of guilt regarding this loss of life. *His blood will be on his own head* was a variation of the formula, 'his blood will be on himself' (33:5; cf. also the requital formula, 9:10). This reflected the outcome forecast in the law (Lev. 20:9, 11–13, 16, 27) by which an individual was held responsible for his own deliberate actions and so had to bear the consequences of his choice.

♦ **33:5** The two courses of action open to the individual who had heard the horn were clearly spelled out. *He had heard the sound of the trumpet but had not taken warning; his blood will be on himself.* The individual had no one but himself to blame for what befell him. He had disregarded the warning which had been given and which he had heard. The second part of the verse set out the alternative positive response in which appropriate action was taken. This was couched in hypothetical terms because it was not in fact the way the individual had reacted. *But ₗifₗ he had taken warning, he would have saved his own life.*[5]

In applying this analogy to the prophets of Israel, it is clear that their message need not be an inflexible pronouncement regarding what was inevitably going to occur. It was rather a statement of what would happen if current circumstances continued to prevail. But the delivery of the prophecy constituted a warning and a plea to individuals or to the nation that they should repent and avert disaster. See the discussion of conditional prophecy in the comments on Chapter 26.

---

3. The verb *nizhār* is a niphal perfect, used in a tolerative sense, 'he lets himself be warned' (cf. 14:3). The pointing of the perfect with *ā* is pausal (cf. 3:21; 33:5 [2×], 6).

4. At this point there is a switch to a *waw*-consecutive imperfect form. Block (1998:237) considers the customary perfect gives way to the customary imperfect.

5. The initial *waw* with a pronoun is disjunctive with adversative force, 'but'. The two verbs are perfects without any conjunction to indicate the conditional sequence, but perfect verbs may be used to convey contrary-to-fact statements (*IBHS* §30.5.4a).

♦ **33:6** A second scenario was then set out in a similar fashion, with the word order again indicating a casuistic legal formulation, *but ⌊as for⌋ the watchman, if he sees*. The situation described earlier (33:2–3a) was presupposed, but now it was developed to expose the consequences of the watchman carelessly performing only half of his duty. The situation was set out in a brief sequence, *he sees the sword coming and does not sound the trumpet and the people are not warned*. In that event the enemy would be able to fall upon an unsuspecting populace. *The sword comes and takes from them a life.* It was not conceded that the one who would die was an innocent victim of another's dereliction of duty. *He has been taken for his own iniquity*, where 'taken' implies 'taken away by death' (cf. 'the sword … takes him', 33:4). 'For his own iniquity' showed the outcome as justified by his personal sin (cf. 3:18). However, it was also the case that *his blood I will inquire for from the hand of the watchman*, which employed a verb synonymous with that found in 3:18, 20; 33:8 (cf. 34:6). The LORD would seek out the delinquent watchman and exact a penalty equivalent to that suffered by the victim of his failure. So the watchman was required to answer not only for himself, but for all lives lost because he had not warned about the impending threat.

Time and again in Israel false prophets had arisen who were oblivious to the spiritual threats facing the nation (ch. 13), but the scenario of the deficient watchman was not developed extensively here, because the focus was on the community's obligation to respond to the genuine warnings which were being issued.

♦ **33:7** The LORD then switched his focus to setting out Ezekiel's personal responsibility: *But ⌊as for⌋ you, son of man.* In saying, *I set you a watchman to the house of Israel*, the LORD reminded him of the terms of his original commission from 3:17,[6] and extended his prophetic ministry in the new circumstances after Jerusalem's fall. This and the following two verses closely echoed 3:17–19. There remained the continuing irony in the situation that the one who appointed the watchman was also the one about whose activity the watchman was to issue the warning.

Even though events had vindicated Ezekiel's previous ministry, they

---

6. On this occasion it is more probable that the perfect verb, *nətattîkā*, 'I have given you', is to be understood as a true past tense than as a performative perfect, 'I ⌊hereby⌋ give you' (Introduction §6.3d), which would imply a second commissioning of Ezekiel to a different role. Instead this was a renewal and continuation of his original appointment.

had not relaxed his obligation to speak faithfully. *When you hear a word from my mouth, you will warn them from me.*

♦ **33:8–9** These verses differed from the earlier charge to Ezekiel as a watchman in that there was no mention of the righteous (3:20–21). Their absence may well reflect the gloomy circumstances prevalent at the fall of Jerusalem.

The LORD continued to impress on Ezekiel the seriousness with which he should pursue his ministry, but, as the message was also addressed to the exiles, it served two further functions. Because so many of them had failed to grasp the prophet's message (33:30–33), the LORD set before them the rationale of Ezekiel's preceding ministry. This would help them understand that the nation had arrived in the sorry state it now found itself in through its intransigence in the face of repeated faithful warnings. It also constituted a solemn admonition to the community regarding their response to the prophet's subsequent ministry. They could not offload onto Ezekiel their personal responsibility. If the prophet failed in his duty, it was still the case that the wicked person would *die for his iniquity* (33:8). If the prophet faithfully executed his commission, whoever did not respond to his call ⌊*to go*⌋ *from his way, to turn from it* in repentance, was also personally responsible and would similarly *die for his iniquity.* Throughout, the outcome for the people was clearly distinguished from that for the prophet, and that is clearly evident in the closing pronouncement where the expressed pronouns 'he' and 'you' hold the two scenarios in tension: *he* ⌊*for his part*⌋ *will die for his iniquity but you* ⌊*for your part*⌋ *will have delivered your life.*

REFLECTION

- How quickly people respond when warning is given of a natural disaster such as a flood or a tempest! But how different the reaction when the warning is of spiritual calamity, and the issues at stake are even more momentous. 'Look you scoffers and be astonished and perish, because I am working a work in your days, a work which you will not at all believe even if someone details ⌊it⌋ to you' (Acts 13:41).
- The metaphor of the prophetic watchman clarifies the differing responsibilities that arise from knowing how God is going to act. Those who have had that truth revealed to them have a duty to tell others as plainly as they can what God has declared to lie ahead, but they are not held responsible for how their hearers react to that message. Paul made this clear in his departing speech to the elders of

the Ephesian church when he said, 'I testify to you this day that I am innocent of the blood of ⌐you¬ all, for I did not hold back from announcing the whole counsel of God to you' (Acts 20:26–27). He had fulfilled his responsibility; his hearers were personally answerable for how they responded to his message. The trumpet had sounded, and those who heard it should react appropriately (cf. Amos 3:6–7).

(2) The Watchman's Message (33:10–20)

The LORD continues to address the prophet, and takes up the matter of the despair of the people whose hopes had been dashed by their changed circumstances (33:10). He does so by repeating the gist of what had been said earlier in chapter 18, but reversing the order of the constituents of his speech so that 33:10–11 correspond to 18:30–32 while 33:12–20 correspond to 18:21–29. This serves to highlight the key statement of 33:11 about the reluctance with which God imposes judgement, and its corollary in the call for repentance. Ezekiel is charged with emphasising the significance of the on-going conduct of each individual (33:12–16). A righteous person who backslides will not be saved by his previous righteousness, but—and this is the message of hope that the despairing exiles needed to hear—the contrary also holds. A wicked person who repents can find life because he has turned away from his sin and does what is right and just.

In the style of a disputation speech, two envisaged responses of the people to the message are presented (33:17a, 20a). They will complain about the LORD's action because they will continue not to grasp that their standing before God is not based on some meritorious balance they have accumulated by their own efforts, but on divine grace. So the passage ends (33:20b) with a solemn word which warns of the judgement of each individual by ascertaining if his conduct gives evidence of his commitment to God.

(a) Repentance, not Despair (33:10–16)

33:10"But ⌐as for¬ you, son of man, say to the house of Israel: Thus you have said, "Our rebellious acts and our sins are upon us, and in them we are rotting away. How then can we live?" 33:11Say to them, "As I live, declares the Lord GOD, I take no pleasure in the death of the wicked ⌐person¬, but rather in a wicked ⌐person¬ turning from his way and living. Turn, turn from your evil ways. Why should you die, O house of Israel? ³³:¹²But ⌐as for⌐ you, son of man, say to the sons of your people: The righteousness of the righteous ⌐person⌐ will not deliver him in the day of his rebellion, and ⌐as for⌐ the wickedness of the wicked ⌐person⌐, he will not be made to stumble by it in the day of his turning from his wickedness. But a righteous ⌐person⌐ will not be able to live by it in the day he sins. ³³:¹³When I say to the righteous ⌐person⌐ that he will surely live, but he trusts upon his righteousness and commits injustice, all his righteous acts will not be remembered and by his injustice which he has committed he will die. ³³:¹⁴And when I say to the wicked ⌐person⌐, 'You will surely die', and he turns from his sin and practises justice and righteousness, ³³:¹⁵⌐if⌐ a wicked ⌐person⌐ restores a pledge, makes restitution for what has been stolen, walks in the statutes of life so as not to commit injustice, ⌐then⌐ he will surely live; he will not die. ³³:¹⁶All his sins which he has committed will not be remembered against him; justice and righteousness he has practised; he will surely live.

♦ **33:10** The absence of any introductory formula indicated that this revelation followed on immediately after the preceding verses. ***But ⌐as for⌐ you, son of man*** retained the focus on Ezekiel who, in his official role as a prophet, was directed to speak to his fellow exiles in their covenant capacity as ***the house of Israel*** (cf. 3:1). In the manner of a disputation speech (see on 11:3), the LORD cited the exiles' point of view. ***Thus you have said*** was followed in Hebrew by a standard expression to introduce direct speech, but which may have the force here of indicating that these were the very words of the people which were being quoted and not merely the gist of their speech.[7]

The community were discouraged by the situation which they recognise they had brought on themselves (***upon us***). ***Our rebellious acts*** (cf. 14:11) ***and our sins*** (cf. 14:13) in effect constituted a confession that they had not remained loyal to the LORD. ***We are rotting away*** pictured the impact of gangrene or some similar infection (Ps. 38:5; Zech. 14:12), using a verb also found in the covenant curse, 'Those who are left among you will rot away in their iniquity in the lands of your enemies, and also for the iniquities of their fathers they

---

7. Elsewhere Ezekiel uses a participle to introduce the speech of the people (8:12; 11:3; 12:27; 13:6), but here he employs the infinitive *lēʾmōr*, 'to say'. While this is a standard marker of direct speech, it may have heightened significance here (Greenberg 1997:673) and in 33:24; 35:12. After *lēʾmōr*, the use of *kî* is either redundant or emphatic, 'certainly' ('surely', NASB, ESV). 'If' (AV, NKJV) is improbable.

will rot away in them' (Lev. 26:39). In terms of the impact of Ezekiel's ministry, 'rot away' had already been used by the LORD (4:17; 24:23), so that for the first time in the prophecy the community were presented as aligning their self-perception with God's verdict regarding them by conceding that they were guilty. This was a hopeful sign of progress in their spiritual condition, but it was not yet 'godly grief' (2 Cor. 7:10) because it was not accompanied by an awareness of divine grace. The rhetorical question, *How then can we live?*, invited a negative response, and disclosed their attitude as one of demoralised hopelessness, which can conceive of no remedy for their condition. 'Live' may connote 'go on living' or 'enjoy life to its fullest extent in fellowship with God'—an outcome viewed as impossible because he had taken offence with them.

♦ **33:11** In this key verse the LORD accepted the accuracy of the Israelites' self-diagnosis, but rejected the implication that their situation was beyond hope of recovery. It may be analysed as containing five components: *asseveration*—'as I live, declares the Lord GOD'; *emphatic negation*—'I take no pleasure in the death of the wicked ⌐person⌐'; *affirmation*—'but rather in a wicked ⌐person⌐ turning from his way and living'; *exhortation*—'turn, turn from your evil ways'; *protestation*—'why should you die?' (adapted from Murray 1955:108).

Their despair could be remedied if they would adopt a correct perception of God's character and his purposes, and submit to him in loyalty. This was vigorously expressed by a divine oath of denial, *As I live, declares the Lord GOD.* It repeated virtually verbatim an earlier assertion (18:23; cf. also 18:32), but with the difference that a rhetorical question was no longer used. Instead, the strong direct avowal, *I take no pleasure in the death of the wicked ⌐person⌐*, provided an indubitable foundation for *a wicked ⌐person⌐ turning* (*šûb*, cf. 18:21) *from his way and living.*

A gospel plea was to be issued: *Turn, turn from your evil ways*. This rare appeal for repentance (cf. 18:30–31) did not sidestep the character and conduct of those addressed: they were indisputably evil. But the divine message of hope was proclaimed in full awareness of that fact. God commanded and urged such individuals to 'turn' in repentance (*šûb*, cf. 18:21). A real, deep-seated change could only come about when they abandoned the ways which they had selected for themselves, and instead chose to proceed as God required.

The LORD countered the people's question of despair (33:10) by posing a further question, *Why should you die, O house of Israel?* This was asked to stir them up to see the folly of adopting any other course of conduct, whether by trying to find resilience through utilising resources they did not possess, or by lapsing into apathetic inertia. The harrowing disaster which divine judgement had imposed on Judah and Jerusalem because of their sin should have led the remnant in Babylon to reassess their attitude. And now the resolution of the exiles' situation had been declared to them, with a guarantee grounded in the character of God himself. Though they deserved to die because of their sin, God's spontaneous love had opened up the way into the future for them. How could they be so blind as to reject it?[8]

♦ 33:12 *But ⌐as for⌐ you* pointed to the significant message which Ezekiel was to deliver regarding human responsibility. He was to remind *the sons of your people* (cf. 33:2), that is, the exilic community, that it was the outcome of a life that determined divine acceptance, not a favourable or unfavourable starting point. *The righteousness of the righteous ⌐person⌐ will not deliver him in the day of his rebellion.* His misconduct would forfeit his good standing before God. *⌐As for⌐ the wickedness of the wicked ⌐person⌐, he will not be made to stumble by it in the day of his turning from his wickedness.* 'By it' referred back to the wickedness which he had formerly perpetrated, and from which he would be liberated by repentance. 'Made to stumble' (cf. stumbling block, 3:20; 18:30) did not point to a temporary loss of balance, but to a fall which had life-threatening consequences. The concluding clause, *But a righteous ⌐person⌐ will not be able to live by it* (that is, because of his former righteousness) *in the day he sins*, repeated what had been said earlier. The temporal expression probably indicated 'whenever he sins', though it might also have conveyed the immediate impact of his sin, 'on that very day'.

This was not a presentation of works righteousness, as though an individual earned his status as righteous through the merit of his works. His status was a divine gift, and the evidence of that was appropriate conduct. 'Yet the one who ends life as a "righteous man" is so through repentance and faith that bears fruit—not through any human efforts to attain righteousness by works' (Hummel 2007:975).

---

8. 'Not only is repentance assumed to be possible, but the question, "why will you die, O house of Israel?" reflects a perplexed frustration at the poor choices the Israelites have made, and continue to make despite the option to turn away that has been offered so many times' (Lapsley 2000a:71).

♦ **33:13** In 33:13-16 examples were given of the principles of 33:12 in action, with many features resembling 18:21-22, 24, but with the case of the fallen rebel dealt with before that of the repentant sinner. Moreover, here and at the start of the next verse, a strong emphasis on divine initiative and control was presented by *when I say.* The first example was concerned with *the righteous ⸢person⸣* to whom God had said that *he will surely live. But* he abused the covenant standing he had been accorded, and put his trust *upon his righteousness*, treating it as something he had personally achieved rather than a gracious endowment. He then *commits* (lit., 'does') *injustice* (see on 3:20) contrary to the precepts of the covenant. In that event *all his righteous acts* (lit., 'all his righteousnesses'[9]) would count for nothing in view of his rebellion. *Will not be remembered* was the personal action of the LORD who holds, or does not hold (33:16), the individual to account. Many righteousnesses could not counterbalance one act of injustice. This was not impersonal, inflexible retribution, but the personal response of the divine King. The danger of relying on one's own righteousness was not considered in chapter 18.

♦ **33:14** Though the fate of the incorrigible backslider was not glossed over, it was the possibility of acceptance for the repentant sinner which received the major emphasis as a means of encouraging the dispirited people. The sinner had been divinely warned, *You will surely die,* but it was envisaged that *he turns from his sin* in repentance which was evidenced by the fact that he *practises* (lit., 'does') *justice and righteousness.* Hummel (2007:962) describes this as a 'standard OT idiom for the sanctification or life of faith of the believer, the sinner who repents' (cf. 18:5). Justice did not refer primarily to social or political processes, but to personal conduct which was just and upright since it conformed to the LORD's commandments.

♦ **33:15** The detail listed of the life of the repentant was intended to evoke a similar commitment from Ezekiel's audience. It was not an exhaustive description of upright conduct, but a selection of three instances which emphasised restitutive behaviour. (1) He *restores a pledge*, that is, what was taken as collateral for a loan (cf. 18:7). There

---

9. The kethib reads *ṣidqātô*, 'his righteousness', but the qere indicates the defectively spelled *ṣidqōtāw*, 'his righteousnesses'. The latter is the less common expression and so to be preferred (cf. 3:20; 18:24). Moreover, a plural noun provides an appropriate subject for the following plural verb *tizzākarnâ*, 'will be remembered'.

were regulations as to what might be taken as a pledge, but what was condemned here was not returning the pledge when the loan was repaid. (2) He **makes restitution for what he has stolen**, which was a wider application of the same principle in respect of what he had robbed others of. (3) He **walks in the statutes of life**. The phrase was unique, though it might well have reflected Leviticus 18:4–5. 'Walks' pointed to these changes as not resulting from isolated pangs of conscience, but of the continuous practice of a different lifestyle. 'Statutes of life' did not imply that observance of the law's demands gave life, but that true repentance was evidenced by respect for God's ordinances, *so as not to commit injustice* (cf. 33:13).

The divine verdict would then be *he will surely live; he will not die.*

♦ **33:16** The implications of the changed life situation of the formerly wicked person were further spelled out. *All his sins*[10] *which he has committed will not be remembered against him* (contrast 33:13). In view was an individual who went beyond formulating resolutions as to reforming his future behaviour; he implemented his intentions. *Justice and righteousness he has practised.* Such credible change warranted the declaration, *He will surely live.* That was the answer to the despairing question of 33:10.

(b) Fair or Unfair? (33:17-20)

> 33:17Yet the sons of your people will say, 'The way of the Lord is not fair'; but ⌊as for⌋ them, their way is not correct. 33:18When a righteous ⌊person⌋ turns from his righteousness and commits injustice, he will die in them, 33:19and when a wicked ⌊person⌋ turns from his wickedness, and practises judgement and righteousness, he will live on account of them. 33:20And you say, 'The way of the Lord is not fair.' Each according to his ways, I will judge you, O house of Israel."'

♦ **33:17** A second reaction in addition to that of 33:10 was then envisaged from Ezekiel's contemporaries in exile, *the sons of your people.* This took the form of an objection which was the same as one they had entertained in the past: *The way of the Lord*[11] *is not fair*

---

10. The kethib has the singular form *ḥaṭṭāʾtô*, 'his sin', but the plural verb *tizzākarnâ*, 'they will be remembered', favours the adoption of the plural form found in the qere, *ḥaṭṭōʾtāw*, 'his sins'.

11. Many Hebrew manuscripts have *yhwh*, 'Yahweh/ the LORD', here rather than *ʾădōnāy*, 'the Lord'. As in 18:25, where the same variation occurs, the unexpected reading, 'the Lord', should be retained.

(18:25, 29). Evidently there were still misconceptions about God's action which needed to be overcome for the community to be ready for divine intervention. As was discussed earlier (18:25), it is difficult to establish the sense of the verb 'to be fair', but it may well have incorporated a complaint about the LORD's actions being unpredictable and not following logically from the facts of the situation. The people continued to misunderstand the nature of divine grace, and considered that it was wrong for a verdict about them to discount their own past behaviour or the fact that they were Israel. Probably they kept bringing forward this allegation to justify their lack of response; they found it incomprehensible that they were being asked to repent (cf. Greenberg 1997:674). It was equally preposterous to them that one slip would wipe out all the good they had been doing previously.

Just as their objection was a carry-over from the past, so the LORD's response to it remained the same. ⌊*As for*⌋ *them, their way is not fair.* Not now using a rhetorical question (18:25, 29), he turned the tables on them with a clear counter-declaration that it was their behaviour which failed to pass the test of rationality. How could they reject an offer which opened up a route to acceptance with their God? Could they not see that he was maintaining both his justice and his grace?

♦ **33:18** Once more God, through the prophet, patiently explained how divine justice operated. *When a righteous* ⌊*person*⌋ *turns from his righteousness and commits injustice* (cf. 33:13), then he has broken the laws of God and has incurred the penalty appropriate to his breach of the covenant requirements. So *he will die in them*, that is, on account of the acts of injustice he had perpetrated.

♦ **33:19** On the other hand, *when a wicked* ⌊*person*⌋ *turns from his wickedness, and practises judgement and righteousness* (cf. 33:14–15), then his repentance would reinstate him in God's favour. *He will live on account of them*, that is, on account of the acts to which his new life gives expression (cf. 18:26).

♦ **33:20** There is a combination here of the second person plural in *you say* and *I will judge you*, and the singular in *each according to his ways.* The people failed to grasp the divine explanation, and maintained their objection to the LORD's grace. Over against their obstinacy, he asserted his kingly rule: *I will judge you* (cf. 7:3). But he would act with discrimination (*each according to his ways*), reflecting the circumstances and motivation of each individual member of the *house of Israel*, his covenant kingdom.

There was, however, no indication of the people's reaction to this message. Did they accept it? Matters were left hanging with the reminder of their individual accountability, and also with the reality of divine acceptance if they abandoned their rebellion and committed their lives to God who is willing to forget a lifetime of disloyalty if only there is repentance.

REFLECTION

- 'In them ['our rebellious acts and our sins'] we are rotting away' (33:10) brings out the loathsome and repulsive nature of sin through the imagery of a festering sore (cf. Ps. 38:5; Zech. 14:12). This makes clear that rebellion against God is not an unfortunate, but static, condition (a benign tumour), but an aggressive and life-threatening complaint. It pollutes the life of the individual; it escalates into increasing putrefaction; it leads to a sub-human mode of existence. It cannot be left untended, but requires intervention and speedy application of an effective remedy. All other seeming sources of relief are spiritual quackery apart from the therapy of the divine physician (Matt. 9:12). He holds the monopoly in such matters, and his help should be urgently sought.
- Those burdened by a sense of sin are reminded that God is not intrinsically hostile to them. They should not yield to bleak despair, as if God renders their situation hopeless. 'Turn from your evil ways' (33:11) is a perpetual reminder that there is the avenue of repentance and the way to life.
- But sorrow over sin, though a healthy spiritual response, is not itself salvation. Paul clearly distinguishes between 'godly grief' and 'worldly grief' (2 Cor. 7:10). What constitutes the difference? It is not primarily a matter of abandoning a defiant attitude towards God, but an acceptance of the reality of grace. Ezekiel's hearers complain about God's way being unfair, and that is because they still think that they have some bargaining power derived from their own conduct or ancestry which enables them to establish a right standing for themselves before God. But 'there is none who does good' (Ps. 14:1; Rom. 3:10–12), and God dismisses all claims to establish a human righteousness as worthless because of the twisted and debased nature of all human thought and conduct. Salvation is a gift of God. 'Not because of works ⌊done⌋ in righteousness, which we ourselves did, but according to his mercy, he saved us' (Titus 3:5).
- But, as the argument of this passage clearly shows, works are not thereby emptied of all significance. Judgement by works is an

essential part of the message of Scripture, both Old and New Testaments. They are not, however, meritorious, but evidence of a heart transformed by divine grace (Matt. 25:31–46; Rev. 20:11–15).

- Restitution of what has been misappropriated (33:15) is always an act of justice towards those who have been victimised. But it also incorporates a public testimony to a changed life and to the one who has changed it. Actions often speak louder than words. 'And Zacchaeus stood and said to the Lord, Behold, the half of my possessions, Lord, I give to the poor. And if I have extorted anything from anyone, I repay it fourfold." And Jesus said to him, "Today salvation has come to this house, since he also is a son of Abraham. For the Son of Man came to seek and to save what was lost" ' (Luke 19:8–10).

(3) The News Arrives (33:21–22)

The central section of the chapter and also of the book is a brief piece of prophetic autobiography in the midst of divine communiques. Ezekiel tells of the day he receives the news that Jerusalem has fallen just as he has been predicting throughout the preceding years of his ministry (33:21). This is an epochal event in the history of the covenant people of God because the city and all its ways are wiped out along with all the hopes based on them.

But the day holds a special significance for Ezekiel. Up to this point, others could question his status as a true prophet because his primary prediction regarding the fall of the city was not yet verified. Now that the unthinkable has occurred just as he foretold, all grounds for doubting his authenticity have been removed. More than that, the LORD has readied the prophet for his subsequent ministry by fulfilling the promise he had made to him in 24:27. He has opened the prophet's mouth (33:22). The exiles struggling to come to terms with the dashing of their hopes for the future will have a prophet among them who will not be restricted in the fulfilment of his duties. He will be able to go in and out among the people, speaking to them personally and urging them to accept the message he has been given for them.

> 33:21And it came about in the twelfth year, in the tenth ⌊month⌋, on the fifth of the month, of our exile, that a fugitive from Jerusalem came to me, saying, 'The city has been struck down!' 33:22Now the hand of the LORD had come upon me on the evening before the fugitive came; and he had opened my mouth before ⌊he⌋ came to me in the morning. And my mouth was opened, and I was no longer without speech.

♦ **33:21** *In the twelfth year, in the tenth ͺmonthͺ, on the fifth of the month, of our exile* corresponds to 8th January 585 B.C. See Introduction §2.4. The phrase 'of our exile' made clear the dating scheme of the book. The city fell on 14th July 586, and was destroyed by fire a month later, so that six months elapsed before the exilic community in Tel-abib received the news. While the journey could have been made much more quickly, given the confused and dangerous conditions which prevailed that was not an improbable lapse of time. However, those who advocate that there was a much shorter siege of Jerusalem which ended in 587 have to account for a delay of eighteen months before the arrival of the news. They therefore adopt 'eleventh year' rather than 'twelfth year', a reading found in some versions.[12]

Elsewhere the date formula was used to introduce direct divine disclosure either in speech or vision, but here it marked the arrival of an individual with the momentous news of Jerusalem's fall. The status of this individual, or whether it was only one person who was involved, is problematic. *A fugitive* (*pālîṭ*) denoted one who eluded an enemy and so escaped from danger, particularly in time of war. Here the term was literally 'the fugitive', which might in this context have conveyed the sense of the individual who had been so designated by God (24:26). But, the term has also been interpreted in a collective sense, 'the refugees' (NASB; Fairbairn 1851:357). This is less likely. It might account for the delay involved compared to Ezra and his company who made a similar journey in the opposite direction in four months (Ezra 7:9). But this is hardly needed. Those deported by the Babylonians would not have left on the very day the city fell, or necessarily a month later, when it was burned. Moreover, the term 'fugitive' was quite distinct from one who was involuntarily deported. A clear instance of its significance was provided in 2 Kings 9:15, 'Let no one go out ͺasͺ a fugitive from the city to go and tell in Jezreel'. As it was improbable that one who had slipped through the Babylonian lines would go to seek refuge in the heartland of the enemy, he had obviously gone there to bring the news to those already there. Had he relatives in Tel-abib? Indeed, was he connected to Ezekiel? But, for safety's sake, he would have shunned the main trade routes and

---

12. English translations do not adopt the reading 'eleventh' as it has scant textual support which is confined to a few Hebrew manuscripts, one early Greek version, and the Peshitta. 'Eleventh' bears all the marks of a secondary attempt to understand the text rather than of an original reading.

contact with imperial officials, and his journey would consequently have been extended. Furthermore, he may well not have known precisely where he was heading. ***To me*** indicated that Ezekiel was not left to hear this news along with others, but was specially sought out by the fugitive.

The city has been struck down/'smitten' (cf. 40:1). The verb was used in contexts of armed conflict to describe infliction of a grievous, generally mortal, blow. So it conveyed the news not only of the capture of the city, but also the physical devastation subsequently wreaked on it and the loss of life involved. This key event in the story line of the Old Testament established Ezekiel's prophetic calling and his prophecies, but those were of minor significance compared to the vindication of the character of God. Now Israel were brought to 'know the LORD' as one who could not be defied with impunity.

♦ **33:22** The conjunction 'and' followed by a non-verb is rendered ***now*** to bring out the fact that this idiom here indicated that what followed was by way of background information. It was a flashback relating to what had previously occurred ***on the evening before the fugitive came*** (24:25–27) when God had once again intervened in Ezekiel's life. ***The hand of the LORD had come upon me*** described the prophet as experiencing personal and powerful divine influence in his conscious existence. Here, however, it was not associated with a visionary encounter (cf. 1:3; 3:22), but was primarily concerned with divine removal of the restriction which had been placed on Ezekiel's mode of ministry. ***He had opened my mouth before ⸢he⸣ came***[13] ***to me in the morning*** obviously related divine action before the arrival of the fugitive who had been explicitly mentioned when the verb 'came' was used earlier in the verse. The primary point being made was not to establish the sequence of events, but God's control over what occurred. Apparently this procedure was adopted to ensure that Ezekiel was prepared to receive the news and for the activity which would follow it. ***And my mouth was opened, and I was no longer without speech.*** This pictured the prophet as ready to engage in an unrestricted ministry under the changed circumstances which prevailed with the fall of the city.

---

13. For *'ad* in the sense of 'before', see *IBHS* §11.2.12b. There is no expressed subject for the infinitive *bô'*, 'coming'. Block (1998:253) suggests *aleph* and *waw* have been accidentally transposed, so that the text reads *b'w*, 'his coming'.

REFLECTION

- God does not operate on the time-scale we perceive. That does not make his action any the less certain, but it does ensure that the myriad events of human existence, which to us seem unrelated, all fit into his overall purpose. Jerusalem had been warned time and again of the outcome which awaited her if she did not abandon her sinful ways. Though some of her kings introduced significant reforms, they usually lapsed on the king's death, and Jerusalem plunged even deeper into the morass she had created for herself. But God will not be mocked indefinitely. In his time disaster struck.
- But, even as he was imposing judgement on his errant people, the LORD was preparing for their future. His commitment to his covenant purposes was not overturned by human sin. He would work in and through the disaster to accomplish his purposes. To that end he had Ezekiel ready as his spokesman. Fulfilment of the warnings he had been giving openly accredited him as a prophet of the LORD, and now in the changed environment after the fall of Jerusalem, he was in a position to continue in that role, but now with a ministry which would lead the people forward to their restoration. The question which remained was that of the extent to which they, despite what had occurred in their national existence, were prepared to learn these lessons and seek to be restored to his favour. God's discipline of his people had once more proved to be both punitive and restorative so that they could truly say, 'For a moment ⌊lasts⌋ his anger, ⌊but⌋ in his favour life ⌊is found⌋; in the evening weeping may take up lodgings, but with morning ⌊there is⌋ joy' (Ps. 30:5; cf. Isa. 54:7-8).

(4) Unrepentant Judah (33:23-29)

While 33:22 is undoubtedly a flashback to what occurred prior to the fugitive's arrival, there is no need to suppose that the remainder of the chapter has to be read as occurring at that point. The date formula of 33:21 marks the start of the record of Ezekiel's ministry subsequent to the fall of Jerusalem, and before the next recorded date in 40:1 some thirteen years later. The two remaining sections of the chapter present the reactions which prevailed at the beginning of that period in the immediate aftermath of the overthrow of Jerusalem.

In this section the focus is on those who had survived the capture of the city, and we are provided with a last look at the inhabitants of the now ruined Jerusalem, who have learned nothing from the calamitous judgement which has befallen them. Their continuing disobedience and contempt is exposed by means of a disputation speech (cf. 11:3) in which the LORD reveals that they are attempting to rebuild their old lives of pious defiance and rebellion against him in the midst of the land ruined by their previous sin (33:23–26). Though they think themselves in possession of the land as the heirs of Abraham, their continuing misconduct will once more bring devastating punishment on them (33:26–29), because there is a fundamental incompatibility between occupation of the LORD's land and violation of his covenant precepts. Because the covenant curses (Lev. 26:14–45; Deut. 28:25–37) are absolute (cf. Lev. 18:24–30; Deut. 4:25–31; 8:19–20), partial depopulation of the land is not an option. All transgressors will be taken from the land they have forfeited by their sin.

> ³³:²³And the word of the LORD came to me, saying, ³³:²⁴"Son of man, those who inhabit these ruined ⌞places⌟ in the land of Israel are saying, "Abraham was one ⌞man⌟, and he possessed the land. But we are many; to us the land has been given as a possession." ³³:²⁵Therefore say to them, "Thus says the Lord GOD: Over the blood you are eating, and your eyes you are lifting up to idols, and blood you are shedding—and the land you will possess? ³³:²⁶You have stood upon your sword, you have committed abomination, and you have each defiled his neighbour's wife—and the land you will possess?" ³³:²⁷You are to say thus to them, "Thus says the Lord GOD: As I live, surely those in the ruined ⌞places⌟ will fall by the sword, and whoever ⌞is⌟ upon the open field I shall give him to the beasts to eat, and those who are in the strongholds and caves will die by the pestilence, ³³:²⁸and I will set the land a desolation and a source of horror, and its proud strength will come to an end, and the mountains of Israel will be desolate with no one crossing ⌞them⌟. ³³:²⁹And they will know that I ⌞am⌟ the LORD when I set the land a desolation and a source of horror because of all the abominations which they have committed."'

♦ **33:23** *And the word of the LORD came to me, saying* introduced a two-part oracle (33:23–29, 30–33), each part of which began with the usual address to Ezekiel as **Son of man** (cf. 2:1). Both parts were also responses to what was being said by the people after the fall of Jerusalem, though the groups involved differ.

♦ **33:24** Ezekiel's immediate audience remained his compatriots from Judah who had been deported in 597 B.C. along with the others who had been forcibly transferred to Babylon after the final collapse of

Jerusalem (2 Kgs. 25:11). However, the situation differed from that after the fall of Samaria when all the surviving population had been transported to a variety of other settlements (2 Kgs. 17:6). Nor had the Babylonians coerced foreigners to come and settle in Judah after the manner of earlier Assyrian practice (2 Kgs. 17:24). ***Those who inhabit these***[14] ***ruined ⌊places⌋ in the land of Israel*** had been some of the poorest people of the land deliberately left behind by the Babylonians to maintain its agriculture, probably with a view to forming a buffer zone of some sort against Egyptian incursions (2 Kgs. 25:12). Equally, many of those whose cities had been demolished and who had escaped the clutches of the Babylonians might have quietly drifted back to live in the ruins (Jer. 40:7-8).

In the manner typical of a disputation speech (cf. 11:3), the LORD informed the prophet of what the remnant back in Judah ***are saying*** (lit., 'are saying, with respect to say'), but it was not immediately obvious with what attitude they were speaking. The mention of Abraham might have indicated the humble resilience of a shattered community which was trying to move forward in reliance upon God, pleading the promise made to Abraham. However, the following verses dispelled any idea of a devoted commitment to the LORD. Rather, viewing themselves as Abraham's heirs was more a pragmatic than a religious argument. They reasoned from the lesser to the greater. ***Abraham was one ⌊man⌋, and he possessed the land.*** He had no offspring when he was brought to Canaan and divinely given the title deeds to the land (Isa. 51:2). ***But we are many; to us the land has been given as a possession.*** 'Possession' (11:15) was connected with a term found in the promise to Abraham regarding the land (Gen. 15:7; 28:4), and related to the right to occupy the property bestowed on them by God (cf. 44:28). Conveniently setting aside their recent massive loss of population, they argued that their numbers far exceeded those associated with Abraham. On its own, they claimed, that entitled them to occupy the land as his heirs. They also thought that because they had survived the catastrophe they had had conferred on them a rightful claim to continue to occupy the land. Their outlook in many respects perpetuated that found earlier in 11:14-15, though the mocking ridicule of the exiles was now absent. They were simply ignored.

♦ **33:25 *Therefore*** introduced the LORD's rejection of their assessment

---

14. Greenberg (1997:684) argues that 'these' should be read with 'inhabitants' rather than 'ruined places': 'these who inhabit ruined places in the land'. The usage would then be contemptuous.

of the situation, which continued into the following verse. *Say to them* was not a directive to speak directly to those in Judah, but an evident rhetorical device by which addressing them would graphically inform Ezekiel's audience regarding the views prevailing in Judah and alert them to avoid adopting similar thinking.

This verse and the next followed a similar pattern in which three sample accusations were directed against the remanent community before an indignant question dismissed their unwarranted claims.

(1) *Over the blood you are eating.* The force of the preposition 'over' (*'al*) is uncertain. If it is rendered 'with', they were directly contravening the long-standing requirement not to eat flesh from which the blood had not been drained (Gen. 9:4; Lev. 17:10–16). An instance of this was recorded using this preposition in 1 Samuel 14:32–33 where Saul's exhausted army ate meat without draining the blood from it. A more sinister interpretation is, however, suggested by the prohibition of Leviticus 19:26, 'You are not to eat over (*'al*) the blood. You are not to seek omens; you are not to be soothsayers.' The collocation may indicate some occult practice, the nature of which is no longer clear (Greenberg 1997:684, but totally dismissed by Fairbairn 1851:355).

(2) *Your eyes you are lifting up to idols.* The posture was that adopted by one looking for help (18:12; Ps. 121:1). For the dismissive terms used for *idols*, see on 6:4. This was indicative of their rejection of the LORD as providing the way forward for them, presumably because, in their misreading of events, he had proved incapable of defending the city, and so they would continue to look for protection and blessing through involvement in idolatrous worship.

(3) *Blood you are shedding.* The role murder had played in the exploitative behaviour prevalent in Jerusalem was exposed in 22:3, 6. The community which had set aside allegiance to the LORD had no qualms in setting aside the social norms of the covenant he had instituted.

And the land[15] *you will possess?* Hebrew questions need not be introduced by an interrogative (cf. 11:3), and in this context an accusatory rhetorical question is appropriate as a translation. It was utterly incongruous that those who defied the requirements of the covenant should entertain the expectation that they would be left to occupy the land.

---

15. The *waw*-disjunctive in *wəhāʾāreṣ*, 'and the land', indicates that this is not a straightforward continuation of the previous statements.

♦ **33:26** The disparity between their conduct and their expectations was then further displayed by three accusations followed by the same indignant question. (1) The expression, ***You have stood upon your sword***, is not found elsewhere, but it indicated to make use of the sword and of associated force the basis of one's security. 'You live by your sword' (Greenberg 1997:685). This was essentially the same as the last item of the triad in the previous verse. The law of the jungle prevailed among the survivors: not right, but might. An instance of the anarchic conditions in Judah was provided by the assassination of Gedaliah (Jer. 41). (2) ***You have committed***[16] ***abomination.*** This covered heinous deviation which caused gross offence to the LORD. Although the term might refer to sexual immorality (e.g., 22:11), as that was clearly the third indictment, it was more probable that idol worship was in view (cf. 5:9), as in the second element of the previous triad. (3) ***You have each defiled his neighbour's wife*** (cf. 18:6, 15; 22:11). It would seem that cultural (never mind covenantal) norms had broken down to such an extent they were engaging in wife swapping.

Again the illustrative triad of transgressions culminated in the accusatory question—***and the land you will possess?*** This was not to dismiss the memory of Abraham and the covenantal promise made to him of his descendants inheriting the land. The accusation was that the remnant in Judah were not acting as Abraham's offspring. Enjoyment of covenant inheritance required adherence to covenant standards, which they had manifestly failed to do. They had learned nothing by the judgement brought on the land, and so the LORD would punish their infidelity.

♦ **33:27** ***You are to say thus to them*** directed Ezekiel to spell out to the survivors in Judah how the LORD would deal with them. The messenger formula, ***Thus says the Lord GOD***, introduced the LORD's answer to the question repeated at the end of the previous two verses. Its solemn nature warranted the affirmation of the divine oath, ***As I live*** (cf. 5:11). The survivors should not think themselves exempt from further attack just because they had already suffered from invasion. ***In the ruined ⌊places⌋*** (*beḥŏrobôt*) and ***by the sword*** (*baḥereb*) were placed next to each other to bring out the assonance between the terms. Three groups were in view. (1) Those who were eking out an existence in the ruined cities ***will fall by the sword***, that is, through

---

16. The *nun* ending on the verb *'ăśîten* makes it appear to be a feminine plural, but it is probably dissimilation for ease of pronunciation before the following word (GKC §44k; Joüon §42f).

military intervention by their enemies. The sword by which they had oppressed (33:26) would be turned against them. (2) As for anyone who was practising subsistence agriculture in *the open field*, the LORD declared *I shall give him to the beasts to eat him*. The prophetic perfect expressed how certain it was that the divine resolution would be carried through (Introduction §6.3b). (3) A third group were those who had sought refuge in naturally inaccessible spots, *in the strongholds and caves*, where, though they escaped human attack, they would *die by the pestilence*. The distributed picture of three locations and three agents of destruction (cf. 5:12; 6:11–12) emphasised how completely the survivors would suffer. There was a further Babylonian campaign, though on a smaller scale, against Judah in 582 B.C. (Jer. 52:30).

♦ **33:28** The toll of destruction to be imposed on the land continued with its becoming *a desolation and a source of horror* (*šəmāmâ ûməšammâ*; cf. 6:14; 33:29; 35:3). The assonance found in this composite expression reinforced the stark reality of how the land would be utterly ravaged. The first term reflected more the objective side of the ruin, and the second, more its psychological impact (cf. *HALOT* 649). As a result of both aspects of this total upheaval, *the pride of its strength will come to an end* (same as 30:18; similar to 7:24; 24:21; 30:6) with the people losing the capacity to boast before others or before God. *The mountains of Israel* (cf. 6:2), a nostalgic reminiscence of the homeland which was so different from the flat plains of Mesopotamia, *will be desolate with no one crossing them*, because the population would have been wiped out.

> What happened to the 'land' of Israel was a concrete symbolical index of an inner spiritual reality, namely, the relative health of the covenantal relationship between Yahweh and his people. When they violated the LORD's trust by their repeated acts of infidelity, his last resort was to startle them into recognition of his righteous, holy nature, will, and purpose by despoiling the politically unstable piece of territory in which they had placed their vain earthly hope. (Wendland 2009:225)

♦ **33:29** The survivors in the land would be compelled to recognise the LORD's sovereignty: *they will know that I ⌐am⌐ the LORD when I set the land a desolation and a source of horror* (cf. 33:28). There was no suggestion that this acknowledgement would be voluntary and lead to reconciliation. It was a belated and forced awareness of the inevitable outcome of intransigent rebellion against God: *because of*

all the abominations which they have committed. In this context 'abominations' covered every aspect of their conduct which was offensive to God. They would learn that the one whom they had dismissed as powerless and irrelevant had eventually exposed their folly by imposing his judgement on them.

REFLECTION
* Those who had survived in the land had learned nothing despite all that had come upon them. Their thinking is clearly set out by those of their number who took Jeremiah with them when they escaped to Egypt. They openly said, '⌐As for⌐ the word which you have spoken to us in the name of the LORD, we are not going to listen to you! But we will certainly do every word which has gone out from our mouth' (Jer. 44:16–17) to indulge in idol worship and disdain the LORD. Though they were prepared at times to dress up their motivation in pious language by referring to Abraham, they were viciously gripped by a determination to have their own way which no amount of temporal chastening could break down. They were those who knew the truth at an intellectual level, who had had the truth repeatedly presented to them, but were hardened to its message, and would be swept away by the LORD.
* The presumption of those who think they know the answers prevents them from hearing the true answer to their predicament which is provided by the LORD. 'O Israel, if you would but listen to me! ... Open your mouth wide, and I will fill it' (Ps. 81:8, 10). 'Take care not to reject him who is speaking. For if those ⌐persons⌐ did not escape when they rejected him who warned ⌐them⌐ on earth, much more ⌐will we not escape if⌐ we turn from him who ⌐warns⌐ from heaven' (Heb. 12:25).

(5) The Exiles' Reaction to Ezekiel (33:30–33)
This section continues the LORD's address to Ezekiel in the aftermath of the fall of Jerusalem, but now he informs him not about the rejected survivors in Judah, but about the reaction of the exilic community where his prophetic ministry is located. Here too the response to the catastrophic overthrow of the city is defective. The deportees accept that the fall of Jerusalem has vindicated Ezekiel's status as a prophet, and they assemble to hear his words (33:30). But Ezekiel is not to be deceived by having a ready audience, for those who gather round him are without spiritual perception (33:31). They do not act on the basis of the prophet's message, but pervert his ministry into a form of

variety show (33:32). Commenting in the light of chapter 37, Renz remarks, 'The prophetic word has, so to speak, gathered "the bones" without yet breathing life into them' (1999:208; see on 37:8). Though the LORD has decreed that the future of his people lies with the exiles, their outlook still has to be transformed. However, there is hope because the LORD announces they will come to realise that Ezekiel is not an entertainer, but a prophet whose word they must truly accept (33:33).

> ³³:³⁰'But ⌊as for⌋ you, son of man, ⌊as for⌋ the sons of your people who are speaking together about you near the walls and in the entrance of the houses, one speaks to another, each to his brother, saying, "Please come and hear what the word is which is coming from the LORD." ³³:³¹And they come to you as people come, and they sit before you—my people!—and they hear your words, but do not do them, for coarse speech they are producing with their mouths ⌊and⌋ after ⌊dishonest⌋ gain their heart is going. ³³:³²And behold you are to them like an erotic song, one with a beautiful voice, or one skilled in playing an instrument; and they hear your words, but are not doing them. ³³:³³But when it comes—behold, it is about to come!—then they will know that a prophet has been in their midst.'

♦ **33:30** The oracle continued with Ezekiel being instructed about the situation on his doorstep in the exilic community where he was resident. ***But ⌊as for⌋ you, son of man*** introduced the insight the LORD gave his emissary regarding ***the sons of your people***, his fellow countrymen who were with him in exile (33:2). Everyone was speaking ***about you***. The AV rendering 'against you', while a possible translation of *bəkā*, failed to capture the situation. Ezekiel, as the prophet whose prophecy had come true, was now a star attraction in the community which was still, however, unable to grasp the spiritual depth of his message. Even so, he had become the talk of the town as they gathered to converse in the shade ***near the walls and in the entrances of the houses. One speaks to another,***[17] ***each to his brother***. His name was on everyone's lips as they urged one another to

---

17. The expression *wədibber-ḥad ʾet-ʾaḥad* is literally 'and one speaks to one', but the construction with which the sentence began is broken off. A plural verb would have been expected, 'The sons of your people who are speaking ... speak one to one.' *ḥad* is an Aramaic form of 'one', and the pointing *ʾaḥad* is used instead of *ʾeḥād* for the sake of assonance.

come and hear what Ezekiel had to say. What a change for the man whose ministry had previously been curtailed by the LORD!

♦ **33:31** *They come to you as people come, and they sit before you* no longer depicted a contingent of a few, select elders, but a substantial congregation. Ezekiel was a popular preacher. But the subject of the first two verbs was delayed, perhaps as an expression of disapproval or bitter irony, *my people!* Their behaviour was far from what the LORD desired to see. 'As people come' indicated in the manner in which an ordinary crowd would gather out of curiosity when something unusual occurred.

Ezekiel was being warned about the dangers of popularity. *They hear your words, but do not do them* (cf. 33:32). There were now crowds round Ezekiel, but he was not getting through to them. This was not the fault of the complexity of his message or his style of communication (contra Block 1998:267); it arose from his hearers' spiritual incapacity. They were unable to move beyond the outward form of what he said; indeed, they perverted it into something else. *For* introduced the evidence of their lack of response. *Coarse speech they are producing with their mouths* was literally, 'Lustfulnesses with their mouth they are making'. The expression used the plural of the noun, 'lust', found in 23:11, where it and the verb from which it was derived obviously referred to inordinate sexual desire. A translation such as 'love' weakens the concept too much. It is improbable that it was to the LORD that 'with their mouths they express devotion' (NIV) or that they flatter the prophet by pretending to be highly appreciative of his message (NRSV). The old Geneva Bible probably caught something of what was involved by its rendering, 'with their mouthes they make iestes', as does 'with lustful talk in their mouths they act' (ESV). It can be easily seen how Ezekiel's message in chapters 16 or 23 could have been turned into matter for coarse, obscene comment or crassly ribald humour. The crowd who gathered were out for a laugh.

After ⌐dishonest⌐ gain their heart is going (cf. 22:13, 27). The prophet's call for change did not impact on an audience which had a prior commitment to the pursuit of material wealth, no matter how it was gained. Self-interest and the indulgence of their own desires desensitised them to Ezekiel's message. They would listen to him, but would still blot out the personal implications of what he said by mocking him.

♦ **33:32** The LORD left Ezekiel in no doubt as to how his ministry was being viewed. *You are to them like an erotic song*, literally 'a song[18] of lustfulnesses' (the same term as 'coarse speech' in 33:31). They regarded Ezekiel's message as simply a titillating or bawdy song performed by *one with a beautiful voice*, or *one skilled in playing an instrument.* This did not imply that Ezekiel sang his message or presented it with musical accompaniment. The point of the comparison was that his proclamation was being treated as a public performance, a matter of entertainment.

The virtual repetition of *they hear your words, but are not doing them* from the previous verse (the form of the verb changed to a participle but the sense was identical) emphasised the divergence between the appearance of piety in gathering to hear the prophet, and the reality of inward resistance to his message. Clearly there was scope for on-going ministry to overcome this gap.

♦ **33:33** *But when it comes—behold, it is about to come!* introduced a new factor into the situation, but it is somewhat puzzling what 'it' would be. If the oracle had originated before the conquest of Jerusalem, then that would have provided an obvious reference for 'it', but the context was clearly subsequent to the fall of the city. One possibility is that 'it', which in Hebrew was a feminine form, pointed to a future critical situation whose character was specified as being anticipated shortly and as inducing a radical change of outlook on the part of the exiles. Following 'your words' in the preceding verse, the event in view was the restoration of their fortunes which now formed the substance of Ezekiel's ministry. It too would be treated by the community as a pleasing illusion until the reality was actualised.

Then they will know introduced a modified form of the recognition formula in which it was not the LORD who was recognised, but Ezekiel as one who was truly his prophet (the term was preposed for emphasis). ***Then they will know that a prophet has been in their midst.*** Whereas their spiritual response to judgement had not been all that it should have been, the coming time of renewal would achieve more. This renewal would not occur because the people would have become more spiritually receptive, but because of the LORD's initiative

---

18. Commentators have found the comparison of Ezekiel to a song too strange to accept. It is possible that *šîr*, 'song', might be taken as an infinitive of the corresponding verb, 'like one who sings lustfulnesses'. Others have achieved a similar rendering by emending to the participial form *šār*, 'singing one'. Most probably the noun 'song' could be used in a metonymous fashion for the one who sang it.

by which he would intervene in their lives for good. This outcome would be a positive result of Ezekiel's ministry as set out in 2:5.

REFLECTION

* Ezekiel was not to misinterpret his sudden popularity and seeming acceptance. The LORD spoke to disabuse him of any idea that might occur to him that his ministry was achieving its goal. He was to continue to set forth God's word faithfully, even though he was mocked for doing so.
* Ezekiel's audience still had their 'minds set on earthly things' (Phil. 3:19). No doubt hearing the prophet speak surrounded by a crowd relieved the tedium of the life in Tel-abib. But merely being present was not what was required. They gave no evidence of awareness of how far their lives were from what God wished to see—of how alienated their hearts had become from God himself. '⌊It is⌋ not the hearers of the law ⌊who are⌋ righteous before God, but the doers of the law will be justified' (Rom. 2:13; cf. Jas. 1:22, 25). There was no evidence of a genuine longing to get to know, and to respond with obedience to, the word of God. To the contrary, its proclamation provided a source of amusement. The imposition of divine judgement had not improved their spiritual perceptivity either. So it is made unarguably clear that there is no hope for the remnant apart from the intervention of divine grace.

B. The Shepherds of Israel (34:1-31)

This chapter contains a sample of the proclamation Ezekiel is authorised to deliver, no longer to convince his exilic audience of the ineluctable devastation of Jerusalem, but instead to allure them with the prospect of restoration. Recovery remains possible even from the ruin which has engulfed the city and from the deportation which they are enduring, and the prophet's message sheds light on the process by which the transformation will occur, especially by setting out a rich picture of what will be accomplished and made available to the ideal, obedient Israel. Throughout it all, however, the LORD's sovereignty dominates matters, since the changed conditions will arise from divine intervention, and will be secured by divine power. Ezekiel's hearers are being cajoled to abandon their spurious spiritual self-sufficiency and to accept God's invitation and gift, and so to participate in this process of restoration.

Though the chapter contains five occurrences of the messenger formula, 'Thus says the Lord GOD' (34:2, 10, 11, 17, 20), they do not appear to function as boundary markers, and it is more appropriate to analyse the chapter along thematic lines. This also suggests a fivefold division, but with somewhat different segments (34:1–10, 11–16, 17–22, 23–24, 25–31). In any event the shepherd theme provides significant thematic continuity throughout the chapter.

The first matter to be tackled in Israel's restoration is the government of the restored people. The term 'shepherd' had been used metaphorically for a ruler, both divine and human, for many centuries throughout the ancient world (Niehaus 2008:34–55), and it was also employed as a designation for the LORD (see on 34:11) and for Israel's kings (see on 34:2). Here the kings of Judah are described as shepherds, but they are not autonomous figures who own their flocks. The LORD has entrusted them with 'my flock', his people over whom he never relinquishes his rights of ownership. Since past rulers have failed in their responsibilities, the LORD has justly punished them, and now he declares that such shepherds will have no further role in ruling his people. Instead the LORD will take action to remedy the situation of the flock which has suffered at their hands (34:1–10).

The oracular presentation then looks forwards. Like a diligent shepherd, the LORD will personally identify and gather his flock, bringing them back to their land and caring for their needs (34:11–16). In particular, the LORD will ensure that there will be no exploitation or oppression within his flock (34:17–22). He will accomplish this by providing them with a shepherd whose David-like characteristics will ensure his obedience to all that God requires of him (34:23–24). That there is now precisely one shepherd (34:23) emphasises the future unity of the people. Moreover, the LORD will instate a covenant of peace with his people in which their land will be bountifully blessed, and foreign aggressors will be removed, so that Israel will enjoy true security and prosperity (34:25–31).

Most critics accept that 34:1–16 (with the exception of 34:7–8) are from the prophet himself, but their views vary on 34:17–31.[19] Still the imagery of shepherd and flock, though less prominent in 34:25–30, pervades all sections and binds the chapter together. Critical positions largely stem from reluctance to allow for a prophet who has presented

---

19. For instance, Zimmerli (1983:212–213) allocates 34:1–15, 34:16 (a link verse), and 34:17–22 to the prophet. Also, 34:23–24 are authentic, though secondary in this position. However, 34:7–8 are later expansions, while 34:25–30(31) are from Ezekiel's disciples. On the other hand, Levenson (1976:84–91) treats the chapter as a unity.

an extensive message of condemnation and judgement to be used subsequently as the carrier of a message of hope and restoration. This is, however, an entirely specious dichotomy. The true prophets were always the heralds of the covenant King, and their message reflected the inherent structure of the covenant: blessings on the obedient, curses on the disobedient.

The denunciation of Judah's kings as shepherds who have failed in their task looks back to a similar earlier passage (Jer. 23:1-6), but the most significant Scriptural links for this chapter are undoubtedly with Jesus' portrayal of himself as the Good Shepherd (see on 34:23-24). There is also a noteworthy similarity to Ezekiel's presentation in chapter 17, particularly as regards the LORD undertaking himself to perform the duties in which his royal appointees have fallen short, and also employing as his agent in this restoration a Messianic figure (cf. Levenson 1976:86-87).

(1) Condemnation of the Corrupt Shepherds (34:1-10)

Though Ezekiel's earlier proclamation has contained glimpses of the coming renewal (11:14-21; 17:22-24; 28:25-26), from now on it becomes his major theme. Even so, it is presented realistically: the future will not immediately become problem-free. But here the groundwork for prospective improvements is laid first of all by looking back and levelling charges against Israel's former shepherds for having exploited their positions and having failed in their duties (34:2-6). They had concentrated on self-aggrandisement and had neglected the needs of the flock—indeed, they had exploited them. There then follows an announcement of what the LORD will impose on the shepherds for their misconduct (34:7-10). They will have no further role in governing God's people. If the exiles were wondering at how their renewal could arise from the sorry wreck of maimed Zedekiah (2 Kgs. 25:7) or the pathetic figure of incarcerated Jehoiachin (2 Kgs. 24:15), who were both with them in Babylon, they need wonder no longer. The era of the kingdom has ended; there will be no place for human monarchs when the exiles return to the land. But the institution of kingship itself is not repudiated. The LORD and his Messiah will fulfil the role of shepherd-king for the people.

(a) Indictment of Israel's Shepherds (34:1-6)

> 34:1And the word of the LORD came to me, saying, 34:2'Son of man, prophesy against the shepherds of Israel. Prophesy and say to them, to the shepherds, "Thus says the Lord GOD: Woe, shepherds of Israel who have been shepherding

themselves! Is it not the flock ⌊that⌋ the shepherds are to shepherd? ³⁴:³The fat you eat and the wool you wear; the well-nourished you slaughter, ⌊but⌋ the flock you do not shepherd. ³⁴:⁴The weak you have not strengthened, and the sick you have not healed, and the broken you have not bandaged, and those driven away you have not brought back, and the lost you have not sought; but with force you have ruled them and with harshness. ³⁴:⁵And they were dispersed because ⌊there was⌋ no shepherd, and they became food for all the beasts of the field, and they dispersed. ³⁴:⁶My flock strayed on all the mountains and upon every high hill, and upon all the face of the earth my flock were dispersed, and no one inquired ⌊for them⌋ and no one sought ⌊them⌋." '

♦ **34:1–2** The oracle was introduced in standard fashion with the word-event formula, and it began with the customary address to Ezekiel as *Son of man.* He was directed to *prophesy against the shepherds of Israel.* The repeated command to prophesy and the two introductory occurrences of 'shepherds' have suggested to some that *to them, to the shepherds* was unnecessarily redundant. Certainly it was unusual in that a different preposition was employed for 'to' in the two phrases, though that might be avoided by rendering, 'Say to them, "To the shepherds thus says the Lord GOD" ' (cf. HCSB, NKJV, NJPS, REB). On the other hand, 'to the shepherds' may be omitted as an instance of dittography (cf. GNB, NIV). However, the two phrases might well have been placed in apposition for emphasis.

Who were 'the shepherds of Israel'? There is no doubt that the usage was a metaphor for those who ruled the covenant people, but there are various possibilities as regards to whom it referred.

(1) Odell has argued for the shepherds being foreign conquerors who ruled and oppressed God's people (2005:423–425). Certainly this helps to explain the presence of chapter 35 and chapters 38–39 in this block of material, and it is not necessarily ruled out by the occurrence of 'my shepherds' (see on 34:8). However, the traditional interpretation of the allegorical language in which the wild beasts included foreign predators remains more plausible (cf. 34:5, 8).

(2) Even when the term shepherds is restricted to Israelites, there is a divergence of emphasis as to whether it is a collective term for the kings who had ruled them over the centuries (or possibly just those of recent generations), or whether the king, the royal court, and leading figures in the community more generally were in view. An exclusively royal reference is more probable in view of the replacement offered, whether in the person of the LORD himself or of one fulfilling the role

of David (34:23), and it also fits in with the views expressed earlier against Judah's self-serving and corrupt monarchs (cf. chs. 17; 19). Strictures against others in leadership roles were expressed in terms of 'fat sheep' (34:20) who formed a group distinct from the shepherd.

The message to be delivered regarding the shepherds began with *woe!* (see on 13:3), which carried with it notice of impending disaster and death for the *shepherds of Israel* because their conduct had been skewed away from uprightness. Throughout the passage the same Hebrew root lay behind the noun 'shepherd' and the verb which described their activity. This repetition leads to somewhat awkward English, though *shepherd* may be employed as a verb in English. It conveys more than 'feed' (NRSV); 'take care of' (NIV) indicates the more general, inclusive scope of their responsibilities. *Who have been shepherding themselves* portrayed shepherds who had been ruthlessly pursuing their own interests (cf. Jude 12). It is inappropriate to go so far as to stress that sheep were, and are, eventually slaughtered, because that is outwith the scope of the comparison embodied in the metaphor. The point was that while the sheep were in their charge shepherds had the duty to provide them with guidance, resources, and general oversight of their well-being. Therefore the challenge was issued: *Is it not the flock ₎that₎ the shepherds are to shepherd?*[20]

♦ **34:3** Mein has pointed out that ancient herding contracts typically specified 'milk products, wool and young animals as belonging to the owner of the flock' (2007:499). Only any surplus which was created over a certain predetermined level became the possession of the hired shepherds. 'Who shepherds a flock and does not eat some of the milk of the flock?' (1 Cor. 9:7). Here, however, the shepherds regarded the whole flock as if it was rightfully their own, and they did not consider themselves answerable to any (in contrast to Jacob in Gen. 31:38–39). Their self-serving policies were described in clauses where the object was placed before the verb for emphasis. Three sins of commission were specified. *The fat you eat* was a particularly heinous offence in Israel because the fat belonged to the LORD (Lev. 3:14–17). If, however, there was a progression in their misdeeds, then the first item might well have been 'consume the milk' (cf. GNB, NIV, NLT).[21] The

---

20. The imperfect verb *yirʿû*, 'they will shepherd', has modal, obligatory force. See Introduction §6.3a.
21. The change envisaged is from *ḥăleb*, 'fat', as in MT, to *ḥālāb*, 'milk', as in the LXX and Vulgate. 'To eat' might be used in the broader sense of 'to consume', or 'milk' might refer to milk products in general, cf. 'curds' (NIV).

change is argued for in that it avoids the first and third sins of commission being identical. However, the first accusation may have referred to eating the fat of an animal, its finest parts, whereas the third referred to the slaughter of fat sheep, the most prized animals in the flock.

The second sin, *the wool you wear*, did not refer to the surplus which would become theirs, but to the produce which belonged to the owner. Thirdly, the *well-nourished*, or 'the fattened ⌜sheep⌝', a collective singular term for the choicest animals of the flock, were slaughtered by them for their own benefit. It is unnecessary to develop a detailed key to the allegory; it is sufficient to see here exploitation of their royal status to the detriment of their subjects and a denial of their obligations to the LORD.

The summary allegation was one of overall failure to display concern for the well-being of the flock: *the flock you do not shepherd.* No 'but' was expressed. The contrast was, however, implied by the juxtaposition of the concluding clause. What was involved in this sin of omission was spelled out in the next verse.

♦ **34:4** There were five items in the catalogue of the shepherds' neglect, where the objects of the verbs were again placed emphatically before the verbs, and the verbs themselves referred to past actions. This was a charge sheet of their remissness. Notice the corresponding positives of what should be done in 34:16. *The weak* and *the sick* render two different forms from the same root which conveyed weakness or exhaustion, possibly brought on by physical illness. The translation chosen reflects the accompanying verb, either *strengthened* or *healed* (cf. 34:16). No action had been taken to maintain the health of the flock, or to treat any injuries. *The broken you have not bandaged.* No care was provided for animals suffering from fractured limbs. Furthermore, *those driven away you have not brought back.* This might have envisaged animals which were frightened by some sudden occurrence or by the presence of a predator. On the other hand, *the lost*[22] were those which had just strayed, and so had become separate from the flock. *You have not sought* brought out the lack of pastoral care on the part of the shepherds. They did not consider it worthwhile to exert themselves to alleviate the predicament of any unfortunate animal.

---

22. Though the verb 'ābad frequently has the sense 'to perish' or 'to be destroyed', when animals are referred to, it conveys rather 'to go astray', 'to become lost', without necessarily implying death (1 Sam. 9:3, 20; Jer. 50:6).

Over against what they had not done, the final clause of the verse set out what the shepherds' course of action had been: **with force you have ruled them and with harshness.** Somewhat surprisingly 'them' was a masculine form whereas the previous terms referring to the sheep had been feminine. Perhaps, the referent of the metaphor began to show through (or else a rare feminine form was avoided). Even on its own 'ruled' (*rādâ*; cf. 29:15) might well have suggested dominance maintained by compulsion, but the addition of 'with force' (here, strength used in a coercive fashion) and 'with harshness' (cf. Exod. 1:13–14; a less common expression for brutal duress) clearly denoted an exploitative rule, which recalled the way the Egyptians had oppressed Israel. It was unacceptable behaviour for an Israelite to treat a fellow member of the covenant community in this fashion (Lev. 25:43, 46, 53); so the rulers had been acting like foreign tyrants and oppressors, and had disregarded the LORD's covenant stipulations.

♦ **34:5** The outcome of this neglect and abuse was that the sheep no longer stayed together cohesively as a flock. Here and at the end of the verse, **they dispersed** (cf. Jer. 10:21) was an active but intransitive verb describing the frightened movement of the sheep. **Because there was no shepherd** meant that there was no one giving true leadership to keep them together (cf. 1 Kgs. 22:17; Matt. 9:36; Mark 6:34). **They became food for all the beasts of the field.** Defenceless and vulnerable, the flock became prey for wild, scavenging animals. The metaphor probably pictured those who, to escape exploitation or death, fled as refugees. The repetition of the earlier verb, **they dispersed**, is viewed with suspicion by many translators. Some read it as the first item in the following verse (LXX, followed by NRSV, ESV); others treat it as an instance of dittography, a mistaken scribal repetition, and omit it (GNB, NEB, NLT). It may, however, be argued that it gives temporal information: 'they dispersed' (cf. AV, NIV, NKJV) occurred at a time when the flock, ravaged by wild beasts, scattered to survive.

♦ **34:6 My flock strayed.**[23] 'My' brought out the LORD's ownership of

---

23. The verb *yišgû* attracts attention for three reasons. (1) It is plural whereas the immediately following subject is singular. Probably this is a construction according to sense with the collective noun *ṣô'nî*, 'my flock'. (2) More striking is the fact that the verb is masculine and the subject feminine, perhaps revealing a shift of focus towards the application of the metaphor to the people. The root, though occurring infrequently, elsewhere has a human subject. (3) The imperfect form of the verb without *waw* is awkward to translate. Possibly the sense is, 'My flock kept straying,' a frequentative use.

the flock; the shepherds were only trustees, who were derelict in their duty. It also contained an element of sympathy towards the people, for, though they were far from guiltless, they had suffered because of the inadequacy and despotism of their rulers. 'My flock' also implied who the true Shepherd of the flock was. The delinquent behaviour of the undershepherds had adversely affected the interests of the true owner of the flock, quite apart from the misery it caused to the sheep. 'Stray' (*šagâ*; the verb occurs only here in Ezekiel) was also used of moral deviance (Ps. 119:10, 21, 118) and for unwitting sin (45:20; Lev. 4:13; Num. 15:22), in which case there may also be an oblique reference to the way in which the unprincipled behaviour of their leaders led not just to the exile but to involvement in idolatry and paganism.

On all the mountains and upon every high hill reflected the terrain of Canaan. **Were dispersed** was now a passive form indicating that others caused the dispersal of the sheep which extended from neighbouring localities to **all the face of the earth**. **No one inquired** and **no one sought** were virtually synonymous, though perhaps 'inquire' (*dāraš*, 34:8, 10, 11) emphasised somewhat more the concern expressed while 'seek' (*biqqēš*, 34:4, 16) focused more on the search undertaken. This depiction involved a marked change from previous characterisations of the people as rebellious and blameworthy.

(b) Judgement on Israel's Shepherds (34:7–10)

> 34:7'Therefore, O shepherds, hear the word of the LORD: 34:8"As I live, declares the Lord GOD, surely because my flock became plunder and my flock became food for all the beasts of the field, because ˻there was˼ no shepherd, and ˻because˼ my shepherds did not inquire for my flock, but the shepherds shepherded themselves and they did not shepherd my flock, 34:9therefore, O shepherds, hear the word of the LORD. 34:10Thus says the Lord GOD: Behold, I am against the shepherds and I will inquire for my flock from their hand, and I will make an end to their shepherding ˻the˼ flock, and the shepherds will no longer shepherd themselves, and I will deliver my flock from their mouths, and they will not become food for them." '

♦ **34:7** The initial *Therefore* with the exhortation, *O shepherds, hear the word of the LORD*, flagged up the following judgement speech against Judah's oppressive rulers.

♦ **34:8** Though the use of the oath formula, *As I live*, drew attention to the gravity of what would be said, the actual content of the oath was delayed until 34:10 by motive clauses introduced by *because*. *Surely* intensified the validity of the grounds for proceeding against the shepherds. *My flock became plunder.* While plunder pertained more to the application of the figure than to the metaphorical picture (cf. 34:22), the thought was restated in metaphorical terms, *my flock became food for all the beasts of the field* (cf. 34:5). Attacks by wild animals on the sheep symbolised enemy attacks on the people. Though the possessives in *my shepherds*[24] and *my flock* pointed to the covenantal dynamics of the accusation, it is significant that 'my flock' was used four times in this verse (cf. 34:6) while 'my shepherds' occurred only once in what was really an instance of irony. Both groups held divinely designated roles, but the deficiencies in the conduct of the shepherds (*did not inquire*; cf. 34:6) rendered them unworthy of their position. They were simply intent on furthering their own interests: *the shepherds shepherded themselves and they did not shepherd my flock* (cf. 34:2).

♦ **34:9-10** *Therefore* introduced the LORD's summons to the shepherds as he delivered his verdict on their performance in their God-given office. The messenger formula, *Thus says the Lord GOD*, prefaced the divine summation of the situation using the opposition formula, *Behold, I am against the shepherds* (cf. 5:8). This was the formal judgement of the royal owner on those who had failed in their allotted duty. Considering the future restoration to the land, the LORD announced his initial action: *I will inquire* (cf. 34:6) *for my flock from their hand.* As the true lord and owner of the flock, he would demand a reckoning from those to whom he had entrusted it, so that accounts might be settled (cf. Matt. 18:23; 25:19). When this exposed their shortcomings, he would deprive them of office. *I will make an end to their shepherding ιthe flockյ.* This would inevitably put a stop to their exploitation of the sheep for their own ends. *The shepherds will no longer shepherd themselves* (cf. 34:2). This was not a repudiation of monarchy in general, but of Israel's kings. However, no mention was made of any further punishment to come on the royal line. It would have been evident to all what had already befallen their former rulers.

---

24. Although the LORD could term the Assyrians 'the rod of my anger' (Isa. 10:5) and the Persian Cyrus 'my shepherd' (Isa. 44:28) when they acted as his agents, the use here of 'my shepherds' argues against Odell's identification of them as foreign rulers (see on 34:2).

The divine initiative to restore the people would in this way bring relief to the flock from internal oppression (as well as external attack, 34:8). ***I will deliver*** (cf. 34:12) ***my flock from their mouths, and they will not become food for them.*** This used the same style of description as for the predators of 34:5, 8, implicitly comparing the shepherds (= the kings) with savage animals who ravaged the flock. The LORD would ensure that royal exploitation would not be a feature of the restoration, and indeed after the exile the Jews did not have native kings.

REFLECTION

- Since the shepherds of Israel were what would nowadays be classified as political figures, thought must be given as to how the teaching of this passage should be understood in the contemporary world. It remains the case that there is a political application in that the 'governing authorities' in the New Testament age are still divinely appointed and hold office as 'God's servant for your good' (Rom. 13:4). However, while Paul's discussion in Romans 13:1–7 is concerned with the relationship between the believer and the civil authorities, the teaching of this passage emphasises the responsibility of rulers before God. They are entrusted with positions of authority, not to advance their personal interests, but to promote what God's word considers to be 'good' by caring for those over whom they rule and furthering their well-being. All exploitative and despotic rule is thereby condemned.

  So there are three basic New Testament principles in this regard. (1) Rulers are answerable to God, and may not enjoin what God forbids, or forbid what God requires. 'We must obey God rather than men' (Acts 5:29). (2) When civil rulers exercise powers which are legitimately theirs, the believer is duty-bound to acknowledge their authority and comply with their regulations (Rom. 13:5). (3) Prayer is to be made 'for kings and all who are in positions of authority, that we may lead a peaceful and quiet life with all godliness and propriety' (1 Tim. 2:2). Since rulers are themselves fallen, and since they rule over a world which is at enmity with God, they need divinely bestowed wisdom to fulfil the mandate that they have been given.

- But additionally in the New Testament the metaphor of shepherding and flocks particularly applies to those who hold positions of leadership in the church. Examples of this may be seen in Christ's words to Peter, such as 'Feed my lambs' (John 21:15), in Paul's exhortation to the Ephesian elders to 'pay careful attention to yourselves and to all the flock in which the Holy Spirit has made you overseers to shepherd the church of God' (Acts 20:28; cf. 'shepherds', Eph. 4:11), and in Peter's advice to elders to 'shepherd the flock of God that is among you' (1 Pet. 5:2).

- Peter's description of how the church of Christ should be governed is a mirror image of the teaching of this passage in that he warns against seeking 'shameful gain' and 'lording it over those in your charge' (1 Pet. 5:2, 3). Too often the cause of Christ is held back and shamed by leaders who forget to act with humility and self-sacrifice in promoting the needs of others. 'Shepherds feeding themselves' (Jude 12) weaken the church and shamefully undermine its testimony. For this God will require that they give an account as those whose work will be subject to testing by fire on the day of reckoning (1 Cor. 3:11–15).

(2) The Good Shepherd (34:11–16)

The LORD's relationship with Israel is often described using the metaphor of a shepherd (Pss. 23:1; 78:52–54; 80:1; Isa. 40:11; Jer. 23:3; Mic. 7:14), and it is in this character that he presents himself as resolving the predicament of the exiled people. Building on his declaration that he would deliver his flock (34:10), this paragraph provides greater detail of his promise that he would solicitously seek his sheep and restore them. His actions will contrast strongly with those of their former rulers (compare, for instance, 34:4 and 34:16). To reverse their irresponsible misconduct requires the direct intervention of the true owner of the flock, the LORD himself.

> 34:11'For thus says the Lord GOD, "Behold I, ⌊even⌋ I myself, will inquire for my flock and scrutinise them. 34:12As a shepherd's scrutiny of his flock in the day when he is in the midst of his flock that had been spread, so I will scrutinise my flock and I will deliver them from all the places where they have been dispersed in a day of clouds and darkness. 34:13And I will bring them out from the peoples and I will gather them from the lands and I will bring them to their land and I will shepherd them on the mountains of Israel, in the valleys and in all the inhabited places of the land. 34:14In good pasture I will shepherd them, and on the mountains of the height of Israel will be their grazing place; there they will lie down in a good grazing place and on lush pasture they will graze on the mountains of Israel. 34:15I myself will shepherd my flock, and I myself will make them lie down, declares the Lord GOD.

³⁴:¹⁶"The lost I will seek, and those driven away I will bring back, and the broken I will bandage, and the weak I will strengthen, but the fat and the strong I will destroy; I will shepherd them with judgement." '

♦ **34:11** *For* linked this use of the messenger formula with the preceding declaration of the LORD's purpose and promise: he himself would act as a true shepherd. The emphatic repetition in ***Behold I, ˌevenˌ I myself*** focused a brilliant spotlight on the LORD, and the false shepherds utterly faded from view. ***Inquire for*** (*dāraš*) repeated the verb which depicted a concerned inquiry after (cf. 34:6, 10)—not withdrawal and abandonment of the downtrodden, but active involvement on their behalf. ***Scrutinise***/ 'inspect'/ 'search through' (*bāqar*) added a different term from those in 34:6, one which was probably drawn from Ezekiel's priestly background to denote a careful examination to establish the condition of something (cf. Lev. 13:36; 19:20; 27:33; Prov. 20:25). The corresponding Aramaic verb occurred in Ezra for careful examination of archives to find a relevant document (Ezra 4:15, 19; 5:17; 6:1). The LORD as the Good Shepherd was not satisfied merely with the presence of the sheep, but also wished to ascertain and ensure that they were in good condition.

♦ **34:12** *A shepherd's scrutiny* repeated the root found in the previous verse, though ***his flock*** employed a noun found only here in Ezekiel, but its meaning was essentially the same as that of the term found elsewhere for flock. ***In the day when he is in the midst of his flock which had been spread***²⁵ described a shepherd's check of his recovered flock to ascertain if any had injuries or were weak, after suffering the trauma of being scattered. The LORD declared that in a similar way, ***I will scrutinise my flock.***

The remainder of the verse described what would temporally occur prior to the scrutiny. ***I will deliver*** (*naṣal*; cf. 3:19) described removal or rescue from a distressing situation, and was reminiscent of the Exodus (Exod. 3:8; 6:6; 12:27). Again the referent of the metaphor was probably made more obvious with the masculine ***them*** (rather than a feminine for 'flock'), though the switch may once more just reflect how uncommon the feminine form was. This new Exodus would, however, be more comprehensive than the departure from Egypt; it

---

25. The feminine plural niphal participle *niprāšôt* appears to qualify the preceding *ṣōʾnô*, 'his flock, spread ones', though its spelling is unusual. As found in MT it comes from the root *pāraš*, 'to explain, declare', but this seems to be a misspelling for *pāraś*, 'to spread' (cf. 17:21).

was envisaged as gathering them *from all the places where they have been dispersed.* This description would cover both deportees and refugees. *A day of clouds and darkness* was a hendiadys for 'a day of dark clouds', and was also language associated with the theophany at Sinai ('darkness', Exod. 20:21; 'clouds and darkness', Deut. 4:11; 5:22), but 'the day' in view here was the time of the LORD's judgement upon Jerusalem (cf. 13:5; 22:24).

♦ **34:13** As in the preceding verse, *them* was a masculine form referring to the people, not the sheep of the metaphor. The three verbs, *bring out, gather, bring to,* would evoke memories of the former Exodus deliverance from Egypt (cf. 20:34–35; 36:24; 37:21), and would have a preliminary fulfilment in the return from the exile, which itself foreshadowed the final gathering of the elect from all the earth (Matt. 24:29–31).

The plurals *peoples ... lands* indicated that more than the deportees in Babylonia were in view, and would have included groups like those in Egypt and elsewhere (Jer. 40:11; 44:1). This would also have included those who were taken from the northern kingdom of Israel to multiple destinations after the fall of Samaria (2 Kgs. 17:6), even though the numbers involved would have been small given how few returned even from Judah after a shorter exile. However, the fact that they would come from so many places heightened the scale of the deliverance that the LORD would effect.

To their land expressed not just the land of their origins, but the resettlement of the covenant people in the land their Overlord had allotted them and where they rightfully belonged. There they would enjoy his provision and his protection. No longer would they be found on the mountains of dispersion (34:6), but *on the mountains of Israel*, one of Ezekiel's favourite phrases for the Promised Land (cf. 6:3). *In the valleys* pictured an ideal setting for a flock with pasture and a water supply. *In all the inhabited places of the land* abandoned the metaphorical reference to sheep and clearly showed that people were in view.

♦ **34:14** The bounty of the LORD's provision was brought out further. *Pasture* was derived from the same root as 'shepherd' and so continued the theme of the chapter. Moreover, it was *good*, fit for purpose and part of the resources made available by their covenant Overlord who *will shepherd them. On the mountains of the height of Israel* may also be rendered on 'Israel's high mountains'. Elsewhere (17:22–23; 20:40) the singular 'mountain' was used (indeed it is found here in the Septuagint and Targum), where it referred specifically to the Temple Mount, but here it was the high land in general. The strategic repetition of these terms reminded the people of all that was attractive in their homeland in contrast to the austere conditions they were currently enduring in the level plains of Babylonia. ***Grazing place*** continued the metaphorical reference to sheep, while ***they will lie down*** reverted to a feminine plural verb form focusing on the sheep as they enjoyed the ***lush pasture*** (cf. Ps. 23:2).

♦ **34:15** *I myself will shepherd my flock* declared that the LORD would be directly responsible for bringing this new state of affairs into existence and maintaining it. This degree of involvement was highlighted by the repetition of the emphatic expression, 'I myself'. Only divine intervention could—and would—provide this relief for the people. ***Make them lie down*** recalled the words of Psalm 23:2, 'In pastures of green grass he makes me lie down'. How much greater his wisdom and foresight than that of the flock! They would have served their own interests best by accepting his provision.

♦ **34:16** The four clauses of the first half of this transitional verse looked back to 34:4a, and mirrored in reverse order the exploitation and cruel negligence critiqued there. But now the aim was to set out the programme of remedial measures engaged in by the true Shepherd who would act with comprehensive care and compassion to reverse the traumas of the past. The repetition of first person verb forms brought out that it was his action which would count. ***The lost I will seek***; no longer would they be left to their own resources as they had been by the self-centred shepherds (34:4, 6; cf. Luke 19:10). ***Those driven away I will bring back***; this Shepherd would actively gather the scattered. ***The broken I will bandage***; he would carefully tend their injuries. ***The weak I will strengthen***. There was an element of compression in this final item which corresponded to the first two clauses of 34:4a. The rendering ***weak*** is probably to be preferred (rather than 'sick' as in 34:4) because the accompanying verb was 'strengthen' rather than 'heal'.

The second half of the verse advanced the presentation by taking up the theme of the following section by mentioning ***the fat***[26] ***and the strong.*** These were feminine singular forms, pointing to typical

---

26. 'The fat' does not occur in the LXX, but that deletion is probably influenced by 34:4 (cf. Allen 1998:157). There is a play between *šāmēn*, 'lush' (34:14), and *šəmēnâ*, 'fat'.

individual sheep from each category. The accompanying verb *I will destroy* was a strong term,[27] which showed how determined the LORD was to rid the flock of them, presumably because their condition reflected the exploitation of others. *I will shepherd them with judgement*. 'Them' was also feminine singular in form. It might agree with the noun 'flock', in which it pointed to how the LORD would supervise them and dispense justice for all. If 'them' had 'the fat' or 'the strong' as its antecedent, then 'judgement' had the narrower sense of condemning them. Either way, the ruthless bullying tactics of the fat and the strong would be curbed in the interests of all being treated equitably.

REFLECTION

- The LORD presents himself elsewhere as the true 'Shepherd of Israel' (Ps. 80:1) who led his flock out of Egypt (Pss. 77:20; 78:52) and who provided for the needs of 'the sheep of his pasture' (Ps. 100:3). Here his restorative shepherding is presented in three cameos.

  (1) *Deliverance*. The LORD will deliver his flock (34:11–13a), gathering the remnant of Israel as he had promised (Mic. 2:12). His care will extend beyond a general call to return and will include a close scrutiny of their location and condition, which will result in their return to the land of his presence.

  (2) *Provision*. The LORD will not then abandon them, but will continue to shepherd them back in the land of Israel (34:13b–16a). His behaviour will be the reverse of the shepherds of Israel who fed themselves. In this his shepherding will conform to the vision presented by Isaiah: 'Like a shepherd he will shepherd his flock; with his arm he will gather the lambs, and will carry ⌊them⌋ in his bosom; he will lead ⌊gently⌋ those that have young' (Isa. 40:11). About this there should be no doubt.

  (3) *Justice*. But shepherding also involves dealing with the problems which will arise within the flock (34:16b, and in the

---

27. The textual evidence varies. *'ašmîd*, 'I will destroy', is supported by the Targum, but other ancient versions (LXX, Vulgate, Peshitta) apparently read *'ešmōr*, 'I will watch' (cf. RSV, following LXX). This change easily arises from confusion of *dalet* and *resh*. If the emendation is followed, it shows the LORD's good shepherding extends to all the members of the flock, and avoids the jarring note of 'I will destroy', but it is precisely that reversal which emphasises the discrimination of the LORD's judgement and provides the transition into the following section.

following section). His benevolence is not to be presumed upon. He will make hard decisions and enforce them. In this picture of what awaited the exiles, the LORD encouraged them to look forward to his coming intervention, and to conform their conduct to his desires.

(3) Divine Intervention in Judgement within the Flock (34:17–22)

This section takes up the theme of the ordering of the state of affairs within the flock, subsequently culminating in the provision of the Messianic shepherd-king in 34:23. The reference to 'judgement' in 34:16 is continued with three occurrences of the verb 'to judge' (34:17, 20, 22), and 'save' in 34:22 parallels 'deliver' in 34:10. However, there is a step forward in the theme. No more is heard of evil shepherds, and the sheep are now directly addressed. There is no elaboration of the form the judgement will take; the focus is on relationships within the community and what the LORD's ordering of their affairs will mean for those who are relieved from oppression.

There are two brief sub-sections. In the first (34:17–19) the LORD addresses all his flock and announces his intention to discriminate in his judgemental intervention. A series of questions is addressed to the powerful and sets out why he will judge them. The second sub-section (34:20–22) focuses more on the LORD's deliverance of the weak among the flock.

The background against which these words were uttered is not known. It does not seem to derive from the anarchic conditions in Judah after the Babylonian victory (Jer. 41–42), but rather from what prevailed within the community in exile. Perhaps the influx of a second set of deportees created tensions. Hummel airs the possibility that there was a reluctance by the earlier exiles to accept the newcomers (2007:1001). It called for considerable self-sacrifice to share their scanty resources with those emaciated survivors of a prolonged siege and lengthy trek to Babylon. Alternatively, some exiles may have attempted to express their former social status by overbearing and domineering conduct towards others (cf. the situation in the restoration community, Neh. 5). It is also possible to envisage that some among the exiles accept Ezekiel's message and repent, which exposes them to intimidation and vexatious behaviour by others who do not share their viewpoint. So it becomes necessary to point out that harassing and oppressing others belongs to the old Jerusalem, and will no longer be tolerated. 'Whoever opposes the divine reinstitution of justice and right relationships in the social order excludes himself from the restored covenant people' (Renz 1999:116).

³⁴:¹⁷'But ⌊as for⌋ you, my flock, thus says the Lord GOD, "Behold, I am about to judge between sheep and sheep, with respect to rams and he-goats. ³⁴:¹⁸Is it too small a thing for you to graze on the good pasture that you must trample the remainder of your pasture with your feet, and to drink of clear water that you muddy what is left with your feet? ³⁴:¹⁹But ⌊as for⌋ my flock, they must graze on what has been trampled by your feet and drink what has been muddied by your feet. ³⁴:²⁰Therefore thus says the Lord GOD to them: Behold I, ⌊even⌋ I myself, will judge between a fat sheep and a lean sheep. ³⁴:²¹Because you have pushed with side and shoulder, and have butted all the weak with your horns until you have dispersed them far and wide, ³⁴:²²I will save my flock and they will no longer become plunder and I will judge between sheep and sheep." '

♦ **34:17** By saying, ***But ⌊as for⌋ you, my flock,*** the LORD turned from those who had failed to discharge properly their leadership roles in Judah to address the whole community in exile. ***I am about to judge*** indicated the LORD's resolve to act to establish justice in the community. 'Judge' was the key term in the paragraph (34:17, 20, 22) and described regulating the people's affairs in accordance with divine standards of justice. ***Between sheep and sheep*** (that is, 'between one sheep and another sheep') repeated a singular noun designating an individual animal. Although the initial 'you' was feminine plural, all were not identical, and justice required a discriminating approach which took into account each member of the flock.

The scope of the LORD's action was then further specified: ***with respect to rams and he-goats.***[28] 'Ram' was a common designation for a human leader, and 'he-goat' was used with a similar sense. It would seem that those who presented themselves as leaders in the exilic community were labelled by these terms (cf. 'fat sheep', 34:20).

♦ **34:18** The rhetorical question constituted the accusation levelled against the behaviour of these self-appointed and self-aggrandising leadership groups. Two analogies were drawn. In the first these dominant animals ***graze on the good pasture*** while at the same time

---

28. Hummel (2007:992) argues that the phrase should be taken as the start of the next verse. He notes that 'between sheep and sheep' in 34:20, 22 is not accompanied by this additional phrase, and that 'you' in this verse is feminine whereas these nouns are masculine and thus fit in with the gender of the verbs in the following verse. But this does not seem necessary.

they ***trample the remainder of your pasture with your feet*** so as to spoil it and prevent others from enjoying it. The second analogy was similar, being expressed in terms of animals drinking at a source of water. ***Clear water***, or 'settled water', was that in which sediment or mud had sunk to the bottom so that there was water fit to drink. The leading animals drank of the clear water, but they would also ***muddy what is left with your feet***, polluting the water from which others had to drink.

♦ **34:19** The conduct of the rams and the he-goats was manifestly detrimental to the interests of ***my flock***, presumably the other members of the community who were left with substandard pasturage and water because of the unsuitable actions of their leaders, whether deliberately or thoughtlessly.

34:20 ***Therefore*** introduced the verdict which Ezekiel as the divine messenger was to relay from the LORD ***to them***, that is, the rams and he-goats. ***Behold I,*** ⌊***even***⌋ ***I myself*** again focused attention on the LORD's action in the situation (cf. 34:11). ***I will judge*** promised intervention to establish just conditions. This would not be merely a matter of imposing sentences on the miscreants; it would equally provide relief for the oppressed (cf. Ps. 82:2–4). In ***between a fat sheep and a lean sheep*** the noun 'sheep' was singular, emphasising the discrimination employed in the judgement. However, the adjectives were feminine (as also in 45:15) rather than the expected masculine. Presumably 'a fat sheep' corresponded to the rams and he-goats who had exploited their position and power to their own advantage, while 'a lean sheep' was one that was oppressed by them.

♦ **34:21–22** The abusive behaviour of the fat sheep (that is, the rams and the he-goats) had included pushing and butting the weak to ensure their own personal access to resources, ***until you have dispersed them far and wide***, where 'dispersed' repeated the term found in 34:5. Because of this the LORD would act to ***save my flock***. 'Save' (*yāšaʿ*, hiphil) emphasised bringing help to those caught up in difficult circumstances and so to rescue them. This echoed 'deliver' in 34:12. ***They will no longer become plunder*** (not 'prey') used the language of human warfare (cf. *NIDOTTE* 1:630) rather than that of the hazards of animal husbandry. However, the concluding remark, ***I will judge between sheep and sheep***, which formed an inclusion with 34:17, reverted to the metaphor of the divine Shepherd and his flock. 'Judge' related to the administration of affairs in an equitable fashion, and was used in a positive sense of settling grievances between individuals to maintain the peace of the realm rather than imposing penalties.

REFLECTION
* There is another side to the metaphor of the divine Shepherd. It is not just a matter of providing for the common needs of the flock; it also involves discriminating assessment of the conduct of those within the flock. The imagery here regarding 'rams and he-goats' (34:17) and 'between a fat sheep and a lean sheep' (34:20) bears obvious resemblances to the description of the final judgement which Jesus gives in terms of a shepherd separating the sheep from the goats (Matt. 25:32–46). The conduct of the members of the flock towards one another is indicative of their relationship with the Shepherd himself. 'As you did it to one of the least of these my brothers, you did it to me' (Matt. 25:40), and 'as you did not do it to one of the least of these, you did not do it to me' (Matt. 25:45). Those with authority or influence are warned to avoid conduct which disadvantages other members of the church, or causes them to leave the fellowship and become dispersed far and wide (34:21).

(4) The Messianic Shepherd (34:23–24)

Only the inclusion detected between 34:17 and 34:22 suggests a degree of separation of 34:23–24 from what precedes. However, the significance of the theme warrants that they be considered separately.

The positive aspect of divine intervention to restore the people includes a further key component in the provision of a shepherd. After regal and divine shepherding, the metaphor is further applied to messianic shepherding, as the true son of the line of David is foreshadowed in less cryptic terms than earlier in Ezekiel. The role envisaged for the Messiah does not conflict with the divine rule, but is an exercise of it as in the previous messianic prophecy in 17:22–24.

The analogy between the Messiah and a shepherd is one which Christ readily applied to himself (Matt. 25:32; Luke 15:3–7; John 10:7–18), and which others also apply to him (Heb. 13:20; 1 Pet. 2:25). He looks for the lost sheep (Matt. 15:24), and sends his apostles to find them (Matt. 10:6; John 21:15–17). It is against the background of imperfect shepherding (34:2–4; John 10:8, 10) that the sterling quality of the perfect Shepherd is appreciated.

34:23⟨And I will set up over them one shepherd, and he will shepherd them, ⌊even⌋ my servant David. He ⌊is the one who⌋ will shepherd them and he ⌊is the one who⌋ will be their shepherd. ³⁴:²⁴And I, the LORD, will be their God, and my servant David ⌊will be⌋ ruler in their midst. I ⌊am⌋ the LORD; I have spoken.'

♦ **34:23** *I will set up* presented the LORD's initiative and authoritative control in instating an individual into an office. The verb 'set up'/'make to stand'/'establish' conveyed the thought of the permanence of the covenant arrangements thus made (cf. 16:60). The gender of *them ... them ... them ... their* alternated between masculine (deriving from the people) and feminine (deriving from the feminine noun 'flock') indicating that use of the metaphor was waning and the concrete situation was coming more into view. *One shepherd* (in contrast to 'I will raise up shepherds over them', Jer. 23:4; possibly a reference to a dynasty) continued to refer to the way this specific individual would tend to the flock and meet their needs. The explicit 'one' (*ʾeḥād*; cf. 37:17) contrasted the conduct of this shepherd with that of the shepherds who failed in their appointed role as well as emphasising his singular, indeed unique, nature which accorded with the unity and oneness of the people over whom he would rule.

The designation *my servant David* was applied to this Shepherd not because he would be David resurrected, but because he would exemplify all the good qualities which David possessed ('a man after his own heart', 1 Sam. 13:14; Acts 13:22–23). He would also be a descendant of David, and thus able to fulfil the requirements of the Davidic covenant which earlier kings had miserably failed to do (chs. 17; 19). This expectation of a Messianic deliverer from the line of David already existed (Hos. 3:5; Isa. 9:7; 16:5; Jer. 30:9), and was further strengthened by this prophecy.

Although 'my servant' used the same noun as that employed for a slave, there was no degradation involved in being accorded this title. Coming from the mouth of God, it was an honorific of the highest order. It had been employed for the patriarchs, Abraham (Gen. 26:24; Ps. 105:6, 42); Isaac (Gen. 24:14); Jacob/Israel (28:25; 37:25; 1 Chron. 16:13), and was extensively used for Moses (e.g., Num. 12:7) and David himself (e.g., 2 Sam. 7:5). The primary implication of the term was obedient compliance with the directions of a superior. So it was said in somewhat repetitious terms, *He ⌊is the one who⌋ will shepherd them and he ⌊is the one who⌋ will be their shepherd.* In his case there would be no disjunction between what he did and the title accorded him. The emphasis in 'servant' was on his faithful discharge of all that was required of him as a royal, mediatorial figure through whom God would channel salvation to his people, while 'shepherd' specified his care and protection of those under him.

♦ **34:24** There would no tension between God's rule and the rule of this coming David. *I, the LORD, will be their God* was the primary link in the covenant bond between God and his people (cf. 37:27), which was not followed here by the corresponding relationship 'and they will be my people', but rather by an expansion of what was involved in the divine dimension of the union: *my servant David ⌊will be⌋ ruler in their midst.* For 'ruler' (*nāśîʾ*), conventionally rendered 'prince', see on 37:25. It was employed here to avoid the negative autocratic overtones of 'king' (see on 7:27), and to emphasise the Davidic servant's rule in humble submission to the LORD from whom he derived his authority. 'In their midst' indicated identification with the people and their interests—living as one of them, as well as being over them. This would fulfil Deuteronomy 17:15, 20, and so avoid the degeneration of the royal status and authority of the one set up 'over them' (34:23) into relentless oppression. *I ⌊am⌋ the LORD; I have spoken* incorporated the announcement formula to guarantee the realisation of this promised provision. What God had solemnly committed himself to would not be thwarted (cf. 5:15).

There was thus a merging of the traditional covenant formula for Israel's relationship with the LORD with an additional term reflecting the promise of the Davidic covenant. What was missing—the people's response reciprocating the relationship—was provided in 34:30–31, after a statement of the blessings of the Messianic regime. In this way closure was brought to the complete picture.

REFLECTION

- Though Ezekiel himself may not yet have appreciated it, in the event divine shepherding and messianic shepherding will prove to be the same thing. When Jesus appropriated the title of 'the good shepherd' (John 10:14), he was claiming to fulfil the requirements not only of this section, but of the preceding section also. Indeed, 'one shepherd' (34:23) spoken by the divine Shepherd intimates that there would be a very close bond between God and the Messiah. It is therefore not surprising that in that context Jesus declared, 'I and the Father are one' (John 10:30).
- The messianic Shepherd would perfectly succeed in the role in which David had achieved only partial success. That David is termed 'my servant' points to adherence to the requirements of God as the constitution under which he ruled and acted. Christ could truly make

the claim, 'I always do the things that are pleasing to him', the one who had sent him (John 8:29), and that he had accomplished the work he had been given to do (John 17:4).
* An important corollary flows from the fact that there is 'one shepherd' (34:23). It is brought out by Christ's statement, 'So there will be one flock and one shepherd' (John 10:16). Fundamentally the church is one because there is only one true God, and therefore all whom he saves and who then serve him are linked by an essential bond to him. Consequently all others who treated the people of God as if they were there to be exploited by them were dismissed by the true Shepherd as thieves and robbers, as strangers (not themselves genuine members of the covenant community), and as hired hands (John 10:1, 5, 12). It is in the light of Christ's status as 'the chief Shepherd' (1 Pet. 5:4) that those who lead in the church are to assess their own status as under-shepherds and so derive the norms for their personal conduct.

(5) The Covenant of Peace (34:25–31)

Presentation of the Messiah as the fulfilment of all that had been foreshadowed by 'my servant David' leads into an elaboration of the blessings which will be enjoyed under his reign. This covenantal provision is presented unconditionally in a passage pervaded by exultant joy at what the LORD has determined to bestow—a future free of danger and overflowing with blessing. This is summarised as 'a covenant of peace' (34:35), a peace which extends far beyond absence of warfare into a scene of pastoral bliss and contentment when the LORD secures the future of his people.

There are three main elements in the presentation of the rejuvenation of the natural realm which will be enjoyed: removal of wild animals (34:25), agricultural fertility (34:26–27a), and deliverance from oppression and attack by the nations (34:27b–28, 29c). This mixture shows that, as well as the natural benefits reflecting the continuing development of the theme of the shepherd and the flock, there are also benefits reflecting the political realities of the time.

The covenant of peace presents one aspect of the LORD's future covenantal administration of the affairs of his people, and enlarges on the picture of the everlasting covenant (16:60), with which it is explicitly identified in 37:26. The covenant of peace is further elaborated on in 36:28–30, 35, and similar themes are found in Hosea 2:18–23. These are the blessings which the LORD will bestow on his obedient people, reflecting the covenant promises of Leviticus 26:1–13 and Deuteronomy 28:2–14.[29]

The alluring picture exhibited in this section is concluded with words of reassurance (34:30–31) regarding the harmony which will prevail in the new covenant arrangements which the LORD will institute. No longer does Ezekiel's presentation end with a dark message of doom and impending judgement. Now he is commissioned to tell of the blessings to be bestowed by the LORD's favour.

However, questions arise as to the fulfilment of this prophecy. Certainly nothing like this occurred in Ezekiel's day, nor did the returning Jews enjoy such complete bliss when they left Babylonia, though elements of it were foreshadowed on that occasion. The provision set out here is only realised in God's eternal blessing for his people, the new Israel comprising Jew and Gentile alike on the basis of a common faith in Jesus as the messianic Shepherd, the son of David, who is also truly God. He alone will bring together all his scattered people so that 'there will be one flock and one shepherd' (John 10:16).

This prophecy shares with the remaining chapters of Ezekiel the phenomenon of prophetic foreshortening. When the LORD discloses to Ezekiel what will come to pass, he does not provide a precise timeline against which events are to be ticked off one by one as they occur. Instead the LORD gives such a vision of the future as will assure his people that he will be faithful to his word and that those who display covenant loyalty to him will receive covenant blessing. The details of when or how this will come to pass are generally beside the point. What matters is that this scenario is divinely guaranteed, and from that perspective it is not of primary importance whether events will transpire in the near future or in the distant future. What is important is that they will definitely be realised: God has spoken. His people, then and now, have to move forward on the pathway of faith, relying on his word, and encouraged by it.

Now, after the epochal events associated with the first coming of Christ, we are in a position to disambiguate the picture somewhat. But the fundamental perspective of faith has not changed. It is not assigning dates to the promises; it is moving forward with assurance in their reliability.

---

29. 'As when dooming Israel Ezekiel used the language of the covenant curses found at the end of the Book of Leviticus (ch. 26), so when describing their future happiness he uses the idiom of the blessings found there' (Greenberg 1987:182).

³⁴:²⁵'And I will make for them a covenant of peace, and I will make an end of evil beasts from the land, and they will dwell securely in the wilderness, and sleep in the woods. ³⁴:²⁶And I will set them and the places round about my hill a blessing, and I will bring down the shower in its time; they will be showers of blessing. ³⁴:²⁷And the trees of the field will give their fruit and the land will give its increase, and they will be upon their land securely. And they will know that I ⌞am⌟ the LORD when I break the bars of their yoke and deliver them from the hand of those who enslaved them. ³⁴:²⁸And they will no longer be plunder for the nations, and the wild beasts will not devour them, and they will dwell securely and there ⌞will be⌟ none to make ⌞them⌟ tremble. ³⁴:²⁹And I will raise up for them a planting place of renown, and they will no longer be victims of famine in the land and they will no longer endure the insults of the nations. ³⁴:³⁰And they will know that I, the LORD their God, ⌞am⌟ with them, and that they, the house of Israel, ⌞are⌟ my people, declares the Lord GOD. ³⁴:³¹But ⌞as for⌟ you my flock, the flock of my pasture, you ⌞are⌟ human; I ⌞am⌟ your God, declares the Lord GOD.'

♦ **34:25** The divine oracle continued and broadened out to include the whole created realm which would be restored in terms of *a covenant of peace* (cf. 37:26, and 'my covenant of peace', Num. 25:12). The harmony which would pervade this renewed world was termed 'peace' (*šālôm*), a condition in which human lives would be brought into harmony with God's requirements so that there would be individual and communal wholeness—indeed, this would spread to all creation. There would be superabundant provision for the people, who would delight in what their Creator and Saviour provided for them.[30]

These renewed arrangements were termed a 'covenant' to denote the binding, perpetual obligation on both parties, God and his people, to maintain the terms inherent in this state of peace between heaven and earth. Even so, it would be provided on the basis of *I will make* (lit., 'cut', the regular expression for covenant making) *for them*, not 'with them'. This would be divine provision instituted by divine initiative, a covenant unconditionally bestowed by divine grace, not on the grounds of human merit.

The phrase, 'a covenant of peace', was also used in Isaiah 54:7–10 with reference to the Noachic covenant as a prototype of the divine

---

30. 'The word *peace* is used to describe the harmony that exists when covenant obligations are being fulfilled and the relationship [between parties] is sound' (Taylor 1969:224).

eschatological settlement, a perspective which was obviously also present in this passage. There are not two different sets of blessing. What is given by sovereign decree continues to be enjoyed by covenant obedience (Lev. 26:3–13), which is guaranteed by the gracious intervention of God and perpetuated by the changes he institutes in his people.

There were three aspects to what the LORD would provide for his people. (1) *I will make an end of evil beasts* (that is, 'dangerous beasts'; cf. 5:17) *from the land.* Eradication of threatening, predatory animals would presage a return to conditions on a par with those which had prevailed in Eden. After the fall, they had been used as agents of divine punishment (5:17; 14:15, 21; 33:27; cf. Isa. 11:6–9; Hos. 2:18). Now the conditional covenant blessings of Leviticus 26:5–6 were presented as of guaranteed fulfilment in the LORD's restoration. *Wilderness ... woods* described two different, and generally, hostile environments, where wild animals were an ever-present threat. But with those animals absent there would be no need to live behind a stockade; it would be possible to *dwell securely* without such protection, and to *sleep* in the open. At this point it is not necessary to detect a reference to foreign aggressors in the evil beasts (but see 34:28). The animals themselves constituted a considerable danger, and their removal got rid of a very real threat (cf. Isa. 35:9). 'Securely' pointed to the confidence they would enjoy, not merely as their subjective perception (contrast 30:9), but soundly based on their trust in the one who provided these benefits for them.

♦ **34:26** (2) The LORD would bless the land with fruitfulness. *I will set them and the places round about my hill a blessing.* 'My hill' was a less common designation of Mount Zion, which was also referred to as a hill in Isaiah 10:32; 31:4. For Ezekiel's avoidance of the term Zion, see on 17:22. 'I will set/give them ... a blessing' implied transformation from something else. In the light of the following reference to 'places', it is more probable that 'them' pointed to the wilderness and woods rather than the people. The fruitfulness evident at these sites would be visible proof of God's favour and intervention.

I will bring down the shower in its time was a collective reference to the rains which normally fell at the beginning (late October to early December) and end (March and April) of the growing season. Without them there would be crop failure and famine. However, timely but unusually heavy rainfall could also spell disaster, and so the LORD added, *They will be showers of blessing.* It was not destructive rainfall that was in view (cf. 13:11, 13; 38:22). The switch to the plural term 'showers' probably arose from assimilation to the covenant blessing, 'I will give/set your showers in their time' (Lev. 26:4; cf. Joel 2:23–24). This was not a picture of human idleness, but of God providing the conditions under which the efforts of the farming community would not suffer setbacks from natural causes.

♦ **34:27** *And the trees of the field will give their fruit and the land will give its increase* (cf. 36:30; Amos 9:13–14) continued to elaborate on the copiousness of the LORD's provision, using words also drawn from Leviticus 26:4 with the clauses reversed. *They will be upon their land securely* (cf. 34:25) described their absence of fear as they enjoyed the provision and protection of the LORD who was their deliverer.

(3) The recognition formula, *And they will know that I ⌊am⌋ the LORD*, was then used to introduce a third divine blessing, the liberation of the people. The covenant people would harbour no doubts as to the source of their changed circumstances. The LORD had intervened on their behalf to *break the bars of their yoke*. 'Yoke' was frequently employed as a symbol for oppression and bondage (cf. 30:18; Isa. 9:4; Jer. 30:8), just as a yoke was placed over the neck of an animal which pulled a plough at the command of the ploughman. The yoke being removed expressed emancipation and freedom (cf. 'I have broken the bars of your yoke and made you walk erect', Lev. 26:13). This deliverance was also expressed in language which reflected the Exodus (see on 20:33–36) as the LORD committed himself to *deliver them from the hand of those who enslaved them* (lit., 'those who do work by means of them'; cf. Lev. 25:46; Jer. 22:13; 30:8; 34:9).

♦ **34:28** This verse expanded on and restated earlier descriptions of blessing. *They will no longer be plunder for the nations* reflected 34:8, 22. *The wild beasts* (lit., 'beasts of the land', cf. 14:15) *will not devour them* reversed the conditions of 34:5, 8, while *they will dwell securely* took up the thought of 34:25, 27. *There ⌊will be⌋ none to make ⌊them⌋ tremble* (cf. 39:26; Lev. 26:6; Jer. 30:10; Mic. 4:4). Since the LORD had removed every threat to their well-being, they would no longer have any reason to experience the emotional and physical reaction of trembling because of attack or adverse circumstances.

♦ **34:29** *I will raise up for them a planting place of renown* (lit., 'of name').³¹ This pointed to the reversal of the LORD's action in bringing desolation on the land, uprooting the people, and taking them off into exile. When they were brought back, it would be to a land which would be famed for its suitability for growing crops and for the abundance of their harvests. Consequently, the people of the LORD would *no longer be victims of famine in the land*, experiencing shortages. 'Victims' was literally 'brought together ones', and probably pictured heaps of corpses of those who had perished through extensive crop failures. That would occur 'no longer' (cf. 12:24).

The prosperity they would enjoy meant that *they will no longer endure the insults of the nations.* The insults were aspersions of disgrace (cf. 36:15), particularly derived from views such as their suffering through famine was the result of the impotence or incompetence of their God. Now the LORD's power would be abundantly evident and their adversaries' mouths would be shut.

♦ **34:30** The concluding two verses set these renewed conditions in the context of God's covenant provision for his people. A modified form of the recognition formula was used to assert that enjoyment of covenant blessing would not be divorced from recognition of the presence of the one who provided those blessings. God's covenant relationship with his people had never been intended to be a distant, arm's length affair. 'I will dwell among the people of Israel and will be their God' (Exod. 29:45). 'I will walk about (*hālak* hithpael; see on 28:14) in your midst, and I will be your God, and you will be my people' (Lev. 26:12). So here that familiar aspect of the covenant bond was stressed. *They will know that I, the LORD their God, ₒamₒ with them.* The more material description of the blessing faded before the spiritual dimension of the covenant of peace.

Moreover, the people would come to recognise their own status. They would know *that they, the house of Israel, ₒareₒ my people.* 'The house of Israel' viewed them as an ideal entity after they had been changed by divine intervention. 'The house of rebelliousness having ceased to exist, the old honorific title regains its validity' (Eichrodt 1970:484). The signature formula, *declares the Lord GOD*, conveyed confirmation that this was not the product of the prophet's wishful thinking but the expression of divine purpose.

---

31. The LXX and the Peshitta replace *ləšēm*, 'for a name', with 'peace' or 'prosperity', by reversing the initial Hebrew letters to form *šālōm*, 'peace'.

♦ **34:31** To round off the oracle the earlier shepherd–sheep imagery was again explicitly employed. The initial *you* was feminine plural, reflecting the gender of 'flock'. ***My flock*** asserted God's sovereign ownership of his people and control of them. ***The flock of my pasture*** viewed them as rightfully dwelling in the land and enjoying its produce. That was then matched by the other side of the covenant formula, by ***I ⌞am⌟ your God***, which was the ultimate foundation of the restoration of Israel.

However, before that there was also the statement, ***you ⌞are⌟ human*** (or, 'mankind', *ʾādām*), where 'you' was a masculine plural form. It seems intrusive, and presumably on those grounds was omitted by the Septuagint (cf. RSV, NRSV). But it did point to the human frailty of the covenant people, and to the condescension of God in entering into such a close and permanent bond with them. Though they were highly privileged by their restoration, they were being warned not to presume on the wonder that 'the dwelling place of God is with man. He will dwell with them, and they will be his people, and God himself will be with them as their God' (Rev. 21:3). This was again accompanied by the assurance conveyed in the signature formula, ***declares the Lord GOD***.

REFLECTION

- This prophecy of the covenant of peace is indirectly messianic. That means that there is no direct mention of the mediatorial figure of the Messiah in it. All the action and provision are related directly to God himself and his initiative in providing for every need of his people. However, it must not be forgotten that this description follows without a break after the introduction of the Messiah in 34:23–24, and all that is said here is the fruit of his completed work. In this way the consummation of the Davidic covenant is merged into the overall provisions of the new covenant which will be God's final provision for his people in Christ.
- 'A covenant of peace' (34:25) describes God's final provision for his people in idyllic terms, as a return to the bliss of Eden in which the natural realm is no longer blighted by the impact of sin (cf. Isa. 11:6–9; Hos. 2:18–23; Joel 3:18). But this harmony in the natural realm is only possible because there has been rapprochement in the spiritual realm. The peace in view is not merely that which arises from the removal of external hazards and human aggression. It is based on the restoration of true covenant relationships between God and his people who 'will know that I, the LORD their God, ⌞am⌟ with

them, and that they, the house of Israel, ⌊are⌋ my people' (34:30). This is nothing other than the peace with God which is established by the work of Christ through whom God was pleased 'to reconcile all things to himself, having made peace by the blood of his cross— whether things on earth or things in heaven' (Col. 1:20).

C. Mount Seir and the Mountains of Israel (35:1–36:15)

At first glance chapter 35 does not seem correctly placed in the prophecy, for it breaks into the presentation of Israel's renewal and restoration by reverting to the theme of judgement upon her enemies. But there are a number of factors which clearly indicate why this oracle has been positioned as it is and has not been included after the prophecy against Edom in 25:12–14.[32]

From a structural viewpoint it must be noted that the introductory formula of 35:1 is not repeated in 36:1, but in 36:16, so that the limits of this section extend beyond chapter 35. From that perspective it is evident that the unusual designation of Edom as Mount Seir has been deliberately employed to set up a contrast between the judgement which is pronounced on Mount Scir (Edom) and the salvation which is extended to the mountains of Israel. Juxtaposing these two prophecies throws into higher relief the deliverance the LORD provides for his people. More than that, these scenarios are two faces of the one coin: as the LORD intervenes to bring salvation to his people, this inevitably involves the imposition of judgement on those who have oppressed his people, and who will do so again unless they are prevented. Just as the judgement against the nations incorporated in the earlier prophecies against them cleared the way for Israel's restoration, the condemnation and overthrow of Edom performs a similar role here. The Edomites infiltrated the territory of Judah after the fall of Jerusalem (see the Introduction to 25:12–14). Their presence there would have been a barrier to the restoration of the covenant people, and so their removal was prophesied.

But there was more than the settlement of territorial boundaries envisaged in this oracle. Edom was characterised by inveterate hostility against Israel (see on 25:12–14). 'At this later point [from chapter 25] Edom's representative role as the quintessence of heathenism becomes clear and the necessity of its destruction as an

---

32. The sevenfold structure of the earlier oracles would not have been upset by the incorporation of additional material immediately after 25:14.

indispensable prelude to Israel's blessedness is correspondingly emphasized' (Woudstra 1968:29). The assistance the LORD in providing for his people includes their future security from all external pressures. It has therefore to be established that he alone rules over the nations of the earth and disposes of his territory as he pleases (Deut. 32:8–9). Edom's conduct challenges that rule, and typifies not only the world's animosity towards the LORD's people, but also its antagonism to all the arrangements he has made throughout his kingdom, because the essential characteristic of 'the world' in an ethical sense is that it has set itself against the LORD himself.

Theology of the Land. Land played a central role in the religious perception of the ancient Near East, and this was also the case for Israel as part of the LORD's covenant provision for his people. Integral to the blessing that they received was the right of residence in his land. Unlike other peoples, Israel belonged in the first instance to God, who in consequence of this granted them tenure of the land. The prevailing cultural model was that the primary relationship was that between a god and the particular territory over which he had control, and his relationship with any people who inhabited that territory was a secondary matter (see on 8:12).

Each tribe and every family were allotted a portion in the land whose borders were guaranteed by God (Num. 34:1–15). God blessed the land as a whole when the people served him faithfully (e.g., Deut. 28:1–6, 8–9, 11–12). But rebellion against their covenant King not only affected the condition of the land, but ultimately undermined their occupancy of it. Those who inhabited God's land had to be pure if they were to retain the privilege of living in the presence of God.

(1) Denunciation of Edom's Treachery (35:1–15)

There is a marked change of tone from the covenant harmony between the LORD and his people with which chapter 34 ends. This section is dominated by the key root *šāmam*, which pictures desolation and the horror to which it gives rise by occurring ten times (35:3 [2×], 4, 7 [2×], 9, 12, 14, 15 [2×]). However, it is no longer the punishment which the LORD imposes on Jerusalem which is in view. The focus is on Mount Seir, whose doom constitutes a warning to every nation and power seeking to assert itself against the LORD and his people. All peoples are under his scrutiny and are liable to judgement for their arrogance and wrongdoing. Moreover, it would be a source of encouragement to Israel to be reminded that, when the LORD intervenes to defend and restore his people, no adversary will be allowed to block the execution of his purpose.

The structure of the prophecy is determined by the fourfold occurrence of the recognition formula, so that after the introductory verses (35:1-2) there are four subsections: 35:3-4, 5-9, 10-12a, 12b-15. Though it is not possible to establish that they were originally uttered together, that seems probable. The two central oracles are judgement oracles structured with 'because ... therefore', while the first and last sections declare the LORD's opposition to mount Seir.

(a) The Desolation of Mount Seir (35:1-4)

> 35:1And the word of the LORD came to me, saying, 35:2'Son of man, set your face against Mount Seir and prophesy against it, 35:3and say to it, "Thus says the Lord GOD: Behold, I am against you, Mount Seir, and I will stretch out my hand against you and I will set you ⌊as⌋ a desolation and a source of horror. 35:4Your cities I will put a site of ruins, and you yourself will be a desolation. And you will know that I ⌊am⌋ the LORD."'

♦ **35:1-2** The message-reception formula marked the start of an oracle, which began with the characteristic divine mode of address to Ezekiel as ***Son of man*** (see on 2:1). The prophet was directed to ***set your face against*** (cf. 6:2), where 'against' (*'al*) denoted with a hostile gaze, and to ***prophesy against it***. This gesture was, of course, for the benefit of Ezekiel's original audience who were being informed of the LORD's opposition to Edom which had recently acted treacherously against Judah (cf. Obad. 11-14; Ps. 137:7; Lam. 4:21). However, the emphasis at this point did not fall on the reason for the LORD's adverse judgement on Edom, but on the fact of it, and its inevitable consequences.

Seir was an ancient term for the mountainous area at the southern end of Transjordanian plateau. Its northern border with Moab was at wadi Zered from where it stretched south to the gulf of Aqaba. The area was originally occupied by the Horites before they were displaced by descendants of Esau (Gen. 14:6; Deut. 2:12, 22). ***Mount Seir*** perhaps referred more particularly to the wooded slopes of mountains lying east of the Arabah (rift valley), which formed Edom's western border, but it could also be used by synecdoche for the whole of Edomite territory.

♦ **35:3** The LORD directed Ezekiel to act as his herald and announce his hostility to Mount Seir (= Edom). This was done using the opposition formula, ***Behold, I am against you*** (cf. 5:8), where 'you' is a masculine singular form, which continues to be used until 35:9b. This divine attitude would be translated into appropriate action, ***I will stretch out my hand against you*** (cf. 6:14). Those whose conduct the LORD condemned could not escape the exercise of God's power in judgement, ***I will set you ⌊as⌋ a desolation and a source of horror*** (as with Judah in 6:14; 33:28–29). The two nouns (*šəmāmâ ûməšammâ*) came from the same root 'to be desolate', 'to be laid waste' (*šāmam*), forms of which appeared ten times in the passage and set its tone.

♦ **35:4** The obliteration of Edom was further predicted in ***Your cities I will put a site of ruins.*** There would be no stronghold left in the land to provide security for the Edomites. ***You yourself will be a desolation*** repeated the thought of the previous verse to emphasise the certainty of the outcome. When it was then said, ***And you will know that I ⌊am⌋ the LORD***, the stark use of the recognition formula conveyed no indication that this would be anything other than a forced recognition of the strength and authority of the one they had so often dismissed and whose people they had belittled.

(b) Punishment of Edomite Atrocities (35:5–9)

Up to this point there has been no specification of Edom's misconduct, but now mention is made of their long-standing antipathy towards Israel and the help they gave in their destruction (35:5). This is followed by the announcement of judgement (35:6–9a), before the recognition formula again concludes the brief paragraph (35:9b). The use of 'perpetual' in 35:5, 9 forms an inclusion round the judgement speech.

> 35:5'Because you had perpetual enmity and gave over the people of Israel to the power of the sword at the time of their calamity, at a time of final punishment, 35:6therefore, as I live, declares the Lord GOD, I will surely make you ⌊into⌋ blood, and blood will pursue you; since you did not hate blood, blood will pursue you. 35:7And I will set Mount Seir a desolation and a source of horror, and I will cut off from it whoever passes through and whoever comes back. 35:8And I will fill its mountains with its slain; in your hills and your valleys and all your riverbeds—those slain by the sword will fall on them. 35:9⌊As⌋ perpetual desolations I will set you, and your cities will not be inhabited. And you will know that I ⌊am⌋ the LORD.'

♦ **35:5 *Because*** introduced this judgement speech by setting out the reasons for the LORD's verdict which was expressed in the following verses. ***You had perpetual enmity*** employed the same expression as had been used for the Philistines' aggressiveness towards the people of God (25:15). Edom's attitude had been perpetuated from the distant past (*'ôlām*, often rendered 'eternal', was also used for time stretching backwards or forwards as far as one cared to look). This dated back to the interaction between Jacob and Esau, 'Esau hated Jacob' (Gen. 27:41), but 'enmity' or 'hatred' also reflected the terms of the protevangelium, when the LORD addressed the serpent with the words, 'I will put enmity between you and the woman' (Gen. 3:15). It was this divinely-imposed enmity between the two seeds which underlay Edom's hostility to Israel, an attitude which they maintained over the ages.

A specific instance of Edom's attitude was evident in their conduct around the time of the fall of Jerusalem. They ***gave over the people of Israel to the power of the sword at the time of their calamity.*** 'The people of Israel' pointed to the covenant status of Judah including the inhabitants of Jerusalem, so that what Edom did to them was in effect action against their Overlord also. 'Gave over' or 'caused to be poured out' with 'blood' understood (cf. AV, NKJV) described Edom's treachery in abandoning Judah in its rebellion against Babylon after participating in the initial conspiracy (cf. Jer. 27:3). Edom left Judah to fend for itself against ***the power of the sword***, that is, the might of Babylon. It was only here that Ezekiel used the word 'calamity' (*'êd*) probably because of its similarity to Edom (*'ĕdôm*, 35:15) especially in the form 'their calamity' (*'êdām*; cf. Jer. 49:8; Obad. 13), whose sound also anticipated 'blood' (*dām*) in the following verse. ***At a time of final punishment*** (cf. 21:25, 29) seems to be a phrase coined by Ezekiel himself. 'Final' (lit. 'of end') referred to the overthrow of Jerusalem when the LORD's patience with Judah had been exhausted. 'Punishment' reflected the third sense of the word for 'iniquity' or 'guilt' (*'āwôn*), namely the penalty imposed as a result of wrongdoing (cf. 4:4).

♦ **35:6** ***Therefore*** introduced the retribution which corresponded to the indictment of the preceding verse. A notable feature of this verse is the fourfold occurrence of 'blood', emphasising the serious loss of life occasioned by Edom's action and the grave sanction which would be imposed on Edom as a result. This was also brought out by the combination of the oath formula and the signatory formula, ***as I live, declares the Lord GOD.*** The LORD would not shrug off Edom's misconduct, but would impose the extreme penalty of forfeiture of life.

*I will surely*³³ *make you ⌜into⌝ blood*³⁴ asserted that a violent catastrophe with loss of life was about to overtake Edom (cf. 16:38). English translations vary in their rendering of this clause, but its general import is clear.

The next clause restated the outcome just envisaged, but using the metaphor of the law of asylum. ***Blood will pursue you.*** In Israel an individual who caused another's death could be pursued for vengeance by his victim's close relative, the avenger, unless the manslayer attained the sanctuary offered by one of the cities of refuge (Num. 35:6–34; Deut. 19:1–13). In terms of the principle enunciated after the Flood, 'Whoever sheds man's blood, by man will his blood be shed' (Gen. 9:6), Edom had wilfully shed blood and was therefore culpable. So here the blood of Edom's victims was personified, and accorded the role of seeking vengeance for the loss of their lives.

Since you did not hate blood, blood will pursue you.³⁵ The Edomites had shown no aversion to lives being lost, and therefore they would not escape pursuit and appropriate reckoning for their conduct. The repetition stressed that the LORD would certainly bring this about.

♦ **35:7** The LORD then spoke not to, but about, Mount Seir as he addressed the exiles. ***I will set Mount Seir a desolation and a source of horror.*** The first noun was another form derived from the root *šāmam* (35:3), but it only occurred here, and may have been no more than a spelling variant. The combination again intensified the wretched barrenness of the outcome. ***Whoever passes through and whoever***

---

33. The *kî* with which the clause begins may not be asseverative ('surely'), but may introduce ('that') the first stated outcome, a construction found in Isa. 49:18; Jer. 22:24; Zeph. 2:9. The expected conjunction *'im-lō'* here introduces the second clause of the statement.

34. The LXX omits the first asseveration, 'I will surely make you into blood, and blood will pursue you', but it is attested in the Targum and Vulgate. Though it does interpose between the oath formula in 35:6a and the announced penalty, this is scarcely reason to omit it.

35. The rendering of the concluding part of the verse reflects that found in most English translations. *'im-lō'* normally introduces an emphatic affirmation (BDB §50a; Joüon §165; cf. 5:11), which would lead to the rendering, 'surely you hated blood', but that does not fit the context. Instead the two elements of the composite conjunction are taken separately with *'im* ('if') being given the sense 'when' or 'since', and the negative taken with the verb. Another approach assumes a metathesis of the first two consonants of the verb, and reads *nāśâ*, 'to bear' rather than *śānē'*, 'to hate', yielding 'you shall bear ⌜the guilt⌝ of blood' (cf. Zimmerli 1983:224; Greenberg 1997:713).

comes back was an instance of a merism (cf. Zech. 7:14; 9:8), which indicated human movement of any sort, not merely that of travellers. The LORD would ***cut off*** from Mount Seir every sign of human life.

♦ **35:8** The description of the LORD's activity in bringing judgement on the land continued with, ***I will fill its mountains with its slain***, where 'its'/'his' refers to Mount Seir, that is, the Edomites. 'The slain' (AV, NIV, ESV) rather than 'its slain' derives from some Septuagint manuscripts, but is an inferior reading. It was not living people who would be found inhabiting the mountains; only corpses would remain to indicate the extent of the catastrophe. Switching back to second person forms (a feature of Hebrew style), it was predicted that ***in your hills and your valleys and all your riverbeds—those slain by the sword will fall on them.*** The listing of specific sites (cf. 6:3; 36:4, 6) added graphic potency to the description of widespread carnage.

♦ **35:9** The LORD further decreed that ⌊as⌋ ***perpetual desolations I will set you***. The plural 'desolations' (a plural of intensity; again derived from *šāmam*, cf. 35:3) pointed to how extensive the devastation would be. 'Perpetual desolations' echoed 'perpetual enmity' (35:5) as the LORD's response. ***Your cities will not be inhabited.***[36] Once more (35:4) the impact of divine judgement on Edom was portrayed in terms of abandoned cities which could no longer afford security to any. This situation would compel Edom to acknowledge whose hand had been at work against them. The recognition formula, ***And you will know that I*** ⌊am⌋ ***the LORD***, had a second person masculine plural subject, whereas a singular 'you' was employed in 35:4, 12, and a third person form in 35:15. It would seem to be addressed not just to the Edomites as a group, but to each individual among them.

(c) Land Grabbing Punished (35:10–12a)

Another judgement speech against Edom adds to the accusations of their perpetual hatred of Israel and of their joy over its downfall the indictment that, after the fall of Jerusalem, they also encroached on Judah's territory. The accusation is again introduced with 'because' (35:10), and the verdict stated after 'therefore' in 35:11. The structure of the remainder of the oracle has been variously analysed. Here the

---

36. The kethib *têšabnâ* is a plene spelling of *tēšabnâ*, 'they will be inhabited' (cf. 29:11), with the fuller spelling possibly being employed to prevent the form being read in the manner suggested by the qere, which has *tāšōbnâ*, 'they will return' (cf. AV), possibly 'they will be restored'.

view is taken that the recognition formula in 35:12a ends the third unit of the oracle, so that it is patterned similarly to 35:5–9. Furthermore, this analysis is reinforced by the record of Edomite speech in 35:12b, which would parallel that in 35:10, so that the two concluding paragraphs have a comparable sequence since the recognition formula recurs at the close of 35:15. However, others point to the messenger formula with which 35:14 begins, and argue that it introduces the final unit of the oracle. On this basis the two cited Edomite speeches (35:10, 12b) form an inclusion around the third paragraph. But that arrangement leaves the recognition formula of 35:12a oddly embedded within that paragraph. Still, on either approach, the theme of judgement against Edom pervades the message.

> 35:10ʹBecause you said, "The two nations and the two lands will be mine and we will take possession of it"—but the LORD was there— 35:11therefore, as I live, declares the Lord GOD, I will deal ⌊with you⌋ according to your anger and according to your jealousy ⌊with⌋ which you acted because of your hatred against them; and I will make myself known among them when I judge you. 35:12aAnd you will know that I ⌊am⌋ the LORD.'

♦ **35:10** A new accusation centred on Edom's unjustifiable intention to occupy the Promised Land. ***Because you said*** (a singular verb) referred to Edom's national policy of overrunning ***the two nations and the two lands***[37], Israel and Judah,[38] so as to make them ***mine***. Various Edomites voiced their target: ***and we will take possession of it*** 'the land' viewed as a whole). Though the political reality to their west had become that of a divided and conquered land, the singular ***it*** showed that their perception of it was still of its previous unity (cf. 37:15–28).

The disjunctive clause, ***but the LORD was there***, indicated that there was an obstacle in the way of Edom fulfilling its strategy. What may well have been prophetic commentary rather than divine speech showed that the Edomites had failed to take account of the LORD's view of the situation. Instead they were acting on the basis of contemporary Near Eastern thought in which the power of a land's patron deity determined its security and prosperity. A defeated land

---

37. The repeated use of ʾet, the object marker, with 'the two nations' and 'the two lands' is unusual in that they form the composite subject of the following verb *tihyenâ*, 'they will be' (cf. *IBHS* §10.3.2b; Joüon §125j (3)).

38. Renz (1999:211) notes how 'people' is avoided. 'Nations' defined political entities and 'lands' described 'territory', but there were not two peoples, but one sadly-divided kinship unit.

implied a defeated deity who could be written off, and whose realm could be raided with impunity. However, although the LORD had removed his people from the land, had permitted it and his Temple to be devastated, and had in the process removed his Glory-presence from it, yet he had not renounced control of the territory. So it remained the case that he alone could bestow possession/inheritance of the land (cf. 11:15). Edom had its own territory (Deut. 2:1–7), and opportunistic claims to the land of Israel were an affront to the LORD and his purposes—purposes which would culminate in 'The LORD is there' (48:35).

♦ **35:11** The combination of the oath and confirmation formulas in ***Therefore, as I live, declares the Lord GOD*** repeated the solemn introduction to the divine verdict found in 35:6. ***I will deal ⌐with you¬ according to your anger and according to your jealousy*** (*qin'â*; here equivalent to 'envy', cf. 5:13) stressed the proportionality of the LORD's retribution against Edom. The Edomites had been driven by anger (cf. Amos 1:11) and jealousy, a spiteful combination which Hummel likens to 'fanaticism' (2007:1022). They ***acted because of your hatred against them***, that is, with unthinking antagonism against Israel and Judah, which had fomented over the centuries.

I will make myself known among them[39] ***when I judge you.*** This referred to 'them', the covenant people, to whom the LORD's judgement upon Edom would provide evidence of his powerful intervention on their behalf against their enemies.

♦ **35:12a** As a result of the same intervention it will also be the case that ***you*** (masculine singular = Edom) ***will know that I ⌐am¬ the LORD.*** Because of what happened to them, Edom would be forced to acknowledge the LORD's sovereign status.

(d) Rejoicing over Edom's Desolation (35:12b–15)

> ³⁵:¹²ᵇ'I have heard all your blasphemies which you uttered against the mountains of Israel, saying, "They have been laid desolate; they have been given to us as food." ³⁵:¹³And you have made great against me with your mouth, and you have multiplied against me your words, ⌐but¬ I myself have heard ⌐it¬. ³⁵:¹⁴Thus says the Lord GOD: When the whole earth rejoices, I will make you a source of horror. ³⁵:¹⁵Like your rejoicing over the inheritance of the house of Israel because it

---

39. The LXX has 'and I will make myself known among you [singular]' (cf. NRSV), which is undoubtedly the easier reading.

was desolate, so I will make you; you will be a source of horror, Mount Seir and all Edom, all of it. And they will know that I ⌊am⌋ the LORD.'

♦ **35:12b** For the division of the verse, see the Introduction to 35:10–12a above. *I have heard* led into a further specification of Edom's sin of which the LORD was aware. *All your blasphemies* employed a root which generally had the sense of speaking disdainfully or insultingly against the LORD. Hezekiah had used a related noun to refer to the Rabshakeh's disrespectful claim that the LORD was as powerless to save his people as other nations' gods had been in the face of Assyrian might (2 Kgs. 19:3 ‖ Isa. 37:3; cf. AV, NKJV). But here the focus of the Edomite speech was not the LORD himself—he had already been dismissed as impotent—but *against the mountains of Israel* (cf. 36:1).

The Edomites were depicted as looking rapaciously at the impoverished, ruined, and largely depopulated land. *They have been laid desolate*, that is, 'they have lost their inhabitants and all their buildings', with the plural subject referring to the *mountains of Israel.*[40] *They have been given* may well indicate their perception that this was done by their own gods, or else by the LORD through his seeming desertion of the land. The opportunity before them seemed to be just theirs for the taking, while *as food* depicted them as intending to devour the resources of the land.

♦ **35:13** Two clauses described the presumptuous speech of the Edomites. *You have made great against me with your mouth*. This may have implied 'made themselves great' (e.g. NRSV) by inflated claims regarding themselves (cf. Obad. 12) and so indirectly deprecating the LORD, but more probably they spoke directly against the LORD in withering and dismissive terms. Either way, they were on a collision course by vaunting themselves against him.

You have multiplied[41] *against me your words.* This implied

---

40. The kethib has the feminine singular form *šāmēmâ*, 'it [the land] has been desolated', which would continue the feminine singular reference 'of it' (35:10) to the land. The qere has the plural form *šāmēmû*, 'they have been desolated', and this is generally preferred in English translations as continuing the immediately preceding reference to 'the mountains of Israel' and also agreeing with the following plural verb, 'they have been given'.

41. The verb *'ātar* (hiphil) ordinarily has the sense 'to make supplication' (to God), but that does not really fit here. On the basis of an Aramaic root, it is suggested that a homonymous root is present here which has the sense 'to be abundant', and hence in the hiphil 'to make abundant' (BDB 801).

excessive, boastful speech, which did not pass unnoticed. *I myself have heard it* picked up the expression at the beginning of the previous verse, and emphasised not only the LORD's awareness of what was occurring but also his attention and interest in the developing situation. Whatever Edom might suppose, he had not been deposed from his superintendence of the affairs of the earth. There was nothing which would escape his scrutiny or evade his assessment.

♦ **35:14** Though the 'therefore' which typically preceded the divine verdict did not occur, it was a modified form of judgement speech which was introduced by the messenger formula, ***Thus says the Lord GOD***. The scope of the divine speech extended beyond Edom's future to anticipate a time *When the whole earth rejoices*. This would be the result of divine intervention to rectify the oppression which existed on earth. But Edom as the enemy of the LORD's people would not be able to join in the otherwise universal celebration of divine salvation. *I will make you a source of horror* (*šəmāmâ*, cf. 35:3), where assonance reinforced the contrast with 'rejoices' (*śāmaḥ*; similarly in the following verse).

♦ **35:15** The retributive correspondence between the offence and the divine penalty was further underlined by the comparison, *like your rejoicing over* (lit., 'with respect to') *the inheritance of the house of Israel*, where 'your rejoicing' was deliberately and ironically contrasted with 'rejoices' in the previous verse. 'Inheritance' (*naḥălâ*) provided the theological clue to the interpretation of the scene. Israel's tenure of the land had been bestowed on them by the LORD (cf. 44:28; Deut. 12:9), and to rejoice in seeing that undone was not merely an exercise in land grabbing or in getting the better of the Israelites, but it betrayed an inner opposition to the whole divine administration of affairs on earth and to the LORD himself. *Because it was desolate* (*šāmam*; cf. 35:3) turned the focus of the comparison from rejoicing to waste and ruin, and linked it to the sentence the LORD pronounced: *so I will make you*.

The physical devastation of the land would be matched by the reaction of those who viewed it because *you will be a source of horror* (*šəmāmâ*, cf. 35:14). *Mount Seir and all Edom, all of it* emphasised that no part of the land would escape the catastrophic penalty that the LORD would impose on it. In the face of such judgement, it was foretold that *they will know that ⌊I⌋ am the LORD*. This concluding occurrence of the recognition formula averred that the Edomites would be forced to acknowledge the LORD's sovereignty and power.[42] It was starkly presented, and did not hold out any hope that their submission would have any element of genuine remorse.

REFLECTION

- Edom's 'perpetual enmity' (35:5) was a display of fanaticism, a deep-seated hostility towards Israel which was passed down unthinkingly from generation to generation. This nursed grudge festered below the level of human rationality, being nurtured by satanic forces intent on frustrating and opposing the purposes of God, especially as they could be seen in his favour extended to his people. Here the doom awaiting such antagonism is set out with no hint of it being averted. However, before his conversion the apostle Paul had been gripped by such a fanatical spirit. 'I persecuted this Way to the death' (Acts 22:4). 'Indeed I myself was convinced that I ought to do many hostile things against the name of Jesus of Nazareth. ... Raging furiously against them I persecuted ⌊them⌋ even to foreign cities' (Acts 26:9, 11). But the former 'blasphemer, persecutor, and insolent antagonist' (1 Tim. 1:13) received mercy.
- There are no double standards with the LORD, as is shown by the parallels between this passage and 6:1–10, addressed to the mountains of Israel. In both passages the hostile-orientation formula is used and a command given to prophesy (6:2; 35:2); the LORD's hand is stretched out against the subjects of the oracle (6:14; 35:3); there will be many slain (6:4, 7; 35:8); cities will lie desolate and in ruins (6:6; 35:4). One difference is that whereas chapter 6 condemns Israel's pagan worship, nothing here is said about Edom's religion. Even so, the LORD's punishment of Edom matched his treatment of Israel. His rule is universal, and his standards do not vary.
- 'It has been said that the prophecies against the nations serve to demonstrate that Yahweh's presence and power are not confined to one nation only, but that he is the nations' Sovereign. There is a sense in which this is true, but this should not be used to obliterate the equally valid truth that Yahweh, by his own volition and by sacred covenant, has attached himself savingly to one people and to one country. Dt. 32:8, 9 represents Yahweh as being both the

---

42. In the earlier part of 35:15 and in 35:14, 'you' is masculine singular, whereas in the recognition formula there is a switch to the third person plural, though the LXX has 'and you will know'. The change to the third person coincides with the focus of Ezekiel's speech moving from Mount Seir to those who are his immediate audience, his fellow exiles, to whom he speaks about Edom in the third person, dropping his rhetorical posture.

sovereign of the nations and the unique Lord of his people' (Woudstra 1968:31). The LORD's devastating judgement upon Edom would be imposed to provide relief and security to his own people.
* The spiritual element underpinning the use of the recognition formula, 'And they will know that I ₓamˌ the LORD,' is not always apparent. In 35:9, 12, however, it clearly conveys the enforced recognition of the LORD's supreme authority and power while retaining a virulent animosity against him. This description corresponds to the LORD subduing the enemies of his people and turning his hand against their foes so that 'those who hate the LORD would feign obedience towards him, and their doom would last for ever' (Ps. 81:15). The fate of Edom is a solemn warning to all those who fail to 'seek the LORD while he may be found; call on him while he is near' (Isa. 55:6). The time will come when the overtures of his grace fall silent and the day of reckoning arrives.
* The LORD's punitive justice will overtake regimes which are hostile to his people and maltreat them. This stands as a reminder to all oppressive regimes which consider themselves at liberty to disregard divine warnings and persecute his people (cf. Ps. 9:19–20).

(2) Reversal of Depredations of Israel's Enemies (36:1–15)

Although in 36:1 the LORD turns to address the prophet, there is no other stylistic indication of a break at this point, certainly not one sufficiently significant to warrant a chapter division. The prophecy continues with the obverse to the preceding section announcing judgement against Mount Seir (Edom) by presenting the salvation which will come to the mountains of Israel.

Even by Ezekiel's standards, the repetition of formulaic speech is noteworthy in this section. The messenger formula, 'Thus says the Lord GOD,' occurs in each verse from 36:2 to 36:7 (and also in 36:13). There are three commands to prophesy (36:1, 3, 6). 'Because' followed by repeated instances of 'therefore' provides an elaborate structure for 36:2–7, and a similar, simpler structure exists in 36:13–14. These and other features have suggested to critics that a later editor composed this passage from by bringing together a number of fragments as well as including accidental repetition or near repetition. However, it is impossible to use modern stylistic criteria to determine ancient authorship. Rather than being a sign of a supplementary and ill-presented farrago, repetition was a device which was often employed for emphasis, and here may well have drawn attention to the extent of the LORD's commitment to Israel's renewal.

In both sub-sections, those addressed are ostensibly the mountains of Israel, but this is a rhetorical device for speaking to Ezekiel's immediate audience, the exiles, about what will happen when the people are restored to the land. First, they are reassured that the LORD will deal with the problem of the hostility of surrounding nations who have ravaged the land (36:1–7). Then he predicts a time of fruitfulness for the mountains of Israel (36:8–15). Restoration will be to a land prepared to receive the returning people (36:8–12). Finally, a short disputation address clarifies the status of the land (36:13–15).

(a) Israel Reassured (36:1–7)

36:1'But ⌐as for⌐ you, son of man, prophesy to the mountains of Israel and say, "O mountains of Israel, hear the word of the LORD. 36:2Thus says the Lord GOD: Because the enemy has said against you, 'Aha!', and 'The ancient heights have become our possession', 36:3therefore prophesy and say, Thus says the Lord GOD: Because of the very fact that they made ⌐you⌐ desolate and trampled you from round about that you might become a possession for the remainder of the nations, and you have been taken up upon the lips of talkers and slandered by people, 36:4therefore, O mountains of Israel, hear the word of the Lord GOD: Thus says the Lord GOD to the mountains and to the hills, to the ravines and to the valleys and to the desolate ruins and to the abandoned cities which have become plunder and derision for the remainder of the nations which ⌐are⌐ from round about. 36:5Therefore thus says the Lord GOD: Surely in the fire of my jealousy I have spoken against the remainder of the nations and against Edom all of it, in that they have given my land to themselves as a possession with wholehearted rejoicing ⌐and⌐ with inner scorn, so that they might empty it for plunder. 36:6Therefore prophesy concerning the land of Israel, and say to the mountains and to the hills, to the ravines and to the valleys, Thus says the Lord GOD: Behold, in my jealousy and in my fury I have spoken because you have borne the insults of nations. 36:7Therefore thus says the Lord GOD: I myself have raised my hand, ⌐saying⌐, Surely, ⌐as for⌐ the nations which are round about you, they themselves will bear their insults." '

♦ **36:1** The message-reception formula was not used to introduce this material (which was thus distinguished from 36:16), and it was therefore intended to be heard in close connection with what preceded, and not as a separate address. It was, however, marked by the transitional formula, ***But ⌐as for⌐ you***, with the standard divine address to the prophet, *son of man* (cf. 2:1). Ezekiel was commanded to turn from Mount Seir and to *prophesy to* (*ʾel*) *the mountains of Israel*. This description had first occurred in 6:2-3, where the mountains were also personified and addressed, but there they had been the site for idolatrous worship. Now the figure of speech was incorporated into a message of consolation and deliverance. 'The mountains of Israel' also looked back to 35:12 and Edom's blasphemous boasting against them, coupled with her rejoicing over the house of Israel (35:15).

There was, however, another factor which motivated using the description, 'the mountains of Israel'. It was a convenient way 'to speak explicitly about the land as a whole rather than about Jerusalem as the representative of the nation' (Renz 1999:110). Jerusalem, and especially the monarchy associated with it, had become so corrupt that it could not be viewed as the foundation for the restored people. The breath of fresh mountain air spreading over their homeland presented suitable imagery for the purged and renewed land where only those truly loyal to the LORD would have right of entry and settlement.

♦ **36:2** An elaboration of the 'because ... therefore' pattern structured 36:2-7, and the messenger formula, ***Thus says the Lord GOD***, was repeated in each of these verses. In this verse 'because' set out the reason for the LORD's intervention to recover his land from its adversaries. The only other occurrence of *the enemy* in Ezekiel was in 39:27, but the term commonly described the psalmist's foes (e.g., Pss. 8:2; 13:2). However, the presence of 'enmity' (35:5), derived from the same root, no doubt accounted for the use of 'enemy' here. The identity of the enemy was not made more specific until 36:5 where it was revealed as including both the remainder of the nations and Edom, who had all behaved similarly in speaking *against you* (*ʿal*). *Aha!* (cf. 25:3; 26:2) conveyed their gloating, malicious glee over Israel's ruin.

The ancient heights have become[43] ***our possession.*** This mirrored Edom's claim in 35:12. Although ***heights*** might designate the high places of pagan worship, that was not its sense here, but simply the physical mountains (cf. Deut. 32:13); also ***ancient*** renders the word often translated 'eternal' (cf. 'perpetual', 35:9). The expression pointed to the stability and permanence of the natural terrain of the land, as distinct from how subject to change were the peoples who

---

43. The verb *hāyətâ* is a feminine singular form although the subject 'heights' is plural. Presumably the noun is being taken as a collective term, and was therefore treated as a virtual singular.

occupied it (cf. expressions in Gen. 49:26; Deut. 33:15; Hab. 3:6). There were long memories of Israel being newcomers in the land. The term 'possession' (*môrāšâ*) had been used of God's grant of tenancy of the land to Israel at the Conquest (cf. 11:15; 33:24). So it was Edom's intention to do to Israel what they had previously done with respect to the Canaanites, and supplant them as occupants of the land. This claim was similar to that of the remaining population which had been left in Judah (33:24). Neither claim was divinely endorsed, and the words of the enemy substantiated the indictment against them.

♦ **36:3** *Therefore* did not here introduce a direct announcement of judgement; this oracle proclaimed salvation for the mountains, which would be achieved by the overthrow of their enemies. Ezekiel was instructed to inform his audience that the LORD would act on their behalf because of what the enemy had done to the mountains, that is, the land of Israel. The divine speech began with an intensified expression *because of the very fact that* (cf. 13:10).[44] There is uncertainty about the identification and meaning of the two verb forms *made ... desolate and crushed*.[45] The first term was almost certainly a form of the verb which Ezekiel often used (*šāmam*, cf. 35:3). At first glance the second verb seems to be derived from a root meaning 'to gasp' or 'to pant', and, when used of animals, 'to pester', but it is more probable that it is to be connected to a similarly spelled word with the sense 'to snap at' or 'to crush' (*šûp*). The term occurred in Genesis 3:15 in the well-known wordplay on the two uses of the verb, the seed of Eve will *crush* the serpent's head while the serpent will *snap at* his heel. Hence it could be seen that those *from round about* the land whose intention it was *that you* (plural) *might become a possession* (cf. 36:2) *for the remainder of the nations* were behaving as the offspring of the serpent in their enmity against the seed of the woman when they acted on their desire to take control of the mountains.

---

44. The implications of the unusual expression *yaʿan bəyaʿan* are not quite clear. It seems to make the causal connection more certain, cf. 'precisely because' (ESV), though many translations do not try to bring out the force of the expression (Joüon §170f (2)). *yaʿan*, 'because', has already occurred in 36:2, and its reoccurrence intensifies the emotionally charged nature of the divine speech.

45. *šammôt*, 'devastated', is most probably a qal infinitive of *šāmam*, 'to devastate', used in a transitive sense. *šāʾōp*, 'trampled', might be an infinite absolute of *šāʾap*, 'to gasp', but with the possibility of Aramaic influence it may also be identified as coming from *šûp*, 'to crush' (cf. Gen. 3:15). Early versions struggled with this expression, and present various interpretations.

'Remainder of the nations' did not signify the survivors of the nations after divine judgement, though this was Ezekiel's usage elsewhere (5:10; 9:8; 11:13); it simply referred to the others who were not part of the covenant community.

As well as suffering from harassment and aggression, the mountains had been vilified by surrounding peoples. *You have been taken up upon the lips of talkers.*[46] The last phrase was literally 'upon lip of tongue', with 'lip' considered as that which produced the sound, whereas 'tongue' focused more on the individuality of the speaker. A similar phrase in Psalm 140:11 was used of a gossip; so here the mountains were portrayed as the theme of idle chatter. The following expression, *slandered by people* (lit., 'slander/ill report of people'), made clear the negative nature of their comments. The same noun was used of the adverse reports of the men sent to reconnoitre Canaan (Num. 13:32; 14:36–37). Possibly what was in view was the Jerusalem theology espoused by Judah in the century before the fall of the city. They had boasted before others that the LORD's presence and protection made their city inviolable to enemy capture, but in the light of events the Edomites were mocking such claims about Jerusalem.

♦ **36:4** Once more, *therefore* drew out another aspect of the situation, rather than announcing punishment on the enemies of Israel. The *mountains of Israel* were again summoned to *hear the word of the Lord GOD* (cf. 36:1). He again spoke *to the mountains and to the hills, to the ravines and to the valleys*, a list which echoed 35:8 regarding Edom, but with a very different outcome in view. Moreover, this list repeated the expression of 6:3 with the obvious intention of reversing the earlier pronouncement of judgement. Since the situation had changed in the meantime and judgement had been imposed, so in cataloguing the features of the land there had to be added *to the desolate ruins* (cf. 33:24) *and to the abandoned cities.* What had earlier been described as 'food' for Israel's enemies (34:8; 35:12) was now explicitly called *plunder.* However, 'plunder' (*baz*) probably incorporates a play on the similarly sounding verb 'to despise' (*bāzâ*), although the term that was in fact used here is *derision* (*laʿag*, cf. 23:32). The land had been subjected to a combination of physical depredation and subjective ridicule.

---

46. The verb *wattēʿălû* is a *forma mixta*, with affinities to both an imperfect niphal, *tēʿālû*, 'you have been taken up', and an imperfect qal, *taʿălû*, 'you came up'. It is difficult to determine the origin of such forms, whether from a dialectal variation or a scribal conflation of two text forms.

♦ **36:5** Again *therefore* and the messenger formula introduced the LORD's reaction to the situation. This was no detached assessment, but another furious blast. *Surely* reinforced the strength of the LORD's statement with an oath. *In the fire of my jealousy* (*qinʾâ*, cf. 5:13) described the LORD's passionate commitment to all the arrangements he had instituted in connection with his covenant and his people, and which he zealously strove to protect and maintain. Accordingly he reassured the mountains (and the exiles) *I have spoken against the remainder of the nations* (cf. 36:4) *and against Edom, all of it*[47] (cf. 35:15). The verb implied not just past action, but the persistence of the royal decree which had been issued. Alternatively, the verb may have had virtually performative status, 'I ⌐hereby⌐ speak' (Introduction §6.3d), and so should be translated as a present (cf. NRSV). At this point Edom was explicitly named because it had taken a lead role in annexing Israelite territory.

The sinful behaviour of the nations was again specified to underline the enormity of their offence and to show that the LORD had taken cognisance of it. In *they have given* the verb was used in a secondary sense of 'to set' or 'to allocate', and hence 'to claim' (cf. 11:15), but this allocation was *to themselves* with blatant disregard of the fact that it remained *my land*. No matter what the LORD had brought on his land and its inhabitants, he had not abandoned his rights over it (cf. 35:10). There was no way it could become *a possession* (cf. 36:2) of others without his permission. But Edom and the nations had not acknowledged any such restrictions and had proceeded *with wholehearted rejoicing* (lit., 'with rejoicing of totality of heart'; for 'heart', see on 36:26). They had also, in the manner of Ammon and Philistia recorded earlier, acted *with inner scorn* (lit., 'with scorn of soul', cf. 25:6, 15). Their gleeful contempt for the LORD and his land required a response. They were not to be permitted to carry out their intention, *so that they might empty it for plunder.*[48] Possibly their plan was to clear the land of any remaining inhabitants by killing or enslaving them, and so occupy it and commandeer its resources.

---

47. The Aramaic spelling of the suffix on *kullāʾ*, 'all of her/it', refers to the land (feminine) of Edom, rather than the people of Edom, which would require a masculine reference.

48. The clause is somewhat obscure in that *migrāšāh* appears to be a noun, 'her/its neighbouring territory' or 'open pasture land' (cf. NIV), but in that case the introductory *ləmaʿan*, 'so that', lacks a following verb. It seems more plausible to take the form as an Aramaic style infinitive with a prefixed *mem* from the root *gāraš*, 'to drive out, to empty'.

♦ **36:6** Most of the contents of this verse repeated what was said elsewhere, though here 'the mountains of Israel' (36:1) was replaced by ***the land of Israel*** (cf. 7:2). ***To the mountains and to the hills, to the ravines and to the valleys*** reflected the specification of 36:4. ***In my jealousy and in my fury I have spoken*** corresponded to the earlier 'in the fire of my jealousy I have spoken' (36:5). ***Because you have borne the insults of nations*** referred to cutting remarks intended to reflect or produce disgrace (cf. 16:52, 54). Whereas 36:5 reiterated the element of plunder in the nations' activities from 'plunder and derision' (36:4), here the latter item was focused on. Both combined to form the basis for the LORD's action.

♦ **36:7** For a last time the introductory words occur, ***Therefore thus says the Lord GOD***. The verb, ***I have raised my hand***, a gesture associated with taking a solemn oath (cf. 20:5), may have reflected a past action with continuing effect, or it may be a performative perfect in that through the prophet's delivery of the message, the LORD 'hereby raises his hand' to give this solemn commitment (Introduction §6.3d). ***Myself*** (the expressed subject of the verb) accentuated the extent of his personal involvement. ***Surely, ⌊as for⌋ the nations which are round about you, they themselves will bear their insults.*** The retribution which would come on them would be proportionate to, and conditioned by, the form of their offence, a theme brought out again in 36:13–14.

REFLECTION
- 'They have given my land to themselves' (36:5). 'They have given' displayed an aspect of mankind's original rebellion against God. The Edomites arrogated to themselves powers and prerogatives which inherently belonged to the Creator. They considered themselves competent to set aside his ordinances and to order their affairs as they saw fit. Moreover, *to themselves* revealed the self-centred motivation which informed their conduct. Though the outward circumstances of humanity have changed substantially over the centuries, the basic paradigm of human sin has been replicated on countless occasions.
- Administration of human justice is ideally presented as a matter of calm, dispassionate judicial assessment—and rightly so. Fallen humanity is susceptible to becoming emotionally involved in evaluating a situation and thus failing to deliver a verdict that is fair. But that does not apply to God. It intensifies his judgements against those who oppose him that his verdict never deviates from what their

sin has incurred, but still because of the personal affront given to him by their conduct, divine justice is administered 'in my jealousy and in my fury' (36:6). It is not cold, detached, indifferent justice that characterises the LORD's treatment of those who transgress his law.

(b) Enjoying the LORD's Favour (36:8–15)

³⁶:⁸'But ⌞as for⌟ you, mountains of Israel, you will produce your branches and you will bear your fruit for my people Israel, for they are close to arriving. ³⁶:⁹For, behold, I am for you, and I will face you, and you will be ploughed and sown. ³⁶:¹⁰And I will multiply human beings upon you, the whole house of Israel, all of it, and the cities will be inhabited and the ruins rebuilt. ³⁶:¹¹And I will multiply upon you human beings and animals, and they will multiply and be fruitful, and I will cause you to dwell as ⌞in⌟ your former times, and I will do good ⌞more⌟ than ⌞in⌟ your beginnings. And you will know that I ⌞am⌟ the LORD. ³⁶:¹²And I will make human beings walk upon you, ⌞even⌟ my people Israel, and they will possess you, and you will be their inheritance, and you will no longer bereave them of children. ³⁶:¹³Thus says the Lord GOD: Because ⌞they⌟ are saying to you, You are devouring human beings, and you have bereaved your nation of children, ³⁶:¹⁴therefore you will no longer devour human beings and you will no longer bereave your nation of children, declares the Lord GOD. ³⁶:¹⁵And I will cause you to hear the insults of the nations no longer, and the reproach of peoples you will bear no longer, and your nation you will make to stumble no longer, declares the Lord GOD.'

♦ **36:8** *But ⌞as for⌟ you* signalled a turn in the prophecy. At last the LORD addressed the *mountains of Israel*, not in terms of being relieved of their oppressors, but as regards the benefits of fruitfulness which would be bestowed on them. *You will produce your branches and you will bear your fruit* from the many plants which would grow from the soil found on their slopes. Much of the land of Israel was, of course, elevated and hilly, but this did not prevent fruit and other trees from growing there. It was 'a land of wheat and barley, of vines and fig trees and pomegranates, a land of olive oil and honey' (Deut. 8:8), and these would again be produced in abundance. *For my people Israel* clarified that this was divine preparation *for they are close to arriving.* There was no acknowledgement that there were any survivors left in the land; the LORD's concern was for those whom he would bring back there. While the people might subsequently maintain the fertility of the land, it had been arranged beforehand by the LORD, just as had been the case when they had entered it after the Exodus. Indeed, the reference to the garden of Eden in 36:35 gives substance to the parallel which Greenberg (1997:719) notes with the creation narrative where the trees were planted before Adam was placed in the garden to keep it (Gen. 2:5–16).

'They are close to arriving' or 'near to coming' did not specify precisely when this would occur, or precisely where they would arrive. The emphasis was rather on the certainty of God's promises being fulfilled, and the lavish arrangements he would make for his people's homecoming. The matter was presented in this way to urge upon Ezekiel's hearers their need to repent and be counted among 'my people Israel' so that they could participate in this grand homecoming whenever it took place.

♦ **36:9** Although *I am for you* (plural, referring to the mountains) renders the same words as 'I am against you' (13:8; cf. 5:8), the difference in orientation, which was present only here, was obvious. It pointed to the great reversal of the condition of the exiles which had been revealed to Ezekiel. *I will face you* ('turn ˻my face˼ to you'), that is, the LORD would no longer hide his face from them in rejection (cf. Deut. 31:17–18), but turn his countenance towards the mountains of Israel in a gracious gesture of favour and acceptance. The language reflected that of the Aaronic benediction (Num. 6:24–26), and also the covenant blessings of Leviticus 26:9, 'I will face you and make you fruitful and multiply you and will confirm my covenant with you.' Previously that outcome had been held before the people as the blessing to be maintained through obedience; now it was to be bestowed on them again by divine grace. *You will be ploughed and sown.* It was still the mountains which were to be treated in this way.

♦ **36:10** The future time of blessing was described in terms of the land being repopulated, *I will multiply human beings* (*’ādām*, cf. 2:1) *upon you. The whole house of Israel, all of it,* was an all-embracing, inclusive expression, probably conveying the incorporation of survivors of the northern kingdom into this future time of blessing, an idea developed in 37:15–28. While recent scholarship has brought out the extent to which the land remained populated during the exile because the poor of the land were not deported (2 Kgs. 25:12), the Biblical perspective was that the land had been emptied of those through whom the covenant promise would be restored. *The cities will*

be inhabited and the ruins rebuilt foretold the reversal of the conditions of 36:4.

♦ **36:11** The thought of the previous verse was then restated and amplified. ***I will multiply upon you human beings and animals*** (two singular collective nouns) described not merely repopulation but replenishment with livestock. No more would be heard of Edom's boast to take possession of them (35:10). ***They will multiply and be fruitful*** is often deleted as a later insertion because the words were omitted in the Septuagint. However, as in 36:8, there was a deliberate echo of the creation narrative in Genesis 1:22, 28, with the order of the verbs reversed, probably because of the initial 'multiply' in this and the preceding verse. The restoration would be a new creation in which the creation mandate would be fulfilled. In ***I will cause you to dwell as ⌊in⌋ your former times*** the 'you' remains ostensibly the mountains of Israel, the location where the LORD had specifically resolved to display his blessing and to be present in fellowship with his people.

But more than restitution of their former condition was promised. The description continued to resonate with creation language in ***I will do good ⌊more⌋ than ⌊in⌋ your beginnings.***[49] 'Beginning' echoes Genesis 1:1, and 'good' echoed the Genesis 1 evaluation formula, 'God saw that it was good' (e.g., Gen. 1:10). The comparative use of the preposition *min*, 'from', or 'than', registered a heightening of divine blessing from anything previously experienced. This also indicated that the prophecy would not be fully exhausted before the Second Coming and entry into heavenly bliss. With each successive wave of blessing towards the consummation of the promise, there would also be a deeper appreciation by the mountains of Israel (= the restored community of God's people) regarding the one who had bestowed all this on them: ***And you will know that I ⌊am⌋ the LORD.***

♦ **36:12** This further description of what the LORD's blessing would involve for the mountains of Israel made clear Israel's participation in this restoration. ***I will make human beings walk upon you.*** Their presence had already been foretold (36:10, 11), but God would grant them more than mere presence in the land. 'Walk' suggests that they would be free to move about, neither slaves whose movements were

---

49. *wəhēṭibōtî*, 'I will do good', involves another *forma mixta*, being a blend of two hiphil forms from cognate roots, *hēṭabtî* from *yāṭab*, 'to be good' (hiphil: 'do good'), and *hăṭîbōtî* from *ṭôb*, 'to be good' (cf. GKC §70e). This does not affect the sense or the allusion to the adjective *ṭôb*, 'good' in Gen. 1.

curtailed by their owners, nor those who were fearful because of enemy hostility. Greenberg (1997:721) relates 'walk' to the perception that legal rights of ownership might be established by walking through the land, just as Abraham had been divinely instructed to 'walk through the length and the breadth of the land' (Gen. 13:17; Josh. 24:3). That certainly fitted in with the explicit identification of those involved as *my people Israel*, the rightful heirs of the land. It also accorded with the declaration, *they will possess you,*[50] *and you will be their inheritance*, where 'you' referred to the mountains. 'Possess' (*yāraš*) indicated being accorded rights of residence and tenure (cf. 36:5), whereas 'inheritance' (*naḥălâ*), a term frequently found in Deuteronomy and Joshua, pointed more to the source of their status, by the grant and disposition of another party (cf. 44:28).

You will no longer bereave them of children, or 'cause them to be childless' (*šākal*), a thought repeated in the two following verses. This unusual expression predicted a reversal of 'I will send against you famine and evil beasts, and they will bereave you' (5:17). Famine and wild animals as agents of divine punishment were viewed as belonging to, and coming from, the mountains and the land. 'No longer' (cf. 12:23) contrasted what had been with what would be. It was repeated twice in 36:14, and three times in 36:15. There would no longer be occasion for God to use the land against the people so as to discipline them for their misconduct.

♦ **36:13** The divine speech in this verse and the next were connected by a 'because ... therefore' formulation which functioned to reinforce the theme of the last clause of 36:12. The land would never again become a threat to those who were permitted to inhabit it.

In the manner of a disputation speech the LORD cited the words or thoughts of others, but not here to refute them (36:14 implicitly acknowledged their accuracy); rather the conditions which gave rise to them would be eliminated. The subject of *are saying* was not specified. Presumably it was those who observed the history of the land and characterised it in this way. *To you* was masculine plural, pointing to the mountains of Israel, but the following references were feminine singular in respect of the land. *You*[51] *are devouring human*

---

50. At this point 'you' becomes singular, whereas earlier in the verse it was a plural form. Both were masculine forms pointing to the mountains or hill country of Israel, and so differed from the feminine forms introduced in 36:13.

51. The qere substitutes the ordinary form of the second person feminine singular pronoun, *'āt*, 'you', for the archaic spelling of the kethib, *'āttî*.

beings reflected the negative report of the faithless spies in Numbers 13:32 when they alleged that the land was an unsuitable and dangerous place to live in, perhaps a reference to famines or to earthquakes. ***You have bereaved your nation*[52] *of children*** used the language of 36:12 to refer to what had happened in the past, with the notable addition of 'your nation'. That referred to the political entity which occupied the territory, and which led to it suffering loss of its population. Although the kinship term 'people' was generally used of Israel as a party in covenant with the LORD, the more political term 'nation' (*gôy*) reflected the covenant promise to Abraham (Gen. 12:2).

♦ **36:14** ***Therefore*** did not here begin a judgemental pronouncement as might have been expected after the preceding 'because' (36:13). Instead it introduced the LORD's restorative provision in the light of all that had been brought on the people through the instrumentality of the land ('you' feminine; cf. 36:6). What had occurred in the past would be definitively superseded. ***You will no longer devour human beings*** (cf. 36:13). The land would become a channel of blessing, not of punishment. ***You will no longer bereave your nation of children*** (cf. 36:12, 13).[53] The people would be permitted to inhabit the land without facing deadly threats.

The signature formula, ***declares the Lord GOD***, concluded this and the following verse to give an emphatic end to the oracle. It may be that this was needed to counter pessimism among the exiles regarding their future and the LORD's intentions for them and to reassure them that they need not doubt his transforming and restoring grace.

♦ **36:15** A resounding threefold promise from the LORD assured the

---

52. The qere has a plural noun, *gôyēyik*, 'your nations', presumably those of north and south (cf. 35:10), whereas the kethib has a singular noun, *gôyēk*, 'your nation', a reading supported by the early versions and also preferred by modern translations. The same qere is repeated in 36:14 and 36:15, and is to be rejected there also.

53. There are two variant readings in this clause. For 'nation'/'nations', see the preceding note. The second variant is difficult to resolve. The kethib reads *təkaššəlî*, 'you will cause to stumble' from the root *kāšal*, whereas the qere transposes the first two consonants to read *təšakkəlî*, 'you will bereave' from the root *šākal*, which has already been used in 36:12, 13. However, in 36:14 the verb 'to stumble' occurs with no marginal variant although several Hebrew manuscripts do have 'you will bereave'. Both the LXX and the Peshitta omit the clause in 36:15. Possibly the repetition of 'devour'/ 'eat' in 36:14 from the preceding verse favours the qere.

land that previous conditions would be eradicated. Each clause ended with an emphatic *no longer* (cf. 36:12) as it was declared that the debilitating features of the past would be swept away by divine power. The common perception in the ancient Near East was that, once a curse was triggered, it took on an existence of its own and could not be reversed. Here it was emphatically declared that, just as the curses of the broken covenant were enacted by the will of the LORD, their continuing imposition was subject to his pleasure and control.

(1) *I will cause you* (feminine singular) *to hear the insults of the nations no longer.* This referred back to the utterances of surrounding groups as they cast Jerusalem's fall and Judah's devastation in their faces (36:6). Changed circumstances would deprive others of any basis for deriding the nation. It is one of the paradoxes of divine intervention that taunts about their disgrace hurled by the nations would be removed, but the people would experience real shame, though not from the mocking invective of their adversaries (cf. 36:26).[54]

(2) *The reproach of peoples you will bear no longer.* The term 'reproach' (*ḥerpâ*; cf. 5:14) summed up the mocking aspersions and disparagement directed at the land. That too would be removed.

(3) *Your nation*[55] *you will make to stumble no longer.* While 'stumble' is a difficult reading, it is not impossible and should not to changed to 'bereave'. But how could the land have caused the nation to stumble, that is, to fall into sin? Perhaps it was through its fruitfulness inducing a spirit of self-reliance which led them to depart from God (cf. Deut. 8:17–18). Zimmerli (1983:239) suggests that this may hint at the exiles perceiving that a new start in the land might be no more successful than the first. So God spoke to avert such despondency by emphasising the radical changes that he would ensure would occur.

---

54. 'Yahweh thus promises to eliminate the insults of the nations occasioned by Israel's shame, which serve no didactic purpose, and worse yet in Ezekiel's view, bring dishonor to Yahweh. The public dimension of shame is to be eliminated in the restoration, a restoration of which the private, inner experience of shame is a cardinal element' (Lapsley 2000b:159).

55. For *gôyēk*, 'your nation', the qere proposes reading *gôyayik*, 'your nations'. For this change, see on 36:13, 14. In this verse there is no change proposed in the qere for *takaššəlî*, 'you will make to stumble'. Hummel (2007:1032, 1044; cf. TEV) argues for the adoption of a variant manuscript reading which does repeat the verb 'bereaved' from the previous two verses, but this reading could hardly be said to be well supported or an obvious piece of terminology either.

REFLECTION
- 'I am for you, and I will face you' (36:5) echoed Israel's prayer for God to 'be gracious to us and bless us and make his face to shine upon us' (Ps. 67:1), itself a reflection of the Aaronic blessing, 'the LORD make his face shine upon you' (Num. 6:25). This described the reality of divine approval and bestowal of blessing. The imagery probably reflected that of being welcomed into a royal court and receiving the favours the king alone could grant a subject. 'In the light of a king's face there is life, and his favour is like the clouds of the late rains' (Prov. 16:15). So here in the description of Israel's restoration there is anticipated 'the time for the restoration of all the things about which God spoke by the mouth of his holy prophets from long ago' (Acts 3:21). Then there will be light, intense and pure, emanating from the presence of God himself (Rev. 21:23–24), accompanied by fruitfulness (Rev. 22:2).
- It is easy to look back and conclude that things are not what they once were. Instead those who take heart from the LORD's promises are exhorted to lay hold of the future summed up in his 'no longer' (36:14–15). The change that the LORD has committed himself to introduce will banish the misery and dejection of living in a fallen world. 'No longer will they hunger, and no longer will they thirst; there will strike them neither the sun nor any burning heat, because the Lamb in the midst of the throne will shepherd them, and he will guide them to springs of waters of life, and God will wipe away every tear from their eyes' (Rev. 7:16–17).

D. A New Heart and a New Spirit (36:16–38)

The LORD continues to set out how he will provide for the restoration of his people. He has indicated that he will provide new leadership (ch. 34) and a secure and renewed land (35:1–36:15). But while those changes are necessary to inaugurate the era ahead, they are not sufficient. It was with the people that the problems had arisen, and it is only as their outlook and conduct is decisively modified that the cycles of spiritual decay seen in the past will be broken. So here the LORD's focus is on how he will redeem and restore Israel.

Structure. The message-reception formula in 36:16 clearly marks the beginning of a new section, which concludes with the recognition formula in 36:38. That a break occurs there is reinforced by the way 37:1 heads the start of a new section.

Within these limits it is possible to identify four paragraphs by the introductory messenger formulas in 36:22, 33, 37. The middle two sections (36:22–32, 33–36) are addressed directly to the house of Israel, whereas the outer segments (36:16–21, 37–38) describe the people in the third person. The closing two sections are briefer than the others, and are often taken as subsequent expansions of earlier material (see on 36:23). However, they do fit in their present context, and, as before, the real question is who did the expanding. There is nothing to debar the prophet from being responsible for this when he collected his oracles into their present form.

Theme. The first section recounts the history of the LORD's relationship with Israel (36:16–21). This might seem to be a topic which has already been exhausted, but apparently the exiles still entertain the notion that the LORD will act for them just because of who they are. Instead it is emphasised that Israel incurred divine wrath because of their sinful conduct which polluted the LORD's land. He has therefore scattered them among the nations, but their presence there has been misinterpreted because it raises questions about the LORD's ability to defend his people. So the background to what follows is based on two premises: the defilement of Israel, and the LORD's vindication of his person and character.

The second, and longest, section begins with a command to the prophet to explain the situation carefully to the remaining covenant community (36:22–32). There is an inclusion round the paragraph, 'Not for your sake am I doing this' (36:22, 32), which encapsulates one of its basic themes. Israel's restoration will be divinely accomplished not because of Israel's worthiness but because of the LORD's desire to correct warped perceptions of who he himself is— which he will do by displaying his holiness and might. Furthermore, it would be irresponsible to return the people to the land without taking steps to remedy their spiritual condition by cleansing them from defilement (36:25, 29) and then by rendering them spiritually responsive. Relocation had to be accompanied by regeneration. They will then be fit to occupy the land (36:28) and enjoy the bounty which the LORD will provide (36:29–30). Even so, they will be contrite over their past conduct (36:31–32).

The third section is a relatively brief résumé of how completely the land will be transformed and of how surrounding nations will come to recognise why all this has befallen Israel (36:33–36).

The culminating, fourth section (36:37–38) pictures the harmony which will then prevail between the LORD and his people, who are once more compared to a flock of sheep. Their numbers will increase, and they will enjoy access to the LORD.

Throughout this section there is a recurrent emphasis that the LORD's action is not motivated by the people's ancestry or their previous status. Their violation of the demands of the covenant has deprived them of pleading for assistance in terms of their past covenant relationship with the LORD. Moreover, they have to recognise that they are incapable of dealing with their own guilt and defilement. They must accept that whatever happens is generated by the spontaneous initiative of God, who for his own reasons is motivated to reinstate and perpetuate the covenant relationship, and to renew the people. While this dependency upon God is humbling (36:31–32), it in fact undergirds the certainty and security of what will be provided precisely because it is not based on human achievement.

(1) For My Holy Name (36:16–21)

This retrospective section breaks the generally optimistic tone of these chapters with its reminder of the comprehensive penalty which has been imposed on the people (cf. ch. 20). This had been the consequence of their far-reaching rebellion, and so restoration required complete spiritual renewal.

It is, however, the astounding message of this unit that, though the punishment of the people had evoked the scorn of the nations against them and, more especially, against their God, he is going to act contrary to all human expectations. What awaits the people is not further punishment and utter annihilation, but restoration because of the LORD's adherence to the covenant commitments he has undertaken. So he will act not because of any merit or redeeming features in the people, but solely on account of his determination to vindicate his holy name (36:21).

> 36:16And the word of the LORD came to me, saying: 36:17'Son of man, ⌞while⌟ the house of Israel were dwelling upon their land, they defiled it with their way and with their deeds; their way was before me like the defilement of menstruation. 36:18And I poured out my fury upon them because of the blood which they had poured out upon the land and for their idols ⌞with which⌟ they had defiled it. 36:19And I dispersed them among the nations and they were scattered in the lands; according to their way and according to their deeds I judged them. 36:20And they came to the nations where they went, and they profaned my holy name when it was said of them, "These ⌞are⌟ the people of the LORD, and from his land they have gone

out?" ³⁶:²¹And I showed pity on account of my holy name which they, the house of Israel, had profaned among the nations where they came.'

♦ **36:16-17** After the message-reception formula at the start of the new section, the LORD addressed Ezekiel in his customary fashion using the vocative, *Son of man* (cf. 2:1). In an instance of the LORD taking his spokesman into his confidence (cf. Amos 3:7), he explained to Ezekiel why the exile had been necessary. He did so because the problems of the past shaped the way in which the restoration would take place. It was also a mark of the LORD's condescension that he couched his message in language which would readily resonate with Ezekiel who had been trained as a priest. Both the content and the form of what was said showed how completely the LORD verbalised his communication to match the mindset of his chosen recipient.

It had to be made clear that the exiles' current situation derived from what had happened ⌊*while*⌋ *the house of Israel were dwelling upon their land.* 'Their' expressed divine recognition that the Israelites had been given the right to occupy the land in terms of the covenant. But that had imposed conditions on their tenure, which they failed to observe. *They defiled it with their way and with their deeds.* 'Way' was a comprehensive term for lifestyle, conduct, while 'deeds' was somewhat more specifically the outward manifestation of their inner disposition, generally in a reprehensible fashion (for the pair, cf. 14:22-23; 20:43-44; 24:14; 36:19).

'Defiled' (*ṭāmēʾ*; cf. 4:14; 20:7) was priestly language for rendering something ritually unclean. The term recurred frequently in the prophecy with various objects: people defiled (or did not defile) themselves (4:14; 14:11; 20:7, 18), the Temple (5:11; 9:7; 23:38), the LORD's holy name (36:20; 43:7-8), or a neighbour's wife (18:6, 11, 15; 22:11; 23:17; 33:26). In the prophecy only in this and the following verse was the land said to be defiled, though the expression was found elsewhere.

One significant discussion of defilement is found in Leviticus 28, where Canaanite practices, such as incest, child sacrifice, homosexuality, and bestiality, were identified as abominations (Lev. 18:29) which caused defilement. The sequence was set out that the Canaanites had become defiled through such conduct, and in that way they had defiled the land, which resulted in the LORD punishing their iniquity by the land vomiting out its inhabitants (Lev. 18:24-25). Despite being warned to avoid such behaviour, Israel had failed to do so, and this had resulted in their expulsion also.

Their way was before me like the defilement of menstruation. While no moral guilt was involved in the uncleanness arising from menstruation, it was used to describe a situation of utter disgust (Lam. 1:9; Ezra 9:11). Moreover, the cultic condition of the woman required separation from the community for a time (Lev. 15:19–24, 25–33). That probably was the point of the comparison. The land had become defiled, but it was not morally culpable, and the appropriate remedy involved separation from it of the people to blame for its condition.

♦ **36:18** Israel's misconduct had aroused the LORD's anger, and so he had ***poured out my fury upon them*** (cf. 7:8) by swamping them with overwhelming calamity. Two reasons were advanced by the LORD for his response. ***Because of the blood which they had poured out upon the land.*** The repetition of 'pour' indicated the reciprocal nature of the LORD's sentence, and fitted in with earlier descriptions of the oppressive loss of life in Jerusalem (e.g., in 22:6, 27) to such an extent that it could rightly be called 'the city of bloodshed' (24:6). As well as this offence involving fellow members of the covenant community, there had been defiance against their covenant King: ***for their idols ⌞with which⌟ they had defiled it*** (cf. ch. 8). For Ezekiel's scatological terminology for 'idols', see on 6:4. Both wilful taking of human life (cf. Num. 35:33–34) and disregard of the sovereign right of God to their exclusive worship had polluted the land.

♦ **36:19** ***So I dispersed them*** (cf. 12:15; 20:23), as a result of which ***they were scattered in the lands.*** Block (1998:347) argues that the fixed period of seven days separation for the menstruant woman was matched by a fixed period of separation for neglect of the appointed sabbatical rests (Lev. 26:34–45; 2 Chron. 36:21). Also, the penalty imposed was proportionate to the offence committed: ***according to their way and according to their deeds I judged them*** (cf. 7:3).

♦ **36:20** Although the equitableness of the divine procedure was evident, it had an unfortunate consequence (cf. 20:9, 14, 22). ***They came*** was in fact a singular verb, 'he came', but the implied subject is the house of Israel (cf. 36:21), and a plural rendering makes for better English.[56] ***To the nations where they went*** was a way of stating generally that they were scattered to various nations (cf. 12:15).

---

56. Many emend on the grounds that *wayyābô'*, 'and he came', has arisen by metathesis from *wayyābō'û*, 'and they came'. Though some manuscripts have this reading, Hebrew idiom permits a change from a collective singular to a plural, and so the text need not be altered (cf. 14:1; 20:38).

The name of the LORD encapsulated all that he had revealed himself to be. In Exodus 34 the proclamation of the name of the LORD was effected by God setting out his character, attributes, person, and purpose (Exod. 34:5–7). 'My *holy* name' was used by metonymy for the LORD himself as the one set apart from all else in his creation. He possessed sovereign power and authority over it, which he exercised with unblemished justice. ***They profaned my holy name*** was employed in Leviticus 20:3; 22:2, 32 (cf. Lev. 18:21; 19:12; 21:6), in reference to deliberate violation of God's express commandments regarding child sacrifice, idolatry, false swearing, and improper behaviour in connection with offerings at the sanctuary. Such actions polluted and defiled God who was their king, and in whose kingdom they resided.

Here, however, the reference was not primarily to any action of the exiles, such as in 12:15–16; 14:22–23. It was their mere presence elsewhere which triggered this profanation *when it was said of them, 'These ⌊are⌋ the people of the LORD, and from his land they have gone out?'* 'The people of the LORD'—an expression found only here in Ezekiel, but equivalent to 'my people'—brought out the bond that existed between them. Consequently, according to the logic of heathendom, Israel's presence in exile was proof of the inadequacy and incompetence of their God who had been unable to protect them and who had been overwhelmed by the gods of other nations. Similar misperception by other peoples had been cited by Moses as an incentive for divine action (Exod. 32:12–13; Num. 14:15–24; cf. also Josh. 7:8–9). Here it formed the basis on which the LORD would act to expose this false interpretation by delivering his people from Babylon. He would not permit his supremacy to be obscured even among the heathen by the continuation of his people in exile. Of course, recourse to this action by the LORD would not have been needed had his people been obedient in the first place. Their conduct had meant that continued residence in the land had not been a valid option, but their presence among the nations was not viable either if the character of the LORD was to be vindicated.

♦ **36:21** *And I showed pity on account of my holy name.* It is not clear that 'show pity' (*ḥāmal*; cf. 5:11) is the most appropriate rendering here. That would point to the LORD's earlier withholding of judgement when he acted with compassion towards them because of his covenant commitment to which he had set his name. However, the context was after the imposition of judgement and the focus was on the LORD's desire to vindicate his name. The meaning of the verb might have extended from 'to have compassion' or 'to spare' to a sense such as 'to act with consideration towards', so that 'I had concern for my holy name' (NIV, ESV) would be a more suitable rendering. That certainly coheres better with **which they, the house of Israel, had profaned among the nations where they came** (cf. 36:20).

REFLECTION

- The essence of divine holiness goes beyond the fact that God's being is transcendent and not physically tied to this world. It also expresses more than the fact that God is morally impeccable and utterly free from any blemish. Ultimately to say 'God is holy' is equivalent to saying 'God is God'. And that is why his concern for his holy name (36:21) is not an exercise in self-centred preening and self-aggrandisement. He is the centre of the universe. The cosmos is the moral and physical realm which he has created. 'I am the LORD, that is my name; and my glory to another I will not give, or my praise to graven images' (Isa. 42:8). To do anything else would be to subvert the very fabric of existence. The attention seeking of human leaders and personalities is mere bombast. When God calls attention to himself, it is to restore a sick world to a healthy engagement with its originator and sustainer.
- Many social welfare programmes foster a debilitating culture of dependency in which recipients crave further, on-going support as their right with no attempt to meet their own responsibilities. It is true that all are recipients of divine welfare: 'the eyes of all look to you, and you give them their food in its season' (Ps. 145:15). But this is accompanied by a stark reminder of human responsibility: 'if anyone is not willing to work, let him not eat' (2 Thess. 3:10).
- It is often argued that the conception of God in Ezekiel is deficient in that nothing is said of God acting in love, or even mercy towards his people (cf. Zimmerli 1983:247–248). But God does care about the response of his people (18:31–32; 33:11), and the stress on their unworthiness to be chosen by him and become recipients of his goodness is designed to provide realistic comfort to those scattered in exile and no longer sure of where they stand. If his provision is 'not for your sake', then it is secure from their failings and failure (36:22). This is a source of true confidence in pleading with God when overwhelmed by a sense of unworthiness, guilt, and shame. Recognition that salvation comes despite human rebellion and incapacity is the greatest tribute which can be paid to the love and

grace of God, and provides a sure ground for pleading with him. 'Help us, O God of our salvation, in the matter of the glory of your name; deliver us and atone for our sins for your name's sake!' (Ps. 79:9).

(2) My Spirit within You (36:22–32)

A correct understanding of this section requires recognition of God's motivation regarding the restoration of Israel, and this is brought out by the terms of the inclusion found in 36:22-23, 32. The action which the LORD will perform on Israel's behalf included their removal from the land of their exile (36:24), and the removal from them of the uncleanness which polluted them (36:24–25). He will also take the initiative in providing spiritual renewal for them so that they will not mar their return but live obediently (36:26–29a). Then in the context of covenant obedience they will enjoy the bounty of the LORD in the land (36:29b–30). The LORD's goodness will evoke from them a spirit of true repentance as they consider their past failure (36:31–32).

The prospect outlined has a number of parallels with 11:14–21, but now the address is more personal ('you' instead of 'them' as in 11:19, but note 11:17). Earlier it was 'one heart' which they would be given (11:19), whereas here it is a 'new heart', and there was nothing previously corresponding to 'my Spirit I will give within you' (36:27).

The overall lesson is the divine initiative in renewing the people. The problem of the desecration of God's holy name is resolved by the cleansing power of the Spirit, and the maintenance of this new life is achieved through the indwelling of the Spirit. 'Yahweh is as serious about creating New Israel as he was about destroying Old Israel. The readers should therefore root their identity not in continuity with the past, but in Yahweh's concern for his name. There is continuity, but it is a continuity of Yahweh's purpose' (Renz 1999:112).

But when is all this achieved? The physical restoration of the Jews to their land after the exile was not accompanied by spiritual renewal such as is described here, though what did happen contained partial depictions of what was yet to be. Indeed the ministry of the Spirit in its fulness was dependent on Christ's completed earthly ministry. Only after he had made atonement could the promised Spirit be bestowed, yet the full extent of the divine redemptive programme and the consummation of these promises still await Christ's return when he will usher in the heavenly kingdom in its totality and will banish for ever the shadows of the present age.

Is it 'distortion by anachronistic individualizing interpretation'

(Joyce 2007:205) to find in these verses the need for personal renewal? Undoubtedly it is appropriate to recognise the corporate dimension of the restoration predicted, just as the judgement imposed on the house of Israel had been an inclusive response to national backsliding and rebellion. Furthermore, it is the case that the corporate dimension of salvation may now be overlooked in presentations of the gospel. However, the condition of the people of God as a whole is the aggregate of their condition individually, and there is no impropriety in understanding the cleansing and renewal in a granular fashion, in which individual sheep in the flock experience divine rebirth so that restoration and revival extend to become characteristic of the flock as a whole.

> 36:22'Therefore say to the house of Israel, "Thus says the Lord God: Not for your sake am I doing ⌊this⌋, O house of Israel, but rather for my holy name which you have profaned among the nations where you have come. 36:23And I will sanctify my great name which has been profaned among the nations, which you profaned in their midst; and the nations will know that I ⌊am⌋ the Lord, declares the Lord God, when I display my holiness in you before their eyes. 36:24And I will take you from the nations and I will gather you from all the lands and I will bring you to your land. 36:25And I will sprinkle clean water upon you and you will be clean; from all your defilements and from all your idols I will cleanse you. 36:26And I will give you a new heart and a new spirit I will give within you, and I will remove the heart of stone from your flesh, and I will give you a heart of flesh. 36:27And my Spirit I will give within you and I will make ⌊it⌋ that in my statutes you will walk and my judgements you will observe and do. 36:28And you will dwell in the land which I gave to your fathers, and you will be my people and I for my part will be your God. 36:29And I will save you from all your defilements; and I will call for grain, and I will multiply it, and I will not set famine upon you. 36:30And I will multiply the fruit of the tree and the increase of the field so that you will no longer receive the reproach of famine among the nations. 36:31And you will remember your evil ways and your doings which ⌊were⌋ not good, and you will loathe yourselves on account of your iniquities and on account of your abominations. 36:32Not for your sake am I doing ⌊this⌋, declares the Lord God. Let ⌊this⌋ be known to you. Be ashamed and feel disgrace because of your ways, O house of Israel." '

♦ **36:22** *Therefore* noted that the LORD moved on from the explanation given to the prophet personally to the public proclamation which he was authorised to make based on the preceding arguments. *Say to the house of Israel* directed his speech to the remanent covenant community, whom he was to address in his capacity as the messenger of their heavenly king: *Thus says the Lord GOD.* They were called on to appreciate the reasons for divine action which were expressed both negatively and positively.

The clause *not for your sake am I doing ⌐this⌐* formed an inclusion with the same expression in 36:32. The original verb was a participle which might be rendered 'am doing' or 'will be doing'. 'Doing' without an expressed object occurred also in 20:9, 14, 22, 24, where God did not act to destroy the people out of concern for his name. Here God would act to restore them, but not directly or primarily out of sympathy for them.

But rather introduced a clear-cut alternative. There was nothing in the character or in the conduct of the Israelites to motivate or earn a favourable response from the LORD's (cf. Ps. 115:1). However, their presence in exile *among the nations where you have come* (36:21) had led to a situation which provided an excuse for the nations to abuse *my holy name* (36:21) as they reckoned the LORD to be a god who, having been defeated by the gods of Babylon, was not as powerful as had been claimed. So God would act in defence of his own interests, just as he had proclaimed through Isaiah, 'I, ⌐even⌐ I, am he who wipes away your acts of rebellion for my sake and I will not remember your sins' (Isa. 43:25).

♦ **36:23** The initial *I will sanctify* (*qādaš* piel) was matched by the later *when I display my holiness* (*qādaš* niphal), both parts of the same verb. The LORD would act to ensure that events did not obscure his unique being and character. *I will sanctify my great name* principally focused on God's supreme power because his action would definitively distinguish ('set apart as holy') his ability to act, and so he would establish that he alone was sovereign even although his name *has been profaned among the nations, which you profaned in their midst* by the very fact of their being there (cf. 36:20).

The result of the LORD's intervention would be that *the nations will know that I ⌐am⌐ the LORD.* This was a significant instance of the recognition formula because here the subjects of 'will know' were clearly identified as 'the nations'. But that does not resolve the question of what type of knowledge would the heathen obtain when

God acted out of concern for his name?[57] The outcome would compel the nations to recognise the supremacy of the LORD. However, such an astonished and overawed reaction need not necessarily lead to humble and obedient submission to the one true God. The signature formula *declares the Lord GOD*, which was not ordinarily employed in the middle of the recognition formula, added emphatic solemnity to the assurance of this result,[58] as well as picking up on the introductory use of the title in 36:22.

The recognition formula was supplemented by *when I display my holiness in you before their eyes*. 'My holiness' was God's essential being and character, which would be exhibited 'in you'[59] (plural here, and throughout to the end of the paragraph). When he delivered Israel, which was the theme of the following verses, they would function as a living testimony to the greatness of the LORD—a testimony which would be inescapably evident *before their eyes*, that is, those of the nations (cf. 20:41).

♦ **36:24** How the LORD would act to restore his people was set out in a chiastic pattern in 36:24–30. The outer elements (36:24, 29b–30) focused on the external change in their circumstances effected by their return to the land, while the core (36:25–29a) dealt with the concomitant spiritual change which would be required. Both were essential components of the return. What advantage could accrue from a return to the LORD's land if the LORD himself could not be present there with his people because their character remained the same as before?

(a) Territorial Restoration. New Exodus terminology (cf. 11:17; 20:34–35, 41–42; 28:25; 29:13, for the Egyptians; 34:13; 37:12, 21;

---

57. 'The Exile is not only a punishment; it is also deeply pedagogical and, at the end of the cleansing process, even revelational. Yahweh will gather his scattered people and return them to their land (Jer 31:10)' (*NIDOTTE* 1:1145).

58. 36:23c–38 is omitted in a major early LXX manuscript (Papyrus 967, 3rd century A.D.), and there are other divergences in the LXX from the MT in this section. However, the Hebrew of the Masada text (1st century A.D.) attests the presence of 36:24–34, all identical with the MT. The LXX variants are therefore to be adjudged as occurring within that textual tradition, and not as witnessing to a divergent earlier Hebrew text (Hummel 2007:1046). For further discussion, see Greenberg (1997:738–40), and Block (1998:337–343). See Crane (2008) for support for P. 967 and also its ordering of the chapters with chs. 38–39 preceding ch. 37.

59. The reading of many Hebrew manuscripts is 'in them', that is, 'in the nations'. This is a weaker reading.

39:27) was used to describe the impending deliverance of Israel from Babylon. The language was especially close to that of 34:13, with the replacement of 'bring out' by 'take', and of 'peoples' by 'nations'. However, leaving Egypt and leaving Babylon both foreshadowed the ultimate Exodus and deliverance which is made possible through the saving death of Jesus Christ (cf. Luke 9:31).

♦ **36:25** *(b) Spiritual Restoration.* With the scattering and dispersal of 36:19 reversed by the new Exodus of 36:24, there remained the problem of the defiled and impure state of the people described in 36:17–18. This too could only be dealt effectively by God himself, and so he also announced, *I will sprinkle clean water upon you and you will be clean.*

'Sprinkle' (*zāraq*) was one of a number of words used in connection with priestly rituals involving sprinkling of blood (e.g., Lev. 1:5, 11; 3:2, 8, 13), in which the liquid was scattered with a sweep of the arm. It did, however, occur twice where water was sprinkled (Num. 19:13, 20). Both these passages dealt with situations involving contact with a corpse, where ritual cleansing was effected by sprinkling with 'water of impurity', that is, water to remove impurity from the affected individual. Here the water that was used was 'clean water', that is, purifying water which brings about cleanness. Words derived from the root 'clean' were used three times in this verse (*ṭāhēr*, 'to be clean, pure') to denote a state opposite to that of defilement.

This particular symbolism was probably chosen to emphasise the divine role in the matter. Other ceremonial cleansings involved an individual washing themselves with water so that they became clean (e.g., Lev. 14:8–9; 15:13; 17:15), but sprinkling had to be carried out by another party. Nor was it the case that a priestly intermediary was envisaged in this passage (contrast the cleansing of the altar in 43:26). The LORD himself would take on the role of priest. Furthermore, the scenarios presented in Numbers 19 involved contact with, and contamination from, what was lifeless. That too fitted in with the spiritual condition of Israel, polluted by the lethal contaminant of idolatry (cf. 24:13; 36:33; 37:23), which had to be removed before they could enjoy life in God's favour.

Only through divine intervention would recovery be possible. *From all your defilements and from all your idols I will cleanse you.*

♦ **36:26** Divine cleansing would not be superficial, but deep-seated. In language reflecting that of 11:19–20a, it was made clear that *I will give* (repeated three times). No one performs a heart transplant operation on himself; the spiritual equivalent of such an operation would be carried out by the divine surgeon. The plural form of the pronoun *you* continued to be used since the people were considered as comprised of so many individuals. What God would graciously provide to sensitise them to his demands and energise them to comply with them was set out in four clauses, three positive and one negative. The clauses were paired, and each had four word units in Hebrew.

'Heart' was used in a number of senses in the Old Testament, though only infrequently of the physical heart (e.g., Jer. 4:19). As a metaphorical extension of its physical sense, 'heart' was on occasions used predominantly of the emotions (cf. 36:5), but even then its wider metaphorical scope was evident. It encompassed the whole inner rational being of an individual. So when *a new heart* was promised, this involved comprehensive renewal of thought patterns, including moral and spiritual discernment, and a person's will, as well as the accompanying emotions. Even so, despite the thoroughness of this renewal of the inner rational and sentient being, the personal identity of those affected would be maintained. They would become renewed, not different, individuals (cf. 36:31).

The word order in the second clause, beginning with *a new spirit* (identical to 11:19) strongly marked that the clause was co-ordinate with the first and that 'spirit' in the first instance referred to a new inner disposition given to the people by the LORD. *Within you* (plural), that is, each one of you, pointed to the interiority of the change (cf. 11:19). There would be a transformation of all that energises and animates an individual's life. This was linked to the presence of the Holy Spirit as the next verse made clear.

Negatively, the LORD promised, *I will remove the heart*[60] *of stone from your flesh* (as in 11:19, but with 'your' instead of 'their'). A heart of stone referred to a cold, unfeeling, obstinate disposition towards God. Kutsko (2000:128–129) proposes that the reference to 'stone' reflects the description of idols as 'wood and stone' (20:32). Israel had become like the idols they worshipped. 'From your flesh' meant no more than 'from your physical body', that which Genesis 2:7 referred to as formed from the dust of the ground. There would be an effective new creation, so that they could respond to God's voice.

---

60. Hebrew uses a singular term such as 'heart' for a part of the body common to a number of individuals. It may be termed a 'conventional collective' (*IBHS* §7.2.1b), and does not imply one national heart, but the disposition of each individual.

The verb form of the final clause in this sequence demonstrated that there would not be a void left by this spiritual heart surgery. The removal of one heart would be followed by the implantation of a radically different heart: *I will give you a heart of flesh* (again as in 11:19, but with 'you' instead of 'them'). This would be one that would be attracted towards God and willingly responded to him and his desires—a heart with fully restored spiritual functionality.

The newness of these arrangements picked up on language found elsewhere in the prophets, particularly the conditions which would prevail under the new covenant as set out in Jeremiah 31:31–34.

♦ **36:27** *My Spirit I will give within you* repeated the terms of the second clause of the preceding verse with 'my' substituted for 'new'. This whole procedure of inner renewal would be effected by God-given power. In 11:20 there had not been an explicit reference to 'my Spirit' as the agent producing such change, but now there was an anticipation of the New Testament revelation of how the third person of the Trinity as the Spirit of God and the Spirit of Christ indwells a believer (Rom. 8:1–17).

Flowing from the LORD's intervention to renew their inner being, there would be conformity at a personal level to the mode of living which God desired and set out in his covenant. *I will make ⌊it⌋ that in my statutes*[61] *you will walk and my judgements you will observe and do* (cf. 5:6). This would not be divine coercion, but effective divine renewal manifesting itself in a close walk with God, and was the equivalent of the new covenant blessing disclosed to Jeremiah: 'I will set my law within them and on their heart I will write it' (Jer. 31:33).

♦ **36:28** The renewed people would also enjoy the covenant privilege of residence in the land, which was here mentioned briefly to prove that their blessings would be in no way truncated. *And you will dwell in the land which I gave to your fathers* (cf. Exod. 6:8). The second Exodus no less than the first would lead to those brought into a right relationship with God living in harmony with his requirements and doing so in the very place where he was pleased to reveal himself. This reinstatement of what the LORD bestowed on his people demonstrated the unity of his purposes over the generations while at the same time addressing the argument from Israel's ancestry which had warped the exiles' spiritual self-perception. What had been given before would be

---

61. 'My statutes' is a masculine plural form *huqqay*, but the use of the masculine, and not the feminine, form is not significant here (contrast 20:25).

given again—and so all would be the product of divine grace, not of any form of human merit.

In this way participation in the bond of the covenant would be restored without any diminution because of sinful disobedience. *You will be my people and I for my part*[62] *will be your God.* This set out the two-sided nature of the covenant relationship between God and his people, with those very terms making clear their respective status, but at the same time indicating the close, personal bond involved through the possessives, 'my' and 'your'—heightened by 'your' as distinct from 'their' (11:20; 37:23, 27). The old bond would be restored (Lev. 26:12). All that was lacking was the divine Glory-presence in their midst, and that omission would be remedied later (43:1–5).

♦ **36:29** This is one of the three places in the prophecy where the verb 'to save' (*yāšaʿ*, hiphil; cf. 34:22; 37:23) was employed. It often referred to release from the clutches of an oppressor, generally external, but also internal. What was pictured here was in effect rescue from themselves: *I will save you from all your defilements.* Their sin was viewed as an overpowering force from which another has to release them, and then to carry out a cleanup of its debilitating traces. This clause may have functioned as a concluding résumé of the LORD's intervention, but it is also possible that it reflected the composite temporal nature of the scene being depicted. Prior to the heavenly consummation of these promises, there would be times of partial fulfilment when relapse of the restored people into sin would still be possible and would require to be dealt with (Hummel 2007:1057; cf. Rom. 7).

(a') Territorial Restoration. I will call for grain and I will multiply it, and I will not set famine upon you. The switch from spiritual deliverance and renewal to material well-being probably reflected the influence of Leviticus where obedience to God's covenant commands was followed by a description of rains in their season (Lev. 26:3–4). Inner obedience and external prosperity were frequently and pervasively linked in the Old Testament. Occupation of the land and enjoyment of its bounty prefigured heavenly bliss and the provision made there. The essential characteristic of both was God's presence and access to him in fellowship.

---

62. The personal pronoun is expressed here and so the usage is emphatic. Only here in Ezekiel is there found the long form of the pronoun (*ʾānōkî*, 'I') rather than the shorter *ʾănî*, which occurs 169 times. Perhaps the older form is deliberately retained in a traditional religious formula.

'Call for grain' or 'summon grain' was an unusual phrase, but it did not envisage others being required to bring it as tribute. This was the divine owner of the land ensuring nothing disturbed its fertility, and providing abundant harvests for those who were his tenants there. God would make certain that it was no longer a devouring or a bereaving land (36:13–15).

♦ **36:30** *I will multiply the fruit of the tree and the increase of the field* (cf. 34:27). By divine action the land would provide abundantly for its inhabitants. In this way the LORD's accomplishment would testify to surrounding nations that he was with his people. *You will no longer receive the reproach of famine among the nations* reflected 36:15 and 34:29. Famine was always a real danger in Canaan, and, if it had occurred, it would have shatter the renewed prosperity of the nation and caused doubts to be raised once more about the power of the LORD, and/or his favour towards his people. But *no longer* ('not again'; cf. 12:24), a feature of restoration oracles, indicated that the conditions which had previously prevailed would come to an end and there would be a radically different future of blessing.

♦ **36:31** The closing two verses of this section took up how the people would respond to the spiritual and material blessing which God would bestow on them. At first sight it may seem surprising that it did not anticipate joy and thankfulness, but shamed realisation of all that had been wrong with their lives. The position of this verse showed that contrition for their sin did not earn their return to the land, but that it was how they should, and would, react when restored by the LORD.

You will remember described a process of reflection stimulated by their return to the land, as they recollected their individual and corporate spiritual history (cf. 20:43; see also 16:53–63). They would then recognise that their conduct had combined *your evil ways and your doings which ⌊were⌋ not good* (cf. 20:25). *Doings* was not the same word as in 36:17, but it came from the same root and had a similar meaning. The result of this review would be that *you will loathe yourselves* (lit., 'feel disgust/revulsion in your face'). Only after divine intervention in their lives would the people be capable of evaluating their former conduct correctly: *on account of your iniquities* (cf. 4:4) *and on account of your abominations* (cf. 5:9).

♦ **36:32** Again the LORD deprived Israel of any ground for self-congratulation in this impending change in their circumstances. The repetition of the thought of 36:21–23 showed how significant the point was, and how liable it was to be misunderstood by the people. *Not for your sake am I doing ⌞this⌟* (cf. 36:22). *Let ⌞this⌟ be known to you.* This was a call for them to conduct an immediate self-examination in the light of God's purpose for their lives. *Be ashamed* and *feel disgrace because of your ways* (cf. 16:52) indicated that the self-loathing of the previous verse was also at present the appropriate response of those who had become spiritually sensitised to all in their conduct which had been at variance with the will of God. However, only after divine intervention would the *house of Israel* be able to comply fully with this divine exhortation.

REFLECTION

- Sin pollutes and defiles, and the resulting lethal and toxic situation can be rectified only by cleansing (36:25; Isa. 4:3–5; Ps. 51:2, 7). In the natural world there are pollutants which bio-degrade, and with the passage of time their deleterious impact is minimised, if not eliminated. This is not, however, the case with the spiritual contamination of sin. Time does not remedy its foul presence or weaken its impact. A thorough purging is needed to deal with the entrenched corruption of human nature, and this is not achieved by the superficial removal of impurities with the duster of human reformation, but by the deep cleansing effected by the divine detergent of sprinkling of clean water. Hence, David's prayer was 'Wash me thoroughly from my iniquity, and from my sin cleanse me!' (Ps. 51:2).
- In discussing the renewal set out in 36:26, John Murray wrote: 'God effects a change which is radical and all-pervasive, a change which cannot be explained in terms of any combination, permutation, or accumulation of human resources, a change which is nothing less than a new creation by him who calls the things that be not as though they were, who spake and it was done, who commanded and it stood fast. This, in a word, is regeneration' (1955:96).
- As regards 36:27, Gordon H. Clark commented: 'Not only does God surgically transplant a heart, but he sees to it that the new heart functions in a satisfactory manner; for with the heart he also implants his Spirit and thus causes his patients to walk according to the Ten Commandments. That is to say, he so controls the volitions of his newly born sons that they walk in his statutes' (1978:38).
- In the light of Paul's usage of the term 'flesh', a 'heart of flesh' (36:26) might suggest human existence apart from God, but that does not correspond to the Old Testament usage of 'flesh'. Here a

heart of flesh is set over against a heart of stone, and the meaning is evidently an inner disposition which is oriented towards God and responsive to him. This is the consequence of the process of conversion in which the new life of the spiritual heart transplant is imparted by God, and immediately the life force that is implanted in that heart gives evidence of its existence. As 36:27 makes clear, this procedure is utterly reliant on the life-imparting work of the Spirit who initiates and maintains the life of faith. 'With fear and trembling work out your own salvation, for it is God who works in you, both to will and to work for ⌊his⌋ good pleasure' (Phil. 2:12–13).

- Ezekiel's fellow exiles were dejected and in despair: 'Our hope has perished' (37:11). They were unable to find any meaning or purpose in their lives, and were effectively living as spiritual zombies, saying No to the life that God gives. But the way in which they wrote themselves off in 37:11 was a totally different response to that portrayed in 36:31–32. It is true that the spiritual outlook in both texts presents a denial of there being any good thing in the individual (cf. 'I know that nothing good dwells in me, that is, in my flesh', Rom. 7:18), but here this is the realisation of faith writing off the past and lamenting over it, while acknowledging the sovereign gift of change given by God. In 37:11 the focus is on the self isolated from God; in 36:31–32 the focus is on the self of the past in the light of how God's action has already impacted on that individual.

(3) Eden Restored (36:33–36)

Both concluding paragraphs of this division take up familiar themes, first that of the future of the land (36:33–36) and then that of the people (36:37–38). The sequence is, however, primarily literary and describes what will happen concurrently. Here it is promised that the land will have its desolation reversed and become a second Eden.

> ³⁶:³³'Thus says the Lord GOD, On the day when I cleanse you from all your iniquities, I will cause the cities to be inhabited and the ruins will be rebuilt. ³⁶:³⁴And the desolate land will be worked instead of being desolate before the eyes of everyone who passes by. ³⁶:³⁵And they will say, "This very land which ⌊was⌋ desolate has become like the garden of Eden, and the cities which ⌊were⌋ ruins, desolate, and razed have been inhabited as strongholds." ³⁶:³⁶And the nations which are left round about you will know that I ⌊am⌋ the LORD; I have rebuilt the razed ⌊places⌋ ⌊and⌋ planted the desolate ⌊place⌋. I ⌊am⌋ the LORD; I have spoken and I will do ⌊it⌋.'

♦ **36:33** The initial clause, *on the day when I cleanse you from all your iniquities*, summarised the change set out in 36:25b. At the time when divine initiative and action would bring about the reversal of the people's spiritual condition, other blessings would follow. Their uncleanness had forced their removal from the land, so their being cleansed would fit them for reinstatement there. Although *to be inhabited* was mentioned here, the question of population growth was reserved until the final oracle, and the primary theme was the divine restoration of the infrastructure of the land (*I will cause*), with *the cities* made fit for occupation once more and *the ruins* no longer lying in heaps, but *rebuilt*.

♦ **36:34** *The desolate land will be worked*. 'Desolate' (*šāmam*, cf. Introduction to ch. 35) was repeated five times in various forms in 36:34–36 to emphasise the bleak scene of devastation which would have prevailed apart from divine restoration. Instead agriculture would be resumed. The translation 'worked' is employed (rather than, say, 'ploughed') to retain the allusion to the original mandate to mankind in Eden where they were required 'to work it and to keep it' (Gen. 2:15). This set the tone for the description of the restoration in the next verse. *Instead of being desolate*, that is, instead of the desolation it in fact already was, it would be visibly and obviously transformed *before the eyes of everyone who passes by* (cf. 5:14; 16:15, 25). The threat of famine would be a thing of the past.

♦ **36:35** *And they will say* was an indefinite plural related to the 'everyone who passes by' of the previous verse. As in 36:20, the prophet was informed of their actual words as they assessed the altered situation before them. They would particularly focus not on the return from the exile or on the spiritual renewal of Israel, but on the physical transformation of the land. *This very land*[63] *which* ⌊*was*⌋ *desolate* through the impact of divine judgement would have *become like the garden of Eden*. Their misconception expressed in 36:20 that the LORD had been unable to provide for the land and its people would be corrected.

Ezekiel had already mentioned Eden (28:13; 31:9, 16, 18), but what was ultimately envisaged here was the eschatological paradise which awaits the people of God (cf. Luke 23:43; Rev. 2:7; Rev. 22). The presentation is the same as that found in Isaiah, 'For the LORD shall

---

63. *hallēzû* is a unique feminine form of a rare demonstrative *hallāz*, which has the effect of reinforcing the demonstrative, 'this very'.

comfort Zion; he shall comfort all her desolate ruins, and shall make her wilderness like Eden and her desert like the garden of the LORD' (Isa. 51:3). The extent of the change was emphasised by the threefold description of the former cities in the land as *ruins* (cf. 36:33), *desolate* (cf. 36:34), *and razed.* The final term implied torn down and left flattened.

What would be particularly striking to these future observers was that the cities would become *strongholds*, fortified and secure. This involved a seeming contrast with 38:11 where future cities would be unwalled. However, the new Jerusalem was portrayed both as walled and with open gates because of the absence of any danger (Rev. 21:12–21, 25). The depictions were all of the same reality: the security of the restored people of God. If these pictures were to be understood as literal prophecies, there would be an inherent paradox in how they could be implemented, but as spiritual metaphors they clearly were in harmony, conveying God's eternal protection and preservation of his people.

♦ **36:36** This verse expressed the dominant fact of this paragraph. The surrounding peoples would be forced by events to revise their views regarding the impotence of the LORD. The exile and the devastation of the land had led them to the conclusion that he was incapable of controlling the situation, and instead they gloated over Israel's demise (36:3–5). Now *the nations which are left*, possibly those of their neighbours who had survived the Babylonian incursions into the area, *will know* the reality of the LORD's power as evidenced in the restoration that would take place, and be compelled to revise their earlier estimates of the significance of events. *I ⌊am⌋ the LORD; I have spoken and I will do it* (cf. 12:25). Nothing could thwart the decree of the King of heaven.

REFLECTION

- We are not to take these scenes of a restored land in an overly literal fashion. They are a word picture for what will happen when the LORD bestows blessing, in ways which can now scarcely be grasped. In Hebrews 11 we are clearly taught that even Old Testament believers understood that the Promised Land, though conveying real blessings to them, was itself symbolic of the far greater blessings which were theirs in heaven. Abraham 'was looking forwards to the city which has the foundations, whose architect and builder is God' (Heb. 11:10), and along with the other patriarchal figures was looking for a heavenly inheritance (Heb. 11:13–16). In the New

Testament the emphasis on the land falls away, but even so Jesus in Mark 10:29–30 uses the picture of receiving 'now in this time houses ... and lands' to communicate an abundance of blessing, while still seeing it consummated in 'the age to come'.
- In this present age there is much evil, and human conduct displays the extent of the opposition of the human heart to God. But there is also the truth, however imperfectly realised, that the new heart is focused on and motivated by the reality of all that will finally be bestowed at the Lord's return. 'I have spoken and I will do it' (36:36) spurs on to faithful continuance until the end.
- It was not easy for the exiles to live in the light of these truths. It still remains difficult to do so. The reality of a coming Day of Judgement is scorned, and the question is sceptically asked, 'Where is the promise of his coming?' (2 Pet. 3:4). But the wonder of that promise and all that it entails continues to lighten the path of faith.

(4) The Flock Increases (36:37–38)

This brief final paragraph addresses another problem to be overcome, that of underpopulation. Enemy incursions decimated the population, and the exiles were few in number. Moreover, when Cyrus permitted the Jews to return from Babylon, not all that many of them in fact wished to do so. This oracle probably speaks to the dejection of those who, while admitting the comprehensive grandeur of what the LORD has outlined for them, feel themselves overwhelmed by the prospect of occupying and working the land because they are so few in number. By reintroducing the metaphor of the people as a flock of sheep, the LORD reminds them that he is the shepherd who will see to the growth of his flock.

> ³⁶:³⁷'Thus says the Lord GOD: ⌞In⌟ this too I will let myself be inquired of by the house of Israel to do ⌞this⌟ for them; I will multiply them as a flock, ⌞one of⌟ people. ³⁶:³⁸As a holy flock, as the flock of Jerusalem at its set feasts, so the ruined cities will become full of human flocks, and they will know that I ⌞am⌟ the LORD.'

♦ **36:37** Once more the messenger formula introduced an announcement of a further change in the condition of restored Israel. ⌞*In*⌟ *this too* (cf. 20:27; 23:38) probably indicated the additional nature of these verses, but the blessing in view was far from incidental. *I will let myself be inquired of by the house of Israel to do ⌞this⌟ for them.* The approaches of the people with requests would no longer be rebuffed (cf. 14:3; 20:3, 31). The covenant King would graciously grant his subjects an audience and accede to the requests they would present to him because harmony would be restored between him and his people. What the people would pray for was what the LORD had already promised in the covenant with Abraham. 'I will surely multiply your offspring as the stars of heaven and as the sand that is on the seashore' (Gen. 22:17; cf. Lev. 26:9). In the light of their renewed covenant fidelity both their persons and their petition would be accepted by him.

I will multiply them as a flock, ⌞one of⌟ people.[64] The imagery of chapter 34 was resumed, and the addition of 'people' emphasised that it was population increase which was specifically in view, not a multiplication of their livestock or their territory.

♦ **36:38** *As a holy flock*, literally 'flock of holinesses', probably used an abstract construction which indicated the status of animals dedicated to the LORD for sacrifice. In one of the rare occurrences of Jerusalem in a positive mode in the prophecy (see on 17:22), the comparison was clarified by *as the flock of Jerusalem at its set feasts*. 'Set feasts' described the three great pilgrimage festivals: Passover, Pentecost (Weeks), and Tabernacles (Sukkot). This incorporated a backward glance at the times when Jerusalem would become very crowded with pilgrims and their offerings. The future blessing did not specifically involve Jerusalem, but spoke more extensively of *the ruined cities* (cf. 36:33). These would no longer lie waste, but would *become full of human flocks* (lit., 'flock of mankind', one consisting of people rather than one owned by them; cf. *IBHS* §9.5.3b). The thronged cities would testify to the LORD's answer to their request, and this would reinforce their perception of his authority and power. *They will know that I ⌞am⌟ the LORD.* The recognition formula fittingly ended this oracle with the bemused and uncertain exiles regaining their assurance of the LORD's effective might and ability, and of his covenant commitment to them.

REFLECTION

• In discussing these prophetic promises it is difficult to disentangle the language used to describe the scene from the reality through which it will be finally realised. This interpretative difficulty is

---

64. The words *kaṣṣōʾn ʾādām* do not form a construct chain ('like a flock of humankind') because the first noun has the article, which is often present in comparisons (*IBHS* §13.5.1f).

intensified as we come to the concluding chapters of the book. Ezekiel was not privileged with detailed information about dates of accomplishment, and his language spoke from the perspective of his own day. The land promise has now become internationalised in that Abraham is presented as 'heir of the world' (Rom. 4:13). Note also the blessing extended to the meek (Matt. 5:5 as compared with Ps. 37:11).

• The picture based on the numbers involved in the flocks around Jerusalem at its set feasts (36:38) reaches its consummation in that 'great multitude that no one could count, from every nation, ⌐from all⌐ tribes and peoples and languages, standing before the throne and before the Lamb' (Rev. 7:9).

E. The Vision of the Dry Bones (37:1-14)

No date is attached to this passage, but it seems to come from several years after the news of the fall of Jerusalem reached Babylonia and shattered the illusory hopes of the exiles. Back then the exiles had begun to pay greater attention to Ezekiel's message, but apparently without any true comprehension of what he was saying (33:30–33). Here they have moved on somewhat in that they accept the justice of God's judgement upon the city, but this has been accompanied by demoralisation and dejection (37:11). The picture Ezekiel is presenting to them of a glorious future (chs. 34; 36) is so remote from their existing condition that they doubt its relevance. The LORD therefore equips his prophet to speak into that situation of gloom and despondency to give new hope by reminding them of his power. By his Spirit he is able to transform what, to a human eye, seems utterly hopeless and beyond recovery. He is not only the God who speaks but also the God who performs (37:14).

Through this message the Israelites are encouraged not to remain detached from God's word of promise and so settle down in apathetic assimilation to the ways of Babylon. The vivid, surreal picture the prophet presents is designed to stimulate the thinking of his audience and draw them out of looking at their situation exclusively from their own perspective and only taking into account human possibilities. That would indeed induce nothing but utter despair. Instead the vision portrays something which goes far beyond their perspective and horizons.

Although it lacks the technical vocabulary which form criticism associates with a vision, that is the most appropriate designation of this section. It is, however, a vision with a difference in that it is not classified among the 'visions of God' (cf. 1:1; 8:3; 40:2), and there is no representation of the divine presence in it. Moreover, the vision is one in which there is a significant level of prophetic involvement as Ezekiel's initial role as a spectator is changed to that of a participant in the scene, even though he is careful to distinguish what he is called on to do from the miraculous transformation which he sees taking place. So Ezekiel does not perform a sign-act (contrast 37:15–20). Rather in his inner consciousness he is a visionary witness to a demonstration of divine power, who has to relay to his audience what God had disclosed to him, along with the divine explanation of what it signified.

It is also worthwhile noting that the two-stage nature of the vision may have conveyed a measure of consolation to Ezekiel regarding his own ministry (see on 37:8).

Structure. The vision proper (37:1–10) is followed by a much modified disputation speech (37:11–14) whose function is to declare the salvation which is coming to the exiled community. In the first ten verses of the chapter Ezekiel describes how the LORD leads him through a visionary scene of scattered, dried human bones (37:1–2). God then conducts a conversation with the prophet regarding the possibility of these bones coming to life again (37:3), and then informs him that he is to announce to the bones the divine programme to remedy their condition (37:4–6). When the prophet does as he has been commanded, the bones first reassemble into skeletons which are clothed with flesh (37:7–8), and then these lifeless corpses are infused by the wind/breath/Spirit, which leads to the presence of a mighty army (37:9–10).

In the second part of the account God explains what Ezekiel has witnessed (37:11–14). First, it is established that the bones represent the exiled community, who are giving up all hope for their future (37:11). Then the LORD declares that he will intervene to bring them to life, no matter how dead they seem to be to themselves. Divine power exercised through the Spirit will transform hopeless despair into new life and grant restoration to the land (37:12–14).

The whole report is carefully structured and vividly developed. There is a very clear inclusion round it, with 'the Spirit of the LORD' (37:1) balancing 'my Spirit' (37:14). There is also a specific form of the verb 'set' found in these opening and closing verses. Furthermore, certain key terms are repeated throughout the section: wind/ breath/ Spirit (*rûaḥ*, ten times), bone (ten times), prophesy (seven times), and live (six times). Also noteworthy is the heightening effect of the repeated use of 'very' in 'very many' (37:2) and 'very dry' (37:2) which matches 'very, very great' (37:10) to form an inclusion round the vision account.

Revivification or Resurrection? Over the centuries this passage has generated much discussion as to whether it teaches the doctrine of the resurrection of the dead. It is, however, necessary to distinguish between an Old Testament belief in the afterlife and what forms the background to this vision.[65] Renz sums up the viewpoint of modern scholarship that what is under consideration in this passage is not 'resurrection to another life but revival within this life (similar to resuscitation, yet of people long dead)' (1999:203). This interpretation can be adopted whatever understanding is advocated of Old Testament teaching regarding individual eschatology. Since the corpses are not resurrected to participate in heavenly glory, the process involved in this vision is more akin to the miracles of revivification in the days of Elijah and Elisha, though after the passage of a much longer period of time (1 Kgs. 17:17–24; 2 Kgs. 4:18–37). The exceedingly large force lives again, like Lazarus (John 11:44), without there being any suggestion that they will subsequently be exempt from death. However, such a display of divine power is not without relevance for appreciating the power of the one who kills and who makes alive (Deut. 32:39; 1 Sam. 2:6).

Moreover, there is another aspect to understanding this vision. It undoubtedly speaks in the first instance to the exiles of their restoration to the land, but the role of the Spirit in the transformation clearly points beyond physical and political reinstatement. Such outward phenomena picture the spiritual renewal which by divine power populates the kingdom of heaven. Those dead in trespasses and sins (Eph. 2:1) are made alive together with Christ (Eph. 2:5).

This visionary experience is not a prophecy foretelling that this would happen in actuality. It does not imply that there is going to be this valley and the bones found in it will come to life and the people will go off and lead ordinary lives. It is a symbolic representation of the truth, and it is the truth symbolised which will be divinely actuated. Just as God was able to initiate life, physical and spiritual, where there was no humanly perceptible potential for its existence, so he is able to

---

65. Old Testament teaching on the afterlife is examined by, for instance, Alexander (1986) and Johnston (2002). The question is more relevant to the interpretation of passages such as 32:17–32.

restore life in its fulness both for a while on earth and throughout eternity. Belief in such a God is of the essence of resurrection faith.

(1) Restored from Death (37:1–10)

The scene is probably that of a battlefield (see on 37:9–10), where there has not only been a defeat, but a humiliating reverse so severe that it has not been possible to bury the dead. Greenberg (1997:748) notes that scenes littered with bones are frequent in Mesopotamian curses and/or victory boasts, and Fensham (1987:59–60) advocates interpreting the dry bones in the light of ancient treaty curses. In Assyrian annals the threat is often incorporated that those who violate treaties will have their slain left to rot in the open field, which was considered to be a disaster of terrifying severity. What the prophet views is not a particular battlefield where Nebuchadnezzar's might has prevailed against Judah, but a visionary scene where the scattered bones remains represent 'the whole house of Israel' (37:11) who are experiencing the curse imposed on covenant breakers (Deut. 28:26).

But the overall theme is recovery from disaster. In the prevailing thought of the day an enacted curse had magical power to hold even the gods in its grasp. But here it is boldly proclaimed that the curse of the broken covenant is invalid and impotent apart from the LORD. He had imposed it, and he retains the power and the prerogative to revoke it and to counteract its effects. What is more, he sovereignly takes the initiative to reverse the desolate and seemingly hopeless doom which has befallen the dry bones.

Moreover, even in this visionary portrayal, Ezekiel is not left as a spectator of what will happen. He becomes an active participant whose proclamation is instrumental in achieving the LORD's purpose. Even so, there is no doubt that the power which is manifested is that of the LORD himself.

⁣³⁷:¹The hand of the LORD came upon me and he brought me out by the Spirit of the LORD and set me down in the midst of the plain; now it ⌊was⌋ full of bones. ³⁷:²And he made me pass by upon them right round about, and behold, ⌊they were⌋ very many upon the surface of the plain, and behold, ⌊they were⌋ very dry. ³⁷:³And he said to me, 'Son of man, can these bones come to life?' And I said, 'Lord GOD, you ⌊are the one who⌋ knows.' ³⁷:⁴And he said to me, 'Prophesy over these bones and say to them, "Dry bones, hear the word of the LORD. ³⁷:⁵Thus says the Lord GOD to these bones: Behold, I am about to cause breath to enter you, and you will live. ³⁷:⁶And I will set sinews upon you and bring up flesh upon you, and I will cover you with skin and set breath in you and you will live; and you will know that I ⌊am⌋ the LORD." ' ⁣³⁷:⁷And I prophesied just as I had been commanded, and there came a noise while I prophesied, and behold! an earthquake, and the bones came near, bone to its bone. ³⁷:⁸And I saw and behold, sinews and flesh came up upon them, and skin covered over upon them from above, but breath was not in them. ³⁷:⁹And he said to me, 'Prophesy to the breath; prophesy, son of man, and say to the breath, "Thus says the Lord GOD: Come from the four winds, O breath, and breathe upon these slain that they may live." ' ³⁷:¹⁰And I prophesied just as I had been commanded, and the breath entered into them and they came alive. And they stood upon their feet, an exceedingly large force.

♦ **37:1** The account began abruptly in Hebrew without any linking construction as was customary. This may have reflected the fact that Ezekiel's personal experience of divine intervention in his life mirrored the LORD's intrusion into human history as portrayed in the vision. It was not possible to establish what factors predisposed the LORD to act in this way. Ultimately divine sovereignty and grace cannot be traced back beyond the exercise of God's will.

Ezekiel described his experience in terms of divine initiative. ***The hand of the LORD came upon me*** (cf. 1:3) also introduced Ezekiel's culminating vision in 40:1. On its own the expression did not indicate that a vision would follow (cf. 33:22), but subsequent references to the Spirit's involvement clearly located the experience in the visionary realm where the prophet received perceptual data not from external observation, or through his own imagination, but through inward induction by divine power. Indeed, that is what was effected by 'the hand of the LORD', an anthropomorphic expression for the exercise of divine power, which here brought this sequence of mental images before the prophet's inner eye.

It was in this inner sphere of personal consciousness that the prophet was aware of the movement implied by ***he brought me out***. Whereas the previous verb 'came' was a feminine form to agree with the gender of 'hand' in Hebrew, this masculine verb clearly indicated that the LORD himself was active. 'Brought out' (*yāṣāʾ*, hiphil; cf. 34:13) had Exodus overtones, which hinted that a parallel might be traced between Ezekiel's experience and what the LORD would provide for the people. ***By the Spirit of the LORD*** would be repetitive if all it signified was by an exercise of divine power. The expression anticipated later Trinitarian revelation regarding the Holy Spirit, the third person of the Trinity. It is not certain how much should be read back into Ezekiel's understanding, but the use of this phrase in a clause where the LORD was the subject was itself remarkable. In the prophecy only here and in 11:5 was the precise expression 'the Spirit of the LORD' employed, linking the two incidents.

The LORD *set me down*[66] indicated a gentle landing *in the midst of the plain*. The term was the same as that found in 3:22–23 in reference to a broad alluvial river plain, not a narrower valley or ravine. The use of the definite article made it highly probable that it designated the same locality as the scene of the second stage of the prophet's initial commissioning, and that it was a locality well known to his audience.

While the plain provided a familiar background, there was a highly distinctive feature in this visionary scenario. *Now it ⌊was⌋ full of bones*. These were not skeletons, still relatively intact, but scattered, separated, disconnected bones such as might be found on a battlefield, some time after the conflict had ended, and where the corpses of the slain had not received a proper burial, but had been left to decay and become carrion for wild beasts and birds. This curse was the destiny of the nation that breached the covenant. 'And your carcass will become food for all birds of the heavens and for the beasts of the earth, and there ⌊will be⌋ no frightening them off' (Deut. 28:26; cf. Jer. 34:20).

♦ **37:2** Care is needed when envisaging, *And he made me pass by*[67]

---

66. The form of the hiphil of *nûaḥ*, 'to rest', used here is without a doubled *nun*, *waynîḥēnî*, and it generally indicates 'give rest to', whereas the second hiphil form with doubled *nun*, which would have been *wayyannîḥēnî*, would normally have the sense 'to set down' (as in 37:14, where along with *rûaḥ*, 'Spirit', it forms an inclusio round the unit). Possibly here and in 40:2 the use of the first hiphil form in the sense of the second form indicates the start of the transition from classical Hebrew forms.

67. Surprisingly the initial verb of the verse *wəheʿĕbîranî*, 'and he made me pass by', is ordinary *waw* with a perfect rather than a *waw*-consecutive imperfect (cf. 37:7, 8, 10; and also 13:6, 8; 17:18; 19:12; 40:24, 35; 41:3, 8, 13, 15; 42:15). Under the influence of Aramaic the use of the *waw*-consecutive construction became less common in later Biblical Hebrew (cf. GKC §112pp; Joüon §119z). On the other hand, the use of this form may be a deliberate off-lining of the event described as not progressing the main narrative. That would be particularly true of first person verbs in accordance with Ezekiel's playing down of his personal role. 'Thus the use of *wəqatal* forms serves to minimise the direct involvement of the prophet. Even the prophet watches what the prophetic word achieves' (Renz 1999:205).

***upon them*ⁿ⁶⁸** need not imply that Ezekiel had to walk on top of the bones. As well as the sense 'over', the preposition 'upon' can convey the thought of 'beside', as in 'he leads me beside quiet waters' (Ps. 23:2), and that may well have applied here. Furthermore, this was a visionary sequence. Contact with the bones of a corpse would be defiling (Num. 19:16), but Ezekiel has no qualms on that score in this visionary experience (contrast 4:14).

The idiom ***right round about*** (*sābîb sābîb*) showed that this was not a casual stroll, but an extensive tour of inspection which the LORD required the prophet to make so that Ezekiel would be deeply impressed by the hopelessness of the situation. There was no possibility of any survivor being found in this scene of past carnage. All hope of recovery was ruled out.

Ezekiel conveyed his surprised reaction to this scene by use of the focus particle, ***behold!*** (also in 37:5, 7, 8), and by the repetition of 'very' (37:10). He was astonished by what was revealed to him, and probably not a little overwhelmed by the magnitude of what he saw ***upon the surface of the plain.*** This was the scene of a large scale tragedy (***very many***) where so much life had been lost that survivors, if there had been any, would have been incapable of interring the fallen (cf. 39:12–16). ***And behold, they were very dry.*** They were bleached white under the eastern sun, and absolutely devoid of any moisture.

♦ **37:3** The LORD then spoke to the prophet to draw out the significance of the scene by asking him, ***Can these bones live?***⁶⁹ That is, was there any possibility that they might come to life again? Divine questions were a feature of visions, used to focus on key features and elicit their meaning (cf. Jer. 1:11, 13; Amos 7:8; 8:2; Zech. 4:1–2, 5). The idea of 'live again' was also implied in 37:5, 6, 9, 10, 14. The restorations to life recorded in the Old Testament were to a natural earthly life, not to the permanence of everlasting life (cf. 1 Kgs. 17:17–24; 2 Kgs. 4:18–37; 13:21), though the power which revivified clearly testified to God's capacity to resurrect.

---

68. 'Them' is a masculine plural suffix referring to the bones, whereas later in the verse both 'many' and 'dry' are feminine plural forms in agreement with the feminine gender of 'bones'. However, in 37:4 and repeatedly thereafter masculine forms are used. This may simply be a sign that later Hebrew preferred masculine forms, or it may anticipate the fact that these bones are indeed to come alive again as men.

69. The imperfect *tiḥyênâ*, 'they will live', has the modal sense, 'they can live' (cf. Joüon §113l).

To a question to which the natural answer was a decided No, the prophet replied with a deferential, **Lord GOD, you ⌐are the one who¬ knows** (cf. John 21:17; Rev. 7:14). If the question had been posed by a human being, Ezekiel would probably have dismissed the idea as ridiculous. But it was the LORD who asked, and the prophet was well aware that his knowledge of what might occur was inferior to that of his questioner. The resuscitations which he would have known about from the Elijah and Elisha narratives would have provided a parallel of sorts. Still those incidents involved the recently dead, not mere bones, totally dried up, and so many of them. But Ezekiel would not limit what the LORD could do; it was not a matter of divine power, but of divine intention.

♦ **37:4** *Restoration Predicted.* The LORD did not respond directly to Ezekiel's answer, but proceeded to describe what he would do. He commissioned the prophet to **prophesy over** (*'al*) **these bones.** This might also be rendered 'to these bones' (NIV). This was the first of three injunctions to prophesy (cf. 37:9, 12) which linked the vision and its explanation. The prophet was no longer a spectator, but had become a participant in the visionary scene—but a participant with a seemingly pointless task. **Say to them, 'Dry bones, hear the word of the LORD.'** Personification of the bones arose from the underlying fact that they represented people. But dry bones could no more hear the prophet than spiritually dead hearts could respond to the divine word.

♦ **37:5** The resolution to this conundrum was provided by what the LORD undertook to do. The LORD's messenger was to announce the outline of the divine revival programme. Previously 'behold' had pointed to what militated against any recovery ('Behold, ⌐they were¬ very dry', 37:2), but now it pointed positively to divine transformation. **Behold, I am about to cause breath to enter you.** 'Breath' renders the Hebrew term *rûaḥ*, a concept of wide scope. It may refer to the Holy Spirit (37:1, 14), the 'spirit' of an individual, as well as his 'breath', and also the 'wind' (37:9). The idea of air in motion was common to the last two terms, and in connection with a human being such breath was indicative of life. A similar range of meaning was associated with the Greek term *pneuma* (cf. John 3:3–8), and context must determine the appropriate rendering. Here 'breath' fits the needs of the lifeless bones. **And you will live**[70] set out the aim of this divine intervention.

---

70. The form *wiḥyîtem*, 'and you will live', rather than an initial *waḥă–*, (also in 37:6, 14) is found with the verb *ḥāyâ*, 'to live' (cf. GKC §63q).

♦ **37:6** A similar description of the assembling of the human body occurred in Job 10:11. Probably the details were just a vivid enactment in the vision and did not reflect specific features of spiritual renewal as in an allegory. The prophecy portrayed a four-stage process of imparting renewed life: sinews on the bones to bind them together; flesh to come on them; skin to cover the flesh—thus reversing the process of physical decomposition—then finally revivification by the impartation of spirit or breath. All would be accomplished by the LORD, with the result that *you* (masculine plural throughout) *will live.*

Technically, the 'you' in the recognition formula, *and you will know that I ⌞am⌟ the LORD*, referred to the bones, but these would be the restored bones. It was not simply a matter of physical renewal. The goal of the process was spiritual perceptivity and commitment. The thought was expanded on in the later explanation (37:13–14). The revivified people would possess true knowledge of God, whom they would no longer underestimate and so write off all hope of restoration. Once God's goal was achieved, they would come to acknowledge that he alone had accomplished this change and was all he claimed to be.

♦ **37:7** *Restoration Accomplished.* As was evident earlier (see Introduction to ch. 4), when God issued commands to him, Ezekiel was content to record the instructions without giving details of his implementation of them. *And I prophesied*[71] *just as I had been commanded* (cf. 12:7; 24:18). This action of God's herald was merely preparatory; the power was the LORD's alone.

What was being described at this point was, however, of such overwhelming significance that Ezekiel did detail the stages by which the silent and static scene before his mind's eye became transformed. *While I prophesied* (*kəhinnābəʾî*, cf. 11:13) showed the prophet to be obedient to the divine command, and an effective instrument in God's hands (cf. 11:5–12). The LORD acted at the same time, and *there came a noise.* The situation had begun to change. Ezekiel delayed the words, *and behold! an earthquake*, for dramatic effect. It is unclear whether the earthquake stirred the bones into action, or whether the action of the bones was so massive that the earth shook as a consequence. It was probably the latter, and the sound was that created by the tremor of their movement. On occasions Ezekiel used the term 'earthquake' (*raʿaš*, cf. Amos 1:1) to refer to human quaking and trembling (12:18; cf. also 38:19–20), and in 3:12–13 he had used 'a sound of a loud rumbling/earthquake' to describe the movement of the cherubim.

---

71. For the perfect form, see the footnote at 37:2.

The bones came near[72] pictured the process as it happened, rather than the result, but ***bone to its bone*** showed that there was orderly reassembling, not a haphazard combination, as the bones were reassociated into skeletons.

♦ **37:8** ***And I saw and behold***[73] catches the amazement of Ezekiel as a spectator when he witnessed what was happening. ***Sinews and flesh came up upon them, and skin covered over upon them from above.***[74] Apparently these two processes occurred from opposite directions. The sinews and flesh 'came up' while 'from above' implied that the skin came down upon the reassembled bodies. Though this transformation was astounding, it was evident that there was one vital feature missing: ***but breath*** (*rûaḥ*, cf. 37:5) ***was not in them.*** They were still corpses, not living beings.

There had been no hint earlier that the process would be two-staged. Had something gone amiss? It would be wrong to suppose that this staggered procedure was the product of Ezekiel's skill as a narrator in heightening the tension in his account of the vision. This was what the LORD disclosed to him. It would seem that two factors were at work. (1) If the first stage of the revival process was embodiment of the bones, then the second might well be characterised as em-*breath*-ment (cf. Wendland 1996:241). It corresponded to the creation account of Genesis 2:7, and reflected the nature of the human constitution. (2) The two stages differentiated between unique divine action and the

---

72. The verb form *wattiqrəbû*, 'and they drew near', is probably to be treated as a feminine form (cf. Job 19:15; Jer. 49:11; GKC §60a, *IBHS* §31.1.1a; Joüon §44da), for which *wattiqrabnâ* might have been expected, rather than as an indication that *ʿeṣem*, 'bone', might be regarded as also being masculine in gender. However, in 'bone to its bone' 'its' is literally 'his'.

73. For the perfect form, see the footnote at 37:2. Renz (1999:204) argues that the construction does not merely reflect a linguistic development here and in 37:7, 10, but that it is deliberately employed to introduce an element of discontinuity, emphasising the role of the prophet as a spectator rather than a messenger. While his obedience facilitates the renewal, it does not in any real way contribute to it. It comes by divine power alone. What the prophet does is at most a prelude to the real exercise of power. He observes, but does not effect, what the prophetic word achieves.

74. The verb *qāram*, 'to cover over', occurs only here and in 37:6, though its meaning is established by cognate terms (*HALOT* 1143). In 37:6 it was transitive, but here it could be either intransitive, 'skin covered over upon them', and so similar in use to the preceding term, or it might be transitive with the LORD as an implicit subject, 'he covered over upon them ⌐with⌐ skin'.

prophetic announcement which could be divinely enabled to accomplish just so much to provide a basis for what was exclusively divine. The dual process also incidentally pointed to the nature of prophetic ministry in general. The halfway house of the lifeless corpses lying on the ground was not failure, but success as regards faithful declaration of the word of the LORD. From this Ezekiel might take encouragement as to the impact of his own ministry (Renz 1999:209), but further divine intervention would be required to complete the renewal.

♦ **37:9** Ezekiel was next instructed to address the breath or wind (*rûaḥ*) rather than the bones as in 37:4–8. The repeated commands implied that this was to be done as a matter of urgency to complete the divinely intended transformation: ***Prophesy to the breath; prophesy, son of man, and say to the breath.*** The term *rûaḥ* (cf. 37:5) may be rendered here 'breath, wind, spirit'. Perhaps it was all three at once, and it is difficult to establish which was the dominant thought at each point in the description. The reference in ***Come from the four winds*** required 'wind' at that point, but 'breath' was possible elsewhere. The breath/wind was to come from every direction simultaneously, a feature which raised the event above any natural phenomenon. Certainly something out of the ordinary was needed because of the nature and magnitude of the task to be carried out. 'Four' was used in a comprehensive sense in 1:6, 17; 10:9; 14:21, but whereas 'to every wind' had been used earlier (cf. 5:10) to describe the scattering of the people, now a centripetal movement was envisaged as the winds rushed together.

Although the Holy Spirit was not directly mentioned in 37:9–10, the Spirit's activity was nonetheless assumed. The wind was composed of the same air which constitutes the breath of an individual, but the coming of the wind did not of itself convey life. ***Breathe*** (*nāpaḥ*) was the same verb as had been used in Genesis 2:7. The finely moulded clay from the divine potter had not become a living being until God *breathed* into it the breath of life. It was the same work of the Spirit that was in view here, particularly in the sequence, body first, then impartation of life. Now there was a people capable of inhabiting the Edenic garden that the LORD had prepared (ch. 36). The desolation caused by their idolatry and the curse embodied in their scattered bones (6:4–6) had been reversed.

Upon these slain introduced a new feature into the situation. Previously nothing had been said about how the bones had met their fate, but here it was made clear that the individuals had not succumbed to a natural death. The possibility of this being the scene of a massacre in battle was reinforced by the use of 'army' in the following verse. *That they may live* did not explain why this change should have been determined by God; it merely stated his sovereign intention in the matter.

♦ **37:10** Once more (37:7) Ezekiel narrated his obedience, *And I prophesied*[75] *just as I had been commanded.* The verb form for 'prophesied' (hithpael of *nābāʾ*) was also used in 13:18, 21 where an improper, magical concept of prophecy was in view. Renz (1999:205) suggests that its use here may have indicated that Ezekiel as a person had to stand somewhat apart from the prophetic word he uttered as it took effect independently of him. *The breath entered into them.* The breath, the spirit, or even the Spirit—all may have been in view— acted in terms of the LORD's command relayed by the prophet, with the outcome that the slain *lived,* that is, came back to life, and gave evidence of this when *they stood upon their feet.* The impact of the Spirit on the bones was similar to the impact on the prophet in 2:2 and 3:24.

The term *force* need not have had a military reference, but Ezekiel did use the term in that sense elsewhere (17:17; 29:18–19; 32:31; 38:4, 15) and that was probably his intention here, reinforcing the scene as one of a battlefield. The concluding note of the vision account, however, was the magnitude of the transformation that God brought about through the Spirit. *A very, very large force* (repeating the term 'very' found twice in 37:2) emphasised the extent and the sheer difficulty of what God had been done 'by the breath (*rûaḥ*) of his mouth' (Ps. 33:6).

REFLECTION
• There is a dualism in the Scripture presentation of the human constitution (Gen. 2:7), but it is not one in which there is a temporary union between an inferior, and discardable, body from below and a superior and imperishable soul divinely imparted from above. Rather true humanity is constituted by an external, visible, tangible existence, accompanied by an internal, intangible inner life. Neither aspect is inferior to the other, and both are divine endowments intended to exist together and to complement each other. That there is now a breach made between them at death is part

---

75. For the perfect form, again see footnote at 37:2.

of the heinous, destructive effects of sin—which will be overcome in the renewed life of the resurrection.
- 'Breath was not in them' (37:8) was also characteristic of idols (Jer. 10:14; Hab. 2:19). For this to be attributed to the bones conveyed at one level the truth that the idol worshippers had become like the idols they served (Ps. 115:8). But primarily it portrayed the physical and spiritual death of the bones. They were therefore unable to remedy their own situation, or even pray about it. It required divine initiative and intervention to transform their situation. That can only come through 'the Spirit who gives life; the flesh provides no help at all' (John 6:63).
- The two-stage process of transformation set out here resembles that which Paul outlines in Romans 10, especially his conclusion, 'So faith comes from hearing, and hearing through the word of Christ' (Rom. 10:17). Just as Ezekiel was divinely commissioned to utter the prophetic word, so too the gospel preacher has to be sent (Rom. 10:15), but the proclamation of the truth, while necessary, is not sufficient to effect change. It is only the Spirit's work that transforms the gospel message from being an aroma of death to death into an aroma of life to life (2 Cor. 2:16).
- Abraham's faith was such that 'he reckoned that God ⌊was⌋ able to raise him [Isaac] even from the dead, from where, even figuratively, he did receive him back' (Heb. 11:19). The faith that lays hold of God's power to revivify is generically identical to the faith that lays hold of his promise to resurrect. It is the same divine power which is operative in both situations.

(2) Interpretation of the Vision (37:11–14)

It is not clear at what point Ezekiel's visionary experience ends because the narrative flows smoothly into divine speech. The symbolism of the bones is clarified (37:11a), and then the attitude of the exilic community is summarised by citing the words they used to express their sense of hopelessness (37:11b). Though this bears a resemblance to the start of a disputation speech (see on 11:3), there is in fact no direct denial of the exiles' self-assessment. Instead, changing the metaphor from a battlefield to a graveyard, the LORD assures the people that he will give them new life and restore them to their land, an outcome which will lead to their recognition of who he is and what he has done (37:12–13). The LORD expressly asserts the role the Spirit will have in this process of transformation (37:14). To dispel their hesitation and despondency, he calls on the people to trust in the declaration he has made about their future. The word of the LORD can be relied on.

While it is true to say that the exiles' viewpoint regarding themselves is not controverted, it must also be noted that it is not simply accepted either. Indeed, it cannot be. Though they do look on themselves as dry bones, something more is true about them: they are bones with a presence in their midst and with a promise regarding their future. The LORD is 'a sanctuary to them for a little while among the lands where they have entered' (11:16), and he has promised to restore them to their land (11:17). In this the exiles differ from the old Jerusalem community which is dead and gone (Renz 1999:200). They should therefore respond with faith to the future God has committed himself to bringing about for them.

> ³⁷:¹¹And he said to me, 'Son of man, ⌊as for⌋ these bones, they ⌊are⌋ the whole house of Israel. Behold, ⌊they⌋ are saying, "Our bones are dried up, and our hope has perished; we are quite cut off." ³⁷:¹²Therefore, prophesy and say to them, "Thus says the Lord GOD: Behold, I am about to open your graves and I will cause you to come up out of your graves, O my people, and I will bring you to the land of Israel. ³⁷:¹³And you will know that I ⌊am⌋ the LORD when I open your graves and bring you up out of your graves, O my people. ³⁷:¹⁴And I will set my Spirit in you and you will live, and I will settle you upon your land, and you will know that I ⌊am⌋ the LORD; I have spoken, and I will do ⌊it⌋, declares the LORD."'

♦ **37:11** The divine conversation with Ezekiel continued as his visionary experience faded, but not before making clear how he as *Son of man*, the LORD's prophetic spokesman, should interpret and declare it. ⌊*As for*⌋ *these bones, they* ⌊*are*⌋ *the whole house of Israel.* 'Are' is a supplement, and is to be taken not as an assertion of identity, but of representation. The comprehensive expression, 'the whole house of Israel', introduced the subject of the remainder of the chapter (as set out in greater detail in the next section). The covenant people of God were essentially one, and as such they would be reunited (cf. 36:10; 39:25; 45:6). Ultimately this included the remnant from the north as well as the south, those deported to Babylon as well as those left in the land and those who had fled as refugees elsewhere. The spiritual condition of all of them was portrayed by the dry, scattered bones.

The focus particle, **behold**, turned the prophet's attention from the details of the vision to that group of the scattered people he knew well in Babylonia. Ezekiel was informed of their attitude regarding what had happened—or, more accurately, reminded of it, for he was well aware of the sentiment that was rife around him. ⌊*They*⌋ *are saying* represented their repeatedly expressed viewpoint, which was summed up in what may have been a three-part lament. There was even a measure of rhyme to their saying as each clause ended in the sound *–nû*, which possibly imparted a mournful tone to their maxim. Each line said essentially the same thing: 'a downcast spirit dries up the bones' (Prov. 17:22).

Our bones are dried up employed a verb from the same root as 'dry' (37:2, 4), thus linking these words to the preceding vision. Lacking moisture they had become lifeless (cf. Ps. 22:14–15). 'Bones' was not used as earlier for skeletal remains, but was a standard Hebrew idiom in which, by synecdoche, 'bones' referred to the whole person, particularly as regards their physical vigour, which was taken to be an index of their mental and spiritual condition. The exiles did not protest their innocence, but lamented their loss of verve and vitality (cf. 33:10; Ps. 32:3–4).

Our hope has perished (cf. 19:5) referred to the false hope they had placed in the inviolability of Jerusalem, about which Ezekiel had warned them for so long. Now that events had not taken the course they expected, they despaired of their survival, and saw no realistic prospect of a prosperous future. So they concluded with absolute bleakness: *we are quite cut off.*[76] They considered themselves for all practical purposes as good as dead. The verb was used of situations such as 'cut off out of the land of the living' (Isa. 53:8), 'cut off from your hand' (Ps. 88:5), and 'Water flowed over my head; I said, "I am cut off" ' (Lam. 3:54). Their catastrophically and judgementally altered circumstances deprived them of all prospect of true life, for the LORD would not intervene in their favour because they had become utterly separated from him. The only course they felt was open to them was to sink, discouraged and defeated, into forlorn listlessness.

♦ **37:12** But to these dejected and downcast people, the LORD acted with sensitive concern when he commanded the prophet to deliver a

---

76. There is a well-known emendation which divides the two words differently (cf. BHS). Instead of *nigzarnû lānû*, 'we are cut off to our detriment' (an ethic dative), it reads *nigzar nôlenû*, 'our thread is cut off', positing a hypothetical form *nāwel*, 'thread', on the basis of a Syriac cognate. Hebrew has its own word for 'thread', and the concept of 'thread [of life]' is not attested elsewhere in the Old Testament.

THE VISION OF THE DRY BONES 283

message from him. The initial ***Therefore***, so often the precursor of judgement, opened up instead a door of hope which was intended to ease them out of their despair. Ezekiel was commanded to ***prophesy and say to them*** (cf. 37:4, 9) in words introduced by the messenger formula. (Though not stated, he presumably first of all communicated the report of the vision given above.)

Behold, I am about to open your graves maintained the underlying description of death for the spiritual condition of the people, but modified the metaphor from that of exposure to that of interment. Such a mutation in the imagery was typical of the movement in visionary experience. It was not indicative of text incorporated from another source. The same scenario was being depicted from a different perspective, but, as before, the vital and vitalising factor was God's action. When their graves were opened, this would not be to inspect their contents, but as a prelude to revivification: ***I will cause you to come up out of your graves.*** Significantly, the LORD addressed them as ***my people***[77] (also in the next verse). Even though they were envisaged as in the grave, the LORD had not abandoned his concern for them and his relationship with them. Moreover, he had a future in view for them. ***I will bring you to the land of Israel*** (cf. 20:42; 34:13; 36:24; 37:21) would be a homecoming indeed. For 'land of Israel', see on 7:2.

♦ **37:13** An expanded form of the recognition formula was used with explicit identification of the subject of the verb. ***And you will know that I ⌊am⌋ the LORD*** showed that the LORD's ultimate concern was spiritual—that the people would acknowledge his sovereign character and power ***when I open your graves and bring you up out of your graves***. More than that, this would all occur within the bond of fellowship summed up by ***my people*** (cf. 37:12). What greater antidote to their disorientation and despair could there be than to be divinely recognised as 'my people', and promised God's powerful and successful intervention on their behalf.

♦ **37:14** There would be a further dimension to the LORD's remedy for his people's despair, not merely dealing with their external circumstances, but providing them with inward renewal and power: ***I***

---

77. The expression 'my people' is often challenged as a later interpolation because it is not found in the Peshitta and most LXX manuscripts, and because it is oddly positioned, not being at the start of the sentence. However, 'my people' is found at the end of 37:13 in the LXX, and its unusual position was obviously climactic.

will set my Spirit in you. This use of *rûaḥ* clarified those of 37:5–6, and developed the thought of the first part of 36:27. Only the inwardly renewing power of the Holy Spirit could transform the people so that ***you will live*** (cf. 37:6, 9), providing not mere existence, but life to its fullest extent. Just as the dry bones had not been left as reassembled and enfleshed skeletons, so the people would have imparted to them new life and power from God.

Their needs would be met in every way. ***I will set you down***, just as Ezekiel had been in the plain (37:1), but now ***upon your land***. 'Land' was literally 'soil', a more evocative term (cf. 7:2). This promise went beyond 37:12, for it was not merely their presence there which was foretold, but their rightful settlement and establishment in territory where they would not be disturbed.

You will know that I ⌞am⌟ the LORD.[78] Again the recognition formula pointed to the people's acknowledgement of the LORD. His greater purpose in all that he had brought on the people would be achieved, in that they would possess clarified spiritual perception regarding the uniqueness of the LORD, the magnitude of his power and the constancy of his commitment. ***I have spoken and I will do ⌞it⌟, declares the LORD*** guaranteed the reliability of the LORD's promises (cf. 12:25) and reinforced this by using the signature formula, albeit in its shorter form (cf. 13:6–7; 16:58). He did not merely speak; his word guaranteed that he would carry out all he had promised.

REFLECTION

- Israel's fearfulness was divinely caused. 'And ⌞as for⌟ those among you who are left, I will bring despondency into their heart in the land of their enemies; and the sound of a rustling leaf will chase them off' (Lev. 26:36). Separated from the LORD, they will be devoid of vigour and will languish in dispirited gloom. This in fact may mark the start of a process of spiritual recovery. They are no longer cocooned by a false perception of their dire condition. No scope for pretence is left to them as their dire prospects hit home. In itself to say 'We wait for light, but behold darkness! for brightness, ⌞but⌟ we walk in gloom' (Isa. 59:9) is not to experience salvation, but it opens the door for divine intervention.
- It is in the face of human impotence and despair (37:11) that the grace and power of God shine forth most clearly. It is when we are

---

78. An alternative rendering is found in the NIV, 'you will know that I the LORD have spoken, and I have done it.' This is possible because there is no verb expressed in the recognition formula.

deprived of earthly support that we perceive the grandeur of God's transforming promises most clearly. Only the one who can truly say, 'I am the resurrection and the life' (John 11:25) can 'swallow up ... the pall that is cast over all peoples, the veil that is spread over all nations' (Isa. 25:7).
- As is often the case, the individual and the corporate dimensions of Scripture promises are here intertwined. For Israel to be collectively transformed through the gift of new life, that change has to be accomplished at the personal level as well. To alter the metaphor to that employed by Peter, each individual of 'those who are elect exiles of the dispersion' (1 Pet. 1:1) through faith in Christ has become a living stone, but corporately they are 'being built up as a spiritual house' (1 Pet. 2:5)—many stones, but one house.
- Gordon H. Clark finds in this chapter an excellent illustration of the five basic Scriptural truths contended for in a Calvinistic presentation of Scripture (1978:39–41). The very dry bones (37:2) are an emblem of mankind's total inability to make any contribution towards their recovery from spiritual death. It is by divine initiative and sovereign choice that the condition of these bones is altered (37:3–5). While God saved all those in the valley, it was only to the bones in the valley that he imparted life, because he had chosen to do so. The bones neither contributed to this process, nor could they hinder it. It was divinely initiated and controlled (37:5–6). After its completion, those given life would recognise who had done this (37:6, 13). God also provides that the people will be saved, cleansed, and enjoy an unbreakable relationship with himself (37:23).

F. Reunion and Restoration (37:15-28)

Although this is a new section of the prophecy, its theme is similar to that of the first part of the chapter, being concerned with the destiny of 'the whole house of Israel' (37:11, 16), not merely the destiny of the tribe of Judah. It looks at the situation which will prevail when the revivified people are restored to their land (37:12, 21).

Now, instead of a visionary report of what awaits the people, Ezekiel is enjoined to present the divine message by means of a sign-act (37:15–19). The prophet is directed to procure two pieces of wood, one of which is to represent Judah and the other Ephraim, that is, the remnants of the northern kingdom. He is then to hold these two pieces of wood in his hand so that they appear as one. This signifies that the restored people will no longer be riven by internal dissension, but will be united and live in harmony. Their restoration will not be to the divided condition of their more immediate past, but will be patterned after the days of David and Solomon.

The prophet is then given an explanation to convey to the people as he holds the pieces of wood in his hand (37:20–28). The restored people will be brought back to the mountains of Israel, the land uniquely theirs. The LORD's message to them emphasises that they will be cleansed (37:23a), in covenantal bond with himself (37:23b), ruled by a Davidic king (37:24), obedient (37:24), multiplied in number (37:26), and all of these arrangements will be for ever (37:25–28). The beneficiaries of the LORD's gracious intervention will be the whole house of Israel, north and south, one nation with one king (37:22). These are the conditions which will prevail under the kingship of the Messiah (37:24–25), during whose reign the blessings of the covenant will be consummated through the presence of the LORD with 'my tabernacle' and 'my sanctuary' being in their midst (37:26–28). The prophecy is of a sanctified people living in harmony with one another, and supremely in harmony with their God.

(1) One in My Hand (37:15–19)

This section involves the last action prophecy in the book, and the only one in connection with Ezekiel's oracles of salvation, and as such it possesses positive overtones. The action of 37:16–17, holding two pieces of wood together so that no join is visible, is explained in 37:18–19, but it also sets the scene for the remainder of the section. Although there is again no record of its performance, there should clearly be no doubt that Ezekiel did carry it out before his fellow exiles, as well as writing it down to benefit them and their offspring in later generations.

> 37:15And the word of the LORD came to me, saying, 37:16'And ⌊as for⌋ you, son of man, take for yourself one piece of wood and write upon it "Belonging to Judah and to the sons of Israel his companions", and take another piece of wood and write upon it, "Belonging to Joseph—Ephraim's piece of wood—and the whole house of Israel his companions." 37:17And bring them together for yourself, one to another, into one piece of wood, and they will become one in your hand. 37:18But when the sons of your people say to you, saying, "Will you not tell us what you ⌊mean⌋ by these?", 37:19speak to them, "Thus says the Lord GOD: Behold, I am about to take Joseph's piece of wood which is in the hand of Ephraim and

the tribes of Israel, his companions, and I will set them upon it, ⌊that is, on⌋ Judah's piece of wood, and I will make them into one piece of wood, and they will become one in my hand."'

♦ **37:15-16** The message-reception formula, *And the word of the LORD came to me*, followed by the LORD's characteristic address to Ezekiel, *And ⌊as for⌋ you, son of man*, once more began a new section of the prophecy. Ezekiel was directed to make suitable preparations for performing a sign-act. *Take for yourself* involved the dative of advantage (ethic dative), the precise force of which is frequently elusive. Here it probably was focused on Ezekiel's involvement in the action (cf. 4:1, 9; 5:1). Presumably he was to hold the pieces of wood (rather than take them and store them somewhere), and was to be directly involved in their use.

One piece of wood used the numeral 'one' (*ʾeḥād*), which was repeated as a correlative 'another' (*ʾeḥād*). It also functioned as a key term in 37:15-19, being used eight times in all (once in the plural!), and repeated again three times in the description of true unity: 'one nation ... one king ... one shepherd' (37:22, 24).

The rendering 'piece of wood' (cf. ESV margin) attempts to be as unspecific as the underlying Hebrew term *ʿēṣ*, which might refer to a 'tree' or 'wood' of any sort, whether used for making some article (15:2-3) or for fuel (15:6; 24:10; 39:10). It could also be used as a collective term for a group of trees (6:13; 31:8; 34:27). In this context there are at least three possible ways to take the term: a stick in general, a specific type of stick—either a sceptre or a shepherd's staff—or a writing-board. The Septuagint rendered it with a word for a stick, which might be royal or pastoral (*rhabdos*), and both those interpretations have found advocates. However, to find here royal associations would imply that the subject of the oracle was an amalgamation of the dynasties of the north and south, and Ezekiel, like the other prophets, only acknowledged the legitimacy of the royal Davidic line of the south. A shepherd's staff has greater plausibility since the concept of 'shepherd' is introduced in 37:24.[79]

A stronger case can be made out for translating it as 'wooden tablet' (REB), which was the rendering favoured by the Targum. There have

---

79. It is difficult to see why a more specialised term was not used if a sceptre or shepherd's crook had been intended. Renz (1999:114) points to the availability of *maṭṭeh*, 'rod' (e.g., 7:10), *šēbeṭ*, 'sceptre' (e.g., 19:11), or even *maqqēl* 'club' (e.g., 39:9).

been preserved from the ancient world writing tablets consisting of two pieces of wood, each with a writing surface covered with wax. These were hinged together so that they could be closed to protect what was written on their inward-facing surfaces (cf. Isa. 8:1; 30:8; Hab. 2:2; Block 1998:400[80]). This would readily fit in with the symbolism of the two pieces of wood being the leaves of the tablet which would have been closed in the prophet's hand.

Even so, it remains best to understand the word simply as a 'stick', which would easily have had sufficient room on a pared surface for the few words which were to be written on it. The words were of greater significance than what they were written on.

The force of the inscription which the prophet was commanded to **write** (either using ink to stain the wood or carving the letters with a knife) is also not completely clear. It may be 'for Judah', 'Judah', or ***belonging to Judah***.[81] There is little difference in meaning between, 'This is Judah' and 'This is Judah's'. There was also represented a further category: ***to the sons of Israel his companions***, a reference to smaller tribes belonging to the covenant people of Israel which had associated with the southern kingdom dominated by Judah.[82] These would have included the tribes of Simeon and Benjamin, as well as priests and Levites residing within Judah's borders (2 Chron. 11:13–14), and others who had left the north at various stages after the breakup of the united kingdom.

The prophet was also commanded to ***take***[83] ***another stick***, and to deal with it in a similar fashion, but now using the inscription,

---

80. Block's further argument (1998:404–405) that the one tablet also contained the text of 37:21–24a and the other that of 37:24b–28 is by his own admission speculative, and unnecessary.

81. The various translations depend on the function of the inseparable preposition *lə*, (1) 'for Judah', 'pertaining to Judah', a *lamed* of reference, the most general rendering; (2) 'Judah' identifying the preposition as a *lamed inscriptionis*, that is, marking a quotation; (3) 'belonging to Judah', a *lamed* of possession. The last is probably the best option in that there is the later phrase, 'Ephraim's piece of wood', and also 'Judah's piece of wood' (37:19), both of which apparently attribute ownership (but note *IBHS* §11.2.10d).

82. Twice in this verse (and again in 37:19), the kethib has *ḥăbērô*, 'his companion', whereas the qere has a more plausible plural form, *ḥăbērâw*, 'his companions'.

83. The fuller form of the imperative *ləqaḥ* is unusual (note the earlier *qaḥ*, 'take'), but it is also found in Exod. 29:1 and Prov. 20:16, and a full form imperfect occurs in 1 Kgs. 17:11. It would seem to be simply a matter of stylistic variation.

Belonging to Joseph. This employed a less common designation for the northern tribes (Amos 5:15; Obad. 18; Pss. 77:15; 78:67). Though both Ephraim and Manasseh were descended from Joseph, it was Ephraim which was the leading tribe in the north, and hence the explanatory phrase, ***Ephraim's piece of wood.*** ***The whole house of Israel his companions*** referred to the other northern tribes. It was recognised that they too remained part of the covenant people, with 'the whole' reflecting the much larger size of the northern division of the people compared to the south. But neither part of the divided people was viewed as constituting Israel on its own.

♦ **37:17** ***Bring them together*** ('bring near', the same verb as 37:7) might have referred to two sticks being held together in a clenched hand covering the join, or two boards of a writing tablet being assembled together either with a wooden hinge pin or by a leather thong. ***They will become one*** employed the plural of the numeral 'one', presumably to indicate a composite unity, but see also the corresponding phrase in 37:19 where the usual singular form occurred presumably because the prophet's action could only achieve a symbolic, composite unity whereas what the LORD would do effectively created a new single entity.

♦ **37:18** ***The sons of your people*** pointed to Ezekiel's fellow countrymen (cf. 33:2). Though the possessive differs from that in 'my people' (37:23), the emphasis is on the prophet's closeness to them, not on any estrangement between the LORD and them. When they witnessed Ezekiel's fulfilment of the divine instructions given to him, the action prophecy would, as was intended, arouse their interest. Again their words were cited to reveal their attitude (cf. 37:11). The LORD predicted that in puzzlement they would quiz the prophet, as to ***what you ⌊mean⌋ by these.*** The idiom was literally, 'What these to you?' (cf. 24:19).

♦ **37:19** The prophet was primed as to how he should ***speak to them*** and explain his conduct. The messenger formula, ***Thus says the Lord GOD,*** proclaimed that Ezekiel was speaking and acting as the LORD's representative, and that he had provided a vivid portrayal of what the LORD himself would do: ***Behold, I***[84] ***am about to take.*** The pieces of

---

84. The personal pronoun *'ănî*, 'I', is expressed here for grammatical reasons, but Wendland (2001:269) notes that its repetition in 37:21, 23, 28 keeps the thematic spotlight fixed upon the LORD as the central character in the text.

wood were mentioned in reverse order to 37:16, with *Joseph's piece of wood* coming first. It was further specified as being that *which is in the hand of Ephraim and the tribes of Israel, his companions.*[85] Ephraim was the tribe which dominated affairs in the north.

I will set them upon it, ˻that is, on˼ Judah's piece of wood. 'Them' referred to the tribes that the piece of wood represented, and it was made clear that 'upon it' designated Judah. The process of reunification was therefore presented in a slightly Judah-centric fashion, but this reflected the historical fact that the northern tribes had broken away from the south. Overall, however, the picture is one of incorporation on an equal basis.

And I will make them into one piece of wood used the singular of the numeral 'one' (cf. 37:17) because when God united the separate entities they would be inseparably bonded together.[86] *They will become one in my hand.* This was a divine promise that the LORD's power ('in my hand') would heal the divisions and remedy the defection from covenant faithfulness which had marred the conduct of his people just as the prophet had symbolised by uniting the two sticks. In this way the fact of effective integration was foretold, but no explanation was yet given of how the LORD would accomplish it; that followed in 37:21–25.

(2) One Nation, One King, One Shepherd (37:20–28)

These verses have fared badly in critical hands, being treated as a wordy amalgamation of various restoration oracles. But these suspicions are unwarranted, and indeed the variety of reconstructions casts doubt on them all.

With the pieces of wood in his hand (37:20), Ezekiel is to relay the divine message of the restoration of Israel (37:21), who will be gathered as a unified nation in their own territory (37:22). They will be purified of all inclination towards idolatry, and so will enter fully into covenant relationship with God (37:23).

An essential feature of their restored unity will be that a descendant of David will rule over them, and this will provide the impetus for their obedience to the demands of the covenant and enjoyment of its

---

85. See note on 37:16 above.

86. Critical commentators detect corruption here because of the intermingled references to tribes and sticks. The LXX and the Vulgate also had difficulty with this verse, but the Hebrew text seems secure no matter how it was later understood.

blessings (37:24–25). The importance of the covenant in this renewed state of affairs underlies the concluding verses which summarise and provide a climax for the whole process (37:26–28). The obedient people will benefit from an increase in their numbers and the divine presence in their midst. Because they have been sanctified by God, this state of affairs will continue for ever.

Fulfilment. Here again there is a prevision of gospel blessings presented in terms which were accessible to the prophet and his contemporaries. The suitability of this Old Testament language for the task in hand was, of course, no accident, since the institutions and history of Israel had been divinely shaped to foreshadow what would be accomplished in Christ. Because of this it is to veer off on an unfortunate interpretive course to start looking for a literalistic fulfilment of what is portrayed here. To some extent after the return from the exile there were individuals from the northern tribes incorporated into Judah: for instance, Anna of the tribe of Asher (Luke 2:36), Saul/ Paul of the tribe of Benjamin (Rom. 11:1), and Levites like Zechariah (Luke 1:5). But that was only a partial fulfilment of what is expressed here.

Nor is this prophecy to be fulfilled through a reappearance of the lost tribes during a future millennium to occupy the Promised Land and build a great temple there. That is to confuse the symbolism of prophetic imagery with the reality of God's spiritual consummation of his provision for his people. The clearest way to understand this and similar passages is to observe the analogy instituted by the manner in which the New Testament treats the prophecy of the New Covenant in Jeremiah 31:31–34. This was originally presented as a promise to both Israel and Judah, in which they were viewed as restored, keeping God's law (as in 37:24 here), and spiritually renewed. But the kingdom is already really, but provisionally, present in the church of Jesus Christ, incorporating Jew and Gentile alike. It is in this that the New Covenant promise is already actualised (Heb. 8:6–13; 10:14–18), and there will be the grand culmination of God's promises at the Second Coming. Then the land promise will not be focused on real estate in the Middle East, but on the new heavens and the new earth. Then the beneficiaries of that promise will not be Israel according to the flesh. It is not that they will be excluded because of their ethnic background. Indeed, it would seem from Romans 11 that ethnic Israel will definitely be represented among their number, but on the same terms and by the same route as all others: faith in Jesus Christ as the alone Saviour. 'If you ⌞are⌟ Christ's, then you are Abraham's seed, heirs according to promise' (Gal. 3:29).

> ³⁷:²⁰'And the pieces of wood upon which you write will be in your hand before their eyes, ³⁷:²¹and speak to them, "Thus says the Lord GOD: Behold, I am about to take the sons of Israel from among the nations where they have gone and I will gather them from round about and I will bring them to their land. ³⁷:²²And I will make them into one nation in the land, on the mountains of Israel, and one king will be king for all of them, and they will no longer be two nations, and they will no longer be divided into two kingdoms any longer. ³⁷:²³And they will no longer defile themselves with their idols and their detestable ⌞things⌟ and with all their rebellious acts, and I will save them from all their dwelling places where they have sinned and I will cleanse them and they will be my people and I for my part will be their God.
> ³⁷:²⁴And my servant David ⌞will be⌟ king over them, and they all will have one shepherd; and they will walk in my judgements and observe my statues and do them. ³⁷:²⁵And they will dwell upon the land which I gave to my servant, to Jacob, in which your fathers dwelled, and they will dwell upon it, they, their sons, and their sons' sons, for ever, and David my servant ⌞will be⌟ their ruler for ever.
> ³⁷:²⁶And I will make with them a covenant of peace; it will be an everlasting covenant with them. And I will set them and multiply them and I will set my sanctuary in their midst for ever. ³⁷:²⁷And my tabernacle will be over them, and I will be their God, and they for their part will be my people. ³⁷:²⁸And the nations will know that I ⌞am⌟ the LORD who am sanctifying Israel, when my sanctuary is in their midst for ever." '

♦ **37:20** After Ezekiel had made the appropriate preparations for performing the sign-act, he was to proceed as the LORD had authorised him. *And the pieces of wood upon which you write will be in your hand* as a symbol of the united people. This was to be a public display *before their eyes* of what the LORD would provide for his people.

♦ **37:21** *Restoration of One Nation.* Ezekiel was once more to address his fellow exiles in his capacity as a divine messenger. They were to be informed on God's behalf that ***I am about to take the sons of Israel.*** 'The sons of Israel' (cf. 2:3) viewed them as the current representatives of the covenant people, rather than being a mere ethnic designation. ***Take*** echoed 37:19 (and also its repeated use in 37:16), and suggested an Exodus-style intervention to remove them ***from*** *among the nations where they have gone* (cf. 36:24). Their dispersal involved more than their presence in Babylon, but it would be divinely reversed. *I will gather them from round about.* This would include the northern tribes which had been displaced elsewhere by the Assyrians (2 Kgs. 17:6; 18:11) as well as various groups of refugees. *I will bring them to their land* promised that God would accomplish their restoration to *their* land where they had divinely bestowed rights of occupation (not of ownership; it remained the LORD's).

♦ **37:22** However, on its own, restoration to the land would not solve the underlying problems which had led to their deportation. The LORD committed himself to sovereign and effective action to constitute the restored people a unity: *I will make them into one nation in the land.* They were already 'one people' (*'am*), but now their political and social cohesion would be established as 'one nation' (*gôy*), not two separate kingdoms. *On the mountains of Israel* is a phrase repeatedly found in Ezekiel (cf. 36:1, 8) to refer to the land of covenant promise, here designated 'the land'. But the earthly land foreshadowed and symbolically represented the heavenly fatherland (Heb. 11:14–16). This promise would not be fully realised apart from Christ and the inheritance he would bestow upon the new Israel, gathered from Jew and Gentile brought into one fold under one shepherd (John 10:16).

The envisaged unity of restored Israel would be effected through the instrumentality of there being one king. *One king will be king for all of them.* In the light of 37:24 this was not a reference to the LORD himself. Ezekiel did not generally use 'king' (*melek*) in a favourable sense, preferring 'leader' (*nāśî'*) when he described Israel's kings. However, here and in 37:24 he did employ *melek*. At this juncture, however, details regarding this king were not spelled out, though in the light of the messianic specification of 34:23–24, the outworking in later verses was not surprising.

And they will no longer be[87] *two nations.* The repetitious nature of 'no longer' (*lō'* ... *'ôd*) and 'any longer' (*'ôd*) emphasised that such a schism could never occur again. It implied that acceptance of the authority and norms of that king would do away with the differences and disputes which fostered disunity.

This description cannot be adequately understood apart from Christ.

---

87. The qere is plural *yihyû*, 'they will be', with the divided kingdoms as the subject. This is read by the early versions and is preferable to the singular form found in the kethib *yihyeh*, 'he/it will be', presumably referring back to 'one nation' earlier in the verse.

The restoration and reunification of Israel after many, but far from all, of them returned from Babylon anticipated greater events in the future. After their reinstatement in the land, Israel did not have a native king of the Davidic line. That had to await the coming of Christ, the nature of whose kingdom is not a matter of political arrangements, but of spiritual organisation. Even so, the unity predicted here has as yet only been imperfectly achieved, and awaits his return and the institution of the heavenly kingdom.

♦ **37:23** *Spiritual Cleansing.* The restored people would not only enjoy political and social cohesion; there would also be religious and spiritual harmony of people living in rapport with one another, but more especially in unison with God. **They will no longer defile themselves** (cf. 14:11) **with their idols** (cf. 6:4) **and their detestable things** (cf. 5:11) **and with all their rebellious acts.** 'Rebellious acts' (cf. 14:11) were those done in deliberate defiance of the known norms of the covenant king. But all that was wrong with rebellious Israel's conduct would be decisively and definitively eliminated. 'No longer' (cf. 37:22) presaged a radical alteration from the past.

There were two actions the LORD would perform to banish any repetition of the people's past. In the first place, *I will save* (cf. *yāšaʿ*, hiphil; 34:22; 36:29). Though only occurring three times in Ezekiel, this major term for salvation denoted deliverance from external enemies, and also deliverance from the inner enslavement to sin.

Though *from all their dwelling places* (MT) is accepted by the AV and NKJV, the phrase seems out of place in this context, and instead 'from all their turnings back/backslidings'[88] may be read with support from some Hebrew and Greek manuscripts. Indeed, the noun *môšab* (ordinarily, 'dwelling') may be have been a variant spelling of *mašûbâ*, 'backsliding', or 'apostasy', a term not found elsewhere in Ezekiel, but a favourite of Jeremiah. Even so, it ought to be noted that the root (*yāšab*) underlying 'dwelling places' did occur three times in 37:25.

The second action which the LORD would perform was: *I will cleanse them.* This verb (*ṭāhar*; cf. 36:25) described the creation of the new heart and new spirit in 36:25, 29, 33—no longer the outward rituals of priestly purification, but the analogous spiritual reality of an inner purity achieved through the work of the Spirit of God (Tit. 3:5).

---

88. Rather than accepting the MT *mikkol môšəbôtêhem*, 'from all their dwelling places', the emended text reads *mikkol mašûbôtêhem*, 'from all their turnings back/backslidings'. The MT may have arisen through metathesis of *waw* and *shin*.

This would lead to the reality encapsulated in the covenant formula: ***they will be my people and I for my part will be their God*** (cf. 11:20; 14:11; 34:30–31). This was repeated in 37:27 in a variant form. It recalled the terms of covenant renewal in 14:11, and was a reversal of the sentence imposed in 5:11. There would be restored the bond of mutuality which was the essence of the covenant relationship, and which had been—and remains—the goal of God's covenant provision.

♦ **37:24** *Davidic Kingship.* ***My servant David*** and ***one shepherd*** already occurred in 34:23–24, but in this verse the term ***king*** was employed rather than 'ruler' as in 34:24 and in 37:25 (cf. 37:22). There was clear identification with the earlier figure through repetition of these phrases, but there was little new information given. 'My servant' was a title of great honour when conferred by the King of kings. His messianic appointee would not rule in a self-serving fashion, intent on advancing his own interests, but would realise the covenant ideal of kingship which had been expressed in Deuteronomy 17:14–20.

The inclusion constituted by the first clause of 37:24 and the last clause of 37:25 strongly suggested that what fell between them was intimately linked with the provision and presence of the messianic king. In effect, what was predicted was that, because the people would acknowledge his authority and respect his directions, ***they will walk in my judgements and observe my statutes and do them*** (cf. 36:27). This would be to conform to the standard of behaviour exhibited by David (1 Kgs. 11:38). Their king's directions would clarify for them what would need to be done, and he himself would provide an example for them to imitate. In this way their fellowship with God would not be marred by contravening the pattern of life which he stipulated for his people.

♦ **37:25** The obedient people would enjoy their occupation of the land. ***They will dwell upon the land which I gave to my servant, to Jacob, in which your fathers dwelled.***[89] The patriarch Jacob (cf. 28:25) had been the recipient of the divine promise of the land (Gen. 28:13–15; 35:11–12), but the original grant had been to Abraham (Gen. 12:7; 13:14–17; 17:1–8). It may be that Jacob, who was renamed Israel, was

---

89. The LXX and Peshitta read 'their fathers', and this is preferred by many translations. The switch in the text from 'their' to 'your' is, however, feasible Hebrew idiom, particularly as 'their fathers' seems to occur in Ezekiel only in reproofs whereas this is promissory (cf. Hummel 2007:1073–1074).

more associated with the unity of the twelve tribes, descended from his sons, whereas Ishmael and Esau were also blood descendants of Abraham. Mention of Jacob and 'your fathers' constituted links with the past which would be reinstated.

They will dwell upon it, they, their sons, and their sons' sons, for ever. 'For ever' (*'ôlām*) did not always denote an eternal situation; it might refer to the distant, but not unlimited, past or future (cf. 25:15; 26:20), or to what was perpetual throughout a period (cf. 35:5, 9). However, the five times the term 'for ever'/'everlasting' (*'ôlām*) occurred in 37:25–28 clearly conveyed the unending duration of the kingdom of the messianic king and the provision he would make for his people. Though the two expressions 'for ever' in this verse were not identical in Hebrew (the first is *'ad-'ôlām*, 'up to for ever', and the second is *lə'ôlām*, 'to for ever'), they were virtually synonymous, with the first perhaps accenting unending progress into the future, and the second viewing eternity as an entity. 'For ever' was characteristic of the Davidic covenant, occurring eight times in 2 Samuel 7, and so providing a lead into the final clause of the verse.

The perpetuity of the enjoyment of covenant blessing was associated with the everlasting dominion of the messianic ruler. **David my servant ⌊will be⌋ their ruler**[90] **for ever.** The eschatological David was here designated **their ruler** (*nāśîʾ*) rather than 'their king' (cf. 37:22, 24). In early times this term had been used of a leader of a tribe (cf. Num. 2–29), and it was employed in Samuel to denote a king without negative absolutist overtones. It would be this leader's faithful adherence as 'my servant' (cf. 2 Sam. 7:5, 8, and David's self reference ten times in 2 Sam. 7:19–29) to the divine requirements which would give effectiveness and success to his role. This term was later used for the leader in connection with the religious life of the community in obedience to God (cf. 44:3).

♦ **37:26** *Covenantal Consummation.* The concluding verses (37:26–28) envisaged the covenantal concord of the community when their loyal and obedient behaviour ensured that they lived in harmony with the LORD and so enjoyed the benefits his rule and protection would lavish upon them. **I will make with them a covenant of peace** brought together various aspects of the prophecy (cf. 34:25). 'Peace' referred to all the good and well-being bestowed by the King through his covenant with his people. **It will be an everlasting covenant with**

---

90. It is of interest that in 34:24 and 37:25 the LXX translated the term *nāśîʾ* by *archōn*, 'leader', rather than by *basileus*, 'king'.

them.[91] 'An everlasting (*'ôlām*, cf. 37:25) covenant' (Gen. 9:16; 17:7, 13, 19; Lev. 24:8) was also claimed for merely human treaties in that their terms were intended to exist in perpetuity. That was one of the distinguishing marks of a covenant as distinct from a contract with a limited term of applicability, but an eternal covenant was only truly achieved in the case of one that was divinely instituted and maintained.[92]

Two features of the covenantal arrangements were set out. The first was the security and increase of the people. ***I will set them*** was used absolutely in the sense of 'I will establish them' (cf. NKJV, NIV), though it may be possible that 'in the land' was to be understood with the verb (ESV; Block 1998:419–420).[93] ***Multiply them*** (cf. 36:10–11, 37). Increased numbers reflected the covenant as a means to realise the creation mandate (cf. Gen. 1:28; 12:1–3; 22:17).

The second feature of the LORD's provision would be his own presence with his people. This introduced the culminating aspect of the restoration, which had not been mentioned hitherto. ***I will set my sanctuary in their midst for ever.*** 'Sanctuary' (*miqdāš*; cf. 5:11; 8:6; 9:6; 23:38–39) viewed the structure as that which was set apart because of the presence of the holy (*qādôš*) God. It was—and is—the greatest act of divine condescension that the God who is apart from his creation should stoop to accommodate to creaturely perception the disclosure of his presence with them. 'In their midst' probably went beyond specifying a geographical location such as once pertained to the tent of meeting in the midst of the wilderness camp (Num. 2:17); it may well have hinted at a degree of familiarity and closeness, while ***for ever*** in final position in this and the concluding verse sealed the perpetuity of the arrangements.

♦ **37:27 *My tabernacle*** (*miškān*) used the term for the sanctuary

---

91. Though *'ōtām* seems to be a form of the direct object marker, it must here be intended as a form of the preposition *'ēt*, 'with'. There is evidence in Kings, Jeremiah and Ezekiel of the two forms being used interchangeably. Cf. the similar expression in 16:60 so that Block (1998:408) suggests that the expression is a dialectal variation.

92. 'We are thereby reminded that covenants in ancient times were typically stated to remain effective "for all future time". After investigating this matter with respect to about 7,500 "eternal" treaties signed between 1500 B.C. and A.D. 1850, an historian reported that the treaties in question lasted an average of two years each!' (Youngblood 1971:42).

93. NRSV follows the Targum and renders, 'I will bless them', rather than 'I will set/give them'.

primarily associated with wilderness period (e.g., Exod. 25:9). It referred to a structure where one resided, and could be used of human tent dwellings. It indicated the immanence of the God who graciously drew near to his people, and who in condescension tented with them in the wilderness. The tabernacle presence was said to be *over them.* Probably a reference to the divine cloud of fire in the wilderness (cf. Isa. 4:5), indicating that the abiding presence of God would cover and protect the people.

Again (cf. 37:23) the mutual relationships of the covenant bond were stressed in terms of the covenant formula: *I will be their God, and they for their part will be my people.*

♦ **37:28** The recognition formula was used to describe the situation at the end of this process of restoration. It will impact on *the nations* who will be compelled to *know that I ⌊am⌋ the LORD* whose presence and power will be obvious in that he would be *sanctifying Israel, when my sanctuary is in their midst for ever.* The distinguishing mark of God's people would be his presence with them, and this in turn would set them apart and mould them into conformity with the requirements of their God.

REFLECTION

- The promises made in this oracle are rich with gospel truth. For instance, there is particular emphasis on the unity of the people of God (37:22). This was a matter which weighed heavily on Christ on the night before his death. He made it a matter of prayer that those who believe in him would 'all be one ... that they may be one even as we ⌊are⌋ one ... I in them and you in me, that they may be completely one, so that the world may know that you sent me and loved them even as you loved me' (John 17:21–23). In essence all who believe in Christ are now integrated into life with him, and share in the oneness of the new life, but there is a sad deficiency when it comes to manifesting that oneness. This stems from imperfect understanding of the truth, which leads to division and tension within the body of Christ. 'Is Christ divided?' (1 Cor. 1:13). A fractured church dishonours God and weakens its witness to the world regarding Christ and God's love.
- The essence of the land promise was that it was the place where God presenced himself with his people in a special way. In the Old Testament 'my sanctuary' (37:26) and 'my tabernacle' (37:27) were physical reminders of his presence. God dwelling with mankind was realised in a more sublime fashion in New Testament times through

the coming of Christ. 'The Word became flesh and tabernacled among us' (John 1:14). This was also attested to by Christ's affirmation that his body is the true temple (John 2:10-22). This temple presence is continued through the indwelling of God in the heart of believers by the Holy Spirit. 'Do you not know that you are God's temple and that God's Spirit dwells in you?' (1 Cor. 3:16; cf. 1 Cor. 6:19). But this process will be completed at the Second Coming when 'the tabernacle of God is with men' (Rev. 21:3), not as a temple building but by God's presence in their midst (Rev. 21:22).

- 'I will cleanse them' (37:23) is the only basis on which those contaminated and defiled by sin can be found in God's presence. 'The blood of Jesus his Son cleanses us from all sin' (1 John 1:7). It is easy to become so accustomed to such Scriptural language that we forget that it is not a natural association of ideas that blood cleanses. It is only through realisation of the sacrificial basis of what is being said that the ideas can be connected and properly understood. The blood is that of a life surrendered in death to pay the penalty for sin, and, once the payment has been made by Christ, it is credited to all those who believe in him and who are thus given a new status in him, cleansed from sin, and drawn ever more into his likeness.
- The dynamic of faithful living underpins 37:24-25. It is as David is the king of the people that their conduct will conform to what God requires and they will enjoy the blessings of the covenant. This is achieved in Christ who is fulfilment of the Davidic promise. No longer do the people of God have his law presented to them merely as external requirements written 'on tablets of stone, but on tablets of human hearts' (2 Cor. 3:3). This is not just a matter of internalisation of the precepts of the law; it derives from a heart attachment to Christ who is the living embodiment of God's law. Those who are devoted to the one who always did his Father's will treasure within themselves what he is like, and seek to be like him. This is one of the great privileges of the New Testament church. How God wishes us to live is presented not only in the divine commandments; it is acted out before us in the person of his Son. He is the living role model to whom all should conform. 'Be imitators of me, as I am of Christ' (1 Cor. 11:1). Paul bestowed the accolade on the Thessalonian church to whom the gospel came 'not only in word but also in power and in the Holy Spirit and with full conviction' that they 'became imitators of us and of the Lord' (1 Thess. 1:5-6).

G. Gog and Magog (38:1-39:29)

In the gruelling conditions of their detention in Babylonia, it would seem that the dispirited exiles are all too conscious of the hostility of the powers of this world which have time and again brought loss of life and loss of property to their people. The LORD therefore extends further encouragement to them: in chapters 38-39 it takes the form of assuring them of his control over the forces of evil, even though they will assail the restored people in their land; in chapters 40-48 there is a presentation of the serenity and orderliness of ideal life in the land centred round the LORD's temple where he is present to receive their worship. The imagery of both scenarios is drawn from the world that the exiles know, but neither state of affairs is tied down to particular dates or events. Rather they are word-pictures of spiritual truth regarding the security of the people of God, to whom these chapters extend the guarantee of divine protection. Even though ferocious nations gather in a hostile alliance to destroy his people and to despoil their land, yet the aggression of their opponents will be under divine control, and the attack they launch will be overthrown by him. So then it is well worthwhile to persevere and to 'strengthen hands that are limp, and make firm knees that tremble. Say to those who are anxious in heart, "Be strong; do not be afraid! Behold your God! ⌞With⌟ vengeance he will come, ⌞with⌟ the recompense of God; he himself will come to save you" ' (Isa. 35:3-4; cf. Heb. 12:12-13).

Structure. Chapters 38 and 39 are demarcated by the word-event formula, 'the word of the LORD came to me' (38:1) and the date formula of 40:1 at the start of the visionary account of God's perfect order which is embodied in the description of the new temple and the new land (chs. 40-48).

Though views differ over the details of the internal structure of these two chapters, it is obvious that there is a sevenfold use of the introductory messenger formula, 'Thus says the Lord GOD' (38:3, 10, 14, 17; 39:1, 17, 25), and this was probably intended to provide markers to identify seven sections in this division of the prophecy spread unevenly between the chapters. On the other hand, it is possible on thematic grounds to analyse the text into a similar number of sections. This is generally achieved by dividing the material into two panels which pivot in a balanced fashion around the chapter division, with chapter 38 dealing with the defeat of Gog and chapter 39 with the disposal of Gog (Block 1992:517; Renz 1999:119).[94] However, the simpler, sevenfold analysis is followed here. It is also worth noting that gain knowledge about God is mentioned seven times in these chapters (38:16, 23; 39:6, 7, 22, 23, 28), though it does not function as a consistent structuring device.

More difficult questions are raised by asking what relationship chapters 38 and 39 bear to what follows and to what precedes them. On the basis that chapter 37 ends with God dwelling in his sanctuary among his people, and the rest of the nations recognising his power, it may plausibly be argued that chapters 38–39 and chapters 40–48 form a closing paired sequence which takes up and elaborates on the themes of 37:26–28 in reverse order. From that perspective it is appropriate to separate chapters 38–39 from chapters 33–37, and consider them along with the concluding chapters of the book.[95]

While this thematic sequence does bring out features of the text, the closing section of chapter 39 strongly indicates a different intention. These verses (39:25–29) present a summary which is oriented towards the themes of preceding chapters, and they fit somewhat awkwardly if chapters 38–48 are taken as the basic block of material. Quite possibly the oracles concerning Gog and Magog were given prior to the vision concerning the temple and the land, and Ezekiel had organised his work in its present form up to 39:29 before being in a position to add the later revelation as a literary appendix. Chapters 33–39 may therefore be suitably viewed as a more interrelated collection of material from his prophetic ministry.

However, other arguments are also brought forward about the appropriateness of where chapters 38–39 are currently located in relation to what precedes them. Given that they deal with the hostility of foreign powers, it is contended that they have an affinity with the oracles against the nations, and should have been located along with them. But there are other places where the conduct and destiny of foreign nations are considered outside chapters 25–32, such as the Ammonites (21:28) and Edom (ch. 35). Moreover, earlier oracles

---

94. Greenberg noted that part of Ezekiel's style was a 'halving' pattern (1983:25–26), and this oracle falls into that category, with 38:1–23 focusing on Yahweh's defeat of Gog and those associated with him, and 39:1–29 largely concerned with the disposal of the corpses of the slain army. Within each section, there is further halving, in that the prophet is issued with renewed commands to speak (38:14; 39:17).

95. A notable instance of this is the volume co-authored by Milgrom and Block (2012), *Ezekiel's Hope: A Commentary on Ezekiel 38–48*.

focused on the current antagonism of the nations neighbouring Israel, whereas the time frame of chapters 38–39 is in the unidentified future, and the enemy in view is a more mysterious figure from afar.

Another approach is to argue that the defeat of Israel's enemies should precede the restoration of chapters 34–37, to which 39:25–29 would form an appropriate introduction, and in that case 37:26–28 would function suitably to lead into the temple vision of chapters 40–48, which decribe the consummation of Israel's recovery. Indeed, there is a Septuagint manuscript (P. 967; second to third century A.D.) with the chapter order 36–38–39–37 (Crane 2008:10), so that there is a straight movement from 37:28 to 40:1. However, it is evident that this sequence is mistaken in that the attack of Gog tells a very different story from the defeat of Israel's enemies prior to their return to the land. Instead it presupposes that the people are already settled securely in the land.[96]

Theme. The storyline of these chapters is fairly clear. It tells of a powerful leader, Gog of the land of Magog, chief ruler of Meshekh and Tubal, who will lead a large and well-equipped army as part of an international alliance intent on crushing Israel. This will occur after the Israelites have returned to their land, and are living there peacefully and prosperously, little suspecting such a sudden attack on them (38:1–10). The aggressors will consider Israel to be easy prey (38:10–14), but they will be unaware that the LORD is directing what happens to achieve his own ends (38:14–16). Even though the LORD had induced the invasion of the northern alliance, when it does occur, he will react with fury against them and they will be utterly routed (38:17–23). Divine intervention will render the weaponry of the invading forces useless, and their slain will be left as carrion on the open fields. Even their homelands will experience catastrophe. In this way the uniqueness and power of the LORD will be demonstrated (39:1–8). The Israelites will be able to despoil their enemies (39:9–10), and it will take seven months for all the dead to be buried and the land cleansed (39:11–16). Another portrayal of the magnitude of the death-toll is given in terms of a banquet which birds and beasts of prey will enjoy as they scavenge the remains of the fallen (39:17–20). This whole incident will convince the nations that the LORD is acting

---

96. Extensive consideration of P. 967 is found in Crane (2008). The manuscript also omits the major pericope (36:23c–38) as well as changing the chapter order. Crane considers P. 967 to preserve the original order, and the MT to reflect changes introduced in the Hasmonean era.

against those who oppose him, and they will also come to appreciate the rationale behind his dealings with his own people (39:21–24). There is a final résumé demonstrating how, and why, the LORD had been at work in the history of Israel, and promising their renewed fellowship with the LORD through the presence of the Spirit (39:25–29).

Identity of Gog. Determining the identity of Gog is closely linked with the mode of interpretation which should be adopted for these chapters. Although many attempts have been made to equate Gog with some figure contemporary with Ezekiel, or subsequent to him, not enough detail is provided to resolve the matter, and this lack of clarity seems to have been deliberate. Whatever the background to the name Gog, it bears a significant resemblance to the Akkadian word for 'darkness' (*gûg*). This sinister figure does not predict any particular individual in the flow of world history, but is a personification of the ruthless antagonism of the forces of evil whenever they gather to oppose the people of God. This does not lead to an ultimate dualism. It is significant that Gog is not accorded the title of king. He is merely the supremo of an international alliance which has to await divine permission before it can assail Israel.

Gog is not to be identified with any historical figure, though the spirit of Gog is evident in many persecutors of the church over the centuries. It is also the case that the details of this prophecy are not to be sought in any particular historical incident, though many aspects of it foreshadow the final cataclysm as foretold by John in Revelation. A literalistic interpretation of these chapters is quite at variance with the presentation of the text, whose purpose is to affirm the perpetuity of restored Israel dwelling in her land (37:25). That in turn is a preview of the unbreakable fellowship between the LORD and his people. The description of a seven month process of interment (39:12) is obviously hyperbolic and symbolic, as is the subsequent sacrificial feast to which LORD invites birds and wild beasts, permitting them to eat the blood and fat usually reserved for himself (39:17–20). This portrait is not susceptible to detailed analysis or literalistic, historical fulfilment. It is a graphic and arresting literary portrayal of complete annihilation.

But that does raise a major question: Why is Gog permitted to attack the people? In particular, if covenantal blessing has been bestowed on them, would not such an invasion be contrary to the promise, 'And I will give peace in the land, and you will lie down, and there ⌊will be⌋ none to make ⌊you⌋ tremble; and I will make an end of evil animals from the land, and a sword will not pass through on your land' (Lev. 26:6)? Though there is restored harmony between the LORD and his people, there continues to be a dark side to the outworking of human history, which is divinely held in check. Clearly these prophecies are predominantly concerned with this interim age before the return of the Lord.

Apocalyptic. The genre of this passage has been subject of much discussion, particularly as regards the appropriateness of the designation 'apocalyptic'. This term is applied to an assortment of literature in which divine intervention leads to a total overthrow of existing structures of human society and government. This occurs in the day of the LORD when he intervenes in cataclysmic judgement to inaugurate the final kingdom of God. The literary genre of apocalyptic developed during the intertestamental period and later, and became characterised by certain stereotyped characteristics, such as a narrative framework with revelatory disclosures of cosmic scope mediated through an angelic figure to a renowned figure of old, and exhibited a deep pessimism about the scope for correcting prevailing conditions apart from their being completely divinely overthrown.

These chapters provided a quarry of material for later writers, both canonical (such as John in Revelation) and extra-canonical. They share the basic premise that resolution of human affairs can only be achieved by unparalleled divine activity. However, as a matter of literary genre Ezekiel's presentation here stops short of what was included in many subsequent writings. In chapters 38–39 there is no angelic narrator, and, though the action involves the overthrow of many hostile nations, it still stops short of universal disintegration, but focuses on the mountains of Israel.

Subsequent Scripture. John later made use of Gog and Magog imagery and of the sequence of the closing chapters of Ezekiel to declare that in the final resolution of earth's history there would be a definitive termination of the troubling hostility of the enemies of God's people (Rev. 20:5–10) before the people come to enjoy final bliss in God's presence (Rev. 21–22).

Both here and in Revelation the lesson being taught is that the overthrow of the powers of darkness is by divine intervention, not by human force. Gog is brought out against God's people only so that the enemy's destruction may finally proclaim the LORD's holiness and assert the security which the LORD affords to his own. As on a previous occasion the LORD affirmed that there would never again be a flood to inundate the earth (Gen. 9:11), here he assures his people that he will not stir up another Babylon against them. Indeed, though a confederacy of ferocious nations plot against them, they will not succeed. Though kings may assemble, they would have no divine warrant to do so, and would be scattered in panic-stricken flight (Ps. 48:4–8). This is the true Zion theology which expresses the security provided for those whose covenant allegiance is genuine, and which anticipates the final consummation (Rev. 20:9).

(1) The Invasion of the Armies of Gog (38:1–9)

> $^{38:1}$And the word of the LORD came to me, saying, $^{38:2}$'Son of man, set your face towards Gog of the land of Magog, the chief ruler of Meshekh and Tubal, and prophesy against him, $^{38:3}$and say, "Thus says the Lord GOD: Behold, I am against you, O Gog, chief ruler of Meshekh and Tubal! $^{38:4}$And I will turn you round and set hooks in your jaws; and I will bring you and all your force out, horses and horsemen, clothed to perfection all of them, a great assembly, ⌊with⌋ shields large and small, all of them wielding swords. $^{38:5}$Persia, Cush and Put with them, all of them ⌊with⌋ shield and helmet, $^{38:6}$Gomer and all its troops, Beth-togarmah ⌊from⌋ the distant north and all its troops—many peoples ⌊are⌋ with you. $^{38:7}$Get ready and keep yourself at the ready, you and all your assembly assembled about you, so that you may become a guard for them. $^{38:8}$After many days you will be summoned; in the latter part of the years you will enter a land brought back from the sword, gathered from many peoples upon the mountains of Israel, which had been a ruin of long-standing; it has been brought out from peoples, and they are dwelling securely, all of them. $^{38:9}$And you will go up, like a storm you will come, you will be like a cloud to cover the land—you and all your troops and many peoples with you." '

38:1–2 For the last time Ezekiel used the message-reception formula to mark the beginning of a major section of his prophecy, and the divine revelation commenced with the characteristic form of address for the prophet, ***Son of man*** (see on 2:1). The hostile-orientation formula, also making its last appearance, was used to determine the posture Ezekiel was to adopt as he delivered this oracle to the exiles. ***Set your face towards*** (see on 6:2) was undoubtedly an inimical gesture in the light of the following command, ***prophesy against him***. So the prophet's attitude was to be a reflection of the LORD's adverse disposition (cf. 38:3).

Ezekiel's stance and message were to be against ***Gog.*** The fact that Gog did occur as a personal name in 1 Chronicles 5:4 corroborates reading the word as a name, but it sheds no light on the identity of the individual named here. Many suggestions have been made over the years, including a second millennium figure in Ugarit, but most commonly Gog has been taken to be a strong king of Lydia in west Asia Minor who died around the middle of the century preceding Ezekiel. He was known to the Greeks as Gyges and to the Assyrians as Gûgu. He was not, however, a particularly significant figure, and it is generally agreed that the primary reference was not to him. While his name could have been used to refer to a king contemporary with Ezekiel (such as Alyattes, the king of Lydia; for other potential candidates, see Zimmerli 1983:300–302; Block 1998:433–435), or even perhaps a coded reference to the Babylonian emperor, it is more probable that his name was borrowed not on account of the character or exploits of the original Gyges, but because he hailed from the ominous north (viewed from the Promised Land), helped by the similarity of his name to the Akkadian term for darkness (*gûg*). He was presented as the ominous leader of an alliance of aggressors who would come against restored Israel.

Gog was said to hail from ***the land of Magog.***[97] Elsewhere in the Old Testament (and also in Rev. 20:7–10) Magog appeared as a personal name, that of the second son of Japheth (Gen. 10:2; 1 Chron. 1:5). Here, however, there was a definite article with Magog, which would be unusual for a personal name.[98] Though no similar name for a country has been found in other ancient Near Eastern sources, it did most probably designate a territory (cf. 39:6). If Magog was a code name (cf. Jeremiah's use of Sheshakh for Babylon, Jer. 25:26), then it too could refer to Babylon, but Babylon was not viewed elsewhere in

---

97. Magog occurs with the article only here. The Targum and Vulgate reflect the MT, but the LXX and Peshitta read 'and the land of Magog': 'Set your face against Gog and the land of Magog, ruler of Ros, Mosech and Thobel, and prophesy against him'. The final 'him' is, however, anomalous, and 38:3 and 39:1 identify Gog as the ruler in both the LXX and MT. Some critics delete 'of the land of Magog' as a later (incorrect) insertion.

98. Another possibility (Tooman 2010:64) is that Gog reflects on the Balaam prophecies where there is predicted that a star (a king) will arise out of Jacob and who will be higher 'than Agag' (*mēʾăgag*). A variety of early textual witnesses including the LXX, Samaritan Pentateuch, and Old Latin have 'than Gog' (*miggôg*). The direction of influence is, however, most probably from this passage on the scribes who were transmitting the text of Numbers.

Ezekiel as the target of divine hostility (see Introduction to chs. 25–32). Josephus identified Magog with the Scythians (*Ant.* 1.123). However, in the light of the following description, it arguably referred to the general area of Anatolia, modern central Turkey. But it was not the location of Magog which was significant, but the way in which it functioned to reinforce the dark and sinister overtones of the name Gog.

Gog was also described as ***the chief ruler of Meshekh and Tubal*** (cf. 38:3; 39:1),[99] though it has to be admitted that this translation is somewhat uncertain.[100] Following the Septuagint, the term rendered 'chief' has been taken by some to be a place name, Rosh (not otherwise known in Scripture). While this cannot be ruled out, the equation of Rosh with Russia is an unwarranted fancy favoured in some circles of prophetic interpretation. The place names, Meshekh and Tubal, were real enough. This was their third appearance in Ezekiel, occurring also in the prosaic Tyrian trading accounts of chapter 27 in reference to lands in the area of Lydia and Cappadocia, and among the defeated warrior kingdoms in Sheol (32:26). They were distant peoples with whom Israel had not had direct contact, but of whose ferocity and barbarity they had heard. Something of their attitude towards these places can be grasped from the words of the pilgrim bemoaning his wretched lot as he returned to Jerusalem. 'Woe to me, that I sojourn in Meshekh, that I dwell together with the tents of Kedar! Too long have I personally had my dwelling together with one who hates peace. I ⌊am for⌋ peace, but when I speak, they ⌊are⌋ for war!' (Ps. 120:5–7). In Revelation 20:8 Gog and Magog were referred to as political powers, deceived by Satan and under his control, who will gather to wage war against the church of Christ.

♦ **38:3** The LORD directed Ezekiel, as his messenger, to convey his

---

99. Wendland (2009:210) suggests that the mention of Meshekh and Tubal here corresponds to 'Meshekh-tubal' in 32:26, and constitutes an example of the structural device of *exclusio* (cf. footnote 1 intro ch. 25), which brackets the dramatic peak of Ezekiel's gospel message in chs. 33–37.

100. The construct chain, *nəśîʾ rōʾš mešek wətubāl*, is unusually formed. It is possible (with most English translations) to take *rōʾš* as an adjectival construct, yielding the sense 'first/head ruler' or 'chief ruler'. Alternatively, there is evidence from Num. 3:32 and 1 Chron. 7:40 that the phrase *nəśîʾ rōʾš* described one of superior rank. So Duguid (1994:22) identifies *rōʾš* not as an adjectival construct, but as a collective noun, so that the sense is 'prince of the chiefs of Meshekh and Tubal'. Another approach is to identify Rosh as a country, and render 'the ruler of Rosh, Meshekh, and Tubal' (LXX; NKJV, REB).

opposition to Gog: ***Behold, I am against you!*** (lit., 'I am towards you', cf. 5:8). The alternative scholarly title for this expression is 'a challenge to a duel' formula, and in the light of 39:3 that is apt here. The ensuing battle was to be a duel between two parties in which Israel played no part until the conflict was over (39:12).

♦ **38:4** The LORD then set out how he would use Gog for his own purposes. Nothing Gog would do would lie outwith the LORD's control: ***I will turn you round*** (*šûb*, polel). The verb (here and in 39:2) poses a problem in that it would ordinarily indicate 'to cause to go back' from a position already reached, but there was no location suggested in the text from which they could be envisaged as moving back, and certainly not the land of Israel where they had not yet arrived. Elsewhere it is rendered 'lead away (enticingly)' (BDB) or 'lead astray' (Isa. 47:10; Jer. 50:6). Possibly the reference here is simply to the motion of turn round or turning away, so that God will induce Gog to leave off whatever else he had intended to do. Without him knowing it, Gog's actions would be controlled by God to accomplish his purpose. ***Set hooks in your jaws*** reflects the action used by the LORD to control the crocodile who was Pharaoh (29:4), and also, more literally, what happened to Manasseh (2 Chron. 33:11). In a similar fashion, Gog would be unwittingly constrained to act in accordance with divine guidance and accomplish not his own purposes, but God's.

I will bring you and all your force out. Gog and his allies would be deployed in battle array in accordance with the LORD's strategy. They would constitute a formidable force of imposing warriors. For ***horses and horsemen***, see 27:14, and for ***clothed to perfection***, see on 23:12. Possibly here the sense was fully equipped with armour, so that they constituted ***a great assembly*** of contingents ready to go to war (cf. the use of 'assembly' in 32: 22, 23 in connection with the Assyrian army). This echoed the 'exceedingly large force' (37:10), but their destinies would be in sharp contrast. For ***with shields large and small***, see on 23:24. The former protected the entire body, while the latter was held in the hand to parry a blow. This force could defend itself as well as mount an attack. ***All of them wielding swords*** (cf. 21:11; 30:21) presented a picture of an imposing, well-equipped, and seemingly insuperable army, brandishing their weapons. Even so, they were all the objects of 'I will bring out' because they would be under ultimate divine control.

♦ **38:5** Gog's allies were then listed, three in this verse, and two in the next, so that along with the two lands he personally controlled, there would be seven nations from the periphery of the world known to Israel drawn up menacingly against her. Seven was also the total number of nations in the oracles against the nations (chs. 25–32), and listed in Sheol in 32:17–32. 'Seven' was also used symbolically twice in 39:9, and in 39:12, 14. Overall the depiction was that of a universal alliance of evil, not some limited local opposition which would be assembled into this vast host.

Persia represented the east. It was still a minor state in Ezekiel's time, but it was a known tribal grouping. Along with Put it provided mercenaries for Tyre (27:10). ***Cush*** represented the south. It was also mentioned in 30:4, 5, and corresponded to the general area of Sudan and Ethiopia. ***Put*** (Libya) to the southwest had been identified as a partner of Tyre in 27:10, and as an ally of Egypt in 30:5. Both Cush and Put were listed in the catalogue of the nations in Genesis 10 (in Gen. 10:6), as were the two nations found in the next verse.

On the basis that 'the distant north' (38:6) referred to the whole of the alliance, critics are inclined to view the names of these allies as later additions to the text. But seven as the number of hostile nations suggests instead that the presentation was rather that of a complete coalition of world forces against Israel. It was again emphasised that they would be not be a hastily mobilised rabble of conscripts, but a well-equipped army, which would constitute a formidable threat, ***all of them ⌊with⌋ shield and helmet.***

♦ **38:6** Two further powers in the alliance were then named. ***Gomer*** had not appeared previously in Ezekiel, but was listed as a brother of Magog, Tubal, and Meshekh in Genesis 10:2, and as the father of Togarmah in Genesis 10:3. Gomer is generally identified with the Cimmerians, a savage tribe from the Ukraine north of the Black Sea, who caused trouble for the Assyrians over an extended period. Eventually they were expelled from their homeland by the Scythians and settled instead in Anatolia. ***Beth-togarmah*** ('house of Togarmah') was listed as a trading partner of Tyre in 27:14. It was probably located on the upper Euphrates, in the southern foothills of the Caucasus, and later became part of Media. ***The distant north***[101]

---

101. Though this expression may be rendered 'the far reaches of Zaphon', a reference to the mythical home of the Canaanite gods, more probably the notion is of geographical distance. It is possible that there are links with Jeremiah's foe from the north (Jer. 1:13–15; 4:6–17; 6:1–30), but more by way of ominous association than through the identity of the foes in view.

certainly applied to Beth-togarmah from Ezekiel's perspective, and probably also to Gomer, but the reference need not be extended backwards to the earlier names. These nations formed part of the northern contingent in the alliance against Israel. In their case the emphasis was not so much on the equipment they possessed, as on their number. The repeated phrase *all its troops* was a distinctively Ezekielian term for military units (cf. 12:14). As a result, counting in all the forces that Gog would have at his disposal, it could be said *many peoples ⌐are⌐ with you*.

♦ **38:7** After Gog had formed this alliance, the fact that it would be held in check for a period was dramatically portrayed by the LORD issuing orders to Gog: *Get ready and keep yourself at the ready.*[102] The singular verbs denoted a primary focus on Gog, but all his coalition troops were involved too: *you and all your assembly assembled about you*. The collective noun 'assembly' (cf. 27:27, 34; 38:4) and the participle 'assembled' (a plural form agreeing with the sense of the collective noun) come from the same root *qāhal*, 'to assemble', 'to gather'. Though they were kitted out, gathered, and eager for action, only when God would permit it could they proceed. In the meantime they must wait.

The sense of the last clause is unclear. The NRSV adopts an old suggestion and renders, 'and hold yourself in reserve for them', understanding the root in a passive sense of 'kept in reserve'. More probably the thought is either 'and be a guard for them', or *so that you may become a guard for them.* 'A guard' did not refer to one on sentry duty to alert the other forces in the alliance, but to one who, as their commander, would himself remain on the watch to deal with any contingencies and oversee the response of the forces under him.

♦ **38:8** *After many days* and *in the latter part of the years* referred to the same period. The urgency with which they were commanded to get ready would not be matched by an immediate engagement. What was to take place was still in the distant future. 'Latter part' (cf. 38:16) pointed to the final period of history in the perspective of the speaker, and was a variant of the prophetic phrase 'in the latter part of the days'

---

102. Two forms of the one verb *kûn* begin the verse: *hikkōn wəhākēn ləkā*. The first verb is a niphal imperative (or possibly an infinitive absolute with imperatival force), used reflexively, 'ready/prepare yourself'. The second verb is a hiphil imperative with the ethic dative adding a reflexive nuance, 'in your own interests make ⌐yourself⌐ ready.'

GOG AND MAGOG   311

for the messianic future (cf. Dan. 2:28; 10:14). Since this made plain that Ezekiel's vision was being directed to that more distant horizon, his contemporaries in exile would be aware that this hostile force did not pose an immediate threat. It referred to the epoch when conditions on earth would have been sweepingly and irrevocable altered by divine intervention.

At that future time, the LORD declared to Gog, *You will be summoned*, or 'mustered', that is, called together for military duty. More specifically, *you will enter a land brought back from the sword.* The land they would invade was one which had been previously the scene of military action, but which had subsequently been rescued from that condition after suffering defeat and decimation. *Gathered from many peoples* described the restoration of the inhabitants of the land after they had scattered in all directions. *Upon the mountains of Israel* (cf. 6:2) finally made it clear that it was Israel which was in view as the target of Gog's activity. *Which had been a ruin of long-standing* referred to the devastated condition of the mountains, which represented the land as whole.

In *it has been brought out from peoples*, 'it' was feminine in reference to the land, which was used by metonymy to refer to its inhabitants. *They are dwelling securely, all of them*[103] did not hint at an unwarranted, presumptuous security (cf. 30:9; 39:6; Isa. 47:8; Jer. 49:31). Rather this was security divinely bestowed upon the people of the covenant (28:26; 34:25; 38:11, 14; 39:26; Lev. 25:18, 19; 26:5). To the eyes of Gog, representing the hostile forces of the world, they would appear to be an easy, unsuspecting target. The time in view still remained in the period of enmity between the two seeds set out in Genesis 3:15. What would come upon the people of God was not divine judgement on their sin, but a period of intense testing imposed by God, which would provide a final demonstration of his commitment to them and protection of them by vanquishing their assailants.

♦ **38:9** Taking advantage of the seeming defencelessness of God's people, Gog would *go up* against them. Two similes were used to describe the hostile advance. *Like a storm you will come*, blowing with tremendous force and demolishing all it encountered. *You will be*

---

103. It is difficult to determine the tenses to be used in translating *hûṣāʾâ* 'it has been brought out' and *wəyāšəbû*, 'and they will dwell/are dwelling'. While the first perfect may reasonably be taken of a past event, the second verb (ordinary *waw* and a perfect) is more problematic. This co-ordinated perfect probably had stative force: 'they began to dwell and still do so.'

like a cloud of dust casting a pall of gloom over the land. Compare Jeremiah's use of 'cloud' and 'come up' for the advance of hostile forces (Jer. 4:13). *To cover the land* ultimately expressed God's purpose in allowing this invasion. All would seem to be lost, as it lay helplessly under enemy control. To escalate this note of vulnerability the massive size of the invading forces was emphasised in terms reminiscent of 38:6—*you and all your troops and many peoples with you.* How could there be recovery from such an aggressor?

REFLECTION

- This forecast of intense opposition was intended to be both realistic and encouraging. God did not play down the fact that hostile forces would assemble against his people. 'In the world you will have tribulation' (John 16:33). However, to focus on that is to open the door to dejection and defeatism. 'But take courage; I have overcome the world' (John 16:33). So too here. Over against the reality of the massed forces of evil, there is to be set the divine word addressed to them, 'I am against you' (38:3), and in the light of that stated opposition from God they cannot succeed. The covenant community are assured of the LORD's protection, and are called on to retain their spiritual nerve until his victory is openly displayed. If they resort to worldly expedients to secure their prosperity, that will in effect be a denial of the LORD, and will result in disaster. 'If you do not remain firm ⌞in faith⌟, indeed you will not remain ⌞at all⌟' (Isa. 7:9).

- Why would God permit his people to suffer from Gog's aggression when they have not committed any obvious sin? This can only be answered in terms of the inscrutable way in which he works to strengthen faith and mature his people. None would argue that training, whether physical or spiritual, is without pain, but being pushed to the limit demands, as well as creates, the capacity for greater trust. The unchallenged life is spiritually weak and flabby. It is only by being thrown in utter dependence on God that we perceive more clearly all that he gives us, and our need for him. '⌞In the⌟ day I am afraid, I for my part put my trust in you' (Ps. 56:3). The training given by facing adverse circumstances in reliance on him heightens the praise rendered to the one who is the deliverer.

- However, the fundamental teaching of these chapters is that attacks on God's people and their consequent suffering do not primarily occur to stimulate faith and increase spiritual resolve—though it is undoubtedly true that they do. While we may feel uncomfortable in recognising it, God permits this spiritual hostility so that he may display his power and gain glory by overwhelming it (38:16, 23; 39:7, 27). He wishes it to be known and acknowledged that he is the God of deliverance, and all else is secondary to the praise and exaltation of his name.

(2) Gog's Plot to Plunder (38:10–13)

Though the LORD will be in control of the situation, it is made clear that Gog and his allies are not being coerced into acting as they do. When the LORD removes his restraining hand from them, they will disclose their inner nature and true character by advancing against the defenceless to pillage and plunder (38:10–12). It will be his own expansionist greed which will impel Gog to act. Moreover, other nations will ask about Gog's motives, probably to see if they too can share in the spoil (38:13).

Many expressions in this description are reminiscent of those found in Jeremiah 49:30–33 in connection with Nebuchadnezzar's attack on Kedar and Hazor. 'He has plotted a plot against you' (Jer. 49:30) compared with 'plot an evil plot' (38:10). 'Arise, go up against a nation which is at ease, which dwells securely ... It has no gates and no gate-bars' (Jer. 49:31) resembles 'I will go up against a land ... those enjoying tranquillity, who dwell securely ... they do not have gate-bars or gates' (38:11). 'Spoil ... plunder' (Jer. 49:32) uses a common pair of synonyms as does 'to despoil spoil and to plunder plunder' (38:12; cf. also Isa. 10:6). The resemblances are not so close as to compel direct dependence. They do, however, suggest that Nebuchadnezzar in many respects was an embodiment of the spirit of Gog.

> ³⁸:¹⁰'Thus says the Lord GOD: And it will come about on that day ⌊that⌋ things will come up upon your mind and you will plot an evil plot. ³⁸:¹¹And you will say, "I will go up against a land of unwalled villages; I will come to those enjoying tranquillity, who dwell securely; all of them are dwelling without a wall and they do not have gate-bar or gates, ³⁸:¹²to despoil spoil and to plunder plunder'"to bring back your hand against ruined places which have been reinhabited and against a people brought together from ⌊the⌋ nations, who have acquired livestock and possessions, who are dwelling at the centre of the earth. ³⁸:¹³Sheba and Dedan and the traders of Tarshish and all its young lions will say to you, "⌊Is it⌋ to despoil spoil you are coming? ⌊Is it⌋ to plunder plunder you have assembled your assembly? to carry off silver and gold? to take livestock and possessions? to despoil great spoil?"'

♦ **38:10** The messenger formula *Thus says the Lord GOD* introduced a new aspect of this future scene, looking at it from a human angle. *It will come about on that day* is unwarrantably identified by Zimmerli (1983:310) as introducing a later expansion to the text. The LORD who is able to disclose the purposes of the heart (1 Cor. 4:5) revealed how Gog would view the situation in the day when divine restraints on his behaviour would be removed (38:8). *Things will come up upon your mind* used the broad term 'things', most often rendered 'words', for the inward articulation of thought. Such ideas would arise spontaneously within Gog's mind, and would reflect his attitude and character. Spurred on by his own evil intentions, Gog *will plot an evil plot* (cf. 11:2), a cognate accusative construction (see on 13:23). Gog's evil would be unleashed when and how the LORD determined, but Gog would still be responsible for it.

♦ **38:11** The details of the scheme which Gog would hatch were given here and in the first part of the next verse. *You will say* presumably had 'to yourself' understood, because what followed was not 'Let us', as if addressing his allies, but 'I will' or 'Let me', in which he formulated his own plan of action. *I will go up against a land of unwalled villages.* 'Go up ... come' repeated verbs from 38:9, indicating how Gog's conduct conformed to that divinely mapped out for him. 'Unwalled villages' (*pərāzôt*; cf. Est. 9:19; Zech. 2:4) were open to predators and enemies, having no protective wall. They would become Gog's victims precisely because they were unsuspecting and posed no threat to the forces which would advance against them. *I will come to those enjoying tranquillity, who dwell securely.* 'Come' was used in a hostile sense, 'attack'. 'Enjoying tranquillity' (*šāqaṭ*, 'to maintain a calm, quiet attitude'; cf. 16:42, 49) and 'dwell securely' (38:8; Jer. 49:31) described the blessings they would possess from the LORD. But those very blessings would make them easy targets for unprovoked, violent assault, since, relying on the LORD's promised safekeeping, they were *dwelling without a wall and they do not have gate-bar or gates.* 'Gates' was a dual noun reflecting the construction of the gate in two parts which were held closed by a wooden bar across them on the inside. This was not the Jerusalem whose walls Nehemiah so courageously and effectively was at pains to re-erect.

♦ **38:12** The sentence continued without a break from the previous verse, and provided a devastating exposé of Gog's motives. His coming would not be to congratulate the settled people on their happy circumstances, but to commit atrocities against them with a view to enriching himself and his allies. Here (and in 38:13) *to despoil spoil and to plunder plunder* reflects the Hebrew use of a verb followed by a cognate noun as its object. The repetition of the roots intensified the expression of the thoroughness and relentlessness with which the looters would set about seizing all that was of value. They were raiders, and would not have permanent occupation and rule in view.

At this point the quotation of Gog's thought changed to the LORD's commentary on Gog's actions addressed to him: *to bring back your*[104] *hand against ruined places.* 'To bring back the hand' was an idiom for 'to strike' (Ps. 81:14; Amos 1:8; Zech. 13:7). The 'ruined places' referred to the devastation and depopulation which the LORD had formerly brought on them (38:8), but now, in accordance with his will they would be places *which have been reinhabited* by *a people brought together from ⌊the⌋ nations.* The returnees had prospered in the land, for they *have acquired* (lit., 'made') *livestock and possessions*, that is, they possessed both domesticated animals and property acquired through trading. This largely agricultural economy was already enjoying divine favour (34:25–31; 36:29–30, 35–36).

Who are dwelling at the centre of the earth. The term *ṭabbûr* occurred elsewhere only in Judges 9:37 in the narrative of Abimelech's downfall where an enemy force was said to be coming down from 'the centre of the earth'/'land' to attack Shechem. The term is often rendered anatomically as 'navel' (LXX), and an allusion is detected to a mythological concept prevalent throughout the ancient world, of a sacred mountain which was the centre of life on earth. However, the term as used here was demythologised, and meant no more than 'in the midst of the nations' (5:5). But it was that central importance in God's workings in history which would provoke Gog's attack. The people's trust and prosperity was a witness to God which Gog instinctively wished to undermine and destroy.

♦ **38:13** The riches to be gained from raiding the land would attract others who, while not attacking Israel, would be very much interested in profiting from the aftermath of Gog's invasion. Their questions (embodying terms already employed) would voice astonishment at Gog's temerity in launching such an attack, but would also express an oblique interest in sharing in the spoils. *Sheba* (cf. 27:22–23), *Dedan* (27:20), and *Tarshish* (cf. 27:12) had been listed among Tyre's trading

---

104. To 'turn my hand' (NIV) follows the LXX, which assumes that Gog's thought continues to be recounted.

partners, who played a major role in the international commerce of the day. Mentioned in a generally east to west order, they were probably a sample of all the economic vultures waiting to see what pickings they could acquire. *All its* (lit., 'her' in reference to Tarshish) ***young lions***[105] indicated its leaders (cf. 19:2–6; 32:2).

REFLECTION

- Gog is not presented as possessing any redeeming qualities. His inner disposition is to attack and plunder the weak and unsuspecting. In this he exemplifies all those who hate the LORD. 'Against your people they concoct crafty plans, and they consult together against your sheltered ones. They say, "Come, let us wipe them out as a nation and let the name of Israel be remembered no more!" ' (Ps. 83:3–4). That is to display the spirit of Satan. 'Your opponent ⌊the⌋ devil prowls around like a roaring lion, seeking someone to devour' (1 Pet. 5:8). Later, John portrays the nations, collectively viewed as Gog and Magog, as deceived by Satan to carry out his purposes (Rev. 20:7–10). In acting in this way, Gog and his associates will display the hostility and blindness of those who are entrenched in their opposition to the LORD. 'But now many nations have banded together against you, saying, "Let her be defiled, and let our eyes gloat on Zion." But they do not know the thoughts of the LORD; and they do not understand his plan, that he has gathered them as sheaves of the threshing floor' (Mic. 4:11–12).
- What a contrast exists between Gog and his allies relentlessly approaching the defenceless and seemingly helpless land to ravage it (38:11–12) and the peoples who flow to Zion and the many nations who come to it for instruction in the law of God (Mic. 4:1–3; cf. Isa. 2:1–4). It is the intent of the heart which determines the moral quality of the same outward, physical action.
- In viewing Judah and Jerusalem as being 'at the centre of the earth' (38:12), Gog's words may have reflected no more than the geographical fact that Israel was situated on the land bridge crossed by trade routes from Europe and Asia before they reached Africa.

---

105. In place of 'young lions' (*kəpîrîm*) the LXX and the Peshitta rendered 'villages', presumably reading some form of *kāpār*, village, with a pronominal suffix, and this is followed by RSV, GNB, NASB and NIV. The Vulgate retains 'lions' (cf. AV, NKJV) and does not attempt to clarify the metaphor, though NRSV offers 'young warriors', which is possible. 'Leading magnates' (REB) conforms to the emendation found in *HALOT* 493 which proposes the more radical emendation, *rōkəlîm*, 'traders' or 'vendors', but that is repetitive.

However, behind that there was the far greater spiritual truth of the position God accorded his people in his purposes. They were, and are, central to the outworking of his kingly rule on earth. Whoever conspired against them, conspired against the LORD himself (Ps. 83:5). Since his people are the focus of his purposes on earth, he cares for them and keeps them as the apple of his eye (cf. Deut. 32:10; Ps. 17:8).

(3) The Divine Purpose (38:14–16)

These verses mostly restate what has been said earlier in the chapter (38:1–9). Indeed the imagery of the storm or cloud in 38:9a and 38:16a may suggest that there is a chiastic pattern reflected in reverse between 38:8–9 and 38:15–16 (cf. Milgrom 2012:16). In that case 38:8 corresponds to 38:16b, and 38:9b to 38:15. The existence of this pattern gives a signal that the attack described in these later verses is still under divine control, as is implied by the initial verb, 'you will be summoned' (38:8).

The key feature of the section is at the end of 38:16. God will not only permit this unholy alliance to advance against his people, but will draw them into doing so, because in that way his own transcendent character will be revealed. Those who invade his land and attack his people who are living in covenant obedience to him will inevitably experience defeat. The power of evil will not be permitted to overcome those who walk in the light. This will lead to universal recognition of the LORD's status and power—something which it is vitally important for Ezekiel to convey to the discouraged exiles, who feel written off and neglected.

> $^{38:14}$'Therefore, prophesy, son of man, and say to Gog, "Thus says the Lord GOD: ⌞Will⌟ it not ⌞be⌟ on that day when my people Israel dwell securely ⌞that⌟ you will know ⌞it⌟? $^{38:15}$And you will come from your place, from the distant north, you and many peoples with you, all of them riding on horses, a great assembly and a large force. $^{38:16}$And you will come up against my people Israel like a cloud to cover the land. In the latter part of the days it will come about that I will bring you against my land so that the nations may know me when I display my holiness through you before their eyes, O Gog." '

♦ **38:14** The link term ***therefore*** integrated this section with the preceding account. It was another component of a cumulative picture, rather than a tell-tale sign of a later expansion of Ezekiel's text. Ezekiel in his capacity as ***son of man***, was to ***prophesy*** and convey to

Gog (and to Ezekiel's immediate audience) God's message describing what would happen *on that day* when Gog would be permitted to act according to his desires. ⌊*Will*⌋ *it not* ⌊*be*⌋ ... ⌊*that*⌋ *you will know* ⌊*it*⌋*?*[106] renders a forceful rhetorical question stressing that when Gog would act, he would do so aware of the situation he would advance against: *my people Israel dwell securely.* 'My people' (cf. 37:27) emphasised the LORD's acknowledgement of his covenant bond with Israel. An attack on Israel would therefore be a declaration of war against their Overlord. 'Dwell securely' (cf. 38:8) described their protected condition maintained by the LORD. Gog and his allies would not be able to claim that they acted through ignorance.

♦ **38:15** *You will come from your place, from the distant north* (cf. 38:6) described Gog's own territory from which he originated. Along the way his allies would gather round him, *you and many peoples with you* (cf. 38:6), as a mobile force well equipped to raid other lands, *all of them riding on horses* (cf. 38:4). Their numbers would intensify the threat they posed as *a great assembly and a large force*, another instance of hendiadys.

♦ **38:16** *You will come up against my people Israel* again stressed the target of their aggression. *Like a cloud to cover the land* (cf. 38:9) presented a scene of a dark, threatening sky, looming oppressively over the land. 'My people' (cf. 38:14), and later 'my land' emphasised the reality of God's identification with them in the bond of the covenant, and thus the ultimate futility of Gog's actions in setting himself against the LORD himself.

There was then expressed the surprising statement of the LORD's role in all this. *In the latter part of the days* possessed a similar eschatological significance as 'in the latter part of the years' (38:8) and looked forwards to the extreme limit of what had been revealed to the prophet. *I will bring you against my land.* It should be observed that this divine action would not be contrary to the promise of security the LORD had given his people because Gog's attack would be divinely

---

106. The verb *tēdāʿ*, 'you will know', is supported by the Peshitta, Targum and Vulgate, but is frequently viewed as a corruption by critical commentators in the light of the LXX rendering 'shall you not be roused?' which could come from *tēʿōr*, 'you rouse youself', with the substitution of *resh* for *daleth*, and the transposition of the last two letters. This is reflected in 'bestir yourself' (RSV) and 'rouse yourself' (NRSV, NLT). However, the MT makes good sense as it stands, and it could easily be the case that the LXX translators misread the Hebrew text they were using, or it might itself have been faulty at this point.

overthrown. The event would reinforce Israel's perception of the LORD's commitment to protect and deliver his people, and thus enhance their faith in him.

More than that, the event was intended to have a key outcome in asserting the character of the LORD to all the nations. *So that the nations may know me* set out God's primary purpose in all this: that he would be duly and universally recognised for what he is as the Sovereign Creator and only God. Only here did the recognition formula take the modified form 'know me' rather than 'know that I am the LORD'. This has led many critical commentators to suppose that this was a later interpolation by a redactor mimicking, but not totally successfully, Ezekiel's customary language. However, that is to propose an unwarranted and improbable straitjacket for Ezekiel's mode of expression. *When I display my holiness* (*qādaš*, niphal; cf. 28:22; 36:23) *through you before their eyes, O Gog*. 'Through' or 'in' Gog, the great antagonist of the LORD and his people, and the complete overthrow imposed on him, the LORD would gain the acknowledgement he desired from other peoples as they witnessed (cf. 20:42; 28:25; 36:23) the encounter and its decisive outcome.

REFLECTION

- Modern 'sensitivities' readily react against the divine programme sketched in 38:16 in which God will bring Gog against Israel so that he may gain universal recognition of himself by his destruction of his enemies. It is solemn and sobering to contemplate the destiny of the wicked, but wishful thinking regarding the end of the impenitent does not alter in the slightest what awaits them. When the LORD removes the restraints he has imposed on Gog and permits him to display his inner motivation, it is so that there is incontrovertible proof of his real nature. Against that disclosure of rejection of the LORD's rule and hatred towards his people, the LORD must display his holiness. To consider such an act of self-vindication and divine vengeance as unworthy of God is to fail in grasping the moral nature of the world in which we live and the absolute and inherent need for God to affirm his supremacy. He is the one who is holy, and whoever or whatever conflicts with him has to face up to that ineluctable fact. His reaction to those who set themselves against him is a divine prerogative. It is not a role model for mankind, but a solemn warning that he requires that 'to me every knee will bow' (Isa. 45:23), whether willingly to the overtures of his grace, or under compulsion through the overwhelming disclosure of his holiness.

(4) The Wrath of the LORD (38:17–23)

There is an introductory query in which the LORD poses a question about Gog's role in the divine purpose (38:17). Unlike other aggressors who came against Israel, Gog has not been divinely appointed to chastise the LORD's people; instead Gog's actions are divinely controlled to bring about his own overthrow. The defeat of this enemy of God is then described in terms of the outpouring of divine wrath when Gog dares to enter the land of God's presence (38:18–20). This will involve both Gog's forces being turned to fight against one another (38:21) and a full display of divine control over the elements to rout the invading hordes (38:22). Through this sweeping reversal of the forces of evil, the LORD will achieve his ultimate purpose of displaying his greatness and inescapable power, and of being decisively recognised among the nations (38:23)—a verse where many expressions mirror those found in 20:5–9; 28:25 and 36:23.

> 38:17'Thus says the Lord GOD: Are you the one of whom I spoke in former days through my servants, the prophets of Israel, who prophesied in those days ⌊for⌋ years that I would bring you against them? 38:18And it will come about in that day, in the day when Gog will come against the land of Israel, declares the Lord GOD, that my fury will come up on my face. 38:19And in my jealousy, in the fire of my rage, I have spoken: Surely in that day there will be a great earthquake upon the land of Israel, 38:20and because of my presence there will quake the fish of the sea and the birds of the heavens and the beasts of the field and every creeping thing which creeps upon the ground and all mankind who are upon the face of the ground; and the mountains will be thrown down, and the cliffs will fall and every wall will fall to the earth. 38:21And I will call for a sword against him on all my mountains, declares the Lord GOD; each man's sword will be against his brother. 38:22And I will enter into judgement with him by pestilence and by blood; and torrential rain and hailstones, fire and brimstone I will shower upon him and upon his troops and upon the many peoples who are with him. 38:23And I will magnify myself, and I will sanctify myself, and I will make myself known in the eyes of many nations; and they will know that I ⌊am⌋ the LORD.'

♦ **38:17** The messenger formula was used to introduce the question designed to provoke thought about the permission the LORD had extended to Gog, *Are you the one?*[107] Many modern interpreters consider the verse awkward in the context, and therefore adjudge it to be a later insertion. Their attention especially focuses on the phrase *my servants, the prophets of Israel*, which they classify as Deuteronomic in the light of the diction of 2 Kings (2 Kgs. 9:7; 17:13, 23; 21:10; 24:2) and Jeremiah (Jer. 7:25; 25:4; 29:19; 35:15; 44:4). That it was only found here in Ezekiel does not provide robust grounds for challenging the genuineness of this passage, and attributing it to an earlier or later date.

More significant is the problem over what answer was expected to the question. God declared that he *spoke in former days through my servants*, giving prophetic warning that there was a foe coming against the people to punish them for their sin. It had indeed been the case that *the prophets of Israel, who prophesied in those days ₍for₎ years*[108] had spoken first of Assyria as 'the rod of my anger' (Isa. 10:5) and of Babylon as the foe from the north (Jer. 1:13–15; 4:5–18; 6:22). Was Gog a further instance of those whom the LORD *would bring ... against them*?

Many commentators consider that the LORD's question implied a positive identification of Gog as a predicted invader, and this was brought out by the NIV (1984) which introduced a negative, 'Are you not the one of whom I spoke?' While there had been no specific earlier prophecies which mentioned Gog, it was argued that this was a case of earlier multi-staged prophecies being only partially fulfilled by Assyria or Babylon. So it is asserted that Gog was the culminating realisation of what had been predicted earlier, and the question could only be answered positively. 'If the author intends that the answer to the rhetorical question attributed to Yahweh be "no," then why pose it at all? Without a positive response, the question has no point' (Darr 2001:1521).

However, a cogent case can be made out for a negative response (cf. Block 1992; 1998:453–456). Assyria and Babylon had been employed by the LORD to chastise his people; Gog's attack would be divinely engineered to rid the cosmos of the hostile powers ranged against the LORD's purposes and against his people. There was no suggestion that Israel had sinned and was being punished. Indeed, while the account

---

107. The LXX, Peshitta, and Vulgate did not translate the interrogative particle in *hā'attâ* ('Are you?'), and a declaration is found in English translations such as REB, NIV (2011).

108. The sequence 'in those days years' is awkward, and the LXX and Peshitta inserted the conjunction 'and' to yield 'those days and years'. More probably 'years' functioned as an accusative of duration, 'for years'.

emphasised Gog's aggression and entry into the land, nothing was said of Israel suffering any casualties or damage to property. No sooner would Gog's actions evidently declare his intention than the LORD would intervene to overwhelm him utterly. A similar sequence is to be found in Revelation 20:7–10 where divine intervention would immediately relieve the camp of the saints and the beloved city. What then was the point of the question? Though Gog and his allies would be permitted to express their enmity and hatred of the LORD's people, neither they nor the people themselves were to interpret this as God setting himself against his people. They would remain secure because they were living in a right relationship with God. Gog was permitted to act as he did so that he would bring about his own destruction, but above all so as to achieve a culminating disclosure of divine greatness and holiness.

♦ **38:18** The LORD proceeded to foretell what would *come about in that day, in the day when Gog will come against the land of Israel.* To 'come against' was to mount an attack upon the land. For 'land of Israel', see on 7:2. The signature formula, *declares the Lord GOD*, authenticated the genuineness of the divine response to this incursion: *my fury will come up on my face*, literally 'on my nose'. Although this anthropomorphic phrase was not found elsewhere, there were similar expressions (2 Sam. 22:9; Pss. 18:8; 78:21, 31), and in particular, 'to cause my wrath to come up' (24:8). Gog's presumptuous attack would inevitably provoke an intense divine reaction.

♦ **38:19–20** The character of the LORD's response was further spelled out: *in my jealousy* (cf. 5:13), that is, his protective zeal to maintain the bond of the covenant, and *in the fire of my rage* (cf. 21:31), his vehement and consuming counteraction to what had offended him. Combinations of terms such as 'fury', 'jealousy', 'fire', and 'rage' occurred frequently (e.g., in Zeph. 1:18; 3:8) to convey the implacable and unavoidable hostility of the LORD to conduct which outraged him. Here his reaction led to the proclamation of a divine decree, *I have spoken*, which took the form of a solemn asseveration. *Surely* ('im-lō') reflected an oath formula asserting the certainty of how the LORD committed himself to respond.

The first aspect of God's intervention would be the occurrence of an earthquake, whose impact was spelled out in considerable detail. *In that day there will be a great earthquake upon the land of Israel.* The nature of this phenomenon can only be appreciated in the light of the expression, *because of my presence* (lit., 'from my face'). The LORD would come to resist his opponents and to provide salvation for his people. His presence would cause all the land to quake, a phenomenon associated with his final intervention in judgement (cf. Hag. 2:6–7; Zech. 14:4–5; Matt. 24:29–31; Mark 13:24–27; Rev. 16:18). Though the epicentre of the earthquake would be in Israel, its shockwaves would spread throughout the world. Indeed, cosmic upheaval would accompany the disclosure of the presence of the LORD (Pss. 18:6–15; 144:5–6; Isa. 24:17–23; Joel 2:10, 30–31; 3:15–16). *There will quake*[109] (from the same root as 'earthquake') *the fish of the sea and the birds of the heavens and the beasts of the field and every creeping thing which creeps upon the ground and all mankind who are upon the face of the ground; and the mountains will be thrown down, and the cliffs*[110] *will fall and every wall will fall to the earth.* The all-encompassing detail, reflecting the created realm as presented in Genesis 1:26, 28; 9:2, was employed to validate the use of 'great' in connection with the earthquake.

These events would all be about greatness. The LORD's adversaries placed their confidence in 'a great assembly and a large force' (38:15), but this display of power would definitively establish whose greatness was greater (cf. 38:23). 'Be thrown down' (cf. 'razed' 13:14) was a passive verb which did not state the agent responsible for the action, but there would be no doubt that it was the LORD's presence which led to the mountains and cliffs losing their stability, and the strong walls defending cities crumbling to the ground.

♦ **38:21** Again, the signature formula confirmed the authenticity of the LORD's declaration, *I will call for a sword against him on all my mountains.*[111] 'On' (*lə*) is more literally 'to' or 'for', but possibly it

---

109. The translation 'there will quake' is adopted to reflect the fact that in Hebrew 'because of my presence' is brought forward for emphasis and placed between the verb and the composite subject.

110. The term 'cliffs' is of uncertain meaning. In its only other occurrence in Song 2:14 it is in parallelism with 'cliff', 'rock', and probably it denoted an inaccessible place. The LXX has 'valleys'. However, the root was cognate with the Arabic for 'step, stair', and Aramaic and Rabbinic Hebrew support the idea of 'terraces' held up by retaining walls which could collapse (Hummel 2007:1114; Milgrom 2012:19). If so, it would then be part of the collapse of manmade, as distinct from natural, structures.

111. The LXX omits the first mention of 'a sword', and has 'all fear' instead of 'for all my mountains', perhaps reading *ləkol-ḥărādâ* instead of *ləkol-hāray ḥereb*. This is reflected in 'I will summon universal terror' (REB) and 'I will summon every kind of terror' (RSV).

here has a distributive force 'throughout'. The 'sword' referred to the LORD's mode of imposing judgement through hostile attack, but who could be called on to attack Gog's coalition when those he was advancing against were peaceful and without means to defend themselves? The LORD would not be at a loss, but would provoke internecine warfare in the intruders' camp: *Each man's sword will be against his brother* (cf. Judg. 7:22; 2 Chron. 20:23; Hag. 2:22). This was one aspect of a war of the LORD, that he could stimulate blind panic in the enemy ranks such that they turned on one another. So Israel's aggressors would be overwhelmed without Israel engaging in any warfare. Nor was there any indication of Israel suffering loss.

♦ **38:22** There were other means that the LORD would use when he fulfilled his declaration, *I will enter into judgement with him*. That is the normal meaning of the idiom, but since the LORD's verdict had already been issued, the sense here was 'I will impose judgement on him'. Three sets of phenomena would be divinely directed against the invading forces. First, *by pestilence and by blood* (cf. 5:17; 28:23) probably was an instance of hendiadys indicating the outbreak of a lethal epidemic. Then, there would also be *torrential rain and hailstones* (cf. 13:11, 13), not here metaphors for judgement, but severe adverse weather conditions which would also cause fatalities (cf. Josh. 10:11; Rev. 16:21. Lastly, the LORD would employ *fire and brimstone* which he would *shower* upon Gog, his armies and *the many peoples who are with him* (cf. 38:6, 9), just as he had showered it down upon Sodom and Gomorrah because of their abominations (Gen. 19:24; Deut. 29:23). The LORD would deploy against Gog a whole range of weapons in this battle to end all battles.

♦ **38:23** This verse reassured God's people that the outcome of the conflict which they would witness would be to God's glory. Three verbs set out the divinely intended consequences of the confrontation with Gog. *I will magnify myself and I will sanctify myself.* These hithpael verbs may have 'estimative-declarative reflexive' force: 'I will show my greatness and I will display my holiness' (*IBHS* §26.2f). 'Magnify' was from the same root as 'great' (38:19), but this victory would not make the LORD great. It would declare what he has always been. In the same way he would use this occasion to exhibit, not create, his holiness (cf. 36:23). Consequently, vanquishing Gog would lead to universal recognition (cf. 38:16). *I will make myself known* (cf. the niphal in 38:16; used of self-disclosure in 20:5, 9; 35:11; 36:23). *In the eyes of many nations* echoed 'many peoples' (38:15).

The overwhelming self-disclosure of who the LORD truly is would compel recognition of his sovereignty. ***Then they will know that I ⌊am⌋ the LORD.*** That every knee would bow before him is the grand aim of all God's purposes disclosed in Scripture.

REFLECTION
- 'God is love' (1 John 4:16) does not negate the reality of divine wrath, because God is of 'purer eyes than to see evil and cannot look at wrong-doing' (Hab. 1:13). No terms are sufficiently strong to express divine revulsion at sin; no warnings against sin and the punishment that awaits it are too extreme as to be unwarranted.
- The power of evil is rampant in this fallen world, and there will be no peace until it is overwhelmed by divine grace or quashed by divine victory. It is an inescapable fact that God's final manifestation of his sovereignty in earth's history involves the judgement of those who remain implacably opposed to him and his purposes. 'Then ⌊comes⌋ the end, when he hands over the kingdom to God the Father, when he has destroyed every rule and every authority and power' (1 Cor. 15:24).
- How then are the LORD's people to respond when confronted by the massed ranks of earthly and Satanic opposition? 'Go, my people; enter your rooms and shut your doors behind you. Hide yourself for a little while until the rage has passed by. For behold, the LORD is about to come out of his place to punish the iniquity of those who dwell on the earth, and the earth will disclose the blood ⌊shed⌋ on it and will no longer cover up those who have been slain on it' (Isa. 26:19–21). The call to the faithful is to stand firm and await the deliverance which the LORD has promised he will accomplish for them (cf. Exod. 14:13–14; Isa. 30:15).

(5) The LORD's Defeat of Gog (39:1–16)
The supremacy of the LORD over Gog and his alliance is hammered home in this section by repetition and expansion of points already made, as well as by introducing certain telling additional features (e.g., 39:6, 9–10). However, some items, such as the LORD's wrath and the earthquake mentioned earlier, do not recur here.

The section is bracketed by the messenger formula in 39:1, and at the start of the following section in 39:17. Within these markers it is possible to identify three paragraphs. In the first (39:1–8), Gog's whole campaign is surveyed, bringing out his helplessness before the LORD. Not just Gog's army in the field is destroyed; the same is true of his homeland (39:6). This will achieve the LORD's purpose of exalting his own name (39:7). In the second paragraph (39:9–10), the Israelites themselves are for the first time accorded a role, for they are to spoil the defeated enemy and burn his weaponry. In the final paragraph (39:11–16), the land is once more purified through an extended process of locating and burying the corpses of the multitudes of the slain strewn throughout the land.

(a) The Slaughter of Gog (39:1–8)

Throughout there is an emphasis on the LORD's action. The repeated use of the recognition formula (39:6, 7) shows that what he does conduces to the fulfilment of his purpose. The certainty of this scenario is reinforced by the repetition of the signature formula (39:5, 8). The LORD's strategy to deal with Gog will be effective.

> ³⁹:¹'And ⌐as for⌐ you, son of man, prophesy against Gog and say, "Thus says the Lord GOD: Behold, I am against you, O Gog, chief ruler of Meshekh and Tubal! ³⁹:²And I will turn you round and lead you on and make you come up from the distant north; and I will bring you against the mountains of Israel. ³⁹:³And I will strike your bow out of your left hand and make your arrows fall from your right hand. ³⁹:⁴Upon the mountains of Israel you will fall—you and all your troops and the peoples who are with you; to birds of prey of every sort and the beasts of the field I will give you as food. ³⁹:⁵Upon the open field you will fall for I myself have spoken, declares the Lord GOD. ³⁹:⁶And I will send fire on Magog and on those who dwell securely in the coastlands; and they will know that I ⌐am⌐ the LORD. ³⁹:⁷But my holy name I will make known in the midst of my people Israel, and I will no longer allow my holy name to be profaned; and the nations will know that I ⌐am⌐ the LORD, the Holy One in Israel. ³⁹:⁸Behold, it is about to come and it shall occur, declares the Lord GOD. That is the day I have spoken about." '

♦ **39:1** The section began with the prophet as *son of man* being issued with a third instruction to prophesy against Gog using the messenger formula. The verse retained a number of elements from 38:2–3 including the identification of **Gog** as **chief ruler of Meshekh and Tubal,** and the opposition formula, **Behold, I am against you,** but there was no mention of Magog, and the hostile orientation formula was not employed. However, there was no diminution in the LORD's settled determination to combat Gog.

♦ **39:2** Once more the LORD set out what he would do to Gog and how he would manipulate his movements. *I will turn you round* probably declared the divine intention to cause Gog to reverse whatever course of action he had intended (see on 38:4). Without Gog and his allies being aware of the LORD's role in it, events and circumstances would induce him to act precisely as the LORD required. So he could say to Gog that he would *lead you on*[112] *and make you come up from the distant north* (cf. 38:15). Not only his initial action but his destination would be divinely controlled. *I will bring you against the mountains of Israel* (cf. 38:8).

♦ **39:3** Having brought Gog to the site where he wished to bring about his destruction, the LORD declared he would proceed to disarm and overwhelm his adversary. *I will strike your bow out of your left hand and make your arrows fall from your right hand.* This expanded on what was stated in 38:1–9 where the invaders were primarily described as horsemen. That they were also archers suggested one of the Scythian tribes from central Asia whose proficiency in this regard was renowned. A right-handed archer would hold his bow in his left hand, and fit an arrow with his right hand. Even so, despite their prowess, the LORD would disarm them (cf. Pss. 37:15; 46:9), and they would be left defenceless.

♦ **39:4** *You and all your troops and the peoples who are with you* reflected the earlier descriptions of the alliance led by Gog (38:6, 9, 22), but their doom was decreed: *Upon the mountains of Israel you will fall.* They would be unable to withstand the forces the LORD would unleash against them, and their mission would be thwarted. Indeed, it would go further than that. They would be subject to a humiliating and catastrophic defeat. *To birds of prey of every sort and the beasts of the field I will give you as food.* Such exposure of the carcasses of the fallen was viewed as a sign of utter disgrace (cf. 29:5). 'Birds of prey of every sort' (lit., 'of every wing') differed from 'birds of the heavens' found elsewhere (29:5; 31:6, 13; 32:4; 38:20) to make

---

112. The derivation and meaning of *wəšiššēʾtîkā* are unclear. While the verb looks like a piel from a root *šāšāʾ*, such a root with the initial consonant repeated is anomalous in Hebrew, and it is more probably a reduplicated form of a root such as *šʾ* or *šwʾ* (GKC §55f). Context would indicate a meaning such as 'show the way', 'lead on' (cf. LXX, Vulgate). The AV, 'leave but a sixth part of thee', follows a medieval Jewish interpretation and assumes a connection with the numeral, *šēš*, 'six', but that is no longer considered plausible.

specific reference to a vast variety of unclean, carrion-eating birds, such as, vultures and ravens. ***The beasts of the field*** described all wild animals, but here flesh-consuming animals were particularly intended, especially scavengers such as hyenas and jackals. The LORD declared that his defeat of Gog would be so swift and overwhelming that there would be no opportunity to bury the fallen. Indeed, there would be none to do so. This would be the fate of those who defiantly set themselves in opposition to the LORD's provision for this people. The description led into the more elaborate account found in 39:17–20, and it also looked back on the different outcome which the LORD instituted for Israel's very dry bones in chapter 37.

♦ **39:5** ***Upon the open field you will fall*** related the end that Gog (and those led by him) would experience, and connected it directly to the divine decree issued against him: ***for I myself have spoken, declares the Lord GOD.*** There would be no way to evade this outcome which had been proclaimed by the ruler of all mankind.

♦ **39:6** At this point the LORD ceased to address Gog through the prophet, and spoke instead about further action he would take against his alliance. ***I will send fire*** employed an idiom which occurred only here in Ezekiel, but which had been repeated extensively in Amos' oracles of judgement (Amos 1:4, 7, 10, 12; 2:2, 5). Fire had already been mentioned as a divine infliction (38:22; Luke 9:54; Rev. 20:9), which destroyed all possessions, whatever their value, as well as posing a major threat to human life. Possibly there were judgemental overtones derived from the overthrow of Sodom and Gomorrah. Here the fire would fall, not on Gog's army, but on ***Magog.*** The reference was to the centre and origin of Gog's domain (cf. 38:2). The fire would also extend to ***those who dwell securely in the coastlands***, a description of the maritime settlements and islands of the Mediterranean from which some of his allies came (Put, 38:5; Tarshish, 38:13). They had previously thought themselves exempt from the setbacks encountered by their forces in the field, and lived with an illusion of security (cf. 30:9). But the LORD's judgement would fall equally on them because of their hostility to him; only those who have become his people would be exempt from his wrath and be able to enjoy real security (34:25; 38:8).

However, the LORD had a purpose in the widespread imposition of judgement. ***They will know that I ⌊am⌋ the LORD.*** The nations and lands which were antagonistic to the LORD would be compelled to acknowledge his sovereignty.

♦ **39:7** This verse functioned as an explanation of the process set out in 39:6. The *but* which introduced it indicated its disjunctive nature, in that Israel's experience through these events will be decisively different from that of the nations. *My holy name I will make to be known in the midst of my people Israel.* The root holy (*qādaš*) is used three times in this verse in connection with the LORD. 'My holy name' (lit., 'name of my holiness'; an adjectival use of the construct) was placed first for emphasis. This summed up all that was distinctive and unique about the LORD. Through the LORD's overthrow of Gog, his allies, and their domains, the covenant people would have a heightened awareness of the awesome sovereignty of their God, who is supreme and is able to remove every rival. This perception would serve to enhance their relationship with him.

I will no longer allow my holy name to be profaned.[113] While this profanation (cf. 13:19) might refer to Israel's direct misconduct against the LORD as in 20:39, that seems out of place in this context. The profanation seems rather to be associated with other peoples having a wrong understanding of the LORD's power and purposes (cf. 36:20–23). Gog's action against the LORD's people was predicated on the assumption that he could be dismissed as weak, ineffective, or unconcerned. Under the conditions which would subsequently prevail, the LORD would no longer (12:24) permit such mistaken notions to be entertained.

Once more the recognition formula was employed to set out the objective of the LORD's action: *the nations will know that I ⌊am⌋ the LORD.* Here, however, the formula was expanded by the addition of the divine epithet, *the Holy One in Israel.* This designation did not occur elsewhere in Ezekiel, but it was very close to Isaiah's designation, 'the Holy One of Israel' (used 25 times throughout his prophecy, e.g., in Isa. 1:4; 5:19, 24; 43:3, 14; 49:7; 60:9, 14) as the one who was set apart from all else and supreme over every other conceivable being, but who had chosen to reveal himself in a unique fashion in Israel. 'In Israel' indicated Ezekiel's priestly turn of mind as shaped by the Shekinah glory, the visible manifestation of divine holiness in the sanctuary both of the Jerusalem Temple and of the final vision. The term was also reflected in the demonic recognition, and that of the disciples, that Jesus is the Holy One of God (Mark 1:24;

---

113. The hiphil *'aḥēl* from *ḥālal* III (BDB), 'to profane, pollute', must have a tolerative sense, though this is usually associated with a niphal (*IBHS* §§23.4f-g, 27.5c).

Luke 4:34; John 6:69). There was here an anticipation of the concluding note of the prophecy, 'The LORD is there' (48:35).

♦ **39:8 Behold** called for attention to be paid to this pronouncement. In ***it is about to come and it shall occur*** the first verb focused on the impending nature of the event, and the second on its certainty (cf. 21:7).[114] The feminine 'it' was used as an abstract form taking in all that was associated with the final divine intervention to overthrow all his enemies. The signature formula, ***declares the Lord GOD,*** further reinforced the guaranteed nature of that event. ***That is the day I have spoken about.*** The day already spoken about was the one on which Gog would be overthrown (38:10, 14, 18). It would be the culminating day of divine intervention, *the* day of the LORD (cf. 7:7; 30:2).

(b) The Spoiling of Gog (39:9–10)

So far the description has focused on the LORD and on the forces of Gog which he overwhelms. It is only after the defeat of their enemies that the Israelites are said to participate in what will occur at that momentous time of divine intervention. Where had they been until this point? Block (1998:465) pictures them as sheltering behind their city walls, taking the term 'cities' (39:9) as implying the existence of defensive structures. Milgrom (2012:22) contends that this creates an unnecessary tension in the passage with 38:10–13 where the people are said to be entirely without city walls. On the basis of Leviticus 25:29 which talks of 'a walled city' and therefore implicitly supposes the existence of 'an unwalled city', it is more probable that the Israelites, as the covenant people, exercised reliance upon the LORD as their defender, and simply remained in their settlements under threat and without visible protection.

> ³⁹:⁹And those who dwell in Israel's cities will go out and kindle ⌊fires⌋ and burn weapons of war, and small and large shields, bow and arrows, and handpikes and javelins; and they will kindle fires with them for seven years. ³⁹:¹⁰And they will not carry pieces of wood from the field nor will they chop ⌊them⌋ from the forests, for with weapons they will kindle fires, and they will despoil those who would spoil them and

---

114. The expression *hinnēh bāʾâ* is an instance of the *futurum instans*, 'it is about to come' (Introduction §6.3c). The final accent on the verb indicates that it is to be read as a participle (not a perfect). The second verb *wənihyātâ* is a niphal perfect, to be understood as a prophetic perfect, 'it shall come about/occur' (Introduction §6.3b).

plunder those who would plunder them, declares the Lord God.

♦ **39:9** There had been no mention of the people of God up to this point, but, once the LORD had triumphed over Gog and his allies, *those who dwell in Israel's cities* would be given a role in the aftermath of his victory. They *will go out and kindle ⌞fires⌟.* Wood was a major constituent in ancient implements of war, and the Israelites task was to destroy them with fire (cf. Isa. 9:5; Ps. 46:9). Rather than *kindle and burn* being an instance of hendiadys (Block 1998:465), it is more probable that this represented a process where a fire was first kindled and then successive loads of weapons were added to it to be burned up (Milgrom 2012:23).[115]

It is unclear whether what followed was a six-item list headed by the generic term *weapons of war* (*nešeq*; used in Ezekiel only in 39:9–10), or whether that was in fact a specific, but unknown, type of weapon. If it was the latter, there would be a catalogue of seven types of weapon, which would correspond with the *seven years* during which *they will kindle fires with them.* Both sevens would have been used to indicate the completeness of what would be done in that the whole weaponry of the enemy would be totally destroyed. For *small and large shields*, with the latter for the whole body, see on 23:24; 38:4. *Handpikes* (lit., 'staff/rod of hand) were thrusting weapons used by infantry, whereas *javelins*/'lances' were throwing weapons, lighter spears, favoured by charioteers. Both had wooden shafts which would easily burn.

♦ **39:10** *They will not carry pieces of wood from the field nor will they chop ⌞them⌟ from the forests, for with weapons they will kindle fires.* The arsenal at the disposal of Gog and his allies would have been so large that the Israelites would not need to gather wood from other sources to kindle ordinary fires throughout the seven year period during which the arms were being destroyed.

There would be a great reversal as the tables were turned on the

---

115. The verb *ûbiʿărû* generally signifies 'to burn up, consume' whereas the second verb *wəhiśśîqû*, from the hiphil of *nāśaq*, would signify 'to kindle'. However, the order 'burn up and kindle' is the wrong sequence. Either the two verbs constitute a hendiadys 'to burn completely' (cf. the one word rendering in the LXX), or else the piel of *bāʿar* is used in the sense 'to kindle' and the second verb may be a form of *śālaq*, 'to kindle, burn' (BDB 969) with an assimilated *lamedh*. The verb provides a sound play with the following *nešeq*, 'weapons of war'.

enemies of God who had seemed to have the upper hand and who had been confident of an easy victory over Israel. Instead, **they will despoil those who would spoil them and plunder those who would plunder them** (cf. 29:19; 38:12–13). This would be a just requital for the looting they had intended to carry out. Possibly this hinted at what had happened at the Exodus (Exod. 3:22; 11:2–3; 12:36), but the terminology there was different. A similar metaphor is employed regarding Christ's work in the New Testament in that he despoiled the devil (Luke 11:22; Eph. 4:8; 1 John 3:8), a process which will be finally complete at his return (1 Cor. 15:25).

(c) The Burial of Gog (39:11–16)

The grand scale of the victory is also emphasised by considering a major problem to which it gives rise. Are the vast numbers of enemy corpses to be left unburied in the open field? Would not this pollute the land? Equally, if they are to be buried, where should this be done? Would it indeed be permissible to inter them within the land of Israel? The answers are divinely given by allotting to Gog a mass burial site within the land, and consigning the corpses there—a process which will be carried out meticulously over seven months to ensure that the land is cleansed.

> 39:11'And it will come about on that day that I will give to Gog a place there, a grave in Israel, ⌊in⌋ the valley of those who pass through, east of the sea, and it will impede those who pass through; and they will bury there Gog and all his multitude, and they will call ⌊it⌋ the Valley of the Multitude of Gog. 39:12And the house of Israel will be burying them for seven months in order to cleanse the land. 39:13And all the people of the land will bury ⌊them⌋, and it will be to their renown on the day when I display my glory, declares the Lord GOD. 39:14And they will appoint men to continuous ⌊employment⌋, passing through the land, burying, with those who pass through, those who are left upon the surface of the land, to cleanse it; at the end of seven months they will search. 39:15And those who pass through will pass through the land, and when anyone sees a human bone, he will erect a marker near it until the buriers bury it in the Valley of the Multitude of Gog. 39:16And indeed the name of the city ⌊was⌋ Multitude, and they will cleanse the land.'

♦ **39:11** *On that day* located the following proceedings as part of what followed in the wake of Gog's attack and overthrow. The divine statement, *I will give*, allocated Gog *a place there*. But it was far from the sort of place the marauding bands had anticipated when they invaded the land. All they would be provided with would be *a grave in Israel*, a site for a war cemetery for the burial of their fallen hordes.

Even though multiple indicators were given for the location of this mass grave, its situation remains disputed, perhaps intentionally so. *In the valley of those who pass through* (*gê hāʿōbərîm*) was not a description used elsewhere, though a similar name, Abarim, occurred in Numbers 27:12; 33:47–48, Jer. 22:20, for a site east of the Jordan in the area of Mount Nebo. Since that Abarim lay in the territory of Moab, this proposal may be dismissed as conflicting with 'in Israel'. Drawing on Ugaritic parallels, Block suggested the rendering 'the valley of those who have passed on' (1998:469). While at first sight appealing, such a reference to the dead in general must be rejected as being out of line with the following repetition of *those who pass through*, which clearly described living travellers whose route was obstructed by the tombs in the valley.

Furthermore, *east of the sea* was doubly ambiguous: did it describe the site of the grave, or the movement of the travellers? was the sea the Mediterranean or the Dead Sea? Locating the graves east of the Mediterranean seems trite because that was true of all Israel; locating the graves east of the Dead Sea conflicts with their location as being in Israel (see Introduction to 47:13–20). Since 'east of the sea' could mean 'facing east ⌞towards⌟ the sea' (cf. Gen. 2:14; 4:16), the description might be of the movement of travellers. This would lead to a rendering such as 'those who pass east through ⌞to⌟ the sea' (cf. NIV 1984), which would locate the valley as west of the Jordan.

This approach accords with what seems the prevailing interpretation of the name. Zimmerli (1983:317) advanced the idea that the Valley of the Multitude of Gog (*gêʾ hămôn gôg*; cf. 39:15) was intended to suggest associations with the Valley of Hinnom (*gêʾ hinnom*), a place of all sorts of abominations, situated southwest of Jerusalem. The latter valley had once before been renamed the Valley of Slaughter (Jer. 7:32), and perhaps the phrase in that verse, 'until there is no room', was here reflected in *it will impede those who pass through*. This expression was literally 'it will muzzle those who pass by' (cf. Deut. 25:4), but in this context the verb was presumably used in a metaphorical sense of hampering the movement of travellers.

Although other locales might be suggested, such as the Jordan Valley, north of the Dead Sea (Hummel 2007:1136), given the lack of a positive identification, the reference may well have been left intentionally vague because what mattered was not where the mass graveyard would be, but that the enemy would be completely slaughtered. *They will bury there Gog and all his multitude.* 'Multitude' or 'horde' (*hāmôn*, cf. 29:19) was used frequently by Ezekiel of foreign armies (31:18; 32:12, 16, 18, 20). The next verse provided clarification of those indicated by 'they'.

♦ **39:12** *The house of Israel will be burying them* showed that this task was allocated to the covenant people, acting as divine agents. Even unburied bodies of criminals would defile the land (Deut. 21:23), so the slain warriors had to be buried even though it took *seven months*. Seven again functioned as a numerical indicator of completeness (cf. 39:14). *In order to cleanse the land* no longer related to the moral impurity arising from the disobedient and idolatrous conduct of the people; this was a matter of cultic purity. The land where the LORD was going to dwell with his people had to be free from all that could besmirch it.

♦ **39:13** *All the people of the land* were the same as 'the house of Israel' (39:12), who were now spiritually renewed. No longer did the term 'the people of the land' designated the group which had earlier played a major role in the corruption of the city (7:27; 12:19; 22:29). In this scenario they would comply with the requirement placed on them: they *will bury ⌊them⌋*. Their diligence in carrying out the tasks assigned to them would not go unnoticed: *it will be to their renown* (lit., 'for a name'; cf. 34:29), approved of and praised by God himself *on the day when I display my glory*. Though this might also be rendered 'when I am glorified', that is, receive glory from others, the sense was probably rather that God would so act that his glory would be made evident by his own action (cf. 28:22). This referred to his overthrow of Gog and his allies.

♦ **39:14** While the disjunctive construction with which this verse began permitted the following description to be an explanation of how the people carried out the mass burials of 39:12–13, in the light of the last clause of the verse it is more probable that what was presented here was a further process instituted to rid the land of every possible trace of contamination after the initial seven-month mass burial. This was an indication of the conscientiousness with which the task was carried out, and the spirit of obedience which would characterise the people.

They (that is, the people of the land) *will appoint men to continuous ⌊employment⌋* (lit., 'men of continuity'). This dedicated task force, appointed by the Israelites as a whole, would have the ongoing remit of locating and appropriately disposing of any undetected human remains. The two participial descriptions, *passing through the land, burying*, did not by itself make clear if one group of the men would carry out both these tasks, or if those involved would be divided into two groups, each with separate responsibilities. However, 39:15 established that it was the latter scenario which was in view.

The phrase *with those who pass through*[116] is problematic. Some suggest that it has been included by scribal error, as it is not witnessed to in the Peshitta or the first hand of the Septuagint. More probably it was omitted precisely because of its difficulty. Block (1998:471) suggests that the phrase was a euphemism for the dead, and was in apposition to *those who are left upon the surface of the land*. However, the sense would seem to indicate co-operation between the two groups in the process of detection and burial, though it might possibly be the case that 'those who pass through' was used again (cf. 39:11) to indicate travellers who were passing by and who were conscripted to help with the task of burying.

♦ **39:15** This verse added further detail to the procedure which would be followed. *Those who pass through will pass through the land.* The first group would have the responsibility of conducting a thorough survey to establish if any remains were unburied. *When anyone sees a human bone, he will erect a marker near it.* Though the predators of 39:4 would have stripped the flesh off the corpses, the bare bones were still present to pollute the land. So if any were found, a distinctive marker would be set up. *Until the buriers bury it in the Valley of the Multitude of Gog* described how the second group would remove the remains to the appointed burial ground and inter them there.

♦ **39:16** In an apparent intrusion into the account of a graveyard, mention was made at this point of a city. *And indeed*[117] *the name of*

---

116. Both participles are preceded by *'et*. If this is the object marker in both instances, the two expressions are in apposition; if the first *'et* is the preposition, 'with', then the passers-by help with the burial of those who are left.

117. Odell (1994:488) notes the presence of the particle *gam* introducing this verse, and suggests as a possible translation, 'Even though the name of the city is Hamonah, they will purify the land.' The verb in the first clause is an English supplement, for which 'was' probably functions better on this reading of the text that this former epithet for the city is now a thing of the past.

the city ⌊was⌋ Multitude, which might be transliterated as Hamonah, an obvious play on the name given to the valley ('Multitude' in 39:11, 15 was Hamon).¹¹⁸ Odell (1994), followed by Block (1998:472), suggests it was the turbulent and rebellious Jerusalem of 5:7–9 and 7:10–14, looked on as the place now purged of every trace of defilement. Alongside its epithet as 'the city of bloodshed' (22:2), it was also designated Hamonah, indicating how it had shared the outlook and characteristics of the invading multitude. However, its actions would prove the change which had occurred and which would eventuate in it being given a new, positive name (48:35). But certainty on the matter is impossible. What would be clear was that *they will cleanse the land*. The task allotted the people in 39:14 would be successfully completed. The way had now been opened up for the LORD to rejoin his people there.

REFLECTION
- While human conflict resolution may for a time mitigate the impact of evil in the world, there can be no lasting peace where repentance and submission to Christ are absent.
- Military might and acquisition of wealth can foster an illusion of security (39:6), but such complacency is unwarranted on the part of those who have opposed themselves to God. Do we not live in a generation to which God is saying as he said to the rich fool, 'Fool! This night your soul is required of you, and the things you have prepared, whose will they be?' (Luke 12:20)?
- It is only after the battle has been engaged and the victory won that the LORD accords a role to the people. Still theirs is a significant contribution to the outworking of the purposes of the one 'who breaks the bow and shatters the spear; he burns the chariots with fire' (Ps. 46:9).

(6) Invitation to a Victory Banquet (39:17–24)
The totality of the wipeout to be experienced by Gog and his allies has already been described in terms of the burning of his weaponry (39:7–10) and the burial of the dead (39:11–16). On a sequential reading of the chapter the slain have already been eaten by predators (39:4), the dead interred (39:11–12), and every single bone buried (39:15), so that the banquet described here would create a paradox. Obviously this

---

118. The form *hămônâ* might be a feminine noun corresponding to *hāmôn*, 'multitude, horde', or it might be that noun with a third feminine singular pronominal suffix spelled without mappiq.

GOG AND MAGOG   337

section is a further, parallel display picturing the aftermath of Gog's overthrow.

The section begins with address to the prophet and the use of the messenger formula (39:17), which is not repeated until 39:25 at the start of the final section. Between those limits there are two paragraphs. In the first (39:17–20) a description is given of a bizarre banquet at which the guests are birds and wild beasts, and the menu consists of the carcasses of the fallen unbelievers and their horses. This is not intended as a literal description, but as a figurative climax to the destruction of Gog, portrayed by using literary special effects. What happens here expands on the description of 39:4, and occurs before all the corpses are buried.

The second paragraph (39:21–24) consists of a résumé of the LORD's action, through which he declares his glory. Alongside Israel's recognition of the LORD (39:22), the nations will realise what his purpose has been in his dealings with his people (39:23–24).

(a) The Grotesque Feast (39:17–20)

> ³⁹:¹⁷'But ⌊as for⌋ you, son of man, thus says the Lord GOD, "Say to birds of every kind and to all the beasts of the field: Assemble and come. Gather together from round about to my sacrifice which I am sacrificing for you, a great sacrifice upon the mountains of Israel, and you will eat flesh and drink blood. ³⁹:¹⁸The flesh of mighty men you will eat, and the blood of the rulers of the earth you will drink—rams, lambs and he-goats, bulls, fat animals of Bashan, all of them. ³⁹:¹⁹And you will eat fat until you are satisfied, and you will drink blood until you are drunk, from my sacrifice which I have sacrificed for you. ³⁹:²⁰And you will be satisfied at my table with horses and chariots, mighty men and all men of war, declares the Lord GOD." '

♦ **39:17** The messenger formula, marking the start of a new unit, ***thus says the Lord GOD***, came unusually early in this verse, before the commissioning of the prophet to speak rather than in its expected position as the authenticating preamble to the words the prophet was to utter. On this occasion he was directed to speak ***to birds of every kind and to all the beasts of the field.*** The invitation would be issued to them: ***Assemble and come.***

Gather together from round about to my sacrifice which I am sacrificing for you. Use of sacrifice to describe the LORD's victory over his foes occurred elsewhere (in connection with Edom in Isa. 34:5–7, and with Nebuchadnezzar's defeat of Pharaoh Neco in Jer.

46:10), but the metaphor was not deployed in as extreme a fashion as here. It was customary for a banquet to be held to celebrate a victory, and the sacrifices offered on such an occasion would be peace (fellowship) offerings, in which parts of the sacrificial victims were returned to the worshipper for consumption in a sacred meal. Here the LORD depicted his victory in terms of the preparation of such a sacrifice, 'my sacrifice which I am sacrificing' (a cognate construction), which he would get ready 'for you', the unclean animals. It would be as though the slaughter of Gog and his allies would occur simply to provide *a great sacrifice upon the mountains of Israel* so that these unclean, wild animals would be provided with a sumptuous meal. This was a surreal twist to a victory banquet shared with his people (Exod. 24:9–11; Isa. 25:6–9). The imagery was taken up in connection with the eschatological victory of Christ in Revelation 19:17–18.

You will eat flesh and drink blood. This was a merism for total consumption of the carcasses, even though consumption of the blood was forbidden in Israel.

♦ **39:18** There could be no doubt about the quality of the repast offered to the animals. The menu for this banquet was set out as: *the flesh of mighty men you will eat, and the blood of rulers of the earth you will drink.* In this context 'the earth' rather than 'the land' is the better rendering of ʾereṣ. The corpses the scavengers would consume were not Israelite, but those of the international coalition.

The well-nourished corpses were likened to the animals used in sacrifice: *rams, lambs and he-goats, bulls, fat animals of Bashan.* Without exception, *all of them* were of the best quality. Bashan was the area east of the Sea of Galilee (equivalent to the modern Golan Heights), renowned for its fertility and for the quality of the livestock bred there (Deut. 32:14; Ps. 22:12; Amos 4:1). While 'rams' and 'goats' had already been used as terms to describe Israel's leaders (34:17), that metaphorical use for rulers was subsidiary here; these animals were mentioned because of their cultic significance.

♦ **39:19** No restrictions were placed on what or how much the LORD's invited guests could consume. *You will eat fat until you are satisfied, and you will drink blood until you are drunk.* Fat was viewed as a delicacy, not something posing a health risk, but in a sacrifice it was generally reserved for the LORD and burnt in the fire (Lev. 3:16–17). Another strange feature of the scene was the implicit invitation to drunkenness which is condemned throughout Scripture. Even though this banquet was provided *from my sacrifice which I have sacrificed for you*, its menu disregarded the commands of the law (see on 39:17).

♦ **39:20** The complete extent of the LORD's victory was highlighted by the fact that the animals *will be satisfied at my table.* Four items for consumption were listed: *horses and chariots, mighty men and all men of war.* These terms were in fact singular nouns used collectively, and they ground the metaphor of this feast in the reality of the overthrow of the enemy. However, even at such a surreal banquet, consumption of 'chariots' was unlikely, and the term was probably used by metonymy for 'horsemen' or 'charioteers'.

(b) Recognition of the Victor (39:21–24)
An alternative analysis of this and the following section derives from the contrast between 'I hid my face from them' (39:23, 24) and 'I will no longer hide my face from them' (39:29) and takes 39:21–24 and 39:25–29 as two panels of a balanced section, each with a chiastic structure (Block 1998:479). However, the chiastic structures are not self-evident, and a case can be made for retaining the analysis of the chapters based on the repetition of the messenger formula (cf. Introduction to ch. 38).

The theme of this paragraph is recognition of the LORD. It begins with the deliverance from Gog and his allies which will function as a disclosure to the nations of the LORD's power and judgement (39:21). His deliverance will provide Israel with a heightened awareness of his sovereignty over them, which will continue from that time forward (39:22). God's action will also clarify for the nations his motives in his previous dealings with his people (39:23–24).

The tone and language of this section and the next are often taken by critics as evidence that they are later additions to Ezekiel's material. But, though the language differs somewhat from that found earlier, the change is not as marked as some have contended. The material Ezekiel presents forms an appropriate conclusion to this sequence of oracles revealed to him.

39:21'And I will set my glory among the nations, and all the nations will see my judgement which I have executed and my hand which I have put on them. 39:22And the house of Israel will know that I ⌊am⌋ the LORD their God from that day and thereafter. 39:23And the nations will know that the house of Israel went into exile for their iniquity, because they acted perfidiously against me, and I hid my face from them, and I gave them into the hand of their foes, and they fell by the sword, all of them. ³⁹:²⁴According to their defilement and according to their rebellious acts I have dealt with them, and I hid my face from them.'

♦ **39:21** The temporal stance in these verses remained that of the great future deliverance from the incursion of Gog and his allies, but looking at it as already accomplished. *I will set my glory* was a different expression from 'I display my glory' (39:13), and perhaps indicated a prolonged disclosure of divine sovereignty and power. *Among the nations* revealed the international scope of the revelation given.

All the nations will see my judgement which I have executed referred to the LORD's imposition of his verdict on Gog for attacking God's vulnerable people. It would be a visible, perceptible matter of fact, which could not be ignored. *My hand which I have put on them*, that is, on the enemy forces as antagonists rather than the nations as spectators. 'Hand' emphasised that what had occurred was a demonstration of divine power. This precise expression occurs only here in Ezekiel, but 'to put hand on' (Ps. 89:25) indicated the use of power to establish something (cf. 2 Kgs. 11:16; 2 Chron. 23:15). The imposition of a just penalty on Gog and the coalition forces linked this paragraph to the preceding oracles (cf. 'from that day' in 39:22).

♦ **39:22** The culmination of one of the goals perceived in Ezekiel's presentation of divine control of history was expressed using the recognition formula with explicit identification of its subject. *And the house of Israel will know that I ⌊am⌋ the LORD their God.* 'The house of Israel' referred to the covenant community who would through these events be brought into a deeper recognition of what it meant to have the LORD as their God. Possibly in this context there was a contrast between the full believing knowledge of God's people and the seeing, but not fully comprehending, perception of the nations in the previous verse.

From that day and thereafter (cf. 43:27) looked back to the LORD's decisive defeat and destruction of Gog and his hordes (39:3–5), but also to what would prevail subsequently. Israel's reaction would not be short-lived, and their recognition of who their God was and what they owed to him would not diminish over time.

♦ **39:23** Alongside Israel's recognition of her covenant God, there would be granted to other peoples an understanding of how God had been active in her history. *And the nations will know* referred to what they would have revealed to them, that Israel's exile had not occurred because of divine weakness and inability to protect her, but because of Israel's sin: *for their iniquity, because they acted perfidiously against me.* 'Iniquity' (cf. 3:18; 4:4) was their deviation from covenant standards. 'Acted perfidiously' (cf. 14:13) related to treacherous behaviour infringing on the sovereign prerogatives of the LORD.

It was the penalty for Israel's disloyalty that they *went into exile* (*gālâ*). This verb was employed here and in 39:28. Elsewhere in Ezekiel the verb was rarely used to describe being exiled (but see 12:3), with 'to scatter' or 'to disperse' being preferred. However, this change in vocabulary (and other similar locutions) is a very slender basis on which to erect the theory of a different author for these verses, one who was a careful, but not quite perfect, mimic of Ezekiel's style (Tooman 2010:54). It is more plausible to see such changes as natural variation, particularly over a number of years. Throughout the prophecy the related nouns for 'exile'/'exiles' (*gôlâ*: 1:1; 3:11, 15; 11:24, 25; 12:3, 4, 7, 11; 25:3; *gālût*: 1:2; 33:21; 40:1) repeatedly occur, as Tooman in fact recognises.

I hid my face from them (cf. 39:24, 29). Though frequent in the Psalms (e.g., Pss. 13:1; 27:9; 104:29), this expression had not occurred hitherto in Ezekiel. It was a common ancient Near Eastern idiom for royal or divine disfavour, and contrasted with expressions such as 'make his face shine on you' and 'lift up his face on you' in the Aaronic blessing (Num. 6:25–26). When a king withheld his favour, calamity would overwhelm his subject, and this had been Israel's experience. *I gave them into the hand of their foes.* The LORD deliberately reacted to his people's unfaithfulness by withdrawing his protection from them and leaving them exposed to enemy attack, so that *they fell by the sword, all of them.*

♦ **39:24** That the course of Israel's history was not to be attributed to deficiencies on the part of the LORD, but to the sinful misconduct of his people, was further brought out by two additional terms describing the offence Israel had given. *Defilement* (cf. 24:13) referred to both how they had acted against God's law, particularly the ceremonial law, and how that had rendered their resultant state one of uncleanness. 'The people's impurity is a cause for God sending them into exile' (Wong 2001:185). Conjoined with this was the imposition of the penalty for the covenant transgression of their *rebellious acts* (cf. 14:11) which they had engaged in contrary to the known will of their legitimate sovereign, so that they breached their sworn commitment of fidelity to their Overlord. *I have dealt with them* (cf. 7:27) was a declaration of the justice with which the LORD had acted *according to*, that is, with a response proportionate to the heinous of the conduct they exhibited. Therefore in connection with those events which caused the nations to conclude that the LORD did not care about breaches of his covenant requirements, or that he was unable to live up to his own covenant commitments, they would be compelled by events to realise that precisely the reverse was the case and that the exile of Israel expressed the LORD's verdict on their flagrant breaches of the covenant, and also his commitment to maintain its standards by imposing the sanctions of the broken covenant on their sin.

I hid my face from them picked up the idiom employed in 39:23 to bring home to them what they brought on themselves by rejecting his rule over them. The policy of rebels was to expect continuing enjoyment of the good provided for them by their King while jettisoning his requirements. But that was inherently flawed and incoherent. If they turned away from him, he would turn from them and make clear to them what their misconduct exposed them to, as had been made clear in the preceding verse.

REFLECTION

- The surreal imagery of this celebratory banquet communicated most effectively that a major victory had been won. This triumphant description is echoed in Revelation 19:17–21 where all the birds of heaven are summoned to 'gather for the great supper of God, to eat the flesh of kings' and of all their subordinates even before battle was engaged. At one level God has already won the victory in Christ. At the cross 'he disarmed the rulers and the authorities and made a public display of them, by triumphing over them in him' (Col. 2:15). No matter what may appear to the contrary, it is already the case that the Christian can join with Paul in affirming, 'In all these ⌊things⌋ we are more than conquerors through him who loved us' (Rom. 8:37). It is the knowledge of the victory which is already won that sustains through the difficulties of this life and the aggression of a defeated but still struggling foe. The day will come when the 'It is finished' of Golgotha (John 19:30) will be taken up in the divine 'It is done' (Rev. 21:6) and 'the one who conquers will have this heritage' (Rev. 21: 7) when all things are made new. Christ's past achievement and the prospect of his heavenly kingdom from which every pernicious foe has been removed serve to strengthen and encourage those on the way to glory.

(7) Restoration of Israel (39:25-29)

This section functions as an epilogue to chapters 33-37 by bringing together the promise of the return of the people to the land, the outpouring of the Holy Spirit on them to secure their spiritual vitality, and their enjoyment of fellowship with their God who has delivered them.

> 39:25"Therefore thus says the Lord GOD, "Now I will restore the fortunes of Jacob and have compassion on the whole house of Israel, and I will be jealous for my holy name. 39:26And they will bear their disgrace and all their perfidy with which they acted against me, when they dwell securely upon their land and there ⌊is⌋ no one to make them afraid. 39:27When I bring them back from the peoples and gather them from their enemies' lands, I will display my holiness through them in the eyes of the many nations. 39:28And they will know that I ⌊am⌋ the LORD their God in that I took them into exile among the nations and I collected them to their land, and I will no longer leave any of them there. 39:29And I will no longer hide my face from them, for I will have poured out my Spirit upon the house of Israel, declares the Lord GOD." '

♦ **39:25** *Therefore* linked this section to the preceding reminders of Israel's sin. Restoration and blessing would only come to them as consequences of the LORD's gracious intervention and settlement of affairs throughout his realm. The messenger formula, ***thus says the Lord GOD***, led immediately into divine speech in which the LORD spoke to the prophet about the people rather than directly to them.

Now brought the time frame of the LORD's speech back from what would take place in the last days into the more immediate future while Israel still remained scattered in exile (39:27).

I will restore the fortunes of used virtually the same idiom as in 16:53 and 29:14.[119] For a discussion of the origin of the phrase and how it should be translated, see on 16:53. The thought was more comprehensive than merely that of return from exile. Ultimately it included a reversal of all the ill consequences of the Fall. ***Jacob***

---

119. The difference in this verse from the earlier occurrences is that it is the hiphil of the verb *šûb* which occurs here, but the hiphil must have the transitive sense, 'cause to come back', 'restore'. The qere form of the noun is *šəbût*, whereas the kethib reads *šəbît* (the same variation as in 16:53). The former form suggests a link with *šûb*, 'to return', whereas the latter form would be associated with *šābâ*, 'to take captive', from which comes the older rendering 'restore the captivity'.

(cf. 37:25) showed that the northern tribes would not be excluded from the restoration which was in view. The reference was also fitting in that in earlier centuries the LORD had brought back Jacob, who had been effectively an exile from the Promised Land when he fled from it to Paddan-Aram in northern Mesopotamia (Gen. 27–33). ***The whole house of Israel*** included all Jacob's offspring in this recapitulation of his experience of restoration.

The LORD stated that he would ***have compassion*** (*rāḥam*), an expression not otherwise found in Ezekiel, but regularly used elsewhere (cf. Exod. 33:19; Isa. 49:13; 54:8; 55:7; 60:10). In this prophecy the term 'to spare' recurred for a sympathetic attitude (*ḥāmal*; 5:11; 7:4, 9; 8:18; 9:5, 10; 16:5; 36:21), but, except for the last of these references, the term was used in a negative sense.[120] The use of 'compassion' here may have reflected the declaration of Deuteronomy: 'For the LORD your God is a compassionate God. He will not abandon you or destroy you or forget the covenant with your fathers which he swore to them' (Deut. 4:31). The one constant factor in all that befell Israel was the unvarying commitment of the LORD to the covenant, out of which in due course his exercise of compassion grew. On that basis alone could it come about that beyond the imposition of penalty there was the possibility of restoration (Lev. 26:40–42; Deut. 30:1–10).

Even so, the LORD was at pains to point out that he was ultimately motivated by a concern for his own sovereign prerogatives. ***I will be jealous for my holy name.*** For divine jealousy, see on 5:13, and for 'my holy name', see on 20:9; 36:20. What was described here was a passionate commitment to the acknowledgement and preservation of his own reputation and character (36:22–23; 39:7).

♦ **39:26** Attention next turned to the people's response to their deliverance and reinstatement. Understanding the nature of that response depends on the identification of the verb with which the verse began. ***They will bear their disgrace*** (or 'shame') was a typical

---

120. The solitary occurrence of 'compassion' here highlights a feature of Ezekiel's message that various terms denoting divine favour are not found, even in passages dealing with the restoration of the people. Thus, concepts such as 'grace' (*ḥēn*) or 'covenant love' (*ḥesed*) are absent, and there is also mention of divine love (*ʾāhab*) or the kinship root for redemption (*gāʾal*). This serves to accentuate the fact that reinstitution of the covenant is not based on any pre-existing relationship or merit, but is solely an act of divine sovereignty. See also on 20:5.

Ezekielian phrase (cf. 16:52, 54; 32:24–25, 30; 34:29; 36:6, 7; 44:13), but many English versions (not AV, NKJV, HCSB, NJPS) render 'they will forget' identifying another root.[121] However, the sequence of shame following deliverance was attested elsewhere (16:61; 20:43; 36:22–32), and it would not be amiss for a holy aversion to their former misconduct to be motivated by the comprehensive bounty of the gracious provision made for them. In *all their perfidy with which they acted perfidiously* the same root was repeated in the noun and the verb (cf. 14:13) to describe their treacherous behaviour towards the LORD. Although the sequence of thought is not obvious in the text, *when they dwell securely upon their land and there ⌊is⌋ no one to make them afraid*[122] did not refer to the same period as 38:8, but to what would prevail after the repulse of Gog.

♦ **39:27** *When I bring them back from the peoples and gather them from their enemies' lands* looked forward to the deliverance the LORD would provide for Israel by removing them from the land of their exile (cf. Lev. 26:36–39) and restoring them to their own land. After the people had exhausted the curses consequent on their covenant disobedience, the LORD would regather them as a new Israel. In doing so he asserted that he would *display my holiness through them* (cf. 38:16). The action he would take would be an open declaration, not of his aversion to their sin, but of his commitment to his word and his power to intervene. *In the eyes of the many nations*[123] again disclosed the universal message that the LORD would convey through the restoration of his people.

♦ **39:28** While the subject of *they will know* might be the nations, the continuing use of the third person plural pronoun to refer to Israel probably indicates that it was their acknowledgement of the LORD

---

121. The versions and the qere take the verb *wənāśû* as a defective form of *wənāśʾû*, 'and they will bear', with the final-*aleph* verb being written as though it were final-*he*. The full spelling with the *aleph* is found in 44:13, 'and they will bear their disgrace'. The alternative rendering treats the word as *wənāšû*, 'and they will forget', from the root *nāšâ*. However, Ezekiel does not use this root elsewhere, and its qal occurs only in Jer. 23:39 and Lam. 3:17.

122. Tenses have to be supplied in translation of both these clauses as the first verb is an infinitive, and the second clause is verbless in Hebrew.

123. This repeats the phrase found in 38:23, but here there is an article with 'nations', though not as would then be expected with the adjective 'many'. Such a lack is rare, and because 'many' is not represented in LXX, many critics delete it as a gloss.

which was involved in this final elaboration of the recognition formula.[124] As they reviewed their national history from the perspective of their final deliverance, they would trace the LORD's purpose throughout it.

(1) *I took them into exile among the nations.* This was not determined by the power of Babylon and its gods, but by the decree of the LORD himself.

(2) *I collected them to their land.* 'Collected them' (cf. 22:21) was a variation on Ezekiel's more usual term 'gather them' (11:17; 20:34, 41; 34:13; 36:24).[125] But notice should be paid to the transformation associated with this collecting which would be conducted in quite a different fashion from 'I will collect you and I will blow upon you with the fire of my rage, and you will be melted in its midst' (22:21).

(3) *I will no longer leave any of them there* in the land of exile. This 'no longer' (cf. 12:24) reflected the radical change of circumstances which would pertain when the LORD completed his restoration of his people. There would be no gaps in those restored to his favour (Deut. 4:30–31; cf. Lev. 26:44–45).

♦ **39:29** The 'no longer' of the new state of affairs of the LORD's people would extend to the reversal of 39:24: *I will no longer hide my face from them.* This anticipated a time of renewed access to their King and enjoyment of fellowship with him, which was further developed in the concluding division of the prophecy.

Translations vary in their understanding of the significance of the conjunction *ʾăšer* which links the clauses in this verse, whether it is temporal 'when' or 'after' (RSV, NRSV, ESV) or causal 'for' (AV, NASB, NKJV, NIV). The latter is more probable. The verb 'I have poured' was used in a future perfect sense, *I will have poured out.* Elsewhere God had talked about pouring out of his wrath (e.g., 7:8; 14:19; 20:8) but, like 'collect' in 39:28, 'pour out' was here used for a radically different action. There had also been earlier promises of the LORD

---

124. The absence of the recognition formula in the concluding division of the book has been used to suggest a difference in authorship, but the picture here is one of Israel having arrived at a true knowledge of their covenant King. What follows is a portrayal of the ideal for the life of the community in the light of that knowledge, and therefore there is naturally no scope for employing the formula.

125. 'To collect' (*kānas*) became more common in post-Biblical Hebrew than 'to gather' (*qābaṣ*). The use of this word reflects Ezekiel's position in the development of the language (Hummel 2007:1132).

regarding the giving of the Spirit in the midst of the people (36:27; 37:14), but those perhaps focused more on internal regeneration and the bestowal of new life to the spiritually dead. Here the idiom highlighted the collective manifestation of the Spirit *upon the house of Israel* (Joel 2:28–29; Zech. 12:10; cf. a similar idiom with different verbs, Isa. 32:15; 44:3). This would be the way in which individually and corporately the great reversal would be accomplished and permanently sealed.

REFLECTION

- The hidden face of the LORD as he averts his gaze from the sin and pollution of his people (39:23–24; cf. Isa. 59:2) denotes the withdrawal of God's favour from his people so that 'many evils and troubles will come upon them' (Deut. 31:17). How fervently David prayed, 'Hide not your face from me' (Ps. 27:9), while imploring God to 'hide your face from my sins' (Ps. 51:9). Now it is promised that the spiritual barrenness and desolation of the hidden face of God will be reversed. 'No longer' again flags up the time of divine renewal and restoration, when his face will not be hidden from his people (39:29) and there will be full enjoyment of fellowship with him.
- The pouring out of God's Spirit (39:29) denotes the lavish endowment of his presence to give new life and vitality to his people. This blessing, which was also envisaged in Joel 2:28–29, has been bestowed upon the followers of Christ since Pentecost (Acts 2:14–21). It is the indwelling Spirit who gives eternal life now and hereafter (Rom. 8:10–11), and his ministry helps maintain a living relationship between the believer and God (Rom. 8:26). In that way the face of God is not averted and his favour is not withdrawn.

VIII. Perfect Order

(40:1–48:35)

OUTLINE

A. The Vision of the Temple (40:1–42:20)
 1. The Vision Unfolds (40:1–4)
 2. The Temple Gateways and Courtyards (40:5–37)
 3. Rooms and Equipment for Preparing the Sacrifices (40:38–43)
 4. Rooms for the Priests (40:44–47)
 5. The Ideal Temple (40:48–41:26)
 6. The Temple Rooms (42:1–20)

B. The Return of the Glory of the LORD (43:1–12)
 1. The Glory Presence (43:1–5)
 2. No Defilement in the King's Presence (43:6–9)
 3. Ezekiel's Task (43:10–12)

C. Ordinances for Temple Worship (43:13–46:24)
 1. The Altar of Burnt Offering (43:13–27)
 2. Closure of the East Gateway (44:1–3)
 3. Ordinances regarding Temple Service (44:4–31)
 4. Apportionment of the Land (45:1–8)
 5. Practical Justice (45:9–17)
 6. The Major Festivals (45:18–25)
 7. Further Regulations for Worship (46:1–15)
 8 Disposition of the Ruler's Property (46:16–18)
 9. The Temple Kitchens (46:19–24)

D. The Life-Giving River (47:1–12)
 1. The River's Source and Growth (47:1–7)
 2. The River's Impact (47:8–12)

E. The Land of Promise (47:13–48:35)
 1. The Boundaries of Israel's Inheritance (47:13–20)
 2. Provision for Sojourners (47:21–23)
 3. Tribal Territories to the North (48:1–7)
 4. The Central District of the Land (48:8–22)
 5. Tribal Territories to the South (48:23–29)

F. 'The LORD Is There' (48:30–35)

VIII. Perfect Order (40:1–48:35)

Twenty-five years have rolled inexorably by, and life for the exiles in Tel-abib (and elsewhere in Babylonia) has maintained its monotonous and dispiriting course. Those deported from Jerusalem in 597 B.C. have had their numbers swollen by new arrivals from the city after its collapse in 586 B.C. Nebuchadnezzar's empire remains as formidable as ever; its iron control over its subjects has not relaxed. Indeed, the emperor's supremacy is further emphasised when an additional contingent of deportees from Judah reaches Babylonia in 581 B.C. (Jer. 52:30). Since then, another eight long years have passed, and Ezekiel's preaching about a revived people, a reunited nation, a bountiful land and restoration to it, and renewed covenantal fellowship with the LORD seems to depict a world which will never come. Indeed, it appears to be a world which is further off than ever for those facing the grim reality of their lives in exile. Will there ever be liberation from the thraldom of Babylon?

Into this gloom the LORD shines light to revive drooping spirits by granting Ezekiel a vision of what he desires for his people. Here is an ideal which should shape their expectations, and a target which they should even now be aiming at. Particularly those in leadership positions in the community should find in this model of how God's kingdom ought to be administered much to challenge their past and present practice, and to ready them for further, dutiful service.

None of the exiles should lose hope because Ezekiel is given a vision for them of what lies ahead. He finishes the story which began with the vision of the Glory of the LORD appearing in Babylonia in chapter 1, and which continued with the further vision of the departure of the Glory from Jerusalem before the destruction of the Temple in chapter 11. The divine promise, 'I will set my sanctuary in their midst for ever' (37:26), will be implemented, and the divine recovery programme for Israel will be completed.

It will not merely incorporate a temple structure of perfect proportions. The LORD tells in chapter 43 of how his Glory will return to the temple and remain with the people, whose life and land will be organised around it. This is the vision of the city whose name will be, 'The LORD is there' (48:35). No matter what their present experiences or feelings are, they are not permanent exiles, and the way to true homecoming in fellowship with their God will be provided for them. These chapters are thus an elaborate, illustrative restatement of the LORD's stated intention, 'And the nations will know that I ⌐am⌐ the

LORD who am sanctifying Israel, when my sanctuary is in their midst for ever' (37:28).

The idiom in which much of this message is announced may seem obscure and alien to a modern reader, but the presentation in these chapters would resonate with its original hearers—and with none more so than the prophet himself. Here is something which draws them to look beyond the troubles which confront them every day and which cast a pall over their lives. The promises of God are sure, and there is a grand future awaiting the people of God—therefore, persevere.

It is also necessary to remember that these chapters present only half the story. Most of the exiles would in effect be viewing a split-screen presentation, one half of which would be their memory of what Jerusalem had been like, and the other half the orderly, secure, and God-honouring portrayal of what Jerusalem ought to resemble (cf. 43:6–11).

Structure. The framework of these chapters is not indicated by formal markers in as clear a fashion as prevailed in the earlier part of Ezekiel's prophecy, but the core structure can be outlined on a thematic basis. First, Ezekiel is transported in vision to a high mountain where he is given a guided tour of a temple complex (40:1–42:20). There follows an account of the LORD's Glory-presence returning to fill the temple (43:1–12). Next directions are given regarding the conduct of worship in this temple, and rules are also set out about access to it and activities to take place within it and in the community at large (43:13–46:24). The prophet is then shown a river of life-giving water which issues from the temple (47:1–12), before directions are set out as to how the land should be apportioned among the twelve tribes (47:13–48:29). The concluding section reverts to a description of the city, and particularly of the gates which permit movement into it and out of it (48:30–34), before the name of the city is revealed in a concluding flourish (48:35).

It is possible to detect other ways in which the content of the vision coheres. One is in terms of an overall outward movement from the temple precincts with the altar at the centre (chs. 40–44) to the surrounding LORD's portion and adjacent related areas of land (chs. 45–46) until the land as a whole is encompassed (chs. 47–48). Another approach is to detect a sequence similar to that of the Pentateuch (Milgrom 2012:61). (1) The LORD's sanctuary is set up in the midst of his people (Exod. 25:1–40:38 || Ezek. 40:1–43:27), culminating in a visual arrival of the Glory-presence (Exod. 40:34–38 || Ezek. 43:1–9).

(2) The maintenance of the sanctuary is delegated to Israel (Lev. 1:1–Num. 10:28 || Ezek. 44:1–46:24). (3) The land is apportioned among the twelve tribes (Num. 34:1–35:34 || Ezek. 47:1–48:35). For a further suggestion, see Levenson 1976:43.

Language and Text. Much of the description includes technical terms, whether those of an architect and builder, or those of a priest. The former set of vocabulary in particular is frequently quite opaque to modern scholarship, rendering various aspects of the envisioned temple uncertain. Indeed, the scribes who transmitted the text were obviously also at a loss to understand items in the text, and as a consequence a significant number of corruptions are encountered in chapters 40–42.

Much twentieth century scholarship was based on a form-critical approach to these chapters (notably Zimmerli 1983). While valuable material is incidentally present in such treatments, the overall approach fragments the text with its identification of layers of activity, alleged remodelling of an original core to suit later conditions, and editorial appendices contributed by Ezekiel's followers. Likening such analysis to picking to pieces a patchwork quilt, Stevenson wryly comments that taking the quilt apart 'would result in a pile of scraps and no more quilt—an engaging pastime, but not much comfort on a cold night. For the text of Ezekiel 40–48, the issue is not that someone pieced together scraps, but that someone wanted a quilt' (1996:7).

Quite so, but paying respect to the claims of the text requires one to say that it did not originate by piecing scraps together, but by God granting the prophet various visionary vistas which had an inherent thematic cohesion. To analyse the text into various sections is not to posit different sources or later adaptations, but to isolate one facet of a complex whole for study while retaining awareness that it is but part of the total, consistent picture.

Setting in the Prophecy and Scripture. Josephus (*Ant.* 10.79) recorded that 'Ezekiel ... left behind him in writing two books concerning these events', and Ellison argues that the only meaning which can be associated with that statement is that the prophecy in its current form was in Josephus' day regarded as two books, the second of which consisted of chapters 40–48 (1956:138).[1] On this basis he contends

---

1. It should be noted, however, that Josephus' statement regarding two books may be understood in other ways. R. K. Harrison used it to argue for a basic division of the prophecy into chs. 1–23 and chs. 24–48 (1969:848–849).

that too close a link should not be assumed between these 'apocalyptic' chapters, which are in measure discontinuous with the preceding part of the prophecy.

It is, however, noteworthy that, despite the differences from earlier material, the concluding vision is well integrated with the rest of the prophecy. The return of the Glory-presence in chapter 43 is unintelligible without the earlier narrative of its departure. Moreover, within the positive message of the restoration in chapters 34–48 there are significant interconnections. In particular, the ideal temple gives greater substance to the sanctuary promised in 37:26–28, and cannot really be divorced from all the blessings promised in earlier passages.

Indeed, it has often been observed that the sequence of chapters 40–48 is adopted in Revelation to set out the development of the end times. A fourfold structure may be detected: the resurrection of God's people (Ezek. 37:1–14 || Rev. 20:4a); the messianic kingdom (Ezek. 37:15–28 || Rev. 20:4b–6); the battle against Gog (Ezek. 38–39 || Rev. 20:7–10); and the concluding vision of the new temple and new Jerusalem with resemblances to Eden and located on a high mountain (Ezek. 40–48 || Rev. 21:1–22:5). The repetition of this pattern makes it unwise to detach Ezekiel 40–48 to any great extent from what precedes. These chapters do indeed present the culmination to Ezekiel's prophetic ministry.

Interpretation. While it is relatively easy to outline the contents of these chapters, it is a major problem to determine how they should be understood. Many theories have been advanced in this regard, and are maintained with considerable fervour. Even so, it is possible to delineate an appropriate hermeneutical framework. This is best done by looking at the main styles of interpretation without becoming enmeshed in the details of any particular presentation.

(a) A Blueprint for the Returning Exiles. Since Ezekiel is told to report all that is disclosed to him to the house of Israel (40:4), one approach has been to consider these chapters, and particularly those concerning the temple with its wealth of detailed measurements, as setting out what the returnees should do when they are brought back to their native land. This approach, however, does not stand up under close scrutiny.

Those who support this view maintain that it is not undermined by the fact that many details pertaining to the structure of the temple are not given. That had also been true regarding the Mosaic Tabernacle, and it was constructed. But the absence of specifications of the height of the structures means that this is far from being an architectural blueprint. While the regulations regarding the priesthood, the conduct of the temple services, and the ordering of the nation's affairs, sacred and secular, could be feasibly implemented, the river of chapter 47 is beyond human creation, and the location of the temple and its surroundings as well as the boundaries of the tribal territories defy the facts of geography (48:1–29). The vision, therefore, does not constitute a viable programme for the exiles to implement.

Moreover, it is apparent that Ezekiel's contemporaries did not view these chapters as a guide to what they should attempt to do in physical reality in Jerusalem. The Temple built on the return from the exile bears no resemblance to the description found here, and there is no evidence that such a discrepancy formed the basis of any prophetic critique of the subsequent behaviour of the people in the post-exilic period.

(b) A Prevision of the Millennium. A dispensationalist approach to Scripture views prophecy as basically a factual account written in advance. Consequently it is argued that since Ezekiel's prophecy has not yet been fulfilled in historical reality, it remains to be implemented either in or by Israel during a glorious period of one thousand years which will intervene just before the consummation of earth's history.

Quite apart from the basic inadequacies of such an overly literal interpretation of Scripture, these chapters pose particular problems for a dispensationalist hermeneutic. For instance, the new temple is described as the scene of repeated sacrificial offerings (e.g., 43:18–27). There was indeed a transitional period after Christ's death when Christian believers, including Paul himself, continued to engage in worship in the Jerusalem Temple. But that Temple and the sacrificial worship associated with it were divinely terminated in A.D. 70. The life of God's people is no longer centred round the elementary teaching of Old Testament times, but on the spiritual realities symbolically represented there. Christ has now offered for all time one unique sacrifice for sins (Heb. 10:12), and the perpetual reality and efficacy of that sacrifice is not to be compromised by any future sacrificing, whether in a millennial temple or in the claimed re-offering of Christ in the Roman Catholic mass.

Dispensationalist scholars have a high regard for Scripture, and they do struggle to reconcile their interpretative schema with these facts, but their best attempts to do so involve suggesting that the millennial sacrifices will be sacramental and commemorative, not propitiatory. Since, however, that is to attach a different significance to those sacrifices from that which was understood by the prophet and his contemporaries (cf. 'to make atonement for them', 45:15), it is in effect an abandonment of the basic 'literal' presuppositions of dispensationalist hermeneutics. Moreover, as has often been pointed out, if the sacrifices are symbolic, then why may the temple not be so also?

Indeed, dispensationalist arguments are only able to make weak allowance for the New Testament evidence that there is at present a temple erected by God in the church of Jesus Christ. It is not a physical building of brick or stone, but it is a real, existing entity (2 Cor. 6:16; Eph. 2:21–22; 1 Pet. 2:5), which transcends the bounds of Old Testament revelation and incorporates believers, Jew and Gentile, who are indwelt by God through the Holy Spirit. It is essentially a spiritual construction which appears in its most sublime form in John's vision of the New Jerusalem where there is no temple because it is all temple (Rev. 21:22), permeated by the presence of, and fellowship with, the Lord God the Almighty and the Lamb.

(c) A Symbolic Presentation. The ordinances and structures of the Old Testament life and worship were divinely instituted vehicles to convey spiritual truth to Israel through outward forms. The concepts and terms embodied in those rituals provide a meaningful reference structure for the prophet and his audience through which it can be communicated to them how the covenant community should function. This is an ideal portrayal of what true holiness involves. It delineates structures which are themselves illustrative guidelines of how the people of God are to enjoy fellowship with their God who is present among them.

To speak of the ideal often induces suspicions that what is being presented is merely notional, a speculative concept which is out of touch and not grounded in reality. Whatever may be the case with humanly generated ideals, such reservations cannot obtain when the envisaged scenario originates from God. A Scriptural example may help to clarify the matter. In Deuteronomy 15:4, Moses tells the Israelites that 'there will be/should not be a poor ⌊person⌋ among you for the LORD will bless you in the land'—that is the ideal—but at the same time Moses does not shrink from declaring the reality which will in fact occur for a variety of reasons, 'there will not cease to be a poor ⌊person⌋ within the land' (Deut. 15:11). Would there be poor in Israel, or not? Obviously, the latter would be the case (cf. Matt. 26:11). Is then the ideal depiction irrelevant and valueless? Far from it. It presents a goal to be striven for even though, through human sin and frailty, it will never be attained until perfected and glorified humanity will be beyond the ravages of this fallen world (Phil. 3:12–14).

So then, Ezekiel is granted a vision from God, and that in itself distances this record from a straightforward description of items and procedures which are physically embodied. There is indeed a familiar physical backdrop in Jerusalem and the Promised Land, just as the plain provided a backdrop for the many bones of 37:1–11, but what is projected onto that background is divine symbolism. While indicating a measure of continuity with previous modes of divine instruction, the ideal portrayal transcends the physicality of the land and teaches the certainty, completeness, and harmony of the restoration God will accomplish. In Revelation, John draws on Ezekiel's categories and concepts, though he sets aside those physical aspects which pertained only to the Old Testament presentation (Rev. 21:1–22:6). This is not to be dismissed as spiritualisation. This is the promise realised in truth and substance. A symbolic approach to this vision is both Scripturally valid and robust.

It is often remarked that a prophet was both a forthteller of God's word and a foreteller of what was yet to be, especially in matters relating to the Messiah. Is this vision then a matter of forthtelling or foretelling? Obviously, a yes/no dichotomy does less than justice to the complexity of the situation, but so does an overemphasis on this vision as foretelling. The primary scope of the message is instruction for the present and the immediate future, both by way of encouragement and by way of illustration of Scriptural norms for the conduct of the covenant community. Though these word pictures are sketched in terms of past realities, the truth they embody is timeless, and of relevance both in the present age and in the heavenly age to come. In this light it is necessary to modify the sentiment expressed by Apóstolo, 'While the initial visions encapsulate the "Israel-that-was," Ezekiel 40–48 projects the vision of the "Israel-to-come' (2008:16). The contrast is rather that between 'the Israel that ought not to have been' and 'the Israel that ought to be'.

It is also pertinent to point out that in Old Testament prophecies the truth God discloses to the prophets frequently involves events which are successively realised before the finale of Christ's Second Coming. In particular, aspects of the truths presented here are imperfectly realised in the church at present, and await heavenly consummation hereafter. These include the realisation of the Immanuel ('God with us') principle, first in the incarnation of Christ and then in the indwelling of the Spirit, and the consequent necessity of a worshipful response to God's presence. There is also the powerful, transforming power of the divine presence bringing life to the barren places of the earth (47:1–12) as well as maintaining heavenly life hereafter. That life is not merely a gift to be enjoyed, but brings with it the responsibility to react appropriately.

Those who oppose a spiritual style of interpretation commonly object that it fails to do justice to many aspects of Ezekiel's presentation, particularly his detailed account of the Temple. If these details are not intended to be the groundwork for an actual building, why are they given? A number of factors may be adduced by way of response. By avoiding vague abstractions, the detail of the vision reinforces the reality of what is portrayed and the expectation of its actualisation. There is a definite design to God's kingdom, which is divinely ordered in every particular element. *All* things should be done decently and in order (1 Cor. 14:40), and they certainly are in the ideal presentation of the kingdom where God carefully controls all that occurs. Every detail in one way or another contributes meaningfully to this presentation, whether by combating past errors, or by emphasising the beauty and perfection of holiness inherent in true worship of the living God.

One can readily agree with Levenson when he writes, 'To "analyze" is, semantically as well as etymologically, "to break up", and to break up this vision into its components is to dissipate its power. The whole of chs. 40–48 is greater than the sum of its parts' (1976:162).

A. The Vision of the Temple (40:1–42:20)

Many have found in Ezekiel's temple vision a programme for human action at some stage in history, but that is to obscure the main point of this description: what is seen is not man-made but divinely provided. The argument to the contrary is often presented in term such as the following:

> The highly specific nature of the description of the Temple, its liturgy and community bespeaks a practical program, not a vision of pure grace. For example, when the text says that eight steps led up to the vestibule of the inner courtyard (Ezek. 40:31), can this be other than a demand that the new Temple be constructed just so? Can this be only description? The fact that God has already constructed the Temple does not mean that man has no role in its construction. On the contrary, what Ezekiel was shown in the divinely constructed model, the *tabnît* like the one David showed Solomon (1 Chr. 28:11–19)' (Levenson 1976:45).

However, in Ezekiel there is no word such as 'pattern' or 'plan' (*tabnît*) used to give instructions (contrast Exod. 25:9, 40; 1 Chron. 28:11–19). This building is displayed not as a heavenly model, but as spiritual reality. It does not await construction by human hands; it is presented as God's complete provision for his people. '… Ezekiel 40–42 is neither instruction for nor narrative of building, but a vision of an already built complex' (Greenberg 1987:218).

More than that, this structure is an assertion of the LORD's kingship. Temples played a major role in ancient Near Eastern culture, where they legitimated royal sovereignty and served as a focal point of society (Stevenson 1996:116). In large measure they subordinated worship of the deity to the needs of the political regime (cf. 43:6–9), and were designed to boost royal prestige through a king claiming that he had the warrant of his god to build his temple. On the contrary, here the vision is granted to a prophet, a divine spokesman; the work has already been carried out by God; the focus of authority and blessing is the temple, not the palace; or rather it is the LORD himself, and not a human leader who eventually appears designated only as a ruler (cf. 44:3). This is the theocracy portrayed in its ideal form.

Furthermore, the temple description does not focus on the costliness of the materials employed in its construction or on the architectural grandeur which it displays. The focus is rather on the creation of spaces, and on keeping them separate (Stevenson 1996:19). In the theocracy there is a well-ordered and stable society maintained around the divine King who is gloriously present in its midst and whose worship is at the heart of its existence.

In rebuttal of the notion that this is a building plan, it is frequently observed that vertical measurements are largely lacking. They are, of course, not needed in establishing boundaries. However, while the only vertical dimensions explicitly stated are those for the exterior wall (40:5), the tables for preparing the sacrifices (40:42), the wooden altar/table (41:22), and, probably, the elevation of the house (41:8), there are repeated indications of elevation given by the presence of stairways for access (40:6, 22, 26, 34, 49). The structures of this vision are far from being fabricated all on one level; there is a heightening towards the divine residence which is at their core.

As has been already remarked, uncertainty surrounds the interpretation of many specific aspects of Ezekiel's vision. Consequently, the figures provided are illustrative, not definitive. Even so, they should prove of assistance in understanding the text.

(1) The Vision Unfolds (40:1–4)

These verses set out the circumstances in which Ezekiel is given in a vision a conducted tour of an ideal temple. The date of his vision is recorded in 40:1, the scene he observes in 40:2, the guide who accompanies him in 40:3, and the mission with which the prophet is entrusted in 40:4.

> ⁴⁰:¹In the twenty-fifth year of our exile, at the beginning of the year, on the tenth of the month, in the fourteenth year after the city was struck down, on this very day, the hand of the LORD came upon me and he brought me there. ⁴⁰:²In the visions of God he brought me to the land of Israel and set me down on a very high mountain and upon it ⌞there was⌟ like a structure of a city to the south. ⁴⁰:³And he brought me there, and behold, ⌞there was⌟ a man ⌞whose⌟ appearance was like the appearance of bronze, and a linen cord ⌞was⌟ in his hand and a measuring rod, and he was standing in the gateway. ⁴⁰:⁴And the man spoke to me, 'Son of man, see with your eyes and with your ears hear, and fix your mind on all that I am causing you to see, for in order to show you ⌞it⌟ you have been brought here. Report all that you are seeing to the house of Israel.'

♦ **40:1** Ezekiel highlighted the significance of the visionary experience he was granted by the extended dating formula with which he began. Since no further indication of the passage of time was given in the concluding chapters of the prophecy, it may well be that this date applied to them all.

The year in which this vision occurred was stated in two forms: ***in the twenty-fifth year of our exile*** and ***in the fourteenth year after the city was struck down*** (cf. 33:21). For an evaluation of this synchronism, see Introduction §2.5. The overlap of these two time periods narrowed the interval down to that between the summer of 573 B.C. and the spring of 572 B.C. However, it is difficult to determine precisely where within that span the vision should be located. ***At the beginning of the year*** (*rō'š haššānâ*) became in later eras a technical designation of New Year's Day, which was the first day of the seventh month in accordance with the civil (autumn) calendar employed by the Jews. However, at this earlier juncture the phrase need not have had that specific reference, and it could well have been used to indicate the beginning of the year in the liturgical (spring) calendar, to which the anniversary calendar Ezekiel employed elsewhere was a close approximation.² Indeed the reference need not have been to a specific day, but more generally to 'the start of the year', either in autumn 573 or spring 572. On the first reckoning *the tenth of the month* would have been 22nd October 573 B.C., but the more probable alternative date is 17th April 572 B.C.

Without endorsing the view that 'the beginning of the year' related to the autumn, and arguing from the facts that the tenth day of the seventh month was the Day of Atonement (Lev. 16:29)—not directly mentioned in Ezekiel—and that in the fiftieth year that day marked the beginning of the year of Jubilee (Lev. 25:9), it is still possible to find Jubilee overtones in the selection of the twenty-fifty year of the exile for the disclosure of this vision. Jeremiah had prophesied that the exile would last seventy years (Jer. 25:11–12; 29:10), and if the start of the exile is calculated from the first deportation in 605 B.C. (Dan. 1:1), then 573/572 B.C. was close to the midpoint of that experience. In the Jubilee year land in Israel was returned to those who had forfeited it. It may well be that twenty-five years carried the suggestion of being halfway towards a Jubilee, a year of liberation (cf. 46:17), quite apart from when the Jubilee was actually celebrated (if at all). In that case the mention of twenty-five years would again strike a hopeful note, echoing the thought of a year of release.

Hummel (2007:1193) also speculates that such an association of twenty-five with the prospect of release might explain why the dimensions of the temple and its compound so frequently involved twenty-five (40:13, 21, 25, 29, 30, 33, 36) and its multiples (e.g., 40:15, 19; 42:16–20), and why the holy section of the land was envisaged as twenty-five thousand cubits long (45:1–6; 48:8–21).

It may also be the case that the date recalled Ezekiel's inaugural vision twenty years earlier when the LORD was pleased to call him as a prophet at the age when he would have entered into the full duties of the priesthood (see on 1:1). Now the LORD marks the time when a priest would formally demit office at the age of fifty years (Num. 4:3, 23, 30) by granting Ezekiel the privileged insights of this priestly vision and a role within it. However, Ezekiel does not at that stage cease to function as a prophet as his reception of the oracle of 29:17–21 two years later testifies.

Three other features of the first part of the verse may also be briefly

---

2. This point is controverted by Young (2006) who argues that the reference is to an autumn festival, indeed to one on the tenth of the month which coincided with a Jubilee year.

noticed. ***Our exile*** was a poignant intrusion of Ezekiel's own experience. He had never forgotten—how could he?—that he was living in a community who were exiles in a strange land. ***The city*** avoided naming Jerusalem even though it was obviously being referred to. Jerusalem's sinful conduct had been so obnoxious that, even in this historical introduction, its name could not be allowed to intrude into the vision of ideal perfection. Throughout this division of the prophecy it was not named as Jerusalem; indeed a new name was finally given to it (48:35). ***On this very day*** (cf. 2:3; 24:2) was an expression of the intensity of Ezekiel's own experience in receiving this vision. The date of the occurrence, just as what was disclosed in it, was unforgettable.

The hand of the LORD came upon me. This again emphasised that it was divine determination and power which occasioned Ezekiel's experience (cf. 1:3; 3:22; 8:1; 37:1). What was revealed to the prophet's inner eye had been disclosed to him by the LORD and was not the product of his own imagination, though the truths presented by means of the vision were divinely communicated in a mode which matched Ezekiel's character and psyche.

Moreover, Ezekiel recorded that ***he brought me.*** This was not described as the action of the LORD's hand (*yād*, a feminine noun), but of the LORD himself (the verb is a masculine form). 'Brought' (*bô'*, 'to come to', 'to enter'; hiphil, 'to bring to') was a key verb in this passage (cf. 40:2) where the prophet's movements were guided by the LORD or by a divine agent. The manner of this bringing was more clearly defined in the following verse.

There (*šāmmâ*; lit., 'to there', but see on 48:35) was also a significant term in this vision. In this context an antecedent might be found in 'the city', but it was probably used in a general sense for the site of the visionary scene about to be disclosed. Moreover, it also formed an inclusion round these chapters in that the name of the restored city was recorded as 'The LORD is there' (*Yahweh šāmmâ*; 48:35).

♦ **40:2** The information given in this verse was of a background nature, expanding on what had been said in 40:1, with the main storyline continuing in 40:3. By using the expression, ***in the visions of God***, Ezekiel linked his experience with what had taken place earlier (1:1; 8:3). The plural 'visions' was probably an intensive form, implying 'visions granted by God'.

He brought me (lit., 'he caused me to come to'; *bô'*, hiphil) repeated the verb of the last clause of 40:1, with the subject 'he' remaining the LORD. The phrase emphasised the divine initiative in, and control over, Ezekiel's experience. Such a *guidance formula* was characteristic of this vision (40:17, 28, 32, 35, 48; 41:1; 42:1; 44:4; 46:19; cf. also 43:5), and other causative verbs of motion were used with a similar sense throughout these chapters, including the following verb *and set me down* (with the same unexpected form as in 37:1), 'he led me' (40:24; 43:1; 47:6), 'he led me out' (42:1, 15; 46:21; 47:2), 'he brought me back' (44:1; 47:1, 6), 'he brought me across/through' (46:21; 47:3, 4), and 'he brought me round' (47:2). 'Set down' implied a smooth and untroubled arrival at the designated spot.

To the land of Israel[3] meant that the prophet experienced a visionary return to the Promised Land, so that the following events were played out against a known background. However, *on a very high mountain* did not correspond to any topographic reality of the land around Jerusalem, but was much more a symbolic representation conveying theological significance. An exalted site was viewed as an appropriate location for the dwelling place of God, and corresponded to Zion as 'the highest of the mountains' (Isa. 2:2–4; Mic. 4:1–3), and to 'a great, high mountain' (Rev. 21:10). Such an elevated location was also a suitable place for receiving visions (cf. Matt. 17:1; Mark 9:2; Luke 9:28; Rev. 21:10). Already the ideal language transcended any present geographical reality and pointed to its conceptual nature as a standard to be attained, embodying truth which would only be completely realised eschatologically.

Upon it, that is on the mountain where he was set down, Ezekiel saw what was *like a structure of a city to the south.* The prophet here reverted to his idiom in chapter 1 where he repeatedly used 'like' or some similar expression to indicate that ordinary language could only approximate the reality of the visionary disclosure. 'Structure' (or, taking the singular noun *mibneh* as a collective term, 'buildings') was found only here, but its root (*bānâ*, 'to build') was well known, and so the sense would not be obscure. But to what did this phrase refer? It is improbable that what caught Ezekiel's eye was the city mentioned in 45:6–7, and again more extensively in chapter 48. Instead laid out before him was the ideal temple which, with its massive wall and gateways, closely resembled ('*like* the structure') a fortified city rather than having the appearance of a typical temple of Ezekiel's times.

---

3. Only here, in 27:17, and in 47:18 does Ezekiel use the expression *'ereṣ yiśrā'ēl*, 'land/territory of Israel', preferring *'ădāmâ yiśrā'ēl*, 'land/ground of Israel' elsewhere (e.g., 7:2; 11:17; 37:12; 38:18–19).

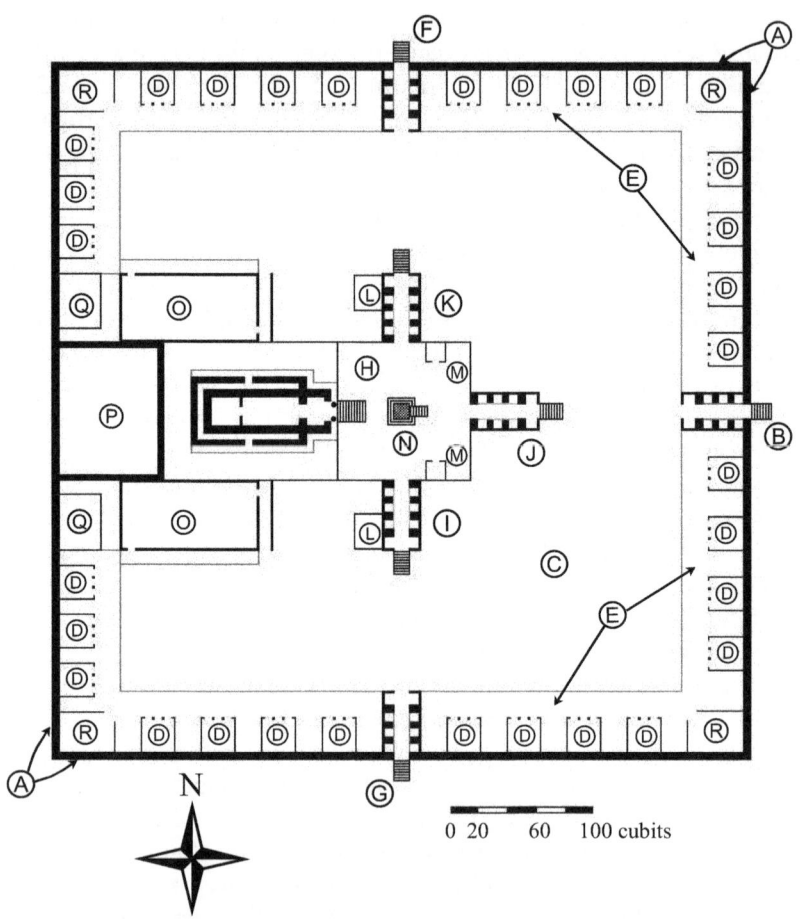

Figure 2. The Temple Complex Revealed to Ezekiel.

Ⓐ	Exterior Wall	40:5
Ⓑ	East Outer Gateway	40:6–16
Ⓒ	Outer Courtyard	40:17
Ⓓ	Outer Courtyard Rooms	40:17
Ⓔ	Pavement	40:18
Ⓕ	North Outer Gateway	40:20–23
Ⓖ	South Outer Gateway	40:24–27
Ⓗ	Inner Courtyard	40:28–47
Ⓘ	South Inner Gateway	40:28–31
Ⓙ	East Inner Gateway	40:32–34
Ⓚ	North Inner Gateway	40:35–37
Ⓛ	Rooms at Inner Gateway	40:36–38
Ⓜ	Rooms in Inner Courtyard	40:44–46
Ⓝ	The Altar	40:47; 43:13–17
Ⓞ	The Priests' Rooms	42:1–11
Ⓟ	The West Building	41:12
Ⓠ	The Priests' Kitchens	46:19
Ⓡ	Kitchens for the Laity	46:22

To the south did not indicate the position of this city-like temple on thesouthern slope of the mountain; instead it reflected the direction from which Ezekiel approached it in vision, that is, he came from the north as would be the case for one arriving at Jerusalem from Babylonia.

♦ **40:3** ***And he brought me there*** repeated the closing words of 40:1 to resume the narrative of the visionary experience. The LORD brought Ezekiel to a location, where, awaiting the prophet's arrival, was ***a man ⌊whose⌋ appearance was like the appearance of bronze.*** At first it had been the LORD himself who had controlled the prophet's movement (40:2, 3), but, with the introduction of this guide (40:3), he took over this role. The guide was clearly distinguished from the LORD in 43:6, but there was no further clue given as to his identity. 'Like the appearance of bronze' was evocative of the gleaming appearance of the living beings in 1:7, but even more so of the individual on the throne in 1:27; 8:2. In the light of the New Testament this figure can be identified as a pre-incarnate appearance of Christ (see Introduction to 1:26–28a). This interpretation is supported by the guide's use of 'son of man' to address the prophet (40:4; 47:6)—the very mode of address which the LORD himself employed. It is difficult to assess the extent to which Ezekiel himself understood the nature of this visionary being.

On the other hand, there are those who identify the man who featured in the vision as 'the angel of the LORD', who repeatedly appears throughout the Old Testament. In favour of this approach is the fact that in John's vision of the New Jerusalem there was also a being with a measuring rod to measure the city (Rev. 21:15–17), and he was apparently the one who was referred to by Jesus as 'my angel' (Rev. 22:16). This angelic figure forbade John from worshipping him and declared himself to be part of the created realm, rather than divine (Rev. 22:8–9). From that perspective, the angelic use of the divine mode of address for the prophet reflected his status as a plenipotentiary ambassador for the LORD, who spoke in his name. However, the created, angelic nature of the Old Testament angel of the LORD is itself a matter of dispute, with many favouring his appearances as being Christophanic in nature. (The matter is discussed extensively in Borland 1978). If this man whose appearance was like the appearance of bronze is identified with the figure *on the throne* who appeared like shining metal (1:26–27), then an appearance of God the Son is established.

Ezekiel's guide carried equipment which showed that he was going to act as a surveyor to measure and define the structures and their contents. This was not primarily a fact-finding role, but an assertion of the LORD's ownership of the temple and his jurisdiction over it. The man carried two items of a surveyor's kit *in his hand*. *A linen cord* referred to material (here, fibres of flax) which had been twisted into thread or rope, and which could then be used to measure long distances probably by means of knots tied every cubit along it (cf. Zech. 2:1–2). There was no mention of this cord even when it came to establishing larger dimensions connected with the temple complex (cf. 42:16–19), but it did come into use in 47:3. *A measuring rod* (lit., 'the reed of measurement', with the article indicating the specific purpose to which it would be put) was an implement for determining shorter distances (40:5).

He was standing in the gateway indicated the guide's awareness of the role assigned to him. Since what was involved was a large building complex resembling a city, 'gateway' (*ša'ar*) is a more accurate rendering than 'gate'. It was not a simple structure pivoting on a set of hinges, but a substantial stone building of some depth as was shortly made clear.

There were three such gateways in the wall of the temple complex, and it is uncertain whether the one referred to here was the northern or the eastern gateway. The northern gateway would fit in with the direction from which Ezekiel arrived, and would account for the movement implied by 'he came' (40:6). On the other hand, there was no suggestion that he brought Ezekiel round from the north gateway to the east one, and perhaps 'in the gateway' had the sense of 'in the general area of the gateway'.

♦ **40:4** *And the man spoke to me* introduced the first speech of the guide, who used the divine idiom, *Son of man* (cf. 2:1) to address Ezekiel. The instructions he issued to him were therefore understood as originating from God himself. Ezekiel was required to *see with your eyes and with your ears hear* (cf. 44:5). These were not two sequential actions, but one combined act of close observation, which would enable the prophet to recall what his guide said to him and what was been disclosed to him. *Fix your mind* (or, 'heart', that is, his whole interior being; see on 11:19) called for more than casual observation; it demanded close inspection with a view to subsequent recall. *All that I am causing you to see* again emphasised that the basis of this report was not human imagination but divine disclosure.

While Ezekiel's experience was intended to familiarise him with this ideal temple (***in order to show you ⌊it⌋ you have been brought here***), it was not to remain a private communication intended solely for Ezekiel's edification. ***Report all that you are seeing to the house of Israel.*** The covenant community in exile were to be informed of the contents of the vision because it was intended to shape their thinking and encourage them to persevere. These instructions were later reflected in 43:11, which thus formed an inclusion round this section.

REFLECTION

- God's presence with his people is the consummating privilege of a right relationship with him. In the wilderness period that reality was symbolised by the Tabernacle, in which God's Glory-presence tented with the people. Later, when the people had settled in the land and were dwelling in permanent structures, Solomon built the Temple so that the LORD might take up residence in their midst. 'The glory of the LORD filled the house of the LORD' (1 Kgs. 8:11). To those who knew the depths of the depravity perpetrated in that Temple so that it then lay in charred ruins, it was a vision of hope to be presented with this portrayal of the ideal temple, and particularly as there was one significant variation from the earlier provision for the divine presence in the midst of the people.

  When God had revealed to Moses the arrangements for the wilderness Tabernacle, he said, 'According to all that I am causing you to see of the pattern of the tabernacle and of the pattern of its furnishings; so you are to make it' (Exod. 25:9). Later, it was David who accumulated the materials for building the Temple, and Solomon who initiated and supervised its construction. Here, neither Ezekiel nor any other being was involved in the erection and equipping of this ideal temple. It was exclusively of divinely provision, a fact which was to be securely grasped by the prophet and reported to the people.

- Without actually naming Zion, the description found here was a virtual counterpart of what was enjoined in Psalm 48:12–14: 'Walk about Zion, go around her, number her towers, set your mind/heart on her ramparts, go through her citadels, that you may tell the next generation that this is God, our God for ever and ever. He will guide us for ever.' By observing what the LORD presented in this vision his people could learn valuable lessons about divine holiness, about the detailed provision God had made for their worship of him, and about how carefully they were to regulate their response to him.

(2) The Temple Gateways and Courtyards (40:5–37)

The elaborate description of the temple revealed to Ezekiel begins with the exterior wall (40:5), and then continues with the east outer gateway (40:6–16), the outer courtyard (40:17–19), the north and south outer gateways (40:20–27), the inner gateways (40:28–37), the rooms and equipment for the preparation of the sacrifices (40:38–43), and the rooms for the priests (40:44–47).

It is possible to compare this description with that of Solomon's Temple in 1 Kings 6–8. This may help fill in missing details, especially for those who take a blueprint approach to the visionary description, but it would also naturally occur to the prophet's audience who were all familiar with the structure which the Babylonians destroyed. However, the two temples reflect radical different power structures. Solomon's Temple was an embodiment of the success of David's royal line. It was 'the house which King Solomon built for the LORD' (1 Kgs. 6:2; cf. 1 Kgs. 8:13), and as such was a lavish tribute celebrating the success and prosperity of the dynasty. In Ezekiel's temple human kingship is demoted (if not eliminated); the temple is the LORD's own provision, and a celebration of his sovereign power. Its extensive symmetry encapsulates the orderliness of his regime, and its many boundaries give structure to the conduct of those who would worship the divine King.

(a) The Exterior Wall (40:5)

Since the prophet is initially situated outside the temple complex, he is immediately aware of the wall which surrounds it (see Fig. 2 A). It is here that the guide begins his activities (Fig. 3 ①), but further details about the exterior wall are given in the concluding subsection of 42:15–20. At this point the focus is on its breadth and width, and on the implement Ezekiel's guide uses to measure it.

> ⁴⁰:⁵And behold, ⌊there was⌋ a wall on the outside of the house right round about ⌊it⌋. And in the man's hand ⌊there was⌋ a measuring rod six cubits long (by the cubit and a span), and he measured the breadth of the structure, one rod, and the height, one rod.

♦ **40:5 *And behold, ⌊there was⌋ a wall.*** As he viewed the structure from outside it, Ezekiel's attention was first of all drawn to the major external feature of the temple compound, its ***wall*** (*ḥômâ*), a term which was used elsewhere in the Old Testament only for a city-wall.

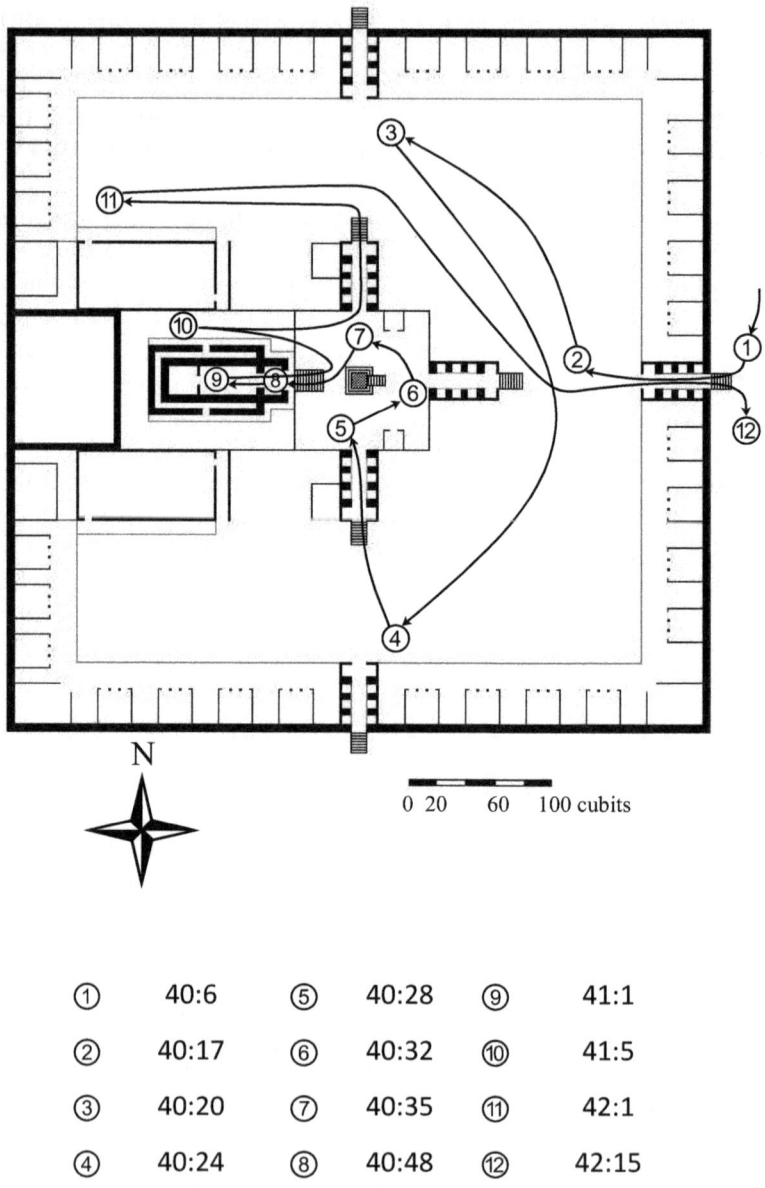

①	40:6	⑤	40:28	⑨	41:1
②	40:17	⑥	40:32	⑩	41:5
③	40:20	⑦	40:35	⑪	42:1
④	40:24	⑧	40:48	⑫	42:15

Figure 3. Ezekiel's Guided Tour (Part 1).

Such a massive structure is unattested for ancient Near Eastern temples. Mention of the wall forms an inclusion with the only other use of the term in the prophecy, at the end of the temple vision (42:20). It was with this structure that the guide began his activities.

The house (*bayit*; cf. 8:14) was the term often applied in the Old Testament to the building which functioned as the earthly dwelling of the heavenly King (e.g., 2 Sam. 7:13). It probably was used in that sense in its twenty other occurrences in chapters 40–42 to refer specifically to the central structure (Milgrom 2012:66), but it also had a wider usage for the whole temple complex ('temple area'; NIV, ESV; cf. 44:11). Either usage would fit this context. The reduplication involved in **right round** (*sābîb sābîb*) was characteristic of Ezekiel's style (otherwise only in 2 Chron. 4:3), but was probably not emphatic, just a variation found in later Hebrew.

In the man's hand ⌊there was⌋ a measuring rod repeated the information provided in 40:3, but with the addition **six cubits ⌊long⌋**, which was further qualified by **by the cubit and a span**. There were various ways of defining a cubit as a measure of length (e.g., 'cubits of the former standard', 2 Chron. 3:3). The ordinary cubit was called in Deuteronomy 3:11 a 'cubit of a man', and was considered to be the distance from the elbow to the tip of the middle finger. It is estimated to be the equivalent of 17.4 inches (44.6 cm) or six spans/handbreadths (four fingers), each of just under 3 inches (about 7.4 cm). There was also a 'long cubit' which was one handbreadth greater at 20.3 inches (52 cm), and which seems to have been regarded as appropriate in sacred and royal contexts, because similar distinctions are attested in Egypt and Babylonia. It was thus made clear that the longer cubit was used in the vision, and the guide's rod was therefore about 2 inches over 10 feet (3.1 m).

The structure (*binyān*, like *mibneh* in 40:2, was derived from *bānâ*, 'to build', and signified 'something built') was the wall, and its **breadth** was found to be **one rod, and the height, one rod.** Since the rod was six cubits, the wall was of square cross-section, around 10.15 feet (3.1 m). This was the exterior height of the wall. Because of the elevation of the outer courtyard which had to be approached up seven steps (40:22, 26), the height of the wall from the inside might have been just under two cubits (around 3.5 feet or 1 m).[4] No hint was given of the material of its construction, but presumably it was stone.

---

4. If the elevation of six cubits in 41:8 corresponds to the ten steps of 40:49 (LXX), then each step had a rise of 0.6 cubits (12.2 in; 31 cm).

Mention of the height of the wall was distinctive in that Ezekiel's description was largely that of a ground plan with no elevation given (see Introduction to 40:1–42:20). While the wall was not sufficiently high as to form a significant defence against military assault, it did constitute an obvious and effective barrier against casual trespass. The temple compound was thus separated from the outside world (cf. 42:20; 43:12), and also by a further surrounding open space (45:2).

(b) The East Outer Gateway (40:6–16)

The eastern gateway is the natural starting point for a tour as the temple, like that of Solomon and Near Eastern temples in general, is oriented towards the east. This had been the exit route taken by the Glory-presence from the Jerusalem Temple (10:19; 11:23), and it will be the gateway through which the LORD will return to this ideal structure (43:4). It is treated in some detail as representative of the other two outer gateways to the north and south, all three of which open directly opposite the altar in the centre.

The guide first measures the entire length of the gateway (40:6–9); next details are given regarding the inner arrangements of the gateway (40:10–12); and then features of the whole structure are recorded in (40:13–15), concluding with a note of internal decorations (40:16). Throughout the description of the gateway it becomes evident that either Ezekiel's guide did not measure all the dimensions of the structure or else the prophet did not consider it necessary to record them. This, combined with the difficulty of interpreting some of the details that are documented, means that reconstructions of this and other structures in the temple compound are not definitive. Enough is recorded to be certain of the main features, but in many respects assumptions have to be made. The extent to which this is so can be seen by comparing the plans produced by different commentators. Still some plan is better than none when it comes to trying to conceive what Ezekiel describes for us here (see Fig. 2 B; Fig. 4).

Gateways control access, and this one is massive. Considerable detail is given about it because the other temple gateways are modelled on it. Ezekiel in his vision may be thought of as following the man who is acting as his tour guide, and obediently noting the dimensions as they are measured and called out (40:4).

> [40:6]And he came to a gateway which faced eastwards, and he went up by its steps and measured the threshold of the gateway, one rod in breadth, and the one threshold, one rod

in breadth. ⁴⁰:⁷And the recess ⌊was⌋ one rod in length and one rod in breadth, and between the recesses five cubits, and the threshold of the gateway near the vestibule of the gateway from the house ⌊was⌋ one rod. ⁴⁰:⁸And he measured the vestibule of the gateway from the house, one rod. ⁴⁰:⁹And he measured the vestibule of the gateway, eight cubits, and its gateposts two cubits, and the vestibule of the gateway ⌊was⌋ from the house. ⁴⁰:¹⁰And the recesses of the gateway eastwards ⌊were⌋ three on this side and three on the other side with the same measurement for the three of them; and ⌊there was⌋ one measurement for the gateposts on either side. ⁴⁰:¹¹And he measured the breadth of the opening of the gateway, ten cubits; the length of the gateway ⌊was⌋ thirteen cubits. ⁴⁰:¹²And there was a border in front of the recesses, one cubit on this side and one cubit on the other side, and ⌊each⌋ recess was six cubits on this side and six cubits on the other side. ⁴⁰:¹³And he measured the gateway from the ceiling of ⌊one⌋ recess to its ceiling; the breadth ⌊was⌋ twenty-five cubits. An opening was opposite an opening. ⁴⁰:¹⁴And he made gateposts, sixty cubits, and to the gatepost of the courtyard the gateway ⌊was⌋ right round about. ⁴⁰:¹⁵And upon the front of the gateway, ⌊that is, at⌋ the entrance, as far as the vestibule of the inner gateway ⌊was⌋ fifty cubits. ⁴⁰:¹⁶And ⌊there were⌋ closable windows to the recesses, and to their posts inwards to the gateways right round about, and similarly for the vestibules; and ⌊there were⌋ windows right round about on the inside; and on ⌊each⌋ post ⌊there were⌋ carved palm trees.

♦ **40:6** *He came to a gateway*.[5] The man may originally have been standing at the east gateway, or he may have escorted Ezekiel to that point (Fig. 3 ①; see on 40:3). Elaborate gateways were not typical of temple complexes, but this description does resemble certain gateways of fortified towns which archaeologists have uncovered, and which may be dated as early as the Solomonic era (Hazor, Gezer, Megiddo). This feature reinforced the city-like appearance of the complex which Ezekiel had described (40:2). *Faced eastwards* (lit., 'its face way of the eastwards') employed Ezekiel's use of 'way/road' to indicate orientation (cf. 8:5). *He went up by its steps*[6] (Fig. 4 a).

---

5. Strangely the term 'gateway' does not here have the article despite the east gateway being the most significant.

6. The qere *bəmaʿălôtāyw*, 'by its steps', spells the masculine singular in its normal full form; the kethib omits the *yodh*, though BHS suggests that it is the singular style of the pronominal suffix that is written in the kethib.

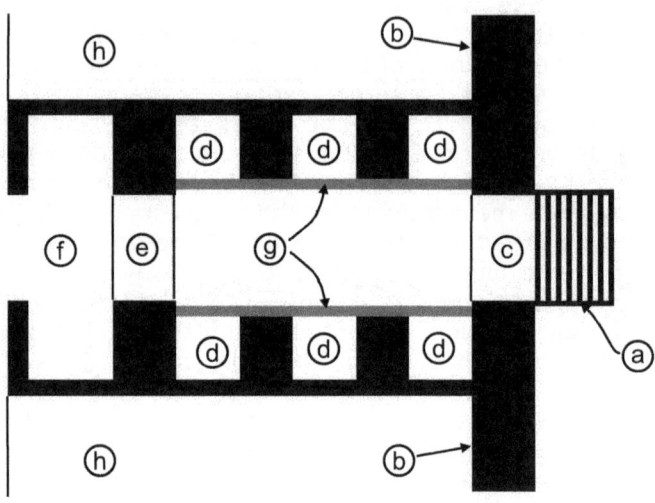

ⓐ	Steps	40:6
ⓑ	Perimeter Wall	40:6
ⓒ	Outer Threshold	40:6
ⓓ	Recesses	40:7, 10
ⓔ	Inner Threshold	40:7
ⓕ	Vestibule	40:9
ⓖ	Border	40:12
ⓗ	Pavement	40:17–18

Figure 4. The Outer East Gateway.

The Massoretic text does not here record how many steps, but the Septuagint has 'seven' to harmonise with 40:22 and 40:26. Clearly the whole structure was constructed on a platform. These steps lay outside the wall in front of it, and at the top of them the threshold through the wall was encountered, which the guide could easily measure once he had ascended the steps.

He measured the threshold of the gateway, one rod in breadth. 'Breadth' here relates to its dimension from east to west ('front to back', NLT). As the threshold (Fig. 4 c) stretched through the wall (Fig. 4 b), it had the same dimension as the wall, somewhat over 10 feet (40:5). *And the one threshold, one rod in breadth.*[7] This seems repetitious, but 'one' was possibly used here as an ordinal to clarify that it is not the second threshold (40:7) which is being described: 'that is, the first threshold, one rod in breadth' (Keil 2002:346). The length (from north to south) of the threshold is not stated but it may be inferred from 40:11.

♦ **40:7** The gateway protruded from inside the wall out into the courtyard. There was therefore space to accommodate various structures within it. Ezekiel first described *the recess*, that is, a typical recess or alcove, because 40:10 makes clear that there were six of them, in a pattern well-known from archaeology (Fig. 4 d). They served as guard posts from which the Levites could monitor those entering the sanctuary to ensure that there were no breaches of decorum (cf. 1 Kgs. 14:28; 2 Chron. 12:11). The sanctity of the holy place had to be preserved from behaviour such as was described in chapter 8. Each recess was a square of *one rod*, that is, six cubits or just over 10 feet. *Between the recesses* apparently referred to the thickness of the walls between these chambers as *five cubits* thick.

The threshold of the gateway near the vestibule of the gateway from the house, that is, at its inner end, viewed from the sanctuary (Fig. 4 e). It had the same width as the first threshold, *one rod*, that is, six cubits, so that the wall separating it from the adjacent recess must have been one cubit thicker than those between the recesses.

---

7. At first sight there seems to be a textual difficulty here in that the text is repetitious. The Peshitta seems to have read 'other (*ʾaḥēr*) threshold' rather than 'one (*ʾeḥād*) threshold', and that is followed by AV, NASB, NKJV. But though there is another threshold into the vestibule in 40:7, mention of its dimensions seems premature here, and many translations (e.g., NIV, REB, ESV) follow the LXX in omitting the phrase in this verse as accidental repetition. The Targum and the Vulgate do, however, reflect the MT.

♦ **40:8** *The vestibule of the gateway* was a larger room outside the inner end of the gateway (Fig. 4 f), with the central passageway continuing to run through it to exit directly into the outer courtyard. There are significant variations in textual traditions. Numerous Hebrew manuscripts, as well as the Peshitta and the Vulgate, omit the last three Hebrew words, *from the house, one rod.* They also omit the first four Hebrew words of 40:9, 'and he measured the vestibule of the gateway', thus apparently recording only one measurement for the vestibule. The measurement of this verse, however, gave the thickness of the separating wall, which was the same as the threshold (40:7).

♦ **40:9** *The vestibule of the gateway* was rectangular, *eight cubits* deep from east to west. The term rendered *gateposts*[8] is of unclear significance, and may describe pillars adjacent to the west wall, but the dimensions given in 40:15 suggest instead that these pillars acted as gateposts and lay at the end of the wall. As the gateposts were sixty cubits high (40:14), the width of *two cubits* would be needed to maintain the integrity of the structure. *The vestibule of the gateway ⌊was⌋ from the house* clarified that it lay within the courtyard, not at the outer entrance where such an entrance hall might have been expected.

♦ **40:10** Having taken the measurements of the previous verse, the guide moved back within the gateway proper. It was noted that *the recesses of the gateway eastwards ⌊were⌋ three on this side and three on the other side*, so that there were six alcoves in all. Also, *with the same measurement for the three of them* showed they were of identical dimensions. Indeed it was further recorded that *⌊there was⌋ one measurement for the gateposts on either side.* The phrase 'on either side' (lit., 'from here … from here') was an Ezekielian idiom. Presumably these gateposts were at the outer entrance to the gateway where the guide obtained the measurements of the next verse.

♦ **40:11** *He measured the breadth of the opening of the gateway* made a straightforward observation that it was *ten cubits*, from north to south. However, *the length of the gateway ⌊was⌋ thirteen cubits* is obscure. One possibility is the ten cubits measured the width of the opening with the additional three cubits accounted for by the posts and

---

8. The qere has the normal pronominal suffix form for a plural noun, *wəʾêlāyw*, 'its gateposts', whereas the kethib has a defectively written form, *wəʾêlāw* (cf. 40:21, 24, 26, 29, 31, 33, 34, 36, 37, where the same variation occurs). For a similar kethib/qere, cf. 40:6.

sockets (Block 1998:518). But why would that be called 'the length'? Zimmerli (1983:349–350) remarks that the 'length' and 'breadth' 'of a measured element are not in terms of the perspective of someone who is passing through, but ... describe quite objectively the longer and shorter dimension of an object to be measured.' So it would seem that here the term 'gateway' was used specifically for the initial entrance, which in total was three cubits greater than the opening because it overlapped the wall at the side of the first threshold, by 1½ cubits on each side.

♦ **40:12** The exact nature of the ***border*** (*gĕbûl*) is not clear, but the same term was used in 43:13 for a low ledge. It might have been a small wall or a slightly raised set of stones ***in front of the recesses*** which would keep those making their way through the gateway from inadvertently straying into the recesses at the side (Fig. 4 g). The border was ***one cubit*** wide. Depending on how far the boundary lay from the recesses, there was from eight to eleven cubits for the central access through the gateway. ⌊***Each*⌋ *recess was six cubits on this side and six cubits on the other side*** essentially reproduced the information given in 40:7a.

♦ **40:13** The guide continued his survey of the property. ***He measured the gateway*** in a different dimension, from north to south. ***From the ceiling of*** ⌊***one***⌋ ***recess to its ceiling*** is not particularly clear, but 'ceiling' is a more probably rendering than 'roof' for *gāg* in this context, because 'roof' might imply that what the guide was providing was an external measurement obtained by going outside onto the top of the structure. Instead the inner dimension of the gateway was taken from where the ceiling and the exterior wall met at the back of one recess straight across the passageway to the corresponding point in the recess opposite. This was feasible since ***an opening was opposite an opening***. Presumably the measurement was taken at ceiling height owing to the presence of the boundary. This yielded a figure for ***the breadth*** of ***twenty-five cubits***, a numeral which frequently occurred in the description of the complex (40:21, 25, 29, 30, 33, 36).

♦ **40:14** Because the meaning of this verse is obscure, many commentators have tended to delete it (for instance, Zimmerli (1983:335) treats it as having arisen through scribal corruption which also affected 40:15–16). The term rendered ***gateposts*** (*'ayil*) has been variously interpreted, but their height of ***sixty cubits*** made it clear that these pillars were more than ordinary gateposts. Indeed ***he made*** (in the sense 'he made it out to be') rather than 'he measured' indicated that the surveyor-guide did not employ his measuring rod to determine their height, but had to use some indirect technique to arrive at this figure. The Vulgate and the Targum support the idea that it was their height which was involved.[9] The height of these gateposts or pillars may seem excessive, but there were somewhat similar structures in Solomon's Temple (1 Kgs. 7:15–22), to make its appearance even more impressive.

♦ **40:15** Again it is difficult to be certain of the details. *Upon the front of the gateway*, that is, presumably from the front of the gateway, indicated one end of the distance being measured, and *as far as the front of the vestibule of the inner gateway* (lit., 'upon with respect to the front') marked the other end of the measurement. This was not a reference to the gateway of the inner courtyard described in 40:28–37, but to the inner end of the outer gateway structure. The measurement was made to the front of the vestibule of the gateway leading inwards, and it came to *fifty cubits.* As Hummel (2007:1176) notes, 'satisfyingly, if one adds up all the measurements already given in 40:6–10, we get a total of fifty cubits'. The figures were 6 cubits for the threshold of the gateway (40:6); 18 cubits for the three side-rooms on each side (40:7, 10); 10 cubits for the two walls between the side-rooms (40:7); 6 cubits for the threshold of the vestibule (40:7); 8 cubits for the vestibule itself (40:9); 2 cubits for the gateposts (40:9). This total made up of various measurements established that the gateway was rectangular.

However, that was not all there was in 40:15, because after 'upon the front of the gateway' there was another word whose grammatical connection with the rest of the verse was not marked, and whose meaning is uncertain because it only occurred here.[10] Taking it as derived from a root meaning 'to come' leads to a translation, *the*

---

9. The LXX seems to have read 'vestibule' (*ʾûlām*) instead of 'gateposts' (*ʾēlîm*), and the ESV and NRSV are based on that, but the dimensions have then also to be modified. The NIV takes the measurement to be that of the circumference of the gateway. Furthermore, the LXX reduced the height to 20 cubits, presumably because 60 cubits seemed doubly excessive for a vestibule.

10. The qere reads *hāʾîtôn*, whereas the kethib interchanges the first two consonants, *hayyōʾtôn*. Reading the qere it is possible to identify the root as *ʾātâ*, 'to come'. However, the term has the article, and so it is not possible to read the three nouns as a construct chain, 'the front of the gateway of the entrance'. Rather it seems to be an appositional usage, '⌊that is, at⌋ the entrance'.

entrance, and it seems to have been added in apposition to the first phrase to clarify where the start of the measurement was.

♦ **40:16** The description in this verse remains obscure. The translation **windows** (*ḥallônôt*) is possibly misleading in that it now suggests a glazed structure. Possibly, 'openings/apertures' would be less misleading. The term was qualified by a word seemingly from a root 'to shut/stop up' (*'āṭam*), so that Block (1998:519, 522–523) envisages niches in the walls shaped like apertures for windows but closed at their outer edges so as to be used as cupboards for storage. More probably the idea was 'closable', that is, with some form of shutter (NRSV) or grating/grille, or perhaps the term indicated an aperture which narrowed towards the outside (RSV).

There are differences of opinion as to where the middle of the verse occurred. The Massoretic text marked it as after ***and similarly for the vestibules,*** but it is often taken to lie before that phrase by commentators. It is difficult to understand the plural 'vestibules', because there was only one vestibule in the entrance gateway, but, when Ezekiel recorded this description, he was aware that these dimensions applied to the other two gateways also. ***On ⌊each⌋ post*** referred to the door posts. ***Carved palm trees*** also featured in the decoration of the temple building itself (41:18).

(c) The Outer Courtyard (40:17–19)

In this brief description there are difficulties in envisaging the scene because of the use of technical terms which are no longer fully understood.

> 40:17And he brought me into the outer courtyard, and behold ⌊there were⌋ rooms and a pavement made for the courtyard right round about; thirty rooms ⌊faced⌋ onto the pavement. 40:18And the pavement ⌊was⌋ at the side of the gateways alongside the length of the gateways; ⌊this was⌋ the lower pavement. 40:19And he measured the breadth from the front of the lower gateway to the front of the inner courtyard from outside, one hundred cubits — on the east and on the north.

♦ **40:17** ***He brought me*** was the first use of the guidance formula with Ezekiel's heaven-appointed escort as its subject (cf. 40:2). The base form of this verb (*bô'* qal) indicated movement towards or into an object, and the causative form employed here (*bô'* hiphil) probably went beyond the thought of 'conducted' to include 'authorised' to move across the boundary between one zone and another (Stevenson 1996:54-56). This was possible because the guide was the LORD's accredited agent, who next escorted Ezekiel *into the outer courtyard* (Fig. 2 C).

Rooms (plural of *liškâ*; Fig. 2 D) was a fairly general term which did not specify their function, shape, or mode of construction. Temple rooms could be used as accommodation for temple officials (1 Chron. 9:33), or as storerooms (Neh. 10:37-39). The fact that kitchens existed in each corner of the courtyard (46:21-24) gives rise to the perception that these rooms functioned as places designated for worshippers to participate in a fellowship offering.

Block (1998:524) plausibly envisages pillared porticoes which could be used for meetings or eating. No mention was made of doors for the rooms, so the structures might well have been open on the side facing the courtyard. However, since a specific number of rooms are mentioned, this may favour the existence of separate chambers rather than a continuous structure. If the open front had pillars to support a roof, that might explain 'the pillars of the courtyard' in 42:6.

No information was given about the arrangement of the rooms apart from *thirty rooms ⌊faced⌋ onto the pavement* (Fig. 2 E). Hummel (2007:1177) suggests that there were four on either side of the north, south and east gateways (that is, eight on each wall), and that the remaining six were found on the west wall on either side of the temple itself (so also Block 1998:525). That is the layout adopted here, though Milgrom argues for ten rooms on each of the north, east and south walls (2012:73). Quite possibly the rooms were positioned right against the external wall so that they could be oriented 'to the pavementwards'.

Not much is known about *the pavement* (*riṣəpâ*), a term which may have indicated that its flagstones were of a superior quality, possibly patterned (cf. Est. 1:6 where it referred a mosaic pavement). *Made*[11] *for the courtyard right round about.* On this basis the view is adopted here that the pavement stretched round all four walls with a break on the west wall.

40:18 ***The pavement ⌊was⌋ at the side of the gateways alongside the***

---

11. The passive participle *'āśûî*, 'made', is masculine whereas 'pavement' (*riṣpâ*, spelled without a *dagesh* in the *pe* to distinguish it from the homonym, 'ember, hot stone') is feminine in form. LXX omitted 'made', but it is repeated in 41:18-20, 25, and Zimmerli (1983:337) suggests it had become a virtual noun used as a technical term.

length of the gateways. The pavement flanked the gateways, running round the perimeter walls. Ezekiel had so far only mentioned one gateway, but he would shortly introduce the other two. Some consider that this statement implied that there was no pavement on the west wall because it did not have a gateway. The view adopted in this regard is presumably influenced by the location assumed for the rooms and other structures mentioned later.

The pavement projected from the outer wall into the outer courtyard as far as the gateways did. Block considers that the presence of the pavement implied that there were at least two levels to the outer courtyard. One was formed by the lower pavement, and the other, not directly referred to, was the slightly raised surface of the rest of the courtyard (Block 1998:525), but this arrangement seems unnecessary. Milgrom argues that the pavement is ignored in taking measurements, and does not imply a differential in height (2012:73). On the other hand a pavement running round all the walls would form a square outer perimeter for the courtyard of 400 cubits (Stevenson 1996:21). The pavement then served as both a boundary marker and a buffer zone between the rooms and the courtyard.

This was the lower pavement. In 40:31, 34, 37 eight steps lead up to the gateways into the inner courtyard. No mention was made of an 'upper' pavement in that courtyard, but perhaps the contrast in view was with 'the place left vacant' round the temple (41:11).

♦ **40:19** The starting point of the next measurement taken by the guide was *from the front of the lower gateway*[12] and its end point was ***to the front of the inner courtyard. From outside*** located the end point more precisely. It would seem to be the innermost edge of the outer gateway to the outermost edge of the inner gateway gate, not the boundary of the inner courtyard. That is confirmed by 40:23 and 40:27. 'Lower gateway' again reflected the difference in height between the two courtyards.

On the east and on the north were traditionally separated in the Massoretic text by a long space from what preceded them. This may have reflected an awareness that words were missing. If so, they may well be those supplied by the Septuagint rendering: 'one hundred cubits to the one which looks to the east. And he brought me up to the

---

12. The form *hattaḥtōnâ*, 'lower', seems to be a feminine adjective which does not agree with the masculine noun *šaʿar*, 'gate', which it modifies. The ending may, however, a directional *he*, so that the sense is 'from the front of the gateway lowerwards'.

north.' Unlike most English translations which ignore the space in the text, Block (1998:524) attempts to do justice to it by translating: 'So far the eastern [gate]; now to the northern [gate]' (cf. ESV margin).

(d) The North and South Gateways (40:20–27)

There is no western gateway behind the Temple itself, the space being taken up by a large building of which little is said (41:12; Fig. 2 P). The two remaining outer gateways, one through the north wall (40:20–23) and the other through the south wall (40:24–27), are constructed in a similar fashion to the east outer gateway. There are, however, a number of verbal variations in the way the structures are described.

> 40:20And ⌞as for⌟ the gateway of the outer courtyard facing northwards, he measured its length and its breadth. 40:21And its recesses ⌞were⌟ three on the one side and three on the other, and its posts and its vestibule were according to the measurements of the first gateway, its length was fifty cubits and its breadth was twenty-five cubits. 40:22And its windows and its vestibule and its palm trees ⌞were⌟ according to the measurements of the gateway facing eastwards, and by seven steps ⌞people⌟ would go up to it, with its vestibule facing them. 40:23And a gateway of the inner courtyard was opposite the gateway towards the north, and he measured from gateway to gateway, one hundred cubits. 40:24And he led me southwards, and behold, ⌞there was⌟ a gateway towards the south; and he measured its posts and its vestibule according to these measurements. 40:25And ⌞there were⌟ windows in it and in its vestibule right round about like these windows; its length ⌞was⌟ fifty cubits and its breadth, twenty-five cubits. 40:26And ⌞there were⌟ seven steps to go up to it, with its vestibule facing them; and it had palm trees on its posts, one on this side and one on the other side. 40:27And the inner courtyard had a gateway towards the south, and he measured from the gateway to the gateway towards the south, one hundred cubits.

♦ **40:20** *The North Gateway.* The specifications of the eastern gateway meant that a summary, differing only in minor respects, sufficed to describe the north outer gateway (Fig. 2 F). No mention was made of the pavement flanking this gate, but its existence was already clear from 40:18. The detail was added in 40:22 that seven steps led up to it from the outer wall, and this was undoubtedly true of the eastern gate too. It was also noted for the first time in 40:23 that the gateways to the inner courtyard were directly opposite those of the outer courtyard.

It is perhaps noteworthy that there was no transitional guidance formula, 'and he brought me', presumably because the prophet's movement did not involve crossing into a different zone. The way in which the prophet was afterwards conducted to all three gateways in the inner courtyard (40:28, 32, 35) renders it almost certain that he was conducted in vision to the north outer gateway also (Fig. 3 ③).

♦ **40:21** Just like *the first gateway*, that is, the eastern gateway, that on the north had *its recesses*.[13] *Twenty-five cubits* was literally 'twenty-five by the cubit', but this was probably just a stylistic change for variety. The dimensions were *according to the measurements of the first gateway.*

♦ **40:22** *Its windows and its vestibule* is often emended to 'the windows of its vestibule' as making better sense.[14] ⌊*People*⌋ *would go up to it* renders an impersonal third person plural construction 'they would go up to it'. *Facing them*[15] did not make clear the reference of 'them', the steps or the people climbing them. It was probably the latter since the pronominal suffix was masculine, and 'steps' was a feminine noun. *By seven steps* indicated the extent to which the courtyard was elevated above ground level outside the perimeter wall. It is probable that each step had a rise of just over a foot so that the total elevation was 7.1 feet (2.2 m; see discussion at 40:49 and 41:8).

40:23 *He measured from gateway to gateway, one hundred cubits* confirmed the distance recorded in 40:19.

♦ **40:24** *The South Gateway.* The description of the south gateway (Fig. 2 G) began with a guidance formula, *and he led me*.[16] While the

---

13. There are three qere/kethib variations in this verse, in each of which the qere substitutes the usual form of a third masculine singular pronominal suffix to a plural noun for the kethib which has either a shortened form of that suffix (without the *yodh*) or a suffix for a singular noun (cf. 40:6). This interchange also occurs in many verses up to 40:38. Here (and in 40:24–26, 29, 31, 33–34, 36) the kethib reading *wəʾēlammô*, 'and its vestibule', is to be preferred to the qere *wəʾēlammāyw*, 'and its vestibules', because there was only one vestibule for each gateway.

14. The change is from *wəḥallônāw wəʾēlammāw* to *wəḥallônê ʾēlammô*.

15. The LXX has 'inside' (cf. RSV, NRSV) but this reads *lipnîmâ* rather than *lipnêhem*, with transposition of the *he* and the *mem*. A similar LXX reading also occurs in 40:26.

16. The verb 'he led me' (*wayyôlikēnî*) is the hiphil of *hālak*, 'to cause to go/walk' (cf. 43:1; 47:6).

verb employed here indicated how his guide directed Ezekiel's path, it did not involve crossing a sacred boundary, but movement within a zone (cf. Stevenson 1996:55). The prophet was close enough to his guide to observe him as he measured and called out the results. *According to these measurements* or 'like these measurements' meant like those of the previous two gateways (cf. 40:28–29, 32–33, 35).

♦ **40:25–27** Various details were repeated from the descriptions of the other gateways to establish that they were identical in shape. *Seven steps to go up to it* was literally, 'steps, seven, its goings up',[17] but the sense is fairly evident (cf. 40:22).

Though various buildings occupied space in the outer courtyard, its basic shape was square. Starting from the north gateway, 50 cubits for the outer gateway which projected into the outer courtyard, 100 cubits from the outer gateway to the inner gateway, and 50 cubits for the north gateway to the inner courtyard totalled 200 cubits. This was replicated on the south, and, combined with the 100 cubit width of the inner courtyard, yielded an overall figure of 500 cubits.

On the east-west axis the calculation was somewhat different. From the east outer gateway across the outer courtyard to the perimeter of the inner courtyard was, similar to the above, 200 cubits. To this had to be added three lengths of 100 cubits for each of the inner courtyard, the temple building, and the west building together with the restricted space. This again yielded a total of 500 cubits.

(e) The Inner Gateways (40:28–37)

There are three gateways which permit access from the outer courtyard to the higher inner courtyard. Each of these inner gateways is situated directly opposite its counterpart in the outer wall. There are, however, significant differences. The gateways in the outer wall lie on the inside of the wall itself, stretching into the outer courtyard; the inner gateways do not intrude into the inner courtyard, but instead extend

---

17. The qere ʿōlôtāyw is plural with a regular suffix form, while the kethib was probably to be read as ʿōlôtāw, with defective spelling. The underlying noun may mean 'staircase' (BDB) and so here 'stairs', or the feminine plural participle could mean 'its going up ones', 'its ascenders', though that meaning it not found elsewhere. Zimmerli (1983:430) suggests the final *he* of *šibʿâ*, 'seven' (a feminine form instead of the expected masculine as the lead term *maʿălâ*, 'step', is feminine) is a scribal error for a *mem* which should have been written as the first letter of the following word, *maʿălôtāyw*, 'its stairs, ways of ascent' (cf. 40:31, 34, 37).

into the outer courtyard (Fig. 2). It is disputed whether the inner gateways were attached to any wall, since none is mentioned round the inner courtyard. However, a retaining wall of some sort (perhaps an earthen embankment) no doubt functioned to support the higher, inner courtyard, though much of it may not have been visible because of structures built against it (e.g., those in 41:10; 42:1). Because the wall round the inner courtyard does not exceed the level of that courtyard, those in the outer courtyard are able to observe the rituals of the altar.

The guardrooms in the inner gateways are not totally redundant. Although all Israelites have right of access to the outer courtyard, only the priests are permitted to access the inner courtyard. However, as regards the visionary scenario, it is concerned with a renewed and obedient people so that the guards' scrutiny would be an act of abundance of caution. No true worshipper would set out to breach the protocols of temple worship. The gateways were therefore also employed for other purposes (40:39–43).

40:28And he brought me into the inner courtyard by the south gateway, and he measured the south gateway according to these measurements. 40:29And its recesses and its posts and its vestibule ⌊were⌋ according to these measurements, and it and its vestibule had windows right round about; ⌊it was⌋ fifty cubits in length and twenty-five cubits in breadth. 40:30And ⌊there were⌋ vestibules right round about, twenty-five cubits long and five cubits broad. 40:31And its vestibule ⌊was⌋ towards the outer courtyard, and ⌊there were⌋ palm trees on its posts; and its stairway ⌊had⌋ eight steps.

40:32And he brought me into the inner courtyard towards the east, and he measured the gateway according to these measurements. 40:33and its recesses, and its posts, and its vestibule ⌊were⌋ according to these measurements, and it and its vestibule had windows right round about; its length ⌊was⌋ fifty cubits and its breadth twenty-five cubits. 40:34And its vestibule ⌊was⌋ towards the outer courtyard and palm trees ⌊were⌋ on its posts, on one side and on the other, and its stairway ⌊had⌋ eight steps.

40:35And he brought me to the north gateway and he measured ⌊it⌋ according to these measurements, 40:36its recesses, its pillars and its vestibule; it had windows right round about. Its length ⌊was⌋ fifty cubits and its breadth twenty-five cubits. 40:37And its posts ⌊were⌋ towards the outer courtyard, and palm trees ⌊were⌋ on its posts on one side and on the other, and its stairway ⌊had⌋ eight steps.

♦ **40:28** *The South Inner Gateway (40:28–31).* The guidance formula, *and he brought me*, related how Ezekiel's guide granted him access in his vision *into the inner courtyard*[18] *by the south gateway* (Fig. 2 I), a more sacred space than the outer courtyard. As a priest, Ezekiel was qualified to cross this boundary and enter the inner courtyard. The south inner gateway was the most convenient point of entry since the guide has last measured the south gateway in the outer wall (Fig. 3).

He measured the south gateway according to these measurements was a somewhat opaque statement, but it seems intended to establish that the inner gateway was identical in size to the outer gateways.

♦ **40:29** *Its recesses and its posts and its vestibule ⌞were⌟ according to these measurements* reiterated the point that its shape and dimensions were equivalent to those attached to the outer wall. It is interesting to note that *it and its vestibule* distinguished between the gateway and the vestibule even though they were both part of the same structure. The fact that both *had windows right round about* implied that the vestibule was not styled as an open portico, but as a building requiring light. *Fifty cubits in length and twenty-five cubits in breadth* corresponded to the earlier dimensions (40:13, 15, 21, 25).

♦ **40:30** This verse is suspect. Note the brackets in the NIV and HCSB. It is missing in the Septuagint and some Hebrew manuscripts. It has no counterpart in the following descriptions of the other two inner gateways. It is difficult to make sense of *vestibules* in respect of one gateway, and the measurements disagree with other information in 40:8–9, 14.

♦ **40:31** This verse noted two differences from the gateways in the outer wall. *Its vestibule ⌞was⌟ towards the outer courtyard* (cf. 40:34, 37). Whereas the gateways in the outer wall projected inwards and had their vestibules at their inner end, the inner gateways projected away from the inner courtyard and lay in the outer courtyard. In this way their vestibules functioned as proper entry chambers, being encountered first by one moving into the inner courtyard. *Palm trees on its posts* were a decorative feature corresponding to the outer gateways (40:16).

A second difference from the outer gateways was that *its stairways ⌞had⌟ eight steps* in contrast to their seven (40:22, 26). On the basis

---

18. Literally, 'a courtyard, the inner ⌞one⌟'. For such an unusual combination, see GKC §126w (cf. 9:2).

previously indicated (40:5), the rise from the outer to the inner courtyard would be just over 8 feet (2.4 m). This increased elevation reflected vertically the gradation of holiness portrayed in other ways in various aspects of the Tabernacle and of Solomon's Temple. The nearer one approached the Holy of Holies, the greater the sanctity.

♦ **40:32–34** *The East Inner Gateway*. **He brought me into the inner courtyard towards the east.** It is unclear how the guidance formula, 'he brought me,' functioned here inasmuch as Ezekiel was already in the inner courtyard (40:28). It may mean that he had been led out by the southern gate and was brought back in, but since in the light of 40:35 that awkward process would require to be repeated, the expression was most probably a resumptive comment. **The gateway** was not specified as the eastern gateway (Fig. 2 J) as the direction had been included earlier.[19]

♦ **40:35–37** *The North Inner Gateway*. A similar description was given of the remaining north inner gateway (Fig. 2 K). The first word in 40:37, **and its gateposts** (*wəʾēlāw*), is rendered 'and its vestibule' (*wəʾēlammô*) by most of the ancient versions, a reading which may well be correct in that it reflects 40:34, and the two words were easily confused. If the emendation is rejected, then the text gave the additional information that there were gateposts at the inner gateways, which would be expected by analogy with the outer gateways.

(3) Rooms and Equipment for Preparing the Sacrifices (40:38–43)

Another stage of the tour now begins but is unmarked by a guidance formula, because the guide and Ezekiel stop at this point (Fig. 3 ⑥) before the guide moves on at 40:47, and Ezekiel's tour resumes in 40:48. For the moment the focus of the vision leaves off consideration of the layout of the temple complex, and takes up particular features of the furnishings in the inner courtyard, and how they are to be used.

Ezekiel notes the existence of a room beside the northern inner gateway and what it was to be used for (40:38). Then a description is given of the tables used to prepare sacrifices (40:39–43). While there is no mention of Ezekiel's guide at this point, he no doubt is the source of the information recorded.

The question arises if the arrangements detailed in this paragraph

---

19. The LXX has 'he brought me into the gate facing east, and he measured it.' This is accepted by many, but Zimmerli (1983:341) prefers to retain the MT as the more difficult reading.

concerning the north gateway are replicated at either or both of the other gateways. Though nothing is explicitly said, the symmetry of the temple layout probably requires that similar facilities existed at the south gateway, but the situation at the east gateway is less certain.

> ⁴⁰:³⁸And ⌊there was⌋ a room and its door at the posts of the gateway; there they are to wash the burnt offering. ⁴⁰:³⁹And in the vestibule of the gateway ⌊there were⌋ two tables on this side and two tables on that side, to slaughter on them the burnt offering and the sin offering and the guilt offering. ⁴⁰:⁴⁰And on the outside wall as one goes up to the door of the north gateway, ⌊there were⌋ two tables, and on the other wall of the vestibule of the gateway ⌊there were⌋ two tables. ⁴⁰:⁴¹Four tables ⌊were⌋ on this side and four tables on that side at the side of the gateway, eight tables on ⌊which⌋ they are to slaughter ⌊offerings⌋. ⁴⁰:⁴²And ⌊there were⌋ four tables of dressed stone for the burnt offering, in length one cubit and a half and in breadth one cubit and a half, and in height one cubit. On them they are to lay the implements with which they are to slaughter the burnt offering and the sacrifice. ⁴⁰:⁴³And ⌊there were⌋ double hooks, an handbreadth ⌊long⌋, set in the house right round about, and on the tables ⌊is to be⌋ the flesh of the offering.

♦ **40:38** There is disagreement as to where this *room* (*liškâ*) was located. *At* ⌊*the*⌋ *posts of the gateway* is literally 'at/in ⌊the⌋ gateposts, the gateways'. Since 40:9 gave the dimensions of the gateposts as two cubits wide, they could not contain a room within them. Some commentators suggest that the phrase should be 'in the vestibule of the gateway' (as in 40:39).[20] However, a room could not really be accommodated in the vestibule because there was no spare space since it had also to contain the tables of 40:40. Keil argued that the chamber was located outside the gateway near one of the gateposts, and that plurals were used to indicate that similar rooms were also found near the other two inner gates (2002:361).This may be supported by the implication of 46:1–2 that the leader's offering was taken in by the east gate. Arguing from the symmetry of the temple that a northern room should be matched by a southern room has some weight, but the location of a single room at the east gateway is inherently asymmetrical. Possibly, the ruler's sacrifice was not processed there.

---

20. The proposed change is from *bəʾêlîm haššəʿārîm*, 'at/in the posts of the gateways', to *bəʾulām haššaʿar*, 'at/in the vestibule of the gateway'.

Tentatively, one might suggest that since the gatepost would stretch from the higher level of the inner courtyard down to that of the outer courtyard, it was in the latter courtyard that there was *a room and its door*, abutting the base of the gateway (Fig. 2 L). Probably the room was where equipment was stored to facilitate the directive that *there they are to wash the burnt offering.* 'They are to wash' renders an imperfect of obligation (Introduction §6.3a), setting out the routine required to prepare a sacrifice. As Ezekiel was conducted round the ideal temple, it was not yet functioning, and the language was prescriptive of what ought to prevail when it became operational. Washing sacrificial animals was prescribed in Leviticus 1:9, 13, and Solomon's Temple had twelve basins for that purpose (2 Chron. 4:6). Although in this verse and in Leviticus it was only mentioned in connection with the burnt offering, it probably took place for the other sacrifices also. Indeed, 'burnt offering' might have been used here by synecdoche for all types of animal sacrifice (40:42).

However, the earlier texts regarding washing relate to the entrails and the lower legs of the victim after it had been slaughtered. Something different was possibly implied here. It may be that this description extended the need for washing to the whole animal, and before it was slaughtered, probably as a matter of physical as well as ceremonial uncleanness. It would seem that the procedure envisaged was that the offerer would bring the animal for the sacrifice to foot of the steps of the northern inner gate, where he would hand it over to the priests. The duty of washing the animal was probably assigned to the Levites (Milgrom 2012:77), who would also ensure the fitness of the animal for sacrifice and, after washing it, would convey the live animal up the steps into the vestibule.

♦ **40:39** Ezekiel seems to have described what he saw while positioned at the top of the staircase. *In the vestibule of the gateway ⌜there were⌝ two tables on this side and two tables on that side.* As the account progresses, it becomes increasingly difficult to determine how many tables were involved and where they were situated, but at this point the reference is clearly to a pair of tables on either side of the central passageway at the head of the stairways before one came to the recesses.

To slaughter on them the burnt offering and the sin offering and the guilt offering. If only the north gateway was used to accomplish this, it might be in conformity with the explicit instruction that sheep or goats were slaughtered on the north side of the altar (Lev. 1:11).

However, an identical arrangement at the south inner gateway is probable with, perhaps, a modified provision for the sacrifices presented by the ruler at the east inner gateway.

Three different types of offering are mentioned. The burnt offering (Lev. 1) was totally burned up on the altar, and no portion was consumed either by the offerer or by the priest. Its significance was both propitiatory (to avert divine wrath) and expiatory (to atone for sin). The sin offering (Lev. 4:1–5:13) was designed to remove the contamination arising from sin and particularly to cleanse the holy place and the equipment used in sacrifices. The guilt offering (Lev. 5:14–6:7) formed a sort of reparation paid as restitution for harm done.

Noticeably absent here was any mention of the peace offering (Lev. 3). It was the one sacrifice where certain parts of the animal were eaten by the worshipper in a meal shared with the officiating priest (Lev. 7:15–16). In that way it crossed a sacred demarcation line, and for that reason it might have been omitted at this juncture (but see on 46:21–24).

♦ **40:40** *On the outside wall* (lit., 'to the shoulder/side outwards') probably referred to the right side of the wall *as one goes up*[21] *to the door of the north gateway* by the eight steps. *On the other wall of the vestibule* would then have referred to the left side. Explicit mention of the north gateway showed that the activities of 40:38–43 took place there, while leaving it an open question if they also occurred at the east and south gateways (but see Lev. 1:10–11). The four tables in this verse were on this understanding located in the outer courtyard at the side of the stairway. No indication was given of whether they touched the stairway or were just close to it, or whether they were parallel or perpendicular to the stairway. Equally, it was not clarified how they were positioned relative to the room of 40:38.

♦ **40:41** This verse summarises 40:39–40 rather than introducing additional tables. *Four tables ⌊were⌋ on this side and four tables on that side of the gateway* with two of each set in the vestibule and two on the lower level next to the stairway. There was therefore a total of *eight tables*. It would seem best to take *on ⌊which⌋ they are to slaughter ⌊offerings⌋* as a general prescription covering the whole process of preparing the sacrificial victims. Block (1998:533)

---

21. Zimmerli (1983:363) considers *lāʿôleh*, 'to one going up', a scribal error for *ləʾulām*, 'for the porch', to parallel the occurrence of the phrase in the second half of the verse (cf. RSV, NRSV), but that seems needlessly speculative.

visualises the outside tables being used to slaughter the animals, and the inside ones for washing, which would fit in with the washing of the legs and entrails in Leviticus 1:9, 13 after the sacrifice had been slaughtered. It may, however, have been the case that the opposite arrangement prevailed here: first and outside the washing, and then secondly and inside the vestibule, the slaughter, though there was probably need for further washing of the entrails.

♦ **40:42** ⌊*There were*⌋ *four tables of dressed stone for the burnt offering.* These do not appear to be different tables from those already mentioned, but it is unclear whether they were those in the vestibule or those below in the courtyard. This is the first mention of the material used in the temple and its precincts. Dressed stone was prepared using hand saws so that it could be made to a precise size. On the basis that mention of the four being of stone implied that the other four were constructed of wood, and that the stone tables were more suited for sacrificing than for washing, their location would be determined by whether or not the animals were already dead before being conveyed up the steps.

'For the burnt offering' was probably a comprehensive usage (40:38), as in the expression 'the altar of burnt offering'.

In length one cubit and a half and in breadth one cubit and a half, so that their top was square. However, in one of the rare references to the height of sacred objects (cf. 41:22; 43:15), it was stipulated *in height one cubit*. This made their surface accessible for preparing the sacrifices, which was probably the reason why their height was specially mentioned.

On them they are to lay[22] *the implements* (lit., 'to/on them and they are to lay' with the prepositional phrase brought forward for emphasis). Most probably they were to leave their tools on the top of the tables to avoid them becoming defiled through contact with the ground. In *with which they would slaughter the burnt offering and the sacrifice*, 'sacrifice' (*zebaḥ*) was used generically, and was equivalent to 'the other sacrifices'.

♦ **40:43** *Double hooks* (a dual form) follows the understanding of the Targum by which the reference was to double-pronged hooks, *an handbreadth* ⌊*long*⌋ (just under 3 inches, about 7.4 cm). These were

---

22. ʾălêhem, with ʾel having the sense of ʿal, 'on them', is brought forward for emphasis. The *waw*-conjunctive plus imperfect, *wəyannînû*, suggests the imperfect is used in an obligatory sense (cf. 40:38).

set in the house right round about, where 'the house' did not refer to the temple area as a whole, but presumably only to the vestibule. In all probability the carcasses would be hung there for skinning and other preparatory work, or while waiting to be offered. An alternative suggestion is that the term should be translated shelves on which pots might be placed, so that there was storage space for the other sacrificial utensils (Milgrom 2012:76).²³

If the hooks were only used for preparatory work, the final clause might be rendered 'while on the tables ⌊is to be⌋ the flesh of the offering', which was ready to be removed to the altar. ***Offering*** (*qorbān*) was the most comprehensive term for sacrifice, described as that which was brought near to God for presentation and offering to him.

(4) Rooms for the Priests (40:44–47)

A new section moves on from the arrangements for sacrifice to rooms reserved for the use of the priests, who are here mentioned for the first time, but who do not actually appear in the vision. A concluding summary of the dimensions of the inner courtyard is provided in 40:47.

> ⁴⁰:⁴⁴And from outside to the inner gateway ⌊were⌋ rooms for singers in the inner courtyard, one at the side of the north gateway facing towards the south, one at the side of the south gateway facing towards the north. ⁴⁰:⁴⁵And he spoke to me, 'This ⌊is⌋ the room which faces towards the south ⌊and is⌋ is for the priests who keep charge of the house, ⁴⁰:⁴⁶and the room which faces towards north is for the priests who keep charge of the altar: they are the sons of Zadok, who from the sons of Levi draw near to the LORD to minister to him.' ⁴⁰:⁴⁷And he measured the courtyard, a hundred cubits in length and a hundred cubits in breadth, foursquare, and the altar ⌊was⌋ in front of the house.

♦ **40:44** The RSV, GNB, and REB, following the Septuagint, have another guidance formula at the beginning of the verse, 'Then he brought me', though this reading is generally rejected. ***And from outside to the inner gateway*** apparently followed the direction of the prophet's observation (at Fig. 3 ⑦) from within the inner north gateway into ***the inner courtyard*** where he observed ***rooms for***

---

23. This would also involve repointing the dual form *wəhašpattayim* to a plural form *haššəpātîm*.

singers, where 'rooms' was the same term as in 40:38, but 'singers' appears to be intrusive. Undoubtedly, choirs had been a feature of temple worship since the days of Solomon (as evidenced by Chronicles), and the more prominent position accorded them in the Second Temple suggested that their role became more prestigious over time. However, it is improbable that the status of singers was such that rooms in this higher courtyard would have been provided for them. Moreover, 'singers' does not fit in with the explanation given by the guide in the following verses. English translations are fairly evenly divided as to whether to retain 'rooms for singers' (AV, NASB, NKJV, NRSV) or to follow the Septuagintal reading 'two rooms' (ESV, NIV, REB, RSV),[24] but the latter is the more probable reading.

As for the rooms themselves (Fig. 2 M), their general location was stated: **one at the side of the north gateway facing towards the south, one at the side of the south**[25] **gateway facing towards the north.** However, no more precise position was given, and no indication of their dimensions.

♦ **40:45** The heavenly guide had last been mentioned in 40:35, and here he spoke to Ezekiel for only the second time (cf. 40:4). That Ezekiel recorded his guide as speaking only a few times accorded greater significance to the explanations he did provide. **The room which faces towards the south** was allocated to **the priests who keep charge of the house** (lit., 'watching ones of watching the house'). Their duties were concerned with 'the house', that is, the inner, temple building itself, rather than the whole temple complex, and would include acting as guardians of the holy space to ensure that its boundaries were not violated or rituals interrupted, as well as maintenance of the fabric of the structure and its associated equipment.

♦ **40:46** The guide then set out the function of **the room which faces towards the north.** It was for **the priests who keep charge of the altar.** The verb 'keep charge' (*šāmar*, 'guard', 'watch over') was the same as

---

24. The change assumes that a *taw* (*štayim*, 'two') has been misread as a *resh* (*šārîm*, 'singers'). The former is read by the LXX, but the Vulgate follows the MT, and the Peshitta supports the consonants of the MT. However, this participle is not used for distinguishing the temple singers. Furthermore, they were classed as Levites and not as priests.

25. The MT reads 'east' (*haqqādîm*; as in AV and NRSV, but not NKJV), but this is at variance with the basic symmetry of the temple layout and there is general agreement that 'south' (*haddārôm*) should be read as was done by the LXX.

for the other group of priests, but the duties assigned to this group were more narrowly defined as those connected with carrying out the rituals associated with the sanctuary. This division of sacred duties reflects that found in Numbers 18:4–5 where the same root occurred: 'They [non-Aaronic Levites] will join with you [Aaron] and keep charge of the tent of meeting for all the service of the tent, and a stranger must not come near you [plural]. And you [plural: Aaronic priests] will keep charge of the holy place and of the altar, that there may never again be indignation on the sons of Israel.' So there was a precedent for the division of priestly duties.

However, the question which arises here is if it was precisely the same arrangement which was envisaged for the ideal temple. Were there two sets of priests with differing responsibilities, or two sets of duties assigned to the one set of priests, being carried out by the same personnel on different occasions? The latter option is to be preferred. The following comment, ***they are the sons of Zadok, who from the sons of Levi draw near to the LORD to minister to him***, is not be confined to the second group of priests so as to distinguish Zadokite priests from the former group of non-Zadokite priests who were assigned only general Levitical (non-sacrificial) duties. In Ezekiel there was a clear demarcation between Zadokite priests and Levites (see on 44:9–31), but that was not what was in view here. Both these rooms were in the inner courtyard, access to which was confined to the Zadokite (sacrificing) priests,[26] who were the only descendants of Aaron permitted to approach the altar. The Levites had duties which included slaying the sacrifices, but not that of offering them, and so their sphere of service went no further than the inner gateways. It was from there that the Zadokite priests took the portions of the slain animals to offer them on the altar.

♦ **40:47** The guide ***measured the courtyard***, that is, the inner courtyard in a similar fashion to his activity in the outer courtyard (40:17–19), to determine that it was ***a hundred cubits in length and a hundred cubits in breadth, foursquare***. Both the dimensions as multiples of five and twenty-five and the square shape were typical of the ordered and balanced layout of the temple precincts. Milgrom argues that there was neither an inner wall nor a pavement surrounding the inner courtyard as they would have served no purpose (2012:43, 82–83).

---

26. The identification of the priests as Zadokite occurs in 40:46; 43:19; 44:15 and 48:11, but it is fanciful to separate out these passages as belonging to some Zadokite source.

There would, however, have been an embankment or a retaining wall of some sort to elevate the inner courtyard (40:31, 34, 37).

The altar ⌊was⌋ in front of the house did not specify precisely where it was sited, but the general assumption is that it was at the centre of the inner courtyard and so at the centre of the whole temple complex (Fig. 2 N). Further details regarding the altar were given in 43:13–17. Its location meant that the altar was accessible only to the Zadokite priests.

(5) The Ideal Temple (40:48–41:26)

This part of the vision contains many details which are obviously patterned after those found in the Tabernacle and in Solomon's Temple. However, the accounts of those structures (Exod. 26:1–31:11; 36:8–39:43; 1 Kgs. 6:1–38; 7:13–51) are theologically sparse. A tripartite arrangement prevails: the vestibule (or porch, or portico), the Holy Place (or the great hall, or the nave), and the Holy of Holies (or inmost room). The decorative features (e.g., cherubim, palm trees) suggest paradise restored, and indicate that the temple will function as the focal point of communication between God and his people as Eden had once done. The return of the Glory to the inmost room (43:5) is an event of the greatest significance in Ezekiel's account of the LORD's dealings with his people.

Certain features of the earlier sanctuaries are not found in this ideal temple. With some, such as the ark of the covenant, it is evident that they have been superseded in these arrangements, but with others it is impossible to tell whether they were in fact absent from the ideal temple or were simply assumed to be there. Yet again some structures may be specifically provided to preclude abuses which had arisen in the Jerusalem Temple (see on 41:12).

(a) The Temple Structure (40:48–41:4)

Solomon's Temple (1 Kgs. 6–7) had a similar layout to that described here with two external free-standing columns and three interior chambers with similar measurements. Significant differences are that the temple in this vision is elevated above the inner courtyard, and that the entrances to each of its chambers get progressively narrower.

40:48 And he brought me to the vestibule of the house and he measured the posts of the vestibule, five cubits on this side and five cubits on the other side; and the breadth of the gateway ⌊was⌋ three cubits on this side and three cubits on

the other side. ⁴⁰:⁴⁹The length of the vestibule ⌊was⌋ twenty cubits, and the breadth eleven cubits, and by the steps which ⌊they⌋ would go up to it, and ⌊there were⌋ pillars by the posts, one on this side and one on the other.
⁴¹:¹And he brought me into the temple, and he measured the posts, six cubits in breadth on this side, and six cubits in breadth on that side—the breadth of the tabernacle. ⁴¹:²And the breadth of the entrance ⌊was⌋ ten cubits and the sides of the entrance ⌊were⌋ five cubits on this side and five cubits on that side; and he measured its length, forty cubits, and ⌊its⌋ breadth, twenty cubits. ⁴¹:³And he went inside and measured a post of the entrance, two cubits, and the entrance, six cubits, and the breadth of the entrance, seven cubits. ⁴¹:⁴And he measured its length, twenty cubits, and ⌊its⌋ breadth, twenty cubits, before the temple, and he said to me, 'This ⌊is⌋ the Holy of Holies.'

♦ **40:48** These verses (40:48–49) could have been selected as the start of a new chapter in that the guide moved to the central temple structure itself, but those who introduced this break obviously thought of the vestibule as a transitional zone, possibly because there was no vestibule in the Tabernacle in the wilderness. Ezekiel did not mention what function was allocated to the vestibule.

The guidance formula, *he brought me* (cf. 40:2), marked a progression to a more sacred level, which involved the prophet being ushered up a flight of steps. *The vestibule of the house* (Fig. 5 ③) was a structure which was located on the highest platform, facing towards the altar. Through it progress could be made into the inner sanctuary.

He measured the posts[27] *of the vestibule, five cubits on this side and five cubits on the other side.* These doorposts were at the entrance to vestibule (cf. 41:1). In *the breadth of the doorway* the term 'doorway' (*šaʿar*) was the same as that rendered 'gateway' earlier (see on 40:3), but that is no longer appropriate because there was no gateway structure adjoining the temple building.

The Massoretic text gives the breadth of the doorway as *three cubits on this side and three cubits on the other side*, but these dimensions do not cohere with the overall structure of the temple. It is therefore necessary to assume that a phrase or line had been omitted from the Hebrew manuscript and to adopt the longer Septuagintal text which reads: 'And the width of the doorway was fourteen cubits, and

---

27. *ʾēl* is to be taken as a defective spelling of *ʾêl*, the construct of *ʾayil*, 'door-post'.

the shoulders/sides of the doorway of the vestibule were three cubits on one side and three cubits on one side.' On that basis the width of the first doorway was 14 cubits. Moving inwards, the next two entrances were progressively narrower at 10 cubits and 6 cubits.

♦ **40:49** *The length of the vestibule ⌊was⌋ twenty cubits, and the breadth eleven cubits.* Again, 'length' and 'breadth' were used simply in the sense of 'longer side' and 'shorter side' (see on 40:11). The two inner sections of the temple were 20 cubits wide from north to south (41:2, 4), and the vestibule had the same width. Furthermore, the 'eleven cubits' of the Massoretic text yields an irresolvable conundrum, whereas the 'twelve cubit' figure found in the Septuagint permits the total length of the structure to be 100 cubits.[28] The breadth of the vestibule was different from the ten cubits of Solomon's Temple (1 Kgs. 6:3).

By the steps which ⌊they⌋ would go up to it. The AV added 'he brought me up' to try to make sense of this expression. The Septuagint read 'ten' (*'eśer*) instead of 'which' (*'ăšer*). In that case there would be ten steps into the temple (cf. 40:22, 26, 31, 34, 37; REB, NRSV, ESV). This would not be an arbitrary figure, and is probably to be adopted: 'by ten steps ⌊they⌋ would go up to it' (Fig. 5 ①). The increase from seven and eight steps between the lower levels would mean that the temple proper was at an elevation of twenty-five steps from the surrounding ground level, and twenty-five was a numeral which occurred frequently in the descriptions of the vision. For the probable rise involved in this ascent, see on 41:8.

There were pillars by the posts, one on this side and one on the other. No indication was given of the nature, function, or precise position of these pillars (Fig. 5 ②). Presumably they corresponded to the free-standing pillars, Jachin and Boaz, in Solomon's Temple (1 Kgs. 7:15–22; 2 Chron. 3:15–17). Block places them in the entranceway to the vestibule, possibly performing some structural function such as supporting the lintel above the entranceway, as archaeological evidence for some contemporary temple structures suggests (1998:542), but they could equally well have been outside the vestibule, flanking it on either side.

---

28. In the light of 41:13, 'eleven' (*'aštê 'eśrēh*) as read by the MT is impossible. The LXX read 'twelve' (*šətēm 'eśrēh*); so NIV, REB, NRSV, ESV. This is one of two places (the other is found in 43:7) where Stevenson (1996) felt compelled to depart from the MT which was otherwise the basis for her study.

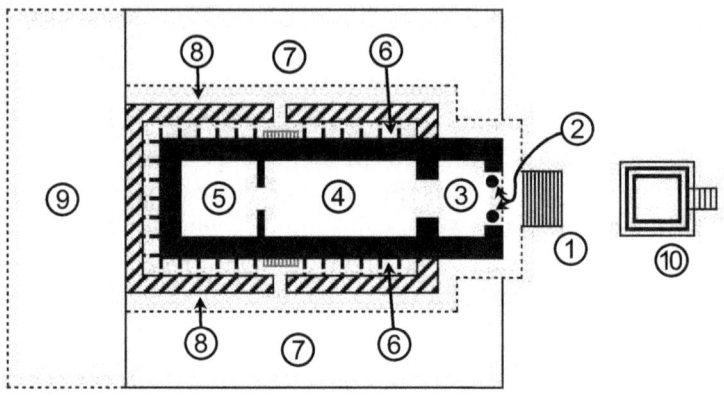

①	Steps	40:49
②	Pillars	40:49
③	Vestibule	40:48
④	The Holy Place	41:1
⑤	The Holy of Holies	41:3
⑥	Side-rooms	41:5
⑦	Vacant Area	41:9
⑧	Pavement	41:11
⑨	Restricted Space	41:12
⑩	The Altar	40:47; 43:13–17

Figure 5. The Temple Building.

♦ **41:1** The guidance formula, *and he brought me* (cf. 40:2), indicated that his guide brought Ezekiel from the vestibule into the more sacred area of the middle chamber of the structure, which was here designated *the temple* (*hêkāl*), a royal term which had occurred earlier (8:16). It was, of course, into the outer chamber of the building that he was taken (Fig. 5 ④).

Again Ezekiel witnessed the guide continuing with his survey. *He measured the posts*, that is, the doorposts at the entrance into the Holy Place, and ascertained that they were *six cubits in breadth on this side, and six cubits in breadth on that side*, and so they were one cubit greater on each side than those leading into the vestibule (40:48) to accommodate the corresponding narrowing of the entrance itself.

The breadth of the tabernacle was apparently a reference to the Tabernacle (tent) of Moses (cf. Num. 11:24, 26; Deut. 31:15). The words are supported by the Peshitta, Vulgate and Targum, and should not be dismissed as an early gloss. There are, however, two possible interpretations. One is that the Tabernacle was six cubits wide. However, it is more generally argued that the Tabernacle was ten cubits wide. More probably, the words should be read with 41:2 as establishing an identity between the Tabernacle and this temple: 'The breadth of the Tabernacle, even the breadth of the entrance, ⌊was⌋ ten cubits'. This comment may have been introduced at this juncture because there was no vestibule in the Tabernacle, and it was only from here on in that the structures corresponded.

♦ **41:2** *The breadth of the entrance ⌊was⌋ ten cubits*, which was larger than that of the entrance to the Holy of Holies (41:3), in accordance with the greater exclusivity the further one advanced into the structure. The walls jutting out from the main side wall were *five cubits* square. The great hall itself was rectangular, with *its length*, that is, its larger dimension being *forty cubits*, and *its breadth, that is, its narrower dimension, twenty cubits*, roughly 68 feet (20.6 m) long from east to west and 34 feet (10.3 m) wide from north to south.

♦ **41:3** *And he went inside* (*bô'*, qal; cf. 40:17[29]). The verb indicated crossing a boundary into a different zone in the temple area, here into

---

29. The expression is often thought to be corrupt as the verb *ûbā'*, 'and he went inside', is *waw*-conjunctive with a perfect rather that a *waw*-consecutive. However, similar use of the perfect has already occurred in 40:20, 24, 35 with the verb *mādad*, 'to measure'. The variant seems to be acceptable to Ezekiel (cf. 37:2).

the Holy of Holies (Fig. 5 ⑤). Significantly, Ezekiel did not say, 'he brought me' (*bô'* hiphil). As a priest, Ezekiel could enter the outer sanctuary, the Holy Place, but even in a visionary experience and that before the return of the Glory of the LORD and the specific dedication of the temple through the divine presence, Ezekiel was debarred from the inner sanctuary. In the Tabernacle the Holy of Holies could only be entered by the high priest once a year on the Day of Atonement (Lev. 16:2–3), but Ezekiel mentions neither high priest nor the Day of Atonement so it may have been that in the ideal regime no human being was to venture here. 'Inside'/'to the insidewards' was a very sparse and unelaborated description. From outside Ezekiel was able to see his guide and to hear him as he called out the measurements.

The guide *measured a post of the entrance, two cubits*, that is, across the thickness of the separating wall. *The entrance, six cubits*, seems unusually to refer to the height of the opening (cf. NASB, NKJV), because otherwise there would be a contradiction with the following, *the breadth of the entrance, seven cubits*.[30]

♦ **41:4** *He measured its length, twenty cubits, and ⌊its⌋ breadth, twenty cubits.* The guide did this *before the temple*, apparently along the wall closer to the Holy Place. This established that the innermost room was perfectly square. No figure was given for its height, but Solomon's Temple had an inmost sanctuary that was a cube of twenty cubits (1 Kgs. 6:20), and it is reasonable to suppose that was the case here also. This symbolised consummate holiness and perfection.

For only the third time, the guide spoke to make the terse comment, *This ⌊is⌋ the Holy of Holies* (*qōdeš haqqŏdāšîm*; lit., 'the holiness of the holinesses'). This Hebrew idiom expressed a superlative, 'Most Holy Place' (cf. 42:13; 43:12; 44:13; 45:3; 48:12). Since the term was used for the corresponding chamber in the Tabernacle (Exod. 26:33–34) and the Temple (1 Kgs. 6:16; 7:50; 8:6; 2 Chron. 3:8, 10), Ezekiel with his priestly training would not have needed such an explanation, but it may have been uttered to indicate the high point of the tour. There was no more sacred depth to be revealed. Ezekiel did not use the term 'inner sanctuary' (*dəbîr*, 1 Kgs. 6:19–23; 8:6, 8) to refer to the Holy of Holies. This chamber was not mentioned again until 45:3.

---

30. If 'the entrance, six cubits' is taken to refer to the width of the entrance rather than its height on the grounds that Ezekiel makes very few references to height, then the text of the LXX has to be followed in the rest of the verse. This gives a longer description analogous to that found in 41:2: 'and the sides of the entrance were seven cubits on one side and seven cubits on the other side.'

THE VISION OF THE TEMPLE

(b) The Side-Rooms (41:5–12)

This paragraph consists mainly of a catalogue of architectural features, many terms of which are obscure and require to be deciphered. In this process corresponding features in 1 Kings 6:5–8 often provide assistance.

⁴¹:⁵And he measured the wall of the house, six cubits, and the width of the side-room, four cubits, right round about the house, round about ⌊it⌋. ⁴¹:⁶And the side-rooms ⌊were⌋ side-room to side-room, three ⌊high⌋, and ⌊there were⌋ thirty on each ⌊storey⌋; and there were ledges in the wall which the house had for the side-rooms right round about that there might be supports, but the supports were not in the wall of the house. ⁴¹:⁷And it widened out and changed direction with increasing height for the side-rooms because the surrounding of the house upwards and upwards ⌊was⌋ right round about with respect to the house; consequently the width of the house was upwards and so from the lowest storey one went up to the highest storey through the one in the middle. ⁴¹:⁸And I saw that the house had height right round about, from the foundation of the side-rooms ⌊was⌋ a full rod, six cubits by the joining. ⁴¹:⁹The breadth of the outer wall of the side-room ⌊was⌋ five cubits. And the vacant area between the side-chambers of the house ⁴¹:¹⁰and the rooms ⌊had⌋ a breadth of twenty cubits round about the house, right round about ⌊it⌋. ⁴¹:¹¹And the entrance of the side-room ⌊was⌋ to the vacant area, one entrance towards the north and another entrance to the south, and the breadth of the site of the vacant area ⌊was⌋ five cubits right round about. ⁴¹:¹²And the building which ⌊was⌋ in front of the restricted space towards the western side ⌊had⌋ a width of seventy cubits; and the wall of the building ⌊was⌋ five cubits in width right round about, and its length ⌊was⌋ ninety cubits.

♦ **41:5** The topic changed without any overt signal, though the use of **and he measured** here and in 41:13 did occur at paragraph boundaries.

The guide next left the interior of the temple, taking Ezekiel with him. They moved to a point where the guide could ascertain the thickness of **the wall** (*qîr*) **of the house**, that is, the side walls of the temple, which had not been included in the specification of the entrances. At **six cubits** these walls were just as thick as the exterior wall around the entire temple compound, though Ezekiel used a different term for that wall (*ḥômâ*; 40:5).

Ezekiel's description then disclosed that the ideal temple conformed to a contemporary pattern of temple building in which there was a second wall surrounding the inner structure (Milgrom 2012:87). This became evident when the guide measured *the width of the side-room, four cubits, right round about the house, round about ⌞it⌟.* The rendering 'side-room' reflects the basic sense of the word 'rib' (*ṣēlāʿ*), sometimes found as a singular (e.g., here and in 41:6, 9, 11), but frequently as a plural form too. It had also been used in connection with Solomon's Temple (1 Kgs. 6:5, 8). These rooms were built outside the temple, but right next to it, with each one having a width of four cubits, though from the nature of their construction it became evident that this applied only to those lying at ground level. They surrounded the temple on all sides except the front (the east). There was no space for a corridor, certainly not on the ground floor level, and so access seems to have been effected from one room directly into the next (Fig. 5 ⑥).

♦ **41:6** *And the side-rooms ⌞were⌟ side-room to*[31] *side-room, three ⌞high⌟, and ⌞there were⌟ thirty on each ⌞storey⌟.* The rooms were situated one above the other in three storeys, with thirty rooms on each level, a total of ninety rooms. Their distribution on each side was not stated: twelve may have been along the longer north and south walls, and six along the shorter western wall, although other arrangements were also possible. *Side-room to side-room* indicated that they were constructed abutting one another.

The relationship between the side-rooms and the temple structure was then described. *There were ledges in the wall which the house had for the side-rooms.* 'Ledges'/ 'things coming' (*bāʾôt*) seems to have been a technical term. The exterior wall of the temple ('the house') was stepped inwards at the level of each storey so that there was a ledge on which the extended beams of the floors/ceilings of the side-rooms might rest so that there were *supports, but the supports were not in the wall of the house.* There was no need to breach the integrity of the wall to insert the ends of the beams for the ceilings of the side-chambers; they merely rested on the ledges. A consequence of this arrangement would be that at the two higher storeys there was additional space in the side-rooms.

♦ **41:7** The specific figures for Solomon's Temple given in 1 Kings 6:6 showed that the side-rooms in the lowest storey were five cubits wide,

---

31. The preposition *ʾel*, 'to', may be used here in the sense of *ʿal*, 'on, upon'.

those in the second storey were six cubits wide, and on the top storey they were seven cubits wide. There was a corresponding reduction in the width of the Temple wall from six cubits at its base to three cubits at its top, and apparently a similar stepped arrangement was in existence in this structure also.

It widened out and changed direction/ 'it was surrounded' referred to the side-rooms.[32] ***With increasing height for the side-rooms*** (lit., 'with respect to upwards, with respect to upwards, with respect to the side-chambers') implied that as one moved upwards each storey of side-chambers became wider.

The surrounding of the house upwards and upwards ⌊was⌋ right round about with respect to the house. The inner sacred building was surrounded (except on the east) by this additional structure.

Consequently the width of the house did not here seem to refer to the width of the temple. Instead 'house', used in the sense of 'building', referred to the additional external construction which consisted of all the side-chambers. ***So from the lowest storey one went up to the highest storey*** indicated that some means of ascending to the upper floors was provided, but gave no specifications as to how that was achieved. Presumably internal stairs or ladders permitted moving to a higher floor. ***Through the one in the middle*** meant that there was no direct, external access to the second or third storey. But why did Ezekiel give these extensive details about what seems a minor detail? His emphasis that to reach the top storey of the side-building one had to pass through the middle storey ruled out the use of an access ramp surrounding the whole building (cf. 1 Kgs. 6:8) and lying outside the sacred structure. Entering the rooms from within the structure helped to prevent violations of its integrity and sanctity.

♦ **41:8** With ***And I saw***, Ezekiel continued his account of what was disclosed to him in the vision while he stood at Figure 3 ⑩. No parallel to the construction in this verse was mentioned in regard to Solomon's Temple in Kings. ***The house had height right round about*** described a platform which elevated the sacred structure to emphasise

---

32. The verb *wərāḥăbâ* 'and it was wide/became wide', is treated by many versions as a noun 'widening'. Also, the Targum reads for *wənāsbâ*, 'it was turned round', a noun equivalent to *məsibbâ*, 'a ramp, a circular passage'. This is adopted by many critics on the assumption that the initial mem of the noun was misread as a nun, and that the final he of the preceding verb should be read as an article on the reconstructed noun, with the sense 'a widening ramp spiralled up to the side-chambers'.

its centrality. ***From the foundation***[33] ***of the side-rooms ... by the joining*** includes technical terms whose meaning remains uncertain. The most plausible interpretation is that this gave the height of the platform as *a full rod, six cubits* above the level of the inner courtyard, and therefore corresponding to the rise of the ten steps (see on 40:49). In that way the base of the temple was elevated by 10.15 feet (3.1 m; cf. 40:6) above the inner courtyard.

♦ **41:9a** This verse really consisted of two separate statements, with the second being part of 41:10. The first clause continued the list of measurements in 41:5. ***The breadth of the outer wall of the side-room ⌊was⌋ five cubits.*** Thus at the level of the platform the whole structure was fifty cubits broad: working inwards on each side, five cubits for the width of the outer wall of the side rooms (41:9), four cubits for the width of the side-rooms (41:5), and six cubits for the thickness of the interior wall of the temple (41:5), totalling fifteen cubits, which when doubled had to have added to it the breadth of the sanctuary at twenty cubits (41:2, 4).

The length of the temple can be determined by working from west to east, beginning at the west end of the outer wall. That wall along with the breadth of the side-rooms and of the interior wall amounted to fifteen cubits, as above. When the twenty cubit length of the Holy of Holies (41:4), the two cubit thickness of the entrance posts (41:3), the forty cubit length of the Holy Place (41:2), the six cubit width of its entrance posts (41:1), and the five cubit width of the posts of the vestibule (40:48) are also taken into account, that gives a running total of eighty-eight cubits. The length of the vestibule, from west to east, has been omitted, and so adopting the Septuagint reading of twelve cubits (40:49), a final total of one hundred cubits is arrived at. In this way it is established that the basic shape of the structure is rectangular with sides in the ratio 2:1, and with dimensions based on multiples of twenty-five.

♦ **41:9b–10** ***And the vacant area*** (*munnāḥ*; Fig. 5 ⑦) ***between***[34] ***the side-rooms which belonged to the house*** (41:9b) began a statement

---

33. The qere *mûsədôt* is from a feminine noun which here apparently means 'foundations'. Some manuscripts only read the qere. The kethibh might have been intended to be *məyussādôt*, a feminine plural pual participle, 'provided with foundations'.

34. *bêt* is here used as a preposition meaning 'between' (cf. Job 8:17; Prov. 8:2), and it is correlative to *bîn*, 'between', at the beginning of the next verb, being a less common synonym of that word.

which was completed in the next verse. Whereas the side-rooms (*ṣēlāʿ*) were clearly those just described as adjoining the sanctuary, **the rooms** (*liškâ*) are to be identified with those more fully delineated in 42:1–11. Their foundations were situated in the outer courtyard, but their superstructure rose in three storeys to the level of the temple platform (Fig. 2 O). The vacant area was **round about the house, right round about ⌞it⌟** with **a breadth of twenty cubits.** For the layout to the rear of the building, see on 41:12.

♦ **41:11** *The entrance of the side-room ⌞was⌟ to the vacant area, one entrance towards the north and another entrance to the south.* The side-rooms were not accessed from the inside of the temple, but through two doors located at some point in its northern and southern walls, from which one passed out into the open space of 41:10b–11. However, it was then stated that *the breadth of the site of the vacant area ⌞was⌟ five cubits right round about*, which differs from the twenty cubits previously mentioned. One plausible way of understanding this is that 'the site' or 'the place' referred to a pavement five cubits wide which formed part of the elevated platform on which the temple stood and which lay beside the outer wall of the temple and of the side-buildings (Fig. 5 ⑧).

♦ **41:12** There was then introduced a further building, a large structure behind the temple to the west (Fig. 2 P). It was described as *the building which ⌞was⌟ in front of the restricted space towards the western side*. The term 'restricted space' (*gizrâ*) came from a root meaning 'to cut off'. It was apparently applied to the continuation of the vacant area (41:9) which lay to the west of the temple building (Fig. 5 ⑨). Not only was it an open, unoccupied space, but it was one to which access was controlled. It was a hundred cubits in length (north to south; 41:13) and twenty cubits wide.

The dimensions of the west building (*binyān*) were given as *a width of seventy cubits* and *its length ⌞was⌟ ninety cubits*, following the usual naming convention (see on 40:11). These were internal measurements, and, since *the wall of the building ⌞was⌟ five cubits in width right round about*, its external dimensions were eighty cubits by one hundred cubits. Inasmuch as the building was against the exterior wall, it is not known if that wall functioned as the rear wall of the building. Presumably the building itself stood at the centre of the west outer wall. It is thus possible to identify at the rear of the temple building a square with sides of one hundred cubits, consisting of the west building and the restricted area. It is not clear where the elevation of the temple platform ended at the rear; the walls of the lower east side of this building might have formed a retaining wall for the inner platforms.

Nothing was said of the function of this building. Later (43:8) it was indicated that various royal administrative buildings had begun to encroach on the sacred space of the Jerusalem Temple (see reconstruction in Volume 1, Fig. 1), and this building may have been intended to prevent such infringement in the ideal temple of Ezekiel's vision. Indeed, the problem may have arisen from more than royal administrative needs. This space and building may also have precluded intrusion by the cults mentioned in chapter 8, particularly if that location was linked to the structure called the 'colonnade' (*parbār*) in 1 Chronicles 26:18 (cf. 'precincts', *parwārim*, associated with sun worship in 2 Kgs. 23:11).

(c) Miscellaneous Measurements (41:13–15a)

The next set of measurements gives dimensions for the temple compound, some of which have already been supplied, and others of which may be inferred.

> 41:13And he measured the house, in length a hundred cubits, and the restricted space and the building and its walls, in length a hundred cubits, 41:14and the breadth of the front of the house to the east and the restricted space, a hundred cubits. 41:15aAnd he measured the length of the building fronting the restricted space which ˻was˼ at its back and its balconies, on this side and on that, a hundred cubits.

♦ **41:13–14** *He measured*[35] *the house* again marked a transition in the description, this time to establish that the sacred central zone could be considered to consist of three squares, each with sides of one hundred cubits. As well as the inner courtyard (40:47), *the house*, that is, the temple and the open area around it measured *in length a hundred cubits.* This was also the length of *the restricted space and the building*[36] *and its walls* behind the temple (41:12). In *the breadth of the front of the house to the east and the restricted space*, the term

---

35. Ordinary *waw* with the perfect is used here (and in 41:15) in *ûmādad*, 'and he measured', instead of the expected *waw*-consecutive with the imperfect, *wayyāmod*, 'and he measured' (41:1-5).

36. In 41:13 there is the only occurrence of *binyâ*, 'building', instead of *binyān*, 'building' (41:12, 15), to refer to the large structure behind (to the west of) the temple.

'the restricted space' was used to refer to what had previously been called 'the vacant area' (41:9). In this way a further dimension of *a hundred cubits* was established.

♦ **41:15a** *And he measured the length of the building fronting the restricted space which* ⌊*was*⌋ *at its back and its balconies*. The building under consideration was most probably not the west building mentioned in 41:12, but that which comprised the rooms of 41:10. 'Fronting' considered this building as viewed from the side of the temple, looking outwards. 'The restricted space' may point to either the open area at the side of the temple, or more narrowly to the area at the rear of the temple, since the priestly rooms overlapped both. *On this side and on that* probably referred to the extent to which the structure containing these rooms extended beyond the restricted space, though it might also have indicated the existence of a southern counterpart which was similarly situated. The length of these buildings was also established as *one hundred cubits*.

However, the meaning of the term rendered 'balconies' (*ʾattîq* or *ʾattûq*)[37] is quite uncertain. Various possibilities have been suggested, such as, 'passageway' or 'corridor' on the basis of Akkadian, or 'ledge' describing the recess of a window frame. Taking into account its other occurrences in Ezekiel (41:16; 42:3, 5), the most plausible notion is that the rooms on the higher floors of these buildings were stepped back with a balcony outside them on top of the floor beneath.

(d) The Temple Interior and Furnishings (41:15b–26)
Since Ezekiel and his guide have earlier left the temple (41:5, 8), this description of its interior and its decorations seems out of place at this point. Translational difficulties abound, and they are intensified by the nature of the text, which is a list of items rather than a sequential account. Moreover, the guide is virtually absent. One might almost have concluded that he had left the prophet for a while in the Holy Place to see what he could for himself, except that he unexpectedly breaks his silence in 41:22.

There is a large space in the Massoretic text between 'a hundred cubits' (41:15a) and 'the inner temple' (41:15b), probably indicating

---

37. The qere reads *wəʾattîqeyhāʾ*, the plural of the noun found in 42:3 (singular, *ʾattîq*) and 41:16 and 42:5 (plural). The kethib, *wəʾattûqeyhāʾ*, is based on a synonym, *ʾattûq*. The form of the third feminine singular suffix used is not attested elsewhere in Hebrew, though it is similar to Aramaic usage.

that before the present versification was added by the Massoretes a new section was identified as beginning here. For a defence of the view that the present versification is superior, see Keil 2002:377–378. Some later verse divisions do not respect the sentence structure either, with 41:16–17, 17–18 and 18–19 flowing across verse breaks.

Ezekiel's description shows that all the interior surfaces of the temple were veneered with wood (41:15b–17a), the vertical surfaces of which were decorated with a carved pattern of alternating cherubim and palm trees (41:17b–20). Mention is also made of the temple doorposts (41:21) and of an altar/table (41:22). The temple doors were two-leaved (41:23–24), and they also were decorated with the standard pattern (41:25). Other parts of the structure were also veneered with wood which had a modified decoration (41:26).

> 41:15bAnd the inner temple and the vestibules of the courtyard, 41:16the thresholds and the closable windows, and the balconies round about the three of them opposite the threshold ⌊were⌋ veneered with wood right round about, and ⌊from⌋ the ground as far as the windows, and the windows were covered, 41:17upon the top of the entrance and as far as the inner house and on the outside. And to all the wall right round about, on the inside and the outside, by measurement, 41:18and there were made cherubim and palm trees, and a palm tree was between a cherub and a cherub. Now each cherub had two faces: 41:19a human face ⌊was⌋ towards the palm tree on one side and the face of a young lion ⌊was⌋ towards the palm tree on the other side. It was made on all the house right round about. 41:20From the ground as far as above the entrance the cherubim and the palm trees ⌊were⌋ made, and ⌊on⌋ the wall of the temple. 41:21⌊As for⌋ the temple, the doorposts were square, and in front of the sanctuary the appearance ⌊was⌋ like the appearance. 41:22The altar ⌊was⌋ of wood, three cubits in height, and its length two cubits; it had corners and its length and its sides ⌊were⌋ of wood; and he spoke to me, 'This is the table which is before the LORD.' 41:23Now the temple and the holy place had two doors, 41:24and the doors had two leaves, two leaves which swung, two for one door and two leaves for the other. 41:25And there were made on them on the doors of the temple cherubim and palm trees just as they had been made for the walls, and a wooden canopy ⌊was⌋ in front of the vestibule outside. 41:26And there ⌊were⌋ closable windows and palm trees on one side and on the other of the sides of the vestibule and the side-rooms of the house and the canopies.

♦ **41:15b–17a** The next sentence began with a list of various features which were ***veneered with wood*** (lit., 'veneer of wood'). The term 'veneer' occurs only here, but an Akkadian cognate suggests that it referred to panelling of some sort which covered the stonework of these features.

Translators differ as to whether each of the three chambers of the temple building were specified by the first three words of the list ('the temple, the inner ⌞sanctuary⌟, the vestibules of the courtyard', e.g., RSV, REB, NIV), or whether only two (e.g., ESV, NKJV, NJPS).[38] On balance Hebrew grammar would favour ***the inner temple*** as a single item, which would describe the great hall and the Most Holy Place. The plural in ***the vestibules of the courtyard*** is also puzzling, and it may be the result of a textual corruption (Milgrom 2012:93). The reference is most probably to the vestibule of the temple, considered as facing the inner courtyard.

The conundrums posed by this list do not cease with the first term in 41:16, ***the thresholds***. These were obviously those encountered in moving into the various chambers of the temple, but would the floor be panelled? Sensing this difficulty, the AV translates *sap* as 'door posts' (cf. 43:8) and is followed by NKJV. But it is undoubtedly the case that the normal meaning of the term is 'threshold'. Since in Solomon's Temple the floor was overlaid with gold (1 Kgs. 6:30), wooden flooring on the threshold is not improbable.

The issues raised by the term ***closable windows*** have already been discussed at 40:16. This feature was also present in the temple building, but see on 41:16b.

The balconies round about the three of them opposite the threshold is quite opaque. It is improbable that there were balconies in the three chambers of the temple, especially so as regards the Holy of Holies. One possible speculation is that the niches of the windows did not have smooth sides, but displayed an inset stepped profile like that of a building with three balconies. 'Opposite the threshold' is omitted in the Septuagint and the Peshitta, and it is frequently deleted as a gloss, probably because it cannot be easily related to the context.

It was emphasised how completely the walls were clad with

---

38. The difference arises from taking *happənîmî* as an adjective agreeing with the preceding 'the temple', or as a noun with the sense 'the innermost' in reference to the Holy of Holies. The absence of the conjunction between the two terms favours the former construal, but then there would be no mention of whether the Holy of Holies was panelled or not.

veneering *right round about*. It started at *the ground* and continued *as far as the windows*, which would have usually been situated high up on the walls, apparently close to ceiling level. The purpose of such windows in temple buildings was to admit light and provide ventilation, not to allow anyone to see out or in, but here it was explicitly stated that *the windows were covered.* Quite what that meant in relation to this structure depended on the relative heights of the inner and outer walls. Possibly the apertures of the windows were also covered with wood because they abutted the side-rooms, or, if the inner walls were much higher, then the window niches may have been panelled. *Upon the top of the entrance and as far as the inner house and on the outside* emphasised how completely the stone inner surface of the great hall and the vestibule was enhanced with panel work. 'Outside' (*ḥîṣôn*) contrasts what is outer or external with what is internal, and may at first suggest that the outer temple walls were panelled, but that is improbable. The contrast in this verse is with the 'inner house', the Holy Place and the Most Holy Place, as distinct from the vestibule (a similar usage occurs in 1 Kgs. 6:29–30; cf. *NIDOTTE* 2:53).

♦ **41:17b–18a** The panelling employed on *all the wall right round about, on the inside and the outside* was not simply plain wood. Instead *by measurement* pointed to carefully sized and proportioned decoration on it. *Were made*[39] showed that there were carved representations of *cherubim and palm trees*, which were in an alternating pattern. 'Cherubim', the same term as found in chapters 9–11, here referred to a likeness of those living beings who were the throne attendants of God.

♦ **41:18b–19** *Now each cherub had two faces.* Earlier Ezekiel's cherubim had four faces (1:6; 10:21), but only two were mentioned here, *a human face* and *the face of a young lion* (cf. 1:10). This was probably because the two dimensional representation of the carvings only permitted two faces to be visible. *It was made on all the house right round about* showed that no vertical surface was left unadorned.

The cherubim and palm-tree style decorations had also been features of Solomon's Temple (1 Kgs. 6:29–35; 7:36), but there was no mention here of Solomon's gold overlays or other embellishments. Such ornamentation was common in ancient Near Eastern art, and the

---

39. The verb is unusual in that it is singular after a composite subject where both terms are plural (cf. 40:17; 41:19).

Old Testament does not explain its significance. Probably the portrayal of cherubim in their role as throne attendants signified all that was associated with the majesty and power of the King of the temple, while the thick foliage of the palm tree and the abundance of its fruit were indicative of the plenty provided by the LORD's rule, and suggested how he would enable his subjects to flourish (Ps. 92:12) and be joyful (Lev. 23:40).

♦ **41:20** The internal wall above the doorway and the inner surface of the external walls were covered with these decorative features. *From the ground as far as above the entrance the cherubim and the palm trees ⌊were⌋ made and ⌊on⌋ the wall of the temple.*[40] The mention of this ornamentation contrasted with how little Ezekiel had to say about such adornment elsewhere, if it existed.

♦ **41:21** ⌊*As for*⌋ *the temple* was an introductory phrase indicating the next item in Ezekiel's catalogue. *The doorposts were square*, literally, 'doorpost of squareness', that is, of square cross-section. 'Doorpost' (*məzûzâ*) referred to the framework at an entrance for supporting the door itself. Later the Hebrew term came to be applied to a small container fixed to the doorpost of a dwelling to give literal adherence to the injunctions of Deuteronomy 6:9; 11:20. Possibly there was a contrast with the five-sided doorposts in Solomon's Temple (1 Kgs. 6:31, NIV84, REB, NASB, ESV).

The Septuagint and the Peshitta took the concluding words of the verse with the following verse: 'Along the front of the Holy Place ⌊was⌋ an appearance like the face of a wooden altar'. The Massoretic text read ⌊*as for*⌋ *the face of the Holy Place, the appearance* ⌊*was*⌋ *like the appearance.* That might have meant that it was also square. However, 'appearance' had been used by Ezekiel (cf. 1:5, 13–14, 16, 26) to describe supernatural entities in terms of things that were more familiar, and that might have been the sense here if 'the appearance like the appearance' described the following 'altar'. It was not quite what it seemed in that it was not an altar, but was in fact a table.

---

40. The dots above every letter in *hahêkāl*, 'the temple', are known as *puncta extraordinaria*. This device occurs on fifteen words of the Old Testament, but its significance is unclear. It predates the Massoretes, and may indicate early scribal uncertainty as to whether the letters should be included. The same word begins the next verse, and the LXX and Vulgate (cf. also the Peshitta) seem to run the two verses together. However, there is really no difficulty in rendering the MT as it stands.

♦ **41:22** It was a matter of surprise that *the altar ⌊was⌋ of wood*, because that was an unsuitable material for an altar on which sacrifices would be burned. *Its length* (*wəʾorkô*) is generally accepted as a copying error for *wəʾadnô*, 'its base' (cf. LXX), because 'length' (cf. AV, NKJV) as such cannot be constructed of wood (Keil 2002:380). Ezekiel's table was significantly different from that in the Tabernacle (Exod. 25:23–30) in that it had been higher than its width (and length). In the Tabernacle the table had been rectangular, two cubits long, one cubit wide, and one and a half cubits high.

He spoke to me indicated that Ezekiel's guide felt it necessary to explain the situation to him. *This is the table which is before the* **LORD**. It was not really an altar, but only had the appearance of such, being in fact what corresponded to the table of the bread of presence (Exod. 25:30; Lev. 24:6; 1 Kgs. 7:48). Why had it been referred to as an altar? It may simply have been that in this renewed temple its shape was similar to that of an altar. The mention of *corners* may have implied 'horns', which were generally connected with altars (Exod. 29:12; 37:25; Lev. 4:7, 18; 1 Kgs. 2:28).

At a more theological level, the statement probably indicated a correspondence with the grain offerings in the same way as the animal offerings were connected to the great altar in the outer courtyard. Nowhere else in the Old Testament, however, was there such a connection made between table and altar, probably to avoid suggesting the heathen belief that the gods needed to be actually fed.[41]

♦ **41:23–24** The terminology employed here was not straightforward, *the temple* was apparently the great hall, and *the holy place* was the inmost sanctuary. As in Solomon's Temple (1 Kgs. 6:31–34), both these chambers had double doors with swinging leaves (the same term is used to describe both the whole door and each leaf). Presumably each half of the door was set in a pivot hole next to the doorpost so that it could swing in either direction.

♦ **41:25** Again *made* (cf. 41:18) seems to have been used in some technical sense to denote carving. This was found *on the doors of the temple*, following the pattern of *cherubim and palm trees just as they had been made for the walls.*

A wooden canopy ⌊was⌋ in front of the vestibule outside. 'Canopy'

---

41. Hummel adds after 'its length two cubits' the phrase 'its width two cubits' found in the LXX, on the grounds that it had been omitted from the Hebrew text through homoioteleuton (2007:1214).

(*'āb*) renders a term which usually means 'a cloud', but presumably the word employed here was a homograph referring to an architectural feature about whose identity there is no certainty. A roof structure of some sort is assumed in most English translations.

♦ **41:26** The vestibule too had *closed windows* (cf. 41:16), but the decor here apparently consisted only of *palm trees*, which were also to be found on *the side-rooms of the house* (cf. 41:5) *and the canopies* (cf. 41:25). This plural may have meant that canopies were also found at the side entrances (Hummel 2007:1215).

(6) The Temple Rooms (42:1–20)

With Ezekiel's description of the temple having come back to the vestibule and side-rooms (41:26), the guide continues his visionary exploration by looking at the rooms set aside for the priests in the outer courtyard and by explaining their purpose (42:1–14). He then brings this part of Ezekiel's experience to a conclusion by establishing the external dimensions of the temple complex (42:15–20).

(a) The Priestly Rooms (42:1–14)

It is readily evident from examining the diagrams provided by various commentators that these verses present considerable difficulties, especially regarding the orientation and layout of the rooms which are described. Rather than unnecessarily multiplying structures, it is preferable to identify the room of 42:1–2 with the set of rooms described in 42:3–9, and to take the whole structure on the north side of the temple to be mirrored on the south side (42:10–12). Finally, the guide explains the purpose of these rooms (42:13–14). This has to be read in conjunction with 44:19 and 46:19–20 to clarify their function and location. They are to be used by the priests to take off their holy apparel after ministering at the altar and to put on other garments before venturing into the outer courtyard, and also for consuming their allotted portions of the sacrifices.

In this connection Milgrom has helpfully observed that the rooms must be in three ascending tiers (not in parallel rows at ground level) so that a priest may enter the block of rooms at a higher level directly from the temple courtyard and after changing his clothing may exit the block from its lowest level into the outer courtyard (2012:43). Adopting that reconstruction does not, however, solve all the conundrums posed by this passage.

⁴²:¹And he led me out to the outer courtyard by the way towards the north, and he brought me to the room which ⌊was⌋ opposite the restricted space, and which ⌊was⌋ opposite the building to the north. ⁴²:²Towards the face of the length (⌊it was⌋ a hundred cubits) ⌊was⌋ the north entrance, and the breadth ⌊was⌋ fifty cubits. ⁴²:³Opposite the twenty ⌊cubits⌋ which ⌊related⌋ to the inner courtyard, and opposite the pavement which ⌊related⌋ to the outer courtyard ⌊were⌋ balcony upon balcony in three ⌊storeys⌋. ⁴²:⁴And in front of the rooms ⌊there was⌋ a walkway of ten cubits in breadth to the inside, a way of one cubit, and their entrances ⌊were⌋ towards the north. ⁴²:⁵Now the upper rooms were narrower because the balconies took space from them compared to the lower and middle ⌊rooms⌋ of the building. ⁴²:⁶For they ⌊were⌋ in three storeys, and they did not have pillars like the pillars of the courtyards; consequently the upper ⌊rooms⌋ were set back from the ground more than the lower or middle ⌊rooms⌋. ⁴²:⁷And ⌊there was⌋ a wall outside alongside the rooms on the way to the outer courtyard, opposite the rooms; its length was fifty cubits. ⁴²:⁸For the length of the rooms which ⌊were⌋ towards the outer courtyard ⌊was⌋ fifty cubits, but behold on the face of the temple ⌊was⌋ a hundred cubits. ⁴²:⁹And under these rooms ⌊was⌋ the entrance from the east as one enters them from the outer courtyard.

⁴²:¹⁰In the breadth of the wall of the courtyard towards the east, in front of the restricted space, and in front of the building, ⌊were⌋ rooms. ⁴²:¹¹and a passage before them like the appearance of the rooms which ⌊were⌋ towards the north; according to their length, so was their breadth; and all their exits, and according to their fashions, and according to their entrances. ⁴²:¹²And according to the entrances of the rooms which ⌊were⌋ towards the south ⌊there was⌋ an entrance at the head of the passage, the passage which is in front of the protecting wall towards the east as one enters them.

⁴²:¹³And he said to me, '⌊As for ⌋ the north rooms ⌊and⌋ the south rooms which ⌊are⌋ opposite the restricted space, they ⌊are⌋ the holy rooms where the priests who draw near to the LORD are to eat the most holy ⌊offerings⌋. There they are to store the most holy ⌊offerings⌋—the grain offering and the sin offering and the guilt offering—for the place ⌊is⌋ holy. ⁴²:¹⁴When the priests enter, they are not to go out from the holy place to the outer courtyard, but there they are to store their garments in which they minister, for they ⌊are⌋ holy; they are to wear other garments when they draw near to that which ⌊is⌋ for the people.'

♦ **42:1** After the loopback to examine (or just to comment on) the decoration of the temple, two guidance formulas (see on 40:17), *and he led me out*[42] and *and he brought me*, served as a reminder that Ezekiel was on a conducted walkabout and was not permitted to wander at will. His tour continued with him being ushered into *the outer courtyard by the way towards the north* (lit., 'the way, the way of the north'). From the inner courtyard he was conducted through the north inner gateway into the outer courtyard, and then led in his vision westwards to the area below the temple building (Fig. 3.11).

Here he was taken *to the room* (*liškâ*, cf. 41:10), a structure which lay *opposite the restricted space* and *opposite the building* (*binyān*), that is, the rear west-building. It is preferable to understand 'room' here as a collective noun for the structure which contained the priestly rooms (Fig. 2 O). For the location of the two features, see on 41:12. Since Ezekiel was in the north of the outer courtyard, the priestly rooms were *to the north* of the central structures.

♦ **42:2** *Towards the face of the length (⌞it was⌟ a hundred cubits)* yielded information that its length was 100 cubits, but, as has been noted before (see on 40:11), 'length' did not specify the orientation of the building. Most probably, it lay west to east along the retaining wall which maintained the higher platforms. However, allowance must be made for the priestly kitchens 'at their extreme western end' (46:19; Fig. 2 Q), though no dimensions were given for them. Since the kitchen-courtyards for preparing the portion for the laity were forty cubits by thirty cubits (46:22; Fig. 2 R), a similar size for the priestly kitchens is not improbable.

On the far wall of the structure was *the north entrance*, permitting access to and from the outer courtyard. *The breadth ⌞was⌟ fifty cubits*. But, as Milgrom notes, if the north and south rooms were considered as one, 'together they would form a square, 100 × 100 cubits—a guarantee of holiness' (2012:99).

♦ **42:3** Further details were then given relating to the location of these priestly rooms as being *opposite the twenty ⌞cubits⌟ which ⌞related⌟ to the inner courtyard*, which was a reference to the 'breadth of twenty cubits round about the house' (41:10). *Opposite the pavement* (*riṣĕpâ*) *which ⌞related⌟ to the outer courtyard* presumably referred to the

---

42. The hiphil of *yāṣāʾ*, 'to bring out' (qal: 'to go out') indicates authorised exit from a special zone (cf. 42:15; 46:21; 47:2), and functions as the opposite of the hiphil of *bôʾ*, 'to bring in' (qal: 'to come in, enter'; see on 40:17).

pavement described in 40:17–18, running along the inside of the outer wall. These rooms were thus located in the outer courtyard, but they were additionally described as **balcony upon balcony** (41:15) **in three ⌊storeys⌋.**[43] Apparently the ground floor balcony was at the level of the outer courtyard, the first floor balcony at the level of the inner courtyard, and the second floor balcony at the level of the temple platform. It was therefore possible for a priest who had served at the altar to enter the priestly building on a higher floor, and having changed his clothing and made his way down through the building to exit on the level of the outer courtyard.

Depending on the point from which the temple was viewed, the location of such buildings may have detracted from the dominance afforded the temple by the elevation of the platform on which it sat. This would, however, have been compensated for to some extent by the terraced profile of the priestly buildings pointing upwards and inwards to the temple proper.

♦ **42:4** Another set of puzzling statements are found in this verse. *In front of the rooms ⌊there was⌋ a walkway (mahălāk) of ten cubits in breadth to the inside.* Rather than 'to the inside' meaning between the rooms and the retaining wall of the inner courtyard, it is preferable to take the reference to be 'to the inside ⌊of the outer courtyard⌋'. These rooms must have immediately abutted the inner platform if the reconstruction outlined above is valid. *A way of one cubit* is generally reckoned to be corrupt, and, following the Septuagint and Peshitta, modern translations substitute, 'a length of one hundred cubits'.[44] If so, that corroborates the length of this building (41:15). *Their entrances ⌊were⌋ towards the north* implied that one could enter the rooms directly from the walkway in front of them.

♦ **42:5–6** Unlike the side-rooms in 41:6 which widened in the higher storeys, in this set of rooms *the upper rooms were narrower because the balconies took space from them compared to the lower and middle ⌊rooms⌋ of the building.* Apparently this applied only to the rooms on the third floor.

---

43. Keil (2002:381, 385) translates 'in the third storey', and takes the balconies as existing on the upmost storey, which would explain why only that one, and not the middle one, is narrowed (42:5-6).

44. In place of *derek 'ammâ 'eḥāt*, 'a way of one cubit', they read *'ōrek mē'â 'ammôt*, 'length of one hundred cubits'. This reading was accepted by Keil (2002:385), but Allen (1998:225–226) prefers a more substantial emendation to read 'and a wall (a cubit thick)', which is further described in 42:7.

Ezekiel offered an explanation as to how this arrangement was contrived. ***They ⌐were⌐ in three storeys*** reiterated (42:3) the point that the priestly rooms were constructed on three levels vertically above one another. Moreover, ***they did not have pillars like the pillars of the courtyards***. However, there has been no previous mention of pillars in connection with the courtyards, but it may be that they supported the roofs of the rooms round the outer walls (40:17), and, since 'courtyards' is plural, the rooms mentioned in 40:44–46 may also have had pillars. However, this set of priestly rooms did not possess pillars, but a setback form of construction was used to provide balconies. ***The upper ⌐rooms⌐ were set back from the ground***, that is, from the outer edge of the structure at its base.

♦ **42:7-8** ***A wall outside alongside to the rooms*** was not part of the structure of the building, but parallel to it and forming an enclosing or boundary wall (*gādēr*, cf. 13:5). Its length of 50 cubits made it more likely that it ran along the east side of the building ***on the way to the outer courtyard, opposite the rooms*** (see 42:9) rather than along the 100 cubits length of the northern side (42:4). Keil records the conjecture that the purpose of this wall was to prevent anyone looking into the rooms along this eastern wall (2002:387). The explanatory clause in 42:8 reinforces this construction, with 'length' being used rather than 'breadth' because of its earlier use in relation to the wall which had the same dimension.

♦ **42:9** ***And under these rooms***[45] related to the east face of the priestly building whose lowest floor was shielded from sight by the wall of 42:7. ***The entrance***[46] ***from the east*** was behind this wall.

♦ **42:10** This and the following two verses described the southern set of priestly rooms. They mirrored those on the north (42:1–9), and it was this symmetry which Ezekiel was concerned to emphasise. ***In the***

---

45. The qere consists of the first two words in *ûmittaḥat hallǝšākôt hāʾēlleh*, 'and from under these rooms', whereas the kethib seems to read *ûmittaḥătāh lǝšākôt hāʾēlleh*, 'and from under it, these rooms'. However, in the kethib the feminine singular suffix would have to refer to the feminine plural noun 'rooms', and the suffix would not be the normal form found with the preposition *taḥat*, 'under'. Furthermore, there is no article with the noun corresponding to that with the demonstrative, as might have been expected. The qere is to be preferred.

46. The kethib, *hammābôʾ*, the entrance, is clearly to be preferred to the qere, *hammēbîʾ*, 'bringing', which would normally be followed by an object specifying what is brought.

breadth of the wall of the courtyard implied that the rooms were within the wall, and their size corresponded to that of the wall (Keil 2002:387–388). However, RSV and Block (1998:562) emend *rōḥab*, 'breadth', to *rō'š*, 'head', and take the phrase with the preceding verse as 'where the outside wall begins' (RSV).

The MT states that the rooms were *derek haqqādîm*, 'towards the east', 'on the east side' (cf. AV, NKJV, NASB), but the Septuagint has 'on the south side' and this is followed by RSV, NIV, ESV. Hummel (2007:1221) argues that the context, especially 'towards the south' (42:12) and 'the northern and southern rooms' (42:13) favour 'south' as the true reading.[47] ***In front of*** was literally 'to the face of' and indicated 'opposite' (cf. *neged* in 42:1).

♦ **42:11** The first clause ***and a passage before them*** might be taken as a separate sentence, 'They also had a passage in front of them', or as attached to the end of the previous verse. However, while the main point was clearly made that the southern rooms were identical to the northern ones, this verse in fact first described the northern rooms. 'According to' might also be 'like', repeated before each of two items to indicate equivalence. ***According to their fashions*** (*mišpāṭ*) employed a term which usually meant 'judgement' or 'justice', but here was obviously used in its extended sense of 'custom', 'recognised order', or 'arrangement'.

♦ **42:12** The passage in 42:11–12 was the counterpart of the walkway in 42:4. ***The passage*** (*derek*) ***which is in front*** gave a more precise specification of the passage which was intended, namely, 'in front of the wall' , but the other term rendered 'protecting' is obscure. Rabbinic tradition understood it as 'appropriate, corresponding' (cf. NRSV, ESV, NIV), but others favour 'protective' or 'intervening'. It corresponded to the wall described in 42:7, while ***towards the east as one enters them*** reflected 42:9.

♦ **42:13** This and the following verse recorded the most extended remarks of the guide in chapters 40–42. He identified and explained in some detail the significance of ***the north rooms and the south rooms ⌊which⌋ are opposite the restricted space.*** They were ***the holy rooms*** which had been set aside for purposes of ritual preparations for worship. The holiness was not inherent in the rooms, but derived from

---

47. Hummel (2007:1221) suggests that *mēhaqqādîm*, 'from the east' (42:9) caused a scribe to write *haqqādîm*, 'the east', instead of *haddārîm*, 'the south', here.

their dedication to God and service at his altar and in the sanctuary. ***The priests who draw near the LORD*** was a technical expression for those priests who were permitted to slay and present the sacrifices (40:46). ***The most holy ⌐offerings¬***[48] referred to the portion of the sacrifices which was not burned on the altar, but which was eaten by the priests themselves as representatives of the LORD (cf. Lev. 21:22). For 'most holy', see on 41:4.

When the priests engaged in sacrificial activity, ***they are to store the most holy ⌐offerings¬*** in these specially designated rooms until they had opportunity to prepare, cook, and eat what was allocated to them. This had to be done in a holy place (Lev. 6:16, 26; 7:6; 10:13), and the portions had to be prepared properly, boiling in the case of meat (Lev. 6:28), or baked without yeast in the case of grain (Lev. 6:17).

The three sacrifices mentioned here, ***the grain offering and the sin offering and the guilt offering***, corresponded to those mentioned in 40:39 except that 'grain offering' replaced the whole burnt offering (from which nothing came to the priests for consumption). The peace offering also was not mentioned. Although a portion of it was given to the priests (Lev. 7:28–36), it was not classed as most holy.

♦ **42:14 *When the priests enter*** (lit., 'in their entering, the priests') used the verb 'enter'/'go in' (*bô'*, cf. 40:17) which denoted passage from one zone of holiness to another. ***They are not to go out from the holy place*** made clear the reference of their entering, and employed the verb 'go out' (*yāṣā'*) in the sense of moving across a boundary into a less holy zone. In their movement into these priestly rooms the priests were to avoid passing ***from the holy place to the outer courtyard.***

There they are to store their garments. The verb repeated that of 42:13 with regard to the most holy offerings. It was for the same reason: ***for they are holy.*** 'They' was a feminine form specifically relating to the garments, and not to the priests. ***They are to wear***[49] ***other garments when they draw near that which is for the people.*** 'Draw near' indicated crossing a boundary of a zone of particular

---

48. The expression *qodšê haqqŏdāšîm*, 'the holy ⌐ones¬ of the holy ⌐ones', is very similar to the expression used for the inmost chamber of the sanctuary, *qōdeš haqqŏdāšîm*, 'the Holy of Holies' (41:4). Both expressions are superlative in their sense.

49. The qere is a perfect form with ordinary *waw*, *wəlābəšû*, 'and they will put on', whereas the kethib is a more emphatic, directive imperfect form without *waw*, *yilbəšû*, 'they are to wear'.

holiness. What was holy must not be allowed to come into contact with what was common or profane (cf. 42:20).

(b) Overall Measurements of the Temple Precincts (42:15-20)
As the prophet is led back to the starting point of his visionary tour (42:15), this section brings closure to the description of the temple precincts by providing summarising measurements of the outer wall (42:20). Further features of the temple compound are described later: the altar (43:13-17) and the kitchens (46:19-24).

The key statement at the end of 42:20—'to separate the holy and the common'—provides insight into the rationale which motivated the layout of the temple precincts and the observations relayed through the prophet.

> ⁴²:¹⁵Now ⌊when⌋ he had finished measuring the inner house, he led me out by way of the gateway which faces towards the east, and he measured it right round about. ⁴²:¹⁶He measured the east side with the measuring rod, five hundred ⌊cubits⌋, ⌊using⌋ rods as the measuring rod, round about. ⁴²:¹⁷He measured the north side, five hundred ⌊cubits⌋, ⌊using⌋ rods as the measuring rod round about. ⁴²:¹⁸The south side he measured, five hundred ⌊cubits⌋, ⌊using⌋ rods as the measuring rod. ⁴²:¹⁹He turned to the west side ⌊and⌋ measured five hundred ⌊cubits⌋, ⌊using⌋ rods as the measuring rod. ⁴²:²⁰On four sides he measured it; it had a wall right round about, in length five hundred ⌊cubits⌋ and in breadth five hundred ⌊cubits⌋ to separate the holy and the common.

♦ **42:15** *He had finished measuring the inner house* indicated the end of the first part of the measuring process which had begun in 40:5. There was then the guidance formula, *he led me out* (cf. 40:2).⁵⁰ The guide escorted Ezekiel *by way of the gateway which faces towards the east*, that is, the east outer gateway, so that both were outside the temple complex (Fig. 3.12). Then *he measured it right round about*, which must in this context have referred to obtaining the exterior measurements of the whole compound.

♦ **42:16-19** The guide began at the east gate and moved to the north, south and west sides. This was the same order as the gates were listed

---

50. The verb here is *wəhôṣîʾanî*, 'and he led me out', using the later construction of *waw*-conjunctive and a perfect verb form rather than the classical *waw*-consecutive imperfect. This occurs in the preceding clause also. In following verses the verbs are asyndetic perfects.

in the description of the new Jerusalem in Revelation 21:13, suggesting it was conceived of as the fulfilment of this passage in Ezekiel. Throughout these verses *side* renders the word *rûaḥ*, elsewhere, 'breath, wind, spirit' (cf. 37:9), but here designating the direction from which the wind would blow on a side.

At first sight it appears that *five hundred*[51] has 'rods' as its unit of measurement, but that would mean that each side was 3,000 cubits, that is, 5,075 feet, almost a mile or 1.6 kilometres, so that the area would be 591 acres (239 ha). This is quite disproportionate to the other measurements given. While many then omit the word 'rods' in each of its three occurrences in these verses, it is preferable to treat the expression as an instrumental use (Block 1998:568), *using rods as the measuring rod*. Then the unit of measurement may be taken as cubits, which would yield sides of 846 feet (258 m), and an area of 16.4 acres (6.5 ha). Both sets of measurements pale into insignificance before the dimensions (including height) attributed to the new Jerusalem of Revelation which is presented as a cube whose edges are 12,000 stadia (1,380 miles, 2,220 kilometres).

♦ **42:20** Back in 40:5 Ezekiel had begun with a description of the wall round the temple complex (which was not at that stage measured), using the term *wall* (*ḥômâ*) which typically described a city wall whose function was to debar those considered undesirable from entering. In an inclusion round the section, that term is now reused and the purpose of the wall stated: *to separate the holy and the common*. These terms (cf. 22:26; 44:23) were standard descriptors respectively of the realm of what was dedicated to the divine and of what was simply the ordinary. It was a primary priestly duty to teach what belonged to either realm and to urge the people to maintain the difference scrupulously (cf. Lev. 10:10–11). Intrusions into the holy of what was not worthy of a place there had dire consequences. So here, to exiles struggling in a pagan environment to maintain any of the ritual laws God had appointed, the message was presented of return to their land yielding them with the opportunity to live in a right fashion before God. This was also an implied indictment of the conduct they had previously displayed there. By despising the holy they had invoked divine wrath upon themselves, and had caused their land and society to become destabilised and destroyed. A strong wall

---

51. The qere has *ḥămēš-mēʾôt*, 'five hundred', which is obviously to be preferred to the kethib which has *ḥămēš-ʾēmôt*, 'five cubits'. The error probably arose through switching of two consonants.

encompassing the sacred precincts was symbolic of the divine preparations to prevent such casual and dangerous commingling of the holy and the common. With the prevention of such intrusions it became possible for the holy God to return and dwell in the midst of his people, and reciprocally for them to enjoy the benefits of his presence secured for them.

REFLECTION

- Failure to appreciate God's distinctiveness is not a uniquely contemporary phenomenon. 'You thought that I am surely like you' (Ps. 50:21) was the divine accusation levelled in Asaph's day when Israel lost sight of the holiness and sovereign power of God. The same forgetfulness is the besetting sin of modern western civilisation. If it thinks of God at all, it domesticates the Almighty into a Santa Claus caricature of unlimited benevolence and genial tolerance. 'There is no fear of God before their eyes' (Rom. 3:18). This description of the ideal meeting place between God and man warns against becoming too comfortable in the presence of God. His ideal dwelling-place on earth is this carefully constructed structure in which his holy presence chamber is elevated and protected from intrusion by elaborate zones of exclusion. It is true that, through Christ, he is approachable as our Father, but we must never lose our sense of awe before him. The ideal temple challenges us with how easy it is to entertain a diminished sense of our privilege in being able to call on him. One is reminded of the title of J. B. Phillips' classic, *Your God Is Too Small*. We must retain an adequate sense of his immensity and his holiness if we are not to warp and impoverish our relationship with him.
- 'To separate the holy and the common' (42:20) brings out how the centrality of separation is embedded in the layout of the temple. Yet it must not be forgotten that this is a temple. It is on earth. As such it prefigures the incarnation of Christ, who is 'holy, innocent, undefiled, separated from sinners, and exalted above the heavens' (Heb. 7:26) and yet who lived among mankind as a temple (John 2:21). So too those who are his are 'in the world' but 'are not of the world' (John 17:11, 16), and are called on to be replicas of that temple existence. 'Do you not know that your body is a temple of the Holy Spirit within you, whom you have from God?' (1 Cor. 6:19). How carefully then we should conduct ourselves in accordance with that holy status! 'God's temple is holy, and you are that temple' (1 Cor. 3:17).

- The holiness of the ideal temple foreshadows the purity of the new Jerusalem into which nothing unclean will ever enter, nor anyone who does what is detestable of false (Rev. 21:27). However, the ideal temple of Ezekiel's vision is still separate from the city. What it depicts is true, but partial symbolism. In the final prevision of heavenly glory the temple and the city merge. There is 'no temple in the city, for its temple is the Lord God Almighty and the Lamb' (Rev. 21:22).

B. The Return of the Glory of the LORD (43:1-12)

The scene has been set, and a detailed account has been given of the imposing grandeur and carefully secured sanctity of the ideal temple. But as yet it remains a lifeless, still presentation. That cannot be allowed to continue for this is the palace of the King whose very being is life itself. So there is now presented to the inner eye of the prophet the arrival of the LORD in all his dynamic glory. His presence elevates what has been a mere ground plan into a vibrant spiritual reality.

But, as Ezekiel's description is at pains to point out, this is not simply a depiction of the arrival of the divine presence; it is the restoration of the Glory-presence of the God of Israel, coming through in 43:4 the same east gate as his presence had been observed to depart by in 10:19 (cf. 11:22–23). God in his mercy visibly re-associates himself with his people whom he will restore. This grand temple bears the marks of his heavenly realm, but it is also designed to facilitate fellowship on earth between Israel and her God.

The stage at which the LORD returns is of some significance. It is before the altar is described and before purification ceremonies are undertaken for it (43:13–27). This ideal temple is divinely provided, and as yet—apart from the prophet—there is no human presence here. So there is no need for cleansing from the polluting impact of human iniquity. Its perfection is not dependent, either in its inauguration or in its perpetuation, on human input. It is of the LORD and, because of that, its continuation is guaranteed.

There are three sections: the return of the Glory (43:1–5); the LORD's demand that there be no defilement (43:6–9); and Ezekiel's task of informing the Israelites so that they may respond correctly (43:10–11). Furthermore, it is possible to detect here the start of a second sequence of movement in Ezekiel's guided tour (Fig. 6). Originally he was escorted from outside the temple precinct to its centre (40:5–41:4) and then back outside again (41:5–42:20). Now he begins outside (43:1), is brought to the centre (43:5), almost goes outside (44:1), and is brought back into the inner courtyard (44:4). Then, after staying there for some time, he is conducted again into the outer courtyard (46:19, 21) before returning to the inner courtyard (47:1) and finally exiting the temple complex (47:2).

(1) The Glory Presence (43:1–5)

> ⁴³:¹And he led me to the gateway, the gateway which was facing towards the east. ⁴³:²And behold, the glory of the God of Israel came from the east, and his voice ⌊was⌋ like the sound of many waters, and the earth shone because of his glory. ⁴³:³And ⌊it was⌋ like the appearance of the appearance which I had seen, like the appearance which I had seen when I came to destroy the city, and the visions ⌊were⌋ like the appearance which I had seen at the river Chebar; and I fell upon my face. ⁴³:⁴And the glory of the LORD came into the house by way of the gateway which faced towards the east. ⁴³:⁵And ⌊the⌋ Spirit lifted me and brought me into the inner courtyard, and behold, the glory of the LORD filled the house.

♦ **43:1** *And he led me* was one of the guidance formulas (cf. 40:2) used of authorised movement. In this instance Ezekiel was already in vision outside the temple complex (42:15), and he was conducted ***to the gateway, the gateway which was facing towards the east.*** From this gateway there was a straight line of access across the outer courtyard, through the inner east gateway, and, crossing the inner courtyard, into the temple itself. This marks the beginning of the second phase of Ezekiel's temple tour (Fig. 6).

♦ **43:2** *And behold* focused attention on a new, significant occurrence. Here it was nothing less than the fact that ***the glory of the God of Israel came from the east.*** This Glory was a visible manifestation of the presence of the LORD himself, who had earlier left the Jerusalem Temple and moved eastwards (11:23). ***His voice ⌊was⌋ like the sound of many waters.*** Since 'voice' (*qôl*) may also be translated as 'sound', there may not have been any verbal communication at that point, but an awesome sound emanating from the Glory-presence in a manner similar to that of 1:24. Here, however, there was no explicit mention of the cherubim, because the focus was on the LORD himself.

The earth shone because of his glory. The audible component of the phenomenon revealed to the inner consciousness of the prophet was accompanied visually by intense brilliance. The association of the

Glory with light and brightness was already noted in 1:4, 13. In this instance the effulgence was such as to cause all surrounding surfaces to coruscate brilliantly (cf. Rev. 21:23, where the illuminating presence is the Lamb himself).

♦ **43:3** This was one of the relatively few occasions on which Ezekiel spoke directly of his own experience, and he emphasised the visual aspect of what was disclosed to him by repeating forms of the root 'to see' (*rāʾâ*) eight times, both as a verb and as the noun 'appearance' (*marʾeh*). ⌊*It was*⌋ *like the appearance of the appearance which I had seen, like the appearance which I had seen.* The duplication involved in these clauses is generally suppressed by translations as an instance of scribal error, but we may perhaps find here another case of repetition arising from Ezekiel's astonishment at what he was being permitted to view, and his difficulty in knowing quite how to represent it. The best he could do was to stress that it was to be identified with what he had previously experienced. Ezekiel recognised that what he was viewing in this vision was to be identified with what he had previously experienced.

More puzzling is the phrase **when I came to destroy the city.** This first person reference was also preserved in the renderings of the Septuagint and the Peshitta. 'Destroy' was from the same root as 'destruction' in 9:1, 6. Also, in 9:8 the prophet had asked the LORD, 'Are you destroying all the remnant of Israel?' If 'I came' is retained, then it would seem that Ezekiel was reflecting on the power of the word of the LORD that he had announced. Keil (2002:395) approved the thought that the prophet destroyed the city ideally by his prophecy of which the fulfilment simply forms the objective reverse side. However, the Vulgate has a third person rendering, 'when he came', as do a few Hebrew manuscripts.[52] This easier reading is adopted by most English translations (not NKJV). But the LORD had not come to Jerusalem on the previous occasion; it was Ezekiel who was brought there. So it would seem that the Massoretic text should be retained.

The visions ⌊***were***⌋ ***like the appearance which I had seen at the river Chebar.*** As well as linking the later phenomenon with the visionary experience of chapters 8–11, Ezekiel linked it to his initial vision (chs. 1–3). 'Visions' (plural, probably a form of *marʾâ*, 'vision'; cf. 1:1; 8:3) pointed to the complex, many-featured nature of what was disclosed to the prophet.

---

52. The difference is of one letter, between *bəbōʾî*, 'when I came' and *bəbōʾô*, 'when he came'.

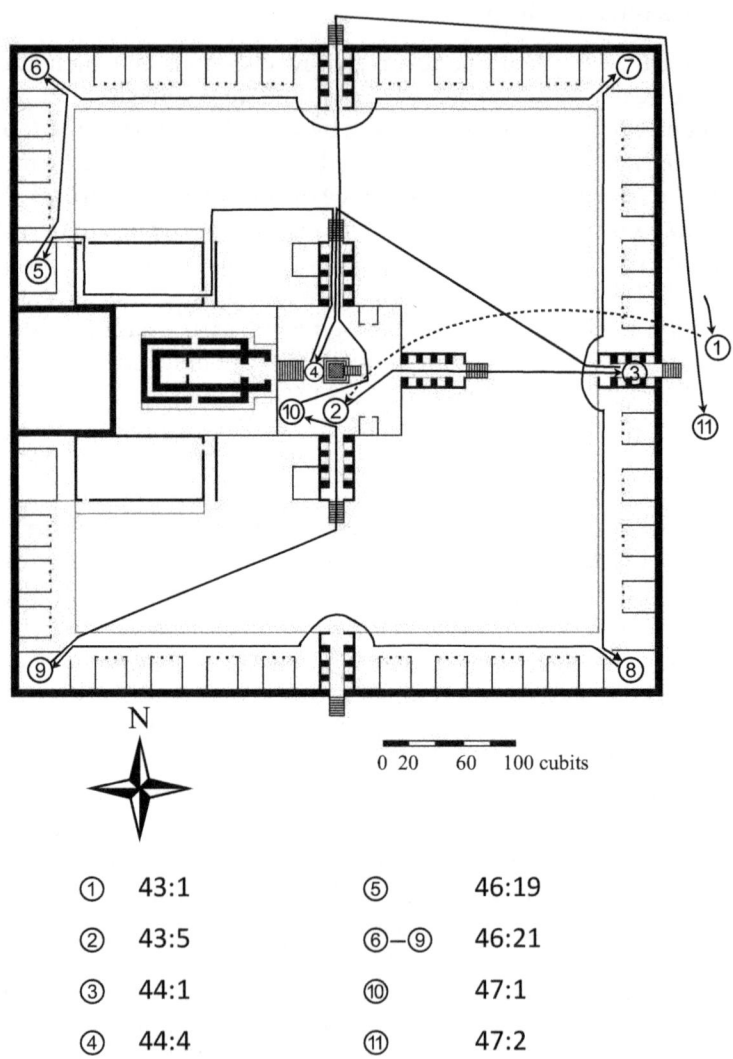

①	43:1	⑤	46:19
②	43:5	⑥–⑨	46:21
③	44:1	⑩	47:1
④	44:4	⑪	47:2

Figure 6. Ezekiel's Guided Tour (Part 2).

I fell upon my face repeated the response of 1:28 and 3:23. Ezekiel's awe and submission had not diminished over the two decades since his first encounter of this sort.

♦ **43:4** ***And the glory of the LORD came into the house by way of the gateway which faced towards the east.*** This unembellished statement may be contrasted with what was said in Exodus 40:34–35 and 1 Kings 8:10–11, and in Ezekiel's earlier descriptions. Possibly this was because of the detail Ezekiel had already supplied about his perception of the Glory-presence. 'The house' referred to the temple building itself, that is, into the Holy of Holies.

♦ **43:5** ⌊***The***⌋ ***Spirit*** who had earlier transported the prophet to a different locality (3:12, 14; 8:3; 11:1, 24; in 40:1 it was the hand of the LORD that did so) was again mentioned when he ***lifted me and brought me into the inner courtyard.*** In this instance the guidance formula, 'brought me' (cf. 40:2), had a feminine subject in agreement with the gender of the Hebrew noun, 'spirit' (cf. 8:3). Ezekiel had been outside the east gateway when he viewed the return of the LORD, but it would appear that he was not permitted to follow the Glory-presence through the gateway. Instead, in the vision the Spirit lifted him off the ground and transported him over the wall and the outer courtyard into the inner courtyard (Fig. 7 ②). That the prophet was able to perceive that ***the glory of the LORD filled the house*** implied that his visionary vantage point was close to the altar, which helps explain why it is discussed in 43:13–27. It also provided the background to the scenario in 44:1 where the east gateway had been closed.

REFLECTION

- There is no clear Scriptural statement that the Glory-presence came into the Temple that was rebuilt in Jerusalem in Zerubbabel's day. It remained a pale reflection of the ideal temple described here until there came the one who could uniquely call the structure in Jerusalem 'my Father's house' (John 2:16). He in himself was the veiled Glory-presence in whom the eye of faith was able to discern 'glory as of the only Son from the Father, full of grace and truth' (John 1:14). In this way he brought greater glory to the rebuilt Temple in fulfilment of the prophecy of Haggai 2:9, but the consummation of that prophecy awaits the New Jerusalem.

(2) No Defilement in the King's Presence (43:6–9)

While the prophet is standing in the inner courtyard, the voice of the LORD emanates from within the sacred structure to declare his intention to remain in the midst of his people (43:6–7a), but also with a warning that the people and their kings should not defile his house again (43:7b–9). This fits in with the twofold perception that his audience would have had when Ezekiel recounted his vision to them. Alongside his presentation of the ideal temple, they would also be aware of what the Jerusalem Temple had been like before it was destroyed, and it was being pointed out to them why that catastrophe had been decreed and what must be done to avert further disasters. As Ellison remarks, 'a vision of the future that does not change the present has failed in its main purpose' (1956:142), though here it is better to think of it as a vision of the ideal rather than a prophecy awaiting literal fulfilment.

> ⁴³:⁶And I heard one speaking to me from the house, while a man was standing beside me. ⁴³:⁷And he said to me, 'Son of man, ⌊this is⌋ the place of my throne and ⌊this is⌋ the place for the soles of my feet where I will reside in the midst of the sons of Israel for ever, and the house of Israel will no longer defile my holy name, they and their kings, by their harlotry and by the corpses of their kings ⌊in⌋ their high places. ⁴³:⁸When they set their threshold by my threshold and their doorpost next to my doorpost, with a wall between me and them, they would defile my holy name by their abominations which they made. So I finished them in my anger. ⁴³:⁹Now let them remove their harlotry and the corpses of their kings far from me, and I will reside in their midst for ever.'

♦ **43:6** In 2:2 Ezekiel had used almost identical wording to *and I heard one speaking to me* when the LORD addressed him directly. On this occasion also the speaker must be the LORD, especially as the voice came *from the house* into which the LORD had just entered. To prevent any mistake in the matter, Ezekiel added the circumstantial clause, *while a man was standing beside me*. The only other being who had participated so far in the vision was Ezekiel's guide, and 'a man' undoubtedly referred to him. Since he did not feature in the rest of the chapter, Ezekiel mentioned that he was 'beside me' to show that the message came directly from the LORD in the temple, and not through the mediation of the guide.

♦ **43:7** The words, *And he said to me, 'Son of man ...'*, were also those used in 2:1 (cf. 2:3; 3:1). ⌐*This is*¬⁵³ *is the place of my throne* was a classical Biblical expression of divine kingship and of the nature of the LORD's presence in the temple (1 Kgs. 8:12–13, 27). When a king set up his throne in a territory, he asserted his jurisdiction over it (cf. Jer. 43:10). *The place for the soles of my feet* was equivalent to 'my footstool' (see on 26:16; cf. Ps. 110:1; Isa. 66:1). *Where I will reside* (lit., 'which I will reside there') used the verb *šākan*, which has the same root as *miškān*, 'tabernacle'. The repetition of 'the place' and the use of 'there' focused on the LORD's royal territorial claim. This Glory-presence did not compromise the omnipresence of God in any way, but was a gracious manifestation of his dwelling *in the midst of the sons of Israel for ever.* The same promise had been expressed using different terminology in 37:26–28 where it was pledged that the sanctuary would be set in the midst of the people.

However, the divine presence in their midst would impose certain restrictions on the Israelites who would have to abjure the conduct which had so displeased God in the past. *The house of Israel will no longer defile my holy name.* 'No longer' marked the new administration of God's rule (cf. 12:24). The use of 'my holy name' (see on 36:20) was related to the promise in Deuteronomy that God would establish one sanctuary where he would 'place his name' or 'cause his name to dwell' (Deut. 12:5, 11; 14:23; 16:2, 6, 11; 26:2). But *they and their kings* alike had not respected the Temple which the LORD had been pleased to designate as his own. The two occurrences of 'kings' (plural of *melek*, cf. 7:27; 12:10; 21:25; 34:23–31) in this verse and a further instance in 43:9 were the only places where this term occurred in chapters 40–48, probably because what was in view were past events stretching back to Solomon building his palace and administrative complex next to the Temple (see Fig. 1 in Volume 1). It is significant that the people and their royal leaders were deemed to be complicit in perpetrating these acts of defilement, and so both were responsible for the judgement which befell them.

---

53. The divine speech begins with a repeated use of *'et-* in a fashion which is difficult to identify. Ezekiel employs the particle in unusual ways in 17:21; 20:16; 35:10; 44:3; 47:17–19 (GKC §117m). English translations render the particle as 'this is', possibly following the Targum. Joüon §125j(5) identifies this as one of the few passages where the particle has a strong meaning equivalent to a pronoun, and so may be translated 'Here is the place.' Keil (2002:396) and Block (1998:575) take it as an instance of the direct object marker brought forward for emphasis, with the phrases being objects of the verb 'will no longer defile'.

Their misconduct was first specified in *by their whoredom* (cf. 23:7), a term which was primarily used of spiritual infidelity through worshipping pagan gods and engaging in the rituals associated with their cult. It could also be used of illegitimate alliances with other nations, which always had religious overtones. This has been developed in chapters 16 and 23, but was of less relevance in this temple context.

The grounds for the second charge against them is less clear because a rendering such as *by the corpses of their kings ˻in˼ their high places* has not gone unchallenged, as the wide variety of English translations attest. 'Their high places' is supported by the Vulgate, Peshitta and Targum, but because there is little evidence that burial sites were associated with the high places of pagan worship (cf. 6:3, 6; 16:16; 20:29), some favour the Septuagint reading of 'in their midst', or 'in their death' as in the NRSV.[54] Otherwise, 'their high places' would be a highly sarcastic reference to the Temple precincts which they had chosen to use for this purpose and so had defiled.

One common interpretation is that what was referred to here was the presence of royal graves in, or near, the Temple. However, there is no Biblical evidence for this. Kings were buried in the city of David (1 Kgs. 2:10; 11:43), but that referred to an area well south of the Temple. Only Manasseh and Amon were reportedly buried in the garden of Uzzah, possibly in palace grounds near the Temple, but still not within it (2 Kgs. 21:18, 26).

Other possibilities include a reference to idolatrous worship since the term rendered 'corpses' (plural of *peger*; cf. 6:5) could also refer to lifeless idols (Lev. 26:30). Other meanings suggested instead of 'corpses' have included 'royal stelae', stone pillars erected in honour of the kings (Ugaritic evidence), or 'offerings for the dead' (based on Akkadian evidence). Apparently, the practice had arisen of commemorating dead kings, whether by stone monuments or by offerings, in the Temple precincts. This had contravened the line between what pertained to the dynasty and what was reserved for the LORD, as was further explored in the following verse.

♦ **43:8** Forgetfulness of the sacred nature of the Temple had been occasioned by the proximity of the royal palace to the Temple. *When they set their threshold by my threshold and their doorpost next to my doorpost.* 'They' referred to the kings, who viewed the Temple as

---

54. The LXX seems to have read *bətôkām* for *bāmôtām* (from *bāmâ*, 'high place') while the NRSV is based on reading *bəmôtām* (from *māwet*, 'death').

a royal chapel. Indeed, it had been constructed as one part of the total royal complex in Jerusalem (cf. 1 Kgs. 6–7; 11). *With a wall between me and them* referred to a wall separating the Temple from royal buildings next to it. This encroachment was remedied in the ideal temple, where there was a clear demarcation of the LORD's palace from that of any earthly ruler and its associated buildings (42:20).

In this way *they would defile[55] my holy name by their abominations which they made.* The comprehensive term, 'abominations' (cf. 5:9, 11; 33:26), summed up the total disgust with the LORD viewed their conduct. A heinous instance of such violation of the sanctity of the Temple had occurred with Manasseh's idolatrous worship of all the host of heaven in the inner and outer courtyards (2 Kgs. 21:5).

So I finished them in my anger was a variation of the expression found in 5:13. Divine patience was eventually exhausted, and judgement was imposed on the LORD's spiritually blind and obstinate vassals.

♦ **43:9** *Now* moved the focus from the behaviour of the past to what should prevail in the future. In the ideal regime characterised by the divine presence (43:7) such conduct was impermissible. It would seem that there were many who were thinking of restoration to the land as a return to the *status quo ante*. God was utterly disparaging of such a misconception.

Ezekiel's audience was exhorted not to repeat the mistakes of their forefathers, but instead to engage in immediate, urgent change of their perception of the future. *Let them remove their whoredom and the corpses of their kings far from me.* No trace of idol worship would be permitted, nor would any intrusion of human vainglory be permitted in the LORD's presence. It was not implied that the people could modify their spiritual outlook to achieve this outcome in their own strength. The declaration was intended to engender a reliance on God to engender such a disposition and to grant the strength to act on it (cf. 18:31; 36:26). To 'remove ... far' was the opposite of 'to bring near' (43:22-24), the verb used for the presentation of sacrificial offerings. True worship would require both what was appropriate to be present and what was inappropriate to be absent.

Under those conditions the divine promise would be realised: *I will reside in their midst for ever.*

---

55. The perfect verb *waṭimmǝʾû*, 'and/then they defiled', may well have habitual force.

REFLECTION

- At the dedication of the Temple, Solomon had reflected on the mode of the LORD's presence there. 'But will God indeed dwell on earth? Behold, heaven and the heaven of heavens cannot contain you; how much less this house which I have built?' (1 Kgs. 8:27). The immensity of God required that his presence was that of a projection of heavenly infinitude into an earthly setting. It was not a matter of identity or interchangeability, but of correspondence through which an analogy could be traced. Old Testament worship typified heavenly realities (Heb. 8:5; 9:23), and through it God graciously presented glimpses of his glory (cf. Exod. 33:20–23).

  But the typical ordinances of Old Testament times passed away with the incarnation of the Son who 'is the radiance of the glory of God and the exact representation of his being' (Heb. 1:3). While in New Testament times the need for physical buildings to function as a temple has completely passed away, such imagery can be used both for earthly (1 Cor. 3:16–17; 6:19; 1 Pet. 2:5) and heavenly realities (Rev. 3:12; 7:15). Hereafter, however, the truth conveyed by the ideal temple is consummated in as direct a form of presence and communication as can exist between God and glorified humanity (Rev. 21:22).

- 'The place of my throne ... the place for the soles of my feet' (43:7) present the LORD as King. Within the Holy of Holies in the Tabernacle and in the first Temple, the ark functioned as the LORD's earthly throne (1 Sam. 4:4; 2 Sam. 6:2; Ps. 80:1) and as his footstool (1 Chron. 28:2; Pss. 99:5; 132:7; Isa. 60:13; Lam. 2:1). In this ideal temple, however, no mention was made of the ark. This seems to be an intentional omission in preparation for the fuller mode of divine presence and dwelling with his people which would occur in Messianic times. Jeremiah 3:16 had promised that then the ark of the covenant would not be remembered or missed, and instead Jerusalem would become the LORD's earthly throne (Jer. 3:17). Again, this is a prevision of Christ.

(3) Ezekiel's Task (43:10–12)

The LORD also spells out the implications of the vision of the ideal temple for Ezekiel's ministry. This is done in words which reflect 40:4, and so they form an inclusion which has a bracketing effect round the intervening material. The description and the measurements of the ideal temple are not a speculative construct pandering to human curiosity. They are designed to encourage the exiles to leave the failures of the past behind and to strive to realise the spiritual possibilities that are disclosed to them.

⁴³:¹⁰⌊As for⌋ you, son of man, tell the house of Israel about the house that they may feel disgrace because of their iniquities, and that they may measure ⌊its⌋ proportions. ⁴³:¹¹And if they feel disgrace because of all that they have done, inform them ⌊about⌋ the plan of the house and its design, and its exits and its entrances, and all its plans and all its statutes, and all its plans and all its laws, and write ⌊them⌋ before their eyes so that they may observe all its plans and all its ordinances and do them.
⁴³:¹²'This ⌊is⌋ the law of the house: upon the top of the mountain all its border right round about ⌊is⌋ most holy. Behold, this ⌊is⌋ the law of the house.'

♦ **43:10** The LORD then proceeded to command Ezekiel in his prophetic role as *son of man* to *tell*[56] *the house of Israel about the house* (cf. 40:4). The vision was not primarily for his personal enlightenment, but was designed to inform and challenge his audience. Presumably, this involved more than setting before them a catalogue of its dimensions, layout, and architectural features. The prophet was to ensure that they learned the spiritual lessons which were being conveyed through this divine disclosure.

In the first place the community was to be spiritually repentant. The presentation of the vision ought to lead to a situation where *they may feel disgrace because of their iniquities.*[57] The contrast between what had prevailed in the Jerusalem Temple and what ideally was the case in the LORD's temple would sensitise their spiritual perception regarding the extent to which their conduct had deviated from the norms expected of the covenant people (for 'iniquity', see on 3:18; 4:4). A similar reaction of disgust at their own conduct was described elsewhere (16:54, 61; 36:32). The spiritually elevating disclosure of the LORD's provision would convict them of their own guilt.

But Ezekiel's communication of the vision he had received had a further end in view: *and ⌊that⌋ they may measure ⌊its⌋ proportions.*

---

56. As regards the significance of the root *nāgad* in the hiphil, Stevenson (1996:14) contends that 'the primary mode is visual rather than oral', and prefers the rendering 'describe' to 'declare' or 'tell'.

57. The result clause is expressed after the volitive 'tell' by ordinary *waw* with the imperfect (*wəyikkāləmû*, 'and let them feel disgrace'). The following verb is *waw*-consecutive perfect with the same sense (*ûmādədû*, 'and let them measure'). For the construction, see *IBHS* §39.2.2.

'Measure' was the verb which had been used for the guide's measuring. This might have been expected to have been stated first—to induce appreciation of their sinfulness as they realised the standard of perfection portrayed. However, what was described here was a subsequent, deepening appreciation grasp of its 'proportions'.[58] This term was rendered 'perfection' in 28:12. The regularity of the pattern and the symmetry of its balance were teaching a lesson about spiritual, not physical, construction. The heavenly architect had designed a structure whose layout merited continuing, close attention. If such careful shapeliness was what informed the ideal temple, the palace of their King, what should the conduct be of the subjects who professed loyalty to this monarch?

◆ **43:11** This verse expanded on the reaction described in the previous verse. The Septuagint had a substantially different text, which amongst other variations replaced the initial conditional clause with a declaration (so also the Vulgate, cf. Block 1998:586–587). However, the Massoretic Text, though unexpected, is more probable. *If they feel disgrace because of all that they have done* envisaged what should happen when they began to respond correctly to Ezekiel's message. He was to enthuse them about the details of the LORD's sovereign ideal. *Inform them*/'make them know' is brought forward in translation before the composite object whose initial position gave it stress. This instruction was a reminder of the teaching duties of prophets and priests as regards the elements of the covenant arrangements which were imposed on Israel. It also echoed the recognition formula (cf. 5:13) regarding the LORD's provision for, and requirements of, his people.

Four times use was made of the noun *plan* ($\d{s}\hat{u}r\hat{a}$), which probably referred to the total external dimensions and form of the temple, whereas *its design*[59] related rather to its internal arrangements. *Its exits and its entrances* emphasised the need for control over access to the

---

58. The LXX, Targum and Peshitta emend *toknît* to *təkûnātô*, 'its arrangement, layout'. This does not greatly affect the meaning. In place of the verb for 'measure' the LXX had 'and its appearance' (as if *ûmādədû* were *ûmiddātô*, 'and its measure') which is adopted by the RSV.

59. 'Design' renders *təkûnâ*, which comes from the root *kāwan*, which in the niphal has the sense 'to be arranged'. In the previous verse 'proportion' rendered *toknît*, which most probably comes from the root *tākan*, 'to determine according to size or weight', so there was a wordplay involved in the use of the terms.

sacred structure so that only authorised persons and personnel could enter the various zones (cf. Rev. 22:14). The highly repetitive *all its plans and all its statutes, and all its plans and all its laws*[60] stressed the need for comprehensive observance of due order. 'Statutes' were permanent ordinances prescribed by the LORD (cf. 5:6), whereas 'laws' tended to be a wider category covering all covenant requirements, moral and ceremonial.

Write ⌊them⌋ before their eyes showed that the prophet was not only to engage in oral teaching but also to leave the legacy which now exists in this book. The prophet's record was not to be hidden, but was to be an accessible reminder so that his ministry of persuasion would extend to subsequent generations. *So that they may observe all its plans and all its statutes and do them.* This was not a command to build this temple structure—something that the Jews never attempted—but to 'observe all its plans', that is, to contemplate the significance of what had been revealed with a view to complying with the teaching embodied in them.

♦ **43:12** *This ⌊is⌋ the law of the house* was not a new covenant, but a renewal of the law first given to Israel. Its requirements had been respected by Solomon with certain adaptations, and in this ideal order some further modifications were introduced, but much remained the same. The aspect which was emphasised here was the separation required round about the temple. *Upon the top of the mountain all its border right round about ⌊is⌋ most holy.* It is improbable that this anticipated the open space of 50 cubits about the temple (45:2). The border demarcated by the wall (40:5) stood by synecdoche for the whole temple area which was separated off from the secular and common. 'Most holy' (*qōdeš qādāšîm*) was a similar expression to that for the Holy of Holies (cf. 41:4), so that the status of the whole temple complex was determined by its most holy area.

Behold, this ⌊is⌋ the law of the house. This may be a conclusion or a title to the following section. Similar phrases in Leviticus were used both to introduce (e.g., Lev. 6:9, 14, 25) and to conclude legislation (e.g., Lev. 7:37; 11:46). On balance, a concluding formula is more probable.

---

60. There are two qere/kethib variations in which the qere substitutes the normal form of a third masculine singular suffix to a plural noun (*ṣûrōtāyw* ... *tôrōtāyw*) for the defective spelling found in the kethib, but this does not affect the meaning, 'its plans ... its laws'.

REFLECTION

- 'Feel disgrace because of their iniquities' (43:10) denotes an aspect of repentance and new spiritual life. What is significant here is that this would be induced not by a depiction of their past conduct to bring out how base it had been. Instead, their changed perception of themselves would result from consideration of the ideal which the LORD set before them. In the light of its purity and perfection, the darkness of their own former conduct would become evident. In many respects this reflects Isaiah's 'Woe is me!' on hearing the angelic choir and seeing the enthroned Lord (Isa. 6:5), or Simon Peter's reaction to Christ, 'Depart from me, for I am a sinful man, O Lord' (Luke 5:8). It was not through a word of condemnation that they were convicted of sin, but by a display of holiness, power, and goodness.
- What in New Testament times corresponds to 'the law of the house' (43:12)? Paul uses the temple analogy to regulate Christian conduct both individually and collectively. Individually, the fact of the Spirit indwelling the body of the believer renders it a temple (1 Cor. 6:19), and that is sufficient motivation for avoiding sexually immoral conduct. The church collectively is a temple through the presence of God's Spirit, and therefore each should take care to build up that temple and not deface it (1 Cor. 3:10–17). The affairs of a congregation should be conducted to nurture it and bring glory to Christ. For instance, it is his presence with his people which alone validates and gives substance to any corporate act of worship, and that necessitates that such worship should be performed in a way that pleases him. There is an abiding reality to the regulative principle which requires that there should be no element of a service which he has not sanctioned. Moreover, while the external aspects of worship are in measure secondary, even they are not to be reckoned as indifferent. The question should always be, What does Christ think of this?

C. Ordinances for Temple Worship (43:13–46:24)

The ideal temple has been scrutinised and the divine Glory-presence has again resumed occupancy of the Holy of Holies. But the temple is not merely a residence; it is a king's palace—what of his subjects? More than that, this King is God—what of his worshippers? In the preceding verses there is the ominous reminder of their need to repent and to 'feel disgrace because of their iniquities ... because of all they have done' (43:10, 11). So here attention turns towards the means by which they may appropriately approach the King in their midst without being repulsed. At the altar they may seek and obtain divine forgiveness for offences they have committed against him.

In the earlier part of Ezekiel's tour little attention is paid to the equipment of the temple, with the exception of the tables for preparing sacrifices (40:39–43), the sacrificial altar (40:47), and of the altar-like table of 41:22. Similarly, not much is said about temple personnel. Now the sacrificial altar is described in detail (43:13–17), and instructions are given for its consecration (43:18–27). After a brief narrative concerning the closure of the east gateway (44:1–3), previous violations of the Temple are exposed (44:4–8) before consideration is given to the priesthood (44:9–31). Ezekiel's visionary vista is then extended to include the apportionment of the land (45:1–8), a theme taken up in greater detail in 47:13–48:29. Attention is also paid to the practicalities of administering justice among the covenant people (45:9–17), the conduct of the major festivals (45:18–25), and of the minor festivals and the prerogatives of the ruler (46:1–18). There is a concluding resumption of the temple tour to visit and describe the kitchens found in the sacred compound (46:19–24).

The arrangements incorporated in Ezekiel's vision of chapters 40–48 differ in various places from those instituted in the Pentateuch, and that divergence is quite noticeable in this section. Many of the sacrifices and rites prescribed for the major festivals in 45:21–25 depart from Pentateuchal precedents, as do those set out for the minor festivals in 46:1–15. For instance, the daily sacrifice is to be offered only in the morning (cf. 46:13–15 in contrast to Num. 28:1–8). There are also noticeable absences from Ezekiel's account. There are no references to the ark, the lampstand or the incense altar. So the ideal temple is described in a fashion which lies part way between the earlier Tabernacle of Moses and the Temple of Solomon, and the final heavenly realisation of all they foreshadowed, as portrayed in the new Jerusalem of Revelation 21, where the limitations of temple structures are done away with, and all live in the presence of God and of the Lamb, and are illumined by them (Rev. 21:22–23).

(1) The Altar of Burnt Offering (43:13–27)
In the ideal temple there are two foci: the Holy of Holies where the Glory-presence dwells, and the altar. Though it is never explicitly stated, it is evident that the altar lies at the centre of the inner courtyard, and consequently of the whole sacred precinct (Fig. 2 N).

For the situation of the altar in relation to the land as a whole, see on 45:1–8. Zimmerli (1983:355) argues that the focus of the temple area is in fact the Holy of Holies. There is a measure of truth in that, but it is better to adopt the view of Stevenson that 'there are two most holy locations in the spatial layout of the House of YHWH' (1996:40). These arrangements make clear that Israel's well-being requires more than the presence of the LORD in their midst; there must also be a means of cleansing the people from impurity so that they can be accepted. The altar, through the sacrifices offered on it, provides for the atonement of sin and for reconciliation with the divine King.

Ezekiel has earlier noted the location of the altar (40:47), and he now describes it (43:13–17) and the rites associated with its consecration (43:18–27). It is noteworthy that in this section there is no mention of Ezekiel's guide, or of the Glory-presence, so recently returned to the temple. More is said about the altar's height than about that of any other artefact.

Altar and Sacrifices. The existence of these features constitutes a major hermeneutical crux for interpreters, especially for those who insist that this altar will be physically embodied on earth. If the new temple has not yet been built, then such literal sacrifices as are described here must be offered after the death of Christ. To maintain that there will ever be circumstances in which the Levitical sacrifices will be reinstituted runs totally counter to the evidence of the New Testament, and especially of Hebrews. Christ has now offered the definitive and final sacrifice, and to introduce sacrifices of any sort— and particularly if they are blood sacrifices—is to challenge and depreciate what he has accomplished. Furthermore, to contend that they are to be thought of as memorials which look retrospectively to the cross breaches an absolutely literal hermeneutic because that is to reinstitute sacrifices with the same name but with a different function. If that were to be the case, the sacrifices and the altar would no longer 'literally' be the same referents as those Ezekiel and his original audience would have understood them to be. Rather these arrangements speak to them and to us because they presented fundamental, underlying spiritual truths in terms that were then accessible to the prophet and his hearers.

(a) The Dimensions of the Altar (43:13–17)
This paragraph describes the altar God himself has provided; it does not prescribe how it should be built. There are no verbs in the Hebrew

text here, and translators into English divulge their interpretation of the passage by the supplements they use. For instance, 'shall be' (ESV) presupposes that there was yet to be built an altar corresponding to this description. Instead the Hebrew style suggests that this is a catalogue of what Ezekiel saw before him in the vision, and there is no implication that it existed, or would exist, in any other form. The text is not divine speech, and the verbal supplements in this paragraph are added in the past tense on the basis that this is Ezekiel's account of what had been revealed to him.

The altar's form possesses a symmetry which matches that of the temple complex as a whole. The exact significance of many of the technical terms employed has been lost over time, and consequently details of any reconstruction of the altar are correspondingly tentative. But the key message is clear. While the LORD's presence is indispensable for the temple to function as a place of worship, there must, in terms of the typical rituals of Old Testament worship, be a duly dedicated altar so that those who approach the LORD may do so in an authorised and acceptable manner. The extensive detail presented by Ezekiel emphasises the importance of the role the altar plays in the functioning of the ideal temple. The description is in two parts, 43:13–15, 16–17.

> ⁴³:¹³ʼAnd these ⌊were⌋ the measurements of the altar in cubits (the cubit ⌊was⌋ a cubit and an handbreadth): ⌊its⌋ trench ⌊was⌋ a cubit, and a cubit ⌊its⌋ breadth, and its border about its edge round about ⌊was⌋ a span; and this ⌊was⌋ the base of the altar. ⁴³:¹⁴From the trench on the ground as far as the lower retaining wall ⌊was⌋ two cubits, and ⌊its⌋ breadth one cubit; and from the small retaining wall as far as the large retaining wall ⌊was⌋ four cubits, and ⌊its⌋ breadth, a cubit. ⁴³:¹⁵And the altar-hearth ⌊was⌋ four cubits, and from the altar-hearth ⌊were⌋ four horns. ⁴³:¹⁶And the altar-hearth ⌊was⌋ twelve cubits long by twelve cubits ⌊in⌋ breadth, foursquare at its four corners. ⁴³:¹⁷And the retaining wall ⌊was⌋ fourteen ⌊cubits⌋ in length by fourteen ⌊cubits⌋ in breadth on its four sides, and the border around it ⌊was⌋ half a cubit, and its trench—a cubit round about; and its steps ⌊were⌋ facing east.

♦ **43:13** The transition from the preceding material was abrupt even if the last clause of 43:12 was a heading to this section. Ezekiel proceeded to give *the measurements of the altar in cubits*, and again repeated the information given in 40:5 that *the cubit ⌊was⌋ a cubit and an handbreadth*, that is, not the ordinary cubit.

The term *trench* (*ḥêq*),[61] which normally means 'bosom' or 'lap', is rendered 'base' in many translations. However, since the lap was viewed as a hollow which could be used to contain material (e.g., Prov. 16:33), it is more probable that this was a gutter round the base of the altar, presumably to catch anything which might spill from the top (Fig. 7 a).[62] *⌊Its⌋ trench ⌊was⌋ a cubit* (lit., 'the cubit') referred to the depth of the gutter, and *a cubit ⌊its⌋ breadth* rendered it of square cross-section. *Its border* (that is, of the trench; cf. 40:12) was a rim about the trench which demarcated the sacred area and provided additional protection against spillage (Fig. 7 b). This extended for *round about* for *a span* on every side of the altar, seemingly as a horizontal piece of the stonework forming the base of the altar.

This ⌊was⌋ the base (*gab*) *of the altar* is often changed, following the Septuagint, into 'the height of the altar' (*gōbah*),[63] and taken with the following verse. Following Dijkstra (1992:28) it is more plausible to take it as referring to the substructure of the altar (Fig. 7 c).

♦ **43:14** The altar was built up in tiers, but the details are unclear, especially the meaning of *ʿăzārâ*, here rendered 'retaining wall', probably a wall of uncut stone to support the altar's superstructure to keep it from collapsing outwards. The interior of the altar would be filled with soil.

The description of the height of the altar started with the distance *from the trench on the ground*, probably from ground level at the border round its edge, and extended *as far as the retaining wall*, that is, to its upper level, a distance which amounted to *two cubits*, where there was a ledge of *one cubit*. Ezekiel then noted that *from the small retaining wall to the large retaining wall* (Fig. 7 d, e), there was a rise of *four cubits*, where again the breadth of the wall formed a ledge one cubit wide.

♦ **43:15** *And the altar-hearth* (Fig. 7 f) represents one term, *harʾēl*,

---

61. The Vulgate and Peshitta divide the words differently, apparently reading *wəḥêqōh ʾammâ*, 'and its gutter ⌊is⌋ a cubit', rather than the somewhat improbable *wəḥêq hāʾammâ*, 'and gutter ⌊is⌋ the cubit'.

62. This understanding may be supported by 1 Kgs. 22:35 where the term probably denotes the shallow lower floor of Ahab's chariot within which his blood collected.

63. Block (1998:592) argues that the text underlying the LXX had wrongly reduplicated the initial *hē* of *hammizbēaḥ*, 'the altar', and it had become attached to the *gab*, 'back'. This would have led to the reading *gōbah*, 'height'. As the harder, but not unintelligible, reading, *gab* is to be preferred.

though subsequent occurrences in this and the following verse were spelled differently.[64] The Septuagint and the Vulgate transliterated the term in all three instances, but it apparently designated the area on the top surface of the altar where the sacrifices were burned. The hearth was *four cubits* higher than the tier below it (43:14b) so that it was flush with the top edge of the retaining wall. However, the overall height of the hearth was further increased by the presence of *four horns* found at its corners (Fig. 7 g). Such projections had also been part of the altar of burnt offering (Exod. 29:12; Lev. 4:25; 16:18) and of the incense altar (Lev. 4:7, 18). Archaeology has established that this feature was common in ancient Near Eastern altars in general. The horns apparently served to keep the sacrifice from falling off the hearth as it burned, but also had a key purificatory role in various sacrificial rites in which they were smeared with blood as part of the stated ritual (see preceding references).

♦ **43:16** The second part of the description of the altar (43:16–17) is often taken as presenting dimensions moving downwards from the top of the altar. However, if that were so, there was the surprising omission of the dimensions of the base, as well as other problems in understanding terms in 43:17. There is therefore some plausibility in Dijkstra's proposal that these were the dimensions of the arrangements at the top level of the altar (1992:29–30).

The horizontal dimensions of the ***altar-hearth*** were first given as ***twelve cubits long by twelve cubits ⌞in⌟ breadth***, which indicated something of the massive size of this structure being equivalent to 20.3 feet (6.24 m) square. Its square shape when seen from above was emphasised by the description, ***foursquare at its four corners*** (lit., 'a square to four of its four'). So the altar-hearth conformed to the basic square paradigm employed throughout the temple complex for what was most holy.

♦ **43:17** ***And the retaining wall ⌞was⌟ fourteen ⌞cubits⌟ in length by fourteen ⌞cubits⌟ in breadth on its four sides***, where 'its' was a feminine form referring to the retaining wall. In terms of the reconstruction offered here the retaining wall rose to the level of the altar-hearth, so that there was a width of a cubit of the wall

---

64. Indeed the following occurrences are themselves spelled in two ways, with a kethib *'ărī'êl*, and a qere *'ărî'ēl*. Both forms may mean 'lion (*'ărî*) of God (*'ēl*)', or if there is a root *'ārâ*, 'to burn', 'fire/hearth of God', in which case the final *lamedh* is simply a nominal afformative.

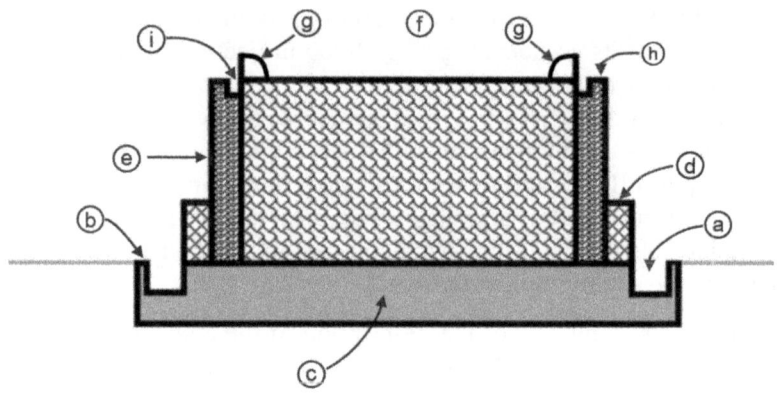

ⓐ	Trench	43:13
ⓑ	Border	43:13
ⓒ	Base	43:13
ⓓ	Small retaining wall	43:14
ⓔ	Large retaining wall	43:14
ⓕ	Altar-hearth	43:15
ⓖ	Horns	43:15
ⓗ	Upper border	43:17
ⓘ	Upper trench	43:17

Figure 7. North–South Cross-section of the Altar.

surrounding the hearth (43:14) which lay within it. Since it here stated that ***the border around it ⌞was⌟ of half a cubit***, it would appear that the top ledge of the upper retaining wall was comprised of the border ***and its trench***, which together measured ***a cubit round about*** (Fig. 6 h, i). This reconstruction, which is based on that proposed by Dijkstra (1992), resolves a number of conundrums, but is still conjectural in many respects. The trench would help prevent material falling off the hearth in a fashion similar to the horns, but would do so even more effectively because it stretched all round the top surface and not just at the corners. It would also channel away any liquids flowing from the burning sacrifice, and it was presumably connected to the lower trench to facilitate this.

In total the altar was 6 cubits high, ignoring the height of the horns, with a base 14 cubits square, or 16 cubits and 2 hands if the substructure was included. Its massive size is not perhaps evident until these figures are expressed in modern units: a height of 10.15 feet (3.12 m) and its base either 23.7 feet (7.3 m) or 27.6 feet (8.5 m) square.

The final clause, ***and its steps***[65] ***⌞were⌟ facing***[66] ***east***, referred to the altar (both 'its' and 'altar' were masculine forms). The existence of steps (Fig. 2 N) raises questions since Exodus 20:26 prohibited steps to ascend the altar, but the portable altar at the Tabernacle had only been three cubits high (4.5 feet, 1.4 m; Exod. 27:1). In Solomon's Temple (2 Chron. 4:1) the altar was ten cubits (17 feet; 5.2 m) high, so that some means of reaching the hearth was required. The presence of the steps on the east meant that when a priest sacrificed he would always be facing the presence chamber of the LORD in the Holy of Holies (contrast the orientation of the sun worshippers in 8:16). It is improbable that the steps stretched along the whole of the east side of the altar, and their highest step would be below the level of the altar-hearth so as to permit the priest who stood on the top step to work at the altar without strain.

(b) The Consecration of the Altar (43:18–27)

Ezekiel has been shown the altar which was divinely prepared, but it is not yet an altar which is in use. Before that can happen, the altar has to

---

65. The form *ûmaʿălōtēhû* has a unique third masculine singular suffix for a feminine plural noun, but the suffix does occur elsewhere with masculine nouns (Joüon §94i).

66. 'Facing' assumes the form to have been a participle *pōnôt*, though the Massoretic text reads an infinitive construct *pənôt*.

be consecrated. This had also taken place with its predecessors, and over a duration of seven days (43:25; Exod. 29:37; 1 Kgs. 8:65).

In giving all these visionary instructions, the LORD directly addressed Ezekiel, according him a status reminiscent of that of Moses, who had been in charge of the construction of the Tabernacle and who, more especially, had been responsible for initiating the priests into their sacred duties (Lev. 8–9).

> ⁴³:¹⁸And he said to me, 'Son of man, thus says the Lord GOD: These ⌊are⌋ the statutes of the altar in the day when it is made to offer burnt offerings upon it and to sprinkle blood upon it. ⁴³:¹⁹And you are to give to the priests the Levites, who are of the offspring of Zadok, who draw near me, declares the Lord GOD, to minister to me, a bull from the herd, for a sin offering. ⁴³:²⁰And you are to take some of its blood and to set ⌊it⌋ upon its four horns and on the four corners of its ledge and on the border round about, and you are to purify it and to make atonement for it. ⁴³:²¹And you are to take the bull for the sin offering and it is to be burned in the appointed part of the house, outside the sanctuary. ⁴³:²²And on the second day you are to offer a male goat without blemish, as a sin offering, and they are to purify the altar just as they purified ⌊it⌋ with the bull. ⁴³:²³When you have finished purifying ⌊it⌋, you are to offer a bull from the herd without blemish and a ram from the flock without blemish. ⁴³:²⁴And you are to offer them before the LORD, and the priests are to throw salt upon them, and to offer them as a burnt offering to the LORD. ⁴³:²⁵For seven days you are daily to make a goat for a sin offering and a bull from the herd and a ram from the flock, ⌊both⌋ without blemish, they will make. ⁴³:²⁶For seven days they are to make atonement for the altar and to cleanse it and to dedicate it. ⁴³:²⁷And when they finish the days, it will come about on the eighth day and thereafter that the priests will make upon the altar your burnt offerings and your peace offerings, and I will accept you, declares the Lord GOD.'

♦ **43:18** The beginning of a new paragraph was indicated here by the direct address to the prophet, ***Son of man***, the messenger formula, ***thus says the Lord GOD***, and the introductory formula, ***These ⌊are⌋ the statutes***. The unit ran on to 43:27 where the signature formula indicated a conclusion. In transmitting these practical directions to the priests Ezekiel functioned like Moses (Lev. 8–9).

And he said to me lacked a stated subject. It was most probably the LORD himself speaking directly to the prophet, though it is possible that these regulations were conveyed through the guide, who had earlier addressed Ezekiel as 'son of man' (40:4) and who might now have used the messenger formula to assure Ezekiel that he was faithfully relaying the dictates of God.

The statutes of the altar in the day when it is made related to the requirements to be followed when the divinely provided altar was 'made', that is, rendered operational by being consecrated through Ezekiel's action in the vision.[67] The altar was designed to function in two main ways: ***to offer burnt offerings upon it and to sprinkle blood upon it.*** For the regulations regarding the burnt offering, see Leviticus 1:3–5. Sprinkling blood was a way of referring to atonement through sacrifice (cf. 36:25; 1 Pet. 1:2).

♦ **43:19** The imperfect Hebrew verb expressed the resolve of a superior (Introduction §6.3a), and throughout this passage this is brought out by using the rendering 'You are to …' in the speech of the divine legislator. However, these verbs were singular in number. While this might have been a generalising idiom ('each one of you', 'you whoever you are'), in this context they seem to have referred to the prophet in the role accorded him of instituting the worship of the ideal temple.

Ezekiel was directed ***to give to the priests the Levites.*** All legitimate priests were Levites in that they members of the tribe of Levi. But there was a further limitation as regards service at the altar of the LORD. As in 40:46, this was restricted to those ***who are of the offspring of Zadok.*** For further information regarding Zadok, see on 44:15. His descendents were the ones who were recognised as those ***who draw near to me.*** As in the description of 42:13, this referred to the priests who had the privilege of offering the sacrifices on the altar, and entering into the sacred building. The use of the signature formula, ***declares the Lord GOD***, as well as its unusual position in the middle of a sentence, highlighted the solemnity of such action as well as affirming the Zadokites' prerogative in the matter.

Ezekiel was to present the sacrificial victim to the recognised priests so that they might ***minister to me***, that is, engage in the designated rituals of the sanctuary. Specifically, he was to give ***a bull from the herd*** (lit., 'a bull, son of herd'; cf. 43:23, 25; 45:18; 46:6). The seemingly redundant stipulation emphasised how carefully the sacrificial requirements were to be adhered to. ***For a sin offering*** (see

---

67. The sense 'becomes operational' is within the range of ʿāśâ, and particularly its niphal (cf. 'prepared for use', *HALOT* 890–891).

on 40:39) showed that the ritual to be enacted was one which removed the defilement caused by sin.

♦ **43:20** The divine directive required the bull to be slain by the other priests, after which Ezekiel, in his superintending role on this occasion, was *to take some of its blood* and perform the priestly function of manipulating the blood. *Set* renders the verb usually glossed as 'to give' (*nātan*). While this verb had a wide range of meaning, in ritual texts it denoted a very deliberate action by which blood or another substance was put in a specific location by daubing or smearing (Gilders 2004:27). In this instance the blood was applied to the altar *upon its four horns and on the four corners of its ledge and on the border round about.* These extremities were selected to represent the whole altar. Probably 'its ledge' referred to the upper ledge, while 'the border round about' was the lower ledge. It is not evident how the horns and corners on the west side of the altar were to be reached.

To modern ears *you are to purify it* seems an odd result of smearing these parts of the altar with blood. However, 'purify' (*ḥāṭāʾ* piel; cf. 'cleanse', 43:26) might more literally be rendered 'de-sin', that is, decontaminate the altar by counteracting the impact of sin on it. *To make atonement for it* signified through the blood of the slain animal that the price had been paid as a penalty for sin (cf. 16:63).

If Ezekiel had experienced frustration and regret that the circumstances of his life had prevented him from ministering at the altar of the Temple, here was compensation in being accorded this key role in consecrating the ideal order which was initiated in his vision.

♦ **43:21** *The bull for the sin offering* was explicitly distinguished from the animal later used in the burnt offering (43:23–24). In ordinary circumstances the flesh of the victim in a sin offering was made available to the priests for consumption (cf. 42:13; 44:29), but in this dedicatory offering other arrangements were to prevail (cf. Exod. 29:14; Lev. 8:17). *It is to be burned* was literally 'and he/one is to burn it' with no specified subject so that a passive construction is preferable in English. Generally this would have been carried out by the priest who offering the sacrifice, but here it might have been intended that Ezekiel himself do so.

Under the Mosaic ritual, if a sin offering was for a priest himself or for the entire congregation, the carcass would be burned outside the camp (Lev. 4:12, 21), and something similar seems to have been involved here. The significance of *in the appointed place of the house* is uncertain. The noun rendered 'appointed place' (*mipqād*) certainly conveyed the idea of authoritative designation by a superior, but it is less certain if the reference is to personnel or to a location. Block argues that this was a duty to be carried out by the duly appointed temple guards (1998:608–609), but the ancient versions and modern translators, probably influenced by the Muster Gate (*šaʿar hammipqād*, Neh. 3:31), favour a place. It was *outside the sanctuary* (*miqdāš*, 'holy place'), with the term being used in an extended sense for the entire temple complex (see on 44:1), as indeed the term, 'the house', was here also (cf. 40:5). So the burning probably took place at an external guardpost or muster point for the temple outwith the temple wall.

♦ **43:22** An unusual aspect of this description was that only in connection with *the second day* was it mentioned that Ezekiel was *to offer a male goat without blemish, as a sin offering* (see on 43:25). 'A male goat' was literally 'a he-goat of the goats', a somewhat redundant expression similar to 'a son of a herd' (43:19). 'Without blemish' was a standing requirement for all sacrificial animals, although it was not specifically mentioned in 43:19. *They will purify the altar just as they purified ⌐it¬ with the bull.* Again the plural subjects were not specified, but it would seem to refer to the priests who carried out this visionary ritual to effect cleansing (see on 43:21).

♦ **43:23** *When you have finished purifying ⌐it¬* referred to the sprinkling of the blood of the sin offerings on the altar. After this, Ezekiel was to *offer a bull from the herd* (see on 43:21) which was now specifically described as *without blemish* as was *a ram from the flock*. As the following verse made clear, they were offered as burnt offerings.

♦ **43:24** This verse is notable for illustrating the distinct and consecutive roles played by the offerer and the priest in connection with Old Testament sacrifice.

(1) *You are to offer them before the LORD* specified Ezekiel's role regarding these burnt offerings as that of presenting or bringing near these animals for sacrifice.

(2) Then the priests were envisaged as taking over for the sacrificial ritual itself. *The priests are to throw salt on them.* This feature was not mentioned above. Indeed Leviticus said nothing about the addition of salt to burnt offerings, though it was required for grain offerings (Lev. 2:13), and perhaps more generally. The purifying and preservative qualities of salt made it an appropriate symbol for the

perpetuity of the covenant arrangements (cf. Num. 18:19; 2 Chron. 13:5). 'Throw' rather than 'sprinkle' probably suggested the use of copious amounts. In this way the priests were also said *to offer them as a burnt offering to the LORD.*

♦ **43:25** The process of consecration lasted *for seven days* and involved execution of the same ritual *daily*. Ezekiel as the offerer was *to make a goat for a sin offering and a bull from the herd and a ram from the flock.* 'Make ... for' was a variant expression for sacrificing, which was employed also in the final verb, *they will make,* where the plural reference was to the priests as the officiants in the sacrificial process. All the sacrifices (the bull and the goat for sin offerings in 43:19–22, and the bull and ram for a burnt offering in 43:23–24) were to be offered on each of the seven days. The spreading of the elements of the ritual over two days as in the description of 43:22 was merely a literary technique for setting out an arrangement which would be carried out sequentially.

♦ **43:26** This verse complemented the preceding account to emphasise that the process of consecration lasted *for seven days* during which time the priests *are to make atonement for the altar* (cf. 43:20).[68] *Cleanse it* (*ṭāhēr*) represented a term used earlier for the purification the LORD effected on the Israelites (cf. 36:25, 33; 37:23). Here it denoted the removal of any defilement caused by sin.

The third activity the priests were to engage in was *to dedicate it.* This use of this idiom was surprising in connection with the altar, for it was literally 'and they are to fill his/its hand',[69] and was employed in relation to the ordination of priests (Exod. 28:41; 29:9, 29, 33, 35; Lev. 8:33; 16:32; 21:10). It seems to have had regard to filling their hands with the portions of the sacrifices allotted to them, and it could be used of installing others into office and bestowing the right to receive its perquisites (cf. Exod. 32:29 with respect to the Levites;

---

68. The MT has an imperfect form here, *yəkappərû*, 'they are to make atonement', but many Hebrew manuscripts (supported by LXX and Peshitta) have a perfect with the conjunction, *wəkippərû*, 'and they will make atonement'. If that reading is followed the last word of 43:25 verse should be taken as the first word of 43:26 to yield, '⌐So⌐ they will do for seven days and they will make atonement'.

69. The kethib has *yādô*, 'his hand', whereas the qere has *yādāyw*, 'his hands'. The idiom for priestly ordination always has a singular, but with either reading the reference is to the altar. The LXX and Targum use a plural 'their hands' as if it was a priestly ordination that was being described (cf. AV).

1 Chron. 29:5 and 2 Chron. 29:31 with respect to the whole assembly of Israel). The altar would thus seem to have been personified and the sacrifices offered to have been regarded as sufficient to render it fit to accomplish its divinely intended purpose.

♦ **43:27** *When they finish the days, it will come about on the eighth day and thereafter* (cf. 39:22) marked the end of the seven days of consecration and the beginning of the stated ritual of the temple and altar which was to be observed from that point onwards. It would then be competent for *the priests* to undertake the sacral routines *upon the altar* which was at the centre of the ceremonies of the ideal temple. Significantly *your burnt offerings and your peace offerings* were expressed using the plural pronoun 'your', as was the following *I will accept you* (cf. 43:19). What was in view was the acceptable worship of the covenant community as a whole. The combination of burnt offerings, dedicated wholly to the LORD, and peace offerings (see on 39:17; 40:39), where there was a sacred meal in which the worshippers participated, represented both aspects of the fellowship which would be promoted by this ideal arrangement.

And I will accept you,[70] *declares the Lord GOD* set out the ultimate goal of God that he and his people should be reconciled through the sacrifices offered. In this Old Testament vision of the ideal covenant community the expressions used were derived from the divine arrangements which had been instituted to teach the people spiritual truths. God would look favourably on the worship offered in accordance with his revealed will but, even so, these things were still merely 'a shadow of the good things to come' (Heb. 10:1). The rituals had anticipated the coming of Christ and the completion of his work. Now that has been achieved in his once for all, final sacrifice, the external rites are obsolete, but the truths which they embodied are gloriously and perfectly finalised in Christ.

REFLECTION

• Once more there are differences of interpretation regarding the precise dimensions or shape of what is described, but they are not of prime importance, though it is relevant to note the altar's substantial size and prominent position. What is key to understanding the section is the theological significance of the altar.

Throughout the ancient world altars could, and did, exist without

---

70. The verb *wərāṣiʾtî* is an Aramaic spelling with *aleph* of *wərāṣîtî*, 'and I will accept'.

a temple, but there was no temple without an altar. Ceremonies to initiate or maintain an appropriate relationship with a god required an altar so that sacrifices could be transformed and sent heavenwards. In this way ancient pagan religions retained something of the early teaching of mankind after the flood (Gen. 8:20–23), though many false ideas accumulated round the practice over the centuries.

The Hebrew term for 'altar' (a sacrifice-place or apparatus) signified a structure on which a sacrifice was offered up to deity. Even so altars could be erected merely as memorials, most notably the altar of witness (Josh. 22:26–27). The patriarchs also erected altars (e.g., Gen. 13:7) to commemorate divine appearances, though in those cases they probably did later sacrifice there. Undoubtedly being used for sacrifice was the dominant function of an altar.

Here in the ideal temple the altar is at the centre of the temple complex, facing the temple itself and the Holy of Holies because sinful mankind cannot present themselves acceptably before the holy and morally perfect God until their sin and rebellion have been atoned for. God cannot brush sin aside as if it is a minor matter. His moral integrity and the moral fabric of this universe he has created require that the dire penalty incurred by sin be paid. This was taught in Old Testament through the blood sacrifices which were instituted. But such sacrifices and an altar has now been superseded by 'the offering of the body of Jesus Christ once for all' (Heb. 10:10).

(2) Closure of the East Gateway (44:1–3)

Ezekiel's vision had started off as a tour of the temple precincts, but initially it had been of a static, non-functioning institution (chs. 40–42). That changed with the return of the Glory-presence and the dedication of the altar (ch. 43). Now two further aspects of the operation of the ideal temple are set out: the closure of the east gateway (44:1–2), and the ruler's role in the worship of the temple (44:3).

> 44:1 And he brought me back by way of the outer gateway of the sanctuary, which faces east, and it was shut. 44:2 And the LORD said to me, 'This gateway is to remain shut; it is not to be opened; and no one is to enter by it for the LORD, the God of Israel, has entered by it, and it is to remain shut. 44:3 As for the ruler, he, the ruler, is to sit in it to eat bread before the LORD; by way of the vestibule of the gateway he is to come in, and by its way he is to go out.'

♦ **44:1** Ezekiel had last recorded his location as the inner courtyard (43:5; Fig. 7 ②), probably close to the altar. *And he brought me back*[71] indicated the resumption of his temple tour and, though Ezekiel did not make it clear that it was his heavenly guide who conducted him, that was most probably the case. Here the guidance formula (see on 40:2) took the form of the hiphil of *šûb*, 'to cause to go back' but, though Ezekiel was escorted *by way of the outer gateway of the sanctuary, which faces east*, when he entered the gateway from the inner (vestibule) end and passed through the gateway moving east, he could not exit because *it was shut.* This referred to the gate at the outer end of the gateway (Fig. 7 ③).

The term 'sanctuary' (*miqdāš*; cf. 43:21) was the prevalent designation for the entire temple complex in this chapter (cf. 44:5, 7, 8, 9, 11, 15, 16) and in the remainder of this section (45:3, 4, 18; 47:12; 48:8, 10, 21), as the place designated and set apart for the divine presence. With the return of the Glory-presence the King was in residence in the temple, which was fulfilling in its intended function.

♦ **44:2** The initial words of the verse were set out in an unusual order (repeated in 44:5), literally, 'and he said to me—the LORD'. This threw emphasis on who it was that was talking, even though the LORD might have been addressing these words through the guiding angel. The absence of 'son of man' in speaking to Ezekiel is to be accounted for by the fact that description follows, rather than a command to the prophet. The status of the LORD was further brought out by the use (only here in Ezekiel) of the full formula, *the LORD, the God of Israel*, which emphasised the exalted status and majesty of the covenant King even though he had graciously taken up residence with his people.

Although *this gateway is to remain shut* was literally 'it will be shut',[72] this did not refer to a future act of closure. The gate had already been closed, and God ordained that it was *not to be opened*. This was not merely a mark of respect to avoid the desecration of the gate by its being used by others *to enter by it, for the LORD, the God of Israel, has entered by it.* It was also a sign that the LORD had no

---

71. In this instance the guidance formula uses the object marker with a pronominal suffix rather than attaching the pronominal suffix directly to the verb. This is merely a stylistic variation.

72. The expression *sāgûr yihyeh* with the passive participle and the imperfect of *hāyâ*, 'to be', expresses the durative aspect of the future (Joüon §121e): 'it will be in a state of having been shut'. Indeed, the imperfect may also have commanding force: 'it must remain shut' (Joüon §113m).

intention of exiting the temple. This circumstance might have incorporated an element of polemic against a Babylonian New Year ritual in which a temple gate that was normally closed was opened to permit the god Marduk's image to be taken out of the compound and then processionally to re-enter it. Whether that comparison was intended or not, the east outer gate was *to remain shut*. Of this ideal temple the LORD truly could say, 'This ⌞is⌟ my resting place for evermore; here I will dwell, for I have desired it' (Ps. 132:14).

♦ **44:3** A switch of focus was then clearly signalled: *As for*[73] *the ruler, he, the ruler.* This was the first occurrence in this vision of a figure who was repeatedly mentioned in subsequent chapters (45:7–9, 16–17, 22; 46:2, 4, 8, 10, 12, 16–18; 48:21–22), but whose precise status was somewhat elusive.

The term 'ruler' (*nāśîʾ*), often rendered 'prince' or 'leader' (cf. 12:10), occurred 128 times in the Old Testament, of which 37 were in Ezekiel, 62 in Numbers, 9 in the rest of the Pentateuch, 13 in Joshua, 2 in Kings, 6 in Chronicles and 1 in Ezra.[74] Outside of Ezekiel the term occurs mainly in descriptions of the pre-monarchic period for recognised chieftains figures who represented their clan or tribe in political and military matters. Under the monarchy the rulers constituted a separate body alongside the king (1 Kgs. 8:1), but with much reduced responsibilities. Though a ruler need not be a king, the king of a small nation might readily be termed a ruler (cf. 26:16).

Ezekiel exhibited a preference for the term 'ruler' to describe Israel's kings, particularly the final kings of Judah (cf. 12:10), probably to bring out their subordination as vassal kings to one emperor or another. A similar notion was apparently involved in the use of the term in this ideal vision. The figure being described was 'a ruler with limited authority, genuinely representative of the people' (Duguid 1994:32–33). In this case, his status was not that of an underling to a worldly emperor, but one who recognised that he was appointed by God and answerable to him.

Views differ as to the relationship, if any, between this ruler and the

---

73. While *ʾet-* normally marks the direct object, it may also be employed with a nominative for emphasis (cf. 43:7; GKC §117m). The emphasis is further strengthened by the repetition of *nāśîʾ*, 'leader'. Though the second occurrence of this is not present in LXX and Peshitta, that is probably for stylistic rather than textual reasons. The Targum and the Vulgate attest the repetition in their text.

74. For further details on kings and rulers, see Duguid 1994:10–57.

messianic figure, 'my servant David' (34:23–24; 37:24–25), who was also termed a 'ruler' (34:24; 37:25). The absence of Davidic overtones in the closing vision suggests to many critical scholars that two different schools of thought were involved, with the ruler or prince being a figurehead, hemmed in by many restrictions. For a summary of critical views, see, for instance, Levenson 1976:57–62.

There are some conservative scholars (e.g., Smith 1993:372–377) who find here a direct messianic prophecy, but that is improbable. This ruler was described as providing animals for sacrifice 'on his own behalf' (45:22) and he was viewed as having sons to whom he would bequeath property (46:16–18). In addition, he is forbidden to take land by oppression (46:18), and his main activity is to receive animals intended for temple offerings and to provide them on appropriate occasions (45:16–17). These features militate against this being a direct prophecy of Christ, but, since any king or ruler who lived up to his God-ordained responsibilities in measure foreshadowed the Messiah to come, the prescribed behaviour of Ezekiel's ruler did possess indirect messianic implications. The vision, however, did not focus on any royal descendant of David, but on the role which the civil ruler of God's people ideally had in the stated worship of the LORD.

The ruler was a privileged figure who was permitted *to sit in it* (the east gateway). Sitting, rather than standing as was usual in worship, marked his enhanced status (cf. 2 Sam. 7:18; Ps. 110:1). Moreover, he alone was allowed *to eat bread before the LORD* in the gateway. In this expression 'bread' was used, as it often was, for food in general, but this was no ordinary meal since it was 'before the LORD' (cf. Exod. 18:12; Deut. 12:7; 14:26). There was no indication of this being a newly introduced ritual in the ideal temple.

Even so, the ruler's subordinate status was strictly controlled. *By way of the vestibule of the gateway he is to come in, and by its way he is to go out.* 'Come in' and 'go out' denote movement across sacred boundaries (cf. 42:1). Though the ruler could occupy the east gateway, he could not enter by its outer gate. Instead, having entered the outer courtyard by either the northern or southern gateway, he was to make his way into the eastern gateway from the inside of the outer courtyard, and he had to leave in the same manner. Moreover, the ruler had no access to the inner courtyard or the altar, though he was privileged to stand at the gatepost of the inner east gateway while the priests offered his sacrifices for him (46:2).

The ruler's authority extended over all twelve tribes, the entire covenant people, but he was not explicitly identified as coming from one particular tribe, or as being from the house of David. He was granted two sections of land in the central zone, separate from the other tribal allotments, but not adjacent to either the temple or the city (45:7). Because of the malpractice of earlier rulers, the ideal ruler's conduct was subjected to various restrictions (43:6–11; 45:8–12; 46:16–18). On the other hand, the ruler was assigned a significant place in the worship of the temple, particularly as regards providing the animals for sacrifice for the nation (45:16–17, 21–25). For the relationship between the ruler and the high priest, see on 44:30.

REFLECTION

- A permanently closed gate could easily be regarded as an ominous sign: No Entry. But that was not the case here. The northern and southern gateways remained open, but the closed east gate was an enduring symbol that God had returned to the ideal temple, and that he was determined that he would remain there permanently. Never again would that gate be opened to let the Glory-presence depart (10:19; 11:23). However, after the return from the exile, there again came a time when Herod's Temple in Jerusalem was levelled by enemy forces (Matt. 24:2). The reality symbolised by the closed gate did not pertain to any physical temple on earth, but to the presence of the Spirit indwelling the church of God. He may be grieved with Christian conduct (Eph. 4:30), individually and collectively, but he will not abandon those who are Christ's.

- Even though the 'ruler' foreshadows Christ only in an indirect fashion, there are two aspects of this ideal figure which are worth emphasising. (1) He is designated by the term 'ruler' because of his willing compliance with the ordinances of God. He is not a figure who is concerned with asserting or exploiting the status accorded him. He recognises that the LORD alone is Israel's real king. His conduct in this regard foreshadowed Christ whose earthly mission was an expression of obedient submission. 'I have come down from heaven, not in order that I should do my own will, but the will of him who sent me' (John 6:38). (2) The duties and privileges accorded the ideal ruler are part of an on-going process whereby there was unfolded to Israel that the roles of king and priest would ultimately merge. This was hinted at in passages such as Psalm 110 and Zechariah 6:12–13, but the tension between the royal and the priestly aspects of the Messiah was not finally resolved until the coming of Christ, who is both 'King of Israel' (John 1:49; 12:13) and our 'great high priest' (Heb. 4:14).

(3) Laws regarding Temple Service (44:4–31)

It is highly significant that these laws regarding temple service are introduced with renewed mention of the Glory-presence resident in the ideal temple (44:4). The regulations are to be viewed as an appropriate response to this manifestation of the LORD, and not merely as a set of ritual requirements to be mechanically performed. Their presence, which extends to 46:18, is not an intrusion of material from another source, but hints at parallels with Moses coming from Sinai with the law of God for the covenant community. Ezekiel performs a similar role in being the one who promulgates the LORD's statutes and laws for the ideal community so that there would be no infringement of the holiness which is appropriate in the LORD's presence.

In the light of previous breaches of the sanctity of the Temple (44:5–8), foreigners are again debarred from the sacred compound (44:9), but two groups are permitted to approach and carry out their roles in the temple: (1) the Levites (44:10–14) and (2) the Zadokites (44:15–16). The function of the Levites in temple ritual is strictly curtailed, but the Zadokite priests are permitted to approach the LORD provided they do not infringe specific requirements (44:15–27). The Zadokites are distinguished by their privileged position among the Israelites (44:28–31).

Originally all members of the tribe of Levi were assigned duties in connection with the sanctuary (Num. 1:50–53), but only Aaron and his sons were 'the anointed priests' who officiated at the altar (Exod. 28:1; Num. 18:7). Zadok was a priest who rose to prominence in the days of David (see on 44:15), and in Ezekiel it is only his descendants who are permitted to serve at the altar. The term Levite is then used both for those from the tribe of Levi not descended from Aaron, and also for those who could claim descent from Aaron, but not from Zadok.

This chapter played a significant role in the history of critical thought because of the way it was exegeted by Wellhausen in the development of the documentary hypothesis.[75] In particular he used it to support his theory that the Zadokite priests, who were in control in the Jerusalem Temple, were a late arrival in Israelite religion, and unconnected to the Levitical priesthood whom they displaced and demoted. He maintained that before Ezekiel's time all Levites had been regarded as priests, and that in this passage the prophet seeks to justify and perpetuate the demotion of the Levitical priests which had

---

75. For further details, see Stevenson 1996:66–78 and McConville 1983.

occurred in the days of Josiah. Stevenson (1996:77) argues that the text 'asserts the past guilt of the House of Israel and the Levites, and the innocence of the Zadokites, but this is not the point of the rhetoric. The rhetorical purpose of this chapter is to give the rules for access to the Holy Place of the future. The distinction is a fine one, but it moves the discussion from the presumption of Levite demotion to the territorial regulation of society.'[76]

While a measure of confusion may exist regarding Zadok's associate in 2 Samuel 8:17 and 2 Samuel 15:24, there is no real reason to doubt that Zadok was descended from Aaron through Eleazar (1 Chron. 6:50–53). It is only by setting aside such information as of questionable reliability that critical scholarship has proposed many elaborate schemes to account for Zadok's prominence.

(a) Previous Violation of the Temple (44:4–8)

> 44:4 And he brought me by way of the north gateway to the front of the house, and I saw and behold, the glory of the LORD filled the house of the LORD, and I fell upon my face. 44:5 And the LORD said to me, 'Son of man, fix your mind on and see with your eyes and with your ears listen to all that I am speaking to you concerning all the statues of the house of the LORD and concerning all its laws, and fix your mind on the entrance to the house with all the exits from the sanctuary. 44:6 And say to the rebellious, to the house of Israel, "Thus says the Lord GOD: You ⌊have gone far⌋ enough with all your abominations, O house of Israel, 44:7 in that you have brought strangers, uncircumcised of heart and uncircumcised of flesh, to be in my sanctuary, to profane my house; when you offered my food, the fat and the blood, they broke my covenant in addition to all your abominations. 44:8 And you have not kept charge of my holy ⌊things⌋, and you put ⌊them⌋ as keepers of my charge in my sanctuary for you." '

♦ **44:4** *He brought me by way of the north gateway* resumed the account of Ezekiel's guided tour as he was conducted from inside the east gateway in the outer courtyard (44:1; Fig. 7 ③) through the inner north gateway into the inner courtyard where he stood at *the front of the house* (Fig. 7 ④). From this position he was once more able to observe that *the glory of the LORD filled the house of the LORD* (cf. 43:5). Ezekiel did not attempt to give a detailed description of the

---

76. For a more extensive discussion of these groups, see Milgrom 2012:141–148.

Glory (cf. 1:26-28; 43:2-3), but recorded that *I fell upon my face*, exhibiting the same reaction of reverent awe that he had previously displayed (1:28; 3:23; 43:3).

It is noteworthy that, in the earlier vision in which the prophet had been brought to the Temple, he had entered the sanctuary through this inner north gateway (8:3) and had then witnessed the people's sins in the Temple—of which he was here again reminded (44:6-8).

♦ **44:5** *And the* LORD *said to me* repeated the unusual word order of 44:2. Though it was once more left unclear whether the LORD spoke directly to Ezekiel, or through the angelic guide, the location and the circumstances strongly suggest the former. This scene may be appropriately compared to Moses on Sinai receiving the law of God (Exod. 24:15-18). In this scene revealed to his inner faculties, Ezekiel enjoyed an audience with the divine King to receive the protocols which must be observed by his loyal people so that their presence would not mar the ideal scenario being presented.

Using the standard form of address for his spokesman, *Son of man* (cf. 2:1), the LORD demanded that he pay particular attention to what was going to be revealed to him. *Fix your mind* (lit., 'set your heart'; cf. 40:4) was an injunction to focus his entire inner faculties on observing all that was revealed to him and to ponder its significance. The paired chiastic injunction, *see with your eyes and with your ears listen* (cf. 40:4), stressed the need for simultaneous, concentrated employment of his faculties to absorb all the LORD was disclosing to him. Unlike 40:4 which emphasised the visual aspect of his visionary experience, here the focus was primarily on what was audible: *all that I am speaking to you concerning all the statutes of the house of the* LORD *and concerning all its laws.*[77] In this description the terms were presented in the reverse order to that found in 43:11. They were concerned with conduct and practices to be maintained within the sacred precincts, with the repeated 'all' emphasising that every aspect had to be taken into account.

Fix your mind on the entrance[78] *to the house with all the exits*

---

77. The qere *tôrōtāyw*, 'its laws', is a plural noun, and the kethib, *twrtw,* is probably to be read as a defectively spelled variant of the same word, *tôrōtāw*.

78. The Vulgate, Peshitta and Targum have a plural 'entrances' to match the following 'exits'. The RSV and NRSV take both nouns to refer to people, 'those who may be admitted' and 'those who are to be excluded', presumably pointing the consonants as hophal participles. If that were the sense, the conjunction *wǝ* would have been expected before *bǝkōl*, 'with all'.

from the sanctuary. As the passage subsequently discussed rightful access to the various zones in the sacred compound, it was not its architecture that Ezekiel was to contemplate, but the carefully structured routes by which admission could be obtained. Probably 'entrance to the house' referred to the single entry point into the central building, and 'exits from the sanctuary' to the various gateways in the courtyard.

♦ **44:6** Against the background of the meticulous layout of the ideal temple so as not to infringe upon the holiness of the LORD, the prophet was directed, *Say to the rebellious* (lit., 'rebellion', cf. the way the noun was twice used in 2:7–8), those who acted with defiant disregard of the LORD's known wishes. Significantly the primary focus of condemnation was the *house of Israel*, the covenant nation as a whole, and not merely its religious leadership, the Levites or the priests. This may be compared to the indictment of the people in 43:7–9 where condemnation of their royal leadership was introduced as a secondary theme. *You ⌊have gone far⌋ enough with all your abominations* (lit., 'much with respect to you from/than all your abominations'; cf. 45:9). This clearly expressed that the LORD's patience with their misconduct had worn out. For 'abominations', see on 5:9, 11; 8:6–17; 16:2; 33:26.

♦ **44:7** In this instance the precise specification of Israel's offence was *in that you have brought strangers* (lit., 'sons of a stranger/strange land') *to be in my sanctuary*, the sacred compound as a whole. Unlike 'foreigner' (7:21; 11:9; 16:32), 'strange' was also used to refer to foreign gods (Deut. 31:16; 32:12; Josh. 24:20, 23; Jer. 8:19). The people had 'brought' (*bô'*, hiphil; cf. 40:2) into the Temple those whose allegiance was to pagan gods in that they had caused or permitted them to cross a boundary of holiness instituted by the LORD. It was not the ethnic origins of the strangers which constituted the offence, but rather their lack of spiritual submission and allegiance to the LORD. *Uncircumcised in heart and uncircumcised in flesh* emphasised the absence of a faith commitment as well as of ceremonial conformity to the requirements of the covenant. Ordinarily in the Old Testament these two were assumed to go together, with the outward sign of circumcision pointing to the inner reality of heart consecration to the LORD (Deut. 10:16; 30:6; Jer. 9:25). The inevitable outcome of such defiant disobedience was *to profane my house* (cf. 23:39).

The main break in the verse is often introduced later in English translations, but the Massoretic pointing directed that the second part of the verse began with *when you offered my food* (*leḥem*, 'bread'), *the fat and the blood*. 'Bread' or 'food' was largely avoided in speaking of Old Testament sacrifices, to avoid the crass pagan conceptions of the deity requiring to consume food (but see Num. 28:2). For fat and blood, see on 44:15. *They broke*[79] *my covenant in addition to all your abominations.* The presence and activity in the palace of the covenant King of those who were not his vassals was obnoxious to him, and was a further aggravation of the detestable conduct of the Israelites. Possibly these strangers had been invited to participate in the meals associated with the peace offerings.

♦ **44:8** *You have not kept charge* (cf. 40:45-46; 44:14-16; 48:11) referred to their failure as regards faithful performance of God's worship according to his prescribed pattern. 'Keep charge' was probably technical vocabulary for guard duty, as specified in Numbers 18:2-7. Here the emphasis was more on the priests as those who should have ensured that the worship of the sanctuary was performed without any breach of the Temple regulations. Not only did their own conduct fall short, but they aggravated the situation in that they *put*[80] strangers *as keepers of my charge in my sanctuary for you.* This implied that the priests had employed foreign guards to whom they delegated their custodial duties at the sanctuary. It may be that this pointed to the role accorded to non-Israelite groups such as the Carites (possibly Anatolian mercenaries) in 2 Kings 11:4, 19. Indeed, since *my holy ⌞things⌟* included anything related to the sacred realm of temple service (cf. 22:8), the alien intrusion may have extended beyond guard duties.

(b) Responsibilities of the Levites (44:9-14)

> 44:9ᵃ "Thus says the Lord GOD: No stranger, uncircumcised in heart and uncircumcised in flesh, is to enter my sanctuary, not even any stranger who ⌞is⌟ in the midst of the sons of Israel. 44:10But rather the Levites who went far from me when Israel strayed, who strayed from me after their idols, they will

---

79. The LXX, Peshitta and Vulgate have a second person plural verb referring to the Israelites. This agrees with the other verb forms in the surrounding context and with the accusation against Israel, not the nations, which is the theme of the passage.

80. 'Put' renders *wattāśîmûn* on the assumption that the *nun* is paragogic. It might, however, be a feminine plural pronominal suffix employed by dissimilation for a masculine form after the preceding *mem*.

bear their iniquity. ⁴⁴:¹¹And they ⌊are to be⌋ ministering in my sanctuary ⌊with⌋ oversight of the gateways of the house, and ⌊to be⌋ ministering ⌊in⌋ the house; they ⌊are the ones who⌋ are to slaughter the burnt offering and the sacrifice for the people, and they ⌊are the ones who⌋ are to stand before them to minister to them. ⁴⁴:¹²Because they would minister to them before their idols and they would become for the house of Israel a stumbling-block of iniquity, on that account I have raised my hand against them, declares the LORD, and they will bear their iniquity. ⁴⁴:¹³And they are not to approach me to act as priests for me or to approach any of my holy ⌊things⌋ ⌊or⌋ to the Holy of Holies; they will bear their disgrace and the abominations which they have done. ⁴⁴:¹⁴And I will appoint them keepers of the charge of the house, for all its work and for all that should be done in it." '

♦ **44:9** This verse was transitional in that its prohibition forbade the laxity of the priests just described, and looked forward to the reinstatement of appropriate temple procedures. The messenger formula, **Thus says the Lord GOD**, however, introduced a new subsection of the divine decrees for the ideal temple and community.

The description of the *stranger* was repeated from 44:7 as being one **uncircumcised in heart and uncircumcised in flesh**, one who was not a member of the covenant community, and so debarred from enjoying its privileges, being both spiritually and ritually unprepared for true worship. They were not *to enter my sanctuary*, which did not refer to the inner holy structure, but to the whole temple complex (see on 44:1).

Not even[81] *any stranger who* ⌊*is*⌋ *in the midst of the sons of Israel.* If there had to be any exemption, it might be supposed that it would have been extended to strangers who were resident in the land. However, their physical and spiritual disqualification debarred them from entering the sanctuary. The language used here was similar in its intent to the need for a new heart and new spirit (11:19; 36:25–26). 'The prohibition here of access to the temple by the uncircumcised may be compared to the eschatological banishment of unbelievers from the new Jerusalem in the eternal state in Rev 22:15' (Hummel 2007:1273).

♦ **44:10 *But rather*** (*kî ʾim*) was a strong adversative, introducing a

---

81. The initial *lamedh* on *ləkol-* may indicate origin, 'belonging to every/any stranger', but it is more likely to function emphatically (GKC §143e; Joüon §125l), indicating the comprehensive scope of the prohibition.

decided contrast, with the alternative implying that, unlike the stranger, the Levites despite their sin were permitted access to, and assigned duties in, the sanctuary. The term, *the Levites*, with no further qualification, designated in Ezekiel's vision all members of the tribe of Levi except those who were descendants of Aaron through the line of Zadok. All these other cultic functionaries, who came exclusively from the tribe of Levi, were assigned an identical status which was lower than that of the Zadokites.

The reason for this lower status was conveyed in the description that they *went far from me when Israel strayed.* 'Went far' or 'were far' (*rāḥaq*; cf. 8:6; 11:15) was here a spatial metaphor from lack of allegiance. Initially when Israel had transgressed in the incident of the Golden Calf, the Levites had remained loyal to the LORD, and were chosen from among the tribes for special divine service (Exod. 32:29; Num. 1:49–53). They had, however, not maintained their initial fidelity, particularly when they *strayed from me after their idols* (cf. 6:4). It is possible that this might have referred to the debased conduct perpetrated by the priests at the shrine in Shiloh (1 Sam. 2:12–17, 22–25, 27–36), leading to the termination of the priesthood in Eli's line. However, a reference to more recent malpractice before and after Josiah's reformation was more probable. Levites had led idolatrous worship throughout Judah at the high places left over from Baal worship. Josiah deposed those priests and desecrated the sites (2 Kgs. 23:5, 8). After his death, however, paganism re-asserted itself (Jer. 2:28; 11:13). There were two aspects to the misconduct of the priests who facilitated such heathen rituals: they themselves were far from the LORD, setting a bad example to the Israelites, and they failed to oppose the idolatry of others. On both counts the LORD said that *they will bear their iniquity* (4:4), that is, the punishment due to their iniquity in that they failed to prevent the violation of proper procedure.

Though critical theory detected here evidence of a dispute after the exile between the Zadokites and other Levitical priests for control over the priesthood, there is no Biblical evidence to support such an hypothesis, which must be discarded. Duguid (1994:77–78), however, argued that the Levites had behaved improperly by straying from the LORD, and then by facilitating Israel's idolatrous worship. For this and for failing to guard the Temple properly they would suffer appropriate divine censure, which would debar them from undertaking the most holy functions.

It was not, however, the case that this represented downgrading of their status as was assumed by Wellhausen and others who accepted his reconstruction of Israelite history. Basing his understanding on a parallel with Leviticus 21:17–23, Duguid argues, 'Exclusion from the altar is thus not necessarily in itself "downgrading". In fact, for the Levites rather the opposite was the case: in spite of their past sin they were still graciously to be restored to the position of privilege and honour which they once held as gatekeepers in the Temple. In a society in which prestige is indicated by one's relationship to the Temple this is no small privilege' (Duguid 1994:78).

♦ **44:11** The divine directive, *they ⌊are to be⌋ ministering*, envisaged the situation as one which would prevail without interruption, possibly even as being resumed and continued from the past (Milgrom 2012:156). Three times the verb 'to minister' (*šārat*, piel) was used in this verse to specify the areas where the non-Zadokite Levites might legitimately serve *in my sanctuary*. There were two main spheres of activity assigned to them.

(1) In connection with preservation of the sanctity of the temple and its ritual, their ministry involved *oversight of the gateways of the house* to prevent improper access.[82] These gateways were those into the outer courtyard from outside; the inner gateways were under the oversight of the Zadokite priests (40:45). As guardians of the outer courtyard, the Levites occupied the guard rooms in the gateways to monitor those who sought access.

(2) *And ⌊to be⌋ ministering ⌊in⌋ the house*, where 'house' again referred to the whole temple precinct (cf. 43:21). This was further specified in respect of two duties, regarding both of which it should be noted that they were oriented towards the worshippers at the temple rather than towards the LORD himself (contrast 44:15).

(a) The first responsibility accorded to the Levites in respect of sacrificial rites was that *they ⌊are the ones who⌋ are to slaughter*[83] *the burnt offering and the sacrifice for the people*, which, when combined, generally stood for all the blood sacrifices (cf. 40:42). In

---

82. Stevenson (1996:64–65) prefers an alternative clausal structure: 'They shall be in my holy place, serving as armed guards at the gates of the house and serving in the house.' This understanding is not reflected in English translations, and, while it makes clear their twofold function, the traditional rendering does so also.

83. Milgrom (2012:155) notes the change in this and the following verb to an imperfect form which he suggests indicates a new role for the Levites as distinct from the participles employed for 'ministering'. The imperfect verbs certainly convey a future obligation imposed on the Levites.

Leviticus 1 and 3 laymen had been allowed to kill their own sacrificial animals, but in the ideal temple they were not allowed into the inner courtyard. After the return from the exile (often referred to as the second Temple period) laymen continued to sacrifice in the Temple, indicating that these regulations were not understood as being operative. Since Ezekiel envisaged a change from previous procedure in which lay persons slaughtered and cooked their own sacrifices, it was the laity who were subjected to restriction here, not the Levites.[84]

(b) Moreover, *they* (the Levites) ⌐*are the ones who*¬ *are to stand before them* (the people) *to minister to them* (the people). The precise duties involved were not specified, but a similar expression was employed earlier when, amongst other privileges, the Levites were appointed 'to stand before the congregation to serve them' (Num. 16:9). As they had slaughtered the sacrificial victims for the people, so after the portions which were offered to the LORD had been burned, those parts which were allocated to the offerer were to be cooked by the Levites. The preparation of the victim for sacrifice took place at the north inner gateway (40:38-43) and the subsequent cooking of portions for the laity in the corners of the outer courtyard (46:21-24). In this way the Levites' activities interposed between Israelite laity and the sacrificing priests as they engaged in their duties, and prevented any encroachment on the inner holy zone.

♦ **44:12** Again the reason for the exclusion of the Levites from the altar was stated: *they would minister* (a frequentative imperfect, indicating the repeated nature of this misconduct) *to them before their idols and they would become*[85] *for the house of Israel a stumbling-block of iniquity.* The emphasis was on past failures, and was presented in such a way as to contrast with the Zadokites. The Levites, as a class of cultic personnel, joined the mass of the people in idol worship (20:30-32; 23:37-39). While 'they' in 'they would become' might refer to the Levites, it is more probable that the idols[86] became a stumbling-block,

---

84. 'A case could be made that the Levites are being "promoted" rather than "demoted" here' (Stevenson 1996:76).

85. The verb *wəhāyû* is not a *waw*-consecutive imperfect expressing a simple consequence, 'and so they became', but following the previous frequentative imperfect it too has frequentative force, 'they kept becoming.'

86. Stevenson (1996:73) challenges the common assumption that it was the Levites who were identified as the stumbling block, noting that the immediately preceding plural noun was in fact 'idols'. Furthermore, 'stumbling-block' occurred elsewhere in Ezekiel with reference to idols and idolatry (7:19; 14:3, 4, 7; 18:30).

since worshipping them promoted further sin and idolatry among the people (cf. Duguid 1994:80).

The outcome of such unfaithful behaviour was that the LORD *raised my hand against them*. While 'raise the hand' could indicate taking an oath (cf. 20:6, 23), this precise expression was not found elsewhere. Here it probably had in view readiness to impose punishment upon them. *Declares the LORD*, the signature formula, pointed to the emphatic decisiveness of his resolve that *they will bear their iniquity*, that is, the penalty of their unfaithfulness (44:10).

♦ **44:13** *And they are not to approach me* restricted their sphere of activity. 'Approach' (*nāgaš*) was used in an idiom for engaging in priestly ministry (Exod. 19:22; Lev. 21:21), drawing close to the presence of the LORD. It was forbidden that they would *act as priests for me* in offering the sacrifices on the altar. Nor were they *to approach any of my holy ⌊things⌋ ⌊or⌋ to the Holy of Holies*. This clearly prohibited the Levites from approaching any object or area which possessed a higher degree of holiness,[87] though what precisely was in view was less certain since 'the Holy of Holies' (cf. 41:4) could also refer to offerings which were 'most holy' (Num. 18:9).

They will bear their disgrace. Hummel (2007:1276) argues that this was not equivalent to 'bear their iniquity/punishment' (cf. 44:10, 12). In 16:52, 54, 63 Ezekiel used 'disgrace' in a context of salvation, not judgement. So here the expression denoted the sense of their unworthiness and hence the renewed gratitude of the truly repentant, who recognised the equity of the penalty imposed on them (Lapsley 2000:145). They would also bear *the abominations which they have done* in that they would acknowledge their previous actions for what they had been and become ashamed of them.

♦ **44:14** In accordance with 44:11 there were positive duties for the Levites to be engaged in, and the description of these was restated.

---

87. 'The Levites are not allowed to serve as priests. The contrast between the territorial access of the priests and the Levites is explicit. The priests stand before YHWH; the Levites stand before the people. The priests guard the guard places of the House Building and the Altar; the Levites guard the gates. The priests have access to the Inner Court; the Levites guard the gates of the Inner Court and slaughter and prepare the offerings in the Inner North Gate, but they do not cross the boundary of the gate to enter the Inner Court. The priests come near the Altar; the Levites do not approach. The priests eat the most holy offerings; there is no mention of offerings for the Levites' (Stevenson 1996:66).

Ordinances for Temple Worship   465

Keepers of the charge of the house involved more than sentry duties at gateways; it included the supervision of all that was required for the activities of the temple as regards the outer courtyard which was their area of responsibility. ***For all its work and for all that should be done in it*** envisaged comprehensive duties as facilitators of the worship, but not as those who engaged in its central act of sacrifice, or who entered the temple building itself.

(c) Responsibilities of the Zadokite Priests (44:15–27)

⁴⁴:¹⁵ˈ "But the priests, the Levites, the sons of Zadok, who kept the charge of my sanctuary when the sons of Israel strayed from me, they ˪are the ones who˩ may draw near to me to minister to me and they may stand before me to offer fat and blood to me, declares the Lord God. ⁴⁴:¹⁶They ˪are the ones who˩ may enter my sanctuary and they ˪are the ones who˩ may come near to my table to minister to me, and they are to keep my charge. ⁴⁴:¹⁷And it will come about that when they enter the gateways of the inner courtyard they are to wear linen garments; wool is not to come upon them while they minister in the gateways of the inner courtyard or in the house. ⁴⁴:¹⁸There are to be linen turbans upon their head, and linen undergarments are to be upon their waists; they are not to put on ˪anything which causes˩ sweat. ⁴⁴:¹⁹And when they go out into the outer courtyard, into the outer courtyard to the people, they are to strip off their garments in which they ˪were˩ ministering and deposit them in the holy rooms and wear other garments; so they will not sanctify the people by their garments. ⁴⁴:²⁰They are not to shave their heads or to let their hair grow long; they are to trim their heads regularly. ⁴⁴:²¹And no priest is to drink wine when he enters the inner courtyard. ⁴⁴:²²They are not to take for themselves as wives a widow or a divorced woman; but rather they may take a virgin from the offspring of the house of Israel or a widow who is a priest's widow. ⁴⁴:²³And they are to teach my people ˪the difference˩ between the holy and the common, and they are to make them know ˪the difference˩ between the unclean and the clean. ⁴⁴:²⁴And about a controversy they ˪are the ones who˩ are to stand to judge; in accordance with my judgements they are to judge it; and my laws and my statutes with respect to all my appointed meetings they are to keep; and my Sabbaths they are to keep holy. ⁴⁴:²⁵And he is not go near a dead person so as to become defiled; but rather, for a father or for a mother or for a son or for a daughter, for a brother or for a sister who is unmarried, they

may defile themselves. ⁴⁴:²⁶And after his cleansing they are to count seven days for him. ⁴⁴:²⁷And in the day when he goes into the holy area, into the inner courtyard to minister in the holy area, he is to offer his sin offering, declares the Lord God." '

♦ **44:15** *But* (a *waw*-disjunctive) changed the theme to consideration of the privileges and duties of *the priests, the Levites, the sons of Zadok* ('righteous'). Although 'the priests, the Levites', was a phrase found repeatedly in Deuteronomy (Deut. 17:9, 18; 18:1; 24:8; 27:9), and could refer to 'all the tribe of Levi' (Deut. 18:1), the addition of 'the sons of Zadok' showed that in Ezekiel's terminology 'priests' was reserved for a particular group within the tribe.

From Israel's earliest days there had been a distinction made between those from the tribe of Levi who were descended from Aaron and those who were not. The non-Aaronite Levites had assigned to them secondary duties at the sanctuary, which, depending on how they were viewed, could leave them classed as priests of a lesser rank. The Aaronites, however, constituted the highest level of priesthood. Of Aaron's four sons, two, Nadab and Abihu perished without heirs (Num. 3:4) because of their infidelity (Lev. 10:1–2), and so all Aaronic priests were descendants of either Eleazar or Ithamar, Aaron's other two sons.

In this vision there was a further stipulation added that only those descended from Zadok were to function as priests in this ideal hierarchy. Zadok was the son of Ahitub, from the line of Phinehas, son of Eleazar (1 Chron. 6:1–8), and rose to prominence in David's reign when he had been one of David's two high priests (2 Sam. 8:17; 15:24–29; 19:11). Abiathar, who functioned jointly as high priest with him, had supported the losing side in the accession crisis, and was deposed and sent into internal exile. Solomon then appointed Zadok as sole high priest (1 Kgs. 1:38–39; 2:35). The high priesthood continued in the line of Zadok down to the time of the exile.

The Zadokites were described as those *who kept the charge of my sanctuary when the sons of Israel strayed from me.* This assessment of the faithfulness of the Zadokites was also recorded in 48:11, but to what did it refer? Certainly in Ezekiel's prophecy the priests were not presented as blameless (7:26; 22:26), and the high priest had been a Zadokite during the period from the division of the kingdom until the fall of Jerusalem. Since the abuses which were described in chapter 8 as existing in the Temple at that time are so much at variance with the exoneration of the Zadokites in this chapter, critical interpreters often suppose that these two accounts must originate with different authors. However, one noticeable feature in chapters 8–11 was the lack of any mention of priests (see on 8:16). Moreover, what was asserted here was the relative, not absolute, faithfulness of the Zadokites. It would seem that they had not promoted the intrusions of paganism into the Temple, though they did acquiesce in them out of deference to royal authority. As a result they had remained comparatively free from the lapses which had blemished other Aaronic lines (cf. Duguid 1994:82).

Consequently, the Zadokites were granted the privilege of being *the ones who,*[88] *may draw near to me.* They were permitted to cross boundaries within the sacred space so as to enter a zone which was closer to where the LORD's Glory-presence was located. In this way, unlike the other Levites who ministered to the people (44:11), the Zadokites were *to minister to me,* employing the term ($šārat$) to denote specifically priestly duties. These included access to the altar and to the holy place. *They may stand before me* indicated the posture of a subordinate who was permitted access to a superior. While this audience might be a one-off favour, in the case of the priests as sanctuary attendants it described their on-going duties of personal service and attendance on the King, waiting for his instructions and being ready to carry them out. In *to offer fat and blood to me,* 'offer' was literally 'to bring near' ($qārab$ hiphil), which was another form of the root 'draw near' ($qārab$ qal) used earlier in 'may draw near'. Their closer approach to the divine presence was a corollary of the duties imposed on them, particularly burning the fat on the altar (Lev. 3:16–17) and sprinkling the blood to decontaminate the holy things (cf. 43:20).

♦ **44:16** The Zadokites were designated as those who *may enter my sanctuary*, not merely the gateways and outer courtyard allowed to the other Levites. They were also those who may *come near to my table to minister to me*. The only table mentioned in the description of this temple was that of 41:22, which was within the Holy Place to which the Zadokite priests alone had access. If, as seems probable, it was the equivalent of the table for the bread of Presence (Exod. 25:23–30),

---

88. The addition of 'are the ones who' attempts to reproduce the emphasis incorporated in the Hebrew text by the presence of $hēmmâ$, 'they'. The grammatical information conveyed by the pronoun is already incorporated in the verb form $yiqrəbu$, 'they will/may draw near', and so the seemingly redundant pronoun focuses somewhat greater attention on the subject of the clause (cf. *IBHS* §16.3.2).

then the priestly duty was that of presenting the bread there. ***They are to keep my charge.*** This may well refer to doing guard duty in the inner courtyard and the sanctuary (cf. 40:45) as distinct from the outer gateways and courtyard (cf. Stevenson 1996:58–60).

♦ **44:17** *(1) Priestly attire (44:17–19).* There then followed various regulations regarding the conduct of the Zadokite priests (44:17–27). Most reflected similar ordinances of the Mosaic code, but with one noteworthy difference. With the absence of any person designated as high priest (see on 44:30), regulations previously prevailing in connection with him were often extended to the priests in general.

The special duties of the Zadokite priests began ***when they enter the gateways of the inner courtyard***. At that point they had to be appropriately dressed. ***They are to wear linen garments*** employed a term for 'linen garments' (*pēšet*), which differed from those used earlier: ordinary linen (*bad*; 9:2–3, 11; 10:2, 6–7), *šēš,* fine linen (16:10; 27:7), and *buṣ,* luxury fine linen (27:16). The variation in the term used was not of significance; what mattered was that ***wool is not to come up upon them while they minister in the gateways of the inner courtyard or in the house.*** This was explained in the next verse.

♦ **44:18** The specification of linen extended to ***turbans upon their head.*** 'Turban', a general term for headgear, was also used for an item of woman's clothing (Isa. 3:20) and for the Israelites generally (24:23), as well as for priests (Exod. 39:28), including Ezekiel himself (24:17).

The use of linen extended to the ***undergarments*** worn by the priests, which were ***upon their waists*** and possibly stretched to their knees (Exod. 28:42). Wearing them was required to avoid indecent exposure as was common in pagan fertility religions.

The reason was then stated for this preference for linen: ***they are not to put on ⌞anything which causes⌟ sweat.*** But that itself was not explained. It may have been that sweat was itself considered to produce uncleanness. More probably it was the reminder that 'sweat' was reckoned to be part of the curse on fallen mankind (a closely related term is used in Gen. 3:19) and, since a priest represented man restored to his original righteousness before God, sweat caused by a heavier material, such as wool, would have been incongruous.

♦ **44:19** The repetition of ***into the outer courtyard*** is absent in some Hebrew manuscripts, and in the Septuagint, the Peshitta, and the Vulgate, and so may be an instance of dittography. When the priests left their official sphere of duty, they were ***to strip off their garments*** *in which they ⌊were⌋ ministering*. They were then to *deposit* their priestly attire *in the holy rooms and wear other garments*. The holy rooms in which their vestments were stored were those described earlier (42:1–14).

This procedure was to be followed *so that they will not sanctify the people by their garments*. In the light of the New Testament 'sanctify' is now usually understood in terms of personal ethical purity, but the Old Testament employs the term more widely. 'Holiness' ('sanctify' is literally 'to cause to be holy') was primarily regarded as a relational concept which described an object or a person as set apart for the service of God. He alone is intrinsically 'holy', but all that came into direct contact with him was withdrawn from ordinary use and set apart as belonging to the sphere of the holy. Such positional holiness could be conveyed by touching a holy object, and the Mosaic law prohibited the congregation in general from coming into contact with the sanctuary and its contents (Exod. 29:37; 30:29; Lev. 6:18, 27). At that stage it had not been specifically mentioned that the priestly garments were a source of such transmitted holiness, but that is made clear here. This touching did not infuse some divine power into those affected, but drew them into the sphere of the holy 'in the sense of becoming subject to cultic restrictions' (*TWOT* 2:787). The fundamental division between the holy and the common was not to be blurred (cf. 46:20).

♦ **44:20** *(2) Priestly hair*. ***They are not to shave their heads or to let their hair grow long*** (lit., 'let loose unkempt hair'). Both extremes were to be avoided, and instead ***they are to trim their heads regularly***. Similar legislation had been introduced under Moses (Lev. 21:5), where there were other regulations, possibly no longer needed because the underlying customs were no longer prevalent. Prohibitions regarding uncut hair were connected with mourning (Lev. 10:6; 21:10), as was the custom of making oneself bald (7:18; 27:31). The rationale behind this prohibition may lie in these customs being associated with pagan worship of the dead, and also being considered as a type of disfigurement, which was to be avoided so that the priests might be without blemish before the LORD (Block 1998:641).

♦ **44:21** *(3) Priestly sobriety*. Abstinence was required of the priests, as in Leviticus 10:9—possibly indicating that it had played a part in the misconduct of Nadab and Abihu which was dealt with in the immediately preceding verses. ***No priest is to drink wine when he enters*** was literally, 'And wine they shall not drink, every/any priest, when they enter'. This was not teetotalism, but maintenance of full control of their faculties while engaged in divine service, lest they sully the sacred space by inappropriate behaviour. Isaiah provided a graphic description of what occurred when such restraint was not observed. 'But ⌊as for⌋ these also, through wine they reeled, and through strong drink they staggered. Priest and prophet reeled through strong drink; they were swallowed up as a result of wine; they staggered as a result of strong drink. They reeled in ⌊their prophetic⌋ vision; they wobbled ⌊when giving a priestly⌋ decision. For all tables are filled with filthy vomit; there is no place ⌊clean⌋.' (Isa. 28:7–8).

♦ **44:22** *(4) Priestly marriage.* Leviticus 21:7 prohibited a priest from marrying a prostitute, a defiled woman, or a divorced woman because a priest was holy to his God. Leviticus 21:14–15 had stricter prohibitions for the high priest who additionally was restricted from marrying a widow, and had to marry an Israelite virgin. The reason given was 'I am the LORD who sanctifies him' (Lev. 21:14) These additional stipulations regarding marriage to *a widow or a divorced woman* were extended here to all the Zadokite priests (Ezekiel made no mention of a high priest), because death was an intrusion into the realm of the holy. The exception in the case of *a widow who is a priest's widow* was probably because she was viewed as already being within the sphere of the holy through her late husband (cf. Lev. 22:13).

♦ **44:23** *(5) Priestly instruction.* In speaking about the functions of the priests, the LORD continued their role as teachers. This had been set out in Leviticus 10:10–11: '⌊You are⌋ to distinguish between the holy and the common, and between the unclean and the clean, and ⌊you are⌋ to teach the sons of Israel all the statutes that the LORD has spoken through (lit., 'by the hand of') Moses' (cf. 22:26; Deut. 33:8–10; Hos. 4:6; Mal. 2:7). The verb *teach* was related to the noun 'law, instruction' (*tôrâ*). As the court attendants of the LORD, the priests were responsible for training the people in what their covenant King required of them.

'Holy' represented what was dedicated to divine service and could therefore properly be brought near to the presence of God, whereas 'common' referred to what belonged to realm of the ordinary. It was still good, but had to be kept at some distance from the divine presence until it underwent a special process of sanctification. What was 'clean' belonged to life as intended by God for his creation (and thus coincided with what was common), whereas 'unclean' implied some loss of life or health, and bore witness to the disruption of the created order by evil. Not only did the ceremonial system of the Old

Testament teach the difference between these conditions, but it also provided the divinely sanctioned remedy for whomever or whatever fell short of the required standards. The ritual ordinances were inherently remedial, designed to save the people from sin and its evil effects and to permit fellowship with God himself. Giving this instruction would constitute a reversion to proper procedure from the previous failure (22:26).

♦ **44:24** *(6) Priestly Adjudication.* A further function of the priesthood, a judicial one, was also continued. **About a controversy** denoted a dispute between members of the community, here one which they had been unable to resolve by themselves and for which they therefore required the services of an arbiter. This role had been assigned to the priests under the Mosaic administration (Deut. 17:8-13; 21:5), though it may have largely lapsed in the period of the kingdom. **Stand to judge**[89] might have reflected a later convention by which the judge stood to pronounce judgement (Isa. 3:13), whereas earlier a judge would sit (cf. Exod. 18:13). More probably, however, 'stand' denoted 'act in an official capacity' rather than saying anything about their physical posture (cf. 2 Chron. 19:8 where the first verb 'appointed' is the hiphil of 'to stand'). **In accordance with my judgements they are to judge it**,[90] that is, the controversy. The standards the priests were required to employ were to be those of the covenant King himself, whose attendants they were. They were not given the right to initiate legislation (nor for that matter was the ruler empowered to do so), but their verdicts were to be according to divine precedents.

It is unclear what demarcation was envisaged as between the priests and the ruler in this ideal setup. Under the monarchy it had been the king or his appointees who constituted a final court of appeal (2 Sam. 15:3-4; 1 Kgs. 3:16-28; Jer. 22:15-16). The ruler would still continue to be responsible for executing 'judgement and righteousness' (45:9), which was the same phrase as was applied to Josiah who 'judged the cause of the afflicted and needy' (Jer. 22:15-16). This would seem to imply that no curtailment of the king's right to administer justice was envisaged. However, 'controversy' or 'law

---

89. The kethib, *lišpōṭ*, 'to judge', is supported by the LXX, Peshitta and Targum over against the qere *ləmišpāṭ*, 'for judgement'.

90. The kethib, *ûšāpəṭuhû*, 'and they will [are to] judge it', and the qere, *yišpəṭûhû*, 'they will [are to] judge', have a different reading of the initial letter and differ in the spelling of the pronominal suffix. The 'and' of the kethib is intrusive here.

suit' (*rîb*) implied that more than clarification of a religious or liturgical matter was in view. Perhaps the difference intended was between what the law meant (a matter for the priests) and how it applied in a particular case (a matter for the leader).

Furthermore, the priests were to be exemplary in meeting the requirements of the law as regards their own conduct, especially in connection with days of sacred observance. ***My laws and my statutes with respect to all my appointed meetings they are to keep; and my Sabbaths they are to keep holy.*** In this way the spiritual leaders of the community would lead by personal example as well as by precept and avoid becoming those who 'preach but do not practise' (Matt. 23:3; cf. Hos. 4:9).

♦ **44:25** *(7) Priestly conduct concerning the dead (44:25–27).* Based on the fact that death is antithetic to the LORD who is life and the giver of life, death was always a reminder of rebellion against him, and constituted a violation of what creation was intended to be. The priest as one who had access to the LORD's presence was therefore to take care not to become ceremonially polluted and so to intrude what was inherently incompatible with the divine purpose into the realm of the holy.

He is not to go[91] ***near a dead person so as to become defiled.*** Perhaps because the behaviour now being scrutinised was unlikely to affect a number of priests simultaneously, the focus switched to an individual priest who was not to approach a corpse (cf. Lev. 21:2–3). ***But rather***, or 'however, instead' (cf. 44:10), permitted exceptions when a close family member died: ***for a father or for a mother or for a son or for a daughter, for a brother or for a sister who is unmarried, they may defile themselves.*** No mention was made of a wife, but that was presumably implied in that she was even more closely related to him than those named. In Leviticus 21:11 the high priest had not been permitted to bury even his father or his mother.

♦ **44:26** After he had contracted ritual defilement through participating in the funeral rites of a close relative, the priest could reinstate his fitness for divine service by a process of ritual purification. ***After his cleansing*** referred to the seven days required by Numbers 19:11–13, and so here that period was probably doubled by the requirement, ***they***

---

91. The verb *yābô'*, 'he will [is to] go', is singular, though the Septuagint, Peshitta and Vulgate have a plural verb, which is also the rendering of most English translations.

are to count*²⁵ *seven days for him. That was probably an impersonal construction equivalent to 'seven days are to be counted for him', although 'they' might have referred to the temple authorities.

♦ **44:27** The LORD's concern for purity and holiness was further emphasised by the requirement for sacrifice after the fortnight of purificatory separation. ***In the day when he goes into the holy area*** marked the resumption of his official duties which required entry ***into the inner courtyard to minister in the holy area.*** 'Holy area' was simply 'the holiness', and while this might refer to the Holy Place, that is the outer chamber of the temple, it was probably used here more extensively of the entire sacred zone to which only the priests had right of entry. All priests (including the high priest, cf. Heb. 5:3; 7:27) were sinful and so, before they could undertake sacred duties, they had to present a sin offering. ***Declares the Lord GOD*** again underscored the significance of ritual sanctity for those who officiated in his sanctuary.

(d) Status of the Zadokite Priests (44:28–31)

> ⁴⁴:²⁸ʼ "And it will be to them for an inheritance ⌊that⌋ I ⌊am⌋ their inheritance, and you will give them no possession in Israel: I ⌊am⌋ their possession. ⁴⁴:²⁹They ⌊are the ones who⌋ may eat the grain offering, the sin offering and the guilt offering, and every dedicated thing in Israel will be theirs. ⁴⁴:³⁰And the first of all the firstfruits of every kind and every heave-offering of every kind from all your heave-offerings will belong to the priests, and the first of your ground grain you will give to the priest so that a blessing may rest on your house. ⁴⁴:³¹⌊As for⌋ any carcass or any torn ⌊animal⌋, ⌊whether⌋ from the birds or from the beasts, the priests are not to eat ⌊it⌋." '

♦ **44:28** Consideration was next given to the property rights and the perquisites of the priests, the first of which was further explored in 45:1–4. The emphasis was on their special status. ***It will be to them for an inheritance that I*** ⌊***am***⌋ ***their inheritance.***⁹³ This echoed the LORD's promise to Aaron, 'In their land you are not to have an inheritance, and a share you are not to have in their midst: I ⌊am⌋ your

---

92. The plural verb is supported by the Vulgate and the Targum, although the Septuagint and Peshitta employ a singular verb which is adopted by RSV and NIV.

93. 'They shall have no inheritance; I am their inheritance' (RSV; cf. REB) reflects the reading of the Vulgate.

share and your inheritance in the midst of the sons of Israel' (Num. 18:20; cf. Num. 18:24; 26:62; Deut. 10:9; 14:27; 18:1–2; Josh. 13:14, 33; 14:3). 'Inheritance' (*naḥălâ*; cf. 35:15) provided part of the core identity of an Israelite as one on whom the LORD had bestowed the right to occupy a portion of the Promised Land. However, there had never been any territory allotted to Levi. Instead their sacred service for the LORD at the sanctuary provided the central focus of their lives.

You will give them no possession in Israel: I ⌐am¬ their possession. 'Possession' (*ʾăḥuzzâ*; cf. 45:5, 6, 7; 46:16, 18; 48:20, 21, 22) primarily referred to the fact of holding and occupying property, no matter in what way one had acquired it, whether as a family legacy or by grant from the monarch himself. Here it was the LORD's gift of direct access to himself in service and for fellowship which was assigned to the priests by virtue of their office. They could access the inner courtyard and were endowed with specific allowances, including portions of some sacrifices (e.g., Deut. 18:1; Josh. 13:14).

♦ **44:29** What was allocated for priestly maintenance was clearly specified. ***They ⌐are the ones who¬ may eat the grain offering, the sin offering and the guilt offering*** (for these offerings, see on 42:13). As these offerings were made to the LORD himself, he was marking the Zadokites' special status by sharing them with them. No mention was made of the burnt offering which was consumed by fire upon the altar so that there was nothing left for human consumption. Also unmentioned were the peace offerings (cf. 43:27; 45:15).

Every dedicated thing in Israel will be theirs. 'Dedicated thing' (*ḥērem*) usually denoted something which was accursed before God and subject to utter destruction (cf. Deut. 7:2–6), but it could also become totally dedicated to divine service (Lev. 27:28–29). Since it could not be redeemed by the donor, it was placed at the disposal of the priests to maintain the sanctuary and its services (Num. 18:14).

♦ **44:30** Three specific categories of offering were listed as belonging to the priests. In acknowledgement of the fact that they occupied the land which belonged to the LORD, Israel were to present the firstfruits of its produce to him (cf. Num. 15:20–21; 18:12; Deut. 26:2, 10). ***The first of all the firstfruits of every kind*** were dedicated to the LORD who was the source of all fruitfulness in the land. The somewhat redundant expression 'first of firstfruits' (cf. Exod. 23:19; 34:26) might have implied the best of the firstfruits or, more probably, emphasised the very first gathered of the ripening crops. These became the property of ***the priests*** (cf. Deut. 18:4).

The second category was *every heave-offering of every kind from all your heave-offerings*. The traditional rendering 'heave-offering' was based on the notion that the word denoted something which the priest would lift up. An alternative understanding views the word as coming from the same root but now used in the sense of that which was reserved or dedicated by an individual by being raised up or lifted out of a whole collection of objects. The word is rendered 'portion' in 45:1, 13; 48:8–9, 20.

The third category was *the first of your ground grain*. The term 'ground grain' was considered by some to indicate 'dough' (LXX, AV) or a sort of porridge, but ground meal used to make such commodities is more probable.

You will give to the priest[94] raises a significant question in relation to these chapters. Is 'the priest' mentioned here the high priest? There seems to be no explicit mention of the high priest in the vision, and it is often argued that the role accorded to the ruler in respect of worship in the ideal temple (see on 44:4) was intended to compensate for that. However, as Duguid (1994:59–64) points out, the high priest did not appear in the earlier chapters of the prophecy either. His survey of the evidence regarding the high priest shows that, while there had been a leading figure among the priests since Mosaic times (most often designated 'the priest', e.g., 1 Sam. 1:9; 1 Kgs. 1:8), there was no single established title for the role in the pre-exilic period. So he argues that 'the priest' in 44:30 and 45:19 was in fact the high priest, and the reason why no prominence was given to the office throughout Ezekiel was that in the pre-exilic period the priest was generally subservient to the king even in matters of internal temple administration and ritual. 'Reforms as well as abuses were introduced at the bidding of the king, not the chief priest. Perhaps the only instance of a chief priest willing to stand up to a king is Azariah's rebuke of Uzziah in 2 Chronicles 26:16ff' (Duguid 1994:63).

So that a blessing may rest upon your house was literally 'to cause to rest a blessing upon your house', in which the subject of the verb was not specified. It might have been God, since he blesses those who are obedient to his requirements, or it might have been the priest invoking divine blessing in response to such a gift (cf. AV).

♦ **44:31** ⌊*As for*⌋ *any carcass or any torn* ⌊*animal*⌋, ⌊*whether*⌋ *from the birds or from the beasts, the priests are not to eat* ⌊*it*⌋. This restriction

---

94. The ESV rendering 'the priests' (cf. 'them' NIV) understands the singular noun *kōhēn*, 'priest', as used collectively.

(cf. 4:14) was part of God's rule for all Israelites (Exod. 22:31; cf. also Deut. 14:21). 'Carcass' probably referred to an animal which had died from natural causes, whereas 'any torn ⌞animal⌟' was one killed by a predator. The prohibition as regards the priests was specifically set out in Leviticus 22:8. While many feel the inclusion of this restriction here is misplaced and should follow the discussion about ritual defilement, it was probable that the contrast was designed to be between what was fit only for wild beasts and what the LORD provided for his people.

REFLECTION

- The employment of strangers to carry out what were regarded as menial tasks connected with the sanctuary (44:7–8) displays an inflated sense of personal importance on the part of Israel in that they considered themselves to be above these things. What task or duty is above any loyal subject of the LORD when it is done for his sake or in the promotion of the cause of his kingdom? How superior was the psalmist's attitude when he said, 'I would choose ⌞to be⌟ a door-keeper in the house of my God rather than to dwell in tents of wickedness' (Ps. 84:10). What matters is not the nature of the task, but avoidance of what is dishonourable so as to be 'useful to the master of the house, ready for every good work' (2 Tim. 2:21). Door-keeping may not attract prestige, but faithful door-keeping is esteemed by the LORD.
- Nothing is more misunderstood by the proponents of modern political correctness than the reality of toleration. It has become a slogan for undifferentiated acceptance of any and every view, so that the ban of 44:9 is instinctively viewed with suspicion as unworthy of God. To the extent that God is thought of at all, it is taken for granted that he will accept any and every person—full stop. But God is not politically correct. He places no barrier on entry into his presence but one—the 'whoever' of John 3:16. There is no tolerance in the courts of heaven for an individual who fails the test of believing in the Son. It is demanded for entry into eternal life.
- The Levites had a chequered history, particularly with their involvement in pagan worship at the high places. Here their past has caught up with them, but through the mercy of God they are not rejected as useless. It is not fitting that they should be in the King's inner courtyard and enter his dwelling, but they are not debarred from serving him as he sees fit. Indeed, their past history may have qualified them all the better to minister to the people (44:11), displaying in their dutiful service the grace of God towards them.

- Scrupulous ritual conduct required of the Zadokite priests would be a perpetual reminder to them and to the worshippers who frequented the ideal temple of the need for careful personal adherence to all the requirements of the law of God. Outward ritual purity was the garb appropriate for those whose inward heart purity came to expression in outward ethical behaviour. The structure of the ideal community devoted to the worship of the LORD is not based on human choice. 'An individual kept doing what was right in his own eyes' (Judg. 21:25) had been tried out before in the days of the judges, and had led to anarchy and national collapse. The true community must adopt as its standard all that is set out by the wisdom of God in his law. 'If you love me, you will keep my commandments' (John 14:15).
- These verses are not to be dismissed as a relic from an era long since obsolete since the Aaronic/Zadokite priesthood was consummated in Christ. Just as Ezekiel's vision saw many of the regulations pertinent to the high priest extended to all the priests, so too in the New Testament church the underlying truths expressed in these ceremonial arrangements are extended to all believers whom he has constituted 'a holy priesthood' and 'a royal priesthood' (1 Pet. 2:5, 9). We too must take care that our conduct does not compromise our role as witnesses to God's mercy extended to us (1 Pet. 2:11–12).

(4) Apportionment of the Land (45:1–8)

Following on from the discussion of the duties and responsibilities of the priests and the arrangements made for their sustenance, there is now a thematically distinct discussion of the way in which the central section of the land would ideally be apportioned. These arrangements are the same as those set out in 48:8–22, where the preceding and succeeding sections (48:1–7; 23–29) are concerned with the tribal allocations which lay to the north and to the south of this central zone of the land. The description that is given bears little relationship to the topography of the land, and is rather couched in terms of spiritual geometry where the various lengths and ratios set out a symmetrical disposition of the various areas, involving five and its multiples, particularly twenty-five. The sanctuary occupies central position (45:2), and around it is an area where the Zadokite priests are to live (45:3–4). North of this, there is a similarly sized area to be occupied by the Levites (45:5), while the city to the south receives territory half that size (45:6). Finally, the residual territory alongside the holy portion is set aside for the use of the ruler (45:7–8).

Throughout this presentation the theme is that of the ordered nature of the ideal organisation of the people of the LORD. The land is his,[95] and he grants the use of it to those who serve him.

> ⁴⁵:¹'And when you allot the land as an inheritance, you are to apportion a portion for the LORD, a holy ⌊portion⌋ from the land, ⌊in⌋ length twenty-five thousand ⌊cubits⌋ ⌊in⌋ length, and ⌊in⌋ breadth ten thousand cubits; it ⌊is⌋ holy in all its border round about. ⁴⁵:²From this there will be for the holy place five hundred by five hundred ⌊cubits⌋ four square round about, with fifty cubits for an open space round about it. ⁴⁵:³And from this measure you are to measure a length of twenty-five thousand ⌊cubits⌋ and a breadth of ten thousand ⌊cubits⌋, and in it will be the sanctuary, the Holy of Holies. ⁴⁵:⁴This ⌊is⌋ the holy ⌊section⌋ of the land; it will be for the priests who minister in the sanctuary, who draw near to minister to the LORD, and it will be for them a place for houses and a holy site for the sanctuary. ⁴⁵:⁵And twenty-five thousand ⌊cubits⌋ in length and ten thousand ⌊cubits⌋ in breadth will be for the Levites who minister in the house, as a possession twenty rooms. ⁴⁵:⁶And you are to give as the possession of the city five thousand ⌊cubits⌋ in breadth and in length twenty-five thousand ⌊cubits⌋, alongside the holy portion; it will be for the whole house of Israel. ⁴⁵:⁷And to the ruler ⌊is to belong⌋ on this side and on that with respect to the holy portion and to the possession of the city, facing the holy portion and facing the possession of the city, westwards on the west side and eastwards on the east side, and its length ⌊is to be⌋ alongside one of the ⌊tribal⌋ shares, from the west boundary to the east boundary. ⁴⁵:⁸With respect to the land it is to be his as a possession in Israel, and my rulers are no longer to oppress my people, but the land they are to give to the house of Israel according to their tribes.'

♦ **45:1** This section began abruptly without any of Ezekiel's formulaic introductions, presumably because it was a continuation of the divine address begun in 44:9. ***When you allot*** was literally 'when you (masculine plural) cause to fall' with 'lot' understood. This idiom (repeated in 47:14, 22; 48:29) was the same as that employed in Joshua 13:6 and 23:4 for the original apportionment of the land. While the details of how this was carried out were not stated (in particular, the precise identity of 'you'), the procedure was not thought of as producing a random outcome, or one determined by fate or chance, but was regarded as a direct expression of God's will on the matter

---

95. For further details on land and inheritance, see Wright 1990:3–70 and Block 2000.

uninfluenced by human manipulation (Prov. 16:33). ***The land as an inheritance*** (cf. 47:22) referred to the land other than the sacred portion which the LORD had reserved in advance and about which he was laying down these separate arrangements.

You are to apportion a portion for the LORD. The rendering reflects the Hebrew use of the hiphil of the verb *rûm*, 'to lift up' and so 'to present' or 'to select', along with a cognate noun *tərûmâ*, 'portion' or 'contribution' (also rendered 'heave-offering' in 44:30; cf. 45:13). Only in Ezekiel was this term used for land (cf. 48:8). The land as a whole was a gift from the LORD, and this was to be acknowledged by 'lifting' from it a tract devoted to his service as a thank-offering. 'You' was plural in this verse, and probably directed the people to ensure that these arrangements were put in place as an acknowledgement on their part of all the benefits that the LORD had provided for them.

A holy ⌊portion⌋ from the land (lit., 'holiness from the land'; cf. 45:4) denoted an area specially dedicated to the LORD's purposes. In specifying its dimensions no unit of measurement was stated apart from the one mention of 'cubits' in 45:2. Keil assumed that all other measurements were in 'rods', each of six cubits (2002:418). That would amount to a length of 48 miles (78 km) in total, virtually the whole distance from the Jordan to the Mediterranean Sea (approximately 56 miles [90 km] at the northern end of the Dead Sea), leaving little, if any, land allotted to the ruler, east and west of the holy sector. Most commentators, therefore, take the measurements to be in cubits, yielding a much smaller holy section ***in length twenty-five thousand ⌊cubits⌋ in length***, that is, about 8.3 miles (13 km). There was a repetition of the specification 'in length'.

The ***breadth*** of the holy section from north to south is problematic in a way that is related to the elasticity of use of the term 'portion'. The Hebrew text stated it to be ***ten thousand cubits***, that is, three miles (5 km), which was the same as that found in 48:9, and the term, 'a portion for the LORD' (found only here), must then refer only to the tract of land allotted to the priests (Fig. 8 A). However, there is a

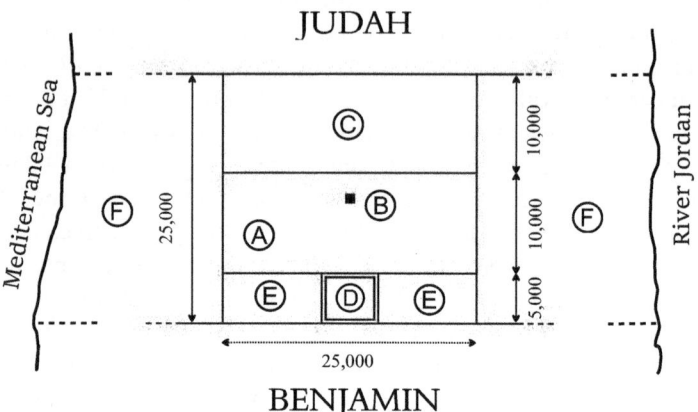

Ⓐ	The Priests' Portion	45:1, 4; 48:8–12
Ⓑ	The Temple Complex	45:2–3; 48:10
Ⓒ	The Levites' Portion	45:5; 48:13–14
Ⓓ	The City	48:15–20
Ⓔ	The City's Possession	45:6–7; 48:15–20
Ⓕ	The Ruler's Portion	45:7; 48:21–22

Figure 8. The Central District of the Land.

variant reading of 'twenty thousand cubits' which is frequently followed in English translations,[96] which would mean that in this verse the LORD's portion referred to both the priestly allocation and the Levitical allocation (which would make better sense of 45:3; Fig. 8 A + C). That is the understanding adopted in the following comments, but whichever reading is followed does not affect the actual distribution. *It is holy in all its border round about,* where 'border' was used to refer to the total territory it enclosed (cf. 43:12).

♦ **45:2** *From this* area designated for the LORD, an allocation was to be made for *the holy place* (lit., 'the holiness'), that is, the temple and its surrounding complex (Fig. 8 B). This was *five hundred by five hundred ⌊cubits⌋ four square round about*, again emphasising the perfection of the arrangement (cf. 42:20). *With fifty cubits for an open space round about it* further set the temple precincts apart with a buffer zone 84.6 foot (26 m) wide around the wall of the temple. The term 'open space' (*migrāš*, cf. 48:15, 17) was often applied to the fields of pasture land about a city, but the sense here was obviously different. This space prevented priestly dwellings from coming too close to the temple area, and thus compromising its holiness.

♦ **45:3** *From this measure* is difficult to understand if the portion of 45:1 was itself ten thousand cubits broad, but if it was twenty thousand cubits, then there is identified here an area amounting to half of that: *a length of twenty-five*[97] *thousand ⌊cubits⌋ and a breadth of ten thousand ⌊cubits⌋.* There was the requirement *you are to measure*, though it is unclear who is being addressed by the singular form of the verb.[98] However, it was made clear that located within the specially

---

96. The LXX reads here (and in 48:9, 13) 'twenty thousand', which is followed by NASB, NIV, ESV. That would refer to the total width of the priests' portion and that of the Levites. It is argued that *'ăśārâ*, 'ten', in the MT is a scribal corruption of an original *'eśrîm*, 'twenty', through confusion of final *mem* and *he*. Certainly such a transmutation is attested elsewhere, but the difference does not affect the sizes of the two portions, only the identification of what was the portion for the LORD. 'Ten thousand' is attested in the Targum, Peshitta and Vulgate.

97. The qere *ḥămiššâ*, 'five', is the expected feminine form of the numeral. The kethib *ḥāmēš* is a masculine form.

98. The singular verb *tāmôd*, 'you are to measure', is unexpected and it is often suggested that this is an instance of metathesis, and that the plural form, *tāmōddû*, should be read instead. However, the MT is supported by the early versions.

measured subdivision *will be the sanctuary (miqdāš), the Holy of Holies* (cf. 41:4).

♦ **45:4** It was then specified that *the holy ⌊section⌋ of the land* described in the preceding verses was *for the priests* (Fig. 8 A). The double designation, *who minister in the sanctuary, who draw near to minister to the LORD*, made it clear that it was the Zadokite priests who were in view (cf. 40:46; 44:15) as distinct from the other Levites (cf. 45:5). They alone were permitted to *draw near to minister to the LORD* by offering sacrifice (cf. 40:46).

This section of land would provide them with *a place for houses*, as well as being *a holy site for the sanctuary*. The latter phrase repeated the term *miqdāš* in two senses, first as 'a holy site', an area dedicated in general to divine service, and then more specifically as the temple sanctuary. So though the priests were to have access to, and use of, the LORD's portion, it was not a tribal allocation to them, but remained specifically the LORD's.

♦ **45:5** There was now designated a second allocation of the central portion which *will be*[99] *for the Levites* (Fig. 8 C). Their lower status was indicated in that they did not occupy the territory which included the Temple. They were, however, those *who minister in the house*, using the same verb as for the priests in 45:4, though the area of their service was limited to the 'house', that is, the temple complex in general (cf. 43:21). They were to occupy this land *as a possession*. While they were given this security of tenure, which was not accorded to the priests, in fact the priests had the greater privilege of having the LORD as their possession (cf. 44:28).

The last phrase of the verse *twenty rooms* (*'eśrîm ləšākōt*) presents a textual crux in that the accommodation was quite inadequate for the number of Levites who would have been involved. This reading does, however, have extensive early support (Targum, Peshitta, Vulgate). Even so the Septuagint reading of 'cities to inhabit' is generally favoured by commentators.[100] However, as Stevenson (1996:85) points out, in Ezekiel's vision there was only one city. It may be that the term 'rooms' was used in a more extended sense to describe the arrangements made for the Levites within the territory allocated to

---

99. The kethib *yihyeh* is preferable to the qere *wəhāyâ*, though the sense is not affected.

100. The implied Hebrew text for 'cities to inhabit' would be *'ārîm lāšebet*, which is obtained by omitting as intrusive the *sin* in *'eśrîm*, 'twenty' and by replacing the *kaph* with a *beth* in *ləšākōt*, with adjustment of the vowels.

them. In any event it was obvious that the former requirement of the priests and Levites occupying cities spread throughout the land was to be given up (Num. 35:1–8), and they were required to live in close proximity to the temple.

There is much discussion as to whether the priestly portion lay north or south of that of the Levites. The order in which they were presented suggests to many that the priestly portion was to the north, as it was mentioned first. Similarly the tribal portions in chapter 48 were described from north to south. However, Ezekiel's descriptions frequently moved from the centre to the periphery. So it is much more probable that here he also began with the central portion, that of the LORD, and then focused northwards on the portion of the Levites before turning south to that of the city. This arrangement recognised the centrality of the LORD's portion, rather than that of the Levites, which would occur if their portion was south of that of the LORD.

It is not totally clear where the temple was located. Given the symmetry of the arrangements, it was certainly within the LORD's portion and most probably at the centre of the entire square of 25,000 cubits. In this way, the square altar in the inner courtyard would also lie at the centre of that square, indicating the centrality of the worship of the LORD in the life of the ideal community. Alternatively, it might have been located at the centre of the priestly portion, in which case it lay 2,500 cubits further south.

♦ **45:6** There remained at the south of the central zone two narrower areas of land which were designated as *the possession of the city*, that is, a communal holding to be used for the well-being of the city, providing space for housing and agriculture (Fig. 8 E). For the city's location in relation to this strip, see 48:15–20. In an unusual stylistic variation (cf. 48:8; Zech. 2:2) the *breadth* of *five thousand ⌞cubits⌟* was stated before the *length* of *twenty-five thousand ⌞cubits⌟*. The orientation of the city's allocation was indicated as *alongside the holy portion*, which described the square which comprised both the LORD's portion and that allocated to the Levites. *It will be for the whole house of Israel* indicated that the city and its environs were not to be dominated by one tribe, but would be for the use of all.

♦ **45:7** The verb to be understood in this sentence may be the same as that in 45:6, 'you are to give', or, more probably, the thought was that of possession, *to the ruler ⌞is to belong⌟*. For the ruler, see on 44:3. He was here assigned a special grant of land because of his official status, something that had not been allocated to earlier kings. This disposition was of two substantial areas, *on this side and on that with respect to the holy portion and to the possession of the city.* These holdings would lie to the east and to the west of the sacred portion (both the priestly and the Levitical portions) and that of the city, and would run *facing* them, that is, contiguous to them, and stretching *westwards on the west side* to the Mediterranean Sea, *and eastwards on the east side*, to the river Jordan and the Dead Sea (Fig. 8 F). The northern and southern boundaries of the ruler's portion would abut the adjoining tribal allocations, Judah's to the north and Benjamin's to the south (cf. 48:7–8, 22–23).

The precise dimensions of the ruler's property were not specified either here or in 48:21. It is, however, fairly clear that its north–south dimension was twenty-five thousand cubits (8.3 miles, 13 km), being equivalent to the sum of priestly allocation (ten thousand cubits; 45:3–4), the Levitical allocation (ten thousand cubits; 45:5) and the allocation to the city (five thousand cubits; 45:6), but with its east–west dimension being irregular.

The ruler needed such land because he was obligated to provide the victims and other material needed for the temple offerings on special occasions (45:17) as well as being the intermediary who received the people's offerings at other times (45:16). So he was here allocated territory adjacent to that of the priests and close to the temple, though not right next to it. The two allocations may well have suggested the double portion of the firstborn (cf. Deut. 21:17).

♦ **45:8** *With respect to the land it is to be his as a possession in Israel* clearly assigned the territory demarcated in 45:7 as the holding of the ruler. This led in to divine reflection on the behaviour of earlier rulers (45:9). It was implied that not having a specific land allocation that corresponded to their royal status had contributed to their corrupt behaviour. They were termed *my rulers,* using the plural of *nāśîʾ* (cf. 44:3; 45:9).[101] The LORD as the covenant Overlord of Israel acknowledged that the earlier kings were duly appointed to office as his representatives. However, they had misused their status to *oppress my people.* 'Oppress' (cf. 18:12; 22:7, 29) indicated social injustice among the covenant people, and here it would seem confiscation of private property was particularly in view (cf. 1 Sam. 8:14, and the incident of Nadab's vineyard, 1 Kgs. 21.)

---

101. 'The rulers of Israel' (REB) follows the LXX in reading *nəśîʾê yiśrāʾēl* rather than *nəśîʾay*, 'my rulers', with the latter term perhaps being mistaken as a scribal abbreviation *nəśîʾê yʺ* for the former.

But the land introduced behaviour contrary to that which had prevailed under earlier monarchs. In ***they are to give*** 'they' presumably referred to future rulers, but 'give' probably did not convey the thought that the rulers had any part in apportioning the land to the house of Israel according to their tribes. 'Give' probably had the sense of 'relinquish' or 'permit to have' (cf. NIV, ESV). The disposition of the land would be determined by the LORD, and the rulers were not to infringe on that arrangement thereafter.

REFLECTION

- The symbolic geography employed in this description certainly has the actual Promised Land as its backcloth, but what is imposed on it is an ideal presentation which is notable for the centrality of the ideal temple, the degree of protection afforded by the various zones about it, and the separation of the temple from the city—a city about which very little is related here. This layout is a pictorial representation to Israel of the need for them to sanctify the Holy One of Jacob and stand in awe at the God of Israel (Isa. 29:23). The necessity of according God the central place in our living with all reverence and obedience has not diminished over the centuries (1 Pet. 3:15).
- The separation of the LORD's portion in the land was a constant reminder that he was its ultimate owner, as he is of the whole created realm. The creation mandate (Gen. 1:28–30) accorded mankind with both rights over the earth and also responsibilities for the way in which it is used, and these have devolved to each succeeding individual and generation. Sadly, short-sightedness and self-focused greed have often sinfully blighted the precious environment and treasures God has placed at the disposal of mankind. The land with the LORD's portion would function as a perpetual corrective to human exploitation and mismanagement.
- The LORD's portion was used to provide for the needs of those who served him in a special way. Those who are appointed to minister about holy things have the right to live from the holy offerings (1 Cor. 9:13). Though Paul voluntarily declined to make use of his rights in that regard, he did not deny that they existed (1 Cor. 9:11–12; 2 Thess. 3:9), and in this ideal arrangement the LORD instituted ample provision for those whom he called to serve him.

(5) Practical Justice (45:9–17)

It is often the case that an effective presentation of the ideal cannot be achieved only by a positive display. What is perfect may well be better understood by contrast with what is currently experienced as flawed and unsatisfactory. So here, in an apostrophe, the LORD begins by addressing Israel's rulers, past and future, and urges them to abandon behaviour that violates the standards of the covenant and to ensure that such misconduct is eradicated from the land. Their personal behaviour in the past is condemned (45:9), and they are to ensure an absence of fraudulent trading practices (45:10–12).

Allied to equitable business standards in the land, appropriate contributions towards the maintenance of temple worship must be made by the people as a whole through the ruler (45:13–16), and also by the ruler personally on stated occasions in sanctuary worship (45:17). The way in which the divine exhortation moves from one area to another envisages that in the ideal society no tension would exist between the liturgical and the ethical. Conformity to the law of God in every sphere of life would be integral to covenant fidelity.

> 45:9'Thus says the Lord GOD: You ⌊have gone far⌋ enough, rulers of Israel! Remove violence and devastation, and execute judgement and righteousness; stop your evictions of my people, declares the Lord GOD. 45:10You are to have honest scales and an honest ephah and an honest bath. 45:11The ephah and the bath are to be the same quantity, so that the bath will carry one-tenth of a homer and the ephah one-tenth of a homer; their measurement is to be according to the homer. 45:12And the shekel ⌊is to be⌋ twenty gerahs; twenty shekels, twenty-five shekels and fifteen shekels is to be a mina for you. 45:13This is the portion which you are to apportion: one-sixth of an ephah from a homer of wheat, and you are to take one-sixth of an ephah from a homer of barley; 45:14and the prescribed amount of oil by the bath of oil, one-tenth of a bath from the kor ⌊which is⌋ ten baths ⌊or⌋ a homer, for ten baths ⌊are⌋ a homer; 45:15and one lamb from the flock, from ⌊every⌋ two hundred, from the well-watered ⌊pastures⌋ of Israel. ⌊These are to be⌋ for grain offerings and for burnt offerings and for peace offerings to make atonement for them, declares the Lord GOD. 45:16All the people of the land are to ⌊give⌋ this portion to the ruler in Israel. 45:17And it is to be on the ruler ⌊to provide⌋ the burnt offerings and the grain offerings and the drink offerings at the feasts and at the new moons and at the Sabbaths, at all the appointed meetings of the house of Israel; he ⌊is the one who⌋ is to provide the sin offerings and the grain offerings and the burnt offerings and the peace offerings to make atonement on behalf of the house of Israel.'

♦ **45:9** A new direct address of the LORD was formally introduced by the messenger formula, *Thus says the Lord GOD* (cf. 2:4), and was further authenticated by use of the signature formula, *declares the Lord GOD* (cf. 5:11). The covenant King addressed those whom he designated as *rulers of Israel.* This continued the use of the expression 'my rulers' (45:8), avoiding the term 'king' for earlier monarchs (cf. 7:27), but also including in the same group those who would govern the people in the future. The term 'ruler' reminded them of their subordinate status before the LORD. He dramatically set before them and before the community that the conduct of rulers was not to be a perpetuation of the misrule which had previously prevailed.

You ⌐have gone far⌐ enough! (lit., 'much with respect to you'; cf. 44:6) declared that earlier malpractice had breached the limits of divine patience. Their behaviour had fallen far short of what was expected of them, and they were commanded to make an end of it.

Remove violence and devastation. The first term ($\d{h}\=am\=as$; cf. 7:11, 23) concentrated on unlawful force employed against the person, whereas 'devastation' ($\v{s}\=od$) zoomed in on offences involving property. But both involved violence, and the two might be considered a hendiadys, equivalent to 'violent lawlessness' (cf. Jer. 6:7; 20:8). In this case it had not been not perpetrated by an enemy, but by those in authority in the land and their associates.

In a reference to the moral and theological aspects of covenant obedience, *execute judgement and righteousness* (cf. 18:5) exhorted that such violations of the covenant rights of the people were to be replaced by the practise and promotion of covenant standards. So the reform programme envisaged was in two parts. It called not merely for removal of abuses (which would result in a vacuum), but also for the institution of approved patterns of conduct. Inasmuch as these commands were addressed to past and future rulers of Israel, the ruler was conceived of as the one who continued to have responsibility for the administration of justice in the civil affairs of the people. This had been the ideal to which David at his best had conformed (2 Sam. 8:15), and later Josiah (Jer. 22:15). In displaying this sort of behaviour these kings had foreshadowed the conduct of the righteous Branch of David (Jer. 23:5).

(a) Economic Practices (45:9b–12). **Stop your evictions of my people.** 'Stop' was literally 'lift up' (*rûm* hiphil; cf. 45:1), probably with the idea of removal of an oppressive burden. The noun rendered 'evictions' occurred only here in the Old Testament, but its root was

used of a divorced woman as one cast out from the family home (cf. Lev. 21:7, 14; 22:13). It is unlikely that unwarranted divorce was in view here; rather it was the forcible ejection of people from occupation of their rightful inheritance (cf. 46:18).

♦ **45:10** There followed a series of particular injunctions designed to secure that right conduct prevailed in the community. Some were addressed particularly to the ruler, but others were for all the people.

Since weights and measures were employed in everyday life to facilitate trading, the use of fraudulent standards was proscribed to ensure that the people were fairly treated by those with whom they were doing business. This was an on-going concern throughout the Old Testament Scriptures (cf. Lev. 19:36; Deut. 25:13–16; Prov. 11:1; 16:11; 20:10, 23; Mic. 6:11). *Honest* was related to the term 'righteousness' in the preceding verse. While this was largely a matter of 'accuracy' (cf. NIV), it extended to ethically appropriate behaviour in every aspect of a transaction. On the *scales* the object to be weighed would be balanced against objects of known weight. As regards volume, there was to be a standard *ephah* for dry goods, such as grain. This would result in a container which would hold about 39 pints (22 litres). The *bath* was used to measure the volume of liquid goods, and it was to be of the same capacity (45:11). The size of these measures had varied over time, and from place to place, but ideally they were to be standardised so that there was no scope for unscrupulous trading. But *you* (plural) *are to have* required transparency regarding what was in use and how they were used throughout the community.

♦ **45:11** It is unclear if this was an attempt to reimpose old measures which had been abandoned, or if it was a reform of existing measures. *The ephah and the bath will be the same volume*, the former for dry goods and the latter for liquids. The use of the article pointed to a typical standard measure. Different styles of container would be used, but their capacity was to be identical (the niphal of the verb corresponding to 'volume' was used of fairness or equity in 18:25, 29; 33:17, 20). It was the *homer* which was to be used as the standard unit. A homer was equivalent to 48 gallons (220 litres), with the ephah and the bath both being a tenth of that amount. These estimated sizes are subject to considerable margins of uncertainty.

♦ **45:12** In this verse what was in view was the weighing, not of the commodity being traded, but of the precious metal which was being given in exchange. As yet coinage had not been introduced. The *gerah* was the smallest weight in use in Israel (about 0.02 ounces or 0.57 g), and so the *shekel* was here computed as about 0.4 ounces (11.4 g). The *mina* was the largest unit mentioned. It was envisaged as being weighed out by using three smaller weights: *twenty shekels, twenty-five shekels and fifteen shekels.*[102] This yielded a total of sixty shekels (24 ounces, 0.68 kilograms), but elsewhere in the Old Testament the mina was reckoned as fifty shekels. Possibly the use of sixty reflected the influence of Babylonian systems of measurement (Block 1998:657), but the larger unit may have theologically reflected a desire for full amounts to be used in the liturgy of the sanctuary.

♦ **45:13** *(b) Provision for Offerings (45:13–17)*. **This is the portion which you** (plural) **are to apportion** introduced directions regarding the various contributions which had to be made to support the regular sacrificial worship of the sanctuary. The term 'portion' (*tərûmâ*) was used earlier in the chapter with respect to a 'portion' of land (45:1, 6, 7), but here it referred to a contribution required from the produce of the LORD's land. **One-sixth of an ephah from a homer of wheat** represented a levy of one-sixtieth (cf. 45:11). **You are to take one-sixth**[103] **of an ephah from a homer of barley** prescribed the same ratio for the required quota of barley.

♦ **45:14 The prescribed amount** (*ḥōq*, cf. 16:27) of olive *oil* was to be measured by **the bath of oil** (lit., 'the bath, the oil'). The measure of a *kor* was apparently less common for either liquid or dry measure, the term occurring only seven times elsewhere, and so there was the explanation of its size, ⌊**which is**⌋ **ten baths** ⌊**or**⌋ **a homer, for ten baths** ⌊**are**⌋ **a homer.** So 1 per cent of the olive oil was to be contributed as compared to 1.6 per cent of the wheat.

♦ **45:15** Lambs were to be contributed at the rate of one from every two hundred (0.5 per cent). It was further required that they be *from the well-watered pastures of Israel.* This was a measure of quality

---

102. The RSV, following the LXX and many commentators, takes the mina as set at the customary fifty shekels. This change is argued for on the basis of unusual features of the expression 'fifteen shekels' which is literally 'ten and five shekel'. Elsewhere 'fifteen' is expressed as 'five and ten', and the singular 'shekel' is employed instead of a plural as in the two preceding weights (though the singular does not violate Hebrew grammar; cf. GKC §97 d, e).

103. The verb *wəšiššîtem*, 'you are to [will] take a sixth' is a denominative piel from *šiššît*, 'a sixth'. Some regard the final *mem* as a scribal error, and simply read the fraction *šiššît*.

control, pointing to well-nourished animals, not those which had been reared in the drier, wilderness zones. It also incorporated a reminder of the fulsome nature of the LORD's provision for the people from which they were to contribute to the maintenance of the temple ritual.

These components were to be provided *for grain offerings and for burnt offerings and for peace offerings.* No mention is made of the sin offering and the guilt offering, but the list was not intended as exhaustive (note the variations in the lists given in 45:17) but representative. *To make atonement for them* (cf. 16:63) reminded them of the goal of these offerings, a goal now consummated in Christ.

♦ **45:16** After the amounts to be supplied had been stipulated, there were set out two special regulations regarding the process of making the contribution. First, *all the people of the land are to ⌊give⌋*[104] *this contribution* (cf. 45:13) *to the ruler in Israel.* 'The people of the land' here (and in 45:22; 46:3, 9: contrast 7:27) designated the whole population viewed as the covenant congregation, of whom none was exempt from this levy. Moreover, they were to present these provisions for the stated offerings, not to the priests, but to the ruler. However, this was not a form of political taxation with the contributions at the disposal of the ruler for his own purposes. Instead, as the next verse made clear, he was to act as the channel through whom the public offerings in the temple were provided.

♦ **45:17** Secondly, the extent to which the ruler's office centred on the sanctuary was set out in the further stipulation: *it is to be on the ruler ⌊to provide⌋.* He was obligated to furnish all the public sacrificial offerings *at the feasts and at the new moons and at the Sabbaths, at all the appointed meetings of the house of Israel.* The two lists of sacrifices in the verse were representative as in 45:15. The major sacrifice omitted was the guilt offering (though it did occur in 40:39; 42:13; 44:29; 46:20), for it was a private, not a public, offering. On the other hand, mention was made of *the drink offerings* (45:17), subsidiary offerings of wine which accompanied other sacrifices.

He ⌊is the one who⌋ is to provide (lit., 'make') laid the duty of furnishing the victims on the ruler (cf. 45:22; 46:2, 7, 13, 14, 15). The purpose of these offerings was specified as *to make atonement on*

---

104. The obligatory imperfect in the expression *yihyû ʾel*, 'they are to be to/towards' indicates the imposition of a duty and responsibility on all the people of the land, as does the corresponding phrase in 45:17 with respect to the ruler: *ʿal-hannāśîʾ yihyeh*, 'on/upon the ruler is to be.'

behalf of the house of Israel (cf. 45:15). The actual sacrificing to deal with Israel's sin (cf. 16:63) would have been carried out by priestly intermediaries, but it is easy to detect here a messianic fusion of the royal and sacerdotal spheres of action. In these ideal arrangements there was no high priest to receive the offerings. Instead the ruler was obligated to fulfil certain aspects of his role. This blurring of the division of the duties involved in these two offices undoubtedly anticipated the work of the Messiah.

REFLECTION

- The ideal society described here is not yet a heavenly one. It still requires the offering of sacrifice because its citizens are still liable to sin and continue to require that atonement be made for their iniquity in accordance with God's requirements so that the penalty they have incurred may be paid and divine justice satisfied. Though such Old Testament offerings have now been definitively superseded by Christ's final offering of himself, the need for its atoning efficacy remains, for 'if we say we have no sin, we deceive ourselves, and the truth is not in us' (1 John 1:8).
- The ideal community was not to be so taken up with 'religious' matters as to forget the need for equitable dealings in the ordinary affairs of life. The prophets had inveighed against those 'made the ephah small and the shekel great, and dealt deceitfully with false balances' (Amos 8:5–6; cf. Mic. 6:10–11) so that those in positions of economic dominance could defraud the poor and uninfluential. The same warnings must be issued still. 'A false balance is an abomination to the LORD, but a just weight is his delight' (Prov. 11:1; cf. Prov. 16:11; 20:10). A commitment to the LORD which does not extend to the market-place is no true commitment at all.
- While it is the case that in New Testament times the spheres of church and state are separated, the standards of morality are the same for both. The world of business and commerce, no less than the affairs of the church, is under divine scrutiny, and scrupulously honest conduct should prevail there also.

(6) The Major Festivals (45:18–25)

Following on from the reference to the festivals of Israelite religion in 45:17, they are extensively discussed in two sections (45:18–25 and 46:1–15), both of which begin with the messenger formula, 'Thus says the Lord GOD'. The first section focuses on the procedure to be followed at the major festivals, while the later section sets out the regulations for the Sabbath and the new moon, and particularly the role to be played by the ruler in connection with them.

The procedures laid out here begin with the institution of a new ceremony for cleansing the sanctuary (45:18–20), followed by revised regulations regarding the Passover (45:21–24) and the feast of Tabernacles (45:25). It is uncertain to what extent whatever is not mentioned is presumed to continue as before or to be abrogated.

> ⁴⁵:¹⁸'Thus says the Lord GOD: In the first ⌞month⌟ on the first of the month, you are to take a bull from the herd without blemish and cleanse the sanctuary. ⁴⁵:¹⁹And the priest is to take some of the blood of the sin offering and set ⌞it⌟ on the doorpost of the house and on the four corners of the ledge of the altar and upon the doorpost of the gateway of the inner courtyard. ⁴⁵:²⁰And you are to act similarly on the seventh of the month because of one who goes astray and because of one who is naive, and you are to make atonement for the house.
> ⁴⁵:²¹In the first month, on the fourteenth day of the month you are to have the Passover; ⌞for⌟ a feast, weeks of days, unleavened bread is to be eaten. ⁴⁵:²²And on that day the ruler is to provide on his own behalf and on behalf of the people of the land a bull for a sin offering. ⁴⁵:²³And on the seven days of the feast he is to provide ⌞as⌟ a burnt offering to the LORD seven bulls and seven rams, ⌞all⌟ without blemish, on each day of the seven days, and ⌞as⌟ a sin offering a he-goat each day. ⁴⁵:²⁴And he is to provide ⌞as⌟ a grain offering an ephah per bull and an ephah per ram, and oil a hin per ephah. ⁴⁵:²⁵In the seventh ⌞month⌟, on the fifteenth day of the month, at the feast, he is to provide according to these ⌞requirements⌟ for seven days according to the sin offering, according to the burnt offering and according to the grain offering, and according to the oil.'

♦ **45:18** *(a) Temple Cleansing (45:18–20)*. Since 45:21 directed that Passover was to be celebrated in the first month, it is clear that in this verse ***in the first ⌞month⌟ on the first of the month*** was reckoned by the traditional calendar of Israel which started in the spring. In ***you are to take***, the Hebrew verb was obligatory and not merely future in its scope (and so with the verbs throughout this section; cf. 40:38). The sacrifice of ***a bull from the herd*** (cf. 43:19) represented a considerable simplification from the offerings required at the beginning of every month under the Mosaic law (Num. 28:11–15), though ***without blemish*** recalled 43:23, 25 and was the standard requirement for sacrifices. However, the purpose of this ceremony, to *cleanse the sanctuary* from the effect of sin (cf. 43:20 with respect to the altar), was different from the monthly sacrifices. Milgrom (2012:149) suggests that 'sanctuary' here is equivalent to the sacred compound of the priests, that is, the inner courtyard and its associated buildings.

It is unclear whether this was intended as a one-off initial event (e.g., Block 1998:662–664), or an annual institution (e.g., Milgrom 2012:199–206). In favour of the former is the singular verb 'you are to take' (cf. 45:20) if it referred to Ezekiel personally, while the references to the Passover would support the view that an annual institution was in view here also. A one-off event might have been patterned after the consecration of the tabernacle on the first day of the year (Exod. 40:2).

♦ **45:19** Though elements of the ritual set out here had parallels in the Pentateuch, in its entirety it was innovative. Hummel (2007:1308) speculates that the blood ritual for New Moons and feasts apart from the Day of Atonement was the same as those for sin offerings for the high priest and for the whole congregation (Lev. 4). In these the priest entered the Holy Place to sprinkle the blood before the curtain and on the incense altar, and then poured the rest of the blood at the base of the sacrificial altar in the courtyard (Lev. 4:5–7, 16–18). As Milgrom notes (2012:209), the blood was not brought within the sanctuary itself, possibly because no human entered within the ideal temple to contaminate it with sin.

In this ideal temple, however, there was no incense altar, and so *the priest* (for the case that this was a reference to the high priest, see on 44:30) was to put *some of the blood of the sin offering ... on the doorpost of the house* (the singular 'doorpost' was probably used collectively; cf. 41:21) *and on the four corners of the ledge of the altar, and upon the doorpost of the gateway* (probably another collective usage for the three gates) *of the inner courtyard.* This was an act to counter and remove the impact of sin (see on 43:20).

♦ **45:20** Nothing was said about what was to occur in the intervening week. On the basis of 43:25–27 it may have been that the rituals were repeated daily. However, what should happen a week later was set out. *You are to act similarly on the seventh of the month.* 'You' was singular, which, if this was a one-off occurrence, might have referred to Ezekiel. This action was to be taken *because of* (causal *min*) two sorts of individual. *One who goes astray* used a verb which ordinarily described wandering livestock, but was applied metaphorically to describe unintentional human sin (this use was found in Lev. 4:13; Num. 15:22). *One who is naive (petî)* was frequently employed in Proverbs to characterise the simple-minded or gullible, one who therefore sinned through ignorance. Though unintended and unwitting sins were to be distinguished from deliberate sin committed 'with a high hand' (Num. 15:30) and were viewed as less heinous, they were nonetheless sin, and required that appropriate countermeasures be employed: *you are to make atonement for the house.*

♦ **45:21** *(b) The Passover (45:21–24). In the first month, on the fourteenth day of the month, you* (plural) *are to have the Passover.* This was its traditional spring date in the first month (Abib, later Nisan, corresponding to March/April). ⌊*For*⌋ *a feast, weeks of days* is an obscure expression, but it was unlikely to extend the Passover season over seven weeks. It seems simply to mean that the feast was to last for seven days (cf. 45:23), and throughout that period *unleavened bread is to be eaten* (cf. Exod. 13:6–7).

♦ **45:22** Although the prescribed routines for these days were similar to those set out in Exodus, the ruler was again given prominence here. Initially the Passover had been a family celebration (Exod. 12), but even before settlement in the land the divine requirement was for a pilgrimage festival involving all males (Exod. 23:14–17; 34:22–23; Deut. 16:16). At times of revival in the kingdom period, reforming kings such as Hezekiah (2 Chron. 30:1–27) and Josiah (2 Chron. 35:1–19) reinstituted the central Passover celebrations and provided the animals for it.

The ruler is to provide on his own behalf ... a bull for a sin offering. This strongly indicated that the ruler was not a direct type of Christ, since the ruler had to sacrifice for his personal sin, as well as providing *on behalf of the people of the land* (cf. 45:17).

♦ **45:23** No mention was made of the Passover lamb, which was killed on the fourteenth day of the first month. Instead on that day (and throughout the festival), the ruler *is to provide* ⌊*as*⌋ *a burnt offering to the* L ORD *seven bulls and seven rams.* All of these were to be *without blemish.* There was also offered ⌊*as*⌋ *a sin offering a he-goat each day.* The Mosaic legislation had required two bulls, a ram, and seven male lambs as a burnt offering as well as a he-goat for a sin offering on each day of the feast of Unleavened Bread following on from the Passover (Num. 28:16–25). These numbers are far lower than those for the sacrifices under Hezekiah and Josiah (2 Chron. 30:24; 35:7).

♦ **45:24** Grain offerings mixed with oil were also a feature of the Mosaic ordinances (Num. 28:20–21), although here the amount of grain was larger and a specific quantity of oil was mandated. A *hin* was about 6.5 pints (3.7 litres). These offerings were therefore heightened from the earlier legislation. The historical background to the Passover in terms of the Exodus was not directly mentioned here, though it may be presumed. The focus was more on maintenance of the holiness of the people and purification from sin.

♦ **45:25** *Tabernacles.* ***In the seventh ₑmonth₃, on the fifteenth day of the month, at the feast*** referred to the Feast of Tabernacles. The ritual prescribed for that feast was to be patterned after what had been previously prescribed. Apparently that did not include the cleansing of the sanctuary (45:18–20), but only the Passover ritual found in 45:21–24, as the fivefold use of *according to* emphasised. The Mosaic ordinances for Tabernacles had not followed such a pattern (Num. 29:12–34). Ezekiel makes no mention of the Feast of Weeks, the Day of Trumpets, the closing eighth day of Tabernacles, or of the Day of Atonement. It may be that the others were assumed to continue as previously, or this more limited set of observances may have represented a scaling down of the liturgical calendar.

REFLECTION

- The frequency with which sacrifices were required in the Mosaic ritual and in these regulations for the ideal temple made it clear to Israel both how deep-seated the problem of human sin is and also how ineffective the partial remedy provided by the offering of animals was. Now that 'the offering of the body of Jesus Christ once for all' (Heb. 10:10) has occurred, the repetitious element in sacrificial worship and the need for the offering of animals have ceased, but that should not be permitted to dull awareness of the fact that sin continues to assail humanity and to pervert human conduct. The atoning and cleansing efficacy of the once-for-all sacrifice needs to be appropriated daily throughout our earthly pilgrimage.
- The profile given in these regulations to the Passover and the Feast of Unleavened Bread emphasised the redemptive nature of this worship and also the perpetual requirement to guard against the presence of sin in the community.

(7) Further Regulations for Worship (46:1–15)

The ideal temple was used on other occasions apart from the Passover and Tabernacles. Consideration is given here to the routines to be followed on the Sabbath, on the first of the month, and on a daily basis. There are variations from the procedures set out in the Mosaic rites, most prominent of which is the role accorded to the ruler.

⁴⁶:¹'Thus says the Lord GOD: The gateway of the inner courtyard which faces east is to be shut for the six working days, but on the Sabbath day it is to be opened and on the day of the new moon it is to be opened. ⁴⁶:²And the ruler is to enter by way of the vestibule of the gateway from outside, and to stand by the doorpost of the gateway. Then the priests are to offer his burnt offering and his peace offering, and he is to bow down at the threshold of the gateway. Then he is to go out, but the gateway is not to be closed until the evening. ⁴⁶:³And the people of the land are to bow down before the LORD at the entrance of that gateway on the Sabbaths and on the new moons. ⁴⁶:⁴And the burnt offering which the ruler offers to the LORD on the Sabbath day ⌞will be⌟ six lambs without blemish and a ram without blemish. ⁴⁶:⁵And the grain offering ⌞will be⌟ an ephah per ram, and the grain offering with the lambs ⌞will be⌟ as much as he chooses, and oil, a hin per ephah. ⁴⁶:⁶And on the day of the new moon ⌞it will be⌟ a bull from the herd without blemish, and six lambs, and a ram; they are to be without blemish. ⁴⁶:⁷And he is to offer an ephah per bull and an ephah per ram ⌞as⌟ a grain offering, and for the lambs as much as he chooses, and oil, a hin per ephah. ⁴⁶:⁸And when the ruler comes in, he is to come in by way of the vestibule of the gateway, and to go out by the same way. ⁴⁶:⁹And when the people of the land come in before the LORD at the appointed meetings, whoever comes in by way of the north gateway to bow down is to go out by way of the south gateway, and whoever enters by way of the south gateway is to go out by way of the north gateway; he is not to return by way of the gateway by which he entered but is to go out by the opposite ⌞gateway⌟. ⁴⁶:¹⁰And the ruler ⌞is to be⌟ in their midst; when they come in, he is to come in, and when they go out, he is to go out.

⁴⁶:¹¹And at the feasts and at the appointed meetings the grain offering is to be an ephah per bull and an ephah per ram and for the lambs as much as he chooses, and oil, a hin per ephah. ⁴⁶:¹²And when the ruler makes a freewill burnt offering or a freewill peace offering to the LORD, and the gateway which faces east is opened for him, then he is to make his burnt offering and his peace offering just as he does on the Sabbath day. Then he is to go out, and the gateway is to be closed after he has gone out.

⁴⁶:¹³And daily you are to offer a year old lamb without blemish

⌊as⌋ a burnt offering to the LORD; you are to offer it each morning. ⁴⁶:¹⁴And you are to offer a grain offering with it each morning, a sixth of an ephah, and oil, a third of a hin, to moisten the fine flour. ⌊It is⌋ a grain offering to the LORD; ⌊they are to be⌋ perpetual ordinances regularly ⌊maintained⌋. ⁴⁶:¹⁵And they are to offer the lamb and the grain offering and the oil each morning ⌊as⌋ a regular burnt offering.'

♦ **46:1** *The East Inner Gateway (46:1–3).* The messenger formula, ***Thus says the Lord GOD***, introduced another section in the development of the visionary scenario which had begun in chapter 40. After the directions for the annual festivals such as the Passover and Tabernacles, consideration was now given to the conduct of temple worship at other times, particularly on the Sabbath and on the day of the new moon. It had earlier been directed that the east gate of the outer courtyard was to be permanently shut (44:1–2), but here the focus was on ***the gateway of the inner courtyard which faces east.*** It too was ***to be shut***[105] but only ***for the six working days***, literally 'days of work', that is, the six weekdays on which work was permitted as enjoined by the fourth commandment in accordance with the pattern set by the LORD's own activity in creation (cf. Exod. 20:8–11). In contrast to what occurred during the week, ***on the Sabbath day***, that is the weekly Sabbath (cf. 20:12), and ***on the day of the new moon*** (the first day of the month in a lunar calendar), the gate ***is to be opened***. At these times the ruler was present to represent the people.

♦ **46:2** Again it is significant that there was no mention of a high priest, but aspects of the role he might have been expected to perform were transferred to ***the ruler*** (see on 44:3), anticipating the merging of the two offices in Christ (see on 45:17). Here he has a supervisory role and his sacrifices were to be offered first, probably because he represented the nation as a whole. While he brought the animals to be offered, the priests performed the actual sacrifice.

As a mark of the status accorded to him, it was laid down that ***the ruler is to enter by way of the vestibule of the gateway from outside.*** This assumed that he was already in the outer courtyard, and granted him the privilege, not extended to ordinary worshippers, of ascending

---

105. The construction *yihyeh sāgûr* is periphrastic (cf. 44:2). The imperfect indicated an obligation (Introduction §6.3a), while the passive participle pointed to the continuing state of 'being shut' rather than to an action to bring that state about. This was a construction which only became common in later Biblical Hebrew.

the eight steps and entering the east inner gateway. Then it would seem that he was allowed to move through it and **stand by the doorpost of the gateway,** at its inner end. 'Doorpost' (*məzûzâ*; 41:21) referred to the framework supporting doors or gates. There were gateposts at the entrance of each inner gateway (40:28-37), and also apparently there were gateposts at the exit of the gateway into the inner courtyard. From there the ruler would see all that was done in the inner courtyard, but the fact that he was stationed there showed that he could not enter the sacred space of the courtyard (the gateway itself being from its position a transitional zone). While he could supervise the sacrificial rituals, he could not personally participate in them.

Once the ruler had taken up his position, **then the priests are to offer his burnt offering and his peace offering.** 'His' might have indicated a personal offering, but it is more probable that it was what he provided on behalf of the people through the contributions they had been directed to make (45:13-17). 'Offer' renders the verb 'to do' (also in 46:15). When the sacrifice was offered, the ruler **is to bow down at the threshold**[106] **of the gateway.** By this action of prostration the ruler would lead the response in worship of the people as a whole. It was not said how long the ruler should maintain this posture before he **is to go out** by the same route by which he entered, retracing his steps down the eastern stairway into the outer courtyard (46:8). However, **the gateway is not to be closed until the evening.** It would remain open for several hours after the ruler had left.

♦ **46:3 The people of the land,** the rest of the community other than the ruler and the priests (cf. 45:16), were also directed to participate in the worship. They were **to bow down before the LORD at the entrance of that gateway,** that is, the east gateway of the inner courtyard. However, the people remained in the outer courtyard. From there they could see much that went on in the inner courtyard because it is improbable that the retaining wall round that courtyard rose above its level. In this they may be thought of as following the ruler's lead in prostrating themselves **before the LORD.** This ritual was to be observed **on the Sabbaths and on the new moons.**

Hummel (2007:1317) argues that 'the correspondence here ... between the worship of the people and the simultaneous worship of the Prince shows that he has a vicarious role. He approaches God more intimately than any of the people can and represents them "before

---

106. The term *miptān* (also in 47:1) is a synonym for the term *sap* used earlier for 'threshold' (40:6-7; 41:16; 43:8).

Yahweh" (44:3), so that, by virtue of his mediation, the people too can worship "before Yahweh" (46:3, 9).'

♦ **46:4** *The Sabbath Offerings (46:4–5)*. **On the Sabbath day** the ruler was to present for sacrifice ***the burnt offering ... to the LORD***. In doing so he was acting on behalf of the community as a whole. The offering of ***six lambs without blemish and a ram without blemish*** was less than that on the festival days (45:21–25), but more than the Mosaic ordinances required (Num. 28:9).

♦ **46:5** The sacrifices were not confined to the burnt offering. There was also to be a ***grain offering*** with ***an ephah per ram*** as its prescribed size. However, for ***the grain offerings with the lambs*** no amount was specified. ***As much as he chooses*** renders 'a gift of his hand', the exact phrase being found only here and in 46:11, though there was a similar expression in 46:7. It might have indicated 'as much as he was able to give' (AV, RSV, ESV), or 'whatever he wished to give' (NKJV, NRSV, NIV). A synonym occurred in 'according to the gift of his hand' (Deut. 16:17), where the context would favour the sense as being that a donation proportionate to the extent to which he had been blessed by the LORD and so was able to provide. The amount of oil, ***a hin per ephah***, repeated the requirement of 45:24.

♦ **46:6** *The New Moon Offerings (46:6–7)*. What was required ***on the day of the new moon***, the first day of the month in Israel's lunar calendar, was reduced in extent from Mosaic provisions set out in Numbers 28:11–15. ***A bull from the herd*** (see on 43:19) ***without blemish***,[107] ***and six lambs, and a ram*** contrasted with the stipulation of 'two bulls from the herd, one ram, seven male lambs a year old without blemish' for the same ceremony in earlier years (Num. 28:11). This reduction constitutes one of the puzzling variations between Ezekiel and the Pentateuch (see also 44:31; 45:18; 45:20).[108] If the quantity to be offered had been increased, that might be explained by

---

107. The plural form *təmîmim* does not agree with the singular *par*, 'bull'. Perhaps the *mem* was wrongly written twice, or the word has been assimilated to the plural form at the end of the verse.

108. A well-known rabbinic tradition reported concerning one Hananiah ben Hezekiah who, when the book of Ezekiel was in danger of being withdrawn from use because of these seeming contradictions, 'brought up three hundred barrels of oil and stayed in the upper room until he had explained away everything' (*b. Menaḥoth* 45a). Unfortunately, the results of his labours have not been preserved.

appealing to the greater sanctity of these ideal arrangements. Did a reduction imply a lesser need for offerings on the part of the restored people?

♦ **46:7** *As much as he chooses* was literally 'according as his hand overtakes/reaches', which probably had the same significance as the similar phrase in 46:5, either whatever amount he choose, or as much as he was able to afford.

♦ **46:8** *Access to the Sacred Precincts (46:8–10).* The arrangements for the passage of worshippers into and through the temple courtyards were detailed. First the ruler was required ***to come in by way of the vestibule of the gateway***. That repeated what had already been said in 46:2 with regard to the east inner gateway, but now it was made clear that he was ***to go out by the same way.*** That forbade him from entering the inner courtyard by one gateway and leaving by another.

♦ **46:9** ***When the people of the land come in before the LORD*** envisaged the congregation gathering to worship in the temple (cf. 45:16). ***At the appointed meetings*** was an inclusive expression covering both the special feast days and the recurrent Sabbath and New Moon ceremonies (but note 46:11). What was in view was not presentation of personal sacrifices, but their presence when sacrifices were brought by the ruler on their behalf. The action of the people was ***to bow down*** in reverent prostration within the sacred precincts, the central gesture of their worship (cf. 46:2, 3).

The movement of the worshippers was carefully controlled. Each had to leave the outer courtyard by the gateway opposite that by which he had entered. ***By the opposite ⌐gateway⌐*** was literally 'his/its opposite', which might mean that he ***is to go out***[109] opposite himself, moving straight ahead and not turning round, or by 'its opposite', that is the facing gateway. Either option was possible, but the direction of movement was the same in either event, and may have been intended to prevent the breach of etiquette involved in turning round and so, at least momentarily, having their backs towards the LORD in the sanctuary (contrast 8:16).

---

109. The qere *yēṣēʾ*, 'he is to go out', agrees with the earlier verbs in the verse which are all singular. The kethib *yēṣəʾû*, 'they are to go out', is plural, and could follow the introductory *ʿam*, 'people', which as a collective noun might be followed by a plural according to sense. The qere, which is in fact the reading of many Hebrew manuscripts and early versions, is more probable. Note also the closing verb in the following verse.

♦ **46:10** *The ruler ⌊is to be⌋ in their midst* associated the ruler's movements with those of the people. ***When they come in*** and ***when they go out*** were literally 'in their coming in' and 'in their coming out'. These expressions are standard Hebrew temporal idioms and are rendered as such by English translations. The possibility, however, must be allowed for here that the three occurrences of the preposition 'in' (*bə*) were intended in the same spatial sense so that what 'in their midst' commanded was not synchronisation of the presence of the ruler and the people, but common adherence to the same pathway. The ruler was to come in/go out where the people did. In this respect the ruler and the people were more closely associated than the priests and the people.

In the Massoretic text the concluding verb in the verse is 'they are to go out', but many Hebrew manuscripts and early versions have ***he is to go out***, which is generally accepted as the reading.

♦ **46:11** *Miscellaneous Regulations (46:11–12)*. This verse generalised the regulations regarding the grain offering for the Sabbaths and New Moons in 46:5, 7 to apply ***at the feasts and at the appointed meetings***. The former was a reference to the pilgrimage festivals; for the latter, see on 46:9. ***As much as he chooses*** (lit. 'a gift of his hand') repeated the idiom found in 46:5.

♦ **46:12** A ***freewill*** offering was one presented in addition to the sacrifices of the stated rites of the sanctuary, and was entirely voluntary and spontaneous (Lev. 22:18–25; Num. 15:1–12). It was often mentioned along with a votive offering made in fulfilment of a vow, which itself was a voluntary obligation though, once made, payment of it was morally binding. Here the possibilities regarding the type of sacrifice which could be presented as a freewill offering were limited to a ***burnt offering*** or a ***peace offering*** (cf. Lev. 22:18, 21; Num. 15:3). ***Just as he does on the Sabbath day*** referred to the manner of sacrificing as prescribed in 46:1–2, though as regards timing the freewill offering could be presented on any suitable day. Since the gateway was ordinarily closed during the week, special arrangements were instituted so that when the ruler presented himself at the east inner gateway to make such an offering, ***the gateway which*** *faces east is to be opened for him.*[110] When he left, *the gateway is to be closed* immediately, and not left open until evening as set out earlier (46:2).

♦ **46:13** *The Daily Offering (46:13–15).* In this and the following verse second person singular verbs are used. The switch is unexpected (but not unprecedented, cf. 45:18, 20), and some early versions (LXX, Vulgate) and English translations (RSV, NRSV) employ third person singular forms. It is unclear whether the ruler, Ezekiel, or the people as a whole are being addressed. Taking up the matter of the daily sacrifices at this juncture followed the precedent of Numbers 28:1–15, and probably it was the ruler's provision that was intended.

The Mosaic ritual specified that a daily burnt offering accompanied by a grain offering and libation was to be offered both morning and evening (Exod. 29:38–40; Num. 28:1–8). Here the repeated mention *each morning* (lit., the distributive expression 'in the morning, in the morning') raises the possibility that the evening offering was abrogated. There was also no mention of the libation required earlier (Exod. 29:40; Num. 28:7–8). Such curtailment, if that was the intention of the text, would have indicated a gradual simplification of the ritual requirements, moving towards the 'once for all' sacrifice of Christ in which all the Mosaic sacrifices found their culmination.

♦ **46:14** Unlike the grain offerings at the feasts (46:5, 7, 11) where the amounts involved were unspecified, here precise quantities were stipulated. *The fine flour* was ground from the inner grain of the wheat with the husks removed, and was required when a grain offering was made (Lev. 2:1). It was to be moistened with drops of oil. While it is possible to take the words *a grain offering to the LORD* with the preceding clause (cf. ESV, HCSB), the Massoretic accents joined it with what followed. Hence the two clauses in the translation: ⌊*It is*⌋ *a grain offering to the LORD;* ⌊*they are to be*⌋ *perpetual ordinances regularly* ⌊*maintained*⌋.

The plural 'perpetual ordinances' occurred only here, and translations generally substitute the more common expression 'a perpetual ordinance' (e.g., in Exod. 12:14, 17; Lev. 16:29, 31, 34). However, the plural may be understood as referring to the burnt

---

110. The expression *ûpātaḥ lô* may mean 'he [that is, the ruler] is to open for himself' and later *wəsāgar*, 'and he is to close'. However, the expressions are more probably instances of unspecified, impersonal subjects 'one is to open', 'one is to close', generally rendered by a passive in English.

offering of 46:13 and the grain offering of this verse. 'Perpetual' (*ʿôlām*) was used here not in the sense of 'everlasting' or 'eternal', but of lasting indefinitely throughout an unspecified period. Such ordinances were undoubtedly abrogated by the consummating self-offering of Christ. *Regularly* or 'repeatedly' (*tāmîd*) was employed frequently in Numbers 28 and 29 to denote a daily occurrence. Indeed in Daniel (Dan. 8:11-13; 11:31; 12:11) 'the *tāmîd*' became the term for the daily sacrifice.

♦ **46:15 *They are to offer*** [111] used the verb 'to make' (*ʿāśâ*), found also in 46:13 and 14, but here the plural subject obviously referred to the priests and so (as in 46:2) this 'making' or 'offering' was actually performed by them rather the plural pointing to those who brought and initiated the sacrifice.

REFLECTION
• The picture of the ideal community that is built up in these verses is one that is characterised by spiritual, not secular, concerns. Their lives are structured round the observances of the sanctuary, so that they are not carried along by the undifferentiated passage of time, but are constantly reminded of the biorhythms of spiritual life in the daily, weekly, monthly, and annual times of worship. These ritual ordinances in their Old Testament form have been done away with (Col. 2:16), but the underlying need to observe the spiritual fabric of our lives remains. 'On the first day of every week' (1 Cor. 16:2) there falls the New Testament equivalent to the Old Testament Sabbath, 'the Lord's day' (Rev. 1:10), no longer hedged about with legalistic restrictions, but with the greater redemptive significance of being specially dedicated to 'the lord of the Sabbath' (Mark 2:28). By 'not neglecting to meet together, as the habit of some is' (Heb. 10:25) on that day, there is set up for the Christian a spiritual rhythm to life, a regular act of reconsecration to the Lord, and the opportunity of 'encouraging one another, and all the more so as you see the day approaching' (Heb. 10:25).
• The regulations enacted here are a reminder of the need that 'all things should be done decently and in order' (1 Cor. 14:40) in the

---

111. The kethib, *wəʿāśû*, 'and they will make', is a *waw*-consecutive, whereas the qere has an imperfect form *yaʿăśû*, 'they will make', probably reflecting a later aversion to the *waw*-consecutive construction. Both verb forms reflect an obligation, and so are translated 'are to make' (Introduction §6.3a).

worship of the Lord. The worship of the ideal temple should reflect the orderliness and harmony of the God whose temple it is.

(8) Disposition of the Ruler's Property (46:16–18)

Ezekiel's vision of the arrangements for worship in the ideal temple have now been concluded, and the two sections which close chapter 46 consist of supplementary material. In the first addition, further prescriptions are set out regarding the ruler's property, which has already been described in 45:7–8, and which will again become the subject in 48:21–22. Three matters are reviewed: a gift by the ruler to one of his sons (46:16), a gift to a subject in general (46:17), and respect for the property rights of others (46:18).

Though the ruler in the ideal constitution envisaged here would have enhanced privileges over against the people as a whole, it would still be the case that he remains a constitutional ruler who is a subject of the covenant King. His freedom of action is therefore circumscribed by the requirements of his Overlord. The passage implies that the past policy of rulers in respect of land occupation and ownership was less than satisfactory. These ideal arrangements all inculcate the need to show respect for the divine distribution of the land. Whoever may presently occupy it, it in reality remains the LORD's, and his disposition of it may not be set aside. The territory allocated to the ruler in the central zone of the land is inalienable, and may not permanently pass out of his family line. Whether the ruler also possessed land in his tribal territory is not mentioned here; indeed, his tribal affiliation is never taken up in Ezekiel's vision.

> 46:16'Thus says the Lord GOD: If the ruler gives a gift to any of his sons, it ⌊will be⌋ his inheritance and will belong to his sons; it ⌊will be⌋ their possession by inheritance. 46:17But if he gives a gift from his inheritance to one of his subjects, then it will be his until the year of release when it will revert to the ruler; it ⌊is⌋ only his inheritance; ⌊as for⌋ his sons—it is to be theirs. 46:18And the ruler is not to take any of the inheritance of the people to oppress them from their possession; from his own possession he is to leave an inheritance to his sons so that none of my people may be dispersed from his possession.'

♦ **46:16** *If the ruler gives a gift to any of his sons* did not explicitly state what the gift consisted of, but mention of *inheritance*, that is, hereditary property, and *possession*, which was primarily the possession of land (cf. 44:28), made it clear what was in view. The ruler was permitted to make a special disposition of the land allotted to him to one of his sons. *It will be his inheritance*,[112] that is, the son's inheritance, and so, as part of his estate, it will in turn *belong to his sons,* that is the son's descendants and heirs. As *their possession by inheritance* no one will have the right to deprive them of it.

♦ **46:17** The second situation envisaged was where the ruler *gives a gift from his inheritance to one of his subjects.* 'From' indicated that what was in view was the donation of some part of his estate. *It will be his until the year of release when it will revert*[113] *to the ruler.* The ruler had, of course, no special grant of land made to him under the Mosaic law. Under the radically different circumstances envisaged in the vision where there was a royal estate consisting of two substantial tracts of land, it was necessary to clarify the terms on which it was held. 'Release' or 'liberty' (*dərôr*) referred to the return of property to the family of its original owners in the Jubilee year (Lev. 25:10), a divinely ordained liberation of the land from a situation of bondage. The term was employed in Isaiah 61:1, 'release to the captives', cited by Christ in Luke 4:18.

'Only' (*ʾak*) seems to function restrictively: *it is only his inheritance.* The ruler had the right to occupy it only because it had been divinely assigned to him, and so it was not competent for him to alienate it. ⌐As for⌐ *his sons—it is to be theirs.* In the Jubilee, tenure of the property would be resumed by the household of the ruler.[114] Such an arrangement would hinder the growth of a bureaucratic class which handed down their positions from generation to generation.

♦ **46:18** The negative influence of many of the depraved kings of Israel

---

112. Following the LXX, many translations (NKJV, NRSV, NIV) insert the preposition 'from' before 'his inheritance', and ignoring the Massoretic accent take it with the preceding clause: 'If the ruler gives a gift to any of his sons *from* his inheritance, it is to belong to his sons.'

113. The verb *wašābat*, 'reverts', is an archaic third person feminine singular qal perfect form (GKC §§44f; 72o). The verb *šûb* was used of the return of Israelites to their ancestral property in the Jubilee regulations (Lev. 25:10, 13, 27, 28, 41).

114. The syntax of the end of the verse is obscure. The LXX read, 'but of the inheritance of his sons, it will be to them.' This involves reading a construct, *naḥălat*, in place of the suffixed form, *naḥălātô*, 'his inheritance'. The latter is, however, the more difficult reading, of which sense can be made by taking *bānāyw*, 'his sons', as a casus pendens, resumed in the following pronominal suffix.

and Judah was again evident (cf. 45:8). There was a close link between a family and its property as one of the components of the LORD's rule of Israel. For the stability and good order of the ideal regime there had to be no return to the corrupt ways of the past. *The ruler is not to take any of the inheritance of the people to oppress them from their possession.* What was in view was royal eviction of people from land which was rightfully theirs. Rather than gaining property in this high-handed fashion to give to his family, through the juxtaposition of the term 'possession' it was stressed that *from his own possession he is to leave an inheritance to his sons.* The ruler was to dispose only of what was rightfully his as a legacy to the next generation. The aim which the LORD had in view was that *none of my people may be dispersed from his possession.* This recalled the language of 34:6, 21. Earlier royal misuse of power had culminated in the scattering of the dispossessed both within the land and as refugees to other countries.

REFLECTION

- In the agrarian economy of Israel, land tenure was at the heart of the social order. Each family had its own small-holding, upon which it depended for its maintenance. Land was also the primary form of capital an individual or family could have. But, beyond the economics of the situation, there lay the divine warrant for distributing the land to the tribes, and through them to the families of the land. It was tempting for a ruler to confiscate land to hand it as a reward to a subordinate, but that was a gross misuse of his power and subversion of the covenant order of the LORD. In the ideal arrangement envisaged here such seizure and misappropriation was explicitly forbidden—a prohibition of economic exploitation which still serves to veto much modern malpractice.

(9) The Temple Kitchens (46:19–24)

Somewhat surprisingly, Ezekiel's temple tour is not yet over. But once the arrangements are in place for sacrifices to be made, attention is given to a further feature of the temple layout which is connected with the way in which portions of the sacrifices are to be consumed. There are two sets of temple kitchens, for the priests (46:19–20) and for the laity (46:21–24), in which these portions are cooked. Much about the exact position and layout of the kitchens is left unclear, but the overall impression is that of the LORD drawing close to his people and having fellowship with them by providing them with a meal.

Ordinances for Temple Worship

(a) Kitchens for the Priests (46:19-20)

⁴⁶:¹⁹And he brought me by the entrance which was at the side of the gateway to the holy rooms of the priests which face north, and behold, there ⌊was⌋ a place at their extreme western end. ⁴⁶:²⁰And he said to me, 'This ⌊is⌋ the place where the priests are to boil the guilt offering and the sin offering ⌊and⌋ where they are to bake the grain offering so that they do not bring them into the outer courtyard to sanctify the people.'

♦ **46:19** *And he brought me* indicates the resumption of Ezekiel's guided tour (cf. 40:3). In 44:4 the guide had brought Ezekiel back to the front of the temple building where he received the divine commands regarding the ideal temple and land (Fig. 7 ④). Now the guide authoritatively conducted the prophet back through the north inner gateway into the outer courtyard. Turning west he approached *the holy rooms*¹¹⁵ *of the priests which face north,* and which were considered as a transitional zone to and from the inner courtyard. Similar holy rooms also faced south, and were described in 42:3-14 and mentioned in 44:19. Ezekiel entered them through their east entrance (described in 42:9), and not through the north facing entrances (cf. 42:4). 'Of the priests' was literally 'to the priests', but the phrase indicated priestly possession of the rooms rather than the priests being presented to Ezekiel.

Behold, there (that is, 'in that position'; Fig. 7 ⑤) drew attention to the specifically designated location set apart for the priestly kitchens, *a place at their extreme*¹¹⁶ *western end.* No more was said about their situation, and it may perhaps have been against the outer wall (Fig. 2 Q). It was called a 'place', not a room or a building, and given that the kitchens for the laity were described as courtyards (46:21), it was probably an open space with hearths.

♦ **46:20** *And he said to me* related that the guide spoke to Ezekiel. He did not describe the architecture of the kitchens; his focus was on the

---

115. 'The holy rooms' is literally 'the rooms the holiness', apparently an adjectival construct chain with the unusual feature of the noun in the construct being determinate (GKC §127 f-g). A similar exception occurs in 43:21, and may be a feature of later Biblical Hebrew, or it may be a scribal error.

116. The kethib *bayyarəkātam*, 'in their rear/far part', has a plural suffix, whereas the qere, *bayyarəkotayim*, is a dual form. The latter is supported by the similar construction in Exod. 26:27; 36:32, and is adopted in the AV ('on the two sides'). Most translations reflect the kethib; the difference is slight.

function for which they were reserved—which related to the portions of sacrifices which the priests were required to consume on the temple premises. The kitchens were provided as *the place where the priests are to boil the guilt offering and the sin offering* (for these offerings, see on 40:39) ⌊*and*⌋ *where they are to bake the grain offering* (see on 44:29; 46:14). The kitchens were equipped with hearths over which meat could be boiled in a pot. The baking would also have been done over the open fire on a flat plate of metal (cf. 4:3).

So that they do not bring them into the outer courtyard to sanctify the people. This was the same undesirable consequence as would have been incurred by exposure to the priests' vestments (44:19). Because of this, the temple was laid out in such a way that the priests could bring whatever portions of the sacrificial items were allotted to them from the vestibules of the north (and south) inner gateway, across the inner courtyard including the space round the temple building, into the priestly rooms, where they would descend to the lowest level before proceeding west to the kitchens. They would then return to the holy rooms where they would consume what had been cooked (42:13). The sin which had been vicariously imposed on the offering had been atoned for by the shedding of its blood, and those portions of the guilt offering and the sin offering which were not burned on the altar were consumed by the priests (cf. Lev. 7:6–7; 6:26; for the grain offering, cf. Lev. 7:9–10).

(b) The Kitchens for the Laity (46:21–24)

> ⁴⁶:²¹Then he led me out to the outer courtyard and brought me across to the four corners of the courtyard, and behold, there was a courtyard in the corner of each courtyard. ⁴⁶:²²In the four corners of the courtyard ⌊were⌋ small courtyards, forty ⌊cubits⌋ in length and thirty ⌊cubits⌋ in breadth; one measure ⌊obtained⌋ for the four of them, set in the corners. ⁴⁶:²³And there was a row ⌊of stones⌋ round about in them, round about the four of them, and hearths had been made at the base of the rows round about. ⁴⁶:²⁴And he said to me, 'These are the kitchens where those who minister in the house are to boil the sacrifice of the people.'

♦ **46:21** The guide then proceeded with the tour, and Ezekiel recorded that *then he led me out to the outer courtyard*, that is, from within the zone of holiness set aside in the outer courtyard for the priests' rooms and kitchens (Fig. 7 ⑤). After that the guide *brought me across to the four corners of the courtyard.* This denoted being conducted ('brought across', movement within a zone) from corner to corner all the way round the outer courtyard (Fig. 7 ⑥–⑨). In this way he was able to observe *a courtyard in the corner of each courtyard* (Fig. 2 R).

♦ **46:22** *In the four corners of the courtyard*, that is, the outer courtyard, there were four courtyards of the same dimensions, *forty ⌊cubits⌋ in length and thirty ⌊cubits⌋ in breadth*, that is, 68 feet by 52 feet (20.6 m × 15.5 m). They were thus rectangular, which was indicative of a lesser degree of holiness in the spiritual geometry of the vision. Also, it was the case that their orientation relative to the temple was not stated.

These courtyards were described by a term ($q\partial ṭurôt$) whose meaning is uncertain. After the rendering of the Septuagint, it has been proposed that $q\partial ṭannôt$, 'small', be read instead, and this is followed by NRSV and ESV, but *enclosed* or 'fenced off', as indicated by the Targum, is more probable (cf. NASB, NIV, HCSB).[117]

The last word in the verse was marked by the Massoretes with *puncta extraordinaria*, supralinear dots, probably indicating that they were suspicious of its authenticity, but not prepared to excise it from the text (cf. 41:20). Moreover, since it is not represented in the Septuagint, Vulgate, or Peshitta, many translations omit it (cf. NRSV, ESV), but its root is related to the word 'corner' earlier in the verse, and a rendering such as *set in the corners* is plausible (cf. NASB, NIV, HCSB).

♦ **46:23** The term *row* was used elsewhere of a row of stones set in a wall (cf. 1 Kgs. 6:36; 7:12), and here it probably referred to some stone structure such as a ledge (NIV) because *hearths had been made*[118] *at the base of the rows round about.* The term for 'hearths' was related to the root 'to boil' (46:20, 24) so that the kitchen was obviously equipped for the use of cauldrons in which the portions of meat from the sacrifices could be boiled.

♦ **46:24** The guide's speech left much to be inferred, but it did emphasise the salient theological point that the meat prepared for the people was kept separate from that for the priests. *These are the*

---

117. Another possibility, derived from a cognate Syriac term, is 'joined', presumably to the walls (cf. AV), but this is less probable as is 'unroofed' (NJPS), which is only to be expected of a courtyard.

118. The form $'ăśûy$ is not plural. For such an uninflected form, compare 40:17; 41:18–19.

kitchens was literally 'house of the boiling ones', where 'house' need imply no more than 'structure', not necessarily a roofed one, and the singular term was probably used collectively for the four courtyards which were regarded as one. ***Those who minister in the house***, that is, in the temple rather than in the kitchens, referred to the Levites and not the Zadokites (cf. 44:9–16), though the same term 'minister' was applied to them also (44:15–17, 19, 27). ***The sacrifice of the people*** was obviously a collective term, which in itself could cover all the sacrifices offered, but in the context must have applied specifically to the fellowship offerings, parts of which were designated for the worshippers to consume in the temple precincts (cf. the description in 2 Chron. 35:11–13).

Kitchens were also a feature of pagan temples, primarily as places where food to feed the gods was cooked. Although not explicitly mentioned elsewhere in Scripture (but note the description of proceedings at the temple in Shiloh, 1 Sam. 2:13–14), temple kitchens were used to prepare food for the worshippers. This most probably was related to the function of the rooms right round the outer courtyard (40:17). They provided accommodation where the worshippers could consume the meat cooked for them.

REFLECTION

- The return of portions of the various types of peace offering to the worshipper is more implied than stated in Scripture, but it seems fairly clear that this was what happened from the description of, say, Deuteronomy 12:18. Involvement in the consumption of those portions of the sacrificial victim not reserved for the LORD or the priests was permitted for the family and household of the worshipper. This feature of the peace offering was shared with 'the sacrifice of the LORD's Passover' (Exod. 12:27), which was closely connected with the peace offering. The consumption of what had been dedicated to the LORD was a mark of restored fellowship with him expressed through a meal enjoyed in the sacred premises. This foreshadowed in many respects the LORD's Supper which, through a joint meal, celebrates that 'Christ, our Passover lamb, has been sacrificed' (1 Cor. 5:7). The commemorative acts of both Testaments derive their significance from sin atoned for, and include a note of triumphant joy: 'You are to rejoice before the LORD your God in all that you put your hand to' (Deut. 12:18).
- So this final aspect of the temple tour was not a footnote, but anticipated joyous fellowship with the LORD. Even so, it is a

description of the ideal. Ezekiel does not record any persons actively engaged in these scenes, only what has been prescribed for them to do. Moreover, though provision for blood rituals is given a prominent place, there is no blood actually shed in the description. These arrangements are accommodated to the situation prevailing in Ezekiel's day, and await the fulness of time for their completion in higher and more perfect forms.

D. The Life-Giving River (47:1-12)

The focus of what is disclosed to Ezekiel now moves out from the temple, which occupies the central position in the community, to consider the land as a whole. It begins with a description of the life-giving river which will flow from the temple through the land and transform it (47:1-12). Consideration is then given to the allocation of territory in the ideal land of promise (47:13-48:29), before the vision culminates with a depiction of the capital city (48:30-35).

Although the terrain of the Holy Land and, in particular, of that portion of it close to Jerusalem provides a backdrop for this vision, it remains a vision in which topography furnishes only a general setting and does not play a determinative role. Key details from real life are employed to paint a vivid picture (e.g., in 47:10-11), but the whole scenario is surreal—which is not the same as unreal. The divine vision is a teaching medium to convey spiritual truth which will encourage and enthuse Ezekiel's contemporaries and all those who await God's provision for his people.

These scenes are incapable of literalistic human fulfilment, and this certainly shows that the vision does not, and is not intended to, provide a realistic blueprint for reconstruction after the return from the exile, or at any later stage. What is pictured here requires divine intervention and power, and is in the truest sense eschatological, in that what is portrayed awaits the inauguration of the final homeland for all the redeemed of the LORD, where what is symbolically promised will be fully realised. For instance, the rapidly increasing volume of water in the river can only be explained supernaturally. The glib suggestion that this might occur naturally with additional water derived from tributaries quite misses the point that it is the water of life which is flowing in this river and that can only have one source, God present with his people as symbolised by the sanctuary. Water from elsewhere would not suffice. It would not only dilute this river; it would pollute it.

The scene divinely disclosed to Ezekiel incorporates elements from various parts of earlier revelation to demonstrate that the river and its impact depict the new creation. The river is portrayed in theological continuity with the river which watered Eden (Gen. 2:10–14). It also bears significant thematic links with two passages in Isaiah (Isa. 8:6–7; 33:20–24). In the first of these, the river is a sign of divine fidelity; in the second, it incorporates the notion of the healing of the infirmities of the people. So here the river is a pledge of the blessedness of the redeemed in the ideal community, anticipating the river of the water of life in the new Jerusalem (Rev. 22:1). In the intermediate stage of the present age, the symbol of the river points to the Spirit's presence and work in the new creation which all those who believe in Christ already experience (John 7:37–39).

The connection between the presence of the Holy Spirit and the fruitfulness of the ideal land had been recognised earlier in Isaiah's prophecy. Depressed circumstances would continue for the people of God 'until the Spirit is poured out on us from on high, and the wilderness becomes a fruitful field and the fruitful field is reckoned a forest' (Isa. 32:15). At a physical level, pouring out of water sustains agricultural growth; and so figuratively, pouring out of the Spirit represents the application of God's superabundant power to produce new inner life in the individual and to sustain it thereafter. At present the realisation of this is to be found in the on-going provision initiated at Pentecost in the spiritual life of the church. The scene will, however, be consummated hereafter in the new heavens and the new earth where unsullied Edenic fruitfulness will prevail in the physical realm, and there will be a corresponding heightened spiritual provision which will be appropriate because of the presence of God incarnate.

Care must be taken in expounding the significance of this life-imparting river. There have been those who have emphasised that the river flows into the Dead Sea, and that the picture of its transforming effects therefore excludes peoples and lands outside of Israel (Darr 1987). Others have envisaged the river as flowing on from there to effect a trans-global transformation back to Edenic conditions. In some respects both characterisations are valid. Ezekiel's ministry was focused on the needs of the exilic community and their restoration to divine favour. However, the vision presented to him did not deny the possibility of saving benefits being extended to other peoples as 47:22–23 amply testify. Even so, salvation for the nations is commonly viewed within the structures of Old Testament revelation as a process whereby others join with Israel. It is therefore improper to suppose that

THE LIFE-GIVING RIVER 513

the river should be envisaged as flowing elsewhere, but equally it is too restrictive to find the realisation of what is portrayed here as confined to Israel after the flesh. In the light of the New Testament Israel is seen in its true character as being essentially not an ethnic or a geographical category, but a spiritual one, 'the Israel of God' (Gal. 6:16), which transcends racial, national, or cultural affiliation and centres on loyalty to Christ as King.

This section may be thought of as composed of two parts, of virtually the same length. First, in 47:1–7 there is a narrative account of the river's source and growth, and then in 47:8–12 there is the guide's explanation of the life-giving impact of the river.

(1) The River's Source and Growth (47:1–7)

> ⁴⁷:¹And he brought me back to the door of the house and, behold, water was going out from under the threshold of the house towards the east, for the front of the house ⌊was⌋ to the east. And the water went out from under the southern side of the house, south of the altar. ⁴⁷:²And he led me out by way of the north gateway and brought me round outside to the outside gateway which faces east, and behold, water was trickling from the south side. ⁴⁷:³When the man went out eastwards with a measuring line in his hand, he measured a thousand cubits and he brought me through the water, water reaching the ankles. ⁴⁷:⁴And he measured a thousand ⌊cubits⌋ and he brought me through the water, water reaching the knees. And he measured a thousand ⌊cubits⌋ and he brought me through water reaching the waist. ⁴⁷:⁵And he measured a thousand ⌊cubits⌋ ⌊and it was⌋ a river which I was not able to pass through, for the water had swollen, water for swimming, a river which could not be passed through. ⁴⁷:⁶And he said to me, 'Have you seen ⌊this⌋, son of man?' And he led me and brought me back ⌊to⌋ the bank of the river. ⁴⁷:⁷When I returned, behold, ⌊there were⌋ on the bank of the river very many trees, on this side and on that.

♦ **47:1** *And he brought me back to the door of the house* related how Ezekiel's guide brought him back (cf. 44:1) from the kitchens in the outer courtyard (Fig. 7 ⑨) to a position in the inner courtyard before the entrance into the temple building (Fig. 7 ⑩). Here Ezekiel was able to observe a phenomenon which had not previously been drawn to his attention and which he presumably had not noticed.

Behold (also in 47:2, 7) captured the element of surprise with which Ezekiel in his vision observed that *water was going out from under* *the threshold of the house towards the east.* The origin of the stream was not stated, but it became visible when it bubbled up under the threshold, which was the massive stone at the base of the door, part of which would have been visible from outside. As Ezekiel also stated that *the water went out from under the southern side of the house, south of the altar*, it is probably indicated that it flowed from the southern side of the threshold. It is unclear if the stream went underground before re-emerging outside the outer wall. If it did, that would have done much to preserve the orderliness and usability of the temple complex which was displayed to the prophet, but this visionary depiction was not subject to ordinary constraints.

It was natural for the water to flow outwards from the temple complex because of its situation on a 'very high mountain' (40:2), and because of the elevation of the temple building itself on the third tier of the terraced arrangement of the compound in which there were ten steps leading down from the temple building itself (40:49), then a further eight steps down from the inner to the outer courtyard (40:31, 34, 37), and finally seven steps on the outside of the perimeter wall (40:22, 26; see also 40:6).

♦ **47:2** *And he led me out by way of the north gateway and brought me round outside to the outside gateway which faces east.* This circuitous route through the outer northern gateway (Fig. 7.11) was necessitated by the fact that the eastern gateway was kept closed. When Ezekiel was escorted round the external perimeter of the temple complex, he was able to observe from the outside that *water was trickling from the south side.* The verb 'trickle' was only found here, and it may well have been formed by onomatopoeia to resemble the sound of bubbling or gurgling water, again possibly from under the ground. The point was that the water was not at this stage copious, though the flow still remained moderate. 'South side' referred to the southern part of the eastern wall, not the southern side of the temple, which would not have been visible from the vicinity of the east outer gateway.

♦ **47:3** *When the man went out eastwards with a measuring line in his hand* indicated that the supernatural guide went ahead of Ezekiel away from the city down towards the Jordan valley and the Dead Sea. The guide had come equipped with measuring instruments, including 'a linen cord' (40:3). He now used this to measure a thousand cubits (about a third of a mile, or half a kilometre). *He brought me through the water* indicated that Ezekiel was escorted to the other (southern) side of the stream. In this way he was able to tell that its depth was now ***water reaching the ankles.***[119]

♦ **47:4** The guide methodically ***measured a thousand ⌊cubits⌋*** further, and again led the prophet through the waters which now reached the knees. Ezekiel had now been brought back to the north side of the stream, but, following the same procedure a further time, he again crossed the river to its southern side and so became aware that waters were now ***reaching the waist.***

♦ **47:5** After the guide had measured yet a further thousand cubits (4,000 cubits in total), the volume of water had become so great that ***⌊it was⌋ a river which I was not able to pass through.*** 'River' does not represent the word *nāhār*, which is usually rendered in this way, but rather *naḥal* which referred to a wadi, a seasonal watercourse which in the heat of summer would be reduced to a trickle or would dry up altogether, but which in the rainy season would be transformed into a rushing stream. However, what was pictured here was a perpetual and copious source of water so that 'river', rather than, say, 'stream', is a more appropriate translation.

Why then was the other term employed (also in 47:6, 7, 9 [2×], 12)? Hummel (2007:1340) notes the similarity in sound (not etymology) between *naḥal*, 'stream, wadi', and *naḥălâ*, 'inheritance' and *nāḥal*, 'to inherit', which occurred frequently in 47:13–48:29. He suggests that the avoidance of the ordinary term for river and the choice of this substitute may have been influenced by this association of sound, which would serve to link the fruitfulness of the inheritance given by God with his provision of water for it. Alternatively, and more probably, *naḥal* was used to indicate the velocity of the water in the stream, as is conveyed by the rendering 'winter torrent' which is sometimes employed. This was not a slow, sluggish flow of water, but one that was sparkling and lively, rushing on with transforming power.

Ezekiel in his vision attempted to ford the river and found himself unable to do so because it had become ***a river which could not be passed through*** and its depth such that it was ***water for swimming.*** It

---

119. The dual noun *'opsayim* occurs only here, from a noun *'ōpes*. Since the closely related noun *'epes* means 'end' or 'extremity', it is easy to propose that the dual refers to the ends of the two legs (note later references to knees and waist). However, the LXX opted to render the phrase *mê 'opsayim* by *hudōr apheseōs*, virtually transliterating the second word and so generating the phrase 'water of forgiveness'. This led to some early writers finding here an anticipation of Christian baptism.

may be implied that the increasing current of the river continued until it reached the Dead Sea. No mention was made of any other river flowing into it, or of another source of water. The river's increased volume was attributable solely to divine power. It may be that this growth is to be compared to that of the Messianic twig which become a large cedar in 17:22-23. A similar growth in the impact of the gospel was predicted in the parables of the mustard seed (Matt. 13:31-32) and the leaven (Matt. 13:33).

♦ **47:6** The guide addressed Ezekiel as *son of man*, using the same term the LORD employed (see on 40:3). The question, *Have you seen ⌐this⌐?* may have exclamatory force (cf. 8:12, 15, 17; Joüon §161b), intended to stir reflection on the copious and increasing flow of water. *He led me* (cf. 40:24) *and brought me back* (cf. 47:1) showed that Ezekiel was still being conducted by the guide, who had again led him into the water to experience that it could not be crossed. So now under the guide's direction the prophet retraced his steps back to *the bank of the river* on the south side of the stream (cf. 47:4).

♦ **47:7** *When I returned* probably indicated that Ezekiel regained the bank of the stream, though it might convey movement up along its course towards the temple. In whatever direction he went, Ezekiel's attention was no longer so concentrated on the river that he noted with surprise in a region which was ordinarily quite barren that *⌐there were⌐ on the bank of the river very many trees, on this side and on that.* Although the Hebrew expression rendered 'very many trees' may also mean 'a very large tree', it is evident in this scene that the noun 'tree' was being used collectively.

(2) The River's Impact (47:8-12)

> ⁴⁷:⁸And he said to me, 'These waters ⌐are⌐ going out to the eastern district and they go down to the ⌐Jordan⌐ valley and enter the sea. When they have been brought out to the sea, then its waters will be healed. ⁴⁷:⁹And it will come about that every living creature which moves about, to everywhere the rivers enter, will live, and there will be very many fish because this water has entered there that they may be healed, and everything will live where the river enters. ⁴⁷:¹⁰And it will come about that fishermen will stand by it from En-gedi to En-eglayim; it will be a place for spreading nets to dry; as regards types their fish will be like the fish of the Great Sea very many. ⁴⁷:¹¹But ⌐as for⌐ its swamps and its marshes, they will not be healed; they will be given over to

salt. ⁴⁷:¹²And by the river there will come up on its bank, upon this side and upon that, every kind of tree ⌊used for⌋ food; its leaf will not wither and its fruit will not come to an end; with respect to ⌊each⌋ of its months it will bear firstfruit because its waters are going out from the sanctuary. And its fruit will be for food and its leaf for healing.'

♦ **47:8** The remainder of this section consists of an explanation of the phenomenon of the life-imparting river. This was provided by the guide who was acting as the LORD's spokesman. ***The eastern district*** may have been a reference to the deepest part of the Jordan valley, particularly just before it entered the Dead Sea. It is unclear if the supernatural stream was presented as flowing directly to the north end of the Dead Sea. The Kidron Valley into which water issuing from the area about the temple would naturally flow runs in a southeastern direction before turning sharply east and joining the Dead Sea well south of the mouth of the Jordan. Hummel (2007:1342) suggests that the present scenario might fit in with the vision that the Mount of Olives was split in two (Zech. 14:4) to permit a channel for the river to run due east. But the vision was not constrained by geographical details, nor was there any indication that the visionary city or the temple were in precisely the same location as their physical counterparts.

The text reads 'to the sea, the having been brought out ones', which may readily be understood to mean, **when they have been brought out to the sea**, that is, when the waters which divinely originated in the temple were constrained by God's power to flow on in ever-increasing volume until they reached the Dead Sea.[120] **Then its waters will be healed**[121] implied that the sterility of the Dead Sea was akin to an affliction with some kind of disease. In 2 Kings 2:21–22 Elisha 'healed' water that was poisonous. So here was a gracious provision of overwhelming power capable of rectifying the previous lifelessness and lack of fertility in the region.

---

120. On the basis of the LXX, 'the water of the breakthrough', many emend *hayyāmâ*, 'the seawards', to *hamayim*, 'the waters', and thus providing a plural noun to go with the participle. The RSV and NRSV have 'the sea of stagnant waters' (cf. the Peshitta), which may also give rise to taking *hammûṣʾîm* from a root *ṣûm*, whose meaning 'to be filthy/polluted' is deduced from cognate languages and related Hebrew terms. The emendation of the participle to *haḥămûṣîm*, 'soured' (from *ḥāmēṣ*, 'to be sour'), is unnecessary.

121. The kethib *wənirpəʾû* is the expected form whereas the qere *wənirpû* is formed as if the verb were final-*he*, not final-*aleph*.

♦ **47:9** The description of the life-imparting properties of the river possessed overtones of the creation account of Genesis 1, particularly in the use of 'living creature' (cf. Gen. 1:20, 21, 24), and of 'moves about' or 'teem, swarm' (cf. Gen. 1:20–21). This was a similar display of the divine endowment of life.

Everywhere the rivers enter had a dual form 'double stream', though this was not reflected in the surrounding references to the river. Though this might be echoed by the two rivers of Zechariah 14:8, Keil (2002:438) takes the dual to indicate a river with a strong current. However, most early versions and later translations use a singular (but not AV or NKJV which have 'rivers'). Perhaps the reference was to the stream from the temple and the Jordan itself.

The impact of the river would be all-encompassing on ***every living creature which moves about*** in that the waters of the Dead Sea would no longer cause their death. Moreover, there would be ***very many fish because this water has entered there that they*** (the waters of the sea) ***may be healed.*** The picture of life and vitality was summed in the statement, ***Everything will live where the river enters.*** The totality of the restorative transformation was emphasised by the threefold repetition of 'every' (*kōl*). The extensive change made the subsequent land allocation more equitable, especially with regard to the arid territory in the south which would again merit the description of being like the Garden of Eden (Gen. 13:10; Milgrom 2012:229).

♦ **47:10** There was then an illustrative example of the extent to which conditions would change. ***Fishermen will stand***[122] ***by it.*** The Dead Sea had been incapable of supporting any life, but the life giving and sustaining power of the river would lead to the formerly incongruous and absurd notion of fishermen plying their trade there.

En-gedi ('spring of goat') still exists as an oasis in the middle of west side of the Dead Sea, which is fed by a spring at the top of a six hundred foot escarpment. ***En-eglaim*** ('spring of two calves') was formerly located just south of Qumran, also on the northwestern shore of the Dead Sea, but as a result of finds in the caves south of Qumran, its location is now considered to be on/near the southeastern shore of the Sea, possibly being the same as the unidentified Eglath-shelishiyah (Isa. 15:5; Jer. 48:34). So the expression 'from En-gedi to En-eglaim' was equivalent to right round the coast of the Dead Sea.

---

122. The kethib reads a qal imperfect *ya'amdû*, 'they will stand', whereas the qere is a perfect *'amədû*, 'they stood', apparently without a *waw-*consecutive which is required for the sense.

The coastline would become *a place for spreading nets to dry* after the day's haul of fish had been brought ashore—a picture of blessing which contrasted with the similar description of Tyre (26:5, 14). The thriving fishery would catch as many types of fish as were found in *the Great Sea*, that is, the Mediterranean. *Types* or 'kinds' was again creational language (cf. Gen. 1:11–12, 21, 24–25). The plural in *their fish* probably referred to the two places just named.

♦ **47:11** The change, though widespread, would be selective in its impact. *Its swamps*[123] (cf. Job 8:11; 40:21) and *its marshes* (or 'pools') referred to the areas at the edge of the Sea, particularly those in its southern section, which would be inundated from time to time, and then dry out in the intense heat to leave a residue consisting predominantly of salt. *They will not be healed; they will be given over to salt* was not a mark of the exclusion of these peripheral zones from the blessing imparted to the Sea. Salt was a highly valued commodity, and this source would be maintained, not lost, in the coming transformation.

♦ **47:12** The description and explanation of the guide returned to the trees growing *by the river ... on its bank, upon this side and upon that* (cf. 47:7). The tree-lined river would sustain *every kind of tree ⌊used for⌋ food* (lit., 'every tree of food'). Again this incorporated a hint of the trees in the creation narrative (Gen. 2:16). *Its leaf will not wither* reflected the description of Psalm 1:3. *Its fruit will not come to an end* decisively reversed the covenant curse of Leviticus 26:20. The distributive expression *with respect to ⌊each⌋ of its months* pictured a never ending succession of the choicest and freshest *firstfruit*. The reason for this phenomenal fruitfulness was that *its waters are going out from the sanctuary.* Only divine power could account for the miraculous blessing of a harvest of fruit every month.

And its fruit will be[124] *for food and its leaf for healing.* This picture recalled Eden (Gen. 2:15–17) and anticipated the eternal

---

123. The kethib *biṣṣō'tāw* has a defective form of the suffix which is spelled in full in the qere *biṣṣō'tāyw*. Both exhibit an Aramaic style plural ending with *aleph* instead of *holem*.

124. The kethib *wəhāyû*, 'and they will be', has a plural form which seems either to treat fruit and leaf as a compound subject, or, in a construction according to sense, to take 'its fruit' as a collective noun. The qere has a singular form, *wəhāyâ*, 'and it will be', which does double duty in the final clause also. This fits in better with the preceding verb forms which are consistently singular.

kingdom (Rev. 22:2–3). Whereas Isaiah 33:24 had hinted at the health to be enjoyed by the citizens of restored Zion, there was here a fuller disclosure of the potential of the created realm when the presence of God was restored among his people. No more would they lack sustenance or be susceptible to the ravages of disease. But the supreme blessing was the spiritual healing which would be imparted. 'No inhabitant will say, "I am sick"; the people who dwell there will be forgiven their iniquity' (Isa. 33:24).

REFLECTION

- The river flowing from the sanctuary is a picture of the abundant blessings enjoyed through the presence and gift of God in the midst of his people. Though God's presence is focused on the inmost chamber of the temple, his gift moves out and grows in volume to meet every need it encounters and to render fruitful even the most blighted territory. This is the Creator's hand restoring his creation and recalls his original provision. 'A river flowed out of Eden to water the garden, and there it divided and became four rivers' (Gen. 2:10), a parallel which is more evocative when it is recognised that Eden, where the LORD God revealed himself, was the prototypical temple (Beale 2004:66–76).

- 'Very many trees' (47:7) was a sign of a land from which the curse of enemy invasion and spoliation had been removed. Not only would trees suffer when a land was wantonly ravaged by marauding troops, but their wood would be specially targeted for siegeworks when cities were blockaded (cf. Deut. 20:19). Whereas when Israel engaged in siege warfare, the LORD required them not to cut down fruit trees, no such limitations would have inhibited the action of the Babylonians. So in contrast to the bleak landscape of the curse, the LORD's gift of new life for the land would furnish trees of every kind to provide food, and their crop would miraculously appear every month because of the fructifying power of the river flowing from the sanctuary. This picture of heightened productivity emphasised the blessings attendant on the LORD's presence with his people.

- The life-giving transformation envisaged here moves beyond the physical realm to spiritual realities: 'its leaf for healing' (47:12). This theme is enlarged on in John's description of the new Jerusalem in which the river of the water of life nurtures the tree of life whose leaves were for the healing of the nations (Rev. 22:1–2). With this every aspect of life is returned to entire physical and spiritual wholesomeness and is properly nurtured through divine blessing.

- A further development of this symbolic teaching was made by Christ when he said, 'Whoever believes in me, as the Scripture has said, "Out of his heart will flow rivers of living water." ' This is explicitly explained as brought about by the Spirit which would be given at Pentecost (John 7:38–39). The traditional reading of these verses considers Christ to anticipate the understanding of the believer as a temple within whom the Holy Spirit will come and reside, so that the believer experiences a full endowment of life and power flowing from the renewed heart within him. 'Whoever drinks of the water that I will give him will never be thirsty again. The water that I will give him will become in him a spring of water welling up to eternal life' (John 4:14). It is less certain that the analogy may additionally be pressed into saying that the Spirit-filled believer is an intermediary from whom the blessing of 'living water'/'the Spirit' flows to others, though that cannot be entirely ruled out, for, to change the metaphor, Christ urged his followers, 'Let your light shine before mankind, so that they may see your good works and glorify your Father who is in heaven' (Matt. 5:16).

E. The Land of Promise (47:13-48:29)

The topic of this penultimate section follows on naturally from the movement outwards from the temple to the Dead Sea in the preceding section. The theme is now the division of the land as a whole, which may in its entirety experience the renewing power of the life-giving river. After setting out the boundaries of the whole of Israel's inheritance (47:13–20), special consideration is given to the situation of foreigners who reside among the people (47:21–23). Then the land allotted to individual tribes is delineated (48:1–7, 23–29) along with that reserved as a holy portion in the centre of the land (48:8–22), and the description culminates in the vision of the eternal city where the LORD will dwell for ever (48:30–35). In all this there are repeated echoes of Moses and Joshua, which suggests that Ezekiel's role in the vision is patterned after theirs.

(1) The Boundaries of Israel's Inheritance (47:13–20)

Since no territory is allocated to the east of the Jordan and to the south of the Sea of Galilee, the boundaries of the land as a whole are substantially similar to those of Numbers 34:1–15, though those of individual tribes frequently differ (cf. 48:1–7, 23–29). However, whereas for the tribes returning from Egypt the first boundary to be established was that in the south, now that the people are deportees in Babylonia the orientation is reversed, and the first boundary is that to the north (47:15–17), followed in clockwise order by the eastern boundary (47:18), the southern boundary (47:19), and the western boundary (47:20). Where possible, geographical entities are used to define the borders: the Great Sea (the Mediterranean) to the west, the river Jordan to the east, the brook of Egypt to the south (see Fig. 9). Elsewhere place names are employed, some of which are now difficult to locate.

> ⁴⁷:¹³Thus says the Lord GOD, 'This ⌊is⌋ the border ⌊by⌋ which you are to divide the land as an inheritance to the twelve tribes of Israel, Joseph ⌊having⌋ two allocations. ⁴⁷:¹⁴And you are to divide it as an inheritance equally in that I raised my hand to give it to your fathers and this land will be allotted to you as an inheritance. ⁴⁷:¹⁵And this ⌊will be⌋ the border of the land: on the north side, from the Great Sea by way of Hethlon as one goes to Zedad, ⁴⁷:¹⁶Hamath, Berothah, Sibraim (which ⌊is⌋ between the border of Damascus and the border of Hamath), Hazer-hatticon (which ⌊is⌋ towards the border of Hauran). ⁴⁷:¹⁷So the border will be from the sea to Hazer-enan (⌊which is on⌋ the border of Damascus) and ⌊as for⌋ the north, northwards ⌊it is⌋ the border of Hamath; and ⌊this will be⌋ the north side. ⁴⁷:¹⁸And on the east side, between Hauran and Damascus; and between Gilead and the land of Israel ⌊will be⌋ the Jordan; you are to measure the border along the eastern sea; and ⌊this will be⌋ the east side. ⁴⁷:¹⁹And on the south side southwards ⌊it will be⌋ Tamar as far as the waters of Meribah-Kadesh, the brook ⌊of Egypt⌋ to the Great Sea, and ⌊this will be⌋ the south side southwards. ⁴⁷:²⁰And on the west side, the Great Sea ⌊will be⌋ the border as far as opposite Lebo-hamath; this ⌊will be⌋ the west side.'

♦ **47:13** The messenger formula, ***Thus says the Lord GOD***, marked the start of the final divine speech which continued to the end of the book, with minor breaks marked by the occurrence of the signature formula at 47:23 and 48:29. ***This ⌊is⌋ the border***[125] indicated that it was within this outer limit that the inheritance would be located. ***Divide ... as an***

---

125. The initial two words of the LORD are represented in the MT as *gēh gəbûl*, 'valley of border/boundary' (cf. the Peshitta), but this seems to involve a double miscopying. Replacing the initial *gimel* by a *zayin* and taking the *he* as the article with the following word leads to the same expression as is found in 47:15, 'This ⌊is⌋ the border'.

inheritance represents the verb *nāḥal*, which was from the same root as the noun 'inheritance', and whose hithpael imperfect was used in a jussive sense with the plural *you* probably referring to the leaders of the community. The term ***inheritance*** (*naḥălâ*; cf. 47:14, 22, 23; 48:29) linked back to the original grant of the land after the Exodus by the LORD, the Israelites' Overlord (e.g., Deut. 4:21). Inasmuch as Israel had not gained the land by their own efforts, but by divine bestowal on those whom he recognised collectively as his son and heir (Exod. 4:22), it was the LORD's prerogative to apportion it among his people on terms of his own choosing. So the ideal arrangements envisaged were the outcome of a new, heightened experience of divine deliverance and benefaction.

The twelve tribes of Israel also harked back to the original entry into the land. Whereas 'the tribes of Israel' (without 'twelve') had occurred only once earlier in describing the reunification of the scattered and divided people (37:19), the phrase was used a further five times before the end of the book (47:21, 22; 48:19, 29, 31) as well as occurrences of 'tribe' (47:23; 48:1, 23). This too was an ideal description which could not be achieved by some ethnic regathering of the scattered and now lost and largely assimilated tribes. The realities of the past were employed in a word picture to portray the security and prosperity which would be extended to the restored covenant community in its entirety. ***Joseph ₍having₎ two allocations*** reflects the understanding of the terse expression 'Joseph, two allocations' in the same way as the Vulgate and the Targum which identified a dual form of the noun as occurring here.[126] The requirement that Joseph was to have a double portion went back to the blessing of Jacob (Gen. 48:5) in which Joseph's two sons, Ephraim and Manasseh, were reckoned to be on a par with their uncles in Jacob's estate (cf. 48:4–5). In this way Joseph effectively received the double portion that was the lot of the firstborn.

To maintain the number twelve in relation to the allocation of the land to the tribes, Levi would not receive an allotment in the same way that the other tribes would, but the priests and Levites would be accommodated in the holy portion as set out in 48:8–22 (cf. 45:1–8; Josh. 14:1–5). In this way they enjoyed the privilege of greater access to the LORD himself. Even so, in the allocation of the twelve gates in 48:30–34, Joseph had only one gate, and Levi was to have a gate.

---

126. This would point *ḥăbālîm* as *ḥăbālayim*. The noun originally meant 'a rope' (cf. 27:24), and by extension the area measured out by a surveyor's line.

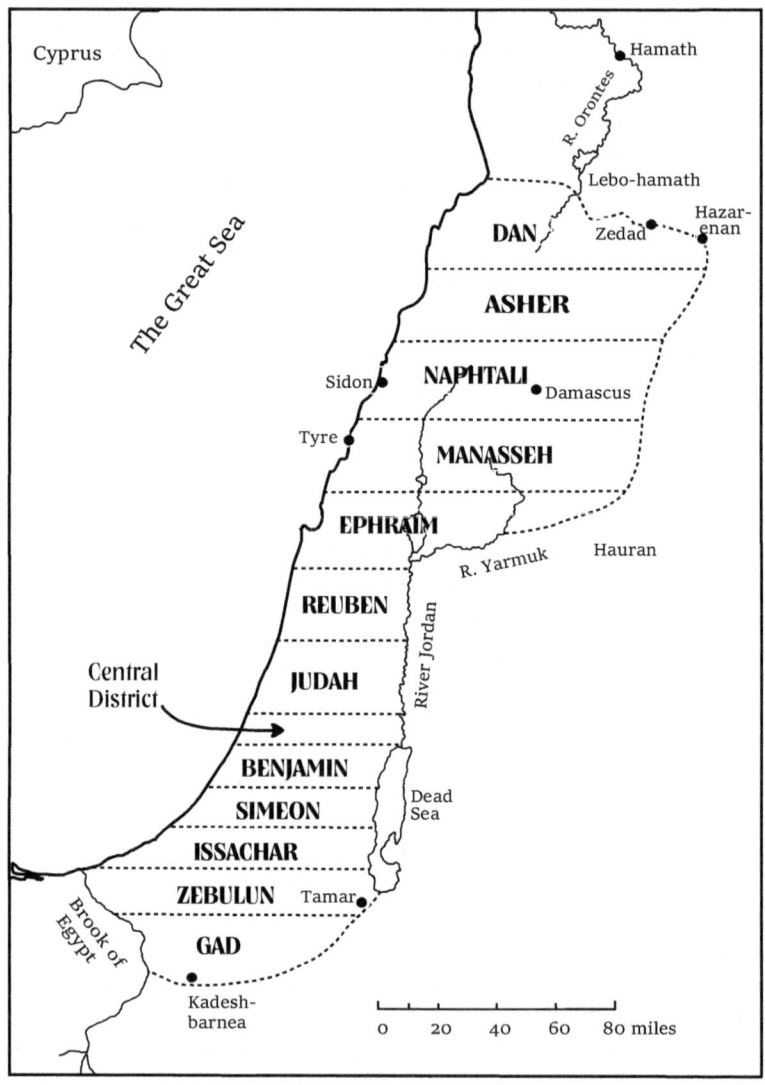

Figure 9. The Tribal Territories.

THE LAND OF PROMISE 525

♦ **47:14** *You are to divide ... as an inheritance* again used the verb of 47:13, while *equally* renders the Hebrew idiom, 'a man like his brother' (cf. Lev. 7:10), which in reference to the tribes required that they were to receive equal portions of the land. For a discussion of what this might mean in practice, see Introduction to 48:1–7.

I raised my hand was a gesture employed in oath-taking (cf. 20:5–6, 15), and the idiom indicated entering into an inviolable commitment. *To your fathers* looked back to the grant of the land to the patriarchs (20:28, 42; Exod. 6:8; Num. 14:30), and pointed to the faithfulness of God in keeping his promises.

This land will be allotted (lit., 'will fall', cf. 45:1) *to you as an inheritance* by divine decree achieved through the casting of lots, a procedure also used in the original division of the land (Num. 33:54; 34:13). Here God announced his provision of the land for the tribes to inhabit, and the use of lots would allow him to control what was allotted to individual families.

♦ **47:15–17** The northern boundary of the land was specified in great detail, reflecting both the orientation of Ezekiel and his audience looking from Babylonia, and the fact that geographical features were inadequate to delineate the fluid and imprecise boundaries in this disputed region. Border checkpoints and frontier lines on maps were, of course, unknown in Ezekiel's time. Moreover, while the places named here were cities of fixed location, the same designation could also be applied to the territory controlled by them, with the result that the border being envisaged might lie some distance from the named city and either include or exclude its territory. Indeed the zone of influence of one city or kingdom probably faded away gradually as that of another began. There is therefore considerable scope for variation in settling where any boundary would lie.

At least *the Great Sea* formed an indisputable reference to the Mediterranean Sea, and so the boundary began on the coast, with precisely where being made somewhat clearer by the terminus specified in 47:20, 'opposite Lebo-hamath'. *By way of Hethlon* involved a place only mentioned here and in 48:1, and any identification is speculative. The location of *Zedad* and later that of *Hazer-enan* at the northern limit of the territory which had been controlled by Damascus were fairly clear (Fig. 9). However, the transition between 47:15 and 47:16 has been variously understood. On the basis of the Septuagint, it has been suggested that the names Zedad and Hamath have been transposed, and *as one goes* (*ləbôʾ*, 'with respect to going') should be read as part of the compound name Lebo-hamath, or 'entrance to Hamath' (cf. REB, ESV, NIV). This is plausible in that *Hamath*, which was mentioned three times in this specification, was a major city-state located 116 miles (187 km) north of Damascus, and it is improbable that Israel's northern boundary was envisaged as lying as far north as that. On the other hand, Lebo-hamath referred to a strategic pass into the Orontes valley into the territory of Hamath from the south, and it marked Israel's northern boundary in periods of territorial expansion (1 Kgs. 8:65; 2 Kgs. 14:25). However, much the same line for the border would obtain if the reference to Hamath was to the southernmost limit of its area of influence.

The references to *Berothah*, *Sibraim*, and *Hazer-hatticon* are now obscure. Indeed the further notes of identification provided indicated that these locations were unfamiliar to the original audience as well. *The border of Hamath* suggested much the same area as Lebo-hamath, at the southern limit of Hamath's zone of control. *The border of Hauran* poses another puzzle. Though Hauran was only mentioned in Scripture at the end of 47:16 and in 47:18, it is known from Egyptian and Assyrian sources that it was a region which lay about a mountain of that name located to the east of Galilee, and that it separated Bashan from the desert. In this context that seems too southerly a location, but *towards the border of Hauran* may indicate the northern limit of the area under its control at that time.

The summary of 47:17 reiterated the line of the northern boundary stretching from the Mediterranean over to *Hazer-enan*, which was specified as being *on the border of Damascus*, that is, at the northern limit of its territory which was also *the border of Hamath* at the south of its territory.

♦ **47:18** The eastern boundary presumably began at or near Hazar-enan (the name is supplied in the RSV). The designations used to describe this section of border were those of areas rather than places so that the border seems to have gone south on the east of the territory controlled by *Damascus* and to the northwest of that of *Hauran*. It is often supposed that it came across westwards to the river Jordan along the line of the river Yarmuk, and then followed the Jordan valley southwards until it came to and went *along the eastern sea* (that is, the Dead Sea; cf. Joel 2:20; Zech. 14:8). So, although the more northerly region of Bashan was incorporated into the ideal land, other territory across the Jordan to the south of Bashan was not. Thus the areas which had been earlier occupied by Reuben, Gad and the half tribe of Manasseh were excluded. This was in line with the original divine allocation (cf. Num. 34:10-12).

The reading *you are to measure* (*tāmōddû*) is often challenged and replaced by 'to Tamar' (either *tāmār* or *tāmārâ*) on the basis of the text of the Septuagint and the Peshitta. This certainly would be supported by the reference to Tamar in 47:19. The location of Tamar is uncertain, but it may have been just to the south-west of the southern end of the Dead Sea (cf. 1 Kgs. 9:18).

♦ **47:19** *On the south side southwards* (found also in 48:28, and with the terms for south reversed at the end of this verse) involved redundancy. The repeated expression, which is also reflected in the Septuagint, was more likely to be idiomatic than an instance of scribal amplification. *Meribah-kadesh*[127] had been the site of Israel's grumbling, Moses' disobedience, and the LORD's abundant provision of water (Num. 20:1-13). The name Meribah means 'strife, contention', and the addition of Kadesh ('Meribah-by-Kadesh', REB) denoted proximity to Kadesh-barnea, the site of a copious spring of water in the north of Sinai. *The brook*[128] ⌊*of Egypt*⌋ is generally identified as the modern wadi el-Arish, the traditional boundary between Israel and Egypt (Josh. 15:4, 47; 1 Kgs. 8:65), which flows into the Mediterranean about fifty miles (80 km) southwest of Gaza.

♦ **47:20** *The west side* was literally 'the side of the sea', that is, the Mediterranean Sea, and the boundary of the land followed the coastline northwards until it reached a point *opposite Lebo-hamath* in the upper valley of the Orontes, so completing a full circle.

REFLECTION
- 'Inheritance' points to what one has rights in typically through heredity, but also by the disposition of property or estate by any testator. The Old Testament inheritance of land by Israel was grounded in the sovereign grant of the covenant King to his loyal subjects. Inheritance continues to be a significant theological

---

127. The MT has the plural form *mərîbôt* rather than the singular *mərîbâ*, which is attested by the Targum, Peshitta and Vulgate as well as some Hebrew manuscripts.

128. The MT has *naḥălâ*, 'inheritance', but that does not fit the context and the form is almost certainly to be derived from *naḥal*, 'brook, wadi', a seasonal watercourse', even though the expected form with *he* of direction would be *naḥlâ*.

concept in the New Testament, but the focus is no longer on real estate in the Middle East. The inheritance now is 'in the kingdom of Christ and God' (Eph. 5:5) and consists of a 'share in the inheritance of the saints in light' (Col. 1:12) as a reward to those who serve the Lord Christ 'in whom we have obtained an inheritance' (Eph. 1:11). At present the seal of the Holy Spirit's presence in the life of the believer acts as 'the guarantee of our inheritance until we acquire possession of it' (Eph. 1:14). So the inheritance is acquired by Christ for his people, and in living union with him through faith we become 'heirs of God and fellow heirs with Christ' (Rom. 8:17) and await the glory that is yet to be revealed.

(2) Provision for Sojourners (47:21–23)

After the external frontiers of the land had been set out, it might be expected that the next step is to establish the tribal allotments within that area. However, before that there is a remarkable insertion in which aliens are granted the same status as native Israelites in the matter of receiving a share of the land in this ideal apportionment. The picture is not quite that of complete equality and lack of differentiation, but it is certainly moving towards the New Testament realisation of 'neither Jew nor Greek' (Gal. 3:28) among the covenant people of God.

Humane treatment of an alien had been part of Israel's institutions since the days of Moses (Exod. 22:21; 23:9; Lev. 19:10, 33–34; 23:22; Deut. 14:29; 24:14–15, 17–22). However, the former regulations still did not incorporate the alien into the tribal structure of the people. In these ideal arrangements they are integrated into the covenant community and permitted to share in the inheritance of the land.

> 47:21'And you are to share this land among yourselves, among the tribes of Israel. 47:22And it will come about that you will cause it to be allotted by lot as an inheritance for yourselves and for the sojourners who are sojourning in your midst, who have begotten sons in your midst, and they will be to you as native-born among the sons of Israel; with you they will allot ⌞it⌟ as an inheritance in the midst of the tribes of Israel. 47:23And it will come about ⌞that⌟ in the tribe with which a sojourner is sojourning, there you will give his inheritance, declares the Lord GOD.'

♦ **47:21** In essence this verse abbreviated information given in 47:13, though using the verb ***share*** (the piel of *ḥālaq*; cf. 48:8) rather than 'divide ... as an inheritance' (the hithpael of *nāḥal*). It may be that the switch to considering resident aliens influenced the avoidance of the verb which associated the land with the covenant inheritance of the people of the LORD. The LORD may distribute his blessings as he pleases, and here there was an extension of the scope of his favour rather than a diminution of what was available to Israel.

♦ **47:22** ***You will cause it to be allotted*** again indicated distribution by lot (cf. 45:1; 47:14), with 'it' referring to the land which was being apportioned. Just as the LORD had determined the tribal boundaries, so the way the lot fell, being controlled by the LORD, would settle family occupation of the land within these tribal boundaries (cf. 47:23).

Conjoining ***for yourselves and for the sojourners who are sojourning in your midst*** showed that the revelation given to Ezekiel was not narrowly and exclusively focused on ethnic Israel. In the ideal society presented in the vision others would come to share what the LORD would give. ***They will be to you as native-born*** (*'ezrāḥ*) ***among the sons of Israel*** employed a term for one born in a territory in which they continued to reside. It occurred only here in Ezekiel, but elsewhere (e.g., Exod. 12:49; Num. 9:14) it was frequently found along with ***sojourner***/'resident alien' (*gēr*) as its counterpart.

It is difficult to translate these terms without introducing modern overtones. 'Sojourner' may imply too transient a residence, whereas 'alien' introduces an unwarranted note of strangeness. The resident alien had rights enshrined in Israel's covenant constitution. For the treatment which it was expected they would be given, see on 14:7; 22:7, 29. Hummel (2007:1358) suggests that 'proselyte' (the term used by the LXX here) or 'convert' might well catch the force of the term. Certainly, ***who have had sons in your midst*** pointed to long-term commitment to residing in Israel so that they could no longer be properly looked on as 'outsiders'.

Although sojourners had been assigned a certain status and measure of security in the community before the exile, they could not own land. Now those who took up permanent residence in Israel, and so identified with the covenant people, were to be granted land tenure rights.

The expression ***with you they will allot ⌊it⌋ as an inheritance*** is literally, 'with you they will fall as an inheritance', but this has no obvious meaning.[129] It is thought by some that the verb should be 'you will allot'. However, the text was now third person, and the obvious

---

129. The verb is *yippəlû*, 'they will fall', but pointing as a hiphil form, *yappilû*, 'they will cause [the lot] to fall', seems more probable.

antecedent for 'they' was 'the sojourners'. The passage may well have been understood as conveying not only the requirement that the sojourners be allotted a portion in the inheritance, but that they participate in the allocation process on an equal footing *in the midst of the tribes of Israel.* On that basis there was here a far-reaching picture of the integration of Israel and the sojourners who would identify with them and their God.

✦ **47:23** *In the tribe with which a sojourner is sojourning, there you will give his inheritance.* The sojourners' allocations of land were to be spread throughout the tribal allocations so that the twelvefold arrangement of the tribes was not disturbed. The sojourner would be assimilated into the tribe where he had been residing.

REFLECTION

- These verses represent a significant expansion of God's constitution for his covenant people. It had already been anticipated in measure in that the foreigner who joined himself to the LORD was forbidden to say, 'The LORD will surely separate me from his people,' and was promised that their worship would become acceptable in the house of the LORD (Isa. 56:3, 6–7). So too here they are guaranteed citizen rights with a share in the land which was a mark of the LORD's covenant favour.
- Paul developed this theme extensively in Ephesians 2:11–3:6. Those who had been 'alienated from the commonwealth of Israel and strangers to the covenants of promise' were so no longer because of the atoning work of Christ. As believers, the Gentiles 'are no longer strangers and sojourners, but you are fellow citizens with the saints and members of the household of God' (Eph. 2:19). There is full inclusiveness 'in Christ' whatever an individual's ethnic background. The church, the new Israel of God, contains an innumerable number 'from every nation—and tribes and peoples and languages' (Rev. 7:9) who have faith in Christ and 'have washed their robes and made them white in the blood of the Lamb' (Rev. 7:14). The ideal set before Ezekiel foreshadowed that universalism which is consummated in Christ.

(3) Tribal Territories to the North (48:1–7)

The allotment of the land among the tribes is an ideal distribution, which is a matter of spiritual geography, not of the actual topology of the land. The overall shape of the land is viewed as being like a parallelogram, with the tribal territories as horizontal strips with straight borders running across it. First, the tribal portions to the north are described (48:1–7), and then there is a separate, lengthy description of the central portion reserved as the sacred district (48:8–22), before the remaining tribes are allocated land to the south of the capital city (48:23–29). See Figure 9 for one visualisation of the result.

This division of the land makes no concessions to the actual topography of the area, which merely serves as a backdrop upon which the ideal allocation is superimposed. The message is conveyed through the picture of the orderliness which will prevail in the arrangements of God's kingdom, and is not intended as a programme that awaits physical enactment in earthly geography at some stage in world history.

The shares allocated to the tribes are not directly related to their territories at any point in Israel's history. Some tribes originally allotted land in the north are here designated as occupying territory in the south, and vice versa. Also, the trans-Jordan tribes (Reuben, Gad and half of Manasseh) are transferred to the west of the Jordan, with no trans-Jordanian territory being allocated. In the original allotment of the land Levi had no distinct possession, only scattered cities (Josh. 21). This is maintained here, with the priests (those descended from Zadok) and the other Levites being accommodated in the central portion. The twelvefold number of the tribes is maintained by granting separate portions to the two Joseph tribes, Ephraim and Manasseh. Their portions are adjacent as befitted their bond as brothers.

The division of the inheritance was to be done 'equally' (47:14), but it is difficult to determine how that equality was envisaged. Certainly the renewal of the land, such as that anticipated in 34:26–27 and 36:29–30, would have meant that there was comparable fertility throughout the territory. Moreover, allocations of land stretching from west to east would encompass all types of terrain within them. Even so an absolute mathematical equality cannot be achieved in terms of acreage or of productivity by means of east–west strips of equal width because of variations in the topography of the area, for instance, the sloping nature of the Mediterranean coast. Indeed, to fit five tribes below the central district requires narrower shares than above it. Also, given the layout of the tribal territories, it is clear that some tribes would be more remote from the sanctuary and the divine presence than others.

All in all, it is best to view the 'equality' of these twelve tribal shares as presenting the message that the new arrangement of their territories would not confer on any one tribe an inherent capacity to exploit or dominate another. These steps would ensure that the LORD's original intention in the covenant disposition of the land would now be achieved in fraternal harmony (Ps. 133:1). The differentiation between the sons of Jacob's wives and the sons of his concubines indicates that the equality in view takes into consideration certain social differences.

A second area of difficulty in envisaging these arrangements comes from the location of the tribal territories in relation to Jerusalem. That the symmetry of the disposition is broken by having seven tribal territories above the central zone and five below strongly suggests that the central zone bears some relationship to Jerusalem, or to the Temple, though the ideal temple is not within the city. However, there is no configuration of the central zone which can completely harmonise with the location of Jerusalem and Solomon's Temple. Again, the ideal arrangement is imposed over a somewhat hazy depiction of the actual physical geography of the land.

Ezekiel's description of the land proceeds tribe by tribe, following the pattern employed at the settlement (Josh. 13–21). Tribal distinctions no longer functioned as they once had, but, even so, as with a new Exodus (20:32–38) and new covenant (34:23–30; 37:21–28), the past provides a template for the future because of the continuity of the overarching purpose of God. One notable innovation is the provision of an allotment for the ruler (48:21–22). However, there is no attempt to recreate Solomon's royal administrative districts (Levenson 1976:113). Indeed, the ruler is not depicted as an administrator, not even in the allocation of the land (see on 45:8).

> ⁴⁸:¹'And these ⌊are⌋ the names of the tribes: from the north border along the way to Hethlon ⌊to⌋ Lebo-hamath ⌊to⌋ Hazer-enan (⌊which is on⌋ the border of Damascus, northwards beside Hamath), they will be his from east side westwards—Dan, one ⌊share⌋. ⁴⁸:²And beside the border of Dan, from east side to west side—Asher, one ⌊share⌋. ⁴⁸:³And beside the border of Asher, from east side to west side—Naphtali, one ⌊share⌋. ⁴⁸:⁴And beside the border of Naphtali, from east side to west side—Manasseh, one ⌊share⌋. ⁴⁸:⁵And beside the border of Manasseh, from east side to west side—Ephraim, one ⌊share⌋. ⁴⁸:⁶And beside the border of Ephraim, from east side to west side—Reuben, one ⌊share⌋. ⁴⁸:⁷And beside the border of Reuben, from east side to west side—Judah, one ⌊share⌋.'

♦ **48:1** A catalogue was presented of the tribes and their allotments, which were described from the northern boundary of the land, moving steadily southwards. Seven tribes would be allotted territory north of the central zone. The northern border of the land, *along the way*[130] *to Hethlon ⌊to⌋ Lebo-hamath ⌊to⌋ Hazer-enan (⌊which is on⌋ the border of Damascus, northwards beside Hamath)*, would become the boundary of Dan (cf. 47:15-17). Lebo-hamath, which meant 'entrance/ approach to Hamath', would lie to the south of Hamath itself (see on 45:15-16). This corresponded to where Dan's boundary used to lie before the decline of the northern kingdom. *They will be his* referred to the areas bounded by the line thus described, with 'his' anticipating the following mention of *Dan*.

From east side westwards (lit., 'seawards') was a form of the phrase which recurred in each of the following descriptions of tribal territory to indicate a line drawn across the land. This was not a realistic description, which might be actually implemented, but an ideal, equal division of the land as was indicated by the repeated closing description: *Dan, one ⌊share⌋*. A case may be made for understanding the repeated numeral 'one' as indicating a list, so that we might render it 'first, second, third, etc.' (cf. Block 1998:719). More probably 'share' should be supplied from 48:8 with the numeral to bring out that each tribe received its due (Keil 2002:446). A similar idiom was employed in 48:31-34 as regards the gates of the city.

The territory allotted to the tribe of Dan had originally been on the Mediterranean coast just north of Judah. However, the hostility of the Amorite inhabitants forced the tribe to relocate to the Upper Jordan Valley, north of the Sea of Galilee (Josh. 19:40-48; Judg. 1:34; 18:1-31). In the envisaged ideal settlement of the land, Dan would retain its northernmost position among the tribes. This also had the effect of locating it, as one of the tribes descended from a concubine of Jacob (in this case Bilhah, Rachel's handmaid, Gen. 30:4-6), more remotely from the sanctuary than the allotments of the tribes descended from one of Jacob's wives. A similar principle underlay the disposition of the tribes according to their ancestry round the Tent of Meeting in Numbers 2.

♦ **48:2** *Asher*, descended from Zilpah, Leah's handmaid (Gen. 30:12-13), was also situated at a distance from the central zone, and in the north as it had previously been. It lay *beside* (*'al*) *the border of Dan*, to

---

130. 'Along' renders the expression *'el-yad*, 'to the hand of', assuming that *'el*, 'to', is used in place of *'al*, 'upon, beside', and that *yād* is used in its secondary sense of 'side'. The phrase is repeated before Hamath where the sense is 'beside'.

its south, and sharing a common straight boundary with it. A similar arrangement configuration prevailed for the borders of the other tribal territories.

♦ **48:3** *Naphtali*, descended from Bilhah, Rachel's handmaid, was the second son of Jacob born to her (Gen. 30:7–8), and the tribe was located, in a fashion similar to the preceding two, at a distance from the central zone, while retaining its position in the north.

♦ **48:4** With *Manasseh*, tribes descended from Jacob's wives came into view, though the next two tribes were in fact named after Jacob's grandsons through Joseph (Gen. 48:5). Four of the tribes from Jacob's wives were located to the north of the central zone, and four to the south. Half of Manasseh as well as the tribes of Reuben and Gad had originally occupied territory east of the Jordan, which they had requested for the purposes of cattle breeding (Num. 32). This area had been outwith the boundaries of the Promised Land (Num. 34:1–15), and, in the event, pressure from Moab and Ammon led to the loss of these tribal regions. Allocation to them of territory west of the Jordan reflected the disposition of the land as ideal and not a reinstatement of the former situation.

♦ **48:5** *Ephraim* was placed next to Manasseh as the other tribe descended from Joseph (Gen. 46:20).

♦ **48:6** *Reuben* would be allocated territory north of Judah, possibly reflecting the fact that he had been Jacob's firstborn son (by Leah; Gen. 29:32), though the tribe had lost its preeminence (Gen. 49:3–4; 1 Chron. 5:1).

♦ **48:7** One of the more surprising features of the allocation of the land was that *Judah* was positioned to the north of the central zone, whereas earlier Judah along with Simeon had occupied the territory to the south of Jerusalem. Previously it had been Benjamin which was located immediately to the north of Jerusalem. Indeed Jerusalem had been technically within Benjaminite territory (Josh. 18:28), but, as it was not captured until the reign of David, it became a city outwith the tribal structures, and very much the city of David, so that its link with Judah could not realistically be broken. 'The hitherto unexplained reversal of Judah and Benjamin is owing to a concern that the royal tribe not oppress the North, that the North have a share in the House of David, and the House of David a share in the North' (Levenson 1976:118). In this way what was pictured was a means of eliminating the sectional rivalries which had contributed to the dissolution of the united kingdom of David and Solomon. The old division of north and south will be banished as meaningless.

(4) The Central District of the Land (48:8–22)

These verses expand on what has already been stipulated in 45:1–8. There the focus had been on the shape and dimensions of the various areas; here it falls more on their boundaries.

After an introduction detailing the dimensions of the central zone (48:8), the district reserved for the LORD is specified in 48:9. This is followed by details of the holy portion allotted to the LORD and occupied by the Zadokite priests (48:10–12) with the sanctuary at its centre; the land allotted to the Levites (48:13–14); the common city property (48:15–20); and the ruler's territory (48:21–22).

Throughout these verses the number twenty-five thousand recurs. It may have symbolic significance comparable to 'the twenty-fifth year' in 40:1, suggesting a turning point in the redemption of God's people (Hummel 2007:1368). The tribe of Levi was not assigned a tribal territory, but was allowed to reside in the central zone. The idea of levitical cities dispersed throughout Israel (Josh. 21) would no longer obtain.

(a) The Priests' Allocation (48:8–12)

> ⁴⁸:⁸⸢And beside the border of Judah, from east side to west side will be the portion which you are to apportion, twenty-five thousand ⌊cubits⌋ in breadth, and in length like one of the ⌊tribal⌋ portions from east side to west side, and the sanctuary will be in its midst. ⁴⁸:⁹The portion which you are to apportion to the LORD ⌊will be⌋ in length twenty-five thousand ⌊cubits⌋ and in breadth ten thousand ⌊cubits⌋. ⁴⁸:¹⁰And to these will be the holy portion, ⌊that is,⌋ to the priests: northwards twenty-five thousand ⌊cubits⌋ and westwards in breadth ten thousand ⌊cubits⌋ and eastwards in breadth ten thousand ⌊cubits⌋ and southwards in length twenty-five thousand ⌊cubits⌋; and the sanctuary of the LORD will be in its midst. ⁴⁸:¹¹⌊It will be⌋ for the priests, whoever has been consecrated, from the sons of Zadok, who have kept my charge, who did not go astray when the sons of Israel went astray as the Levites went astray. ⁴⁸:¹²And it will be their special portion from the portions of the land, most holy, at the border of the Levites.

♦ **48:8** *Alongside the border of Judah* indicated that immediately to the south of Judah's tribal allocation, *from east side to west side*, that is, stretching from the river Jordan to the Mediterranean Sea in the same way as the tribal allocations, would be *the portion which you are to apportion* (Fig. 9). This referred to the entire central district of the land, and introduced the key word in this section, namely, *tərûmâ*, 'portion' or 'reserve' (REB), along with the verb 'apportion' from the same root, in the form which conveyed the sense 'to cause to be high, to lift up, to dedicate' (*rûm*, hiphil; cf. 45:1). This signified specially separating a part from a whole. In this instance, since the LORD had sovereignly granted tenure of the whole land to the people, they in turn were to reserve a special portion of it which was to be designated for his service. It thus was often described in this passage as 'holy' (48:10, 12, 18, 20, 21).

Twenty-five thousand ⌞cubits⌟ in breadth. The breadth was the shorter measurement of the central zone from north to south. Throughout these verses no unit of measurement was specified, though it is generally taken that the reference was to the cubit (the long cubit of 20.3 inches [52 cm]; cf. 40:5). In that case 25,000 cubits would be about 8 miles (13 km). Keil (2002:447), however, took the unit of measurement to be the measuring rod of the guide, which was 6 cubits long (40:5), but for the difficulties that causes, see on 45:1.

In length[131] ***like one of the ⌞tribal⌟ shares from east side to west side***. The length described here was the longer (unspecified) distance from the Jordan to the Mediterranean, so that the area under consideration was the whole of the central district, within which lay the square holy portion of 45:1 (see Fig. 8). 'Shares' (*ḥēleq*) was used for the tribal territories to differentiate them from the central portion and its divisions.

The sanctuary will be in its midst.[132] The centrality of the sanctuary (*miqdāš*) was more precisely specified in 48:10, but its location was what gave significance to the central zone of the land. The LORD's palace on earth was to be at the geographical and, more significantly, the spiritual heart of the nation's life (Fig. 8 B).

♦ **48:9** The Hebrew text differs from the Greek text as to which part of

---

131. 'Like' (*kə*) may well have been used not to institute a comparison but to assert identity or equality, 'equal to one of the tribal portions'.

132. The masculine suffix on *bətôkô*, 'in its midst', refers to the feminine noun *tərûmâ*, 'portion', but the gender of the suffix has been rendered masculine through the influence of the intervening masculine noun *ḥēleq*, 'portion'. Similar instances of grammatical attraction occur in 48:10 and in the qere of 48:15, 21.

The Land of Promise

the central zone was delimited here, though the variation does not affect the overall disposition of the area. Consultation of Figure 8 helps understanding of what was said. ***The portion which you are to apportion*** had specifically added here ***to the LORD*** (as in 45:1), and referred to part of the entire central belt. ***In length twenty-five thousand ⌊cubits⌋*** (8 miles; 13 km) measured it from east to west, and ***in breadth ten thousand ⌊cubits⌋*** (3 miles; 5 km) measured it from north to south. On that basis the area under review is that of Figure 8 A. However, the Septuagint gave the breadth as 'twenty thousand' which would identify the LORD's portion as consisting of areas A and C in Figure 8. Hummel (2007:1370) prefers the Massoretic text since only the priests' allotment is designated 'most holy' (48:12), because it contains the sanctuary, whereas when the Levites' land was later taken into consideration the designation is simply 'holy' (48:14b). Most English translations, however, consider that renders the text repetitious as the same dimensions would then be restated in 48:10. On balance it may be preferable to adopt the Septuagintal text, and view the text as narrowing successively from the central belt as a whole (48:8), to the LORD's portion (48:9), to the holy portion occupied by the Zadokite priests (48:10–12).

♦ **48:10** ***And to these will be the holy portion***. It was not immediately evident to whom 'to these' referred, and presumably that was why the further specification ***to the priests*** was added. The dimensions of the portion in view were specified as a rectangle of ***twenty-five thousand ⌊cubits⌋*** in length (***northwards*** and ***southwards*** respectively as one looked there from the centre to its perimeter), and ***ten thousand ⌊cubits⌋*** in breadth (again as one looked ***westwards*** and ***eastwards*** to those boundaries; see Fig. 8 A).

And the sanctuary of the LORD will be in its midst repeated the closing thought of 48:8 with the addition of 'of the LORD'. However, in this verse it was the holy portion which was in view. In mathematical terms that would centre the sanctuary 15,000 cubits south of the northern boundary of the central zone. However, 'in its midst' might not have been intended in quite that sense. The symmetrical nature of the vision possibly favoured the temple being at the centre of the square zone in the middle of the central district, and thus 2,500 cubits further north than that, as marked in Figure 8. On either construal, what was paramount was the theological significance of the arrangement: the LORD's presence was ideally the central and controlling feature of the life of the nation.

♦ **48:11** Again it was emphasised that use of the LORD's portion was restricted to *the sons of Zadok* in recognition of their past loyalty (cf. 43:19; 44:15). Here they were described as *the priests, whoever has been consecrated*[133], that is, specially set apart to serve the LORD in his inner sanctuary.

♦ **48:12** The paragraph marker before this verse in the Massoretic text denoted the beginning of a new paragraph here even though the thought flowed on. *And it will be* had as its subject the 'portion' apportioned to the LORD in 48:9. *Their* (lit., 'for them') referred to the priests, who were given the privilege of occupying the territory around the temple. *Special portion* renders a unique noun ($tərûmîyâ$) which was obviously closely linked to the frequently repeated 'portion' ($tərûmâ$; 48:8), and may simply have been a variant spelling of that term. If it did have additional significance, it must have derived from the fact that it was distinguished *from all the portions of the land*, and its status described as *most holy* ($qōdeš\ qŏdāšîm$, cf. 41:4).

The portions of the land referred to the components of the central zone in their entirety. *At the border of the Levites* marked a transition from the most holy portion to the territorial assignment to the Levites, which was merely 'holy' (48:14). While some argue that this phrase required the Levites' portion to be to the south of the priests' portion, that is improbable. The dominating factor was undoubtedly the position of the temple within the priests' portion, and the other portions were described working out from there in terms of comparative sanctity, not in terms of physical situation.

(b) The Levites' Allocation (48:13–14)

> ⁴⁸:¹³And the Levites ⌊will have a portion⌋ alongside the border of the priests: twenty-five thousand ⌊cubits⌋ in length and in breadth ten thousand ⌊cubits⌋; the whole length ⌊is to be⌋ twenty-five thousand ⌊cubits⌋ and the breadth ten thousand ⌊cubits⌋. ⁴⁸:¹⁴And they are not to sell any of it nor is one to exchange ⌊any of it⌋; and one is not to alienate the best part of the land, for it is holy to the LORD.

---

133. The Hebrew text is literally 'for the priests, the one consecrated (*hamquddāš*) from the sons of Zadok', in which the plural term is followed by a singular qualification. However, it is not necessary to transpose the *mem* of the following preposition to the end of the pual participle to yield a plural form. The singular may be understood in a distributive sense, 'whoever has been consecrated'.

♦ **48:13** In the first part of the verse *will have a portion*, or some equivalent phrase, is required to complete the sense of the allocation which was *alongside* (*ləʿummat*) that of the priests. From east to west it was to be *twenty-five thousand ⌊cubits⌋ in length*, while its breadth from north to south was to be *ten thousand ⌊cubits⌋* (Fig. 8 C). Adding that to the 10,000 cubits of the priests' portion (48:9–10), and the 5,000 cubits of the city (48:15) yielded a north to south total of 25,000 cubits, so that there was a square zone in the middle of the central district (48:20).

In the Hebrew text the second part of the verse repeated, with the addition of *whole*, the first part of the verse including the phrase *the breadth ten thousand ⌊cubits⌋* (cf. NASB, NIV, NLT). It is puzzling that these dimensions should be duplicated virtually verbatim. However, there is Septuagintal evidence for reading 'twenty thousand' (*ʿeśrîm ʾelep*) instead of *ten thousand* (*ʿaśeret ʾălāpîm*). In that case (cf. 45:1 and 48:9) 'whole' referred to the dimensions of the LORD's portion (Fig. 8 A + C) rather than repeating those of the Levites' portion (Fig. 8 C; cf. RSV, NRSV, ESV).

♦ **48:14** The interpretation embodied in the Massoretic text implied that these regulations pertained only to the Levites' administration of their tract of land of ten thousand cubits breadth, but Hummel (2007:1372), despite following the Massoretic text in the preceding verse, argues that the restrictions applied to the priests also, which would be the natural assumption following the Septuagintal reading of 'twenty thousand cubits' in 48:13b. The text may refer only to the disposition of the land allocated to the Levites, or its requirements may also have been applicable to the district which was assigned to the Zadokite priest. Either understanding is possible since neither verb had a stated subject; indeed, the first was plural (*they are not to sell*) and the second was singular, *nor is one to exchange ⌊any of it⌋*.[134] Also, the phrase *the best part of the land* may also be rendered 'the

---

134. The translation assumes that *mimmennû*, 'from it', is to be understood with the second verb also. That verb, *yārēd*, is a singular jussive hiphil, 'let one exchange'. The Peshitta and Vulgate read a plural verb, while the LXX has a singular verb, but identifies a different root. While the singular may just be a stylistic variation for an unspecified subject, the switch may emphasise the individual nature of the transactions being considered. It is more difficult to account for the jussive form. That it too may simply be a stylistic variation is supported by the fact that the accompanying negative is *lōʾ*, and not the regular *ʾal*, which would be expected if a jussive sense were attached to the word.

firstfruits of the land' (cf. 44:30), in which case it might more readily refer to the priests' portion. It had been surrendered as a tithe to the LORD to be disposed of and used as he decreed. This would fit in with the clause, *for it is holy* (lit., 'holiness') *to the LORD*, as a reference to the temple being in the centre of the priests' portion (see on 48:10b).

Under consideration here was a matter not taken up in 45:1–8, the possibility of sale or transfer of property. The theme reflected that of the Mosaic regulations for property in the Levitical cities scattered throughout the land (Lev. 25:32–34). Such property might be sold for a limited time, but had to be returned in the Jubilee year. The regulations here were stricter. *One is not to alienate*,[135] that is, cause its ownership to pass over into the hands of one who is not a member of the family. No sale or transfer was possible because ultimately that section of the land had been dedicated to the LORD. All the land was his, and the central portion had been returned to him to be allocated to the priests and Levites.

(c) The City (48:15–20)

The city, which is not named, is not within the territorial allocation of any tribe, but is equally accessible to each of them by means of their designated gateways (48:30–34). All the tribes have a role in the functioning of the city, and thus those who come from them are accorded access to the surrounding portions of land to encamp on or to maintain themselves.

> 48:15And the five thousand ⌊cubits⌋ which remain in the breadth facing the twenty-five thousand ⌊cubits⌋ ⌊will be⌋ for the city's ordinary use, for habitation and for open space, and the city will be in the midst of it. 48:16And these ⌊will be⌋ its measurements: the north side four thousand five hundred ⌊cubits⌋, and the south side four thousand five hundred ⌊cubits⌋, and the east side four thousand five hundred ⌊cubits⌋, and the west side four thousand five hundred ⌊cubits⌋. 48:17And the city will have open space: northwards two hundred and fifty ⌊cubits⌋, and southwards two hundred and fifty ⌊cubits⌋, and eastwards two hundred and fifty ⌊cubits⌋, and westwards two hundred and fifty ⌊cubits⌋. 48:18And that which remains in length alongside the holy portion ⌊will be⌋ ten thousand ⌊cubits⌋

---

135. The kethib *wəlōʾ yaʿăbûr*, 'and it is not to be alienated', is a masculine, intransitive qal form with 'the best of the land' to be taken as its subject, even though both these nouns are feminine. The qere *wəlōʾ yaʿăbîr* is a transitive hiphil form with an unspecified subject, 'and one is not to alienate.'

eastwards, and ten thousand ⌊cubits⌋ westwards, and it will be alongside the holy portion. And its produce will be bread for those who work in the city. ⁴⁸:¹⁹And ⌊as for⌋ whoever works in the city, those from all the tribes of Israel will work it. ⁴⁸:²⁰The whole portion ⌊will be⌋ twenty-five thousand ⌊cubits⌋ by twenty-five thousand ⌊cubits⌋, four square; you are to apportion the holy portion in addition to the possession of the city.

♦ **48:15** This section gives further details regarding 'the possession of the city' which had been previously mentioned in 45:6-7 (the term itself is found in 48:20). This comprised the oblong to the south of the allocations to the priests and the Levites, and combined with them to form a square in the centre of the land (Fig. 8). *The five thousand ⌊cubits⌋ which remain in the breadth facing the twenty-five thousand ⌊cubits⌋* incorporated the expression 'which remain' or 'that which remains', which was used with different referents (cf. 48:18, 21). Apparently it here described a square area in the middle of the remaining rectangle (Fig. 8 D), and located it as contiguous with the southern border of the priests' portion.

The LORD decreed that the allocation ⌊*will be*⌋ *for the city's ordinary use* (lit., 'common for the city'). 'Common' (*ḥōl*) could be used in a negative sense for what lacked sanctity, but here its connotations were neutral: it was simply what was ordinary. As such, it could be used by those who did not hold any special status in the community for two purposes: *for habitation and for open space.* It was clearly intended that the city should be populated. While the term 'open space' occurred in 45:2 for an unused barrier zone about the temple, that is implausible here. What may have been indicated was permission to use this space for purposes such as accommodating the tents of worshippers attending major feasts at the temple. Additionally, 'open space' could be employed in the sense of 'pastureland', for instance the land found around the Levitical cities (Lev. 25:34; Num. 35:2–5). This supplemented the agricultural zones provided in 48:18.

Separation between the zone for habitation and the open space was achieved by the requirement that *the city will be in the midst of it,*[136] that is, of the lower square.

---

136. The kethib for the last word in the verse may be vocalised as *bətôkōh*, an alternative spelling of the qere, *bətôkô*, 'in its midst', that is, of the earlier 'which remain' (a masculine singular form). If the kethib were vocalised as *bətôkāh*, then the feminine suffix might point to the special portion or to the land, both feminine forms, but those are quite improbable options.

♦ **48:16** In *its measurements* the suffix 'its' was feminine, agreeing with 'the city' at the end of the previous verse. Listing the dimension of each side separately as *four thousand five hundred ⌞cubits⌟*,[137] emphasised the symmetrical shape of the city as about 1.4 miles (2.3 km) square. If the units had been rods (see on 48:8), then the city would have been 8.6 miles (14 km) square.

♦ **48:17** Like the dimensions of the city in the preceding verse, the dimensions of the *open space* (cf. 48:15) were also listed separately for each side to emphasise its symmetry. The *two hundred and fifty ⌞cubits⌟* on each side added to the 4,500 cubits for the city gave a square with sides of 5,000 cubits for the city and its pastureland combined.

♦ **48:18** *That which remains* (cf. 48:15) here referred to two areas, one to the east and the other to the west of the city and its pastureland (Fig. 8 E). Each was a rectangle, *ten thousand ⌞cubits⌟ eastwards and ten thousand ⌞cubits⌟ westwards* on either side of the city, with the remaining side of five thousand cubits. *It will be alongside the holy portion* (that is, the portion allotted to the priests to its north). *And its produce*[138] *will be bread for those who work in the city*. Clearly the land was designated for growing crops. The identity of the workers was clarified somewhat in the following verse.

♦ **48:19** It was specified that those who would work in the city would be drawn *from all the tribes of Israel.* Quite what was envisaged is obscure. It may have been that individuals from all the tribes would be selected by lot to come and dwell permanently in the city (in a fashion similar to that recorded in Neh. 11:1–2), or that some rotational system of workers was envisaged. *Will work it* suggested an agricultural labour force, with 'it' (masculine) looking back to 'that which remains'.

♦ **48:20** The first half of the verse summarised the preceding verses and indicated that the combined territory occupied by the priests' portion, the Levites' portion, and the area for the city and its hinterland

---

137. In the dimensions of the south side of the square, after the word *ḥămēš*, 'five', the consonants *ḥmš* are repeated in the MT without any vowels, and with a marginal note 'one of eight [words] written but not read', identifying the letters as an instance of scribal dittography.

138. The variation between the kethib *təbûʾātōh* and the qere *təbûʾātô*, both of which mean 'its produce', is merely one of the spelling of the masculine pronominal suffix.

comprised a perfect square of ***twenty-five thousand ⌊cubits⌋ by ⌊twenty-five⌋ thousand cubits four square***.[139] ***The whole portion*** used the term more narrowly than in 48:8, 12, where it included the ruler's tracts as well. The final clause, ***you are to apportion the holy portion in addition to the possession of the city*** indicated that the city's portion was required to make up the square. It was the southernmost of the three allocations which comprised the central square of the land. The Levitical portion lay furthest to the north; the portion allocated to the priests and including the temple occupied the middle of the zone; and finally the portion designated for the city and its inhabitants was located to the south.

(d) The Ruler's Territory (48:21–22)

> ⁴⁸:²¹And what remains ⌊will be⌋ the ruler's, on this side and on that of the holy portion and of the possession of the city, facing the twenty-five thousand ⌊cubits⌋ of the portion as far as the eastern border, and westwards facing the twenty-five thousand ⌊cubits⌋ along the border westwards alongside the ⌊tribal⌋ shares; ⌊it will be⌋ the ruler's. And the holy portion and the sanctuary of the house will be in its midst. ⁴⁸:²²And from the possession of the Levites and from the possession of the city ⌊which are⌋ in the midst of what will be the ruler's; between the border of Judah and the border of Benjamin will be the ruler's.'

♦ **48:21** There was one outstanding matter to be considered in the disposition of the land in the central district. Since the holy zone was only 25,000 cubits from east to west, it did not reach either the river Jordan on the east or the Mediterranean on the west. ***What remains*** referred to the two substantial outlying portions of ground ***on this side and on that of the holy portion and of the possession of the city***. These formed the western border of the eastern portion, and the eastern border of the western portion alongside ***the ⌊tribal⌋ shares*** which were located on their northern and southern borders (Fig. 8 F). These outlying portions were allocated as ***the ruler's***, as had been set out in 45:7–8.

---

139. *rəbîʿît*, here represented by 'four square', elsewhere means 'one-quarter'. The Massoretic text is generally emended to a pual participle, *mərubbāʿ*, 'foursquare' (found in 40:47; 45:2) or to a qal passive participle, *rəbuʿâ* (found in 41:21), either of which appears to have been the reading of the ancient versions, which also diverge from the Massoretic punctuation.

And the holy portion and the sanctuary of the house will be in its midst.[140] 'In its midst' referred to 'that which remains', so that the two outlying portions belonging to the ruler abutted the 'holy portion', that is, the priests' land with the temple within it.

♦ **48:22** The territories allotted to the ruler were further described as stretching out *from the possession of the Levites and from the possession of the city*, so that these areas were sandwiched *in the midst of what will be the ruler's*. Looking at the disposition of the ruler's portion from a north to south perspective, *between the border of Judah and the border of Benjamin will be the ruler's*. The term 'possession' which was used of these allocations probably indicated their lesser status compared to the 'holy portion' in which the temple was situated. Mention of the 'border of Benjamin' to the south led into resumption of the description of the tribal territories.

(5) Tribal Territories to the South (48:23–29)

> ⁴⁸:²³'And ⌊as for⌋ the rest of the tribes, from east side to west side—Benjamin one ⌊share⌋. ⁴⁸:²⁴And beside the border of Benjamin, from east side to west side—Simeon one ⌊share⌋. ⁴⁸:²⁵And beside the border of Simeon, from east side to west side—Issachar one ⌊share⌋. ⁴⁸:²⁶And beside the border of Issachar, from east side to west side—Zebulun one ⌊share⌋. ⁴⁸:²⁷And beside the border of Zebulun, from east side to west side—Gad one ⌊share⌋. ⁴⁸:²⁸And beside the border of Gad at the south side southwards, the border will be from Tamar to the waters of Meribah-kadesh, the brook ⌊of Egypt⌋, to the Great Sea. ⁴⁸:²⁹This ⌊is⌋ the land which you are to allot for an inheritance to the tribes of Israel, and these ⌊are⌋ their shares, declares the Lord GOD.'

♦ **48:23** The listing of the tribal portions resumed from 48:7 and covered *the rest of the tribes*, proceeding southwards from the central zone (Fig. 9). The territory of **Benjamin** would be switched from north of the temple and city to their south. This might reflect the meaning of the name Benjamin, 'son of the right hand', where 'right' was also used to refer to the south. Its proximity to the central zone probably reflected the fact that Jerusalem had originally lain within its territory.

---

140. The qere *bətôkô* and the kethib vocalised as *bətôkōh* (cf. 48:15) would have the masculine suffix referring to 'what remains'. Vocalising the kethib with a feminine suffix, *bətôkāh*, would refer to the entire portion.

♦ **48:24** Next in order southwards was the territory allotted to *Simeon*, descended from Jacob's second son by Leah (Gen. 29:33). This tribe had originally occupied land situated in the south, almost completely surrounded by Judah. Over the years it had lost much of its tribal identity, but it was here given full status in the envisaged restoration.

♦ **48:25-26** The two tribes of *Issachar* (descended from Leah's fifth son to Jacob, Gen. 30:18) and *Zebulun* (descended from Leah's sixth son to Jacob, Gen. 30:20) were also repositioned to the south of the sacred zone, most probably to increase the number of the tribes to the south and so to accentuate the centrality of the holy portion in the restored nation.

♦ **48:27-28** The tribe of *Gad* was descended from the son of Zilpah, the handmaid of Leah (Gen. 30:11), and so it was allocated a position distant from the central zone (cf. 48:1-3). The southern border of the land was once more delineated since it coincided with the southern border of Gad's territory in this ideal arrangement. For *Tamar, the waters of Meribah-kadesh*, and *the brook ⌊of Egypt⌋*, see on 47:19.

♦ **48:29** The catalogue concluded with a summary statement of the arrangements laid out in 47:13-48:28, with *this ⌊is⌋ the land* referring to 47:13-23, and *these ⌊are⌋ their shares* referring to 48:1-28. Both the *inheritance to the tribes of Israel* and *shares* emphasised that this ideal disposition of the land expressed the sovereign will of the LORD, to which he annexed the signature formula, *declares the Lord GOD.*

REFLECTION

- The apportionment of the land brought out the inclusiveness of the LORD's provision. There was a place for every tribe, and none was excluded. This is a theme which is taken up in the vision granted to John of those sealed by divine appointment (Rev. 7:4-8). But it is also to be noted that the allotment of the tribal territories was done with discrimination. In this illustrative model respect was paid to the social origins of each tribe. Differential treatment on that basis has been superseded in New Testament times, but distinctions are still made among the people of God. All who are Christ's will be saved, but those who have built on the foundation of Christ that which survives the testing of the final Day will be rewarded (1 Cor. 3:12-15). 'Each will receive his wages according to his labour' (1 Cor. 3:8). It is on that basis that John exhorts the believer to take care to 'win a full reward' (2 John 8). The ideal disposition of the land, symbolising the place of divine fellowship, here provides one model for conceiving what that fulness might consist of—closer access to the Lord's presence.

F. 'The LORD Is There.' (48:30–35)

In the final section of the prophecy, which is still covered by the messenger formula of 47:13, the LORD turns his attention to 'the city', of which little has been said so far, and defines the access of the tribes to the city, with each tribe having its own gateway (48:30–34). No previous name for the city is indicated. Indeed, only once does the name Jerusalem occur in oracles of restoration (36:38)—and even then in an indirect fashion. However, the city is clearly the ideal counterpart of the earthly Jerusalem, whose behaviour had been the focus of condemnation in the earlier sections of the book. Consequently, the city whose 'name is defiled' (22:5) does not merit mention in the new order; instead, it has to be renamed (48:35). Even so, by being presented in this final, climactic position, the city is declared to be in some sense the goal and fulfilment of the ideal order—not as a matter of geography, but because of the abiding presence of the LORD.

Critics have tended to view the final verses as an addendum by another hand to make up for the lack of an explicit Zion theology in Ezekiel, as contrasted with, say, Isaiah. However, the return here to 'the city' mirrors the initial description 'resembling a city' (40:2). The temple and the city are not to be divorced in that in 43:1–12 the LORD came to take up his abode in the temple, but here it is the city which will be known as 'The LORD is there'. Scripture finally reintegrates the two concepts, not with the temple in the city, but with the city being identified as all temple (Rev. 21:22). So, in this visionary context no problem arises from the temple lying to the north of the city.

In the wilderness period the tribes were grouped around the Tabernacle, but the order in Numbers 2 is not followed here. Earlier the tribes to the north were Dan, Asher, and Naphtali; to the east, Judah, Issachar, and Zebulun; to the south, Reuben, Simeon, and Gad; and to the west, Ephraim, Manasseh, and Benjamin, while the tribe of Levi were allocated to a buffer zone immediately around the Tabernacle. Here the six tribes related to Leah are arranged on the north and south, three of the sons of Jacob's concubines on the west, with Joseph and Benjamin, the sons of Rachel on the east along with Dan, a son of the concubine Bilhah.

⁴⁸:³⁰ 'And these ⌊will be⌋ the outer bounds of the city: on the north side, four thousand five hundred ⌊cubits⌋ by measure,

⁴⁸:³¹and the gateways of the city (ₗnamedₗ after the names of the tribes of Israel): three gateways on the north, the gateway of Reuben, one; the gateway of Judah, one; the gateway of Levi, one; ⁴⁸:³²and on the east side, four thousand five hundred ₗcubitsₗ, three gateways, the gateway of Joseph, one; the gateway of Benjamin, one; the gateway of Dan, one; ⁴⁸:³³and on the south side four thousand five hundred ₗcubitsₗ by measure, three gateways, the gateway of Simeon, one, the gateway of Issachar one; the gateway of Zebulun, one. ⁴⁸:³⁴On the west side, four thousand five hundred ₗcubitsₗ, their gateways three: the gateway of Gad, one; the gateway of Asher, one; the gateway of Naphtali, one. ⁴⁸:³⁵Round about ₗit will beₗ eighteen thousand ₗcubitsₗ. And the name of the city from ₗthatₗ day ₗwill beₗ, The LORD is there.'

♦ **48:30** The section began with the formal ***These ₗwill beₗ the outer bounds of the city.*** For similar titles using 'these ₗwere/are/will beₗ', compare 43:13; 48:1, 16. 'Outer bounds' rather than 'exits' attempts to catch the sense of the term which frequently occurs in Numbers 34 and Joshua 15–19 for 'ways out from' or 'outer limits of'.[141] This coheres with the fact that each description here began with the length of that side (as a limit) before mentioning the gates that would be there.

On the north side, four thousand five hundred ₗcubitsₗ by measure stipulated the length of a boundary. The measurement itself had already been given in 48:16, and amounted to about 1.4 miles (2.3 km) for each side of the square city.

♦ **48:31** ***The gateways of the city*** introduced a new feature of the scene. Multiple gateways to a city, while not unknown in the ancient world, were nonetheless far from common because the gateway constituted a weak point in the city's defences. Whereas the temple gateways had primarily restricted access, these were designed to afford it. Their number probably also conveyed the thought that there would be no external threat so that the presence of the gateways did not undermine the city's security.

It is explained that the gateways were named ***after the names of the tribes of Israel.*** This required that there be twelve gates corresponding to the twelve tribes, though here the tribes were reckoned differently from the disposition of the land. Levi was included as a tribe and, to compensate for this, Joseph was reckoned as one tribe with no separate

---

141. The term found here is *tôṣā'ôt*, whereas elsewhere the plural of *môṣā'*, 'exit, is found (42:11; 43:11; 44:5). Both are derived from *yāṣā'*, 'to go out'.

mention of Ephraim or Manasseh, the two tribes descending from Joseph's sons. But the symmetry of the arrangement with three gates on each side, and with the repeated *one* recalling its use earlier in the chapter presented a scene in which parity of treatment was emphasised (cf. Rev. 21:12–13). Though there was no explicit mention of city walls, that was virtually implied by the term 'city' itself ('She had a great and high wall and twelve gates', Rev. 21:12).

Earlier Jerusalem had gates named after tribes to whose territory they afforded access (e.g., the Ephraim Gate, 2 Kgs. 14:13; the Benjamin Gate, Jer. 37:13; 38:7). To some extent that may have been a factor in the nomenclature here (Judah and Reuben to the north, and Simeon, Issachar and Zebulun to the south). Another factor was the grouping of the names. On the north, the three most important tribes descended from Leah, Jacob's first wife—the first born ***Reuben***; the tribe with the messianic promise, ***Judah***; and the priestly tribe of ***Levi***.

♦ **48:32** The description then moved to the *east side*, which had the standard measurement of *four thousand five hundred ⌊cubits⌋*, and where there were also *three gateways*. The tribes mentioned here were descended from the two sons of Rachel, ***Joseph*** and ***Benjamin***, along with ***Dan***, descended from Rachel's maid, Bilhah. Dan's tribal territory was in the extreme north, and in fact Dan is omitted from the list of tribes in Revelation 7:5–8. The Joseph tribes of Manasseh and Ephraim had their territory in the north of the land.

48:33 *On the south side* the standard measurement of the boundary was maintained, and there were found the gates of the other three Leah tribes, facing their brethren's gates to the north: ***Simeon, Issachar, Zebulun.*** On the north side the order from west to east is first born, fourth born, third born; here on the south side it is second born, fifth born, sixth born, assuming the naming went clockwise in the same way as the description of the walls.

♦ **48:34–35a** The west side, which was taken up last, may have been the least favoured side: ***Gad, Asher, Naphtali.*** There were three tribes descended from Jacob's concubines: the first two from Zilpah and the last from Bilhah.

There was a variation in the fourth description in the phrase, ***their gateways three***, with the addition of 'their', for which there was no clear antecedent, and the textual evidence varies.[142]

---

142. 'Their' is supported by the Targum and the Vulgate, but not the Septuagint or the Peshitta which read 'three gateways'.

Round about ⌞it will be⌟ eighteen thousand ⌞cubits⌟, the sum of the four lengths of the four walls, concluded the description of the city.

♦ **48:35b** Then, in a grand climax, the city itself was renamed, indicating the essence of its function. *From ⌞that⌟ day* referred to the return of the LORD to the temple (43:1–5) and the closure of the east gateway (44:1–2). In this ideal presentation the truth embodied in symbolic form by the closed gate was that once the LORD had taken up his residence with his people his presence would not be revoked. Consequently, the place of his presence with them could then be appropriately designated, ***The* LORD *is there*** (*YHWH šāmmâ*; traditionally Jehovah Shammah).

Though *there* (*šammâ*) in earlier Hebrew was more appropriately rendered 'to there', the ending had largely lost its directional force by Ezekiel's time and often simply conveyed the sense, 'there' (as in 23:3; 32:29–30). Note that 'there' had been used in 40:1, where the fall of the old city had been recorded, so that there was a verbal and thematic inclusion round this visionary presentation. Through divine intervention, the city of rebellion and bloodshed had been ideally replaced by the city of divine presence. In the vision this city was the only settlement of that sort in the restored, ideal land, reflecting the uniqueness of the LORD and his presence among his people.

REFLECTION
- It is a remarkable feature of Biblical portrayals of the redemptive and transformative power of God that the city is so insistently used to depict the culmination of salvation history. The city arose from the endeavours of Cain, the first murderer, to reverse the divine sentence on his sin, 'You will be a fugitive and a wanderer on the earth' (Gen. 4:11). He also expressed defiant rejection of the security afforded to him by the mark God placed on him (Gen. 4:15), and in an act of unfaith sought security by building a city (Gen. 4:17). Though the line of Cain and the cities they founded utilised the gifts of God's common grace to advance civilisation, it was a civilisation without God and so inherently doomed. One part of the Bible story is that of the cities that failed: Babel, Sodom, Nineveh, Babylon, Rome, and particularly here in Ezekiel, Jerusalem, the city of bloodshed. But rather than abandon the city as an embodiment of the overweening pride of fallen mankind, it is a measure of the extent of God's grace that he cleanses and renews even this aspect of human rebellion against his rule. The city is presented as the goal of the spiritual pilgrim's journey, and the epitome of heavenly bliss for

those with faith like Abraham's and who look forwards 'to the city that has foundations, whose architect and builder is God' (Heb. 11:10).
- There are two key elements in the concluding part of Ezekiel's vision: the presence of the covenant people, and the presence of the God of the covenant. Here the twelve gates into the city emphasise that all the tribes of Israel enjoy equal rights of access there. It would not be dominated by one tribe as the earthly Jerusalem had been by Judah, nor was it 'the city of David'. A similar visual presentation of the spiritual reality of equal access for all the people of God to his presence was set out in the closing chapters of Revelation where the description in part draws on that of Isaiah 54:12, but is even more evidently modelled on Ezekiel 48. The redeemed city provides a model of humanity functioning harmoniously in pursuit of what life should truly accomplish to the praise of the Creator.
- But of even greater significance as regards the heavenly city is the divine presence there. The most surprising feature of John's account of the new Jerusalem is that he apparently denies what is central to Ezekiel's vision. John saw no temple in the city (Rev. 21:22). But that was because the Glory-presence of God, which had previously been confined to the temple, now permeated the whole city with its lustre, rendering a temple redundant. As has often been remarked, it will not be a case of no temple, but of all temple. The heavenly city suffused with the light emanating from the Lord God the Almighty and the Lamb will be the supreme realisation of all that is encapsulated in its name, The LORD is there.

WORKS CITED

Alexander, T. D.
1986 'The Old Testament View of Life After Death', *Themelios* 11: 41–46.

Allen, L.C.
1987 'Ezekiel 24:3–14: A Rhetorical Perspective', *Catholic Biblical Quarterly* 49: 404–14.
1992 'The Structuring of Ezekiel's Revisionist History Lesson (Ezekiel 20:3–31)', *Catholic Biblical Quarterly* 54: 448–62.
1993 'The Structure and Intention of Ezekiel I', *Vetus Testamentum* 43: 145–61.
1998 *Ezekiel 20–48* (Word Biblical Commentary; Dallas: Word).
2002 *Ezekiel 1–19* (Word Biblical Commentary; Dallas: Word).

Apóstolo, S.S.S.
2008 'Imagining Ezekiel', *Journal of Hebrew Scriptures* 8/13.

Beale, G.K.
2008 *We Become What We Worship: A Biblical Theology of Idolatry* (Downers Grove, Ill.: IVP Academic).

Beale, G.K.
2004 *The Temple and the Church's Mission: A Biblical Theology of the Dwelling Place of God* (New Studies in Biblical Theology; Leicester: Apollos).

Beare, F.W.
1970 *The First Epistle of Peter* (Oxford: Blackwell).

Beentjes, P.C.
1996 'What a Lioness Was Your Mother: Reflections on Ezekiel 19', in B. Becking and M. Dijkstra (eds.), *On Reading Prophetic Texts: Gender-Specific and Related Studies in Memory of Fokkelien Van Dijk-Hemmes* (Leiden: Brill): 21–35.

Block, D.I.
1988 'Text and Emotion: A Study in the 'Corruption' in Ezekiel's Inaugural Vision (Ezekiel 1:4–28)', *Catholic Biblical Quarterly* 50: 418–42.
1989 'The Prophet of the Spirit: The Use of Rwḥ in the Book of Ezekiel', *Journal of the Evangelical Theological Society* 32: 27–49.
1991 'Ezekiel's Boiling Cauldron: A Form-Critical Solution to Ezekiel xxiv 1–14', *Vetus Testamentum* 41: 12–37.

	1992	'Gog in Prophetic Tradition: A New Look at Ezekiel xxxviii 17 ', *Vetus Testamentum* 42: 154–72.
	1995	'Bringing Back David: Ezekiel's Messianic Hope', in P.E. Satterthwaite, R.S.Hess and G.J.Wenham (eds), *The Lord's Anointed: Interpretation of Old Testament Messianic Texts* (Carlisle/Grand Rapids: Paternoster/Baker): 167–88.
	1997	*The Book of Ezekiel: Chapters 1–24* (The New International Commentary on the Old Testament; Grand Rapids, Michigan: Eerdmans).
	1998	*The Book of Ezekiel: Chapters 25–48* (The New International Commentary on the Old Testament; Grand Rapids, Michigan: Eerdmans).
	2000a	'Divine Abandonment: Ezekiel's Adaptation of an Ancient Near Eastern Motif', in M.S. Odell and J.T. Strong (eds.), *The Book of Ezekiel: Theological and Anthropological Perspectives* (Atlanta: Society of Biblical Literature): 15–42.
	2000b [1988]	*The Gods of the Nations: Studies in Ancient Near Eastern National Theology.* (ETS Studies; second edition, Grand Rapids/Leicester: Baker/Apollos).

Boadt, L.
    1990   'The Function of the Salvation Oracles in Ezekiel 33–37', *Hebrew Annual Review* 12: 1–21.

Borland, J.A.
    1978   *Christ in the Old Testament* (Chicago: Moody Press; rprt. Christian Focus).

Brownlee, W.H.
    1986   *Ezekiel 1–19* (Word Biblical Commentary; Waco, TX: Word).

Bruce, F.F.
    1954   *Commentary on the Book of the Acts* (New International Commentary on the New Testament; Grand Rapids: Eerdmans).

Calvin, J.
    1989   *Commentary on the First Twenty Chapters of the Book of the Prophet Ezekiel, Volume 2* (T. Myers, trans.; Grand Rapids: Eerdmans).
    1994   *Ezekiel (Chapters 1–12)* (D. Foxgrover and D. Martin, trans.; Grand Rapids, Mich./Carlisle, UK: Eerdmans/Paternoster).

Chisholm, R.B., Jr.
    2002   *Handbook on the Prophets* (Grand Rapids: Baker).

Clark, G.H.
- 1978 — *Predestination in the Old Testament* (Phillipsburg, N.J.: Presbyterian and Reformed).

Crane, A.S.
- 2008 — *Israel's Restoration: A Textual-Comparative Exploration of Ezekiel 36–39* (Leiden: Brill).

Darr, K.P.
- 1987 — 'The Wall Around Paradise: Ezekelian Ideas About the Future', *Vetus Testamentum* 37: 271–79.
- 1992 — 'Ezekiel's Justifications of God: Teaching Troubling Texts', *Journal for the Study of the Old Testament* 55: 97–117.
- 1994 — 'Ezekiel Among the Critics', *Currents in Research: Biblical Studies* 2: 9–24.
- 2001 — 'The Book of Ezekiel: Introduction, Commentary, and Reflections', in *The New Interpreter's Bible* (Nashville: Abingdon Press): VI: 1073–1607.

Davidson, A.B.
- 1893 — *The Book of the Prophet Ezekiel, with Notes and Introduction* (The Cambridge Bible for Schools and Colleges; Cambridge: Cambridge University Press).

Davis, E.F.
- 1989 — *Swallowing the Scroll: Textuality and the Dynamics of Discourse in Ezekiel's Prophecy* (Bible and Literature; Sheffield: Almond Press).

Day, J.
- 2000 — *Yahweh and the Gods and Goddesses of Canaan* (JSOT Supplement Series; London: Sheffield Academic Press).

Dijkstra, M.
- 1992 — 'The Altar of Ezekiel: Fact or Fiction?' *Vetus Testamentum* 42: 22–36.

Duguid, I.M.
- 1994 — *Ezekiel and the Leaders of Israel* (Supplements to Vetus Testamentum; Leiden: Brill).

Dumbrell, W.J.
- 1984 — *Covenant and Creation: An Old Testament Covenantal Theology* (Exeter: Paternoster Press).

Eichrodt, W.
- 1970 — *Ezekiel: A Commentary* (Old Testament Library; London: SCM Press).

Ellison, H.L.
- 1956 — *Ezekiel: The Man and His Message* (Exeter: Paternoster Press).

Fairbairn, P.
    1851   *Ezekiel and the Book of His Prophecy* (Edinburgh: T & T Clark).
    1865   *Prophecy Viewed in Respect to Its Distinctive Nature, Its Special Function, and Proper Interpretation* (Edinburgh: T & T Clark).
    1964 [1865] *The Interpretation of Prophecy* (rprt., second ed.; London: Banner of Truth).
    1975 [1864] *The Typology of Scripture* (rprt., Welwyn, Herts.: Evangelical Press).

Fensham, F.C.
    1987   'The Curse of the Dry Bones in Ezekiel 37:1–14 Changed to a Blessing of Resurrection', *Journal of Northwest Semitic Languages* 13: 59–60.

Ferguson, P.
    2006   'A Proof Text for Inerrancy or Fallibility of the Old Testament?' *Bible and Spade* 19: 47–58.

Friebel, K.G.
    1999   *Jeremiah's and Ezekiel's Sign-Acts: Rhetorical Nonverbal Communication* (Sheffield: Sheffield Academic Press).

Galambush, J.
    1992   *Jerusalem in the Book of Ezekiel: The City as Yahweh's Wife* (Atlanta, Georgia: Scholars Press).

Gilders, W.K.
    2004   *Blood Ritual in the Hebrew Bible: Meaning and Power* (Baltimore and London: John Hopkins UP).

Greenberg, M.
    1983a   *Ezekiel 1–20: A New Translation with Introduction and Commentary* (The Anchor Bible; New York: Doubleday).
    1983b   '*MSRT HBRYT*, "The Obligation of the Covenant," in Ezekiel 20:37', in C.L. Meyers and M. O'Connor (eds.), *The Word of the Lord Shall Go Forth: Essays in Honor of David Noel Freedman in Celebration of His Sixtieth Birthday* (Winona Lake, Indiana: Eisenbrauns): 37–46.
    1987   'The Design and Themes of Ezekiel's Program of Restoration', in J.L. Mays and P.J. Achtemeier (eds.), *Interpreting the Prophets* (Philadelphia: Fortress Press).
    1997   *Ezekiel 21–37: A New Translation with Introduction and Commentary* (Anchor Bible; New York: Doubleday).

Hals, R.M.
    1989   *Ezekiel* (The Forms of Old Testament Literature; Grand Rapids, Michigan: Eerdmans).

Hamilton, J.M., Jr
2010 *God's Glory in Salvation Through Judgment: A Biblical Theology* (Wheaton: Crossway).

Harrison, R.K.
1969 *Introduction to the Old Testament* (Leicester, England: Inter-Varsity Press).

Heiser, M.S.
2015 *The Unseen Realm: Recovering the Supernatural Worldview of the Bible* (Bellingham, WA: Lexham Press).

Hengstenberg, E.W.
1869 *The Prophecies of the Prophet Ezekiel Elucidated* (Edinburgh: T & T Clark).

Holladay, W.L.
2001 'Had Ezekiel Known Jeremiah Personally?' *Catholic Biblical Quarterly* 63: 31–34.

Hummel, H.D.
2005 *Ezekiel 1–20* (Concordia Commentary; St Louis, Missouri: Concordia).
2007 *Ezekiel 21–48* (Concordia Commentary; St Louis, Missouri: Concordia).

Hutton, R.R.
2009 'Are the Parents Still Eating Sour Grapes? Jeremiah's Use of the Mašal in Contrast to Ezekiel', *Catholic Biblical Quarterly* 71: 275–85.

Jenson, R.W.
2009 *Ezekiel* (SCM Theological Commentary on the Bible; London: SCM).

Johnston, P.S.
2002 *Shades of Sheol: Death and Afterlife in the Old Testament* (Leicester: Inter-Varsity Press).

Joyce, P.M.
1989 *Divine Initiative and Human Response in Ezekiel* (JSOT Supplement Series; Sheffield: Sheffield Academic Press).
2007 *Ezekiel: A Commentary* (Library of Hebrew Bible/Old Testament Studies; New York/London: T & T Clark).

Kaiser, W.C., Jr.
1978 *Toward an Old Testament Theology* (Grand Rapids, Mich.: Zondervan).
1995 *The Messiah in the Old Testament* (Carlisle: Paternoster).

Keil, C.F.
2002 [1876] 'Biblical Commentary on the Prophecies of Ezekiel', in *Commentary on the Old Testament* by C.F. Keil and F. Delitzsch. (rprt. Peabody, MA: Hendrickson): 9.1–480.

Kidner, D.
1973 *Psalms 1–72: An Introduction and Commentary* (Tyndale Old Testament Commentaries; Downers Grove, IL: InterVarsity).

Kitchen, K.A.
1966 *Ancient Orient and Old Testament* (Downers Grove, Ill.: InterVarsity).

Kohn, R.L.
2002 *A New Heart and a New Soul: Ezekiel, the Exile and the Torah* (JSOT Supplement Series; London/New York: Sheffield Academic Press).
2003 'Ezekiel at the Turn of the Century', *Currents in Biblical Research* 2: 9–31.

Kutsko, J.F.
2000 *Between Heaven and Earth: Divine Presence and Absence in the Book of Ezekiel* (Winona Lake, Indiana: Eisenbrauns).

Lapsley, J.E.
2000a *Can These Bones Live?: The Problem of the Moral Self in the Book of Ezekiel* (Berlin: Walter de Gruyter).
2000b 'Shame and Self-Knowledge: The Positive Role of Shame in Ezekiel's View of the Moral Self', in M.S. Odell and J.T. Strong (eds.), *The Book of Ezekiel: Theological and Anthropological Perspectives* (Atlanta: Society of Biblical Literature): 143–73.

Levenson, J.D.
1976 *Theology of the Program of Restoration of Ezekiel 40–48* (Harvard Semitic Monograph Series; Atlanta, Georgia: Scholars Press).

Lyons, M.A.
2010 'Transformation of Law: Ezekiel's Use of the Holiness Code (Leviticus 17–26)', in W.A. Tooman and M.A. Lyons (eds.), *Transforming Visions: Transformations of Text, Tradition, and Theology in Ezekiel* (Eugene, Oregon: Pickwick): 1–32.

Mackay, J.L.
2004 *Jeremiah* (2 vols. Mentor Commentary; Fearn, Ross-shire: Christian Focus).

Malamat, A.
 1968 'The Last Kings of Judah and the Fall of Jerusalem. An Historical-Chronological Study', *Israel Exploration Journal* 18: 137–55.

Matties, G.H.
 1990 *Ezekiel 18 and the Rhetoric of Moral Discourse* (SBL Dissertation Series; Atlanta, Georgia: Scholars Press).

McConville, J.G.
 1983 'Priests and Levites in Ezekiel: A Crux in the Interpretation of Israel's History', *Tyndale Bulletin* 34: 3–31.

McKeating, H.
 1993 *Ezekiel* (Sheffield: Almond Press).

Mein, A.
 2007 'Profitable and Unprofitable Shepherds: Economic and Theological Perspectives on Ezekiel 34', *Journal for the Study of the Old Testament* 31: 493–504.

Milgrom, J.
 2012 *Ezekiel's Hope: A Commentary on Ezekiel 38–48: Jacob Milgrom and Daniel I. Block in Conversation* (Eugene, OR: Cascade Books).

Mol, J.
 2009 *Collective and Individual Responsibility: A Description of Corporate Personality in Ezekiel 18 and 20* (Leiden: Brill).

Murray, J.
 1955 *Redemption Accomplished and Applied* (Grand Rapids: Eerdmans).

Newsom, C.A.
 1984 'A Maker of Metaphors: Ezekiel's Oracles Against Tyre', *Interpretation* 38: 151–64.

Niehaus, J.J.
 2008 *Ancient Near Eastern Themes in Biblical Theology* (Grand Rapids, Mich.: Kregel).

Odell, M.S.
 1992 'The Inversion of Shame and Forgiveness in Ezekiel 16.59–63', *Journal for the Study of the Old Testament* 56: 101–12.
 1994 'The City of Hamonah in Ezekiel 39:11–16: The Tumultuous City of Jerusalem', *Catholic Biblical Quarterly* 56: 479–89.
 1998a 'The Particle and the Prophet: Observations on Ezekiel II 6', *Vetus Testamentum* 48: 425–32.

1998b	'You Are What You Eat: Ezekiel and the Scroll', *Journal of Biblical Literature* 117: 229–48.
2000	'Genre and Persona in Ezekiel 24:15–24', in M.S. Odell and J.T. Strong (eds.), *The Book of Ezekiel: Theological and Anthropological Perspectives* (Atlanta: Society of Biblical Literature): 195–219.
2005	*Ezekiel* (Smyth & Helwys Bible Commentary; Macon, Georgia: Smyth and Helwys).

Oehler, G.F.
1883   *Theology of the Old Testament* (Trans. and Ed. G.E. Day; New York; London: Funk & Wagnalls).

Ortlund, R.C., Jr.
1996   *Whoredom: God's Unfaithful Wife in Biblical Theology* (New Studies in Biblical Theology; Leicester: Apollos).

Parker, R.A., and Dubberstein, W.H.
1956   *Babylonian Chronology, 626 B.C.–A.D. 75* (Providence, Rhode Island: Brown University Press).

Peels, H.G.L.
2003   *Shadow Sides: The Revelation of God in the Old Testament* (Carlisle: Paternoster).

Peterson, B.N.
2012   *Ezekiel in Context: Ezekiel's Message Understood in Its Historical Setting of Covenant Curses and Ancient Near Eastern Mythological Motifs* (Princeton Theological Monograph Series Book; Eugene, Oregon: Pickwick).

Raabe, P.R.
2010   'Transforming the International Status Quo: Ezekiel's Oracles Against the Nations', in W.A. Tooman and M.A. Lyons (eds.), *Transforming Visions: Transformations of Text, Tradition, and Theology in Ezekiel* (Eugene, Oregon: Pickwick): 187–207.

Renz, T.
1999   *The Rhetorical Function of the Book of Ezekiel* (Leiden: Brill).
2000   'Proclaiming the Future: History and Theology in Prophecies Against Tyre', *Tyndale Bulletin* 51: 17–58.

Roberts, J.J.M.
1971   'The Hand of Yahweh', *Vetus Testamentum* 21: 244–51.

Robertson, O.P.
1980   *The Christ of the Covenants* (Grand Rapids, Mich.: Baker).

Rooker, M.F.
1998   'The Use of the Old Testament in the Book of Ezekiel', *Faith and Mission* 15: 45–50.

Rowley, H.H.
   1953   'The Book of Ezekiel in Modern Study', *Bulletin of John Rylands Library* 36: 146–90 [Reprinted in *Men of God: Studies in Old Testament History and Prophecy*. London, Nelson 1963:169–210.].
   1956   *The Faith of Israel: Aspects of Old Testament Thought* (London: SCM).

Schwartz, B.J.
   2000   'Ezekiel's Dim View of Israel's Restoration', in M.S. Odell and J.T. Strong (eds.), *The Book of Ezekiel: Theological and Anthropological Perspectives* (Atlanta: Society of Biblical Literature): 43–67.

Sloane, A.
   2008   'Aberrant Textuality? The Case of Ezekiel the (Porno) Prophet', *Tyndale Bulletin* 59: 53–76.

Smith, J.E.
   1993   *What the Bible Teaches About the Promised Messiah* (Nashville, Tenn.: Thomas Nelson).

Smith-Christopher, D.L.
   2004   'Ezekiel in Abu Ghraib: Rereadng Ezekiel 16:37–39 in the Context of Imperial Conquest', in S.L. Cook and C.L. Patton (eds.), *Ezekiel's Hierarchical World: Wrestling with a Tiered Reality* (Atlanta: Society of Biblical Literature): 141–57.

Stevenson, K.R.
   1996   *Vision of Transformation: The Territorial Rhetoric of Ezekiel 40–48* (Society of Biblical Literature Dissertation Series; Atlanta: Scholars Press).

Stiebert, J.
   2002   *The Construction of Shame in the Hebrew Bible: The Prophetic Contribution* (JSOT Supplement; London: Sheffield Academic Press).

Strine, C.A.
   2012   'The Role of Repentance in the Book of Ezekiel: A Second Chance for the Second Generation', *Journal of Theological Studies* 63: 467–91.

Stuart, D.
   2002   *Hosea-Jonah* (Word Biblical Commentary; Dallas: Word).

Taylor, J.B.
   1969   *Ezekiel: An Introduction and Commentary* (Tyndale Old Testament Commentaries; London: Tyndale Press).

Taylor, S.G.
    1966   'A Reconsideration of the 'Thirtieth Year' in Ezekiel 1:1', *Tyndale Bulletin* 17: 119–20.

Tooman, W.A.
    2010   'Transformation of Israel's Hope: The Reuse of Scripture in the Gog Oracles', in W.A. Tooman and M.A. Lyons (eds.), *Transforming Visions: Transformations of Text, Tradition, and Theology in Ezekiel* (Eugene, Oregon: Pickwick): 50–110.

Udd, K.J.
    2005   'Prediction and Foreknowledge in Ezekiel's Prophecy Against Tyre', *Tyndale Bulletin* 56: 25–41.

Van Groningen, G.
    1990   *Messianic Revelation in the Old Testament* (Grand Rapids, Mich.: Baker).

Viguier, P.P.-L.
    2013   *The Glory of God: A Biblical Theology* (Bellingham, WA: Lexham Press).

Vos, G.
    1975 [1948]   *Biblical Theology: Old and New Testaments* (Edinburgh: Banner of Truth).

Waymeyer, M.
    2016   'Words of God and Words of Man: Inerrancy and Dual Authorship', in J. MacArthur (ed.), *The Inerrant Word* (Wheaton, Ill.: Crossway): 288–303.

Wendland, E.R.
    1996   'Text Analysis and the Genre of Jonah (Part 1)', *Journal of the Evangelical Theological Society* 39: 191–206.
    2001   '"Can These Bones Live Again?": A Rhetoric of the Gospel in Ezekiel 33–37, Part II', *Andrews University Seminary Studies* 39: 241–72.
    2009   *Prophetic Rhetoric: Case Studies in Text Analysis and Translation* (LaVergne, TN: Xulon Press).

Williamson, P.R.
    2007   *Sealed with an Oath* (Nottingham: Apollos).

Wilson, R.R.
    1972   'An Interpretation of Ezekiel's Dumbness', *Vetus Testamentum* XXII(1): 91–104.

Wong, K.L.
    2001   *The Idea of Retribution in the Book of Ezekiel* (Leiden: Brill).
    2003   'Profanation/Sanctification and the Past, Present and Future of Israel in the Book of Ezekiel', *Journal for the Study of the Old Testament* 28: 210–39.

Woudstra, M.H.
- 1968   'Edom and Israel in Ezekiel', *Calvin Theological Journal* 3: 21-35.
- 1971   'The Everlasting Covenant in Ezekiel 16:59-63', *Calvin Theological Journal* 6: 22-48.

Wright, C.J.H.
- 1990   *God's People in God's Land: Family, Land and Property in the Old Testament* (Carlisle: Paternoster Press).

York, A.D.
- 1977   'Ezekiel I: Inaugural and Restoration Visions?' *Vetus Testamentum* 27: 82-98.

Young, E.J.
- 1952   *My Servants the Prophets* (Grand Rapids, Mich.: Eerdmans).
- 1965   *The Book of Isaiah: Volume 1, Chapters 1–18* (Grand Rapids, Mich.: Eerdmans).

Young, R.C.
- 2004   'When Did Jerusalem Fall?' *Journal of the Evangelical Theological Society* 47: 21-38.
- 2006   'Ezekiel 40:1 as a Corrective for Seven Wrong Ideas in Biblical Interpretation', *Andrews University Seminary Studies* 44: 265-83.

Youngblood, R.
- 1971   *The Heart of the Old Testament* (Grand Rapids, Mich.: Baker).

Zimmerli, W.
- 1969   'The Message of the Prophet Ezekiel', *Interpretation* 23: 131-57.
- 1979   *Ezekiel 1: A Commentary on the Book of the Prophet Ezekiel, Chapters 1–24* (Hermeneia; Philadelphia: Fortress Press).
- 1982 [1953]   'I Am Yahweh', in W.A. Brueggemann (ed.), *I Am Yahweh* (Atlanta: John Knox Press): 1-28.
- 1982 [1954]   'Knowledge of God According to the Book of Ezekiel', in W.A. Brueggemann (ed.), *I Am Yahweh* (Atlanta: John Knox Press): 29-98.
- 1983   *Ezekiel 2: A Commentary on the Book of the Prophet Ezekiel, Chapters 25–48* (Hermeneia; Philadelphia: Fortress Press).

SUBJECT INDEX

abominations 1:192, 432
Abraham 2:185
adoption formula 1:437
Adam 2:77, 79
adultery 1:462
Alexander the Great 2:32, 42
allegorical fable 1:485
altar 2:450
  of burnt offering 2:437
Ammon/Ammonites 1:498, 639–40; 2:16, 534
Amorites 1:433, 468; 2:533
announcement formula 1:199, 201, 573
apocalyptic 1:38; 2:304
apostrophe 1:378
Asherah 1:207, 261, 280
Assyria/Assyrians 1:15, 17, 51, 164, 321, 343, 454, 646, 680–81, 685, 692, 694; 2:129, 153
  alliance with 1:454
  object lesson from 2:126
atonement 1:483
autobiography 1:32, 68
avoidance of terms 1:570; 2:344

Babylon 1:67, 490
  alliance with 1:455
  coded reference 1:639
  omission of 2:15, 148
  overthrow predicted 1:643
because ... therefore 1:191; 2:17
blood 1:242, 646
bones 2:282
bow 1:102
brook of Egypt 2:527, 545
burnt offering 2:390

Cambyses 2:103
Canaanite religion 1:207, 218, 261, 448, 451, 520, 591, 654

case law 1:35, 143, 392, 519; 2:168
cedar 1:489, 506; 2:55, 126, 129
Chaldea/Chaldeans 1:75, 333, 352, 455, 686, 692
chariot-throne 1:92–93, 133, 285, 297, 332
Chebar 1:71, 75, 154, 306, 308; 2:425
cherub/cherubim 1:85–86, 91–93, 285, 305, 333; 2:82, 410
child sacrifice 1:449, 588, 594
choose
  avoidance of 1:570
chronology 1:18, 69, 709; 2:181, 360
date formula 1:69, 255, 564, 708; 2:36, 96, 107, 123, 127, 141, 149, 181, 360
city personified 1:427
city, the ideal 2:540
  dimensions of 2:542
  gates of 2:547
  name of 2:549
  situation of 2:483, 541
clean 2:470
cleansing, spiritual 2:257, 294
common 2:470, 541
cosmic tree 2:126, 130
covenant 1:40, 45
  Abrahamic 1:223; 2:12
  blessing 1:45, 48–49, 51, 80, 180, 201, 212, 328, 407; 2:214, 263
  curse 1:45–48, 80, 204, 408, 586, 718; 2:12, 184
  Davidic 2:213
  everlasting 1:480; 2:297
  fidelity 1:572
  of peace 2:216, 296
  presence of the LORD 1:41; 2:297
  with Noah 1:102; 2:216

Subject Index

covenant formula 1:40, 330; 2:295
cubit 2:371
cup 1:696; 2:295
curse
  ANE perception of 2:245, 271
Cush 2:103, 113, 116, 309

Dan
  original territory 2:533
Daniel 1:25, 410; 2:71
daughter
  used of towns 1:454; 2:42
David 2:212, 295
day of the LORD 1:221, 228, 231; 2:111
Dead Sea 2:517
Dedan 2:27, 61, 315
defilement 2:249
deportation, of rebels 1:17; 2:185
detestable things 1:195
Deuteronomy, influence of 1:34, 218
disputation speech 1:312–13
divination 1:360, 371, 632
drink offerings 1:591

eagle 1:89, 488
Eden 2:77, 80, 133, 138, 264, 512
Edom/Edomites 1:478; 2:25, 60, 157, 221, 223, 231, 238
Egypt 2:93
  alliance with 1:452–53
  Babylonian invasion 2:95
  crocodile, symbol for 2:97
  historical background 2:94–95
  religion of 1:269
  restoration of 2:94, 104–5
Elam/Elamites 2:154
elders 1:278
  in exile 1:17, 255, 394, 565
  in Jerusalem 1:245, 256, 269, 311
En-gedi 2:518
evil 1:201, 227

exclusio 2:13n1
exiles
  conditions encountered by 1:17–18, 343
  dejection of 2:173, 282
  expectations of 1:81, 160, 406, 565; 2:166
Exodus 1:572
  new 1:327, 572, 599; 2:205, 256, 259
  reversal of 1:283
Ezekiel
  age of 1:70
  belittled by hearers 1:127, 613; 2:191
  call of 1:27, 67, 105
  character of 1:29, 122, 128, 134, 178, 292, 354, 724
  early years of 1:24, 178
  forbidden to mourn 1:722
  and Jeremiah 1:26–28
  later life 1:28–29
  like Moses 1:103; 2:444, 455, 457, 521
  location of ministry 1:31
  meaning of name 1:74
  prophet 1:27n4
  speechlessness of 1:156, 731; 2:182
  wife of 1:720
  wordplay on name 1:128, 136

firstborn 1:589
focus particle 1:82
fugitive 1:731; 2:181
futurum instans 1:62

Gedaliah 1:270
glory 1:43, 103
Glory-cloud 1:262, 286–87, 298, 300, 307, 311, 333
  departure of 1:286, 297, 332
  return of 2:424

God
  avoidance of term (Elohim) 1:72
  my holy name 1:605
  name of 1:42, 574
Gog 2:303, 306
grain offering 2:419
guidance formula 2:363
guilt offering 2:390
Gyges 2:306

halving 1:35, 485; 2:301n94
Hamonah 2:336
heart 1:329, 367; 2:70, 258
  of flesh 1:330; 2:259
  new 1:541; 2:258
  of stone 1:330; 2:258
heave offering 1:606
hendiadys 1:520; 2:62
Herodotus 2:74, 95, 98
high place 1:207
high priest 2:475, 491
historical parable 2:77
Hittites 1:433, 467
holy 1:43; 2:552
Holy of Holies 2:400
Holy One in Israel 2:329
Holy Spirit 1:59, 96, 109, 154, 259, 311, 315; 2:259, 272, 275, 278, 284, 346–47, 512
hostile-orientation formula 1:205
hubris 2:74

'I', repetition of 1:192
idols 1:209, 448
Immanuel principle 1:191
imperfect of obligation 1:61
inclusion 1:68; 2:13n1
individual responsibility 1:147, 511; 2:175
inheritance 2:473, 523, 527
interest 1:522
Israel
  border of 1:318
  conduct in Egypt 1:569, 676
  election of 1:570
  Ezekiel's use of 1:111
  hard of heart 1:113
  historical review 1:568
  house of 1:123, 170
  increased population 2:267
  land of 1:222
  mountains of 1:205; 2:235, 240
  my people 1:624
  population increase 2:297
  rebellion of 1:112, 114, 342, 496, 573, 579–80, 584, 586, 590, 593, 597, 711
  remnant of 1:184, 213, 292, 352
  restoration of fortunes 1:475; 2:91, 205, 240, 343
  sons of 1:111
  spiritual state of 1:342
  unity of restored people 2:289, 293

Jaazaniah
  son of Azzur 1:311
  son of Shaphan 1:270, 280
jealousy
  statue of 1:261, 263
Jehoahaz 1:219, 547
Jehoiachin 1:16, 73, 489, 550
Jehoiakim 1:16, 550
Jehovah-makkeh 1:230
Jehovah-meqaddesh 1:579
Jehovah Shammah 2:549
Jehu 1:680
Jeremiah 1:26–28
Jerusalem 1:431, 679
  arrival of news of fall 2:208
  city of bloodshed 1:646
  corruption in 1:254, 713
  date of fall 1:18
  depiction of siege 1:163
  foreign alliances 1:452
  Hamonah 2:336

Subject Index

judgement of 1:415
marking of inhabitants 1:287
nakedness of 1:461
name avoided 2:362, 546
privileged status of 1:188
rebellion of 1:188
wife of the LORD 1:425
Job 1:410
Josephus 1:61, 278n17, 639; 2:16, 95, 125, 307, 353
Josiah 1:15
Jubilee year 1:70, 236; 2:361n2, 505n113, 540
judge 1:567; 2:209

kethib 1:59
king/kings
  avoidance of term 1:245, 349, 546, 651; 2:487
  criticism of 1:651; 2:195, 429, 487

lament 1:121, 544; 2:47, 53, 75
land
  apportionment of 2:477, 521
  resettlement in 1:55, 328; 2:295
  significance of loss 1:272; 2:228
  theology of 2:222
Lebanon 1:489
Lebo-hamath 2:525, 533
Levites 2:461
  land allocated to 2:482
Leviticus
  influence of 1:34, 407
lion 1:89, 546, 667; 2:142, 410
litotes 1:530
living beings 1:87
Lord (Adonai) 1:42, 113, 1:376n24
LORD 1:42, 114
  Glory of 1:43–44, 104
  hand of 1:75
  holiness of 1:43
  house of 1:275

  jealousy of 1:199, 262, 693; 2:238–39, 322, 344
  kingship of 1:34, 101, 597, 599; 2:359
  name of 1:386n32; 2:251
  oath of 1:571
  presence with his people 2:297
  reaction to Israel's sin 1:214
  return of 2:424, 451
  who sanctifies 1:579
  wrath of 1:235
Lord GOD 1:42, 113
lots, casting of 1:632, 714; 2:478, 525
Lud 2:56, 113

Magog 2:306
Manasseh 1:15, 455
marriage 1:678
merism 1:217, 612
merkabah 1:78
Meshekh 2:59, 307
Meshekh-tubal 2:155
message-reception formula 1:74, 144
messenger formula 1:113
Messiah in Ezekiel 1:57
Moab/Moabites 1:583; 2:21, 223, 333, 534
Molech 1:450
mythology 2:76

name, my holy 1:605; 2:251
nations, misperceptions of 2:251
Nebuchadnezzar 1:15–17, 67, 496, 631; 2:41, 95, 106, 117
  attacking Tyre 2:41
  campaign against Jerusalem 1:631
  invasion of Egypt 2:95, 108, 116, 125
  king of Babylon 2:41
  siege of Tyre 2:107
Negeb 1:612

Nile	2:97, 102, 117	false	1:364, 366
Nineveh	1:646	fulfilment of	1:596; 2:34, 215
niphal tolerativum	1:62	inspiration	1:11, 33
no longer	1:193, 360; 2:245	lack of temporal perspective	2:35
Noah	1:70, 410	messianic	1:57, 505, 637; 2:109, 211, 295
oath formula	1:194	multi-staged fulfilment	2:35
official	1:245–46, 311	not history written beforehand	2:34
officials	1:669	prophetess	1:381
Oholah	1:677	prophetic perfect	1:62
Oholibah	1:677	prophets	1:666, 670
opposition formula	1:191	false	1:364, 403
oracle	1:12	protevangelium	2:225
oracles against the nations	2:11	proverb	1:358–59, 467, 488, 514, 614, 711
Passover	2:494	Put	2:57, 113–14, 309
Pathros	2:104, 119		
peace	1:377	qere	1:59
peace offerings	2:338		
Pelatiah	1:312, 319	Rabbah	1:631; 2:19
people of the land	1:246, 670	Rahab	2:94, 105
performative perfect	1:62	rainbow	1:102
Persia	2:56, 309	recognition formula	1:114, 198
conquest of Egypt	2:103	absence of	2:346n124
Peshitta	1:60	refining silver	1:661
Pharaoh		repentance	1:540, 558; 2:174
Ahmose	2:95	requital formula	1:294
Hophra	1:498–99; 2:94	resident alien	2:529
meaning of	2:96	resumptive exposition	1:37
Psammetichus II	1:252, 492, 498	resurrection	2:270
Philistines	1:454, 478; 2:29	retributive equivalence	1:49
Phoenicia	2:157	revenge	2:26
Phoenicians	2:32	revivification	2:270
polygamy	1:678	rhetorical question	1:372
pornography	1:428	Riblah	1:219, 318
possession	2:236, 474	riddle	1:488
priests	1:244, 277, 668	river, life-giving	2:511
ordination of	2:448	Rosh	2:307
training of	1:25, 70	ruler	1:349, 666; 2:452
prophecy		disposition of property	2:504
conditional	2:34, 45	land allocated to	2:483, 543
early positive passages	1:322, 352, 405, 474, 478, 504, 603	privileges of	2:453, 497

SUBJECT INDEX 567

typical role of 453, 491, 494, 497

Saba 1:703
Sabbath 1:578, 582
  offerings 2:499
Samaria 1:468, 471, 679; 2:185
sanctuary 1:265; 2:297
  for a little while 1:327
  sanctuaries 1:616; 2:86
Satan 2:77
scroll 1:118–121
Seir 2:22, 223
self-loathing 1:214, 481, 483, 608; 2:261
Septuagint 1:60
P. 967 1:363; 2:256n58, 302
servant
  of the LORD 2:212
Shaddai 1:98–99
Shamash 1:278
Shaphan 1:270
Shekinah 1:286, 298, 300; 2:329
Sheol 2:136, 148, 152
shepherd 2:194
  divine 1:600; 2:200, 204
  human 2:196, 2:201
  messianic 2:211
Sidon 2:32–33, 56, 87, 157
sign-acts 1:161
signature formula 1:195
sin offering 2:390
social injustice in Israel 1:52, 293, 652, 654–55
Sodom 1:299, 406, 468, 471; 2:324
sojourner 1:400, 652; 2:528
son of man 1:107
song
  of the cauldron 1:709
  of the cup 1:696
  of the sword 1:620
soul 1:148, 385
spirit
  new 1:329, 541; 2:258

spirit/wind 1:82, 135; 2:275
statutes, not good 1:586
stumbling-block 1:150, 239, 626; 2:463
sun worship 1:278
sword 1:182, 317, 610, 619; 2:1159
  song of 1:620
symbolic actions 1:162

Tabernacles, feast of 2:495
Tammuz 1:274
Targum 1:60, 70
Tarshish 1:94; 2:58, 63, 315
Tel-abib 1:136
Teman 1:612; 2:27
temple
  significance of 1:274; 2:359
temple, ideal 2:395
  altar in 2:395, 437, 450
  cleansing of 2:493
  gateway 2:372, 382, 384
  guide in 2:366
  Holy of Holies 2:400
  interpretation of 2:354
  kitchens of 2:506
  priestly rooms 2:413
  sacrifices 2:389, 438
  sanctuary structure 2:395
  table in 2:412
  vertical measurements 2:359, 397
  wall of 2:369
Temple, Jerusalem 1:259
theophany 1:81
  Christophany 1:100–01, 256; 2:366
therefore 1:190
topheth 1:450
Tubal 2:59, 307
twelve tribes 2:523, 547
Tyre 1:498; 2:31
  compared to merchant ship 2:52
  daughters of 2:39

history of 2:31
king of 2:68
siege of 2:107
situation of 2:31
slave trade 2:59
trading network 2:57

uncircumcised 1:454; 2:74, 139, 151
unclean 2:470
unmarked question 1:313, 465, 526
Ushu 2:31

vengeance 2:26
vine 1:421, 425, 491, 555
visions of God 1:72, 259; 2:269, 362
Vulgate 1:60

watchman 1:145; 2:166
  responsibility of 1:148, 150; 2:170
wheel/wheelwork 1:94, 298, 304
whoredom 1:51, 214, 427, 445, 676
wife of Ezekiel 1:720
wilderness 1:557, 562, 577, 677, 703; 2:217, 297, 546
  of the peoples 1:600

yoke 2:121, 218

Zadok 2:466
Zadokite priests 2:394, 445, 466
  conduct of 2:468
  duties of 2:467
  privileges of 2:473
  territory occupied by 482
Zaphon 1:507
Zedekiah 1:16, 73, 349, 491, 496, 502, 547, 550, 635
Zephaniah, influence of 1:34, 665

Zion 1:507, 603, 605; 2:217, 305, 363, 368, 520, 546
Zion theology 1:51, 165, 187, 314, 339, 366, 431, 443, 623, 634, 641, 698; 2:546

INDEX OF SCRIPTURES QUOTED

Genesis
1:10	2:242
2:9	2:133
2:10	2:520
3:5	1:698, 2:70, 74
3:8	1:99
3:15	2:31
4:11	2:549
6:9	1:410
6:13	1:221, 224, 233
9:6	2:160, 226
12:3	1:598, 706; 2:12
12:7	1:223
13:17	2:243
15:16	1:468
15:17	1:85
18:25	1:520
18:32	1:406
21:15	1:435
22:17	2:267
27:41	2:225
35:11	1:111
49:9	1:547
49:10	1:637
49:11	1:555

Exodus
3:5	1:605
7:5	1:220
12:12	2:119
12:27	2:510
15:3	1:619
15:18	1:599
17:15	1:230
19:5–6	1:45
19:6	1:188, 706
19:8	1:196
20:3	1:211, 572
20:5–6	1:518
20:7	1:386
20:13	1:650
24:17	1:43
25:9	2:368
29:45	1:41; 2:219
31:14	1:582
32:10	1:579
33:20	1:43
33:23	1:104

Leviticus
1:1	1:287
1:2	1:404
10:10–11	2:470
11:44	1:178
16:21	1:483
18:5	1:524
18:18	1:678
19:4	1:521
19:16	1:654
19:17	1:157
19:26	2:186
19:30	1:653
20:6	1:383
21:14	2:470
25:29	2:330
26:4	2:218
26:6	1:202; 2:304
26:9	2:241
26:12	1:41; 2:219
26:13	2:218
26:17	1:205
26:19	1:727
26:22	1:202, 413
26:25	1:202, 413–14, 622
26:26	1:180, 410
26:27–28, 33	1:425
26:29	1:193
26:30	1:207
26:31	1:200
26:32–33	1:356
26:33	1:184, 586
26:36	2:284
26:39	1:180; 2:174
26:44–45	1:185

Numbers
6:25	2:246
6:25–26	2:341
7:89	1:286
11:5	1:675
14:34	1:170
15:30	2:494
15:39	1:572
16:28	1:368
17:8	1:232
18:4–5	2:394
18:20	2:474
23:9	1:602
28:11	2:499

Deuteronomy
4:11	1:83
4:15	1:100
4:24	1:84
4:28	1:598
4:29	1:565–66
4:31	2:344
6:6	1:308
7:7–8	1:436
7:9–10	1:415
8:8	2:240
8:17	1:247, 656
10:16	1:542

11:9	1:223	10:27	1:442	11:4	1:273
11:12	1:273	11:36	1:187	12:2	1:329
12:18	2:510	14:15	1:223	14:1	1:368; 2:179
15:4	2:356	14:23	1:218	16:10, 11	2:160
15:11	2:356			18:10	1:308
16:17	2:499	**2 Kings**		19:12	1:595
17:16	1:502	6:32	1:255	20:7	1:273
18:9, 14	1:387	9:15	2:181	23:2	2:206, 274
18:22	1:359; 2:34	16:18	1:455	25:2–3	1:476
22:9	1:490n110	21:7	1:261	27:9	2:347
22:24	1:655	25:1	1:23	30:5	1:732; 2:183
24:16	1:518	25:4	1:351	33:6	2:279
28:7	1:680			33:9	1:437
28:25	1:628	**1 Chronicles**		40:4	2:105
28:26	2:273	28:18	1:92	46:5	1:51
29:4	1:342			46:9	2:336
29:16	1:598	**2 Chronicles**		48:7	2:67
30:6	1:542	30:5	1:458	48:12–14	2:368
31:17	2:347	33:7, 15	1:261	50:21	2:422
31:21	1:586	36:9	1:73	51:2	2:262
32:16, 21a	1:262	36:10	1:21	51:4	1:215
32:23	1:201	36:13	1:502	51:9	2:347
32:35	2:27			56:3	2:312
		Ezra		67:1	2:246
Judges		1:2	1:104	68:5	1:653
21:25	2:477	2:59	1:137	78:4	1:656
		8:17	1:137	78:7	1:657
1 Samuel				78:38	1:581
2:9	1:519	**Job**		79:4	1:649
8:5, 20	1:597	1:1	1:410	80:1	2:207
8:7	1:597	1:8	1:410	81:8, 10	2:189
13:14	2:212	1:21	1:724	81:15	2:233
26:19	1:325	4:8	1:720	83:3–4	2:316
		9:33	1:157	84:10	2:476
2 Samuel		13:1	1:130	88:5	2:282
7:14–15	1:504	31:1	1:690	89:44	1:625
				96:13	1:619
1 Kings		**Psalms**		97:2	1:83
6:2	2:369	2:6	1:507	100:3	2:207
8:11	2:368	5:5	1:312	103:10	1:582
8:27	1:332, 334; 2:432	8:5	1:92	106:23	1:371

109:16	1:389	**Ecclesiastes**		59:2	1:166
112:7	2:49	8:11	2:122	63:10	1:59
115:2–3	1:104	10:17	1:107	65:2	1:543
116:12	1:458				
120:5–7	2:307	**Isaiah**		**Jeremiah**	
121:1, 2	1:521	1:9	1:185	1:8	1:117
122:6	1:380	5:20	1:151, 593	1:9	1:118
130:3	1:371	5:21	2:75	1:18	1:116
132:13	1:440	6:1	1:100	2:23	1:431
132:14	2:452	6:5	1:608; 2:436	3:11	1:472
132:17	2:109	6:8	1:106	5:21	1:342
136:1	1:562	6:10	1:342	6:1	1:236
137:1	1:13, 76	6:11	1:293	6:14	1:244
139:7	1:96	7:9	2:312	6:17	1:146, 148
145:15	2:252	7:14	1:58	7:17–19	1:261
146:3	1:553	7:20	1:181	11:13	1:254, 456
147:20	1:650	9:4	1:231	15:16	1:118, 124
		10:5	1:644	18:7–8	1:362
Proverbs		10:12	1:644	18:18	1:244
1:29–31	1:406	22:5	1:229	20:2	1:283
5:21	1:97	25:7	2:285	21:9–10	1:501
6:28	1:50	26:19–21	2:325	22:15–16	2:471
11:1	2:491	30:7	2:94	22:20, 22	1:430
11:4	1:239	31:3	2:105	23:4	2:212
11:14	1:245	32:15	2:512	23:23–24	1:96
13:15	1:690	33:14	1:302	27:6	2:45, 110
14:12	1:539	33:24	2:520	27:11	2:45
15:3	1:97	35:3–4	2:300	28:8	2:11
16:5	2:75	36:6	2:100	29:6	1:382
16:15	2:246	37:29	1:549	29:9	1:111
16:18	2:139	40:11	2:207	29:19	1:110
16:33	1:714	42:8	1:44; 2:122, 252	31:33	2:259
17:5	2:40	43:25	2:255	36:2	1:124
17:17	2:105	45:23	2:319	44:16–17	2:189
17:22	2:282	51:3	2:265	46:28	2:25
18:24	2:105	52:1	1:649	49:30, 31, 32	2:313
20:22	2:27	53:4–5	1:230		
22:6	1:527	53:6	1:405	**Lamentations**	
24:17–18	2:21	53:8	2:282	1:1	1:200
25:4	1:664	55:6	2:233	1:2	2:105
28:9	1:402	56:3, 6–7	2:530	2:9	1:244

2:15	1:442	**Nahum**		**Mark**	
3:33	1:543	3:10	1:242	2:27	1:582
3:44	1:166			2:28	2:503
3:54	2:282	**Habakkuk**		4:9	1:159
		1:13	2:325	10:29–30	2:266
Daniel		2:3	1:364	13:22	1:391
4:9	2:71	2:4	1:536		
4:37	1:509			**Luke**	
7:9–10	1:85	**Zephaniah**		1:69	2:109
7:9	1:93	1:14	1:228	4:16–30	2:35
7:13	1:100, 108	1:18	1:239	5:8	2:436
12:3	1:257	3:3 ,5	1:647	10:25	1:729
		3:3	1:667, 1:669	10:37	1:730
Hosea		3:4	1:668	12:20	2:336
1:2	1:678	3:5	1:672	12:20–21	2:68
1:9	1:130	3:8	1:672	12:48	1:189
2:16	1:592			13:3, 5	2:51
2:20	1:266	**Zechariah**		13:5	1:619
4:12	1:405	2:5	1:117	18:11	1:673
8:9	1:430	7:3	1:21	19:8–10	2:180
8:13	1:172	7:5	1:21	21:32	2:28
11:8	1:294			24:27	1:57
		Matthew			
Amos		4:10	1:212	**John**	
3:2	1:187; 2:23	5:13	1:707	1:14	1:104–5; 2:299, 427
5:4	1:567	5:16	2:521		
5:5	1:567	5:45	2:106	1:49	2:454
5:18, 20	1:229	7:13	1:275	2:16	2:427
7:2, 4	1:291	8:20	1:174	2:21	1:105
8:2	1:223	8:22	1:725	3:16	1:543
8:5	2:491	10:38	1:174	3:19	1:650
		11:15	1:158	4:14	2:521
Jonah		12:8	1:582	4:23	1:334
2:7	1:214	13:32	1:509	7:52	1:67
3:4	2:35	15:14	1:504	6:38	2:454
4:10	1:107	25:21	1:524	6:63	2:280
		25:40	2:211	7:38	2:521
Micah		25:45	2:211	8:12	1:650
2:1	1:312	26:52	1:356; 2:160	8:29	2:214
3:3	1:316			8:33	1:435
4:11–12	2:316			10:14	2:213
7:8	2:25				

Index of Scriptures Quoted

10:16	2:214–15	4:13	2:268	10:3–4	1:495
10:28, 29	1:536	5:5	1:478	10:4	1:628
10:30	2:213	5:6, 10	1:436	11:2–3	1:683
11:25	2:285	5:19	1:536	11:2	1:266
12:13	2:454	7:12	1:590	12:4	1:84
14:15	1:575; 2:477	7:18	2:263	12:9	1:356
14:27	1:381	8:1	1:415		
14:29	1:732	8:17	2:528	**Galatians**	
15:13	2:105	8:31	2:40	3:28	2:528
16:33	2:312	8:37	2:342	3:29	2:292
17:11, 16	2:422	10:6	1:581	6:7–8	1:720
17:21–23	2:298	10:17	2:280	6:7	1:295
19:30	2:342	11:12, 15	1:602	6:10	1:474
21:15	2:202	12:17, 19	2:28	6:16	2:93, 513
		13:4	2:202		
Acts		13:14	1:402	**Ephesians**	
2:24–32	2:160	16:20	2:31	1:11	2:528
2:39	1:414			1:14	2:528
3:21	2:246	**1 Corinthians**		2:1	1:542
5:29	2:202	1:13	2:298	2:3	1:436
7:39	1:676	1:24	1:582	2:19	2:530
7:42	1:587	1:27–29	1:332	4:11	2:203
7:48	1:332	3:8	2:545	5:2	1:484
7:53	1:575	3:15	1:148	5:5	2:528
8:4	1:151	3:16	2:299	5:27	1:672
12:20–23	2:75	3:17	2:422		
13:41	2:171	5:7	2:510	**Philippians**	
16:13	1:71	6:19	2:422	2:12–13	2:263
20:26–27	2:172	9:7	2:197	3:19	2:193
20:28	2:203	10:12	1:266, 458		
22:4	2:232	11:1	2:299	**Colossians**	
26:9, 11	2:232	14:40	2:503	1:5	1:553
		15:24	1:225; 2:325	1:12	2:528
Romans		16:2	2:503	1:20	2:221
1:24, 26, 28	1:589			1:22	1:266
2:11	1:698	**2 Corinthians**		2:15	1:619; 2:342
2:12	1:248	3:3	2:299	4:6	1:158
2:13	2:193	5:21	1:673		
3:10–12	2:179	6:14, 16	1:263	**1 Thessalonians**	
3:18	2:422	7:10	1:558; 2:174, 179	1:5–6	2:299
3:25	1:484				

2 Thessalonians
1:7–8	2:28
1:9	1:589
2:11–12	1:403
3:10	2:252

1 Timothy
1:13	2:232
2:2	1:554; 2:202
2:4	1:543
6:17	1:473, 656

2 Timothy
2:19	1:290, 536
2:21	2:476
3:16	1:11

Titus
Titus 3:5 1:484; 2:179

Hebrews
1:3	2:432
3:7–8, 13	1:159
4:14	2:454
7:25	1:673
7:26	2:422
10:1	2:449
10:10	2:450, 495
10:25	2:503
11:10	2:265, 550
11:19	2:280
12:2	1:478
12:11	1:501
12:23	1:589
12:25	1:720; 2:189

James
1:13–14	1:405
2:18, 22	1:525
4:3	1:567
4:13–14	2:40

1 Peter
1:1	1:602; 2:93, 285
1:4	2:93
1:14	1:194
2:5	2:285, 477
2:9	2:477
4:17–18	2:12
4:17	1:290
5:2,3:203	
5:2	1:374; 2:203
5:4	2:214
5:6	1:501
5:8	2:316

2 Peter
1:10	1:537
1:21	1:11
3:4	2:266

1 John
1:5	1:216
1:7	2:299
1:8	2:491
2:15–16	1:679
2:15	1:215
2:16	1:215, 381, 690
4:1	1:280, 373
4:16	1:465; 2:325
5:21	1:211

2 John
8	2:545

Jude
12	2:203
23	1:568

Revelation
1:7	2:122
1:10	2:5034
2:5	1:335
2:6	1:568
2:20	1:212
2:21	2:122
3:19	2:93
4:6, 8	1:305
4:6	1:98
5:9	1:609
7:4	1:290
7:9	2:268, 530
7:14	2:530
7:16–17	2:246
19:11	1:619
19:15	1:619
19:17–21	2:342
21:3	2:226, 299
21:6	2:342
21:7	2:343
21:12	2:548
21:22–23	1:105
21:22	2:423, 427
21:27	1:607
22:3–4	1:336

INDEX OF HEBREW WORDS

א

ʾădāmâ	1:223
ʾădōnāy	1:113
ʾāhab	1:460
ʾāwen	1:312
ʾeḥād	2:287
ʾāsap	1:328
ʾôpan	1:298
ʾereṣ	1:223, 346
ʾôt	1:346

ב

bayit	1:274; 2:371
bāḥar	1:570
ben-ʾādām	1:107
binyān	2:371
biqʿâ	1:154
biqqēš	2:200
bāqar	2:204
bôš	1:472

ג

gābāh	1:471; 2:70
gādap	1:591
gôy	2:293
gālâ	1:461; 2:341
gôlâ	1:71; 2:341
galgal	1:298
gillûlîm	1:209
gālût	1:73; 2:341

ד

dəmût	1:87
derek	1:264
dāraš	1:396; 2:200, 204

ה

hāyâ	1:74, 1:145
hêkāl	1:276
hāmôn	1:233; 2:108
hinnēh	1:82

ז

zābaḥ	1:591
zānâ	1:427, 445, 676
zāraq	1:299; 2:257
zārâ	1:183–84

ח

ḥašmal	1:84
ḥārôn	1:235
ḥāṭāʾ	1:150, 409; 2:445
ḥātat	1:117
ḥayyâ	1:87
ḥelʾâ	1:713
ḥālal	1:385
ḥēmâ	1:134
ḥōq	1:320
ḥuqqâ	1:189
ḥittît	2:48

ט

ṭāhar	1:718
ṭāhēr	2:277, 448
ṭāmēʾ	1:195, 385, 573; 2:249
ṭumʾâ	1:718

י

yākaḥ	1:156
yāṣāʾ	1:572
yāraš	2:243
yāšaʿ	1:148; 2:260

כ

kālâ	1:198
kālam	1:472
kāʿas	1:279

ל

lōʾ ... ʿôd	1:193, 360
lākēn	1:190
ləmaʿan	1:180
ləʿênê	1:177

מ

mibneh	2:363
mihmād	1:722
maʿal	1:409
məʿat	1:327
môpēt	1:346
miqdāš	1:195, 265; 2:297
mārâ	1:114
mārad	1:112
marʾeh	1:87
merkābâ	1:92
māšāl	1:358, 488
mišpāṭ	1:188

נ

nābîʾ	1:27n4
nāgîd	2:69
nûaḥ	1:198
naḥălâ	2:231, 243
nāḥam	1:198
nākâ	1:230
nepeš	1:516, 688
naṣal	1:148; 2:204
nāśîʾ	1:245, 349; 2:452
nātan	1:145

ס		ר	
sāḥar	2:59	rādâ	2:113
sēmel	1:261	rûaḥ	2:275
		rāḥam	2:344
ע		rākal	2:53
ʿāgab	1:681	rāʾâ	1:369
ʿāwel	1:149	riṣĕpâ	2:380
ʿāwōn	1:147, 168	rāšāʿ	1:147
ʿălîlâ	1:607		
ʿôlām	2:225, 296	שׂ	
ʿam	2:293	śar	1:245, 311
ʿānān	1:83		
ʿēṣ	2:287	שׁ	
		šāʾaṭ	2:22
פ		šûb	1:149, 266n11, 399, 534, 540
pālîṭ	1:213; 2:195		
pāqad	1:282, 689		
pārar	1:480	šādad	2:146
pāšaʿ	1:112	šadday	1:99
pûṣ	1:326n52	šāḥaṭ	1:450
		šûṭ	1:478
צ		šāwʾ	1:360
ṣādaq	1:472	šālaḥ	1:110
ṣaddîq	1:149	šālôm	1:244, 377; 2:216
		šāmam	1:137, 208, 355; 2:222
ק			
qābaṣ	1:328		
qādaš	2:255	šāpaṭ	1:318
qādôš	2:297	šiqqûṣîm	1:195
qāhāl	1:705	šārat	1:598
qôl	1:98		
qînâ	1:545	ת	
qinʾâ	1:199	tāwek	1:71n3
qereb	1:669n63	təhôm	2:130
qorbān	1:591	tannîm	2:142
qûm	1:480	tôʿēbôt	1:192
qešet	1:102	tôrâ	1:244
		tərûmâ	1:606; 2:479